INTERNATIONAL CRIMINAL LAW

Documents Supplement

Jordan J. Paust

M. Cherif Bassiouni

Michael Scharf

Leila Sadat

Jimmy Gurulé

Bruce Zagaris

ISBN 978-1-61163-365-8

Carolina Academic Press

International Criminal Law
Documents Supplement

Jordan J. Paust
University of Houston Law Center

M. Cherif Bassiouni
DePaul University College of Law

Michael Scharf
Case Western Reserve
School of Law

Leila Sadat
Washington St. Louis
School of Law

Jimmy Gurulé
Notre Dame Law School

Bruce Zagaris
of the D.C. Bar

Carolina Academic Press
Durham, North Carolina

ISBN: 978-1-61163-365-8
LCCN: 2012954323

Carolina Academic Press
700 Kent Street
Durham, North Carolina 27701
Telephone (919) 489-7486
Fax (919) 493-5668
www.cap-press.com

Printed in the United States of America

Contents

Table of Abbreviations

Can. T.S.	Canadian Treaty Series
G.A.	General Assembly
GAOR	General Assembly Official Records
L.N.T.S.	League of Nations Treaty Series
O.A.S.	Organization of American States
O.A.U.	Organization of African Unity
Stat.	U.S. Statutes at Large
T.I.A.S.	Treaties and Other International Acts Series
T.S.	Treaty Series
U.N.T.S.	United Nations Treaty Series
U.S.T.	United States Treaties and Other International Agreements
Y.B.U.N.	Yearbook of the United Nations

United States Constitution

(extracts)

Article I.

Section 1. All legislative Powers herein granted shall be vested in a Congress of the United States, which shall consist of a Senate and House of Representatives.

Section 8. [1] The Congress shall have Power To lay and collect Taxes, Duties, Imposts and Excises, to pay the Debts and provide for the common Defence and general Welfare of the United States; but all Duties, Imposts and Excises shall be uniform throughout the United States;

[2] To borrow money on the credit of the United States;

[3] To regulate Commerce with foreign Nations, and among the several States, and with the Indian Tribes;

[4] To establish an uniform Rule of Naturalization, and uniform Laws on the subject of Bankruptcies throughout the United States;

[5] To coin Money, regulate the Value thereof, and of foreign Coin, and fix the Standard of Weights and Measures;

[6] To provide for the Punishment of counterfeiting the Securities and current Coin of the United States;

[7] To Establish Post Offices and Post Roads;

[8] To promote the Progress of Science and useful Arts, by securing for limited Times to Authors and Inventors the exclusive Right to their respective Writings and Discoveries;

[9] To constitute Tribunals inferior to the supreme Court;

[10] To define and punish Piracies and Felonies committed on the high Seas, and Offences against the Law of Nations;

[11] To declare War, grant Letters of Marque and Reprisal, and make Rules concerning Captures on Land and Water;

[12] To raise and support Armies, but no Appropriation of Money to that Use shall be for a longer Term than two Years;

[13] To provide and maintain a Navy;

[14] To make Rules for the Government and Regulation of the land and naval Forces;

[15] To provide for calling forth the Militia to execute the Laws of the Union, suppress Insurrections and repel Invasions;

[16] To provide for organizing, arming, and disciplining, the Militia, and for governing such Part of them as may be employed in the Service of the United States, reserving to the States respectively, the Appointment of the Officers, and the Authority of training the Militia according to the discipline prescribed by Congress; ...

[18] To make all Laws which shall be necessary and proper for carrying into Execution the foregoing Powers, and all other Powers vested by this Constitution in the Government of the United States, or in any Department or Officer thereof.

Section 9.

[2] The privilege of the Writ of Habeas Corpus shall not be suspended, unless when in Case of Rebellion or Invasion the public Safety may require it.

[3] No Bill of Attainder or ex post facto Law shall be passed.

Section 10.

[1] No State shall enter into any Treaty, Alliance, or Confederation; grant Letters of Marque and Reprisal....

[3] No State shall, without the Consent of Congress, ... enter into any Agreement or Compact with another State, or with a foreign Power or engage in War, unless actually invaded, or in such imminent Danger as will not admit of delay.

Article II.

Section 1. [1] The executive Power shall be vested in a President of the United States of America.

[8] Before he enter on the Execution of his Office, he shall take the following Oath or Affirmation:—"I do solemnly swear (or affirm) that I will faithfully execute the Office of President of the United States, and will to the best of my Ability, preserve, protect and defend the Constitution of the United States."

Section 2. [1] The President shall be Commander in Chief of the Army and Navy of the United States, and of the militia of the several States, when called into the actual Service of the United States; he may require the Opinion, in writing, of the principal Officer in each of the Executive Departments, upon any Subject relating to the Duties of their respective Offices, and he shall have Power to grant Reprieves and Pardons for Offenses against the United States, except in Cases of Impeachment.

[2] He shall have Power, by and with the Advice and Consent of the Senate to make Treaties, provided two thirds of the Senators present concur; and he shall nominate, and by and with the Advice and Consent of the Senate, shall appoint Ambassadors, other public Ministers and Consuls, Judges of the supreme Court, and all other Officers of the United States, whose Appointments are not herein otherwise provided for, and which shall be established by Law; but the Congress may by Law vest the Appointment of such inferior Officers, as they think proper, in the President alone, in the Courts of Law, or in the Heads of Departments....

Section 3.... [H]e shall receive Ambassadors and other public Ministers; he shall take Care that the Laws be faithfully executed, and shall Commission all the Officers of the United States.

Article III.

Section 1. The judicial Power of the United States, shall be vested in one supreme Court, and in such inferior Courts as the Congress may from time to time ordain and establish....

Section 2. [1] The judicial Power shall extend to all Cases, in Law and Equity, arising under this Constitution, the Laws of the United States, and Treaties made, or which shall be made, under their Authority;—to all Cases affecting Ambassadors, other public Ministers and Consuls;—to all Cases of admiralty and maritime Jurisdiction;—to Controversies to which the United States shall be a Party;—to Controversies between two or more States;—between a State and Citizens of another State;—between Citizens of different States;—between Citizens of the same State claiming Lands under the Grants of different States, and between a State, or the Citizens thereof, and foreign States, Citizens or Subjects.

[2] In all Cases affecting Ambassadors, other public Ministers and Consuls, and those in which a State shall be a Party, the supreme Court shall have original Jurisdiction. In all the other Cases before mentioned, the supreme Court shall have appellate Jurisdiction, both as to Law and Fact, with such Exceptions, and under such Regulations as the Congress shall make.

Article VI.

[2] This Constitution, and the Laws of the United States which shall be made in Pursuance thereof; and all Treaties made, or which shall be made, under the Authority of the United States, shall be the supreme Law of the Land; and the Judges in every State shall be bound thereby, any Thing in the Constitution or Laws of any State to the Contrary notwithstanding.

Amendment X.

The powers not delegated to the United States by the Constitution, nor prohibited by it to the States, are reserved to the States respectively, or to the people.

Charter of the United Nations
T.S. 993, 59 Stat. 1031, 1976 Y.B.U.N. 1043 (June 26, 1945)

WE THE PEOPLES OF THE UNITED NATIONS DETERMINED to save succeeding generations from the scourge of war, which twice in our lifetime has brought untold sorrow to mankind, and to reaffirm faith in fundamental human rights, in the dignity and worth of the human person, in the equal rights of men and women and of nations large and small, and to establish conditions under which justice and respect for the obligations arising from treaties and other sources of international law can be maintained, and to promote social progress and better standards of life in larger freedom,

AND FOR THESE ENDS to practice tolerance and live together in peace with one another as good neighbours, and to unite our strength to maintain international peace and security, and to ensure by the acceptance of principles and the institution of methods, that armed force shall not be used, save in the common interest, and to employ international machinery for the promotion of the economic and social advancement of all peoples,

HAVE RESOLVED TO COMBINE OUR EFFORTS TO ACCOMPLISH THESE AIMS Accordingly, our respective Governments, through representatives assembled in the city of San Francisco, who have exhibited their full powers found to be in good and due form, have agreed to the present Charter of the United Nations and do hereby establish an international organization to be known as the United Nations.

Chapter I. Purposes and Principles

Article 1

The Purposes of the United Nations are:

1. To maintain international peace and security, and to that end: to take effective collective measures for the prevention and removal of threats to the peace, and for the suppression of acts of aggression or other breaches of the peace, and to bring about by peaceful means, and in conformity with the principles of justice and international law, adjustment or settlement of international disputes or situations which might lead to a breach of the peace;

2. To develop friendly relations among nations based on respect for the principle of equal rights and self-determination of peoples, and to take other appropriate measures to strengthen universal peace;

3. To achieve international co-operation in solving international problems of an economic, social, cultural, or humanitarian character, and in promoting and encouraging respect for human rights and for fundamental freedoms for all without distinction as to race, sex, language, or religion; and

4. To be a centre for harmonizing the actions of nations in the attainment of these common ends.

Article 2

The Organization and its Members, in pursuit of the Purposes stated in Article 1, shall act in accordance with the following Principles.

1. The Organization is based on the principle of the sovereign equality of all its Members.

2. All Members, in order to ensure to all of them the rights and benefits resulting from membership, shall fulfil in good faith the obligations assumed by them in accordance with the present Charter.

3. All Members shall settle their international disputes by peaceful means in such a manner that international peace and security, and justice, are not endangered.

4. All Members shall refrain in their international relations from the threat or use of force against the territorial integrity or political independence of any state, or in any other manner inconsistent with the Purposes of the United Nations.

5. All Members shall give the United Nations every assistance in any action it takes in accordance with the present Charter, and shall refrain from giving assistance to any state against which the United Nations is taking preventive or enforcement action.

6. The Organization shall ensure that states which are not Members of the United Nations act in accordance with these Principles so far as may be necessary for the maintenance of international peace and security.

7. Nothing contained in the present Charter shall authorize the United Nations to intervene in matters which are essentially within the domestic jurisdiction of any state or shall require the Members to submit such matters to settlement under the present Charter; but this principle shall not prejudice the application of enforcement measures under Chapter VII.

Chapter III. Organs

Article 7

1. There are established as the principal organs of the United Nations: a General Assembly, a Security Council, an Economic and Social Council, a Trusteeship Council, an International Court of Justice, and a Secretariat.

2. Such subsidiary organs as may be found necessary may be established in accordance with the present Charter.

Article 8

The United Nations shall place no restrictions on the eligibility of men and women to participate in any capacity and under conditions of equality in its principal and subsidiary organs.

Chapter IV. The General Assembly

Composition

Article 9

1. The General Assembly shall consist of all the Members of the United Nations.

2. Each Member shall have not more than five representatives in the General Assembly.

Functions and Powers

Article 10

The General Assembly may discuss any questions or any matters within the scope of the present Charter or relating to the powers and functions of any organs provided for in the present Charter, and, except as provided in Article 12, may make recommendations to the Members of the United Nations or to the Security Council or to both on any such questions or matters.

Article 12

1. While the Security Council is exercising in respect of any dispute or situation the functions assigned to it in the present Charter, the General Assembly shall not make any recommendations with regard to that dispute or situation unless the Security Council so requests....

Article 13

1. The General Assembly shall initiate studies and make recommendations for the purpose of:

    a. promoting international cooperation in the political field and encouraging the progressive development of international law and its codification;

    b. promoting international cooperation in the economic, social, cultural, educational, and health fields, and assisting in the realization of human rights and fundamental freedoms for all without distinction as to race, sex, language, or religion.

2. The further responsibilities, functions, and powers of the General Assembly with respect to matters mentioned in paragraph 1 (b) above are set forth in Chapters IX and X.

Article 14

Subject to the provisions of Article 12, the General Assembly may recommend measures for the peaceful adjustment of any situation, regardless of origin, which it deems likely to impair the general welfare or friendly relations among nations, including situations resulting from a violation of the provisions of the present Charter setting forth the Purposes and Principles of the United Nations.

Article 22

The General Assembly may establish such subsidiary organs as it deems necessary for the performance of its functions.

Chapter V. The Security Council Composition

Article 23

1. The Security Council shall consist of fifteen Members of the United Nations. The Republic of China, France, the Union of Soviet Socialist Republics, the United Kingdom of Great Britain and Northern Ireland, and the United States of America shall be permanent members of the Security Council. The General Assembly shall elect ten other Members of the United Nations to be non-permanent members of the Security Council, due regard being specially paid, in the first instance to the contribution of Members of the United Nations to the maintenance of international peace and security and to the other purposes of the Organization, and also to equitable geographical distribution.

2. The non-permanent members of the Security Council shall be elected for a term of two years. In the first election of the non-permanent members after the increase of the membership of the Security Council from eleven to fifteen, two of the four additional members shall be chosen for a term of one year. A retiring member shall not be eligible for immediate re-election.

3. Each member of the Security Council shall have one representative.

Functions and Powers

Article 24

1. In order to ensure prompt and effective action by the United Nations, its Members confer on the Security Council primary responsibility for the maintenance of international peace and security, and agree that in carrying out its duties under this responsibility the Security Council acts on their behalf.

2. In discharging these duties the Security Council shall act in accordance with the Purposes and Principles of the United Nations. The specific powers granted to the Security Council for the discharge of these duties are laid down in Chapters VI, VII, VIII, and XII.

3. The Security Council shall submit annual and, when necessary, special reports to the General Assembly for its consideration.

Article 25

The Members of the United Nations agree to accept and carry out the decisions of the Security Council in accordance with the present Charter.

Chapter VI. Pacific Settlement of Disputes

Article 33

1. The parties to any dispute, the continuance of which is likely to endanger the maintenance of international peace and security, shall, first of all, seek a solution by negotiation, enquiry, mediation, conciliation, arbitration, judicial settlement, resort to regional agencies or arrangements, or other peaceful means of their own choice.

2. The Security Council shall, when it deems necessary, call upon the parties to settle their dispute by such means.

Article 34

The Security Council may investigate any dispute, or any situation which might lead to international friction or give rise to a dispute, in order to determine whether the continuance of the dispute or situation is likely to endanger the maintenance of international peace and security.

Chapter VII. Action with Respect to Threats to the Peace, Breaches of the Peace, or Acts of Aggression

Article 39

The Security Council shall determine the existence of any threat to the peace, breach of the peace, or act of aggression and shall make recommendations, or decide what measures shall be taken in accordance with Articles 41 and 42, to maintain or restore international peace and security.

Article 40

In order to prevent an aggravation of the situation, the Security Council may, before making the recommendations or deciding upon the measures provided for in Article 39, call upon the parties concerned to comply with such provisional measures as it deems necessary or desirable. Such provisional measures shall be without prejudice to the rights, claims, or position of the parties concerned. The Security Council shall duly take account of failure to comply with such provisional measures.

Article 41

The Security Council may decide what measures not involving the use of armed force are to be employed to give effect to its decisions, and it may call upon the Members of the United Nations to apply such measures. These may include complete or partial interruption of economic relations and of rail, sea, air, postal, telegraphic, radio, and other means of communication, and the severance of diplomatic relations.

Article 42

Should the Security Council consider that measures provided for in Article 41 would be inadequate or have proved inadequate, it may take such action by air, sea, or land forces as may be necessary to maintain or restore international peace and security. Such action may include demonstrations, blockade, and other operations by air, sea, or land forces of Members of the United Nations.

Article 43

1. All Members of the United Nations, in order to contribute to the maintenance of international peace and security, undertake to make available to the Security Council, on its call and in accordance with a special agreement or agreements, armed forces, assistance, and facilities, including rights of passage, necessary for the purpose of maintaining international peace and security.

2. Such agreement or agreements shall govern the numbers and types of forces, their degree of readiness and general location, and the nature of the facilities and assistance to be provided.

3. The agreement or agreements shall be negotiated as soon as possible on the initiative of the Security Council. They shall be concluded between the Security Council and

Members or between the Security Council and groups of Members and shall be subject to ratification by the signatory states in accordance with their respective constitutional processes....

Article 45

In order to enable the United Nations to take urgent military measures, Members shall hold immediately available national air-force contingents for combined international enforcement action. The strength and degree of readiness of these contingents and plans for their combined action shall be determined, within the limits laid down in the special agreement or agreements referred to in Article 43, by the Security Council with the assistance of the Military Staff Committee.

Article 48

1. The action required to carry out the decisions of the Security Council for the maintenance of international peace and security shall be taken by all the Members of the United Nations or by some of them, as the Security Council may determine.

2. Such decisions shall be carried out by the members of the United Nations directly and through their action in the appropriate international agencies of which they are members.

Article 49

The Members of the United Nations shall join in affording mutual assistance in carrying out the measures decided upon by the Security Council.

Article 50

If preventive or enforcement measures against any state are taken by the Security Council, any other state, whether a Member of the United Nations or not, which finds itself confronted with special economic problems arising from the carrying out of those measures shall have the right to consult with the Security Council with regard to a solution of those problems.

Article 51

Nothing in the present Charter shall impair the inherent right of individual or collective self-defence if an armed attack occurs against a Member of the United Nations, until the Security Council has taken measures necessary to maintain international peace and security. Measures taken by Members in the exercise of this right of self-defence shall be immediately reported to the Security Council and shall not in any way affect the authority and responsibility of the Security Council under the present Charter to take at any time such action as it deems necessary in order to maintain or restore international peace and security.

Chapter VIII. Regional Arrangements

Article 52

1. Nothing in the present Charter precludes the existence of regional arrangements or agencies for dealing with such matters relating to the maintenance of international peace and security as are appropriate for regional action, provided that such arrangements or agencies and their activities are consistent with the Purposes and Principles of the United Nations.

2. The Members of the United Nations entering into such arrangements or constituting such agencies shall make every effort to achieve pacific settlement of local disputes through

such regional arrangements or by such regional agencies before referring them to the Security Council.

3. The Security Council shall encourage the development of pacific settlement of local disputes through such regional arrangements or by such regional agencies either on the initiative of the states concerned or by reference from the Security Council.

4. This article in no way impairs the application of Articles 34 and 35.

Article 53

1. The Security Council shall, where appropriate, utilize such regional arrangements or agencies for enforcement action under its authority. But no enforcement action shall be taken under regional arrangements or by regional agencies without the authorization of the Security Council, with the exception of measures against any enemy state, as defined in paragraph 2 of this Article, provided for pursuant to Article 107 or in regional arrangements directed against renewal of aggressive policy on the part of any such state, until such time as the Organization may, on request of the Governments concerned, be charged with the responsibility for preventing further aggression by such a state.

2. The term enemy state as used in paragraph 1 of this article applies to any state which during the Second World War has been an enemy of any signatory of the present Charter.

Article 54

The Security Council shall at all times be kept fully informed of activities undertaken or in contemplation under regional arrangements or by regional agencies for the maintenance of international peace and security.

Chapter IX. International Economic and Social Cooperation

Article 55

With a view to the creation of conditions of stability and well-being which are necessary for peaceful and friendly relations among nations based on respect for the principle of equal rights and self-determination of peoples, the United Nations shall promote:

a. higher standards of living, full employment, and conditions of economic and social progress and development;

b. solutions of international economic, social, health, and related problems; and international cultural and educational cooperation; and

c. universal respect for, and observance of, human rights and fundamental freedoms for all without distinction as to race, sex, language, or religion.

Article 56

All Members pledge themselves to take joint and separate action in cooperation with the Organization for the achievement of the purposes set forth in Article 55.

Article 57

1. The various specialized agencies, established by intergovernmental agreement and having wide international responsibilities, as defined in their basic instruments, in economic, social, cultural, educational, health, and related fields, shall be brought into relationship with the United Nations in accordance with the provisions of Article 63.

2. Such agencies thus brought into relationship with the United Nations are hereinafter referred to as specialized agencies.

Article 58

The Organization shall make recommendations for the coordination of the policies and activities of the specialized agencies.

Article 59

The Organization shall, where appropriate, initiate negotiations among the states concerned for the creation of any new specialized agencies required for the accomplishment of the purposes set forth in Article 55.

Article 60

Responsibility for the discharge of the functions of the Organization set forth in this Chapter shall be vested in the General Assembly and, under the authority of the General Assembly, in the Economic and Social Council, which shall have for this purpose the powers set forth in Chapter X.

Chapter X. The Economic and Social Council

Composition

Article 61

1. The Economic and Social Council shall consist of fifty-four Members of the United Nations elected by the General Assembly.

2. Subject to the provisions of paragraph 3, eighteen members of the Economic and Social Council shall be elected each year for a term of three years. A retiring member shall be eligible for immediate re-election.

3. At the first election after the increase in the membership of the Economic and Social Council from twenty-seven to fifty-four members, in addition to the members elected in place of the nine members whose term of office expires at the end of that year, twenty-seven additional members shall be elected. Of these twenty-seven additional members, the term of office of nine members so elected shall expire at the end of one year, and of nine other members at the end of two years, in accordance with arrangements made by the General Assembly.

4. Each member of the Economic and Social Council shall have one representative.

Functions and Powers

Article 62

1. The Economic and Social Council may make or initiate studies and reports with respect to international economic, social, cultural, educational, health, and related matters and may make recommendations with respect to any such matters to the General Assembly, to the Members of the United Nations, and to the specialized agencies concerned.

2. It may make recommendations for the purpose of promoting respect for and observance of, human rights and fundamental freedoms for all.

3. It may prepare draft conventions for submission to the General Assembly, with respect to matters falling within its competence.

4. It may call, in accordance with the rules prescribed by the United Nations, international conferences on matters falling within its competence.

Article 63

1. The Economic and Social Council may enter into agreements with any of the agencies referred to in Article 57, defining the terms on which the agency concerned shall be

brought into relationship with the United Nations. Such agreements shall be subject to approval by the General Assembly.

2. It may coordinate the activities of the specialized agencies through consultation with and recommendations to such agencies and through recommendations to the General Assembly and to the Members of the United Nations.

Article 64

1. The Economic and Social Council may take appropriate steps to obtain regular reports from the specialized agencies. It may make arrangements with the Members of the United Nations and with the specialized agencies to obtain reports on the steps taken to give effect to its own recommendations and to recommendations on matters falling within its competence made by the General Assembly.

2. It may communicate its observations on these reports to the General Assembly.

Article 65

The Economic and Social Council may furnish information to the Security Council and shall assist the Security Council upon its request.

Article 66

1. The Economic and Social Council shall perform such functions as fall within its competence in connection with the carrying out of the recommendations of the General Assembly.

2. It may, with the approval of the General Assembly, perform services at the request of Members of the United Nations and at the request of specialized agencies.

3. It shall perform such other functions as are specified elsewhere in the present Charter or as may be assigned to it by the General Assembly.

Voting

Article 67

1. Each member of the Economic and Social Council shall have one vote.

2. Decisions of the Economic and Social Council shall be made by a majority of the members present and voting.

Article 68

The Economic and Social Council shall set up commissions in economic and social fields and for the promotion of human rights, and such other commissions as may be required for the performance of its functions.

Article 69

The Economic and Social Council shall invite any Member of the United Nations to participate, without vote, in its deliberations on any matter of particular concern to that Member.

Article 70

The Economic and Social Council may make arrangements for representatives of the specialized agencies to participate, without vote, in its deliberations and in those of the commissions established by it, and for its representatives to participate in the deliberations of the specialized agencies.

Article 71

The Economic and Social Council may make suitable arrangements for consultation with nongovernmental organizations which are concerned with matters within its competence. Such arrangements may be made with international organizations and, where appropriate, with national organizations after consultation with the Member of the United Nations concerned.

Article 72

1. The Economic and Social Council shall adopt its own rules of procedure, including the method of selecting its President.

2. The Economic and Social Council shall meet as required in accordance with its rules, which shall include provision for the convening of meetings on the request of a majority of its members.

Chapter XIV. The International Court of Justice

Article 92

The International Court of Justice shall be the principal judicial organ of the United Nations. It shall function in accordance with the annexed Statute, which is based upon the Statute of the Permanent Court of International Justice and forms an integral part of the present Charter.

Article 93

1. All Members of the United Nations are *ipso facto* parties to the Statute of the International Court of Justice.

2. A state which is not a Member of the United Nations may become a party to the Statute of the International Court of Justice on conditions to be determined in each case by the General Assembly upon the recommendation of the Security Council.

Article 94

1. Each Member of the United Nations undertakes to comply with the decision of the International Court of Justice in any case to which it is a party.

2. If any party to a case fails to perform the obligations incumbent upon it under a judgment rendered by the Court, the other party may have recourse to the Security Council, which may, if it deems necessary, make recommendations or decide upon measures to be taken to give effect to the judgment.

Article 95

Nothing in the present Charter shall prevent Members of the United Nations from entrusting the solution of their differences to other tribunals by virtue of agreements already in existence or which may be concluded in the future.

Article 96

1. The General Assembly or the Security Council may request the International Court of Justice to give an advisory opinion on any legal question.

2. Other organs of the United Nations and specialized agencies, which may at any time be so authorized by the General Assembly, may also request advisory opinions of the Court on legal questions arising within the scope of their activities.

Chapter XV. The Secretariat

Article 97

The Secretariat shall comprise a Secretary-General and such staff as the Organization may require. The Secretary-General shall be appointed by the General Assembly upon the recommendation of the Security Council. He shall be the chief administrative officer of the Organization.

Article 98

The Secretary-General shall act in that capacity in all meetings of the General Assembly, of the Security Council, of the Economic and Social Council, and of the Trusteeship Council, and shall perform such other functions as are entrusted to him by these organs. The Secretary-General shall make an annual report to the General Assembly on the work of the Organization.

Article 99

The Secretary-General may bring to the attention of the Security Council any matter which in his opinion may threaten the maintenance of international peace and security.

Article 100

1. In the performance of their duties the Secretary-General and the staff shall not seek or receive instructions from any government or from any other authority external to the Organization. They shall refrain from any action which might reflect on their position as international officials responsible only to the Organization.

2. Each Member of the United Nations undertakes to respect the exclusively international character of the responsibilities of the Secretary-General and the staff and not to seek to influence them in the discharge of their responsibilities.

Article 101

1. The staff shall be appointed by the Secretary-General under regulations established by the General Assembly.

2. Appropriate staffs shall be permanently assigned to the Economic and Social Council, the Trusteeship Council, and, as required, to other organs of the United Nations. These staffs shall form a part of the Secretariat.

3. The paramount consideration in the employment of the staff and in the determination of the conditions of service shall be the necessity of securing the highest standards of efficiency, competence, and integrity. Due regard shall be paid to the importance of recruiting the staff on as wide a geographical basis as possible.

Chapter XVI. Miscellaneous Provisions

Article 102

1. Every treaty and every international agreement entered into by any Member of the United Nations after the present Charter comes into force shall as soon as possible be registered with the Secretariat and published by it.

2. No party to any such treaty or international agreement which has not been registered in accordance with the provisions of paragraph 1 of this article may invoke that treaty or agreement before any organ of the United Nations.

Article 103

In the event of a conflict between the obligations of the Members of the United Nations under the present Charter and their obligations under any other international agreement, their obligations under the present Charter shall prevail.

Article 104

The Organization shall enjoy in the territory of each of its Members such legal capacity as may be necessary for the exercise of its functions and the fulfillment of its purposes.

Article 105

1. The Organization shall enjoy in the territory of each of its Members such privileges and immunities as are necessary for the fulfillment of its purposes.

2. Representatives of the Members of the United Nations and officials of the Organization shall similarly enjoy such privileges and immunities as are necessary for the independent exercise of their functions in connection with the Organization.

3. The General Assembly may make recommendations with a view to determining the details of the application of paragraphs 1 and 2 of this article or may propose conventions to the Members of the United Nations for this purpose.

Statute of the International Court of Justice

T.S. No. 993, 59 Stat. 1055 (June 26, 1945)

Article 34

1. Only states may be parties in cases before the Court.

2. The Court, subject to and in conformity with its Rules, may request of public international organizations information relevant to cases before it, and shall receive such information presented by such organizations on their own initiative.

3. Whenever the construction of the constituent instrument of a public international organization or of an international convention adopted thereunder is in question in a case before the Court, the Registrar shall so notify the public international organization concerned and shall communicate to it copies of all the written proceedings.

Article 35

1. The Court shall be open to the states parties to the present Statute.

2. The conditions under which the Court shall be open to other states shall, subject to the special provisions contained in treaties in force, be laid down by the Security Council, but in no case shall such conditions place the parties in a position of inequality before the Court.

3. When a state which is not a Member of the United Nations is a party to a case, the Court shall fix the amount which that party is to contribute towards the expenses of the Court. This provision shall not apply if such state is bearing a share of the expenses of the Court.

Article 36

1. The jurisdiction of the Court comprises all cases which the parties refer to it and all matters specially provided for in the Charter of the United Nations or in treaties and conventions in force.

2. The states parties to the present Statute may at any time declare that they recognize as compulsory *ipso facto* and without special agreement, in relation to any other state accepting the same obligation, the jurisdiction of the Court in all legal disputes concerning:

   a. the interpretation of a treaty;

   b. any question of international law;

   c. the existence of any fact which, if established, would constitute a breach of an international obligation;

   d. the nature or extent of the reparation to be made for the breach of an international obligation

3. The declarations referred to above may be made unconditionally or on condition of reciprocity on the part of several or certain states or for a certain time.

4. Such declarations shall be deposited with the Secretary-General of the United Nations, who shall transmit copies thereof to the parties to the Statute and to the Registrar of the Court.

5. Declarations made under Article 36 of the Statute of the Permanent Court of International Justice and which are still in force shall be deemed, as between the parties to the present Statute, to be acceptances of the compulsory jurisdiction of the International Court of Justice for the period which they still have to run and in accordance with their terms.

6. In the event of a dispute as to whether the Court has jurisdiction the matter shall be settled by the decision of the Court.

Article 37

Whenever a treaty or convention in force provides for reference of a matter to a tribunal to have been instituted by the League of Nations, or to the Permanent Court of International Justice, the matter shall, as between the parties to the present Statute, be referred to the International Court of Justice.

Article 38

1. The Court, whose function is to decide in accordance with international law such disputes as are submitted to it, shall apply:

   a. international conventions, whether general or particular, establishing rules expressly recognized by the contesting states;

   b. international custom, as evidence of a general practice accepted as law;

   c. the general principles of law recognized by civilized nations;

   d. subject to the provisions of Article 59, judicial decisions and the teachings of the most highly qualified publicists of the various nations, as subsidiary means for the determination of rules of law.

2. This provision shall not prejudice the power of the Court to decide a case *ex aequo et bono,* if the parties agree thereto.

Article 53

1. Whenever one of the parties does not appear before the Court, or fails to defend its case, the other party may call upon the Court to decide in favor of its claim.

2. The Court must, before doing so, satisfy itself, not only that it has jurisdiction in accordance with Articles 36 and 37, but also that the claim is well founded in fact and law.

Article 55

1. All questions shall be decided by a majority of the judges present.

2. In the event of an equality of votes, the President or the judge who acts in his place shall have a casting vote.

Article 59

The decision of the Court has no binding force except between the parties in respect of that particular case.

Article 60

The judgment is final and without appeal. In the event of dispute as to the meaning or scope of the judgment, the Court shall construe it upon the request of any party.

Article 62

1. Should a state consider that it has an interest of a legal nature which may be affected by the decision in the case, it may submit a request to the Court to be permitted to intervene.

2. It shall be for the Court to decide upon this request.

Article 65

1. The Court may give an advisory opinion on any legal question at the request of whatever body may be authorized by or in accordance with the Charter of the United Nations to make a request.

2. Questions upon which the advisory opinion of the Court is asked shall be laid before the Court by means of a written request containing an exact statement of the question upon which an opinion is required, and accompanied by all documents likely to throw light upon the question.

Declaration on Principles of International Law Concerning Friendly Relations and Co-Operation Among States in Accordance with the Charter of the United Nations

October 24, 1970, U.N. G.A. Res. 2625, 25 U.N. GAOR, Supp. No. 28, at 121, U.N. Doc. A/8028 (1971)

Preamble

The General Assembly,

Reaffirming in the terms of the Charter of the United Nations that the maintenance of international peace and security and the development of friendly relations and co-operation between nations are among the fundamental purposes of the United Nations,

Recalling that the peoples of the United Nations are determined to practice tolerance and live together in peace with one another as good neighbours,

Bearing in mind the importance of maintaining and strengthening international peace founded upon freedom, equality, justice and respect for fundamental human rights and of developing friendly relations among nations irrespective of their political, economic and social systems or the levels of their development,

Bearing in mind also the paramount importance of the Charter of the United Nations in the promotion of the rule of law among nations,

Considering that the faithful observance of the principles of international law concerning friendly relations and co-operation among States and the fulfillment in good faith of the obligations assumed by States, in accordance with the Charter, is of the greatest importance for the maintenance of international peace and security and for the implementation of the other purposes of the United Nations,

Convinced that the strict observance by States of the obligation not to intervene in the affairs of any other State is an essential condition to ensure that nations live together in peace with one another, since the practice of any form of intervention not only violates the spirit and letter of the Charter, but also leads to the creation of situations which threaten international peace and security,

Recalling the duty of States to refrain in their international relations from military, political, economic or any other form of coercion aimed against the political independence or territorial integrity of any State,

Considering it essential that all States shall refrain in their international relations from the threat or use of force against the territorial integrity or political independence of any State, or in any other manner inconsistent with the purposes of the United Nations,

Considering it equally essential that all States shall settle their international disputes by peaceful means in accordance with the Charter,

Reaffirming, in accordance with the Charter, the basic importance of sovereign equality and stressing that the purposes of the United Nations can be implemented only if States enjoy sovereign equality and comply fully with the requirements of this principle in their international relations,

Convinced that the subjection of peoples to alien subjugation, domination and exploitation constitutes a major obstacle to the promotion of international peace and security,

Convinced that the principle of equal rights and self-determination of peoples constitutes a significant contribution to contemporary international law, and that its effective application is of paramount importance for the promotion of friendly relations among States, based on respect for the principle of sovereign equality,

Convinced in consequence that any attempt aimed at the partial or total disruption of the national unity and territorial integrity of a State or country or at its political independence is incompatible with the purposes and principles of the Charter,

Considering the provisions of the Charter as a whole and taking into account the role of relevant resolutions adopted by the competent organs of the United Nations relating to the content of the principles,

Considering the progressive development and codification of the following principles:

(a) The principle that States shall refrain in their international relations from the threat or use of force against the territorial integrity or political independence of any State, or in any other manner inconsistent with the purposes of the United Nations,

(b) The principle that States shall settle their international disputes by peaceful means in such a manner that international peace and security and justice are not endangered,

(c) The duty not to intervene in matters within the domestic jurisdiction of any state, in accordance with the Charter,

(d) The duty of States to co-operate with one another in accordance with the Charter,

(e) The principle of equal rights and self-determination of peoples,

(f) The principle of sovereign equality of States,

(g) The principle that States shall fulfill in good faith the obligations assumed by them in accordance with the Charter, so as to secure their more effective application within the international community, would promote the realization of the purposes of the United Nations.

Having considered the principles of international law relating to friendly relations and co-operation among States,

1. *Solemnly proclaims* the following principles:

The principle that States shall refrain in their international relations from the threat or use of force against the territorial integrity or political independence of any State, or in any other manner inconsistent with the purposes of the United Nations

Every State has the duty to refrain in its international relations from the threat or use of force against the territorial integrity or political independence of any State, or in any other manner inconsistent with the purposes of the United Nations. Such a threat or use of force constitutes a violation of international law and the Charter of the United Nations and shall never be employed as a means of settling international issues.

A war of aggression constitutes a crime against the peace for which there is responsibility under international law.

In accordance with the purposes and principles of the United Nations, States have the duty to refrain from propaganda for wars of aggression.

Every State has the duty to refrain from the threat or use of force to violate international boundaries of another State or as a means of solving international disputes, including territorial disputes and problems concerning frontiers of States.

Every State likewise has the duty to refrain from the threat or use of force to violate international lines of demarcation, such as armistice lines, established by or pursuant to an international agreement to which it is a party or which it is otherwise bound to respect. Nothing in the foregoing shall be construed as prejudicing the positions of the parties concerned with regard to the status and effects of such lines under their special regimes or as affecting their temporary character.

States have a duty to refrain from acts of reprisal involving the use of force.

Every State has the duty to refrain from any forcible action which deprives peoples referred to in the elaboration of the principle of equal rights and self-determination of their right to self-determination and freedom and independence.

Every State has the duty to refrain from organizing or encouraging the organization of irregular forces or armed bands, including mercenaries, for incursion into the territory of another State.

Every State has the duty to refrain from organizing, instigating, assisting or participating in acts of civil strife or terrorist acts in another State or acquiescing in organized activities within its territory directed towards the commission of such acts, when the acts referred to in the present paragraph involve a threat or use of force.

The territory of a State shall not be the object of military occupation resulting from the use of force in contravention of the provisions of the Charter. The territory of a State shall not be the object of acquisition by another State resulting from the threat or use of force. No territorial acquisition resulting from the threat or use of force shall be recognized as legal. Nothing in the foregoing shall be construed as affecting:

(a) Provisions of the Charter or any international agreement prior to the Charter regime and valid under international law; or

(b) The powers of the Security Council under the Charter....

Nothing in the foregoing paragraphs shall be construed as enlarging or diminishing in any way the scope of the provisions of the Charter concerning cases in which the use of force is lawful....

The duty of States to co-operate with one another in accordance with the Charter

States have the duty to co-operate with one another, irrespective of the differences of their political, economic and social systems, in the various spheres of international relations, in order to maintain international peace and security and to promote international economic stability and progress, the general welfare of nations and international cooperation free from discrimination based on such differences.

To this end:

(a) States shall co-operate with other States in the maintenance of international peace and security;

(b) States shall co-operate in the promotion of universal respect for, and observance of, human rights and fundamental freedoms for all, and in the elimination of all forms of racial discrimination and all forms of religious intolerance;

(c) States shall conduct their international relations in the economic, social, cultural technical and trade fields in accordance with the principles of sovereign equality and non-intervention,

(d) States Members of the United Nations have the duty to take joint and separate action in co-operation with the United Nations in accordance with the relevant provisions of the Charter.

States should co-operate in the economic, social and cultural fields as well as in the field of science and technology and for the promotion of international cultural and educational progress. States should cooperate in the promotion of economic growth throughout the world, especially that of the developing countries.

The principle of equal rights and self-determination of peoples

By virtue of the principle of equal rights and self-determination of peoples enshrined in the Charter of the United Nations, all peoples have the right freely to determine, without external interference their political status and to pursue their economic, social and cultural development, and every State has the duty to respect this right in accordance with the provisions of the Charter.

Every State has the duty to promote, through joint and separate action, realization of the principle of equal rights and self-determination of peoples, in accordance with the provisions of the Charter, and to render assistance to the United Nations in carrying out the responsibilities entrusted to it by the Charter regarding the implementation of the principle, in order:

(a) To promote friendly relations and co-operation among States, and

(b) To bring a speedy end of colonialism, having due regard to the freely expressed will of the peoples concerned;

and bearing in mind that subjection of peoples to alien subjugation, domination and exploitation constitutes a violation of the principle, as well as a denial of fundamental human rights, and is contrary to the Charter.

Every State has the duty to promote through joint and separate action universal respect for and observance of human rights and fundamental freedoms in accordance with the Charter.

The establishment of a sovereign and independent State, the free association or integration with an independent State or the emergence into any other political status freely determined by a people constitute modes of implementing the right of self-determination by that people.

Every State has the duty to refrain from any forcible action which deprives peoples referred to above in the elaboration of the present principle of their right to self-determination and freedom and independence. In their actions against, and resistance to, such forcible action in pursuit of the exercise of their right to self-determination, such peoples are entitled to seek and to receive support in accordance with the purposes and principles of the Charter.

The territory of a colony of other Non-Self-Governing Territory has, under the Charter, a status separate and distinct from the territory of the State administering it; and such separate and distinct status under the Charter shall exist until the people of the colony or Non-Self-Governing Territory have exercised their right of self-determination in accordance with the Charter, and particularly its purposes and principles.

Nothing in the foregoing paragraphs shall be construed as authorizing or encouraging any action which would dismember or impair, totally or in part, the territorial integrity or political unity of sovereign and independent States conducting themselves in compliance with the principle of equal rights and self-determination of peoples as described above and thus possessed of a government representing the whole people belonging to the territory without distinction as to race, creed or colour.

Every State shall refrain from any action aimed at the partial or total disruption of the national unity and territorial integrity of any other State or country.

The principle of sovereign equality of States

All States enjoy sovereign quality. They have equal rights and duties and are equal members of the international community, notwithstanding differences of an economic, social, political or other nature.

In particular, sovereign equality includes the following elements:

(a) States are judicially equal;

(b) Each State enjoys the rights inherent in full sovereignty;

(c) Each State has the duty to respect the personality of other States;

(d) The territorial integrity and political independence of the State are inviolable;

(e) Each State has the right freely to choose and develop its political, social, economic and cultural systems;

(f) Each State has the duty to comply fully and in good faith with its international obligations and to live in peace with other states.

The principle that States shall fulfill in good faith the obligations assumed by them in accordance with the Charter

Every State has the duty to fulfil in good faith the obligations assumed by it in accordance with the Charter of the United Nations....

GENERAL PART

2. *Declares* that:

In their interpretation and application the above principles are interrelated and each principle should be construed in the context of the other principles.

Nothing in this Declaration shall be construed as prejudicing in any manner the provisions of the Charter or the rights and duties of Member States under the Charter or the rights of peoples under the Charter, taking into account the elaboration of these rights in this Declaration.

3. *Declares further* that:

The principles of the Charter which are embodied in this Declaration constitute basic principles of international law, and consequently appeals to all States to be guided by these principles in their international conduct and to develop their mutual relations on the basis of the strict observance of these principles.

North Atlantic Treaty
34 U.N.T.S. 243, T.I.A.S. No. 1964, 63 Stat. 2241 (1949)

The Parties to this Treaty reaffirm their faith in the purposes and principles of the Charter of the United Nations and their desire to live in peace with all peoples and all governments.

They are determined to safeguard the freedom, common heritage and civilization of their peoples, founded on the principles of democracy, individual liberty and the rule of law.

They seek to promote stability and well-being in the North Atlantic area.

They are resolved to unite their efforts for collective defense and for the preservation of peace and security.

They therefore agree to this North Atlantic Treaty:

Article 1

The Parties undertake, as set forth in the Charter of the United Nations, to settle any international disputes in which they may be involved by peaceful means in such a manner that international peace and security, and justice, are not endangered, and to refrain in their international relations from the threat or use of force in any manner inconsistent with the purposes of the United Nations.

Article 2

The Parties will contribute toward the further development of peaceful and friendly international relations by strengthening their free institutions, by bringing about a better understanding of he principles upon which these institutions are founded, and by promoting conditions of stability and well-being. They will seek to eliminate conflict in their international economic policies and will encourage economic collaboration between any or all of them.

Article 3

In order more effectively to achieve the objectives of this Treaty, the Parties, separately and jointly, by means of continuous and effective self-help and mutual aid, will maintain and develop their individual and collective capacity to resist armed attack.

Article 4

The Parties will consult together whenever, in the opinion of any of them, the territorial integrity, political independence or security of any of the Parties is threatened.

Article 5

The Parties agree that an armed attack against one or more of them in Europe or North America shall be considered an attack against them all; and consequently they agree that, if such an armed attack occurs, each of them, in exercise of the right of individual or collective self-defense recognized by Article 51 of the Charter of the United Nations, will assist the Party or Parties so attacked by taking forthwith, individually and in concert with the other Parties, such action as it deems necessary, including the use of armed force, to restore and maintain the security of the North Atlantic area.

Any such armed attack and all measures taken as a result thereof shall immediately be reported to the Security Council. Such measures shall be terminated when the Security Council has taken the measures necessary to restore and maintain international peace and security.

Article 6

For the purpose of Article 5 an armed attack on any one or more of the Parties is deemed to include an armed attack on the territory of any of the Parties in Europe or North America..., on the islands under the jurisdiction of any Party in the North Atlantic area north of the Tropic of Cancer or on the vessels or aircraft in this area of any of the Parties.

Article 7

This Treaty does not affect, and shall not be interpreted as affecting, in any way the rights and obligations under the Charter of the Parties which are members of the United Nations, or the primary responsibility of the Security Council for the maintenance of international peace and security.

Article 9

The Parties hereby establish a council, on which each of them shall be represented, to consider matters concerning the implementation of this Treaty. The council shall be so organized as to be able to meet promptly at any time. The council shall set up such subsidiary bodies as may be necessary; in particular it shall establish immediately a defense committee which shall recommend measures for the implementation of Articles 3 and 5.

Article 11

This Treaty shall be ratified and its provisions carried out by the Parties in accordance with their respective constitutional processes....

Resolution on the Definition of Aggression

December 14, 1974, U.N. G.A. Res.3314, 29 U.N. GAOR, Supp. (No. 31) 142, U.N. Doc. A/9631, Annex (1975)

The General Assembly,

Basing itself on the fact that one of the fundamental purposes of the United Nations is to maintain international peace and security and to take effective collective measures for the prevention and removal of threats to the peace, and for the suppression of acts of aggression or other breaches of the peace,

Recalling that the Security Council, in accordance with Article 39 of the Charter of the United Nations, shall determine the existence of any threat to the peace, breach of the peace or act of aggression and shall make recommendations, or decide what measures shall be taken in accordance with Articles 41 and 42, to maintain or restore international peace and security.

Recalling also the duty of States under the Charter to settle their international disputes by peaceful means in order not to endanger international peace, security and justice,

Bearing in mind, that nothing in this Definition shall be interpreted as in any way affecting the scope of the provisions of the Charter with respect to the functions and powers of the organs of the United Nations.

Considering also that, since aggression is the most serious and dangerous form of the illegal use of force, being fraught, in the conditions created by the existence of all types of weapons of mass destruction, with the possible threat of a world conflict and all its catastrophic consequences, aggression should be defined at the present stage,

Reaffirming the duty of States not to use armed force to deprive peoples of their right to self-determination, freedom and independence, or to disrupt territorial integrity,

Reaffirming also that the territory of a State shall not be violated by being the object, even temporarily, of military occupation or of other measures of force taken by another State in contravention of the Charter, and that it shall not be the object of acquisition by another State resulting from such measures or the threat thereof,

Reaffirming also the provisions of the Declaration on Principles of International Law concerning Friendly Relations and Co-operation among States in accordance with the Charter of the United Nations,

Convinced that the adoption of a definition of aggression ought to have the effect of deterring a potential aggressor, would simplify the determination of acts of aggression and the implementation of measures to suppress them and would also facilitate the protection of the rights and lawful interests of, and the rendering of assistance to, the victim,

Believing that, although the question whether an act of aggression has been committed must be considered in the light of all the circumstances of each particular case, it is nevertheless desirable to formulate basic principles as guidance for such determination,

Adopts the following Definition of Aggression.

Article 1

Aggression is the use of armed force by a State against the sovereignty, territorial integrity or political independence of another State, or in any other manner inconsistent with the Charter of the United Nations, as set out in this Definition....

Article 2

The first use of armed force by a State in contravention of the Charter shall constitute *prima facie* evidence of an act of aggression although the Security Council may, in conformity with the Charter, conclude that a determination that an act of aggression has been committed would not be justified in the light of other relevant circumstances, including the fact that the acts concerned or their consequences are not a sufficient gravity.

Article 3

Any of the following acts, regardless of a declaration of war, shall, subject to and in accordance with the provisions of article 2, qualify as an act of aggression:

(a) The invasion or attack by the armed forces of a State of the territory of another State, or any military occupation, however temporary, resulting from such invasion or attack, or any annexation by the use of force of the territory of another State or part thereof;

(b) Bombardment by the armed forces of a State against the territory of another State or the use of any weapons by a State against the territory of another State;

(c) The blockade of the ports or coasts of a State by the armed forces of another State;

(d) An attack by the armed forces of a State on the land, sea or air forces, or marine and air fleets of another State;

(e) The use of armed forces of one State which are within the territory of another State with the agreement of the receiving State, in contravention of the conditions provided for in the agreement or any extension of their presence in such territory beyond the termination of the agreement;

(f) The action of a State in allowing its territory, which it has placed at the disposal of another State, to be used by that other State for perpetrating an act of aggression against a third State;

(g) The sending by or on behalf of a State of armed bands, groups, irregulars or mercenaries, which carry out acts of armed force against another State of such gravity as to amount to the acts listed above, or its substantial involvement therein.

Article 4

The acts enumerated above are not exhaustive and the Security Council may determine that other acts constitute aggression under the provisions of the Charter.

Article 5

1. No consideration of whatever nature, whether political, economic, military or otherwise, may serve as a justification for aggression.

2. A war of aggression is a crime against international peace. Aggression gives rise to international responsibility.

3. No territorial acquisition or special advantage resulting from aggression is or shall be recognized as lawful.

Article 6

Nothing is this Definition shall be construed as in any way enlarging or diminishing the scope of the Charter, including its provisions concerning cases in which the use of force is lawful.

Article 7

Nothing in this definition, and in particular Article 3, could in any way prejudice the right to self-determination, freedom and independence, as derived from the Charter, of peoples forcibly deprived of that right and referred to in the Declaration on Principles of International Law concerning Friendly Relations and Cooperation among States in accordance with the Charter of the United Nations, particularly peoples under colonial and racist regimes or other forms of alien domination; nor the right of these peoples to struggle to that end and to seek and receive support, in accordance with the principles of the Charter and in conformity with the above-mentioned Declaration.

Article 8

In their interpretation and application the above provisions are interrelated and each provision should be construed in the context of the other provisions.

Resolutions Regarding Afghanistan and Iraq
U.N. Security Council Resolution 1373
(28 Sept. 2001)

The Security Council,

Reaffirming its resolutions 1269 (1999) of 19 October 1999 and 1368 (2001) of 12 September 2001,

Reaffirming also its unequivocal condemnation of the terrorist attacks which took place in New York, Washington, D.C., and Pennsylvania on 11 September 2001, and expressing its determination to prevent all such acts,

Reaffirming further that such acts, like any act of international terrorism, constitute a threat to international peace and security,

Reaffirming the inherent right of individual or collective self-defence as recognized by the Charter of the United Nations as reiterated in resolution 1368 (2001),

Reaffirming the need to combat by all means, in accordance with the Charter of the United Nations, threats to international peace and security caused by terrorist acts,

Deeply concerned by the increase, in various regions of the world, of acts of terrorism motivated by intolerance or extremism,

Calling on States to work together urgently to prevent and suppress terrorist acts, including through increased cooperation and full implementation of the relevant international conventions relating to terrorism,

Recognizing the need for States to complement international cooperation by taking additional measures to prevent and suppress, in their territories through all lawful means, the financing and preparation of any acts of terrorism,

Reaffirming the principle established by the General Assembly in its declaration of October 1970 (resolution 2625 (XXV)) and reiterated by the Security Council in its resolution 1189 (1998) of 13 August 1998, namely that every State has the duty to refrain from organizing, instigating, assisting or participating in terrorist acts in another State or acquiescing in organized activities within its territory directed towards the commission of such acts,

Acting under Chapter VII of the Charter of the United Nations,

1. *Decides* that all States shall:

(a) Prevent and suppress the financing of terrorist acts;

(b) Criminalize the wilful provision or collection, by any means, directly or indirectly, of funds by their nationals or in their territories with the intention that the funds should be used, or in the knowledge that they are to be used, in order to carry out terrorist acts;

(c) Freeze without delay funds and other financial assets or economic resources of persons who commit, or attempt to commit, terrorist acts or participate in or facilitate the commission of terrorist acts; of entities owned or controlled directly or indirectly by such persons; and of persons and entities acting on behalf of, or at the direction of such persons and entities, including funds derived or generated from property owned or controlled directly or indirectly by such persons and associated persons and entities;

(d) Prohibit their nationals or any persons and entities within their territories from making any funds, financial assets or economic resources or financial or other related services available, directly or indirectly, for the benefit of persons who commit or attempt to commit or facilitate or participate in the commission of terrorist acts, of entities owned or controlled, directly or indirectly, by such persons and of persons and entities acting on behalf of or at the direction of such persons;

2. *Decides also* that all States shall:

(a) Refrain from providing any form of support, active or passive, to entities or persons involved in terrorist acts, including by suppressing recruitment of members of terrorist groups and eliminating the supply of weapons to terrorists;

(b) Take the necessary steps to prevent the commission of terrorist acts, including by provision of early warning to other States by exchange of information;

(c) Deny safe haven to those who finance, plan, support, or commit terrorist acts, or provide safe havens;

(d) Prevent those who finance, plan, facilitate or commit terrorist acts from using their respective territories for those purposes against other States or their citizens;

(e) Ensure that any person who participates in the financing, planning, preparation or perpetration of terrorist acts or in supporting terrorist acts is brought to justice and ensure that, in addition to any other measures against them, such terrorist acts are established as serious criminal offences in domestic laws and regulations and that the punishment duly reflects the seriousness of such terrorist acts;

(f) Afford one another the greatest measure of assistance in connection with criminal investigations or criminal proceedings relating to the financing or support of terrorist acts, including assistance in obtaining evidence in their possession necessary for the proceedings;

(g) Prevent the movement of terrorists or terrorist groups by effective border controls and controls on issuance of identity papers and travel documents, and through measures for preventing counterfeiting, forgery or fraudulent use of identity papers and travel documents;

3. *Calls upon* all States to:

(a) Find ways of intensifying and accelerating the exchange of operational information, especially regarding actions or movements of terrorist persons or networks; forged or falsified travel documents; traffic in arms, explosives or sensitive materials; use of communications technologies by terrorist groups; and the threat posed by the possession of weapons of mass destruction by terrorist groups;

(b) Exchange information in accordance with international and domestic law and cooperate on administrative and judicial matters to prevent the commission of terrorist acts;

(c) Cooperate, particularly through bilateral and multilateral arrangements and agreements, to prevent and suppress terrorist attacks and take action against perpetrators of such acts;

(d) Become parties as soon as possible to the relevant international conventions and protocols relating to terrorism, including the International Convention for the Suppression of the Financing of Terrorism of 9 December 1999;

(e) Increase cooperation and fully implement the relevant international conventions and protocols relating to terrorism and Security Council resolutions 1269 (1999) and 1368 (2001);

(f) Take appropriate measures in conformity with the relevant provisions of national and international law, including international standards of human rights, before granting refugee status, for the purpose of ensuring that the asylum seeker has not planned, facilitated or participated in the commission of terrorist acts;

(g) Ensure, in conformity with international law, that refugee status is not abused by the perpetrators, organizers or facilitators of terrorist acts, and that claims of political motivation are not recognized as grounds for refusing requests for the extradition of alleged terrorists;

4. *Notes* with concern the close connection between international terrorism and transnational organized crime, illicit drugs, money-laundering, illegal arms-trafficking, and illegal movement of nuclear, chemical, biological and other potentially deadly materials, and in this regard *emphasizes* the need to enhance coordination of efforts on national, subregional, regional and international levels in order to strengthen a global response to this serious challenge and threat to international security;

5. *Declares* that acts, methods, and practices of terrorism are contrary to the purposes and principles of the United Nations and that knowingly financing, planning and inciting terrorist acts are also contrary to the purposes and principles of the United Nations;

6. *Decides* to establish, in accordance with rule 28 of its provisional rules of procedure, a Committee of the Security Council, consisting of all the members of the Council, to monitor implementation of this resolution, with the assistance of appropriate expertise, and *calls upon* all States to report to the Committee, no later than 90 days from the date of adoption of this resolution and thereafter according to a timetable to be proposed by the Committee, on the steps they have taken to implement this resolution;

7. *Directs* the Committee to delineate its tasks, submit a work programme within 30 days of the adoption of this resolution, and to consider the support it requires, in consultation with the Secretary-General;

8. *Expresses* its determination to take all necessary steps in order to ensure the full implementation of this resolution, in accordance with its responsibilities under the Charter;

9. *Decides* to remain seized of this matter."

Public Law 107-40 (Sept. 18, 2001)
Authorization for Use of Military Force
Joint Resolution

To authorize the use of United States Armed Forces against those responsible for the recent attacks launched against the United States.

Whereas, on September 11, 2001, acts of treacherous violence were committed against the United States and its citizens; and

Whereas, such acts render it both necessary and appropriate that the United States exercise its rights to self-defense and to protect United States citizens both at home and abroad; and

Whereas, in light of the threat to national security and foreign policy of the United States posed by these grave acts of violence; and

Whereas, such acts continue to pose an unusual and extraordinary threat to the national security and foreign policy of the United States; and

Whereas, the President has authority under the Constitution to take action to deter and prevent acts of international terrorism against the United States:

Now, therefore, be it

Resolved by the Senate and House of Representatives of the United States of America in Congress assembled,

Section 1. Short Title.

This joint resolution may be cited as the "Authorization for Use of Military Force."

Section 2. Authorization for Use of United States Armed Forces.

(a) In General. — That the President is authorized to use all necessary and appropriate force against those nations, organizations, or persons he determines planned, authorized, committed, or aided the terrorist attacks that occurred on September 11, 2001, or harbored such organizations or persons, in order to prevent any future acts of international terrorism against the United States by such nations, organizations or persons.

(b) War Powers Resolution Requirements. —

(1) Specific statutory authorization. — Consistent with section 8 (a) (1) of the War Powers Resolution, the Congress declares that this section is intended to constitute specific statutory authorization within the meaning of section 5 (b) of the War Powers Resolution.

(2) Applicability of other requirements. — Nothing in this resolution supercedes any requirement of the War Powers Resolution.

U.N. Security Council Resolution 678
(Nov. 29, 1990)

The Security Council, ...

Acting under Chapter VII of the Charter,

1. *Demands* that Iraq comply fully with resolution 660 (1990) [re: immediate withdrawal from Kuwait] and all subsequent relevant resolutions, and decides, while maintaining all its decisions, to allow Iraq one final opportunity, as a pause of goodwill, to do so;

2. *Authorizes* Member States co-operating with the Government of Kuwait, unless Iraq on or before 15 January 1991 fully implements, as set forth in paragraph 1 above, the foregoing resolutions, to use all necessary means to uphold and implement resolution 660 (1990) and all subsequent relevant resolutions and to restore international peace and security in the area;

3. *Requests* all States to provide appropriate support for the actions undertaken in pursuance of paragraph 2 of the present resolution ... ;

5. *Decides* to remain seized of the matter.

U.N. Security Resolution 1441
(8 Nov. 2002)

The Security Council,

Recalling all its previous relevant resolutions, in particular its resolutions 661 (1990)..., 678 (1990)..., 686 (1991)..., 687 (1991)..., 688 (1991)..., 707 (1991)..., 715 (1991)...,

986 (1995)..., and 1284 (1999) of 17 December 1999, and all the relevant statements of its President,

Recalling also its resolution 1382 (2001) of 29 November 2001 and its intention to implement it fully,

Recognizing the threat Iraq's non-compliance with Council resolutions and proliferation of weapons of mass destruction and long-range missiles poses to international peace and security,

Recalling that its resolution 678 (1990) authorized Member States to use all necessary means to uphold and implement its resolution 660 (1990) of 2 August 1990 and all relevant resolutions subsequent to resolution 660 (1990) and to restore international peace and security in the area,

Further recalling that its resolution 687 (1991) imposed obligations on Iraq as a necessary step for achievement of its stated objective of restoring international peace and security in the area, ...

Deploring also that the Government of Iraq has failed to comply with its commitments pursuant to resolution 687 (1991) with regard to terrorism, pursuant to resolution 688 (1991) to end repression of its civilian population and to provide access by international humanitarian organizations to all those in need of assistance in Iraq, and pursuant to resolutions 686 (1991), 687 (1991), and 1284 (1999) to return or cooperate in accounting for Kuwaiti and third country nationals wrongfully detained by Iraq, or to return Kuwaiti property wrongfully seized by Iraq,

Recalling that in its resolution 687 (1991) the Council declared that a ceasefire would be based on acceptance by Iraq of the provisions of that resolution, including the obligations on Iraq contained therein,

Determined to ensure the full and immediate compliance by Iraq without conditions or restrictions with its obligations under resolution 687 (1991) and other relevant resolutions and recalling that the resolutions of the Council constitute the governing standard of Iraqi compliance, ...

Determined to secure full compliance with its decisions,

Acting under Chapter VII of the Charter of the United Nations,

1. *Decides* that Iraq has been and remains in material breach of its obligations under relevant resolutions, including resolution 687 (1991), in particular through Iraq's failure to cooperate with United Nations inspectors and the IAEA, and to complete the actions required under paragraphs 8 to 13 or resolution 687 (1991);

2. *Decides*, while acknowledging paragraph 1 above, to afford Iraq, by this resolution, a final opportunity to comply with its disarmament obligations under relevant resolutions of the Council; and accordingly decides to set up an enhanced inspection regime with the aim of bringing to full and verified completion the disarmament process established by resolution 687 (1991) and subsequent resolutions of the Council;

3. *Decides* that, in order to begin to comply with its disarmament obligations, in addition to submitting the required biannual declarations, the Government of Iraq shall provide to UNMOVIC, the lARA, and the Council, not later than 30 days from the date of this resolution, a currently accurate, full, and complete declaration of all aspects of its programmes to develop chemical, biological, and nuclear weapons, ballistic missiles, and other delivery systems such as unmanned aerial vehicles and dispersal systems designed

for use on aircraft. including any holdings and precise locations of such weapons, components, sub-components, stocks of agents, and related material and equipment, the locations and work of its research, development and production facilities, as well as all other chemical, biological, and nuclear programmes, including any which it claims are for purposes not related to weapon production or material;

4. *Decides* that false statements or omissions in the declarations submitted by Iraq pursuant to this resolution and failure by Iraq at any time to comply with, and cooperate fully in the implementation of, this resolution shall constitute a further material breach of Iraq's obligations and will be reported to the Council for assessment in accordance with paragraphs 11 and 12 below;

5. *Decides* that Iraq shall provide UNMOVIC and the IAEA immediate, unimpeded, unconditional, and unrestricted access to any and all, including underground, areas, facilities, buildings, equipment, records, and means of transport which they wish to inspect, as well as immediate, unimpeded, unrestricted, and private access to all officials and other persons whom UNMOVIC or the IAEA wish to interview in the mode or location of UNMOVIC's or the IAEA's choice pursuant to any aspect of their mandates; further decides that UNMOVIC and the IAEA may at their discretion conduct interviews inside or outside of Iraq, may facilitate the travel of those interviewed and family members outside of Iraq, and that, at the sole discretion of UNMOVIC and the IAEA, such interviews may occur without the presence of observers from the Iraqi Government; and instructs UNMOVIC and requests the IAEA to resume inspections no later than 45 days following adoption of this resolution and to update the Council 60 days thereafter; ...

8. *Decides* further that Iraq shall not take or threaten hostile acts directed against any representative or personnel of the United Nations or the IAEA or of any Member State taking action to uphold any Council resolution;

9. *Requests* the Secretary-General immediately to notify Iraq of this resolution, which, binding on Iraq, demands that Iraq confirm within seven days of that notification its intention to comply fully with this resolution; and demands further that Iraq cooperate immediately, unconditionally, and actively with UNMOVIC and the IAEA;

10. *Requests* all Member States to give full support to UNMOVIC and the IAEA in the discharge of their mandates, including by providing any information related to prohibited programmes or other aspects of their mandates, including on Iraqi attempts since 1998 to acquire prohibited items, and by recommending sites to be inspected, persons to be interviewed, conditions of such interviews, and data to be collected, the results of which shall be reported to the Council by UNMOVIC and the IAEA;

11. *Directs* the Executive Chairman of UNMOVIC and the Director-General of the IAEA to report immediately to the Council any interference by Iraq with inspection activities, as well as any failure by Iraq to comply with its disarmament obligations, including its obligations regarding inspections under this resolution;

12. *Decides* to convene immediately upon receipt of a report in accordance with paragraphs 4 or 11 above, in order to consider the situation and the need for full compliance with all of the relevant Council resolutions in order to secure international peace and security;

13. *Recalls*, in that context, that the Council has repeatedly warned Iraq that it will face serious consequences as a result of its continued violations of its obligations;

14. *Decides* to remain seized of the matter.

Convention Against the Recruitment, Use, Financing and Training of Mercenaries
2163 U.N.T.S. 75 (1989)

Article 1 ...

2. A mercenary is also any person who, in any other situation:

(a) Is specially recruited locally or abroad for the purpose of participating in a concerted act of violence aimed at:

(i) Overthrowing a Government or otherwise undermining the constitutional order of a State; or

(ii) Undermining the territorial integrity of a State;

(b) Is motivated to take part therein essentially by the desire for significant private gain and is prompted by the promise or payment of material compensation;

(c) Is neither a national nor a resident of the State against which such an act is directed;

(d) Has not been sent by a State on official duty; and

(e) Is not a member of the armed forces of the State on whose territory the act is undertaken.

Article 2

Any person who recruits, uses, finances or trains mercenaries, as defined in article 1 of the present Convention, commits an offence for the purposes of the Convention.

Article 3

1. A mercenary, as defined in article 1 of the present Convention, who participates directly in hostilities or in a concerted act of violence, as the case may be, commits an offence for the purposes of the Convention.

2. Nothing in this article limits the scope of application of article 4 of the present Convention.

Article 4

An offence is committed by any person who:

(a) Attempts to commit one of the offences set forth in the present Convention;

(b) Is the accomplice of a person who commits or attempts to commit any of the offences set forth in the present Convention.

Article 5

1. States Parties shall not recruit, use, finance or train mercenaries and shall prohibit such activities in accordance with the provisions of the present Convention.

2. States Parties shall not recruit, use, finance or train mercenaries for the purpose of opposing the legitimate exercise of the inalienable right of peoples to self-determination, as recognized by international law, and shall take, in conformity with international law, the appropriate measures to prevent the recruitment, use, financing or training of mercenaries for that purpose.

3. They shall make the offences set forth in the present Convention punishable by appropriate penalties which take into account the grave nature of those offences.

Article 6

States Parties shall cooperate in the prevention of the offences set forth in the present Convention, particularly by:

(a) Taking all practicable measures to prevent preparations in their respective territories for the commission of those offences within or outside their territories, including the prohibition of illegal activities of persons, groups and organizations that encourage, instigate, organize or engage in the perpetration of such offences;

(b) Coordinating the taking of administrative and other measures as appropriate to prevent the commission of those offences.

Article 7

States Parties shall cooperate in taking the necessary measures for the implementation of the present Convention.

Article 8

Any State Party having reason to believe that one of the offences set forth in the present Convention has been, is being or will be committed shall, in accordance with its national law, communicate the relevant information, as soon as it comes to its knowledge, directly or through the Secretary-General of the United Nations, to the States Parties affected.

Article 9

1. Each State Party shall take such measures as may be necessary to establish its jurisdiction over any of the offences set forth in the present Convention which are committed:

(a) In its territory or on board a ship or aircraft registered in that State;

(b) By any of its nationals or, if that State considers it appropriate, by those stateless persons who have their habitual residence in that territory.

2. Each State Party shall likewise take such measures as may be necessary to establish its jurisdiction over the offences set forth in articles 2, 3 and 4 of the present Convention in cases where the alleged offender is present in its territory and it does not extradite him to any of the States mentioned in paragraph 1 of this article.

3. The present Convention does not exclude any criminal jurisdiction exercised in accordance with national law.

Article 10

1. Upon being satisfied that the circumstances so warrant, any State Party in whose territory the alleged offender is present shall, in accordance with its laws, take him into custody or take such other measures to ensure his presence for such time as is necessary to enable any criminal or extradition proceedings to be instituted. The State Party shall immediately make a preliminary inquiry into the facts.

2. When a State Party, pursuant to this article, has taken a person into custody or has taken such other measures referred to in paragraph 1 of this article, it shall notify without delay either directly or through the Secretary-General of the United Nations:

(a) The State Party where the offence was committed;

(b) The State Party against which the offence has been directed or attempted;

(c) The State Party of which the natural or juridical person against whom the offence has been directed or attempted is a national;

(d) The State Party of which the alleged offender is a national or, if he is a stateless person, in whose territory he has his habitual residence;

(e) Any other interested State Party which it considers it appropriate to notify.

3. Any person regarding whom the measures referred to in paragraph 1 of this article are being taken shall be entitled:

(a) To communicate without delay with the nearest appropriate representative of the State of which he is a national or which is otherwise entitled to protect his rights or, if he is a stateless person, the State in whose territory he has his habitual residence;

(b) To be visited by a representative of that State.

4. The provisions of paragraph 3 of this article shall be without prejudice to the right of any State Party having a claim to jurisdiction in accordance with article 9, paragraph 1 (b), to invite the International Committee of the Red Cross to communicate with and visit the alleged offender.

5. The State which makes the preliminary inquiry contemplated in paragraph 1 of this article shall promptly report its findings to the States referred to in paragraph 2 of this article and indicate whether it intends to exercise jurisdiction.

Article 11

Any person regarding whom proceedings are being carried out in connection with any of the offences set forth in the present Convention shall be guaranteed at all stages of the proceedings fair treatment and all the rights and guarantees provided for in the law of the State in question. Applicable norms of international law should be taken into account.

Article 12

The State Party in whose territory the alleged offender is found shall, if it does not extradite him, be obliged, without exception whatsoever and whether or not the offence was committed in its territory, to submit the case to its competent authorities for the purpose of prosecution, through proceedings in accordance with the laws of that State. Those authorities shall take their decision in the same manner as in the case of any other offence of a grave nature under the law of that State.

Article 13

1. States Parties shall afford one another the greatest measure of assistance in connection with criminal proceedings brought in respect of the offences set forth in the present Convention, including the supply of all evidence at their disposal necessary for the proceedings. The law of the State whose assistance is requested shall apply in all cases.

2. The provisions of paragraph 1 of this article shall not affect obligations concerning mutual judicial assistance embodied in any other treaty.

Article 14

The State Party where the alleged offender is prosecuted shall in accordance with its laws communicate the final outcome of the proceedings to the Secretary-General of the United Nations, who shall transmit the information to the other States concerned.

Article 15

1. The offences set forth in articles 2, 3 and 4 of the present Convention shall be deemed to be included as extraditable offences in any extradition treaty existing between States Parties. States Parties undertake to include such offences as extraditable offences in every extradition treaty to be concluded between them.

2. If a State Party which makes extradition conditional on the existence of a treaty receives a request for extradition from another State Party with which it has no extradition treaty, it may at its option consider the present Convention as the legal basis for extradition in respect of those offences. Extradition shall be subject to the other conditions provided by the law of the requested State.

3. States Parties which do not make extradition conditional on the existence of a treaty shall recognize those offences as extraditable offences between themselves, subject to the conditions provided by the law of the requested State.

4. The offences shall be treated, for the purpose of extradition between States Parties, as if they had been committed not only in the place in which they occurred but also in the territories of the States required to establish their jurisdiction in accordance with article 9 of the present Convention....

Universal Declaration of Human Rights
U.N. G.A. Res. 217A, 3 U.N. GAOR, U.N. Doc. A/810, at 71 (1948)

Preamble

Whereas recognition of the inherent dignity and of the equal and inalienable rights of all members of the human family is the foundation of freedom, justice and peace in the world,

Whereas disregard and contempt for human rights have resulted in barbarous acts which have outraged the conscience of mankind, and the advent of a world in which human beings shall enjoy freedom of speech and belief and freedom from fear and want has been proclaimed as the highest aspiration of the common people,

Whereas it is essential, if man is not to be compelled to have recourse, as a last resort, to rebellion against tyranny and oppression, that human rights should be protected by the rule of law,

Whereas it is essential to promote the development of friendly relations between nations,

Whereas the peoples of the United Nations have in the Charter reaffirmed their faith in fundamental human rights, in the dignity and worth of the human person and in the equal rights of men and women and have determined to promote social progress and better standards of life in larger freedom,

Whereas Member States have pledged themselves to achieve, in cooperation with the United Nations, the promotion of universal respect for and observance of human rights and fundamental freedoms,

Whereas a common understanding of these rights and freedoms is of the greatest importance for the full realization of this pledge.

Now Therefore, The General Assembly *proclaims this universal declaration of human rights* as a common standard of achievement for all peoples and all nations, to the end that every individual and every organ of society, keeping this Declaration constantly in mind, shall strive by teaching and education to promote respect for these rights and freedoms and by progressive measures, national and international, to secure their universal and effective recognition and observance, both among the peoples of Member States themselves and among the peoples of territories under their jurisdiction.

Article 1

All human beings are born free and equal in dignity and rights. They are endowed with reason and conscience and should act towards one another in a spirit of brotherhood.

Article 2

Everyone is entitled to all the rights and freedoms set forth in this declaration, without discrimination of any kind, such as race, colour, sex, language, religion, political or other opinion, national or social origin, property, birth or other status.

Furthermore, no distinction shall be made on the basis of the political, jurisdictional or international status of the country or territory to which a person belongs, whether it be independent, trust, non-self-governing or under any other limitation of sovereignty.

Article 3

Everyone has the right to life, liberty and the security of person.

Article 4

No one shall be held in slavery or servitude; slavery and the slave trade shall be prohibited in all their forms.

Article 5

No one shall be subjected to torture or to cruel, inhuman or degrading treatment or punishment.

Article 6

Everyone has the right to recognition everywhere as a person before the law.

Article 7

All are equal before the law and are entitled without any discrimination to equal protection of the law. All are entitled to equal protection against any discrimination in violation of this Declaration and against any incitement to such discrimination.

Article 8

Everyone has the right to an effective remedy by the competent national tribunals for acts violating the fundamental rights granted him by the constitution or by law.

Article 9

No one shall be subjected to arbitrary arrest, detention or exile.

Article 10

Everyone is entitled in full equality to a fair and public hearing by an independent and impartial tribunal, in the determination of his rights and obligations and of any criminal charge against him.

Article 11

1. Everyone charged with a penal offence has the right to be presumed innocent until proved guilty according to law in a public trial at which he has had all the guarantees necessary for his defense.

2. No one shall be held guilty of any penal offence on account of any act or omission which did not constitute a penal offence, under national or international law, at the time when it was committed. Nor shall a heavier penalty be imposed than the one that was applicable at the time the penal offence was committed.

Article 12

No one shall be subjected to arbitrary interference with his privacy, family, home or correspondence, nor to attacks upon his honour and reputation. Everyone has the right to the protection of the law against such interference or attacks.

Article 13

1. Everyone has the right to freedom of movement and residence within the borders of each State.

2. Everyone has the right to leave any country, including his own, and to return to his country.

Article 14

1. Everyone has the right to seek and to enjoy in other countries asylum from persecution.

2. This right may not be invoked in the case of prosecutions genuinely arising from non-political crimes or from acts contrary to the purposes and principles of the United Nations.

Article 15

1. Everyone has the right to a nationality.

2. No one shall be arbitrarily deprived of his nationality nor denied the right to change his nationality.

Article 16

1. Men and women of full age, without any limitation due to race, nationality or religion, have the right to marry and to found a family. They are entitled to equal rights as to marriage, during marriage and at its dissolution.

2. Marriage shall be entered into only with the free and full consent of the intending spouses.

3. The family is the natural and fundamental group unit of society and is entitled to protection by society and the State.

Article 17

1. Everyone has the right to own property alone as well as in association with others.

2. No one shall be arbitrarily deprived of his property.

Article 18

Everyone has the right to freedom of thought, conscience and religion; this right includes freedom to change his religion or belief, and freedom, either alone or in community with others and in public or private, to manifest his religion or belief in teaching, practice, worship and observance.

Article 19

Everyone has the right to freedom of opinion and expression; this right includes freedom to hold opinions without interference and to seek, receive and impart information and ideas through any media and regardless of frontiers.

Article 20

1. Everyone has the right to freedom of peaceful assembly and association.

2. No one may be compelled to belong to an association.

Article 21

1. Everyone has the right to take part in the government of his country, directly or through freely chosen representatives.

2. Everyone has the right official access to public service in his country.

3. The will of the people shall be the basis of the authority of government; this will shall be expressed in periodic and genuine elections which shall be by universal and equal suffrage and shall be held by secret vote or by equivalent free voting procedures.

Article 22

Everyone, as a member of society, has the right to social security and is entitled to realization, through national effort and international cooperation and in accordance with the organization and resources of each State, of the economic, social and cultural rights indispensable for his dignity and the free development of his personality.

Article 23

1. Everyone has the right to work, to free choice of employment, to just and favorable conditions of work and to protection against unemployment.

2. Everyone, without any discrimination, has the right to equal pay for equal work.

3. Everyone who works has the right to just and favourable remuneration ensuring for himself and his family and existence worthy of human dignity, and supplemented, if necessary, by other means of social protection.

4. Everyone has the right to form and to join trade unions for the protection of his interests.

Article 24

Everyone has the right to rest and leisure, including reasonable limitation of working hours and periodic holidays with pay.

Article 25

1. Everyone has the right to a standard of living adequate for the health and well-being of himself and of his family, including food, clothing, housing and medical care and necessary social services, and the right to security in the event of unemployment, sickness, disability, widowhood, old age or other lack of livelihood in circumstances beyond his control.

2. Motherhood and childhood are entitled to special care and assistance. All children, whether born in or out of wedlock, shall enjoy the same social protection.

Article 26

1. Everyone has the right to education. Education shall be free, at least in the elementary and fundamental stages. Elementary education shall be compulsory. Technical and professional education shall be made generally available and higher education shall be equally accessible to all on the basis of merit.

2. Education shall be directed to the full development of the human personality and to the strengthening of respect for human rights and fundamental freedoms. It shall promote understanding, tolerance and friendship among all nations, racial or religious groups, and shall further the activities of the United Nations for the maintenance of peace.

3. Parents have a right to choose the kind of education that shall be given to their children.

Article 27

1. Everyone has the right freely to participate in the cultural life of the community, to enjoy the arts and to share in scientific advancement and its benefits.

2. Everyone has the right to the protection of the moral and material interests resulting from any scientific, literary or artistic production of which he is the author.

Article 28

Everyone is entitled to a social and international order in which the rights and freedoms set forth in this Declaration can be fully realized.

Article 29

1. Everyone has duties to the community in which alone the free and full development of his personality is possible.

2. In the exercise of his rights and freedoms, everyone shall be subject only to such limitations as are determined by law solely for the purpose of securing due recognition and respect for the rights and freedoms of others and of meeting the just requirements of morality, public order and the general welfare in a democratic society.

3. These rights and freedoms may in no case be exercised contrary to the purposes and principles of the United Nations.

Article 30

Nothing in this Declaration may be interpreted as implying for any States, group or person any right to engage in any activity or to perform any act aimed at the destruction of any of the rights and freedoms set forth herein.

International Covenant on Civil and Political Rights (ICCPR)
999 U.N.T.S. 171 (Dec. 9, 1966)

Preamble

The States Parties to the present Covenant,

Considering that, in accordance with the principles proclaimed in the Charter of the United Nations, recognition of the inherent dignity and of the equal and inalienable rights of all members of the human family is the foundation of freedom, justice and peace in the world,

Recognizing that these rights derive from the inherent dignity of the human person,

Recognizing that, in accordance with the Universal Declaration of Human Rights, the ideal of free human beings enjoying civil and political freedom and freedom from fear and want can only be achieved if conditions are created whereby everyone may enjoy his civil and political rights, as well as his economic, social and cultural rights,

Considering the obligation of States under the Charter of the United Nations to promote universal respect for, and observance of, human rights and freedoms,

Realizing that the individual, having duties to other individuals and to the community to which he belongs, is under a responsibility to strive for the promotion and observance of the rights recognized in the present Covenant,

Agree upon the following articles:

Part I

Article 1

1. All peoples have the right of self-determination. By virtue of that right they freely determine their political status and freely pursue their economic, social and cultural development.

2. All peoples may, for their own ends, freely dispose of their natural wealth and resources without prejudice to any obligations arising out of international economic co-operation, based upon the principle of mutual benefit, and international law. In no case may a people be deprived of its own means of subsistence.

3. The States Parties to the present Covenant, including those having responsibility for the administration of Non-Self-Governing and Trust Territories, shall promote the realization of the right of self-determination, and shall respect that right, in conformity with the provisions of the Charter of the United Nations.

Part II

Article 2

1. Each State Party to the present Covenant undertakes to respect and to ensure to all individuals within its territory and subject to its jurisdiction the rights recognized in the present Covenant, without distinction of any kind, such as race, colour, sex, language, religion, political or other opinion, national or social origin, property, birth or other status.

2. Where not already provided for by existing legislative or other measures, each State Party to the present Covenant undertakes to take the necessary steps, in accordance with its constitutional processes and with the provisions of the present Covenant, to adopt such legislative or other measures as may be necessary to give effect to the rights recognized in the present Covenant.

3. Each State Party to the present Covenant undertakes:

(a) To ensure that any person whose rights or freedoms as herein recognized are violated shall have an effective remedy, notwithstanding that the violation has been committed by persons acting in an official capacity;

(b) To ensure that any person claiming such a remedy shall have his right thereto determined by competent judicial, administrative or legislative authorities, or by any other competent authority provided for by the legal system of the State, and to develop the possibilities of judicial remedy;

(c) To ensure that the competent authorities shall enforce such remedies when granted.

Article 3

The States Parties to the present Covenant undertake to ensure the equal right of men and women to the enjoyment of all civil and political rights set forth in the present Covenant.

Article 4

1. In time of public emergency which threatens the life of the nation and the existence of which is officially proclaimed, the States Parties to the present Covenant may take measures derogating from their obligations under the present Covenant to the extent strictly required by the exigencies of the situation, provided that such measures are not incon-

sistent with their other obligations under international law and do not involve discrimination solely on the ground of race, colour, sex, language, religion or social origin.

2. No derogation from Articles 6, 7, 8 (paragraphs 1 and 2), 11, 15, 16 and 18 may be made under this provision.

3. Any State Party to the present Covenant availing itself of the right of derogation shall immediately inform the other States Parties to the present Covenant, through the intermediary of the Secretary-General of the United Nations, of the provisions from which it has derogated and of the reasons by which it was actuated. A further communication shall be made, through the same intermediary, on the date on which it terminates such derogation.

Article 5

1. Nothing in the present Covenant may be interpreted as implying for any State, group or person any right to engage in any activity or perform any act aimed at the destruction of any of the rights and freedoms recognized herein or at their limitation to a greater extent than is provided for in the present Covenant.

2. There shall be no restriction upon or derogation from any of the fundamental human rights recognized or existing in any State Party to the present Covenant pursuant to law, conventions, regulations or custom on the pretext that the present Covenant does not recognize such rights or that it recognizes them to a lesser extent.

Part III

Article 6

1. Every human being has the inherent right to life. This right shall be protected by law. No one shall be arbitrarily deprived of his life.

2. In countries which have not abolished the death penalty, sentence of death may be imposed only for the most serious crimes in accordance with the law in force at the time of the commission of the crime and not contrary to the provisions of the present Covenant and to the Convention on the Prevention and Punishment of the Crime of Genocide. This penalty can only be carried out pursuant to a final judgment rendered by a competent court.

3. When deprivation of life constitutes the crime of genocide, it is understood that nothing in this article shall authorize any State Party to the present Covenant to derogate in any way from any obligation assumed under the provisions of the Convention on the Prevention and Punishment of the Crime of Genocide.

4. Anyone sentenced to death shall have the right to seek pardon or commutation of the sentence. Amnesty, pardon or commutation of the sentence of death may be granted in all cases.

5. Sentence of death shall not be imposed for crimes committed by persons below eighteen years of age and shall not be carried out on pregnant women.

6. Nothing in this article shall be invoked to delay or to prevent the abolition of capital punishment by any State Party to the present Covenant.

Article 7

No one shall be subjected to torture or to cruel, inhuman or degrading treatment or punishment. In particular, no one shall be subjected without his free consent to medical or scientific experimentation.

Article 8

1. No one shall be held in slavery; slavery and the slave trade in all their forms shall be prohibited.

2. No one shall be held in servitude.

3. (a) No one shall be required to perform forced or compulsory labour;

(b) Paragraph 3(a) shall not be held to preclude, in countries where imprisonment with hard labour may be imposed as a punishment for a crime, the performance of hard labour in pursuance of a sentence to such punishment by a competent court;

(c) For the purpose of this paragraph the term "forced or compulsory labour" shall not include:

(i) Any work or service, not referred to in sub-paragraph (b), normally required of a person who is under detention in consequence of a lawful order of a court, or of a person during conditional release from such detention;

(ii) Any service of a military character and, in countries where

conscientious objection is recognized, any national service required by law of conscientious objectors;

(iii) Any service exacted in cases of emergency or calamity threatening the life or well-being of the community;

(iv) Any work or service which forms part of normal civil obligations.

Article 9

1. Everyone has the right to liberty and security of person. No one shall be subjected to arbitrary arrest or detention. No one shall be deprived of his liberty except on such grounds and in accordance with such procedure as are established by law.

2. Anyone who is arrested shall be informed, at the time of arrest, of the reasons for his arrest and shall be promptly informed of any charges against him.

3. Anyone arrested or detained on a criminal charge shall be brought promptly before a judge or other officer authorized by law to exercise judicial power and shall be entitled to trial within a reasonable time or to release. It shall not be the general rule that persons awaiting trial shall be detained in custody, but release may be subject to guarantees to appear for trial, at any other stage of the judicial proceedings, and, should occasion arise, for execution of the judgment.

4. Anyone who is deprived of his liberty by arrest or detention shall be entitled to take proceedings before a court, in order that court may decide without delay on the lawfulness of his detention and order his release if the detention is not lawful.

5. Anyone who has been the victim of unlawful arrest or detention shall have an enforceable right to compensation.

Article 10

1. All persons deprived of their liberty shall be treated with humanity and with respect for the inherent dignity of the human person.

2. (a) Accused persons shall, save in exceptional circumstances, be segregated from convicted persons and shall be subject to separate treatment appropriate to their status as unconvicted persons;

(b) Accused juvenile persons shall be separated from adults and brought as speedily as possible for adjudication.

3. The penitentiary system shall comprise treatment of prisoners the essential aim of which shall be their reformation and social rehabilitation. Juvenile offenders shall be segregated from adults and be accorded treatment appropriate to their age and legal status.

Article 11

No one shall be imprisoned merely on the ground of inability to fulfil a contractual obligation.

Article 12

1. Everyone lawfully within the territory of a State shall, within that territory, have the right to liberty of movement and freedom to choose his residence.

2. Everyone shall be free to leave any country, including his own.

3. The above-mentioned rights shall not be subject to any restrictions except those which are provided by law, are necessary to protect national security, public order (*ordre public*), public health or morals or the rights and freedoms of others, and are consistent with the other rights recognized in the present Covenant.

4. No one shall be arbitrarily deprived of the right to enter his own country.

Article 13

An alien lawfully in the territory of a State Party to the present Covenant may be expelled therefrom only in pursuance of a decision reached in accordance with law and shall, except where compelling reasons of national security otherwise require, be allowed to submit the reasons against his expulsion and to have his case reviewed by, and be represented for the purpose before, the competent authority or a person or persons especially designated by the competent authority.

Article 14

1. All persons shall be equal before the courts and tribunals. In the determination of any criminal charge against him, or of his rights and obligations in a suit at law, everyone shall be entitled to a fair and public hearing by a competent, independent and impartial tribunal established by law. The Press and the public may be excluded from all or part of a trial for reasons of morals, public order (*ordre public*) or national security in a democratic society, or when the interest of the private lives of the parties so requires, or to the extent strictly necessary in the opinion of the court in special circumstances where publicity would prejudice the interests of justice; but any judgment rendered in a criminal case or in a suit at law shall be made public except where the interest of juvenile persons otherwise requires or the proceedings concern matrimonial disputes or the guardianship of children.

2. Everyone charged with a criminal offence shall have the right to be presumed innocent until proved guilty according to law.

3. In the determination of any criminal charge against him, everyone shall be entitled to the following minimum guarantees, in full equality:

(a) To be informed promptly and in detail in a language which he understands of the nature and cause of the charge against him;

(b) To have adequate time and facilities for the preparation of his defence and to communicate with counsel of his own choosing;

(c) To be tried without undue delay;

(d) To be tried in his presence, and to defend himself in person or through legal assistance of his own choosing; to be informed, if he does not have legal assistance, of this right; and to have legal assistance assigned to him, in any case where the interests of justice so require, and without payment by him in any such case if he does not have sufficient means to pay for it;

(e) To examine, or have examined, the witnesses against him and to obtain the attendance and examination of witnesses on his behalf under the same conditions as witnesses against him;

(f) To have the free assistance of an interpreter if he cannot understand or speak the language used in court;

(g) Not to be compelled to testify against himself or to confess guilt.

4. In the case of juvenile persons, the procedure shall be such as will take account of their age and the desirability of promoting their rehabilitation.

5. Everyone convicted of a crime shall have the right to his conviction and sentence being reviewed by a higher tribunal according to law.

6. When a person has by a final decision been convicted of a criminal offence and when subsequently his conviction has been reversed or he has been pardoned on the ground that a new or newly discovered fact shows conclusively that there has been a miscarriage of justice, the person who has suffered punishment as a result of such conviction shall be compensated according to law, unless it is proved that the non-disclosure of the unknown fact in time is wholly or partly attributable to him.

7. No one shall be liable to be tried or punished again for an offence for which he has already been finally convicted or acquitted in accordance with the law and penal procedure of each country.

Article 15

1. No one shall be held guilty of any criminal offence on account of any act or omission which did not constitute a criminal offence, under national or international law, at the time when it was committed. Nor shall a heavier penalty be imposed than the one that was applicable at the time when the criminal offence was committed. If, subsequent to the commission of the offence, provision is made by law for the imposition of a lighter penalty, the offender shall benefit thereby.

2. Nothing in this article shall prejudice the trial and punishment of any person for any act or omission which, at the time when it was committed, was criminal according to the general principles of law recognized by the community of nations.

Article 16

Everyone shall have the right to recognition everywhere as a person before the law.

Article 17

1. No one shall be subjected to arbitrary or unlawful interference with his privacy, family, home or correspondence, nor to unlawful attacks on his honour and reputation.

2. Everyone has the right to the protection of the law against such interference or attacks.

Article 18

1. Everyone shall have the right to freedom of thought, conscience and religion. This right shall include freedom to have or to adopt a religion or belief of his choice, and free-

dom, either individually or in community with others and in public or private, to manifest his religion or belief in worship, observance, practice and teaching.

2. No one shall be subject to coercion which would impair his freedom to have or to adopt a religion or belief of his choice.

3. Freedom to manifest one's religion or beliefs may be subject only to such limitations as are prescribed by law and are necessary to protect public safety, order, health, or morals or the fundamental rights and freedoms of others.

4. The States Parties to the present Covenant undertake to have respect for the liberty of parents and, when applicable, legal guardians to ensure the religious and moral education of their children in conformity with their own convictions.

Article 19

1. Everyone shall have the right to hold opinions without interference.

2. Everyone shall have the right to freedom of expression; this right shall include freedom to seek, receive and impart information and ideas of all kinds, regardless of frontiers, either orally, in writing or in print, in the form of art, or through any other media of his choice.

3. The exercise of the rights provided for in paragraph 2 of this article carries with it special duties and responsibilities. It may therefore be subject to certain restrictions, but these shall only be such as are provided by law and are necessary:

(a) For respect of the rights or reputations of others;

(b) For the protection of national security or of public order (*ordre public*), or of public health or morals.

Article 20

1. Any propaganda for war shall be prohibited by law.

2. Any advocacy of national, racial or religious hatred that constitutes incitement to discrimination, hostility or violence shall be prohibited by law.

Article 21

The right of peaceful assembly shall be recognized. No restrictions may be placed on the exercise of this right other than those imposed in conformity with the law and which are necessary in a democratic society in the interests of national security or public safety, public order (*ordre public*), the protection of public health or morals or the protection of the rights and freedoms of others.

Article 22

1. Everyone shall have the right to freedom of association with others, including the right to form and join trade unions for the protection of his interests.

2. No restrictions may be placed on the exercise of this right other than those which are prescribed by law and which are necessary in a democratic society in the interests of national security or public safety, public order (*ordre public*), the protection of public health or morals or the protection of the rights and freedoms of others. This article shall not prevent the imposition of lawful restrictions on members of the armed forces and of the police in their exercise of this right.

3. Nothing in this article shall authorize States Parties to the International Labour Organization Convention of 1948 concerning Freedom of Association and Protection of the

Right to Organize to take legislative measures which would prejudice, or to apply the law in such a manner as to prejudice, the guarantees provided for in that Convention.

Article 23

1. The family is the natural and fundamental group unit of society and is entitled to protection by society and the State.

2. The right of men and women of marriageable age to marry and to found a family shall be recognized.

3. No marriage shall be entered into without the free and full consent of the intending spouses.

4. States Parties to the present Covenant shall take appropriate steps to ensure equality of rights and responsibilities of spouses as to marriage, during marriage and at its dissolution. In the case of dissolution, provision shall be made for the necessary protection of any children.

Article 24

1. Every child shall have, without any discrimination as to race, colour, sex, language, religion, national or social origin, property or birth, the right to such measures of protection as are required by his status as a minor, on the part of his family, society and the State.

2. Every child shall be registered immediately after birth and shall have a name.

3. Every child has the right to acquire a nationality.

Article 25

Every citizen shall have the right and the opportunity, without any of the distinctions mentioned in Article 2 and without unreasonable restrictions:

(a) To take part in the conduct of public affairs, directly or through freely chosen representatives;

(b) To vote and to be elected at genuine periodic elections which shall be by universal and equal suffrage and shall be held by secret ballot, guaranteeing the free expression of the will of the electors;

(c) To have access, on general terms of equality, to public service in his country.

Article 26

All persons are equal before the law and are entitled without any discrimination to the equal protection of the law. In this respect, the law shall prohibit any discrimination and guarantee to all persons equal and effective protection against discrimination on any ground such as race, colour, sex, language, religion, political or other opinion, national or social origin, property, birth or other status.

Article 27

In those States in which ethnic, religious or linguistic minorities exist, persons belonging to such minorities shall not be denied the right, in community with the other members of their group, to enjoy their own culture, to profess and practice their own religion, or to use their own language.

Part IV

Article 28

1. There shall be established a Human Rights Committee (hereafter referred to in the present Covenant as the Committee). It shall consist of eighteen members and shall carry out the functions hereinafter provided.

2. The Committee shall be composed of nationals of the States Parties to the present Covenant who shall be persons of high moral character and recognized competence in the field of human rights, consideration being given to the usefulness of the participation of some persons having legal experience.

3. The members of the Committee shall be elected and shall serve in their personal capacity.

Article 29

1. The members of the Committee shall be elected by secret ballot from a list of persons possessing the qualifications prescribed in Article 28 and nominated for the purpose by the State Parties to the present Covenant.

2. Each State Party to the present Covenant may nominate not more than two persons. These persons shall be nationals of the nominating State.

3. A person shall be eligible for renomination.

Article 30

1. The initial election shall be held no later than six months after the date of the entry into force of the present Covenant.

2. At least four months before the date of each election to the Committee, other than an election to fill a vacancy declared in accordance with Article 34, the Secretary-General of the United Nations shall address a written invitation to the States Parties to the present Covenant to submit their nominations for membership of the Committee within three months.

3. The Secretary-General of the United Nations shall prepare a list in alphabetical order of all the persons thus nominated, with an indication of the States Parties which have nominated them, and shall submit it to the States Parties to the present Covenant no later than one month before the date of each election.

4. Elections of the members of the Committee shall be held at a meeting of the States Parties to the present Covenant convened by the Secretary-General of the United Nations at the Headquarters of the United Nations. At that meeting, for which two thirds of the States Parties to the present Covenant shall constitute a quorum, the persons elected to the Committee shall be those nominees who obtain the largest number of votes and an absolute majority of the votes of the representatives of States Parties present and voting.

Article 31

1. The Committee may not include more than one national of the same State.

2. In the election of the Committee, consideration shall be given to equitable geographical distribution of membership and to the representation of the different forms of civilization and of the principal legal systems.

Article 32

1. The members of the Committee shall be elected for a term of four years. They shall be eligible for re-election if renominated. However, the terms of nine of the members elected at the first election shall expire at the end of two years; immediately after the first election, the names of these nine members shall be chosen by lot by the Chairman of the meeting referred to in Article 30, paragraph 4.

2. Elections at the expiry of office shall be held in accordance with the preceding articles of this part of the present Covenant.

Article 33

1. If, in the unanimous opinion of the other members, a member of the Committee has ceased to carry out his functions for any cause other than absence of a temporary character, the Chairman of the Committee shall notify the Secretary-General of the United Nations, who shall then declare the seat of that member to be vacant.

2. In the event of the death or the resignation of a member of the Committee, the Chairman shall immediately notify the Secretary-General of the United Nations, who shall declare the seat vacant from the date of death or the date on which the resignation takes effect.

Article 34

1. When a vacancy is declared in accordance with Article 33 and if the term of office of the member to be replaced does not expire within six months of the declaration of the vacancy, the Secretary-General of the United Nations shall notify each of the States Parties to the present Covenant, which may within two months submit nominations m accordance with Article 29 for the purpose of filling the vacancy.

2. The Secretary-General of the United Nations shall prepare a list in alphabetical order of the persons thus nominated and shall submit it to the States Parties to the present Covenant. The election to fill the vacancy shall then take place in accordance with the relevant provisions of this part of the present Covenant.

3. A member of the Committee elected to fill a vacancy declared in accordance with Article 33 shall hold office for the remainder of the term of the member who vacated the seat on the Committee under the provisions of that article.

Article 35

The members of the Committee shall, with the approval of the General Assembly of the United Nations, receive emoluments from United Nations resources on such terms and conditions as the General Assembly may decide, having regard to the importance of the Committee's responsibilities.

Article 36

The Secretary-General of the United Nations shall provide the necessary staff and facilities for the effective performance of the functions of the Committee under the present Covenant.

Article 37

1. The Secretary-General of the United Nations shall convene the initial meeting of the Committee at the Headquarters of the United Nations.

2. After its initial meeting, the Committee shall meet at such times as shall be provided in its rules of procedure.

3. The Committee shall normally meet at the Headquarters of the United Nations or at the United Nations Office at Geneva.

Article 38

Every member of the Committee shall, before taking up his duties, make a solemn declaration in open committee that he will perform his functions impartially and conscientiously.

Article 39

1. The Committee shall elect its officers for a term of two years. They may be re-elected.

2. The Committee shall establish its own rules of procedure, but these rules shall provide, *inter alia*, that:

(a) Twelve members shall constitute a quorum;

(b) Decisions of the Committee shall be made by a majority vote of the members present.

Article 40

1. The States Parties to the present Covenant undertake to submit reports on the measures they have adopted which give effect to the rights recognized herein and on the progress made in the enjoyment of those rights:

(a) Within one year of the entry into force of the present Covenant for the States Parties concerned;

(b) Thereafter whenever the Committee so requests.

2. All reports shall be submitted to the Secretary-General of the United Nations, who shall transmit them to the Committee for consideration. Reports shall indicate the factors and difficulties, if any, affecting the implementation of the present Covenant.

3. The Secretary-General of the United Nations may, after consultation with the Committee, transmit to the specialized agencies concerned copies of such parts of the reports as may fall within their field of competence.

4. The Committee shall study the reports submitted by the States Parties to the present

Covenant. It shall transmit its reports, and such general comments as it may consider appropriate, to the States Parties. The Committee may also transmit to the Economic and Social Council these comments along with the copies of the reports it has received from States Parties to the present Covenant.

5. The States Parties to the present Covenant may submit to the Committee observations on any comments that may be made in accordance with paragraph 4 of this article.

Article 41

1. A State Party to the present Covenant may at any time declare under this article that it recognizes the competence of the Committee to receive and consider communications to the effect that a State Party claims that another State Party is not fulfilling its obligations under the present Covenant. Communications under this article may be received and considered only if submitted by a State Party which has made a declaration recognizing in regard to itself the competence of the Committee. No communication shall be received by the Committee if it concerns a State Party which has not made such a declaration. Communications received under this article shall be dealt with in accordance with the following procedure:

(a) If a State Party to the present Covenant considers that another State Party is not giving effect to the provisions of the present Covenant, it may, by written communication, bring the matter to the attention of that State Party. Within three months after the receipt of the communication, the receiving State shall afford the State which sent the communication an explanation or any other statement m writing clarifying the matter, which should include, to the extent possible and pertinent, reference to domestic procedures and remedies taken, pending, or available in the matter.

(b) If the matter is not adjusted to the satisfaction of both States Parties concerned within six months after the receipt by the receiving State of the initial communication, either State shall have the right to refer the matter to the Committee, by notice given to the Committee and to the other State.

(c) The Committee shall deal with a matter referred to it only after it has ascertained that all available domestic remedies have been invoked and exhausted in the matter, in conformity with the generally recognized principles of international law. This shall not be the rule where the application of the remedies is unreasonably prolonged.

(d) The Committee shall hold closed meetings when examining communications under this article.

(e) Subject to the provisions of sub-paragraph (c), the Committee shall make available its good offices to the States Parties concerned with a view to a friendly solution of the matter on the basis of respect for human rights and fundamental freedoms as recognized in the present Covenant.

(f) In any matter referred to it, the Committee may call upon the States Parties concerned, referred to in sub-paragraph (b), to supply any relevant information.

(g) The States Parties concerned, referred to in sub-paragraph (b), shall have the right to be represented when the matter is being considered in the Committee and to make submissions orally and/or in writing.

(h) The Committee shall, within twelve months after the date of receipt of notice under sub-paragraph (b), submit a report:

(i) If a solution within the terms of sub-paragraph (e) is reached, the Committee shall confine its report to a brief statement of the facts and of the solution reached;

(ii) If a solution within the terms of sub-paragraph (e) is not reached, the Committee shall confine its report to a brief statement of the facts; the written submissions and record of the oral submissions made by the States Parties concerned shall be attached to the report. In every matter, the report shall be communicated to the States Parties concerned.

2. The provisions of this article shall come into force when ten States Parties to the present Covenant have made declarations under paragraph 1 of this article. Such declarations shall be deposited by the States Parties with the Secretary-General of the United Nations, who shall transmit copies thereof to the other States Parties. A declaration may be withdrawn at any time by notification to the Secretary-General. Such a withdrawal shall not prejudice the consideration of any matter which is the subject of a communication already transmitted under this article; no further communication by any State Party shall be received after the notification of withdrawal of the declaration has been received by the Secretary-General, unless the State Party concerned has made a new declaration.

Article 42

1. (a) If a matter referred to the Committee in accordance with Article 41 is not resolved to the satisfaction of the States Parties concerned, the Committee may, with the prior consent of the States Parties concerned, appoint an ad hoc Conciliation Commission (hereinafter referred to as the Commission). The good offices of the Commission shall be made available to the States Parties concerned with a view to an amicable solution of the matter on the basis of respect for the present Covenant;

(b) The Commission shall consist of five persons acceptable to the States Parties concerned. If the States Parties concerned fail to reach agreement within three months on all or part of the composition of the Commission, the members of the Commission concerning whom no agreement has been reached shall be elected by secret ballot by a two-thirds majority vote of the Committee from among its members.

2. The members of the Commission shall serve in their personal capacity. They shall not be nationals of the States Parties concerned, or of a State not party to the present Covenant, or of a State Party which has not made a declaration under Article 41.

3. The Commission shall elect its own Chairman and adopt its own rules of procedure.

4. The meetings of the Commission shall normally be held at the Headquarters of the United Nations or at the United Nations Office at Geneva. However, they may be held at such other convenient places as the Commission may determine in consultation with the Secretary-General of the United Nations and the States Parties concerned.

5. The secretariat provided in accordance with Article 36 shall also service the commissions appointed under this article.

6. The information received and collated by the Committee shall be made available to the Commission and the Commission may call upon the States Parties concerned to supply any other relevant information.

7. When the Commission has fully considered the matter, but in any event not later than twelve months after having been seized of the matter, it shall submit to the Chairman of the Committee a report for communication to the States Parties concerned:

(a) if the Commission is unable to complete its consideration of the matter within twelve months, it shall confine its report to a brief statement or the status of its consideration of the matter;

(b) if an amicable solution to the matter on the basis of respect for human rights as recognized in the present Covenant is reached, the Commission shall confine its report to a brief statement of the facts and of the solution reached;

(c) if a solution within the terms of sub-paragraph (b) is not reached, the Commission's report shall embody its findings on all questions of fact relevant to the issues between the States Parties concerned, and its views on the possibilities of an amicable solution of the matter. This report shall also contain the written submissions and a record of the oral submissions made by the States Parties concerned;

(d) if the Commission's report is submitted under subparagraph (c), the States Parties concerned shall, within three months of the receipt of the report, notify the Chairman of the Committee whether or not they accept the contents of the report of the Commission.

8. The provisions of this article are without prejudice to the responsibilities of the Committee under Article 41

9. The States Parties concerned shall share equally all the expenses of the members of the Commission in accordance with estimates to be provided by the Secretary-General of the United Nations.

10. The Secretary-General of the United Nations shall be empowered to pay the expenses of the members of the Commission, if necessary, before reimbursement by the States Parties concerned, in accordance with paragraph 9 of this article.

Article 43

The members of the Committee, and of the ad hoc conciliation commissions which may be appointed under Article 42, shall be entitled to the facilities, privileges and immunities of experts on mission for the United Nations as laid down in the relevant sections of the Convention on the Privileges and Immunities of the United Nations.

Article 44

The provisions for the implementation of the present Covenant shall apply without prejudice to the procedures prescribed in the field of human rights by or under the constituent instruments and the conventions of the United Nations and of the specialized agencies and shall not prevent the States Parties to the present Covenant from having recourse to other procedures for settling a dispute in accordance with general or special international agreements in force between them.

Article 45

The Committee shall submit to the General Assembly of the United Nations, through the Economic and Social Council, an annual report on its activities.

Part V

Article 46

Nothing in the present Covenant shall be interpreted as impairing the provisions of the Charter of the United Nations and of the constitutions of the specialized agencies which define the respective responsibilities of the various organs of the United Nations and of the specialized agencies in regard to the matters dealt with in the present Covenant.

Article 47

Nothing in the present Covenant shall be interpreted as impairing the inherent right of all peoples to enjoy and utilize fully and freely their natural wealth and resources.

Part VI

Article 48

1. The present Covenant is open for signature by any State Member of the United Nations or member of any of its specialized agencies, by any State Party to the Statute of the International Court of Justice, and by any other State which has been invited by the General Assembly of the United Nations to become a party to the present Covenant.

2. The present Covenant is subject to ratification. Instruments of ratification shall be deposited with the Secretary-General of the United Nations.

3. The present Covenant shall be open to accession by any State referred to in paragraph 1 of this article.

4. Accession shall be effected by the deposit of an instrument of accession with the Secretary-General of the United Nations.

5. The Secretary-General of the United Nations shall inform all States which have signed this Covenant or acceded to it of the deposit of each instrument of ratification or accession.

Article 49

1. The present Covenant shall enter into force three months after the date of the deposit with the Secretary-General of the United Nations of the thirty-fifth instrument of ratification or instrument of accession.

2. For each State ratifying the present Covenant or acceding to it after the deposit of the thirty-fifth instrument of ratification or instrument of accession, the present Covenant

shall enter into force three months after the date of the deposit of its own instrument of ratification or instrument of accession.

Article 50

The provisions of the present Covenant shall extend to all parts of federal States without any limitations or exceptions.

Article 51

1. Any State Party to the present Covenant may propose an amendment and file it with the Secretary-General of the United Nations. The Secretary-General of the United Nations shall thereupon communicate any proposed amendments to the States Parties to the present Covenant with a request that they notify him whether they favor a conference of States Parties for the purpose of considering and voting upon the proposals. In the event that at least one third of the States Parties favors such a conference, the Secretary-General shall convene the conference under the auspices of the United Nations. Any amendment adopted by a majority of the States Parties present and voting at the conference shall be submitted to the General Assembly of the United Nations for approval.

2. Amendments shall come into force when they have been approved by the General Assembly of the United Nations and accepted by a two-thirds majority of the States Parties to the present Covenant in accordance with their respective constitutional processes.

3. When amendments come into force, they shall be binding on those States Parties which have accepted them, other States Parties still being bound by the provisions of the present Covenant and any earlier amendment which they have accepted.

Article 52

Irrespective of the notifications made under Article 48, paragraph 5, the Secretary-General of the United Nations shall inform all States referred to in paragraph 1 of the following particulars:

(a) Signatures, ratifications and accessions under Article 48;

(b) The date of the entry into force of the present Covenant under Article 49 and the date of the entry into force of any amendments under Article 51.

Article 53

1. The present Covenant, of which the Chinese, English, French, Russian and Spanish texts are equally authentic, shall be deposited in the archives of the United Nations.

Second Optional Protocol, Aiming at the Abolition of the Death Penalty

U.N. G.A. Res. 44/128, 44 U.N. GAOR,
Supp. No. 49, at 206, U.N. Doc. A/44/49 (1989)

The States Parties to the present Protocol,

Believing that abolition of the death penalty contributes to enhancement of human dignity and progressive development of human rights,

Recalling Article 3 of the Universal Declaration of Human Rights, adopted on 10 December 1948, and Article 6 of the International Covenant on Civil and Political Rights, adopted on 16 December 1966,

Noting that Article 6 of the International Covenant on Civil and Political Rights refers to abolition of the death penalty in terms that strongly suggest that abolition is desirable,

Convinced that all measures of abolition of the death penalty should be considered as progress in the enjoyment of life,

Desirous to undertake hereby an international commitment to abolish the death penalty,

Have agreed as follows:

Article 1

1. No one within the jurisdiction of a State Party to the present Protocol shall be executed.

2. Each State party shall take all necessary measures to abolish the death penalty within its jurisdiction.

Article 2

1. No reservation is admissible to the present Protocol, except for a reservation made at the time of ratification or accession that provides for the application of the death penalty in time of war pursuant to a conviction for a most serious crime of a military nature committed during wartime.

2. The State Party making such a reservation shall at the time of ratification or accession communicate to the Secretary-General of the United Nations the relevant provisions of its national legislation applicable during wartime.

3. The State Party having made such a reservation shall notify the Secretary-General of the United Nations of any beginning or ending of a state of war applicable to its territory.

Article 3

The States Parties to the present Protocol shall include in the reports they submit to the Human Rights Committee, in accordance with Article 40 of the Covenant, information on the measures that they have adopted to give effect to the present Protocol.

Article 4

With respect to the States Parties to the Covenant that have made a declaration under Article 41, the competence of the Human Rights Committee to receive and consider communications when a State Party claims that another State Party is not fulfilling its obligations shall extend to the provisions of the present Protocol, unless the State Party concerned has made a statement to the contrary at the moment of ratification or accession.

Article 5

With respect to the States Parties to the first Optional Protocol to the International Covenant on Civil and Political Rights adopted on 16 December 1966, the competence of the Human Rights Committee to receive and consider communications from individuals subject to its jurisdiction shall extend to the provisions of the present Protocol, unless the State Party concerned has made a statement to the contrary at the moment of ratification or accession.

Article 6

1. The provisions of the present Protocol shall apply as additional provisions to the Covenant.

2. Without prejudice to the possibility of a reservation under Article 2 of the present Protocol, the right guaranteed in Article 1, paragraph 1, of the present Protocol shall not be subject to any derogation under Article 4 of the Covenant.

Article 9

The provisions of the present Protocol shall extend to all parts of federal States without any limitations or exceptions....

American Declaration of the Rights and Duties of Man
OAS Res. XXX (1948), OAS Off. Rec. SEA/Ser. L/V/I.4 Rev. (1965)

Preamble

All men are born free and equal, in dignity and in rights, and, being endowed by nature with reason and conscience, they should conduct themselves as brothers one to another.

The fulfillment of duty by each individual is a prerequisite to the rights of all. Rights and duties are interrelated in every social and political activity of man. While rights exalt individual liberty, duties express the dignity of that liberty.

Duties of a juridical nature presuppose others of a moral nature which support them in principle and constitute their basis.

Inasmuch as spiritual development is the supreme end of human existence and the highest expression thereof, it is the duty of man to serve that end with all his strength and resources.

Since culture is the highest social and historical expression of that spiritual development, it is the duty of man to preserve, practice and foster culture by every means within his power.

And, since moral conduct constitutes the noblest flowering of culture, it is the duty of every man always to hold it in high respect.

Chapter One. Rights

Article I. Every human being has the right to life, liberty and the security of his person.

Article II. All persons are equal before the law and have the rights and duties established in this Declaration, without distinction as to race, sex, language, creed or any other factor.

Article III. Every person has the right freely to profess a religious faith, and to manifest and practice it both in public and in private.

Article IV. Every person has the right to freedom of investigation, of opinion, and of the expression and dissemination of ideas, by any medium whatsoever.

Article V. Every person has the right to the protection of the law against abusive attacks upon his honor, his reputation, and his private and family life.

Article VI. Every person has the right to establish a family, the basic element of society, and to receive protection therefor.

Article VII. All women, during pregnancy and the nursing period, and all children have the right to special protection, care and aid.

Article VIII. Every person has the right to fix his residence within the territory of the state of which he is a national, to move about freely within such territory, and not to leave it except by his own will.

Article IX. Every person has the right to the inviolability of his home.

Article X. Every person has the right to the inviolability and transmission of his correspondence.

Article XI. Every person has the right to the preservation of his health through sanitary and social measures relating to food, clothing, housing and medical care, to the extent permitted by public and community resources.

Article XII. Every person has the right to an education, which should be based on the principles of liberty, morality and human solidarity.

Likewise every person has the right to an education that will prepare him to attain a decent life, to raise his standard of living, and to be a useful member of society.

The right to an education includes the right to equality of opportunity in every case in accordance with natural talents, merit and the desire to utilize the resources that the state or the community is in a position to provide.

Every person has the right to receive, free, at least a primary education.

Article XIII. Every person has the right to take part in the cultural life of the community, to enjoy the arts, and to participate in the benefits that result from intellectual progress, especially scientific discoveries.

He likewise has the right to the protection of his moral and material interests as regards his inventions or any literary, scientific or artistic works of which he is the author.

Article XIV. Every person has the right to work, under proper conditions, and to follow his vocation freely, in so far as existing conditions of employment permit.

Every person who works has the right to receive such remuneration as will, in proportion to his capacity and skill, assure him a standard of living suitable for himself and for his family.

Article XV. Every person has the right to leisure time, to wholesome recreation, and to the opportunity for advantageous use of his free time to his spiritual, cultural and physical benefit.

Article XVI. Every person has the right to social security which will protect him from the consequences of unemployment, old age, and any disability arising from causes beyond his control that make it physically or mentally impossible for him to earn a living.

Article XVII. Every person has the right to be recognized everywhere as a person having rights and obligations, and to enjoy the basic civil rights.

Article XVIII. Every person may resort to the courts to ensure respect for his legal rights. There should likewise be available to him a simple, brief procedure whereby the courts will protect him from acts of authority that, to his prejudice, violate any fundamental constitutional rights.

Article XIX. Every person has the right to the nationality to which he is entitled by law and to change it, if he so wishes, for the nationality of any other country that is willing to grant it to him.

Article XX. Every person having legal capacity is entitled to participate in the government of his country, directly or through his representatives, and to take part in popular elections, which shall be by secret ballot, and shall be honest, periodic and free.

Article XXI. Every person has the right to assemble peaceably with others in a formal public meeting or an informal gathering, in connection with matters of common interest of any nature.

Article XXII. Every person has the right to associate with others to promote, exercise and protect his legitimate interests of a political, economic, religious, social, cultural, professional, labor union or other nature.

Article XXIII. Every person has a right to own such private property as meets the essential needs of decent living and helps to maintain the dignity of the individual and of the home.

Article XXIV. Every person has the right to submit respectful petitions to any competent authority, for reasons of either general or private interest, and the right to obtain a prompt decision thereon.

Article XXV. No person may be deprived of his liberty except in the cases and according to the procedures established by pre-existing law.

No person may be deprived of liberty for nonfulfillment of obligations of a purely civil character.

Every individual who has been deprived of his liberty has the right to have the legality of his detention ascertained without delay by a court, and the right to be tried without undue delay, or otherwise, to be released. He also has the right to humane treatment during the time he is in custody.

Article XXVI. Every accused person is presumed to be innocent until proved guilty.

Every person accused of an offense has the right to be given an impartial and public hearing, and to be tried by courts previously established in accordance with pre-existing laws, and not to receive cruel, infamous or unusual punishment.

Article XXVII. Every person has the right, in case of pursuit not resulting from ordinary crimes, to seek and receive asylum in foreign territory, in accordance with the laws of each country and with international agreements.

Article XVIII. The rights of man are limited by the rights of others, by the security of all, and by the just demands of the general welfare and the advancement of democracy.

Chapter Two. Duties

Article XXIX. It is the duty of the individual so to conduct himself in relation to others that each and every one may fully form and develop his personality.

Article XXX. It is the duty of every person to aid, support, educate and protect his minor children, and it is the duty of children to honor their parents always and to aid, support and protect them when they need it.

Article XXXI. It is the duty of every person to acquire at least an elementary education.

Article XXXII. It is the duty of every person to vote in the popular elections of the country of which he is a national, when he is legally capable of doing so.

Article XXXIII. It is the duty of every person to obey the law and other legitimate commands of the authorities of his country and those of the country in which he may be.

Article XXXIV. It is the duty of every able-bodied person to render whatever civil and military service his country may require for its defense and preservation, and, in case of public disaster, to render such services as may be in his power.

It is likewise his duty to hold any public office to which he may be elected by popular vote in the state of which he is a national.

Article XXXV. It is the duty of every person to cooperate with the state with respect to social security and welfare, in accordance with existing circumstances.

Article XXXVI. It is the duty of every person to pay the taxes established by law for the support of public services.

Article XXXVII. It is the duty of every person to work, as far as his capacity and possibilities permit, in order to obtain the means of livelihood or to benefit his community.

Article XXXVIII. It is the duty of every person to refrain from taking part in political activities that, according to law, are reserved exclusively to the citizens of the state in which he is an alien.

American Convention on Human Rights
OAS Treaty Ser. No. 36 (1969), 144 U.N.T.S. 123

Preamble

The American states signatory to this present Convention,

Reaffirming their intention to consolidate in this hemisphere, within the framework of democratic institutions, a system of personal liberty and social justice based on respect for the essential rights of man;

Recognizing that the essential rights of man are not derived from one's being a national of a certain state, but are based upon attributes of the human personality, and that they therefore justify international protection in the form of a convention reinforcing or complementing the protection provided by the domestic law of the American states;

Considering that these principles have been set forth in the Charter of the Organization of American States, in the American Declaration of the Rights and Duties of Man, and in the Universal Declaration of Human Rights, and that they have been reaffirmed and refined in other international instruments, worldwide as well as regional in scope;

Reiterating that, in accordance with the Universal Declaration of Human Rights, the ideal of free men enjoying freedom from fear and want can be achieved only if conditions are created whereby everyone may enjoy his economic, social, and cultural rights, as well as his civil and political rights; and

Considering that the Third Special Inter-American Conference (Buenos Aires, 1967) approved the incorporation into the Charter of the Organization itself of broader standards with respect to economic, social, and educational rights and resolved that an inter-American convention on human rights should determine the structure, competence, and procedure of the organs responsible for these matters,

Have agreed upon the following:

Part I. State Obligations and Rights Protected

Chapter I. General Obligations

Article 1. Obligation to Respect Rights

1. The States Parties to this Convention undertake to respect the rights and freedoms recognized herein and to ensure to all persons subject to their jurisdiction the free and full exercise of those rights and freedoms, without any discrimination for reasons of race, color, sex, language, religion, political or other opinion, national or social origin, economic status, birth, or any other social condition.

2. For the purposes of this Convention, "person" means every human being.

Article 2. Domestic Legal Effects

Where the exercise of any of the rights or freedoms referred to in Article 1 is not already ensured by legislative or other provisions, the States Parties undertake to adopt, in accordance with their constitutional processes and the provisions of this Convention, such legislative or other measures as may be necessary to give effect to those rights or freedoms.

Chapter II. Civil and Political Rights

Article 3. Right to Juridical Personality

Every person has the right to recognition as a person before the law.

Article 4. Right to Life

1. Every person has the right to have his life respected. This right shall be protected by law, and, in general, from the moment of conception. No one shall be arbitrarily deprived of his life.

2. In countries that have not abolished the death penalty, it may be imposed only for the most serious crimes and pursuant to a final judgment rendered by a competent court and in accordance with a law establishing such punishment, enacted prior to the commission of the crime. The application of such punishment shall not be extended to crimes to which it does not presently apply.

3. The death penalty shall not be reestablished in states that have abolished it.

4. In no case shall capital punishment be inflicted for political offences or related common crimes.

5. Capital punishment shall not be imposed upon persons who, at the time the crime was committed, were under 18 years of age or over 70 years of age; nor shall it be applied to pregnant women.

6. Every person condemned to death shall have the right to apply for amnesty, pardon, or commutation of sentence, which may be granted in all cases. Capital punishment shall not be imposed while such a petition is pending decision by the competent authority.

Article 5. Right to Humane Treatment

1. Every person has the right to have his physical, mental, and moral integrity respected.

2. No one shall be subjected to torture or to cruel, inhuman, or degrading punishment or treatment. All persons deprived of their liberty shall be treated with respect for the inherent dignity of the human person.

3. Punishment shall not be extended to any person other than the criminal.

4. Accused persons shall, save in exceptional circumstances, be segregated from convicted persons, and shall be subject to separate treatment appropriate to their status as unconvicted persons.

5. Minors while subject to criminal proceedings shall be separated from adults and brought before specialized tribunals, as speedily as possible, so that they may be treated in accordance with their status as minors.

6. Punishments consisting of deprivation of liberty shall have as an essential aim the reform and social readaptation of the prisoners.

Article 6. Freedom from Slavery

1. No one shall be subject to slavery or to involuntary servitude, which are prohibited in all their forms, as are the slave trade and traffic in women.

2. No one shall be required to perform forced or compulsory labor. This provision shall not be interpreted to mean that, in those countries in which the penalty established for certain crimes is deprivation of liberty at forced labor, the carrying out of such a sentence imposed by a competent court is prohibited. Forced labor shall not adversely affect the dignity or the physical or intellectual capacity of the prisoner.

3. For the purposes of this article the following do not constitute forced or compulsory labor:

(a) work or service normally required of a person imprisoned in execution of a sentence or formal decision passed by the competent judicial authority. Such work or service shall be carried out under the supervision and control of public authorities, and any persons performing such work or service shall not be placed at the disposal of any private party, company, or juridical person;

(b) military service and, in countries in which conscientious objectors are recognized, national service that the law may provide for in lieu of military service;

(c) service exacted in time of danger or calamity that threatens the existence or the well-being of the community; or

(d) work or service that forms part of normal civil obligations.

Article 7. Right to Personal Liberty

1. Every person has the right to personal liberty and security.

2. No one shall be deprived of his physical liberty except for the reasons and under the conditions established beforehand by the constitution of the State Party concerned or by a law established pursuant thereto.

3. No one shall be subject to arbitrary arrest or imprisonment.

4. Anyone who is detained shall be informed of the reasons for his detention and shall be promptly notified of the charge or charges against him.

5. Any person detained shall be brought promptly before a judge or other officer authorized by law to exercise judicial power and shall be entitled to trial within a reasonable time or to be released without prejudice to the continuation of the proceedings. His release may be subject to guarantees to assure his appearance for trial.

6. Anyone who is deprived of his liberty shall be entitled to recourse to a competent court, in order that the court may decide without delay on the lawfulness of his arrest or detention and order his release if the arrest or detention is unlawful. In States Parties whose laws provide that anyone who believes himself to be threatened with deprivation of his liberty is entitled to recourse to a competent court in order that it may decide on the lawfulness of such threat, this remedy may not be restricted or abolished. The interested party or another person in his behalf is entitled to seek these remedies.

7. No one shall be detained for debt. This principle shall not limit the orders of a competent judicial authority issued for nonfulfillment of duties of support.

Article 8. Right to a Fair Trial

1. Every person has the right to a hearing, with due guarantees and within a reasonable time, by a competent, independent, and impartial tribunal, previously established by law, in the substantiation of any accusation of a criminal nature made against him or for the determination of his rights and obligations of a civil, labor, fiscal, or any other nature.

2. Every person accused of a criminal offense has the right to be presumed innocent so long as his guilt has not been proven according to law. During the proceedings, every person is entitled, with full equality, to the following minimum guarantees:

(a) the right of the accused to be assisted without charge by a translator or interpreter, if he does not understand or does not speak the language of the tribunal or court;

(b) prior notification in detail to the accused of the charges against him;

(c) adequate time and means for the preparation of his defense;

(d) the right of the accused to defend himself personally or to be assisted by legal counsel of his own choosing, and to communicate freely and privately with his counsel;

(e) the inalienable right to be assisted by counsel provided by the state, paid or not as the domestic law provides, if the accused does not defend himself personally or engage his own counsel within the time period established by law;

(f) the right of the defense to examine witnesses present in the court and to obtain the appearance, as witnesses, of experts or other persons who may throw light on the facts;

(g) the right not to be compelled to be a witness against himself or to plead guilty; and

(h) the right to appeal the judgment to a higher court.

3. A confession of guilt by the accused shall be valid only if it is made without coercion of any kind.

4. An accused person acquitted by a nonappealable judgment shall not be subjected to a new trial for the same cause.

5. Criminal proceedings shall be public, except insofar as may be necessary to protect the interests of justice.

Article 9. Freedom from Ex Post Facto Laws

No one shall be convicted of any act or omission that did not constitute a criminal offense, under the applicable law, at the time it was committed. A heavier penalty shall not be imposed than the one that was applicable at the time the criminal offense was committed. If subsequent to the commission of the offense the law provides for the imposition of a lighter punishment, the guilty person shall benefit therefrom.

Article 10. Right to Compensation

Every person has the right to be compensated in accordance with the law in the event he has been sentenced by a final judgment through a miscarriage of justice.

Article 11. Right to Privacy

1. Everyone has the right to have his honor respected and his dignity recognized.

2. No one may be the object of arbitrary or abusive interference with his private life, his family, his home, or his correspondence, or of unlawful attacks on his honor or reputation.

3. Everyone has the right to the protection of the law against such interference or attacks.

Article 12. Freedom of Conscience and Religion

1. Everyone has the right to freedom of conscience and religion. this right includes freedom to maintain or to change one's religion or beliefs, and freedom to profess or dis-

seminate one's religion or beliefs either individually or together with others, in public or in private.

2. No one shall be subject to restrictions that might impair his freedom to maintain or to change his religion or beliefs.

3. Freedom to manifest one's religion and beliefs may be subject only to the limitations prescribed by law that are necessary to protect public safety, order, health, or morals, or the rights or freedoms of others.

4. Parents or guardians, as the case may be, have the right to provide for the religious and moral education of their children or wards that is in accord with their own convictions.

Article 13. Freedom of Thought and Expression

1. Everyone shall have the right to freedom of thought and expression. This right shall include freedom to seek, receive, and impart information and ideas of all kinds, regardless of frontiers, either orally, in writing, in print, in the form of art, or through any other medium of his choice.

2. The exercise of the right provided for in the foregoing paragraph shall not be subject to prior censorship but shall be subject to subsequent imposition of liability, which shall be expressly established by law to the extent necessary in order to ensure:

(a) respect for the rights or reputations of others; or

(b) the protection of national security, public order, or public health or morals.

3. The right of expression may not be restricted by indirect methods or means, such as the abuse of government or private controls over newsprint, radio broadcasting frequencies, or equipment used in the dissemination of information, or by any other means tending to impede the communication and circulation of ideas and opinions.

4. Notwithstanding the provisions of paragraph 2 above, public entertainments may be subject by law to prior censorship for the sole purpose of regulating access to them for the moral protection of childhood and adolescence.

5. Any propaganda for war and any advocacy of national, racial, or religious hatred that constitute incitements to lawless violence or to any other similar illegal action against any person or group of persons on any grounds including those of race, color, religion, language, or national origin shall be considered as offenses punishable by law.

Article 14. Right of Reply

1. Anyone injured by inaccurate or offensive statements or ideas disseminated to the public in general by a legally regulated medium of communication has the right to reply or make a correction using the same communications outlet, under such conditions as the law may establish.

2. The correction or reply shall not in any case remit other legal liabilities that may have been incurred.

3. For the effective protection of honor and reputation, every publisher, and every newspaper, motion picture, radio, and television company, shall have a person responsible, who is not protected by immunities or special privileges.

Article 15. Right of Assembly

The right of peaceful assembly, without arms, is recognized. No restrictions may be placed on the exercise of this right other than those imposed in conformity with the law and necessary in a democratic society in the interest of national security, public safety, or public order, or to protect public health, or morals or the rights or freedoms of others.

Article 16. Freedom of Association

1. Everyone has the right to associate freely for ideological, religious, political, economic, labor, social, cultural, sports, or other purposes.

2. The exercise of this right shall be subject only to such restrictions established by law as may be necessary in a democratic society, in the interest of national security, public safety, or public order, or to protect public health or morals or the rights and freedoms of others.

3. The provisions of this article do not bar the imposition of legal restrictions, including even deprivation of the exercise of the right of association, on members of the armed forces and the police.

Article 17. Rights of the Family

1. The family is the natural and fundamental group unit of society and is entitled to protection by society and the state.

2. The right of men and women of marriageable age to marry and to raise a family shall be recognized, if they meet the conditions required by domestic laws, insofar as such conditions do not affect the principle of nondiscrimination established in this Convention.

3. No marriage shall be entered into without the free and full consent of the intending spouses.

4. The States Parties shall take appropriate steps to ensure the equality of rights and the adequate balancing of responsibilities of the spouses as to marriage, during marriage, and in the event of its dissolution. In case of dissolution, provision shall be made for the necessary protection of any children solely on the basis of their own best interests.

5. The law shall recognize equal rights for children born out of wedlock and those born in wedlock.

Article 18. Right to a Name

Every person has the right to a given name and to the surnames of his parents or that of one of them. The law shall regulate the manner in which this right shall be ensured for all, by the use of assumed names if necessary.

Article 19. Rights of the Child

Every minor child has the right to the measures of protection required by his condition as a minor on the part of his family, society, and the state.

Article 20. Right to Nationality

1. Every person has the right to a nationality.

2. Every person has the right to the nationality of the state in whose territory he was born if he does not have the right to any other nationality.

3. No one shall be arbitrarily deprived of his nationality or of the right to change it.

Article 21. Right to Property

1. Everyone has the right to the use and enjoyment of his property. The law may subordinate such use and enjoyment to the interest of society.

2. No one shall be deprived of his property except upon payment of just compensation, for reasons of public utility or social interest, and in the cases and according to the forms established by law.

3. Usury and any other form of exploitation of man by man shall be prohibited by law.

Article 22. Freedom of Movement and Residence

1. Every person lawfully in the territory of a State Party has the right to move about in it and to reside in it subject to the provisions of the law.

2. Every person has the right to leave any country freely, including his own.

3. The exercise of the foregoing rights may be restricted only pursuant to a law to the extent necessary in a democratic society to prevent crime or to protect national security, public safety, public order, public morals, public health, or the rights or freedoms of others.

4. The exercise of the rights recognized in paragraph 1 may also be restricted by law in designated zones for reasons of public interest.

5. No one can be expelled from the territory of the state of which he is a national or be deprived of the right to enter it.

6. An alien lawfully in the territory of a State Party to this Convention may be expelled from it only pursuant to a decision reached in accordance with law.

7. Every person has the right to seek and be granted asylum in a foreign territory, in accordance with the legislation of the state and international conventions, in the event he is being pursued for political offenses or related common crimes.

8. In no case may an alien be deported or returned to a country, regardless of whether or not it is his country of origin, if in that country his right to life or personal freedom is in danger of being violated because of his race, nationality, religion, social status, or political opinions.

9. The collective expulsion of aliens is prohibited.

Article 23. Right to Participate in Government

1. Every citizen shall enjoy the following rights and opportunities:

(a) to take part in the conduct of public affairs, directly or through freely chosen representatives;

(b) to vote and to be elected in genuine periodic elections, which shall be by universal and equal suffrage and by secret ballot that guarantees the free expression of the will of the voters; and

(c) to have access, under general conditions of equality, to the public services of his country.

2. The law may regulate the exercise of the rights and opportunities referred to in the preceding paragraph only on the basis of age, nationality, residence, language, education, civil and mental capacity, or sentencing by a competent court in criminal proceedings.

Article 24. Right to Equal Protection

All persons are equal before the law. Consequently, they are entitled, without discrimination, to equal protection of the law.

Article 25. Right to Judicial Protection

1. Everyone has the right to simple and prompt recourse, or any other effective recourse, to a competent court or tribunal for protection against acts that violate his fundamental rights recognized by the constitution or laws of the state concerned or by this Convention, even though such violation may have been committed by persons acting in the course of their official duties.

2. The States Parties undertake:

(a) to ensure that any person claiming such remedy shall have his rights determined by the competent authority provided for by the legal system of the state;

(b) to develop the possibilities of judicial remedy; and

(c) to ensure that the competent authorities shall enforce such remedies when granted.

Chapter III. Economic, Social, and Cultural Rights

Article 26. Progressive Development

The States Parties undertake to adopt measures, both internally and through international cooperation, especially those of an economic and technical nature, with a view to achieving progressively, by legislation or other appropriate means, the full realization of the rights implicit in the economic, social, educational, scientific, and cultural standards set forth in the Charter of the Organization of American States as amended by the Protocol of Buenos Aires.

Chapter IV. Suspension of Guarantees, Interpretation, and Application

Article 27. Suspension of Guarantees

1. In time of war, public danger, or other emergency that threatens the independence or security of a State Party, it may take measures derogating from its obligations under the present Convention to the extent and for the period of time strictly required by the exigencies of the situation, provided that such measures are not inconsistent with its other obligations under international law and do not involve discrimination on the ground of race, color, sex, language, religion, or social origin.

2. The foregoing provision does not authorize any suspension of the following articles: Article 3 (Right to Juridical Personality), Article 4 (Right to Life), Article 5 (Right to Humane Treatment), Article 6 (Freedom from Slavery), Article 9 (Freedom from Ex Post Facto Laws), Article 12 (Freedom of Conscience and Religion), Article 17 (Rights of the Family), Article 18 (Right to a Name), Article 19 (Rights of the Child), Article 20 (Right to Nationality), and Article 23 (Right to Participate in Government), or of the judicial guarantees essential for the protection of such rights.

3. Any State Party availing itself of the right of suspension shall immediately inform the other States Parties, through the Secretary General of the Organization of American States, of the provisions the application of which it has suspended, the reasons that gave rise to the suspension, and the date set for the termination of such suspension.

Article 28. Federal Clause

1. Where a State Party is constituted as a federal state, the national government of such State Party shall implement all the provisions of the Convention over whose subject matter it exercises legislative and judicial jurisdiction.

2. With respect to the provisions over whose subject matter the constituent units of the federal state have jurisdiction, the national government shall immediately take suitable measures, in accordance with its constitution and its laws, to the end that the competent authorities of the constituent units may adopt appropriate provisions for the fulfillment of this Convention.

3. Whenever two or more States Parties agree to form a federation or other type of association, they shall take care that the resulting federal or other compact contains the

provisions necessary for continuing and rendering effective the standards of this Convention in the new state that is organized.

Article 29. Restrictions Regarding Interpretation

No provision of this Convention shall be interpreted as:

(a) permitting any State Party, group, or person to suppress the enjoyment or exercise of the rights and freedoms recognized in this Convention or to restrict them to a greater extent than is provided for herein;

(b) restricting the enjoyment or exercise of any right or freedom recognized by virtue of the laws of any State Party or by virtue of another convention to which one of the said states is a party;

(c) precluding other rights or guarantees that are inherent in the human personality or derived from representative democracy as a form of government; or

(d) excluding or limiting the effect that the American Declaration of the Rights and Duties of Man and other international acts of the same nature may have.

Article 30. Scope of Restrictions

The restrictions that, pursuant to this Convention, may be placed on the enjoyment or exercise of the rights or freedoms recognized herein may not be applied except in accordance with laws enacted for reasons of general interest and in accordance with the purpose for which such restrictions have been established.

Article 31. Recognition of Other Rights

Other rights and freedoms recognized in accordance with the procedures established in Articles 76 and 77 may be included in the system of protection of this Convention.

Chapter V. Personal Responsibilities

Article 32. Relationship Between Duties and Rights

1. Every person has responsibilities to his family, his community, and mankind.

2. The rights of each person are limited by the rights of others, by the security of all, and by the just demands of the general welfare, in a democratic society.

Part III. Means of Protection

Chapter VI. Competent Organs

Article 33

The following organs shall have competence with respect to matters relating to the fulfillment of the commitments made by the States Parties to this Convention:

(a) the Inter-American Commission on Human Rights, referred to as "The Commission"; and

(b) the Inter-American Court of Human Rights, referred to as "The Court."

Chapter VII. Inter-American Commission on Human Rights

Section 1. Organization

Article 34

The Inter-American Commission on Human Rights shall be composed of seven members, who shall be persons of high moral character and recognized competence in the field of human rights.

Article 35

The Commission shall represent all the member countries of the Organization of American States.

Article 36

1. The Members of the Commission shall be elected in a personal capacity by the General Assembly of the Organization from a list of candidates proposed by the governments of the member states....

Section 2. Functions

Article 41

The main functions of the Commission shall be to promote respect for and defense of human rights. In the exercise of its mandate it shall have the following functions and powers:

(a) to develop an awareness of human rights among the peoples of America;

(b) to make recommendations to the governments of the member states, when it considers such action advisable, for the adoption of progressive measures in favor of human rights within the framework of their domestic law and constitutional provisions as well as appropriate measures to further the observance of those rights;

(c) to prepare such studies or reports as it considers advisable in the performance of its duties;

(d) to request the governments of the member states to supply it with information on the measures adopted by them in matters of human rights;

(e) to respond, through the General Secretariat of the Organization of American States, to inquiries made by the member states on matters related to human rights and, within the limits of its possibilities, to provide those states with the advisory services they request;

(f) to take action on petitions and other communications pursuant to its authority, under the provisions of Article 44 through 51 of this Convention; and

(g) to submit an annual report to the General Assembly of the Organization of American States.

Article 42

The States Parties shall transmit to the Commission a copy of each of the reports and studies that they submit annually to the Executive Committees of the Inter-American Economic and Social Council and the Inter-American Council for Education, Science, and Culture, in their respective fields, so that the Commission may watch over the promotion of the rights implicit in the economic, social, educational, scientific, and cultural standards set forth in the Charter of the Organization of American States as amended by the Protocol of Buenos Aires.

Article 43

The States Parties undertake to provide the Commission with such information as it may request of them as to the manner in which their domestic law ensures the effective application of any provisions of this Convention.

Section 3. Competence

Article 44

Any person or group of persons, or any nongovernmental entity legally recognized in one or more member states of the Organization, may lodge petitions with the Commission containing denunciations or complaints of violation of this Convention by a State Party.

Article 45

1. Any State Party may, when it deposits its instrument of ratification of or adherence to this Convention, or at any later time, declare that it recognizes the competence of the Commission to receive and examine communications in which a State Party alleges that another State Party has committed a violation of a human right set forth in this Convention.

2. Communications presented by virtue of this article may be admitted and examined only if they are presented by a State Party that has made a declaration recognizing the aforementioned competence of the Commission. The Commission shall not admit any communication against a State Party that has not made such a declaration.

3. A declaration concerning recognition of competence may be made to be valid for an indefinite time, for a specified period, or for a specific case.

4. Declarations shall be deposited with the General Secretariat of the Organization of American States, which shall transmit copies thereof to the member states of that Organization.

Article 46

1. Admission by the Commission of a petition or communication lodged in accordance with Articles 44 or 45 shall be subject to the following requirements:

(a) that the remedies under domestic law have been pursued and exhausted, in accordance with generally recognized principles of international law;

(b) that the petition or communication is lodged within a period of six months from the date on which the party alleging violation of his rights was notified of the final judgment;

(c) that the subject of the petition or communication is not pending before another international procedure for settlement; and

(d) that, in the case of Article 44, the petition contains the name, nationality, profession, domicile, and signature of the person or persons or of the legal representative of the entity lodging the petition.

2. The provisions of paragraphs 1 (a) and 1 (b) of this article shall not be applicable when:

(a) the domestic legislation of the state concerned does not afford due process of law for the protection of the right or rights that have allegedly been violated;

(b) the party alleging violation of his rights has been denied access to the remedies under domestic law or has been prevented from exhausting them; or

(c) there has been unwarranted delay in rendering a final judgment under the aforementioned remedies.

Article 47

The Commission shall consider inadmissible any petition or communication submitted under Articles 44 or 45 if:

(a) any of the requirements indicated in Article 46 has not been met;

(b) the petition or communication does not state facts that tend to establish a violation of the rights guaranteed by this Convention;

(c) the statements of the petitioner or of the state indicate that the petition or communication is manifestly groundless or obviously out of order; or

(d) the petition or communication is substantially the same as one previously studied by the Commission or by another international organization.

Section 4. Procedure

Article 48

1. When the Commission receives a petition or communication alleging violation of any of the rights protected by this Convention, it shall proceed as follows:

(a) If it considers the petition or communication admissible, it shall request information from the government of the state indicated as being responsible for the alleged violations and shall furnish that government a transcript of the pertinent portions of the petition or communication. This information shall be submitted within a reasonable period to be determined by the Commission in accordance with the circumstances of each case.

(b) After the information has been received, or after the period established has elapsed and the information has not been received, the Commission shall ascertain whether the grounds for the petition or communication still exist. If they do not, the Commission shall order the record to be closed.

(c) The Commission may also declare the petition or communication inadmissible or out of order on the basis of information or evidence subsequently received.

(d) If the record has not been closed, the Commission shall, with the knowledge of the parties, examine the matter set forth in the petition or communication in order to verify the facts. If necessary and advisable, the Commission shall carry out an investigation, for the effective conduct of which it shall request, and the state concerned shall furnish to it, all necessary facilities.

(e) The Commission may request the states concerned to furnish any pertinent information and, if so requested, shall hear oral statements or receive written statements from the parties concerned.

(f) The Commission shall place itself at the disposal of the parties concerned with a view to reaching a friendly settlement of the matter on the basis of respect for the human rights recognized in this Convention.

2. However, in serious and urgent cases, only the presentation of a petition or communication that fulfills all the formal requirements of admissibility shall be necessary in order for the Commission to conduct an investigation with the prior consent of the state in whose territory a violation has allegedly been committed.

Article 49

If a friendly settlement has been reached in accordance with paragraph 1 (f) of Article 48, the Commission shall draw up a report, which shall be transmitted to the petitioner and to the States Parties to this Convention, and shall then be communicated to the Secretary General of the Organization of American States for publication. This report shall contain a brief statement of the facts and of the solution reached. If any party in the case so requests, the fullest possible information shall be provided to it.

Article 50

1. If a settlement is not reached, the Commission shall, within the time limit established by its Statute, draw up a report setting forth the facts and stating its conclusions. If the report, in whole or in part, does not represent the unanimous agreement of the members of the Commission, any member may attach to it a separate opinion. The written and oral statements made by the parties in accordance with paragraph 1 (e) of Article 48 shall also be attached to the report.

2. The report shall be transmitted to the states concerned, which shall not be at liberty to publish it.

3. In transmitting the report, the Committee may make such proposals and recommendations as it sees fit.

Article 51

1. If, within a period of three months from the date of the transmittal of the report of the Commission to the states concerned, the matter has not either been settled or submitted by the Commission or by the state concerned to the Court and its jurisdiction accepted, the Commission may, by the vote of an absolute majority of its members, set forth its opinion and conclusions concerning the question submitted for its consideration.

2. Where appropriate, the Commission shall make pertinent recommendations and shall prescribe a period within which the state is to take the measures that are incumbent upon it to remedy the situation examined.

3. When the prescribed period has expired, the Commission shall decide by the vote of an absolute majority of its members whether the state has taken adequate measures and whether to publish its report.

Chapter VIII. Inter-American Court of Human Rights

Section 1. Organization

Article 52

1. The Court shall consist of seven judges, nationals of the member states of the Organization, elected in an individual capacity from among jurists of the highest moral authority and of recognized competence in the field of human rights, who possess the qualifications required for the exercise of the highest judicial functions in conformity with the law of the state of which they are nationals or of the state that proposes them as candidates.

2. No two judges may be nationals of the same state.

Article 55

1. If a judge is a national of any of the States Parties to a case submitted to the Court, he shall retain his right to hear the case.

2. If one of the judges called upon to hear a case should be a national of one of the States Parties to the case, any other State Party in the case may appoint a person of its choice to serve on the Court as an *ad hoc* judge.

3. If among the judges called upon to hear a case none is a national of any of the States Parties to the case, each of the latter may appoint an *ad hoc* judge.

4. An *ad hoc* judge shall possess the qualifications indicated in Article 52.

5. If several States Parties should have the same interest in a case, they shall be considered as a single party for purposes of the above provisions. In case of doubt, the Court shall decide.

Article 56

Five judges shall constitute a quorum for the transaction of business by the Court.

Article 57

The Commission shall appear in all cases before the Court....

Article 60

The Court shall draw up its Statute which it shall submit to the General Assembly for approval. It shall adopt its own Rules of Procedure.

Section 2. Jurisdiction and Functions

Article 61

1. Only the States Parties and the Commission shall have the right to submit a case to the Court.

2. In order for the Court to hear a case, it is necessary that the procedures set forth in Articles 48 to 50 shall have been completed.

Article 62

1. A State Party may, upon depositing its instrument of ratification or adherence to this Convention, or at any subsequent time, declare that it recognizes as binding, *ipso facto,* and not requiring special agreement, the jurisdiction of the Court on all matters relating to the interpretation or application of this Convention.

2. Such declaration may be made unconditionally, on the condition of reciprocity, for a specified period, or for specific cases. It shall be presented to the Secretary General of the Organization, who shall transmit copies thereof to the other member states of the Organization and to the Secretary of the Court.

3. The jurisdiction of the Court shall comprise all cases concerning the interpretation and application of the provisions of this Convention that are submitted to it, provided that the States Parties to the case recognize or have recognized such jurisdiction, whether by special declaration pursuant to the preceding paragraphs, or by a special agreement.

Article 63

1. If the Court finds that there has been a violation of a right or freedom protected by this Convention, the Court shall rule that the injured party be ensured the enjoyment of his right or freedom that was violated. It shall also rule, if appropriate, that the consequences of the measure or situation that constituted the breach of such right or freedom be remedied and that fair compensation be paid to the injured party.

2. In cases of extreme gravity and urgency, and when necessary to avoid irreparable damage to persons, the Court shall adopt such provisional measures as it deems pertinent in matters it has under consideration. With respect to a case not yet submitted to the Court, it may act at the request of the Commission.

Article 64

1. The member states of the Organization may consult the Court regarding the interpretation of this Convention or of other treaties concerning the protection of human

rights in the American States. Within their spheres of competence, the organs listed in Chapter X of the Charter of the Organization of American States, as amended by the Protocol of Buenos Aires, may in like manner consult the Court.

2. The Court, at the request of a member state of the Organization, may provide that state with opinions regarding the compatibility of any of its domestic laws with the aforesaid international instruments.

Article 65

To each regular session of the General Assembly of the Organization of American States the Court shall submit, for the Assembly's consideration, a report on its work during the previous year. It shall specify, in particular, the cases in which a state has not complied with its judgments, making any pertinent recommendations.

Section 3. Procedure

Article 66

1. Reasons shall be given for the judgment of the Court.

2. If the judgment does not represent in whole or in part the unanimous opinion of the judges, any judge shall be entitled to have his dissenting or separate opinion attached to the judgment.

Article 67

The judgment of the Court shall be final and not subject to appeal. In case of disagreement as to the meaning or scope of the judgment, the Court shall interpret it at the request of any of the parties, provided the request is made within ninety days from the date of notification of the judgment.

Article 68

1. The States Parties to the Convention undertake to comply with the judgment of the Court in any case to which they are parties.

2. That part of a judgment that stipulates compensatory damages may be executed in the country concerned in accordance with domestic procedure governing the execution of judgments against the state.

Article 69

The parties to the case shall be notified of the judgment of the Court and it shall be transmitted to the States Parties to the Convention....

Protocol to the American Convention on Human Rights to Abolish the Death Penalty
OAS T.S. No. 73, OAS G.A. Res. 1042, 20th Sess. (8 June 1990)

Article 1

The States Parties to this Protocol shall not apply the death penalty in their territory to any person subject to their jurisdiction.

Article 2

1. No reservations may be made to this Protocol. However, at the time of ratification or accession, the States Parties to this instrument may declare that they reserve the right

to apply the death penalty in wartime in accordance with international law, for extremely serious crimes of a military nature.

2. The State Party making this reservation shall, upon ratification or accession, inform the Secretary General of the Organization of American States of the pertinent provisions of its national legislation applicable in wartime, as referred to in the preceding paragraph.

3. Said State Party shall notify the Secretary General of the Organization of American States of the beginning or end of any state of war in effect in its territory.

Statute of the Inter-American Commission on Human Rights
reprinted in Basic Documents pertaining to Human Rights in the Inter-American System, OAS Doc. OEA/Ser. L.V/II.82, doc. 6, rev. 1, at 93 (1992)

I. Nature and Purposes

Article 1

1. The Inter-American Commission on Human Rights is an organ of the Organization of the American States, created to promote the observance and defense of human rights and to serve as consultative organ of the Organization in this matter.

2. For the purposes of the present Statute, human rights are understood to be:

a. The rights set forth in the American Convention on Human Rights, in relation to the States Parties thereto;

b. The rights set forth in the American Declaration of the Rights and Duties of Man, in relation to the other member states.

II. Membership and Structure

Article 2

1. The Inter-American Commission on Human Rights shall be composed of seven members, who shall be persons of high moral character and recognized competence in the field of human rights.

2. The Commission shall represent all the member states of the Organization.

Article 3

1. The members of the Commission shall be elected in a personal capacity by the General Assembly of the Organization from a list of candidates proposed by the governments of the member states....

Article 6

The members of the Commission shall be elected for a term of four years and may be reelected only once. Their terms of office shall begin on January 1 of the year following the year in which they are elected.

Article 7

No two nationals of the same state may be members of the Commission.

Article 8

1. Membership on the Inter-American Commission on Human Rights is incompatible with engaging in other functions that might affect the independence or impartiality of the member or the dignity or prestige of his post on the Commission.

2. The Commission shall consider any case that may arise regarding incompatibility in accordance with the provisions of the first paragraph of this article, and in accordance with the procedures provided by its Regulations. If the Commission decides, by an affirmative vote of a least five of its members, that a case of incompatibility exists, it will submit the case, with its background, to the General Assembly for decision.

3. A declaration of incompatibility by the General Assembly shall be adopted by a majority of two thirds of the member states of the Organization and shall occasion the immediate removal of the member of the Commission from his post, but it shall not invalidate any action in which he may have participated.

Article 9

The duties of the members of the Commission are:

1. Except when justifiably prevented, to attend the regular and special meetings the

Commission holds at its permanent headquarters or in any other place to which it may have decided to move temporarily.

2. To serve, except when justifiably prevented, on the special committees which the

Commission may form to conduct on-site observations, or to perform any other duties within their ambit.

3. To maintain absolute secrecy about all matters which the Commission deems confidential.

4. To conduct themselves in their public and private life as befits the high moral authority of the office and the importance of the mission entrusted to the Commission.

Article 12

1. In those member states of the Organization that are Parties to the American Convention on Human Rights, the members of the Commission shall enjoy, from the time of their election and throughout their term of office, such immunities as are granted to diplomatic agents under international law. While in office, they shall also enjoy the diplomatic privileges required for the performance of their duties.

2. In those member states of the Organization that are not Parties to the American Convention on Human Rights, the members of the Commission shall enjoy the privileges and immunities pertaining to their posts that are required for them to perform their duties with independence.

3. The system of privileges and immunities of the members of the Commission may be regulated or supplemented by multilateral or bilateral agreements between the Organization and the member states....

III. Headquarters and Meetings

Article 16

1. The headquarters of the Commission shall be in Washington, D.C.

2. The Commission may move to and meet in the territory of any American State when it so decides by an absolute majority of votes, and with the consent, or at the invitation of the government concerned.

3. The Commission shall meet in regular and special sessions, in conformity with the provisions of the Regulations.

Article 17

1. An absolute majority of the members of the Commission shall constitute a quorum.

2. In regard to those States that are Parties to the Convention, decisions shall be taken by an absolute majority vote of the members of the Commission in those cases established by the American Convention on Human Rights and the present Statute. In other cases, an absolute majority of the members present shall be required.

3. In regard to those States that are not Parties to the Convention, decisions shall be taken by an absolute majority vote of the members of the Commission, except in matters of procedure, in which case, the decisions shall be taken by simple majority.

IV. Functions and Powers

Article 18

The Commission shall have the following powers with respect to the member states of the Organization of American States:

a. to develop an awareness of human rights among the peoples of the Americas;

b. to make recommendations to the governments of the states on the adoption of progressive measures in favor of human rights in the framework of their legislation, constitutional provisions and international commitments, as well as appropriate measures to further observance of those rights;

c. to prepare such studies or reports as it considers advisable for the performance of its duties;

d. to request that the governments of the states provide it with reports on measures they adopt in matters of human rights;

e. to respond to inquiries made by any member state through the General Secretariat of the Organization on matters related to human rights in the state and, within its possibilities, to provide those states with the advisory services they request;

f. to submit an annual report to the General Assembly of the Organization, in which due account shall be taken of the legal regime applicable to those States Parties to the American Convention on Human Rights and of that system applicable to those that are not Parties;

g. to conduct on-site observations in a state, with the consent or at the invitation of the government in question; and

h. to submit the program-budget of the Commission to the Secretary General, so that he may present it to the General Assembly.

Article 19

With respect to the States Parties to the American Convention on Human Rights, the Commission shall discharge its duties in conformity with the powers granted under the Convention and in the present Statute, and shall have the following powers in addition to those designated in Article 18:

a. to act on petitions and other communications, pursuant to the provisions of Articles 44 to 51 of the Convention;

b. to appear before the Inter-American Court of Human Rights in cases provided for in the Convention;

c. to request the Inter-American Court of Human Rights to take such provisional measures as it considers appropriate in serious and urgent cases which have not yet been submitted before it for consideration, whenever this becomes necessary to prevent irreparable injury to persons;

d. to consult the Court on the interpretation of the American Convention on Human Rights or of other treaties concerning the protection of human rights in the American states;

e. to submit additional draft protocols to the American Convention on Human Rights to the General Assembly, in order to progressively include other rights and freedoms under the system of protection of the Convention; and

f. to submit to the General Assembly, through the Secretary General, proposed amendments to the American Convention on Human Rights, for such action as the General Assembly deems appropriate.

Article 20

In relation to those member states of the Organization that are not parties to the American Convention on Human Rights, the Commission shall have the following powers, in addition to those designated in Article 18:

a. to pay particular attention to the observance of the human rights referred to in Articles I, II, III, IV, XVIII, XXV, and XXVI of the American Declaration of the Rights and Duties of Man;

b. to examine communications submitted to it and any other available information, to address the government of any member state not a Party to the Convention for information deemed pertinent by this Commission, and to make recommendations to it, when it finds this appropriate, in order to bring about more effective observance of fundamental human rights; and

c. to verify, as a prior condition to the exercise of the powers granted under subparagraph b above, whether the domestic legal procedures and remedies of each member state not a Party to the Convention have been duly applied and exhausted.

V. Secretariat

Article 21

1. The Secretariat services of the Commission shall be provided by a specialized administrative unit under the direction of an Executive Secretary. This unit shall be provided with the resources and staff required to accomplish the tasks the Commission may assign to it.

2. The Executive Secretary, who shall be a person of high moral character and recognized competence in the field of human rights, shall be responsible for the work of the Secretariat and shall assist the Commission in the performance of its duties in accordance with the Regulations.

3. The Executive Secretary shall be appointed by the Secretary General of the Organization, in consultation with the Commission. Furthermore, for the Secretary General to be able to remove the Executive Secretary, he shall consult with the Commission and inform its members of the reasons for his decision.

VI. Statute and Regulations

Article 22

1. The present Statute may be amended by the General Assembly.

2. The Commission shall prepare and adopt its own Regulations, in accordance with the present Statute.

Article 23

1. In accordance with the provisions of Articles 44 to 51 of the American Convention on Human Rights, the Regulations of the Commission shall determine the procedure to be followed in cases of petitions or communications alleging violation of any of the rights guaranteed by the Convention, and imputing such violation to any State Party to the Convention.

2. If the friendly settlement referred to in Articles 44 to 51 of the Convention is not reached, the Commission shall draft, within 180 days, the report required by Article 50 of the Convention.

Article 24

1. The Regulations shall establish the procedure to be followed in cases of communications containing accusations or complaints of violations of human rights imputable to States that are not Parties to the American Convention on Human Rights....

African [Banjul] Charter on Human and Peoples' Rights
1520 U.N.T.S. 217 (1981)

Preamble

The African States members of the Organization of African Unity, parties to the present convention entitled "Banjul Charter on Human and Peoples' Rights,"

Recalling Decision 115 (XVI) of the Assembly of Heads of State and Government at its Sixteenth Ordinary Session held in Monrovia, Liberia, from 17 to 20 July 1979 on the preparation of "a preliminary draft on an African Charter on Human and Peoples' Rights providing *inter alia* for the establishment of bodies to promote and protect human and peoples' rights";

Considering the Charter of the Organization of African Unity, which stipulates that "freedom, equality, justice and dignity are essential objectives for the achievement of the legitimate aspirations of the African peoples";

Reaffirming the pledge they solemnly made in Article 2 of the said Charter to eradicate all forms of colonialism from Africa, to coordinate and intensify their cooperation and efforts to achieve a better life for the peoples of Africa and to promote international cooperation having due regard to the Charter of the United Nations and the Universal Declaration of Human Rights;

Taking into consideration the virtues of their historical tradition and the values of African civilization which should inspire and characterize their reflection on the concept of human and peoples' rights;

Recognizing on the one hand, that fundamental human rights stem from the attributes of human beings, which justifies their international protection and on the other hand that the reality and respect of peoples' rights should necessarily guarantee human rights;

Considering that the enjoyment of rights and freedom also implies the performance of duties on the part of everyone;

Convinced that it is henceforth essential to pay particular attention to the right to development and that civil and political rights cannot be dissociated from economic, social and cultural rights in their conception as well as universality and that the satisfaction of economic, social and cultural rights is a guarantee for the enjoyment of civil and political rights;

Conscious of their duty to achieve the total liberation of Africa, the peoples of which are still struggling for their dignity and genuine independence, and undertaking to eliminate colonialism, neo-colonialism, apartheid, zionism and to dismantle aggressive foreign military bases and all forms of discrimination, particularly those based on race, ethnic group, colour, sex, language, religion or political opinion;

Reaffirming their adherence to the principles of human and peoples' rights and freedoms contained in the declarations, conventions and other instruments adopted by the Organization of African Unity, the Movement of Non-Aligned Countries and the United Nations;

Firmly convinced of the duty to promote and protect human and peoples' rights and freedoms taking into account the importance traditionally attached to these rights and freedoms in Africa;

Have agreed as follows:

Part I. Rights and Duties

Chapter I. Human and Peoples' Rights

Article 1

The Member States of the Organization of African Unity parties to the present Charter shall recognize the rights, duties and freedoms enshrined in this Charter and shall undertake to adopt legislative or other measures to give effect to them.

Article 2

Every individual shall be entitled to the enjoyment of the rights and freedoms recognized in the present Charter without distinction of any kind such as race, ethnic group, colour, sex, language, religion, political or any other opinion, national and social origin, fortune, birth or other status.

Article 3

1. Every individual shall be equal before the law.

2. Every individual shall be entitled to equal protection of the law.

Article 4

Human beings are inviolable. Every human being shall be entitled to respect for his life and the integrity of his person. No one may be arbitrarily deprived of this right.

Article 5

Every individual shall have the right to the respect of the dignity inherent in a human being and to the recognition of his legal status. All forms of exploitation and degradation of man, particularly slavery, slave trade, torture, cruel, inhuman or degrading punishment or treatment shall be prohibited.

Article 6

Every individual shall have the right to liberty and to the security of his person. No one may be deprived of his freedom except for reasons and conditions previously laid down by law. In particular, no one may be arbitrarily arrested or detained.

Article 7

1. Every individual shall have the right to have his cause heard. This comprises:

   a. The right to an appeal to competent national organs against acts violating his fundamental rights as recognized and guaranteed by conventions, laws, regulations and customs in force;

b. The right to be presumed innocent until proved guilty by a competent court or tribunal;

c. The right to defence, including the right to be defended by counsel of his choice;

d. The right to be tried within a reasonable time by an impartial court or tribunal.

2. No one may be condemned for an act or omission which did not constitute a legally punishable offence at the time it was committed. No penalty may be inflicted for an offence for which no provision was made at the time it was committed. Punishment is personal and can be imposed only on the offender.

Article 8

Freedom of conscience, the profession and free practice of religion shall be guaranteed. No one may, subject to law and order, be submitted to measures restricting the exercise of these freedoms.

Article 9

1. Every individual shall have the right to receive information.

2. Every individual shall have the right to express and disseminate his opinions within the law.

Article 10

1. Every individual shall have the right to free association provided that he abides by the law.

2. Subject to the obligation of solidarity provided for in Article 29 no one may be compelled to join an association.

Article 11

Every individual shall have the right to assemble freely with others. The exercise of this right shall be subject only to necessary restrictions provided for by law in particular those enacted in the interest of national security, the safety, health, ethics and rights and freedoms of others.

Article 12

1. Every individual shall have the right to freedom of movement and residence within the borders of a State provided he abides by the law.

2. Every individual shall have the right to leave any country including his own, and to return to his country. This right may only be subject to restrictions provided for by law for the protection of national security, law and order, public health or morality.

3. Every individual shall have the right, when persecuted, to seek and obtain asylum in other countries in accordance with the laws of those countries and international conventions.

4. A non-national legally admitted in a territory of a State Party to the present Charter may only be expelled from it by virtue of a decision taken in accordance with the law.

5. The mass expulsion of non-nationals shall be prohibited. Mass expulsion shall be that which is aimed at national, racial, ethnic or religious groups.

Article 13

1. Every citizen shall have the right to participate freely in the government of his country, either directly or through freely chosen representatives in accordance with the provisions of the law.

2. Every citizen shall have the right of equal access to the public service of his country.

3. Every individual shall have the right of access to public property and services in strict equality of all persons before the law.

Article 14

The right to property shall be guaranteed. It may only be encroached upon in the interest of public need or in the general interest of the community and in accordance with the provisions of appropriate laws.

Article 15

Every individual shall have the right to work under equitable and satisfactory conditions and shall receive equal pay for equal work.

Article 16

1. Every individual shall have the right to enjoy the best attainable state of physical and mental health.

2. States Parties to the present Charter shall take the necessary measures to protect the health of their people and to ensure that they receive medical attention when they are sick.

Article 17

1. Every individual shall have the right to education.

2. Every individual may freely take part in the cultural life of his community.

3. The promotion and protection of morals and traditional values recognized by the community shall be the duty of the State.

Article 18

1. The family shall be the natural unit and basis of society. It shall be protected by the State which shall take care of its physical health and morals.

2. The State shall have the duty to assist the family which is the custodian of morals and traditional values recognized by the community.

3. The State shall ensure the elimination of every discrimination against women and also ensure the protection of the rights of the women and the child as stipulated in international declarations and conventions.

4. The aged and the disabled shall also have the right to special measures of protection in keeping with their physical and moral needs.

Article 19

All peoples shall be equal; they shall enjoy the same respect and shall have the same rights. Nothing shall justify the domination of a people by another.

Article 20

1. All peoples shall have the right to existence. They shall have the unquestionable and inalienable right to self-determination. They shall freely determine their political status and shall pursue their economic and social development according to the policy they have freely chosen.

2. Colonized or oppressed peoples shall have the right to free themselves from the bonds of domination by resorting to any means recognized by the international community.

3. All peoples shall have the right to the assistance of the States Parties to the present Charter in their liberation struggle against foreign domination, be it political, economic or cultural.

Article 21

1. All peoples shall freely dispose of their wealth and natural resources. This right shall be exercised in the exclusive interest of the people. In no case shall a people be deprived of it.

2. In case of spoliation the dispossessed people shall have the right to the lawful recovery of its property as well as to an adequate compensation.

3. The free disposal of wealth and natural resources shall be exercised without prejudice to the obligation of promoting international economic cooperation based on mutual respect, equitable exchange and the principles of international law.

4. States Parties to the present Charter shall individually and collectively exercise the right to free disposal of their natural wealth and natural resources with a view to strengthening African unity and solidarity.

5. States Parties to the present Charter shall undertake to eliminate all forms of foreign economic exploitation particularly that practiced by international monopolies so as to enable their peoples to fully benefit from the advantages derived from their natural resources.

Article 22

1. All peoples shall have the right to their economic, social and cultural development with due regard to their freedom and identity and in the equal enjoyment of the common heritage of mankind.

2. States shall have the duty, individually or collectively, to ensure the exercise of the right to development.

Article 23

1. All peoples shall have the right to national and international peace and security. The principles of solidarity and friendly relations implicitly affirmed by the Charter of the United Nations and reaffirmed by that of the Organization of African Unity shall govern relations between States.

2. For the purpose of strengthening peace, solidarity and friendly relations, States Parties to the present Charter shall ensure that:

    a. any individual enjoying the right of asylum under Article 12 of the present Charter shall not engage in subversive activities against his country of origin or any other State Party to the present Charter;

    b. their territories shall not be used as bases for subversive or terrorist activities against the people of any other State Party to the present Charter.

Article 24

All peoples have the right to a general satisfactory environment favourable to their development.

Article 25

States Parties to the present Charter shall have the duty to promote and ensure through teaching, education and publication, the respect of the rights and freedoms contained in the present Charter and to see to it that these freedoms and rights as well as corresponding obligations and duties are understood.

Article 26

States Parties to the present Charter shall have the duty to guarantee the independence of the Courts and shall allow the establishment and improvement of appropriate national institutions entrusted with the promotion and protection of the rights and freedoms guaranteed by the present Charter.

Chapter II. Duties

Article 27

1. Every individual shall have duties towards his family and society, the State and other legally recognized communities and the international community.

2. The rights and freedoms of each individual shall be exercised with due regard to the rights of others, collective security, morality and common interest.

Article 28

Every individual shall have the duty to respect and consider his fellow beings without discrimination, and to maintain relations aimed at promoting, safeguarding and reinforcing mutual respect and tolerance.

Article 29

The individual shall also have the duty:

1. To preserve the harmonious development of the family and to work for the cohesion and respect of the family, to respect his parents at all times, to maintain them in case of need;

2. To serve the national community by placing his physical and intellectual abilities at its service;

3. Not to compromise the security of the State whose national or resident he is;

4. To preserve and strengthen social and national solidarity, particularly when the latter is threatened;

5. To preserve and strengthen the national independence and the territorial integrity of his country and to contribute to its defence in accordance with the law;

6. To work to the best of his abilities and competence, and to pay taxes imposed by law in the interest of the society;

7. To preserve and strengthen positive African cultural values in his relations with other members of the society, in the spirit of tolerance, dialogue and consultation and, in general, to contribute to the promotion of the moral well being of society;

8. To contribute to the best of his abilities, at all times and at all levels, to the promotion and achievement of African unity.

Part II. Measures of Safeguard

Chapter I. Establishment and Organization of the African Commission on Human and Peoples' Rights

Article 30

An African Commission on Human and Peoples' Rights, hereinafter called "the Commission," shall be established within the Organization of African Unity to promote human and peoples' rights and ensure their protection in Africa.

Chapter II. Mandate of the Commission

Article 45

The functions of the Commission shall be:

1. To promote Human and Peoples' Rights and in particular:

a. To collect documents, undertake studies and researches on African problems in the field of human and peoples' rights, organize seminars, symposia and conferences, disseminate information, encourage national and local institutions concerned with human and peoples' rights, and should the case arise, give its views or make recommendations to Governments.

b. To formulate and lay down principles and rules aimed at solving legal problems relating to human and peoples' rights and fundamental freedoms upon which African Governments may base their legislations.

c. Co-operate with other African and international institutions concerned with the promotion and protection of human and peoples' rights.

2. Ensure the protection of human and peoples' rights under conditions laid down by the present Charter.

3. Interpret all the provisions of the present Charter at the request of a State Party, an institution of the OAU or an African organization recognized by the OAU.

4. Perform any other tasks which may be entrusted to it by the Assembly of Heads of State and Government.

Chapter III. Procedure of the Commission

Article 46

The Commission may resort to any appropriate method of investigation; it may hear from the Secretary-General of the Organization of African Unity or any other person capable of enlightening it.

Communication from States

Article 47

If a State Party to the present Charter has good reasons to believe that another State Party to this Charter has violated the provisions of the Charter, it may draw, by written communication, the attention of that State to the matter. This communication shall also be addressed to the Secretary-General of the OAU and to the Chairman of the Commission. Within three months of the receipt of the communication, the State to which the communication is addressed shall give the enquiring State written explanation or statement elucidating the matter. This should include as much as possible relevant information relating to the laws and rules of procedure applied and applicable and the redress already given or course of action available.

Article 48

If within three months from the date on which the original communication is received by the State to which it is addressed, the issue is not settled to the satisfaction of the two States involved through bilateral negotiation or by any other peaceful procedure, either State shall have the right to submit the matter to the Commission through the Chairman and shall notify the other States involved.

Article 49

Notwithstanding the provisions of Article 47, if a State Party to the present Charter considers that another State Party has violated the provisions of the Charter, it may refer the matter directly to the Commission by addressing a communication to the Chairman, to the Secretary-General of the Organization of African Unity and the State concerned.

Article 50

The Commission can only deal with a matter submitted to it after making sure that all local remedies, if they exist, have been exhausted, unless it is obvious to the Commission that the procedure of achieving these remedies would be unduly prolonged.

Article 51

1. The Commission may ask the States concerned to provide it with all relevant information.

2. When the Commission is considering the matter, States concerned may be represented before it and submit written or oral representation.

Article 52

After having obtained from the States concerned and other sources all the information it deems necessary and after having tried all appropriate means to reach an amicable solution based on the respect of Human and Peoples' Rights, the Commission shall prepare, within a reasonable period of time from the notification referred to in Article 48, a report stating the facts and its findings. This report shall be sent to the States concerned and communicated to the Assembly of Heads of State and Government.

Article 53

While transmitting its report, the Commission may make to the Assembly of Heads of State and Government such recommendations as it deems useful.

Article 54

The Commission shall submit to each Ordinary Session of the Assembly of Heads of State and Government a report on its activities.

Other Communications

Article 55

1. Before each Session, the Secretary of the Commission shall make a list of the communications other than those of States Parties to the present Charter and transmit them to the Members of the Commission, who shall indicate which communications should be considered by the Commission.

2. A communication shall be considered by the Commission if a simple majority of its members so decide.

Article 56

Communications relating to human and peoples' rights referred to in Article 55 received by the Commission, shall be considered if they:

1. indicate their authors even if the latter request anonymity,

2. are compatible with the Charter of the Organization of African Unity or with the present Charter,

3. are not written in disparaging or insulting language directed against the State concerned and its institutions or to the Organization of African Unity,

4. are not based exclusively on news disseminated through the mass media,

5. are sent after exhausting local remedies, if any, unless it is obvious that this procedure is unduly prolonged,

6. are submitted within a reasonable period from the time local remedies are exhausted or from the date the Commission is seized of the matter, and

7. do not deal with cases which have been settled by these States involved in accordance with the principles of the Charter of the United Nations, or the Charter of the Organization of African Unity or the provisions of the present Charter.

Article 57

Prior to any substantive consideration, all communications shall be brought to the knowledge of the State concerned by the Chairman of the Commission.

Article 58

1. When it appears after deliberation of the Commission that one or more communications apparently relate to special cases which reveal the existence of a series or serious or massive violations of human and peoples' rights, the Commission shall draw the attention of the Assembly of Heads of State and Government to these special cases.

2. The Assembly of Heads of State and Government may then request the Commission to undertake an in-depth study of these situations and make a factual report, accompanied by its findings and recommendations.

3. A case of emergency duly noticed by the Commission shall be submitted by the latter to the Chairman of the Assembly of Heads of State and Government who may request an in-depth study.

Article 59

1. All measures taken within the provisions of the present Chapter shall remain confidential until such a time as the Assembly of Heads of State and Government shall otherwise decide.

2. However, the report shall be published by the Chairman of the Commission upon the decision of the Assembly of Heads of State and Government.

3. The report on the activities of the Commission shall be published by its Chairman after it has been considered by the Assembly of Heads of State and Government.

Chapter IV. Applicable Principles

Article 60

The Commission shall draw inspiration from international law on human and peoples' rights, particularly from the provisions of various African instruments on human and peoples' rights, the Charter of the United Nations, the Charter of the Organization of African Unity, the Universal Declaration of Human Rights, other instruments adopted by the United Nations and by African countries in the field of human and peoples' rights as well as from the provisions of various instruments adopted within the Specialized Agencies of the United Nations of which the parties to the present Charter are members.

Article 61

The Commission shall also take into consideration, as subsidiary measures to determine the principles of law, other general or special international conventions, laying down rules expressly recognized by member states of the Organization of African Unity, African practices consistent with international norms on human and peoples' rights, customs generally accepted as law, general principles of law recognized by African states as well as legal precedents and doctrine.

Article 62

Each State Party shall undertake to submit every two years, from the date the present Charter comes into force, a report on the legislative and other measures taken with a view to giving effect to the rights and freedoms recognized and guaranteed by the present Charter. . . .

Protocol to the African Charter on Human and Peoples' Rights on the Establishment of an African Court on Human and Peoples' Rights

(Adopted by the 34th Ordinary Session of the Assembly of Heads of State and Government meeting in Ouagadougou, Burkina Faso from 8–10 June 1998. In a signing ceremony held thereafter, at the same venue, thirty Member States signed the Protocol)

The Member States of the Organization of African Unity hereinafter referred to as the OAU, States Parties to the African Charter on Human and Peoples' Rights:

Considering that the Charter of the Organization of African Unity recognizes that freedom, equality, justice, peace and dignity are essential objectives for the achievement of the legitimate aspirations of the African peoples;

Noting that the African Charter on Human and Peoples' Rights reaffirms adherence to the principles of human and peoples' rights, freedoms and duties contained in the declarations, conventions and other instruments adopted by the Organization of African Unity, and other international organizations;

Recognizing that the twofold objective of the African Charter on Human and Peoples' Rights is to ensure on the one hand promotion and on the other protection of human and peoples' rights, freedoms and duties;

Recognizing further, the efforts of the African Commission on Human and Peoples' Rights in the promotion and protection of human and peoples' rights since its inception in 1987;

Recalling resolution AHGIRe5.230 (XXX) adopted by the Assembly of Heads of State and Government in June 1994 in Tunis, Tunisia, requesting the Secretary-General to convene a Government experts' meeting to ponder, in conjunction with the African Commission, over the means to enhance the efficiency of the African Commission and to consider in particular the establishment of an African Court on Human and Peoples' Rights;

Noting the first and second Government legal experts' meetings held respectively in Cape Town, South Africa (September, 1995) and Nouakchott, Mauritania (April, 1997), and the third Government Legal Experts meeting held in Addis Ababa, Ethiopia (December, 1997), which was enlarged to include Diplomats;

Firmly convinced that the attainment of the objectives of the African Charter on Human and Peoples' Rights requires the establishment of an African Court on Human and Peoples' Rights to complement and reinforce the functions of the African Commission on Human and Peoples' Rights.

Have agreed as follows:

Article 1. Establishment of the Court

There shall be established within the Organization of African Unity an African Court on Human and Peoples' Rights (hereinafter referred to as "the Court"), the organization, jurisdiction and functioning of which shall be governed by the present Protocol.

Article 2. Relationship between the Court and the Commission

The Court shall, bearing in mind the provisions of this Protocol, complement the protective mandate of the African Commission on Human and Peoples' Rights (hereinafter referred to as "the Commission") conferred upon it by the African Charter on Human and Peoples' Rights (hereinafter referred to as "the Charter").

Article 3. Jurisdiction

1. The jurisdiction of the Court shall extend to all cases and disputes submitted to it concerning the interpretation and application of the Charter, this Protocol and any other relevant Human Rights instrument ratified by the States concerned.

2. In the event of a dispute as to whether the Court has jurisdiction, the Court shall decide.

Article 4. Advisory Opinions

1. At the request of a Member State of the OAU, the OAU, any of its organs, or any African organization recognized by the OAU, the Court may provide an opinion on any legal matter relating to the Charter or any other relevant human rights instruments, provided that the subject matter of the opinion is not related to a matter being examined by the Commission.

2. The Court shall give reasons for its advisory opinions provided that every judge shall be entitled to deliver a separate or dissenting decision.

Article 5. Access to the Court

1. The following are entitled to submit cases to the Court:

   a. The Commission;

   b. The State Party which has lodged a complaint to the Commission.

   c. The State Party against which the complaint has been lodged at the Commission;

   d. The State Party whose citizen is a victim of human rights violation;

   e. African Intergovernmental Organizations.

2. When a State Party has an interest in a case, it may submit a request to the Court to be permitted to join.

3. The Court may entitle relevant Non Governmental Organizations (NGOs) with observer status before the Commission and individuals to institute cases directly before it, in accordance with article 34 (6) of this Protocol.

Article 6. Admissibility of Cases

1. The Court, when deciding on the admissibility of a case instituted under article 5 (3) of this Protocol, may request the opinion of the Commission which shall give t as soon as possible.

2. The Court shall rule on the admissibility of cases taking into account the provisions of article 56 of the Charter.

3. The Court may consider cases or transfer them to the Commission.

Article 7. Sources of Law

The Court shall apply the provisions of the Charter and any other relevant human rights instruments ratified by the States concerned.

Article 8. Consideration of Cases

The Rules of Procedure of the Court shall lay down the detailed conditions under which the Court shall consider cases brought before it, bearing in mind the complementarity between the Commission and the Court.

Article 9. Amicable Settlement

The Court may try to reach an amicable settlement in a case pending before it in accordance with the provisions of the Charter.

Article 10. Hearings and Representation

1. The Court shall conduct its proceedings in public. The Court may, however, conduct proceedings in camera as may be provided for in the Rules of Procedure.

2. Any party to a case shall be entitled to be represented by a legal representative of the party's choice. Free legal representation may be provided where the interests of justice so require.

3. Any person, witness or representative of the parties, who appears before the Court, shall enjoy protection and all facilities, in accordance with international law, necessary for the discharging of their functions, tasks and duties in relation to the Court.

Article 11. Composition

1. The Court shall consist of eleven judges, nationals of Member States of the OAU, elected in an individual capacity from among jurists of high moral character and of recognized practical, judicial or academic competence and experience in the field of human and peoples' rights.

2. No two judges shall be nationals of the same State.

Article 12. Nominations

1. States Parties to the Protocol may each propose up to three candidates, at least two of whom shall be nationals of that State.

2. Due consideration shall be given to adequate gender representation in the nomination process.

Article 13. List of Candidates

1. Upon entry into force of this Protocol, the Secretary-General of the OAU shall request each State Party to the Protocol to present, within ninety (90) days of such a request, its nominees for the office of judge of the Court.

2. The Secretary-General of the OAU shall prepare a list in alphabetical order of the candidates nominated and transmit it to the Member States of the OAU at least thirty days prior to the next session of the Assembly of Heads of State and Government of the OAU hereinafter referred to as "the Assembly".

Article 14. Elections

1. The judges of the Court shall be elected by secret ballot by the Assembly from the list referred to in Article 13 (2) of the present Protocol.

2. The Assembly shall ensure that in the Court as a whole there is representation of the main regions of Africa and of theft principal legal traditions.

3. In the election of the judges, the Assembly shall ensure that there is adequate gender representation.

Article 15. Term of Office

1. The judges of the Court shall be elected for a period of six years and may be re-elected only once. The terms of four judges elected at the first election shall expire at the end of two years, and the terms of four more judges shall expire at the end of four years.

2. The judges whose terms are to expire at the end of the initial periods of two and four years shall be chosen by lot to be drawn by the Secretary-General of the OAU immediately after the first election has been completed.

3. A judge elected to replace a judge whose term of office has not expired shall hold office for the remainder of the predecessor's term.

4. All judges except the President shall perform their functions on a part-time basis. However, the Assembly may change this arrangement as it deems appropriate.

Article 16. Oath of Office

After their election, the judges of the Court shall make a solemn declaration to discharge their duties impartially and faithfully.

Article 17. Independence

1. The independence of the judges shall be fully ensured in accordance with international law.

2. No judge may hear any case in which the same judge has previously taken part as agent, counsel or advocate for one of the parties or as a member of a national or international court or a commission of enquiry or in any other capacity. Any doubt on this point shall be settled hy decision of the Court.

3. The judges of the Court shall enjoy, from the moment of theft election and throughout their term of office, the immunities extended to diplomatic agents in accordance with international law.

4. At no time shall the judges of the Court be held liable for any decision or opinion issued in the exercise of theft functions.

Article 18. Incompatibility

The position of judge of the Court is incompatible with any activity that might interfere with the independence or impartiality of such a judge or the demands of the office, as determined in the Rules of Procedure of the Court.

Article 19. Cessation of Office

1. A judge shall not be suspended or removed from office unless, by the unanimous decision of the other judges of the Court, the judge concerned has been found to be no longer fulfilling the required conditions to be a judge of the Court.

2. Such a decision of the Court shall become final unless it is set aside by the Assembly at its next session.

Article 20. Vacancies

1. In case of death or resignation of a judge of the Court, the President of the Court shall immediately inform the Secretary General of the Organization of African Unity, who shall declare the seat vacant from the date of death or from the date on which the resignation takes effect.

2. The Assembly shall replace the judge whose office became vacant unless the remaining period of the term is less than one hundred and eighty (180) days.

3. The same procedure and considerations as set out in Articles 12, 13 and 14 shall be followed for the filling of vacancies.

Article 21. Presidency of the Court

1. The Court shall elect its President and one Vice-President for a period of two years. They may be re-elected only once.

2. The President shall perform judicial functions on a full-time basis and shall reside at the seat of the Court.

3. The functions of the President and the Vice-President shall be set out in the Rules of Procedure of the Court.

Article 22. Exclusion

If a judge is a national of any State which is a party to a case submitted to the Court, the judge shall not hear the case.

Article 23. Quorum

The Court shall examine cases brought before it, if it has a quorum of at least seven judges.

Article 24. Registry of the Court

1. The Court shall appoint its own Registrar and other staff of the registry from among nationals of Member States of the OAU according to the Rules of Procedure.

2. The office and residence of the Registrar shall be at the place where the Court has its seat.

Article 25. Seat of the Court

1. The Court shall have its seat at the place determined by the Assembly from among States parties to this Protocol. However, it may convene in the territory of any Member State of the OAU when the majority of the Court considers it desirable, and with the prior consent of the State concerned.

2. The seat of the Court may be changed by the Assembly after due consultation with the Court.

Article 26. Evidence

1. The Court shall hear submissions by all parties and if deemed necessary, hold an enquiry. The States concerned shall assist by providing relevant facilities for the efficient handling of the case.

2. The Court may receive written and oral evidence including expert testimony and shall make its decision on the basis of such evidence.

Article 27. Findings

1. If the Court finds that there has been violation of a human or peoples' right, it shall make appropriate orders to remedy the violation, including the payment of fair compensation or reparation.

2. In cases of extreme gravity and urgency, and when necessary to avoid irreparable harm to persons, the Court shall adopt such provisional measures as it deems necessary.

Article 28. Judgment

1. The Court shall render its judgment within ninety (90) days of having completed its deliberation.

2. The judgment of the Court decided by majority shall be final and not subject to appeal.

3. Without prejudice to sub-article 2 above, the Court may review its decision in the light of new evidence under conditions to be set out in the Rules of Procedure.

4. The Court may interpret its own decision.

5. The judgement of the Court shall be read in open court, due notice having been given to the parties.

6. Reasons shall be given for the judgement of the Court.

7. If the judgment of the Court does not represent, in whole or in part, the unanimous decision of the judges, any judge shall be entitled to deliver a separate or dissenting opinion.

Article 29. Notification of Judgment

1. The parties to the case shall be notified of the judgment of the Court and it shall he transmitted to the Member States of the OAU and the Commission.

2. The Council of Ministers shall also be notified of the judgment and shall monitor its execution on behalf of the Assembly.

Article 30. Execution of Judgment

The States parties to the present Protocol undertake to comply with the judgment in any case to which they are parties within the time stipulated by the Court and to guarantee its execution.

Article 31. Report

The Court shall submit to each regular session of the Assembly, a report on its work during the previous year. The report shall specify, in particular, the cases in which a State has not complied with the Court's judgment.

Article 32. Budget

Expenses Of the Court, emoluments and allowances for judges and the budget of its registry, shall be determined and borne by the OAU, in accordance with criteria laid down by the OAU in consultation with the Court.

Article 33. Rules of Procedure

The Court shall draw up its Rules and determine its own procedures. The Court shall consult the Commission as appropriate.

Article 34. Ratification

1. This Protocol shall be open for signature and ratification or accession by any State Party to the Charter.

2. The instrument of ratification or accession to the present Protocol shall be deposited with the Secretary-General of the OAU.

3. The Protocol shall come into force thirty days after fifteen instruments of ratification or accession have been deposited.

4. For any State Party ratifying or acceding subsequently, the present Protocol shall come into force in respect of that State on the date of the deposit of its instrument of ratification or accession.

5. The Secretary-General of the OAU shall inform all Member States of the entry into force of the present Protocol.

6. At the time of the ratification of this Protocol or any time thereafter, the State shall make a declaration accepting the competence of the Court to receive cases under article 5 (3) of this Protocol. The Court shall not receive any petition under article 5 (3) involving a State Party which has not made such a declaration.

7. Declarations made under sub-article (6) above shall be deposited with the Secretary General, who shall transmit copies thereof to the State parties.

Article 35. Amendments

1. The present Protocol may be amended if a State Party to the Protocol makes a written request to that effect to the Secretary-General of the OAU. The Assembly may adopt, by simple majority, the draft amendment after all the States Parties to the present Protocol have been duly informed of it and the Court has given its opinion on the amendment.

2. The Court shall also be entitled to propose such amendments to the present Protocol as it may deem necessary, through the Secretary-General of the OAU.

3. The amendment shall come into force for each State Party which has accepted it thirty days after the Secretary-General of the OAU has received notice of the acceptance.

Arab Charter on Human Rights
League of Arab States (May 22, 2004)

Based on the faith of the Arab nation in the dignity of the human person whom God has exalted ever since the beginning of creation and in the fact that the Arab homeland is the cradle of religions and civilizations whose lofty human values affirm the human right to a decent life based on freedom, justice and equality,

In furtherance of the eternal principles of fraternity, equality and tolerance among human beings consecrated by the noble Islamic religion and the other divinely-revealed religions,

Being proud of the humanitarian values and principles that the Arab nation has established throughout its long history, which have played a major role in spreading knowledge between East and West, so making the region a point of reference for the whole world and a destination for seekers of knowledge and wisdom,

Believing in the unity of the Arab nation, which struggles for its freedom and defends the right of nations to self-determination, to the preservation of their wealth and to development; believing in the sovereignty of the law and its contribution to the protection of universal and interrelated human rights and convinced that the human person's enjoyment of freedom, justice and equality of opportunity is a fundamental measure of the value of any society,

Rejecting all forms of racism and Zionism, which constitute a violation of human rights and a threat to international peace and security, recognizing the close link that exists between human rights and international peace and security, reaffirming the principles of the Charter of the United Nations, the Universal Declaration of Human Rights and the provisions of the International Covenant on Civil and Political Rights and the International Covenant on Economic, Social and Cultural Rights, and having regard to the Cairo Declaration on Human Rights in Islam,

The States parties to the Charter have agreed as follows:

Article 1

The present Charter seeks, within the context of the national identity of the Arab States and their sense of belonging to a common civilization, to achieve the following aims:

1. To place human rights at the centre of the key national concerns of Arab States, making them lofty and fundamental ideals that shape the will of the individual in Arab States and enable him to improve his life in accordance with noble human values.

2. To teach the human person in the Arab States pride in his identity, loyalty to his country, attachment to his land, history and common interests and to instill in him a culture of human brotherhood, tolerance and openness towards others, in accordance with universal principles and values and with those proclaimed in international human rights instruments.

3. To prepare the new generations in Arab States for a free and responsible life in a civil society that is characterized by solidarity, founded on a balance between awareness of rights and respect for obligations, and governed by the values of equality, tolerance and moderation.

4. To entrench the principle that all human rights are universal, indivisible, interdependent and interrelated.

Article 2

1. All peoples have the right of self-determination and to control over their natural wealth and resources, and the right to freely choose their political system and to freely pursue their economic, social and cultural development.

2. All peoples have the right to national sovereignty and territorial integrity.

3. All forms of racism, Zionism and foreign occupation and domination constitute an impediment to human dignity and a major barrier to the exercise of the fundamental rights of peoples; all such practices must be condemned and efforts must be deployed for their elimination.

4. All peoples have the right to resist foreign occupation.

Article 3

1. Each State party to the present Charter undertakes to ensure to all individuals subject to its jurisdiction the right to enjoy the rights and freedoms set forth herein, without distinction on grounds of race, colour, sex, language, religious belief, opinion, thought, national or social origin, wealth, birth or physical or mental disability.

2. The States parties to the present Charter shall take the requisite measures to guarantee effective equality in the enjoyment of all the rights and freedoms enshrined in the present Charter in order to ensure protection against all forms of discrimination based on any of the grounds mentioned in the preceding paragraph.

3. Men and women are equal in respect of human dignity, rights and obligations within the framework of the positive discrimination established in favour of women by the Islamic Shariah, other divine laws and by applicable laws and legal instruments. Accordingly, each State party pledges to take all the requisite measures to guarantee equal opportunities and effective equality between men and women in the enjoyment of all the rights set out in this Charter.

Article 4

1. In exceptional situations of emergency which threaten the life of the nation and the existence of which is officially proclaimed, the States parties to the present Charter may take measures derogating from their obligations under the present Charter, to the extent strictly required by the exigencies of the situation, provided that such measures are not inconsistent with their other obligations under international law and do not involve discrimination solely on the grounds of race, colour, sex, language, religion or social origin.

2. In exceptional situations of emergency, no derogation shall be made from the following articles: article 5, article 8, article 9, article 10, article 13, article 14, paragraph 6, article 15, article 18, article 19, article 20, article 22, article 27, article 28, article 29 and article 30. In addition, the judicial guarantees required for the protection of the aforementioned rights may not be suspended.

3. Any State party to the present Charter availing itself of the right of derogation shall immediately inform the other States parties, through the intermediary of the Secretary-General of the League of Arab States, of the provisions from which it has derogated and of the reasons by which it was actuated. A further communication shall be made, through the same intermediary, on the date on which it terminates such derogation.

Article 5

1. Every human being has the inherent right to life.

2. This right shall be protected by law. No one shall be arbitrarily deprived of his life.

Article 6

Sentence of death may be imposed only for the most serious crimes in accordance with the laws in force at the time of commission of the crime and pursuant to a final judgment rendered by a competent court. Anyone sentenced to death shall have the right to seek pardon or commutation of the sentence.

Article 7

1. Sentence of death shall not be imposed on persons under 18 years of age, unless otherwise stipulated in the laws in force at the time of the commission of the crime.

2. The death penalty shall not be inflicted on a pregnant woman prior to her delivery or on a nursing mother within two years from the date of her delivery; in all cases, the best interests of the infant shall be the primary consideration.

Article 8

1. No one shall be subjected to physical or psychological torture or to cruel, degrading, humiliating or inhuman treatment.

2. Each State party shall protect every individual subject to its jurisdiction from such practices and shall take effective measures to prevent them. The commission of, or participation in, such acts shall be regarded as crimes that are punishable by law and not subject to any statute of limitations. Each State party shall guarantee in its legal system redress for any victim of torture and the right to rehabilitation and compensation.

Article 9

No one shall be subjected to medical or scientific experimentation or to the use of his organs without his free consent and full awareness of the consequences and provided that ethical, humanitarian and professional rules are followed and medical procedures are observed to ensure his personal safety pursuant to the relevant domestic laws in force in each State party. Trafficking in human organs is prohibited in all circumstances.

Article 10

1. All forms of slavery and trafficking in human beings are prohibited and are punishable by law. No one shall be held in slavery and servitude under any circumstances.

2. Forced labor, trafficking in human beings for the purposes of prostitution or sexual exploitation, the exploitation of the prostitution of others or any other form of exploitation or the exploitation of children in armed conflict are prohibited.

Article 11

All persons are equal before the law and have the right to enjoy its protection without discrimination.

Article 12

All persons are equal before the courts and tribunals. The States parties shall guarantee the independence of the judiciary and protect magistrates against any interference, pressure or threats. They shall also guarantee every person subject to their jurisdiction the right to seek a legal remedy before courts of all levels.

Article 13

1. Everyone has the right to a fair trial that affords adequate guarantees before a competent, independent and impartial court that has been constituted by law to hear any criminal charge against him or to decide on his rights or his obligations. Each State party shall guarantee to those without the requisite financial resources legal aid to enable them to defend their rights.

2. Trials shall be public, except in exceptional cases that may be warranted by the interests of justice in a society that respects human freedoms and rights.

Article 14

1. Everyone has the right to liberty and security of person. No one shall be subjected to arbitrary arrest, search or detention without a legal warrant.

2. No one shall be deprived of his liberty except on such grounds and in such circumstances as are determined by law and in accordance with such procedure as is established thereby.

3. Anyone who is arrested shall be informed, at the time of arrest, in a language that he understands, of the reasons for his arrest and shall be promptly informed of any charges against him. He shall be entitled to contact his family members.

4. Anyone who is deprived of his liberty by arrest or detention shall have the right to request a medical examination and must be informed of that right.

5. Anyone arrested or detained on a criminal charge shall be brought promptly before a judge or other officer authorized by law to exercise judicial power and shall be entitled to trial within a reasonable time or to release. His release may be subject to guarantees to appear for trial. Pre-trial detention shall in no case be the general rule.

6. Anyone who is deprived of his liberty by arrest or detention shall be entitled to petition a competent court in order that it may decide without delay on the lawfulness of his arrest or detention and order his release if the arrest or detention is unlawful.

7. Anyone who has been the victim of arbitrary or unlawful arrest or detention shall be entitled to compensation.

Article 15

No crime and no penalty can be established without a prior provision of the law. In all circumstances, the law most favorable to the defendant shall be applied.

Article 16

Everyone charged with a criminal offence shall be presumed innocent until proved guilty by a final judgment rendered according to law and, in the course of the investigation and trial, he shall enjoy the following minimum guarantees:

1. The right to be informed promptly, in detail and in a language which he understands, of the charges against him.

2. The right to have adequate time and facilities for the preparation of his defense and to be allowed to communicate with his family.

3. The right to be tried in his presence before an ordinary court and to defend himself in person or through a lawyer of his own choosing with whom he can communicate freely and confidentially.

4. The right to the free assistance of a lawyer who will defend him if he cannot defend himself or if the interests of justice so require, and the right to the free assistance of an interpreter if he cannot understand or does not speak the language used in court.

5. The right to examine or have his lawyer examine the prosecution witnesses and to a defense according to the conditions applied to the prosecution witnesses.

6. The right not to be compelled to testify against himself or to confess guilt.

7. The right, if convicted of the crime, to file an appeal in accordance with the law before a higher tribunal.

8. The right to respect for his security of person and his privacy in all circumstances.

Article 17

Each State party shall ensure in particular to any child at risk or any delinquent charged with an offence the right to a special legal system for minors in all stages of investigation, trial and enforcement of sentence, as well as to special treatment that takes account of his age, protects his dignity, facilitates his rehabilitation and reintegration and enables him to play a constructive role in society.

Article 18

No one who is shown by a court to be unable to pay a debt arising from a contractual obligation shall be imprisoned.

Article 19

1. No one may be tried twice for the same offence. Anyone against whom such proceedings are brought shall have the right to challenge their legality and to demand his release.

2. Anyone whose innocence is established by a final judgment shall be entitled to compensation for the damage suffered.

Article 20

1. All persons deprived of their liberty shall be treated with humanity and with respect for the inherent dignity of the human person.

2. Persons in pre-trial detention shall be separated from convicted persons and shall be treated in a manner consistent with their status as unconvicted persons.

3. The aim of the penitentiary system shall be to reform prisoners and effect their social rehabilitation.

Article 21

1. No one shall be subjected to arbitrary or unlawful interference with regard to his privacy, family, home or correspondence, nor to unlawful attacks on his honour or his reputation.

2. Everyone has the right to the protection of the law against such interference or attacks.

Article 22

Everyone shall have the right to recognition as a person before the law.

Article 23

Each State party to the present Charter undertakes to ensure that any person whose rights or freedoms as herein recognized are violated shall have an effective remedy, notwithstanding that the violation has been committed by persons acting in an official capacity.

Article 24

Every citizen has the right:

1. To freely pursue a political activity.

2. To take part in the conduct of public affairs, directly or through freely chosen representatives.

3. To stand for election or choose his representatives in free and impartial elections, in conditions of equality among all citizens that guarantee the free expression of his will.

4. To the opportunity to gain access, on an equal footing with others, to public office in his country in accordance with the principle of equality of opportunity.

5. To freely form and join associations with others.

6. To freedom of association and peaceful assembly.

7. No restrictions may be placed on the exercise of these rights other than those which are prescribed by law and which are necessary in a democratic society in the interests of national security or public safety, public health or morals or the protection of the rights and freedoms of others.

Article 25

Persons belonging to minorities shall not be denied the right to enjoy their own culture, to use their own language and to practice their own religion. The exercise of these rights shall be governed by law.

Article 26

1. Everyone lawfully within the territory of a State party shall, within that territory, have the right to freedom of movement and to freely choose his residence in any part of that territory in conformity with the laws in force.

2. No State party may expel a person who does not hold its nationality but is lawfully in its territory, other than in pursuance of a decision reached in accordance with law and after that person has been allowed to submit a petition to the competent authority, unless compelling reasons of national security preclude it. Collective expulsion is prohibited under all circumstances.

Article 27

1. No one may be arbitrarily or unlawfully prevented from leaving any country, including his own, nor prohibited from residing, or compelled to reside, in any part of that country.

2. No one may be exiled from his country or prohibited from returning thereto.

Article 28

Everyone has the right to seek political asylum in another country in order to escape persecution. This right may not be invoked by persons facing prosecution for an offence under ordinary law. Political refugees may not be extradited.

Article 29

1. Everyone has the right to nationality. No one shall be arbitrarily or unlawfully deprived of his nationality.

2. States parties shall take such measures as they deem appropriate, in accordance with their domestic laws on nationality, to allow a child to acquire the mother's nationality, having due regard, in all cases, to the best interests of the child.

3. No one shall be denied the right to acquire another nationality, having due regard for the domestic legal procedures in his country.

Article 30

1. Everyone has the right to freedom of thought, conscience and religion and no restrictions may be imposed on the exercise of such freedoms except as provided for by law.

2. The freedom to manifest one's religion or beliefs or to perform religious observances, either alone or in community with others, shall be subject only to such limitations as are prescribed by law and are necessary in a tolerant society that respects human rights and freedoms for the protection of public safety, public order, public health or morals or the fundamental rights and freedoms of others.

3. Parents or guardians have the freedom to provide for the religious and moral education of their children.

Article 31

Everyone has a guaranteed right to own private property, and shall not under any circumstances be arbitrarily or unlawfully divested of all or any part of his property.

Article 32

1. The present Charter guarantees the right to information and to freedom of opinion and expression, as well as the right to seek, receive and impart information and ideas through any medium, regardless of geographical boundaries.

2. Such rights and freedoms shall be exercised in conformity with the fundamental values of society and shall be subject only to such limitations as are required to ensure respect for the rights or reputation of others or the protection of national security, public order and public health or morals.

Article 33

1. The family is the natural and fundamental group unit of society; it is based on marriage between a man and a woman. Men and women of marrying age have the right to marry and to found a family according to the rules and conditions of marriage. No marriage can take place without the full and free consent of both parties. The laws in force regulate the rights and duties of the man and woman as to marriage, during marriage and at its dissolution.

2. The State and society shall ensure the protection of the family, the strengthening of family ties, the protection of its members and the prohibition of all forms of violence or abuse in the relations among its members, and particularly against women and children. They shall also ensure the necessary protection and care for mothers, children, older persons and persons with special needs and shall provide adolescents and young persons with the best opportunities for physical and mental development.

3. The States parties shall take all necessary legislative, administrative and judicial measures to guarantee the protection, survival, development and well-being of the child in an atmosphere of freedom and dignity and shall ensure, in all cases, that the child's best interests are the basic criterion for all measures taken in his regard, whether the child is at risk of delinquency or is a juvenile offender.

4. The States parties shall take all the necessary measures to guarantee, particularly to young persons, the right to pursue a sporting activity.

Article 34

1. The right to work is a natural right of every citizen. The State shall endeavor to provide, to the extent possible, a job for the largest number of those willing to work, while ensuring production, the freedom to choose one's work and equality of opportunity without discrimination of any kind on grounds of race, colour, sex, religion, language, political opinion, membership in a union, national origin, social origin, disability or any other situation.

2. Every worker has the right to the enjoyment of just and favourable conditions of work which ensure appropriate remuneration to meet his essential needs and those of his family and regulate working hours, rest and holidays with pay, as well as the rules for the preservation of occupational health and safety and the protection of women, children and disabled persons in the place of work.

3. The States parties recognize the right of the child to be protected from economic exploitation and from being forced to perform any work that is likely to be hazardous or to interfere with the child's education or to be harmful to the child's health or physical, mental, spiritual, moral or social development. To this end, and having regard to the relevant provisions of other international instruments, States parties shall in particular:

(a) Define a minimum age for admission to employment;

(b) Establish appropriate regulation of working hours and conditions;

(c) Establish appropriate penalties or other sanctions to ensure the effective endorsement of these provisions.

4. There shall be no discrimination between men and women in their enjoyment of the right to effectively benefit from training, employment and job protection and the right to receive equal remuneration for equal work.

5. Each State party shall ensure to workers who migrate to its territory the requisite protection in accordance with the laws in force.

Article 35

1. Every individual has the right to freely form trade unions or to join trade unions and to freely pursue trade union activity for the protection of his interests.

2. No restrictions shall be placed on the exercise of these rights and freedoms except such as are prescribed by the laws in force and that are necessary for the maintenance of national security, public safety or order or for the protection of public health or morals or the rights and freedoms of others.

3. Every State party to the present Charter guarantees the right to strike within the limits laid down by the laws in force.

Article 36

The States parties shall ensure the right of every citizen to social security, including social insurance.

Article 37

The right to development is a fundamental human right and all States are required to establish the development policies and to take the measures needed to guarantee this right. They have a duty to give effect to the values of solidarity and cooperation among them and at the international level with a view to eradicating poverty and achieving economic, social, cultural and political development. By virtue of this right, every citizen has the right to participate in the realization of development and to enjoy the benefits and fruits thereof.

Article 38

Every person has the right to an adequate standard of living for himself and his family, which ensures their well-being and a decent life, including food, clothing, housing, services and the right to a healthy environment. The States patties shall take the necessary measures commensurate with their resources to guarantee these rights.

Article 39

1. The States parties recognize the right of every member of society to the enjoyment of the highest attainable standard of physical and mental health and the right of the citizen to free basic health-care services and to have access to medical facilities without discrimination of any kind.

2. The measures taken by States parties shall include the following:

(a) Development of basic health-care services and the guaranteeing of free and easy access to the centres that provide these services, regardless of geographical location or economic status.

(b) Efforts to control disease by means of prevention and cure in order to reduce the mortality rate.

(c) Promotion of health awareness and health education.

(d) Suppression of traditional practices which are harmful to the health of the individual.

(e) Provision of the basic nutrition and safe drinking water for all.

(f) Combating environmental pollution and providing proper sanitation systems;

(g) Combating drugs, psychotropic substances, smoking and substances that are damaging to health.

Article 40

1. The States parties undertake to ensure to persons with mental or physical disabilities a decent life that guarantees their dignity, and to enhance their self-reliance and facilitate their active participation in society.

2. The States parties shall provide social services free of charge for all persons with disabilities, shall provide the material support needed by those persons, their families or the families caring for them, and shall also do whatever is needed to avoid placing those persons in institutions. They shall in all cases take account of the best interests of the disabled person.

3. The States parties shall take all necessary measures to curtail the incidence of disabilities by all possible means, including preventive health programmes, awareness raising and education.

4. The States parties shall provide full educational services suited to persons with disabilities, taking into account the importance of integrating these persons in the educational system and the importance of vocational training and apprenticeship and the creation of suitable job opportunities in the public or private sectors.

5. The States parties shall provide all health services appropriate for persons with disabilities, including the rehabilitation of these persons with a view to integrating them into society.

6. The States patties shall enable persons with disabilities to make use of all public and private services.

Article 41

1. The eradication of illiteracy is a binding obligation upon the State and everyone has the right to education.

2. The States parties shall guarantee their citizens free education at least throughout the primary and basic levels. All forms and levels of primary education shall be compulsory and accessible to all without discrimination of any kind.

3. The States parties shall take appropriate measures in all domains to ensure partnership between men and women with a view to achieving national development goals.

4. The States parties shall guarantee to provide education directed to the full development of the human person and to strengthening respect for human rights and fundamental freedoms.

5. The States parties shall endeavour to incorporate the principles of human rights and fundamental freedoms into formal and informal education curricula and educational and training programmes.

6. The States parties shall guarantee the establishment of the mechanisms necessary to provide ongoing education for every citizen and shall develop national plans for adult education.

Article 42

1. Every person has the right to take part in cultural life and to enjoy the benefits of scientific progress and its application.

2. The States parties undertake to respect the freedom of scientific research and creative activity and to ensure the protection of moral and material interests resulting from scientific, literary and artistic production.

3. The States parties shall work together and enhance cooperation among them at all levels, with the full participation of intellectuals and inventors and their organizations, in order to develop and implement recreational, cultural, artistic and scientific programmes.

Article 43

Nothing in this Charter may be construed or interpreted as impairing the rights and freedoms protected by the domestic laws of the States parties or those set forth in the international and regional human rights instruments which the states parties have adopted or ratified, including the rights of women, the rights of the child and the rights of persons belonging to minorities.

Article 44

The states parties undertake to adopt, in conformity with their constitutional procedures and with the provisions of the present Charter, whatever legislative or non-legislative measures that may be necessary to give effect to the rights set forth herein.

Article 45

1. Pursuant to this Charter, an "Arab Human Rights Committee", hereinafter referred to as "the Committee" shall be established. This Committee shall consist of seven members who shall be elected by secret ballot by the states parties to this Charter.

2. The Committee shall consist of nationals of the states parties to the present Charter, who must be highly experienced and competent in the Committee's field of work. The members of the Committee shall serve in their personal capacity and shall be fully independent and impartial.

3. The Committee shall include among its members not more than one national of a State party; such member may be re-elected only once. Due regard shall be given to the rotation principle.

4. The members of the Committee shall be elected for a four-year term, although the mandate of three of the members elected during the first election shall be for two years and shall be renewed by lot.

5. Six months prior to the date of the election, the Secretary-General of the League of Arab States shall invite the States parties to submit their nominations within the following three months. He shall transmit the list of candidates to the States parties two months prior to the date of the election. The candidates who obtain the largest number of votes cast shall be elected to membership of the Committee. If, because two or more candidates have an equal number of votes, the number of candidates with the largest number of votes exceeds the number required, a second ballot will be held between the persons with equal numbers of votes. If the votes are again equal, the member or members shall be selected by lottery. The first election for membership of the Committee shall be held at least six months after the Charter enters into force.

6. The Secretary-General shall invite the States parties to a meeting at the headquarters of the League of Arab States in order to elect the member of the Committee. The

presence of the majority of the States parties shall constitute a quorum. If there is no quorum, the Secretary-General shall call another meeting at which at least two-thirds of the States parties must be present. If there is still no quorum, the Secretary-General shall call a third meeting, which will be held regardless of the number of States parties present.

7. The Secretary-General shall convene the first meeting of the Committee, during the course of which the Committee shall elect its Chairman from among its members, for a two-year term which may be renewed only once and for an identical period. The Committee shall establish its own rules of procedure and methods of work and shall determine how often it shall meet. The Committee shall hold its meetings at the headquarters of the League of Arab States. It may also meet in any other State party to the present Charter at that party's invitation.

Article 46

1. The Secretary-General shall declare a seat vacant after being notified by the Chairman of a member's:

(a) Death;

(b) Resignation; or

(c) If, in the unanimous, opinion of the other members, a member of the Committee has ceased to perform his functions without offering an acceptable justification or for any reason other than a temporary absence.

2. If a member's seat is declared vacant pursuant to the provisions of paragraph 1and the term of office of the member to be replaced does not expire within six months from the date on which the vacancy was declared, the Secretary-General of the League of Arab States shall refer the matter to the States parties to the present Charter, which may, within two months, submit nominations, pursuant to article 45, in order to fill the vacant seat.

3. The Secretary-General of the League of Arab States shall draw up an alphabetical list of all the duly nominated candidates, which he shall transmit to the States parties to the present Charter. The elections to fill the vacant seat shall be held in accordance with the relevant provisions.

4. Any member of the Committee elected to fill a seat declared vacant in accordance with the provisions of paragraph 1 shall remain a member of the Committee until the expiry of the remainder of the term of the member whose seat was declared vacant pursuant to the provisions of that paragraph.

5. The Secretary-General of the League of Arab States shall make provision within the budget of the League of Arab States for all the necessary financial and human resources and facilities that the Committee needs to discharge its functions effectively. The Committee's experts shall be afforded the same treatment with respect to remuneration and reimbursement of expenses as experts of the secretariat of the League of Arab States.

Article 47

The States parties undertake to ensure that members of the Committee shall enjoy the immunities necessary for their protection against any form of harassment or moral or material pressure or prosecution on account of the positions they take or statements they make while carrying out their functions as members of the Committee.

Article 48

1. The States parties undertake to submit reports to the Secretary-General of the League of Arab States on the measures they have taken to give effect to the rights and freedoms

recognized in this Charter and on the progress made towards the enjoyment thereof. The Secretary-General shall transmit these reports to the Committee for its consideration.

2. Each State party shall submit an initial report to the Committee within one year from the date on which the Charter enters into force and a periodic report every three years thereafter. The Committee may request the States parties to supply it with additional information relating to the implementation of the Charter.

3. The Committee shall consider the reports submitted by the States parties under paragraph 2 of this article in the presence of the representative of the State party whose report is being considered.

4. The Committee shall discuss the report, comment thereon and make the necessary recommendations in accordance with the aims of the Charter.

5. The Committee shall submit an annual report containing its comments and recommendations to the Council of the League, through the intermediary of the Secretary-General.

6. The Committee's reports, concluding observations and recommendations shall be public documents which the Committee shall disseminate widely.

Article 49

1. The Secretary-General of the League of Arab States shall submit the present Charter, once it has been approved by the Council of the League, to the States members for signature, ratification or accession.

2. The present Charter shall enter into effect two months from the date on which the seventh instrument of ratification is deposited with the secretariat of the League of Arab States.

3. After its entry into force, the present Charter shall become effective for each State two months after the State in question has deposited its instrument of ratification or accession with the secretariat.

4. The Secretary-General shall notify the States members of the deposit of each instrument of ratification or accession.

Article 50

Any State party may submit written proposals, though the Secretary-General, for the amendment of the present Charter. After these amendments have been circulated among the States members, the Secretary-General shall invite the States parties to consider the proposed amendments before submitting them to the Council of the League for adoption.

Article 51

The amendments shall take effect, with regard to the States parties that have approved them, once they have been approved by two-thirds of the States parties.

Article 52

Any State party may propose additional optional protocols to the present Charter and they shall be adopted in accordance with the procedures used for the adoption of amendments to the Charter.

Article 53

1. Any State party, when signing this Charter, depositing the instruments of ratification or acceding hereto, may make a reservation to any article of the Charter, provided

that such reservation does not conflict with the aims and fundamental purposes of the Charter.

2. Any State party that has made a reservation pursuant to paragraph 1 of this article may withdraw it at any time by addressing a notification to the Secretary-General of the League of Arab States.

European Convention for the Protection of Human Rights and Fundamental Freedoms

213 U.N.T.S. 221, Eur. T.S. No. 5 (1950), revised by Protocol 11

The Governments signatory hereto, being Members of the Council of Europe,

Considering the Universal Declaration of Human Rights proclaimed by the General Assembly of the United Nations on 10 December 1948;

Considering that this Declaration aims at securing the universal and effective recognition and observance of the Rights therein declared;

Considering that the aim of the Council of Europe is the achievement of greater unity between its Members and that one of the methods by which that aim is to be pursued is the maintenance and further realisation of Human Rights and Fundamental Freedoms;

Reaffirming their profound belief in those Fundamental Freedoms which are the foundation of justice and peace in the world and are best maintained on the one hand by an effective political democracy and on the other by a common understanding and observance of the Human Rights upon which they depend;

Being resolved, as the Governments of European countries which are like-minded and have a common heritage of political traditions, ideals, freedom and the rule of law, to take the first steps for the collective enforcement of certain of the Rights stated in the Universal Declaration,

Have agreed as follows:

Article 1. Obligation to respect human rights

The High Contracting Parties shall secure to everyone within their jurisdiction the rights and freedoms defined in Section I of this Convention.

Section I. Rights and Freedoms

Article 2. Right to life

1. Everyone's right to life shall be protected by law. No one shall be deprived of his life intentionally save in the execution of a sentence of a court following his conviction of a crime for which this penalty is provided by law.

2. Deprivation of life shall not be regarded as inflicted in contravention of this article when it results from the use of force which is no more than absolutely necessary:

a. in defence of any person from unlawful violence;

b. in order to effect a lawful arrest or to prevent the escape of a person lawfully detained;

c. in action lawfully taken for the purpose of quelling a riot or insurrection.

Article 3. Prohibition of torture

No one shall be subjected to torture or to inhuman or degrading treatment or punishment.

Article 4. Prohibition of slavery and forced labour

1. No one shall be held in slavery or servitude.

2. No one shall be required to perform forced or compulsory labour.

3. For the purpose of this article the term "forced or compulsory labour" shall not include:

a. any work required to be done in the ordinary course of detention imposed according to the provisions of Article 5 of this Convention or during conditional release from such detention;

b. any service of a military character or, in case of conscientious objectors in countries where they are recognized, service exacted instead of compulsory military service;

c. any service exacted in case of an emergency or calamity threatening the life or well-being of the community;

d. any work or service which forms part of normal civic obligations.

Article 5. Right to liberty and security

1. Everyone has the right to liberty and security of person. No one shall be deprived of his liberty save in the following cases and in accordance with a procedure described by law;

a. the lawful detention of a person after conviction by a competent court;

b. the lawful arrest or detention of a person for non-compliance with the lawful order of a court or in order to secure the fulfilment of any obligation prescribed by law;

c. the lawful arrest or detention of a person effected for the purpose of bringing him before the competent legal authority on reasonable suspicion of having committed an offence or when it is reasonably considered necessary to prevent his committing an offence or fleeing after having done so;

d. the detention of a minor by lawful order for the purpose of educational supervision or his lawful detention for the purpose of bringing him before the competent legal authority;

e. the lawful detention of persons for the prevention of the spreading of infectious diseases, of persons of unsound mind, alcoholics or drug addicts or vagrants;

f. the lawful arrest or detention of a person to prevent his effecting an unauthorized entry into the country or of a person against whom action is being taken with a view to deportation or extradition.

2. Everyone who is arrested shall be informed promptly, in a language which he understands, of the reasons for his arrest and of any charge against him.

3. Everyone arrested or detained in accordance with the provisions of paragraph 1(c) of this article shall be brought promptly before a judge or other officer authorised by law to exercise judicial power and shall be entitled to trial within a reasonable time or to release pending trial. Release may be conditioned by guarantees to appear for trial.

4. Everyone who is deprived of his liberty by arrest or detention shall be entitled to take proceedings by which the lawfulness of his detention shall be decided speedily by a court and his release ordered if the detention is not lawful.

5. Everyone who has been the victim of arrest or detention in contravention of the provisions of this article shall have an enforceable right to compensation.

Article 6. Right to a fair trial

1. In the determination of his civil rights and obligations or of any criminal charge against him, everyone is entitled to a fair and public hearing within a reasonable time by an independent and impartial tribunal established by law. Judgment shall be pronounced publicly but the press and public may be excluded from all or part of the trial in the interest of morals, public order or national security in a democratic society, where the interests of juveniles or the protection of the private life of the parties so require, or to the extent strictly necessary in the opinion of the court in special circumstances where publicity would prejudice the interests of justice.

2. Everyone charged with a criminal offence shall be presumed innocent until proved guilty according to law.

3. Everyone charged with a criminal offence has the following minimum rights:

a. to be informed promptly, in a language which he understands and in detail, of the nature and cause of the accusation against him;

b. to have adequate time and facilities for the preparation of his defence;

c. to defend himself in person or through legal assistance of his own choosing or, if he has not sufficient means to pay for legal assistance, to be given it free when the interests of justice so require;

d. to examine or have examined witness against him and to obtain the attendance and examination of witnesses on his behalf under the same conditions as witnesses against him;

e. to have the free assistance of an interpreter if he cannot understand or speak the language used in court.

Article 7. No punishment without law

1. No one shall be held guilty of any criminal offence on account of any act or omission which did not constitute a criminal offence under national or international law at the time it was committed.

2. This article shall not prejudice the trial and punishment of a person for any act or omission which at the time when it was committed, was criminal according to the general principles of law recognized by civilized nations.

Article 8. Right to respect for private and family life

1. Everyone has the right to respect for private and family life, his home and his correspondence.

2. There shall be no interference by a public authority with the exercise of this right except such as is in accordance with the law and is necessary in a democratic society in the interests of national security, public safety or the economic well-being of the country, for the prevention of disorder or crime, for the protection of health or morals, or for the protection of the rights and freedoms of others.

Article 9. Freedom of thought, conscience and religion

1. Everyone has the right to freedom of thought, conscience and religion; this right includes freedom to change his religion or belief and freedom, either alone or in community with others and in public or private, to manifest his religion or belief, in worship, teaching, practice and observance.

2. Freedom to manifest one's religion or belief shall be subject only to such limitations as are prescribed by law and are necessary in a democratic society in the interests of public order, health or morals, or for the protection of the rights and freedoms of others.

Article 10. Freedom of expression

1. Everyone has the right to freedom of expression. This right shall include freedom to hold opinions and to receive and impart information and ideas without interference by public authority and regardless of frontiers. This article shall not prevent States from requiring the licensing of broadcasting, television or cinema enterprises.

2. The exercise of these freedoms, since it carries with it duties and responsibilities, may be subject to such formalities, conditions, restrictions or penalties as are prescribed by law and are necessary in a democratic society, in the interests of national security, territorial integrity or public safety, for the prevention of disorder or crime, for the protection of the reputation or rights of others, for preventing the disclosure of information received in confidence, or for maintaining the authority and impartiality of the judiciary.

Article 11. Freedom of assembly and association

1. Everyone has the right to freedom of peaceful assembly and to freedom of association with others, including the right to form and to join trade unions for the protection of his interests.

2. No restrictions shall be placed on the exercise of these rights other than such as are prescribed by law and are necessary in a democratic society in the interests of national security or public safety for the prevention of disorder or crime, for the protection of health or morals or for the protection of the rights and freedoms of others. This article shall not prevent the imposition of lawful restrictions on the exercise of these rights by members of the armed forces, of the police or the administration of the State.

Article 12. Right to marry

Men and women of marriageable age have the fight to marry and to found a family, according to the national laws governing the exercise of this right.

Article 13. Right to an effective remedy

Everyone whose rights and freedoms as set forth in this Convention are violated shall have an effective remedy before a national authority notwithstanding that the violation has been committed by persons acting in an official capacity.

Article 14. Prohibition of discrimination

The employment of the rights and freedoms as set forth in this Convention shall be secured without discrimination on any ground such as sex, race, colour, language, religion, political or other opinion, national or social origin, association with a national minority, property, birth or other status.

Article 15. Derogation in time of emergency

1. In time of war or other public emergency threatening the life of the nation any High Contracting Party may take measures derogating from its obligations under this Convention to the extent strictly required by the exigencies of the situation, provided that such measures are not inconsistent with its other obligations under international law.

2. No derogation from Article 2, except in respect of deaths resulting from lawful acts of war, or from Articles 3, 4 (paragraph 1) and 7 shall be made under this provision.

3. Any High Contracting Party availing itself of this right of derogation shall keep the Secretary General of the Council of Europe fully informed of the measures which it has taken and the reasons therefor. It shall also inform the Secretary General of the Council of Europe when such measures have ceased to operate and the provisions of the Convention are again being fully executed.

Article 16. Restrictions on political activity of aliens

Nothing in Articles 10, 11, and 14 shall be regarded as preventing the High Contracting Parties from imposing restrictions on the political activity of aliens.

Article 17. Prohibition of abuse of rights

Nothing in this Convention may be interpreted as implying for any State, group or person any right to engage in any activity or perform any act aimed at the destruction of any of the rights and freedoms set forth herein or at their limitation to a greater extent than is provided for in the Convention.

Article 18. Limitation on use of restrictions on rights

The restrictions permitted under this Convention to the said rights and freedoms shall not be applied for any purpose other than those for which they have been prescribed.

Protocol No. 6 to the European Convention for the Protection of Human Rights and Fundamental Freedoms (excerpt)
Eur. T.S. 114

Article 1

The death penalty shall be abolished. No one shall be condemned to such penalty or executed.

Article 2

A State may make provisions in its law for the death penalty in respect of acts committed in time of war or of imminent threat of war; such penalty shall be applied only in the instances laid down in the law and in accordance with its provisions. The State shall communicate to the Secretary General of the Council of Europe the relevant provisions of that law.

Article 3

No derogation from the provisions of this Protocol shall be made under Article 15 of the Convention.

Article 4

No reservation may be made under Article 64 of the Convention in respect of the provisions of this Protocol.

Instructions for the Government of Armies of the United States in the Field, General Orders No. 100 (1863)
(the 1863 Lieber Code)

Article 11

The law of war does not only disclaim all cruelty and bad faith concerning engagements concluded with the enemy during war, but also the breaking of stipulations solemnly contracted by the belligerents in time of peace, and avowedly intended to remain in force in case of war between the contracting powers.

It disclaims all extortions and other transactions for individual gain; all acts of private revenge, or connivance in such acts.

Offenses to the contrary shall be severely punished, and especially so if committed by officers....

Article 13

Military jurisdiction is of two kinds: First, that which is conferred and defined by statute; second, that which is derived from the common law of war.... The character of the courts which exercise these jurisdictions depends upon the local laws of each particular country....

Article 14

Military necessity, as understood by modern civilized nations, consists in the necessity of those measures which are indispensable for securing the ends of the war, and which are lawful according to the modern law and usages of war.

Article 15

Military necessity admits of all direct destruction of life and limb of armed enemies, and other persons whose destruction is incidentally unavoidable in the armed contests of the war; it allows the capturing of every armed enemy, and every enemy of importance to the hostile government, or of particular danger to the captor; it allows all destruction of property, and obstruction of the ways and channels of traffic, travel, or communication, and of all withholding of sustenance or means of life from the enemy; of the appropriation of whatever an enemy's country affords necessary for the subsistence and safety of the army, and of such deception as does not involve the breaking of good faith either positively pledged, regarding agreements entered into during the war, or supposed by the modern laws of war to exist. Men who take up arms against one another in public war do not cease on this account to be moral beings, responsible to one another and to God.

Article 16

Military necessity does not admit of cruelty — that is the infliction of suffering for the sake of suffering or for revenge, nor of maiming or wounding except in fight, nor of torture to extort confessions. It does not admit of the use of poison in any way, nor the wanton devastation of a district. It admits of deception, but disclaims acts of perfidy; and, in general, military necessity does not include any act of hostility which makes the return to peace unnecessarily difficult.

Article 17

War is not carried on by arms alone. It is lawful to starve the hostile belligerent, armed or unarmed, so that it leads to the speedier subjection of the enemy.

Article 18

When a commander of a besieged place expels the noncombatants, in order to lessen the number of those who consume his stock of provisions, it is lawful, though an extreme measure, to drive them back, so as to hasten on the surrender....

Article 21

The citizen or native of a hostile country is thus an enemy, as one of the constituents of the hostile state or nation, and as such is subjected to the hardships of war.

Article 22

Nevertheless, as civilization has advanced during the last centuries, so has likewise steadily advanced, especially in war on land, the distinction between the private individual belonging to a hostile country and the hostile country itself, with its men in arms. The principle has been more and more acknowledged that the unarmed citizen is to be spared in person, property, and honor as much as the exigencies of war will admit.

Article 23

Private citizens are no longer murdered, enslaved, or carried off to distant parts, and the inoffensive individual is as little disturbed in his private relations as the commander of the hostile troops can afford to grant in the overruling demands of a vigorous war....

Article 34

As a general rule, the property belonging to churches, to hospitals, or other establishments of an exclusively charitable character, to establishments of education, or foundations for the promotion of knowledge, whether public schools, universities, academies of learning or observatories, museums of the fine arts, or of a scientific character–such property is not to be considered public property ... [for seizure or appropriation]; but it may be taxed or used when the public service may require it.

Article 35

Classical works of art, libraries, scientific collections, or precious instruments, such as astronomical telescopes, as well as hospitals, must be secured against all avoidable injury, even when they are contained in fortified places whilst besieged or bombarded.

Article 36

If such works of art, libraries, collections, or instruments belonging to a hostile nation or government, can be removed without injury, the ruler of the conquering state or nation may order them to be seized and removed for the benefit of the said nation. The ultimate ownership is to be settled by the ensuing treaty of peace.

In no case shall they be sold or given away, if captured by the armies of the United States, nor shall they ever be privately appropriated, or wantonly destroyed or injured.

Article 37

The United States acknowledge and protect, in hostile countries occupied by them, religion and morality; strictly private property; the persons of the inhabitants, especially those of women; and the sacredness of domestic relations. Offenses to the contrary shall be rigorously punished....

Article 44

All wanton violence committed against persons in the invaded country, all destruction of property not commanded by the authorized officer, all robbery, all pillage or sacking, even after taking a place by main force, all rape, wounding, maiming, or killing of such inhabitants, are prohibited under the penalty of death, or such other severe punishment as may seem adequate for the gravity of the offense.

A soldier, officer or private, in the act of committing such violence, and disobeying a superior ordering him to abstain from it, may be lawfully killed on the spot by such superior.

Article 45

All captures and booty belong, according to the modern law of war, primarily to the government of the captor....

Article 47

Crimes punishable by all penal codes, such as arson, murder, maiming, assaults, highway robbery, theft, burglary, fraud, forgery, and rape, if committed by an American soldier in a hostile country against the inhabitants, are not only punishable as at home, but in all cases in which death is not inflicted, the severer punishment shall be preferred....

Article 49

A prisoner of war is a public enemy armed or attached to the hostile army for active aid, who has fallen into the hands of the captor ...

All soldiers, of whatever species of arms; all men who belong to the rising en masse of the hostile country; all those who are attached to the army for its efficiency and promote directly the object of the war, except such as are hereinafter provided for ... are prisoners of war ...

Article 56

A prisoner of war is subject to no punishment for being a public enemy, nor is any revenge wreaked upon him by the intentional infliction of any suffering, or disgrace, by cruel imprisonment, want of food, by mutilation, death, or other barbarity.

Article 57

So soon as a man is armed by a sovereign government and takes the soldier's oath of fidelity, he is a belligerent; his killing, wounding, or other warlike acts are not individual crimes or offenses. No belligerent has a right to declare that enemies of a certain class, color, or condition, when properly organized as soldiers, will not be treated by him as public enemies.

Article 58

The law of nations knows no distinction of color, and if an enemy of the United States should enslave and sell any captured persons of their army, it would be a case of the severest retaliation, if not redressed upon complaint.

The United States cannot retaliate by enslavement; therefore death must be the retaliation for this crime against the law of nations.

Article 59

A prisoner of war remains answerable for his crimes committed against the captor's army or people....

Article 62

All troops of the enemy known or discovered to give no quarter in general, or to any portion of the army, receive none.

Article 63

Troops who fight in the uniform of their enemies, without any plain, striking, and uniform mark of distinction of their own, can expect no quarter....

Article 65

The use of the enemy's national standard, flag, or other emblem of nationality, for the purpose of deceiving the enemy in battle, is an act of perfidy by which they lose all claim to the protection of the laws of war....

Article 68

... Unnecessary or revengeful destruction of life is not lawful.

Article 70

The use of poison in any manner, be it to poison wells, or food, or arms, is wholly excluded from modern warfare. He that uses it puts himself out of the pale of the law and usages of war.

Article 71

Whoever intentionally inflicts additional wounds on an enemy already wholly disabled, or kills such an enemy, or who orders or encourages soldiers to do so, shall suffer death, if duly convicted, whether he belongs to the Army of the United States, or is an enemy captured after having committed his misdeed....

Article 76

Prisoners of war shall be fed upon plain and wholesome food, whenever practicable, and treated with humanity.

They may be required to work for the benefit of the captor's government, according to their rank and condition.

Article 77

A prisoner of war who escapes may be shot or otherwise killed in his flight, but neither death nor any other punishment shall be inflicted upon him simply for his attempt to escape....

Article 79

Every captured wounded enemy shall be medically treated, according to the ability of the medical staff....

Article 81

Partisans are soldiers armed and wearing the uniform of their army, but belonging to a corps which acts detached from the main body for the purpose of making inroads into the territory occupied by the enemy. If captured, they are entitled to all the privileges of the prisoner of war.

Article 82

Men, or squads of men, who commit hostilities, whether by fighting, or inroads for destruction or plunder, or by raids of any kind, without commission, without being part and portion of the organized hostile army, and without sharing continuously in the war, but do so with intermitting returns to their homes and avocations, or with the occasional assumption of the semblance of peaceful pursuits, divesting themselves of the character or appearance of soldiers—such men, or squads of men, are public enemies, and therefore, if captured, are not entitled to the privileges of prisoners of war, but shall be treated summarily as highway robbers or pirates.

Article 83

Scouts, or single soldiers, if disguised in the dress of the country or in the uniform of the army hostile to their own, employed in obtaining information, if found within or lurking about the lines of the captor, are treated as spies, and suffer death....

Article 101

While deception in war is admitted as a just and necessary means of hostility, and is consistent with honorable warfare, the common law of war allows even capital punishment for clandestine or treacherous attempts to injure an enemy, because they are so dangerous, and it is so difficult to guard against them....

Article 148

The law of war does not allow proclaiming either an individual belonging to the hostile army, or a citizen, or a subject of the hostile government, an outlaw, who may be slain without trial by any captor, any more than the modern law of peace allows such intentional outlawry; on the contrary, it abhors such outrage.... Civilized nations look with horror upon offers of rewards for the assassination of enemies as relapses into barbarism.

Hague Convention (No. IV) Respecting the Laws and Customs of War on Land, and Annex

done at The Hague, Oct. 18, 1907
36 Stat. 2277, T.S. No. 539, 1 Bevans 631

Preamble

... Considering that, while seeking means to preserve peace and prevent armed conflicts between nations, it is likewise necessary to bear in mind the case where an appeal to arms may be brought about by events which their solicitude could not avert;

Animated by the desire to serve, even in this extreme case, the interests of humanity and the ever progressive needs of civilization;

Thinking it important, with this object, to revise the general laws and customs of war, either with a view to defining them with greater precision or to confining them within such limits as would mitigate their severity as far as possible;

Have deemed in necessary to complete and render more precise in certain particulars the work of the First Peace Conference, which, following on the Brussels Conference of 1874, and inspired by the ideas dictated by a wise and generous forethought, adopted provisions intended to define and govern the usages of war on land.

According to the views of the High Contacting Parties, these provisions, the wording of which has been inspired by the desire to diminish the evils of war, so far as military requirements permit, are intended to serve as a general rule of conduct for the belligerents in their mutual relations and in their relations with the inhabitants.

It has not, however, been found possible at present to concert Regulations covering all the circumstances which arise in practice;

On the other hand, the High Contracting Parties clearly do not intend that unforeseen cases should, in the absence of a written undertaking, be let to the arbitrary judgment of military commanders.

Until a more complete code of the laws of war has been issued, the High Contracting Parties deem it expedient to declare that, in cases not included in the Regulations adopted by them, the inhabitants and the belligerents remain under the protection and the rule of the principles of the law of nations, as they result from the usages established among civilized peoples, from the laws of humanity, and from the dictates of the public conscience.

They declare that it is in this sense especially that Articles 1 and 2 of the Regulations adopted must be understood....

Who, after having deposited their full powers, found in good and due form, have agreed upon the following:

Article 1

The Contracting Parties shall issue instructions to their armed land forces which shall be in conformity with the Regulations respecting the Laws and Customs of War on Land, annexed to the present Convention.

Article 2

The provisions contained in the Regulations referred to in Article 1, as well as in the present Convention, do not apply except between Contracting Powers, and then only if all the belligerents are parties to the Convention.

Article 3

A belligerent party which violates the provisions of the said Regulations shall, if the case demands, be liable to pay compensation. It shall be responsible for all acts committed by persons forming part of its armed forces....

Annex to the Convention.

Regulations Respecting the Laws and Customs of War on Land

Section I. On Belligerents.

Chapter I. The Qualifications of Belligerents.

Article 1

The laws, rights, and duties of war apply not only to armies, but also to militia and volunteer corps fulfilling the following conditions:

1. To be commanded by a person responsible for his subordinates;

2. To have a fixed distinctive emblem recognizable at a distance;

3. To carry arms openly; and

4. To conduct their operations in accordance with the laws and customs of war.

In countries where militia or volunteer corps constitute the army, or form part of it, they are included under the denomination "army."

Article 2

The inhabitants of a territory which has not been occupied, who, on the approach of the enemy, spontaneously take up arms to resist the invading troops without having had time to organize themselves in accordance with Article 1, shall be regarded as belligerents if they carry arms openly and if they respect the laws and customs of war.

Article 3

The armed forces of the belligerent parties may consist of combatants and noncombatants. In the case of capture by the enemy, both have a right to be treated as prisoners of war.

Chapter II. Prisoners of War.

Article 4

Prisoners of war are in the power of the hostile Government, but not of the individuals or crops who capture them.

They must be humanely treated.

All their personal belongings, except arms, horses, and military papers, remain their property.

Article 5

Prisoners of war may be interned in a town, fortress, camp, or other place, under obligation not to go beyond certain fixed limits; but they can only be placed in confinement as an indispensable measure of safety and only while the circumstances which necessitate the measure continue to exist....

Article 20

After the conclusion of peace, the repatriation of prisoners of war shall be carried out as quickly as possible.

Chapter III. The Sick and Wounded.

Article 21

The obligations of belligerents with regard to the sick and wounded are governed by the Geneva Convention [of 1906].

Section II. Hostilities.

Chapter I. Means of Injuring the Enemy, Sieges, and Bombardments.

Article 22

The right of belligerents to adopt means of injuring the enemy is not unlimited.

Article 23

In addition to the prohibitions provided by special Conventions, it is especially forbidden:

(a) To employ poison or poisoned weapons;

(b) To kill or wound treacherously individuals belonging to the hostile nation or army;

(c) To kill or wound an enemy who, having laid down his arms, or having no longer means of defence, has surrendered at discretion;

(d) To declare that no quarter will be given;

(e) To employ arms, projectiles, or material of such as nature as to cause unnecessary suffering;

(f) To make improper use of a flag of truce, of the national flag, or of the military insignia and uniform of the enemy, as well as the distinctive badges of the Geneva Convention;

(g) To destroy or seize the enemy's property, unless such destruction or seizure be imperatively demanded by the necessities of war;

(h) To declare abolished, suspended, or inadmissible in a court of law the rights and actions of the nationals of the hostile party.

A belligerent is likewise forbidden to compel the nationals of the hostile party to take part in the operations of war directed against their own country, even if they were in the belligerent's service before the commencement of the war.

Article 24

Ruses of war and the employment of measures necessary for obtaining information about the enemy and the country are considered permissible.

Article 25

The attack or bombardment, by whatever means, of towns, villages, dwellings, or buildings which are undefended is prohibited.

Article 26

The officer in command of an attacking force must, before commencing bombardment, except in cases of assault, do all in his power to warn the authorities.

Article 27

In sieges and bombardments all necessary steps must be taken to spare, as far as possible, buildings dedicated to religion, art, science, or charitable purposes, historic monuments, hospitals, and places where the sick and wounded are collected, provided they are not being used at the time for military purposes.

It is the duty of the besieged to indicate the presence of such buildings or places by distinctive and visible signs, which shall be notified to the enemy beforehand.

Article 28

The pillage of a town or place, even when taken by assault, is prohibited.

Section III. Military Authority Over the Territory of the Hostile State.

Article 42

Territory is considered occupied when it is actually placed under the authority of the hostile army.

The occupation extends only to the territory where such authority has been established and can be exercised.

Article 43

The authority of the legitimate power having in fact passed into the hands of the occupant, the latter shall take all the measures in his power to restore, and ensure, as far as possible, public order and safety, while respecting, unless absolutely prevented, the laws in force in the country.

Article 44

A belligerent is forbidden to force the inhabitants of occupied territory to furnish information about the army of the other belligerent, or about its means of defence.

Article 45

It is forbidden to compel the inhabitants of occupied territory to swear allegiance to the hostile Power.

Article 46

Family honour and rights, the lives of persons, and private property, as well as religious convictions and practice, must be respected.

Private property cannot be confiscated.

Article 47

Pillage is formally forbidden.

Article 48

If, in the territory occupied, the occupant collects the taxes, dues, and tolls imposed for the benefit of the State, he shall do so, as far as is possible in accordance with the rules of assessment and incidence in force, and shall in consequence be bound to defray the expenses of the administration of the occupied territory to the same extent as the legitimate Government was so bound.

Article 49

If, in addition to the taxes mentioned in the above article, the occupant levies other money contributions in the occupied territory, this shall only be for the needs of the army or of the administration of the territory in question.

Article 50

No general penalty, pecuniary or otherwise, shall be inflicted upon the population on account of the acts of individuals for which they cannot be regarded as jointly and severally responsible.

Article 51

No contribution shall be collected except under a written order, and on the responsibility of a Commander-in-chief.

The collection of the said contribution shall only be effected as far as possible in accordance with the rules of assessment and incidence of the taxes in force.

For every contribution a receipt shall be given to the contributors....

Article 53

An army of occupation can only take possession of cash, funds, and realizable securities which are strictly the property of the State, depots of arms, means of transport, stores and supplies, and, generally, all movable property belonging to the State, which may be used for operations of the war.

All appliances, whether on land, at sea, or in the air, adapted for the transmission of news, or for the transport of persons or things, exclusive of cases governed by naval law, depots of arms, and, generally, all kinds of ammunition of war, may be seized, even if they belong to private individuals, but must be restored and compensation fixed when peace is made.

Article 54

Submarine cables connecting an occupied territory with a neutral territory shall not be seized or destroyed except in the case of absolute necessity. They must likewise be restored and compensation fixed when peace is made.

Article 55

The occupying State shall be regarded only as administrator and usufructuary of public buildings, real estate, forests, and agricultural estates belonging to the hostile State, and situated in the occupied country. It must safeguard the capital of these properties, and administer them in accordance with the rules of usufruct.

Article 56

The property of municipalities, that of institutions dedicated to religion, charity and education, the arts and sciences, even when State property, shall be treated as private property.

All seizure of, destruction or wilful damage done to institutions of this character, historic monuments, works of art and science, is forbidden, and should be made the subject of legal proceedings.

List of War Crimes Prepared by the Commission on the Responsibility of the Authors of the War and on Enforcement of Penalties, Presented to the Preliminary Peace Conference

Paris, 29 March 1919
(members: Belgium, British Empire, France, Greece, Italy,
Japan, Poland, Roumania, Serbia, United States)

1. Murder and massacres—systematic terrorism.

2. Putting hostages to death.

3. Torture of civilians.

4. Deliberate starvation of civilians.

5. Rape.

6. Abduction of girls and women for the purpose of enforced prostitution.

7. Deportation of civilians.

8. Internment of civilians under inhuman conditions.

9. Forced labour of civilians in connection with the military operations of the enemy.

10. Usurpation of sovereignty during military occupation.

11. Compulsory enlistment of soldiers among the inhabitants of occupied territory.

12. Attempts to denationalize the inhabitants of occupied territory.

13. Pillage.

14. Confiscation of property.

15. Exaction of illegitimate or of exorbitant contributions and requisitions.

16. Debasement of the currency and issue of spurious currency.

17. Imposition of collective penalties.

18. Wanton devastation and destruction of property.

19. Deliberate bombardment of undefended places.

20. Wanton destruction of religious, charitable, educational and historic buildings and monuments.

21. Destruction of merchant ships and passenger vessels without warning and without provision for the safety of passengers and crew.

22. Destruction of fishing boats and relief ships.

23. Deliberate bombardment of hospitals.

24. Attack and destruction of hospital ships.

25. Breach of other rules relating to the Red Cross.

26. Use of deleterious and asphyxiating gases.

27. Use of explosive or expanding bullets and other inhuman appliances.

28. Directions to give no quarter.

29. Ill-treatment of wounded and prisoners of war.

30. Employment of prisoners of war on unauthorized works.

31. Misuse of flags of truce.

32. Poisoning of wells.

[Item added by the War Crimes Commission]

33. Indiscriminate mass arrests.

Geneva Convention Relative to the Treatment of Prisoners of War of 12 August 1949 (GPW)
75 U.N.T.S. 135, 6 U.S.T. 3316, T.I.A.S. No. 3364

Part I. General Provisions

Article 1

The High Contracting Parties undertake to respect and to ensure respect for the present Convention in all circumstances.

Article 2

In addition to the provisions which shall be implemented in peacetime, the present Convention shall apply to all cases of declared war or of any other armed conflict which may arise between two or more of the High Contracting Parties, even if the state of war is not recognized by one of them.

The Convention shall also apply to all cases of partial or total occupation of the territory of a High Contracting Party, even if the said occupation meets with no armed resistance.

Although one of the Powers in conflict may not be a party to the present Convention, the Powers who are parties thereto shall remain bound by it in their mutual relations. They shall furthermore be bound by the Convention in relation to the said Power, if the latter accepts and applies the provisions thereof.

Article 3

In the case of armed conflict not of an international character occurring in the territory of one of the High Contracting Parties, each party to the conflict shall be bound to apply, as a minimum, the following provisions:

(1) Persons taking no active part in the hostilities, including members of armed forces who have laid down their arms and those placed *hors de combat* by sickness, wounds, detention, or any other cause, shall in all circumstances be treated humanely, without any adverse distinction founded on race, colour, religion or faith, sex, birth or wealth, or any other similar criteria.

To this end, the following acts are and shall remain prohibited at any time and in any place whatsoever with respect to the above-mentioned persons:

(a) violence to life and person, in particular murder of all kinds, mutilation, cruel treatment and torture;

(b) taking of hostages;

(c) outrages upon personal dignity, in particular, humiliating and degrading treatment;

(d) the passing of sentences and the carrying out of executions without previous judgment pronounced by a regularly constituted court, affording all the judicial guarantees which are recognized as indispensable by civilized peoples.

(2) The wounded and sick shall be collected and cared for.

An impartial humanitarian body, such as the International Committee of the Red Cross, may offer its services to the Parties to the conflict.

The Parties to the conflict should further endeavor to bring into force, by means of special agreements, all or part of the other provisions of the present Convention.

The application of the preceding provisions shall not affect the legal status of the Parties to the conflict.

Article 4

A. Prisoners of war, in the sense of the present Convention, are persons belonging to one of the following categories, who have fallen into the power of the enemy:

1. Members of the armed forces of a Party to the conflict, as well as members of militias or volunteer corps forming part of such forces.

2. Members of other militias and members of other volunteer corps, including those of organized resistance movements, belonging to a Party to the conflict and operating in or outside their own territory, even if this territory is occupied, provided that such militias or volunteer corps, including such organized resistance movements, fulfil the following conditions:

a. that of being commanded by a person responsible for his subordinates;

b. that of having a fixed distinctive sign recognizable at a distance;

c. that of carrying arms openly;

d. that of conducting their operations in accordance with the laws and customs of war.

3. Members of regular armed forces who profess allegiance to a government or an authority not recognized by the Detaining Power....

6. Inhabitants of a non-occupied territory, who on the approach of the enemy spontaneously take up arms to resist the invading forces, without having had time to form themselves into regular armed units provided they carry arms openly and respect the laws and customs of war....

C. This article shall in no way affect the status of medical personnel and chaplains as provided for in Article 33 of the present Convention.

Article 5

The present Convention shall apply to the persons referred to in Article 4 from the time they fall into the power of the enemy and until their final release and repatriation.

Should any doubt arise as to whether persons, having committed a belligerent act and having fallen into the hands of the enemy, belong to any of the categories enumerated in

Article 4, such persons shall enjoy the protection of the present Convention until such time as their status has been determined by a competent tribunal.

Article 6

In addition to the agreements expressly provided for in Articles 10, 23, 28, 33, 60, 65, 66, 67, 72, 73, 109, 110, 118, 119, 122 and 132, the High Contracting Parties may conclude other special agreements for all matters concerning which they may deem it suitable to make separate provision. No special agreement shall adversely affect the situation of prisoners of war, as defined by the present Convention, nor restrict the rights which it confers upon them....

Article 7

Prisoners of war may in no circumstances renounce in part or in entirety the rights secured to them by the present Convention, and by the special agreements referred to in the foregoing article, if such there be ...

Part II. General Protection of Prisoners of War

Article 12

Prisoners of war are in the hands of the enemy Power, but not of the individuals or military units who have captured them. Irrespective of the individual responsibilities that may exist, the Detaining Power is responsible for the treatment given them.

Prisoners of war may only be transferred by the Detaining Power to a Power which is a party to the Convention and after the Detaining Power has satisfied itself of the willingness and ability of such transferee Power to apply the Convention. When prisoners of war are transferred under such circumstances, responsibility for the application of the Convention rests on the Power accepting them while they are in its custody.

Nevertheless, if that Power fails to carry out the provisions of the Convention in any important respect, the Power by whom the prisoners of war were transferred shall, upon being notified by the Protecting Power, take effective measures to correct the situation or shall request the return of the prisoners of war. Such requests must be complied with.

Article 13

Prisoners of war must at all times be humanely treated. Any unlawful act or omission by the Detaining Power causing death or seriously endangering the health of a prisoner of war in its custody is prohibited, and will be regarded as a serious breach of the present Convention. In particular, no prisoner of war may be subjected to physical mutilation or to medical or scientific experiments of any kind which are not justified by the medical, dental or hospital treatment of the prisoner concerned and carried out in his interest.

Likewise, prisoners of war must at all times be protected, particularly against acts of violence or intimidation and against insults and public curiosity.

Measures of reprisal against prisoners of war are prohibited.

Article 14

Prisoners of war are entitled in all circumstances to respect for their persons and their honour.

Women shall be treated with all the regard due to their sex and shall in all cases benefit by treatment as favourable as that granted to men.

Prisoners of war shall retain the full civil capacity which they enjoyed at the time of their capture. The Detaining Power may not restrict the exercise, either within or without its own territory, of the rights such capacity confers except in so far as the capacity requires.

Article 15

The Power detaining prisoners of war shall be bound to provide free of charge for their maintenance and for the medical attention required by their state of health.

Article 16

Taking into consideration the provisions of the present Convention relating to rank and sex, and subject to any privileged treatment which may be accorded to them by reason of their state of health, age or professional qualifications, all prisoners of war shall be treated alike by the Detaining Power, without any adverse distinction based on race, nationality, religious belief or political opinions, or any other distinction founded on similar criteria.

Part III. Captivity

Section I. Beginning of Captivity

Article 18

All effects and articles of personal use, except arms, horses, military equipment and military documents, shall remain in the possession of prisoners of war, likewise their metal helmets and gas masks and like articles issued for personal protection. Effects and articles used for their clothing or feeding shall likewise remain in their possession, even if such effects and articles belong to their regulation military equipment.

At no time should prisoners of war be without identity documents. The Detaining Power shall supply such documents to prisoners of war who possess none.

Badges of rank and nationality, decorations and articles having above all a personal or sentimental value may not be taken from prisoners of war.

Sums of money carried by prisoners of war may not be taken away from them except by order of an officer, and after the amount and particulars of the owner have been recorded in a special register and an itemized receipt has been given, legibly inscribed with the name, rank and unit of the person issuing the said receipt. Sums in the currency of the Detaining Power, or which are changed into such currency at the prisoner"s request, shall be placed to the credit of the prisoner"s account as provided in Article 64.

The Detaining Power may withdraw articles of value from prisoners of war only for reasons of security; when such articles are withdrawn, the procedure laid down for sums of money impounded shall apply.

Such objects, likewise sums taken away in any currency other than that of the Detaining Power and the conversion of which has not been asked for by the owners, shall be kept in the custody of the Detaining Power and shall be returned in their initial shape to prisoners of war at the end of their captivity.

Article 19

Prisoners of war shall be evacuated, as soon as possible after their capture, to camps situated in an area far enough from the combat zone for them to be out of danger.

Only those prisoners of war who, owing to wounds or sickness, would run greater risks by being evacuated than by remaining where they are, may be temporarily kept back in a danger zone.

Prisoners of war shall not be unnecessarily exposed to danger while awaiting evacuation from a fighting zone.

Article 20

The evacuation of prisoners of war shall always be effected humanely and in conditions similar to those for the forces of the Detaining Power in their changes of station.

The Detaining Power shall supply prisoners of war who are being evacuated with sufficient food and potable water, and with the necessary clothing and medical attention. The Detaining Power shall take all suitable precautions to ensure their safety during evacuation, and shall establish as soon as possible a list of the prisoners of war who are evacuated.

If prisoners of war must, during evacuation, pass through transit camps, their stay in such camps shall be as brief as possible....

Section II. Internment of Prisoners of War

Chapter I. General Observations.

Article 22

Prisoners of war may be interned only in premises located on land and affording every guarantee of hygiene and healthfulness. Except in particular cases which are justified by the interest of the prisoners themselves, they shall not be interned in penitentiaries.

Prisoners of war interned in unhealthy areas, or where the climate is injurious for them, shall be removed as soon as possible to a more favourable climate.

The Detaining Power shall assemble prisoners of war in camps or camp compounds according to their nationality, language and customs, provided that such prisoners shall not be separated from prisoners of war belonging to the armed forces with which they were serving at the time of their capture, except with their consent.

Article 23

No prisoner of war may at any time be sent to, or detained in areas where he may be exposed to the fire of the combat zone, nor may his presence be used to render certain points or areas immune from military operations.

Prisoners of war shall have shelters against air bombardment and other hazards of war, to the same extent as the local civilian population. With the exception of those engaged in the protection of their quarters against the aforesaid hazards, they may enter such shelters as soon as possible after the giving of the alarm. Any other protective measure taken in favor of the population shall also apply to them.

Detaining Powers shall give the Powers concerned, through the intermediary of the Protecting Powers, all useful information regarding the geographical location of prisoner of war camps.

Whenever military considerations permit, prisoner of war camps shall be indicated in the day-time by the letters PW or PG, placed so as to be clearly visible from the air. The Powers concerned may, however, agree upon any other system or marking. Only prisoner of war camps shall be marked as such.

Article 24

Transit or screening camps of a permanent kind shall be fitted out under conditions similar to those described in the present Section, and the prisoners therein shall have the same treatment as in other camps.

Chapter II. Quarters, Food and Clothing of Prisoners of War.

Chapter III. Hygiene and Medical Attention.

Chapter IV. Medical Personnel and Chaplains Retained to Assist Prisoners of War.

Article 33

Members of the medical personnel and chaplains while retained by the Detaining Power with a view to assisting prisoners of war, shall not be considered as prisoners of war. They shall, however, receive as a minimum the benefits and protection of the present Convention, and shall be granted all facilities necessary to provide for the medical care of, and religious ministration to prisoners of war....

Chapter V. Religious, Intellectual and Physical Activities.

Chapter VI. Discipline.

Chapter VII. Transfer of Prisoners of War After Their Arrival in Camp.

Section III. Labour of Prisoners of War

Section IV. Financial Resources of Prisoners of War

Section V. Relations of Prisoners of War with the Exterior

Section VI. Relations Between Prisoners of War and the Authorities

Chapter I. Complaints of Prisoners of War Respecting the Conditions of Captivity.

Chapter II. Prisoner of War Representatives.

Chapter III. Penal and Disciplinary Sanctions.

I. General Provisions

Article 82

A prisoner of war shall be subject to the laws, regulations and orders in force in the armed forces of the Detaining Power; the Detaining Power shall be justified in taking judicial or disciplinary measures in respect of any offence committed by a prisoner of war against such laws, regulations or orders. However, no proceedings or punishments contrary to the provisions of this Chapter shall be allowed.

Article 83

In deciding whether proceedings in respect of an offence alleged to have been committed by a prisoner of war shall be judicial or disciplinary, the Detaining Power shall ensure that the competent authorities exercise the greatest leniency and adopt, wherever possible, disciplinary rather than judicial measures.

Article 84

A prisoner of war shall be tried only by a military court, unless the existing laws of the Detaining Power expressly permit the civil courts to try a member of the armed forces of the Detaining Power in respect of the particular offence alleged to have been committed by the prisoner of war.

In no circumstances whatever shall a prisoner of war be tried by a court of any kind which does not offer the essential guarantees of independence and impartiality as generally recognized, and, in particular, the procedure of which does not afford the accused the rights and means of defence provided for in Article 105.

Article 85

Prisoners of war prosecuted under the laws of the Detaining Power for acts committed prior to capture shall retain, even if convicted, the benefits of the present Convention.

Article 86

No prisoner of war may be punished more than once for the same act or on the same charge.

Article 87

Prisoners of war may not be sentenced by the military authorities and courts of the Detaining Power to any penalties except those provided for in respect of members of the armed forces of said Power who have committed the same acts....

Collective punishment for individual acts, corporal punishment, imprisonment in premises without daylight and, in general, any form of torture or cruelty, are forbidden.

No prisoner of war may be deprived of his rank by the Detaining Power, or prevented from wearing his badges.

II. Disciplinary Sanctions

III. Judicial Proceedings

Article 99

No prisoner shall be tried or sentenced for an act which is not forbidden by the law of the Detaining Power or by international law, in force at the time the said act was committed.

No moral or physical coercion may be exerted on a prisoner of war in order to induce him to admit himself guilty of the act which he is accused.

No prisoner of war may be convicted without having had an opportunity to present his defence and the assistance of a qualified advocate or counsel.

Article 102

A prisoner of war can be validly sentenced only if the sentence has been pronounced by the same courts according to the same procedure as in the case of members of the armed forces of the Detaining Power, and if, furthermore, the provisions of the present Chapter have been observed.

Article 104

In any case in which the Detaining Power has decided to institute judicial proceedings against a prisoner of war, it shall notify the Protecting Power as soon as possible and at least three weeks before the opening of the trial....

Article 105

The prisoner of war shall be entitled to assistance by one of his prisoner comrades, to defence by a qualified advocate or counsel of his own choice, to the calling of witnesses and, if he deems it necessary, to the services of a competent interpreter. He shall be advised of these rights by the Detaining Power in due time before the trial.

Failing a choice by the prisoner of war, the Protecting Power shall find him an advocate or counsel, and shall have at least one week at its disposal for the purposes....

The advocate or counsel conducting the defence on behalf of the prisoner of war shall have at his disposal a period of two weeks at least before the opening of the trial, as well as the necessary facilities to prepare the defence of the accused. He may, in particular, freely visit the accused and interview him in private. He may also confer with any witnesses for the defence, including prisoners of war. He shall have the benefit of these facilities until the term of appeal or petition has expired.

Particulars of the charge or charges on which the prisoner of war is to be arraigned, as well as the documents which are generally communicated to the accused by virtue of the laws in force in the armed forces of the Detaining Power, shall be communicated to the accused prisoner of war in a language which he understands, and in good time before the opening of the trial. The same communication in the same circumstances shall be made to the advocate or counsel conducting the defence on behalf of the prisoner of war.

The representatives of the Protecting Power shall be entitled to attend the trial of the case, unless, exceptionally, this is held *in camera* in the interest of State security. In such a case the Detaining Power shall advise the Protecting Power accordingly.

Article 106

Every prisoner of war shall have, in the same manner as the members of the armed forces of the Detaining Power, the right of appeal or petition from any sentence pronounced upon him, with a view to the quashing or revising of the sentence or the reopening of the trial. He shall be fully informed of his right to appeal or petition and of the time limit within which he may do so.

Article 108

Sentences pronounced on prisoners of war after a conviction has become duly enforceable, shall be served in the same establishments and under the same conditions as in the case of members of the armed forces of the Detaining Power. These conditions shall in all cases conform to the requirements of health and humanity.

A woman prisoner of war on whom such a sentence has been pronounced shall be confined in separate quarters and shall be under the supervision of women....

Part IV. Termination of Captivity

Section I. Direct Repatriation and Accommodation in Neutral Countries

Section II. Release and Repatriation of Prisoners of War at the Close of Hostilities

Article 118

Prisoners of war shall be released and repatriated without delay after the cessation of active hostilities....

Article 119

Prisoners of war against whom criminal proceedings for an indictable offence are pending may be detained until the end of such proceedings, and, if necessary, until completion of the punishment. The same shall apply to prisoners of war already convicted for an indictable offence....

Part VI. Execution of the Convention

Section I. General Provisions

Article 126

Representatives or delegates of the Protecting Powers shall have permission to go to all places where prisoners of war may be, particularly to places of internment, imprisonment and labour, and shall have access to all premises occupied by prisoners of war; they shall also be allowed to go to the places of departure, passage and arrival of prisoners who are being transferred. They shall be able to interview the prisoners, and in particular the prisoners' representatives, without witnesses, either personally or through an interpreter....

Article 127

The High Contracting Parties undertake, in time of peace as in time of war, to disseminate the text of the present Convention as widely as possible in their respective countries, and, in particular, to include the study thereof in their programmes of military and, if possible, civil instruction, so that the principles thereof may become known to all their armed forces and to the entire population.

Any military or other authorities, who in time of war assume responsibilities in respect of prisoners of war, must possess the text of the Convention and be specially instructed as to its provisions.

Article 128

The High Contracting Parties shall communicate to one another through the Swiss Federal Council and, during hostilities, through the Protecting Powers, the official translations of the present Convention, as well as the laws and regulations which they may adopt to ensure the application thereof.

Article 129

The High Contracting Parties undertake to enact any legislation necessary to provide effective penal sanctions for persons committing, or ordering to be committed, any of the grave breaches of the present Convention defined in the following article.

Each High Contracting Party shall be under an obligation to search for persons alleged to have committed, or to have ordered to be committed, such grave breaches, and shall bring such persons, regardless of their nationality, before its own courts. It may also, if it prefers, and in accordance with the provisions of its own legislation, hand such persons over for trial to another High Contracting Party concerned, provided such High Contacting Party has made out a *prima facie* case.

Each High Contracting Party shall take measures necessary for the suppression of all acts contrary to the provisions of the present Convention other than grave breaches defined in the following article.

In all circumstances, the accused persons shall benefit by safeguards of proper trial and defence, which shall not be less favourable than those provided by Article 105 and those following of the present Convention.

Article 130

Grave breaches to which the preceding article relates shall be those involving any of the following acts, if committed against persons or property protected by the Convention: wilful killing, torture or inhuman treatment, including biological experiments, wilfully causing great suffering or serious injury to body or health, compelling a prisoner of war to serve in the forces of the hostile Power, or wilfully depriving a prisoner of war of the rights to fair and regular trial prescribed in this Convention.

Article 131

No High Contracting Part shall be allowed to absolve itself or any other High Contracting Party of any liability incurred by itself or by another High Contracting Party in respect of breaches referred to in the preceding article.

Article 132

At the request of a Party to the conflict, an enquiry shall be instituted, in a manner to be decided between the interested Parties, concerning any alleged violation of the Convention.

If agreement has not been reached concerning the procedure for the enquiry, the Parties should agree on the choice of an umpire who will decide upon the procedure to be followed.

Once the violation has been established, the Parties to the conflict shall put an end to it and shall repress it with the least possible delay....

Geneva Convention Relative to the Protection of Civilian Persons in Time of War of August 12, 1949 (GC)
75 U.N.T.S. 287, 6 U.S.T. 3516, T.I.A.S. No. 3365

Article 1

The High Contracting Parties undertake to respect and to ensure respect for the present Convention in all circumstances.

Article 2

In addition to the provisions which shall be implemented in peacetime, the present Convention shall apply to all cases of declared war or of any other armed conflict which may arise between two or more of the High Contracting Parties, even if the state of war is not recognized by one of them.

The Convention shall also apply to all cases of partial or total occupation of the territory of a High Contracting Party, even if the said occupation meets with no armed resistance.

Although one of the Powers in conflict may not be a party to the present Convention, the Powers who are parties thereto shall remain bound by it in their mutual relations. They shall furthermore be bound by the Convention in relation to the said Power, if the latter accepts and applies the provisions thereof.

Article 3

In the case of armed conflict not of an international character occurring in the territory of one of the High Contracting Parties, each party to the conflict shall be bound to apply, as a minimum, the following provisions:

(1) Persons taking no active part in the hostilities, including members of armed forces who have laid down their arms and those placed *hors de combat* by sickness, wounds, detention, or any other cause, shall in all circumstances be treated humanely, without any adverse distinction founded on race, colour, religion or faith, sex, birth or wealth, or any other similar criteria.

To this end, the following acts are and shall remain prohibited at any time and in any place whatsoever with respect to the above-mentioned persons:

(a) violence to life and person, in particular murder of all kinds, mutilation, cruel treatment and torture;

(b) taking of hostages;

(c) outrages upon personal dignity, in particular, humiliating and degrading treatment;

(d) the passing of sentences and the carrying out of executions without previous judgment pronounced by a regularly constituted court, affording all the judicial guarantees which are recognized as indispensable by civilized peoples.

(2) The wounded and sick shall be collected and cared for.

An impartial humanitarian body, such as the International Committee of the Red Cross, may offer its services to the Parties to the conflict.

The Parties to the conflict should further endeavor to bring into force, by means of special agreements, all or part of the other provisions of the present Convention.

The application of the preceding provisions shall not affect the legal status of the Parties to the conflict.

Article 4

Persons protected by the Convention are those who, at a given moment and in any manner whatsoever, find themselves, in case of a conflict or occupation, in the hands of a Party to the conflict or Occupying Power of which they are not nationals.

Nationals of a State which is not bound by the Convention are not protected by it. Nationals of a neutral State who find themselves in the territory of a belligerent State, and nationals of a co-belligerent State, shall not be regarded as protected persons while the State of which they are nationals has normal diplomatic representation in the State in whose hands they are.

The provisions of Part II are, however, wider in application, as defined in Article 13.

Persons protected by the Geneva Convention for the Amelioration of the Condition of the Wounded and Sick in Armed Forces in the Field of August 12, 1949, or by the Geneva Convention for the Amelioration of the Condition of Wounded, Sick and Shipwrecked Members of Armed Forces at Sea of August 12, 1949, or by the Geneva Convention Relative to the Treatment of Prisoners of War of August 12, 1949, shall not be considered as protected persons within the meaning of the present Convention.

Article 5

Where, in the territory of a Party to the conflict, the latter is satisfied that an individual protected person is definitely suspected of or engaged in activities hostile to the security of the State, such individual person shall not be entitled to claim such rights and privileges under the present Convention as would, if exercised in the favor of such individual person, be prejudicial to the security of such State.

Where in occupied territory an individual protected person is detained as a spy or saboteur, or as a person under definite suspicion of activity hostile to the security of the Occupying Power, such person shall, in those cases where absolute military security so requires, be regarded as having forfeited rights of communication under the present Convention.

In each case, such persons shall nevertheless be treated with humanity, and in case of trial, shall not be deprived of the rights of fair and regular trial prescribed by the present Convention. They shall also be granted the full rights and privileges of a protected person under the present Convention at the earliest date consistent with the security of the State or Occupying Power, as the case may be.

Article 6

The present Convention shall apply from the outset of any conflict or occupation mentioned in Article 2.

In the territory of Parties to the conflict, the application of the present Convention shall cease on the general close of military operations.

In the case of occupied territory, the application of the present Convention shall cease one year after the general close of military operations; however, the Occupying Power shall be bound, for the duration of the occupation, to the extent that such Power exercises the functions of government in such territory, by the provisions of the following articles of the present Convention: 1 to 12, 27, 29 to 34, 47, 49, 51, 52, 53, 59, 61 to 77, 143.

Protected persons whose release, repatriation or re-establishment may take place after such dates shall meanwhile continue to benefit by the present Convention.

Article 7

In addition to the agreements expressly provided for in Articles 11, 14, 15, 17, 36, 108, 109, 132, 133 and 149, the High Contracting Parties may conclude other special agreements for all matters concerning which they may deem it suitable to make separate provision. No special agreement shall adversely affect the situation of protected persons, as defined by the present Convention, nor restrict the rights which it confers upon them.

Protected persons shall continue to have the benefit of such agreements as long as the Convention is applicable to them, except where express provisions to the contrary are contained in the aforesaid or in subsequent agreements, or where more favourable measures have been taken with regard to them by one or other of the Parties to the conflict.

Article 8

Protected persons may in no circumstances renounce in part or in entirety the rights secured to them by the present Convention, and by the special agreements referred to in the foregoing article, if such there be....

Article 10

The provisions of the present Convention constitute no obstacle to the humanitarian activities which the International Committee of the Red Cross or any other impartial humanitarian organization may, subject to the consent of the Parties to the conflict concerned, undertake for the protection of civilian persons and for their relief....

Part II. General Protection of Populations Against Certain Consequences of War

Article 13

The provisions of Part II cover the whole of the populations of the countries in conflict, without any adverse distinction based, in particular, on race, nationality, religion or political opinion, and are intended to alleviate the sufferings caused by war.

Article 16

The wounded and sick, as well as the infirm, and expectant mothers, shall be the object of particular protection and respect.

As far as military considerations allow, each Party to the conflict shall facilitate the steps taken to search for the killed and wounded, to assist the shipwrecked and other persons exposed to grave danger, and to protect them against pillage and ill-treatment.

Article 17

The Parties to the conflict shall endeavour to conclude local agreements for the removal from besieged or encircled areas, of wounded, sick, infirm, and aged persons, children and maternity cases, and for the passage of ministers of all religions, medical personnel and medical equipment on their way to such areas.

Article 18

Civilian hospitals organized to give care to the wounded and sick, the infirm and maternity cases, may in no circumstances be the object of attack, but shall at all times be respected and protected by the Parties to the conflict....

Article 23

Each High Contracting Party shall allow the free passage of all consignments of medical and hospital stores and objects necessary for religious worship intended only for civilians of another High Contracting Party, even if the latter is its adversary. It shall likewise permit the free passage of all consignments of essential foodstuffs, clothing and tonics intended for children under fifteen, expectant mothers and maternity cases.

The obligation of a High Contracting Party to allow the free passage of consignments indicated in the preceding paragraph is subject to the condition that this Party is satisfied that there are no serious reasons for fearing:

    a. that the consignments may be diverted from their destination,

    b. that the control may not be effective, or

    c. that a definite advantage may accrue to the military efforts or economy of the enemy through the substitution of the above-mentioned consignments for goods which would otherwise be provided or produced by the enemy or through the release of such material, services or facilities as would otherwise be required for the production of such goods....

Article 24

The Parties to the conflict shall take the necessary measures to ensure that children under fifteen, who are orphaned or are separated from their families as a result of the war, are not left to their own resources, and that their maintenance ... [is] facilitated in all circumstances....

Article 25

All persons in the territory of a Party to the conflict, or in a territory occupied by it, shall be enabled to give news of a strictly personal nature to members of their families, wherever they may be, and to receive news from them. This correspondence shall be forwarded speedily and without undue delay....

Article 26

Each Party to the conflict shall facilitate enquiries made by members of families dispersed owing to the war, with the object of renewing contact with one another and of meeting, if possible. It shall encourage, in particular, the work of organizations engaged on this task provided they are acceptable to it and conform to its security regulations.

Part III. Status and Treatment of Protected Persons

Section I. Provisions Common to the Territories of the Parties to the
Conflict and to Occupied Territories

Article 27

Protected persons are entitled, in all circumstances, to respect for their persons, their honour, their family rights, their religious convictions and practices, and their manners and customs. They shall at all times be humanely treated, and shall be protected especially against all acts of violence or threats thereof and against insults and public curiosity.

Women shall be especially protected against any attack on their honour, in particular against rape, enforced prostitution, or any form of indecent assault.

Without prejudice to the provisions relating to their state of health, age and sex, all protected persons shall be treated with the same consideration by the Party to the conflict in whose power they are, without any adverse distinction based, in particular, on race, religion or political opinion.

However, the Parties to the conflict may take such measures of control and security in regard to protected persons as may be necessary as a result of the war.

Article 28

The presence of a protected person may not be used to render certain points or areas immune from military operations.

Article 29

The Party to the conflict in whose hands protected persons may be, is responsible for the treatment accorded to them by its agents, irrespective of any individual responsibility which may be incurred.

Article 30

Protected persons shall have every facility for making application to the Protecting Powers, the International Committee of the Red Cross, the National Red Cross (Red Crescent, Red Lion and Sun) Society of the country where they may be, as well as to any organization that might assist them.

These several organizations shall be granted all facilities for that purpose by the authorities, within the bounds set by military or security considerations.

Apart from the visits of the delegates of the Protecting Powers and of the International Committee of the Red Cross, provided for by Article 143, the Detaining or Occupying Powers shall facilitate as much as possible visits to protected persons by the representatives of other organizations whose object is to give spiritual aid or material relief to such persons.

Article 31

No physical or moral coercion shall be exercised against protected persons, in particular to obtain information from them or from third parties.

Article 32

The High Contracting Parties specifically agree that each of them is prohibited from taking any measure of such a character as to cause the physical suffering or extermination of protected persons in their hands. This prohibition applies not only to murder, torture, corporal punishment, mutilation and medical or scientific experiments not necessitated by the medical treatment of a protected person, but also to any other measures of brutality whether applied by civilian or military agents.

Article 33

No protected person may be punished for an offence he or she has not personally committed. Collective penalties and likewise all measures of intimidation or of terrorism are prohibited.

Pillage is prohibited.

Reprisals against protected persons and their property are prohibited.

Article 34

The taking of hostages is prohibited.

Section II. Aliens in the Territory of a Party to the Conflict

Article 35

All protected persons who may desire to leave the territory at the outset of, or during a conflict, shall be entitled to do so, unless their departure is contrary to the national interests of the State....

Article 42

The internment or placing in assigned residence of protected persons may be ordered only if the security of the Detaining Power makes it absolutely necessary....

Article 43

Any protected person who has been interned or placed in assigned residence shall be entitled to have such action reconsidered as soon as possible by an appropriate court or administrative board designated by the Detaining Power for that purpose. If the internment or placing in assigned residence is maintained, the court or administrative board shall periodically, at least twice yearly, give consideration to his or her case with a view to the favourable amendment of the initial decision, if circumstances permit.

Unless the persons concerned object, the Detaining Power shall, as rapidly as possible, give the Protecting Power the names of any protected persons who have been interned or subjected to assigned residence, or who have been released from internment or assigned residence. The decisions of the courts or boards mentioned in the first paragraph of the present Article shall also, subject to the same conditions, be notified as rapidly as possible to the Protecting Power.

Article 44

In applying the measures of control mentioned in the present Convention, the Detaining Power shall not treat as enemy aliens exclusively on the basis of their nationality *de jure* of an enemy State, refugees who do not, in fact, enjoy the protection of any government.

Article 45

Protected persons shall not be transferred to a Power which is not a party to the Convention.

This provision shall in no way constitute an obstacle to the repatriation of protected persons, or to their return to their country of residence after the cessation of hostilities.

Protected persons may be transferred by the Detaining Power only to a Power which is a party to the present Convention and after the Detaining Power has satisfied itself of the willingness and ability of such transferee Power to apply the present Convention. If protected persons are transferred under such circumstances, responsibility for the application of the present Convention rests on the Power accepting them, while they are in its custody. Nevertheless, if that Power fails to carry out the provisions of the present Convention in any important respect, the Power by which the protected persons were transferred shall, upon being so notified by the Protecting Power, take effective measures to correct the situation or shall request the return of the protected persons. Such request must be complied with.

In no circumstances shall a protected person be transferred to a country where he or she may have reason to fear persecution for his or her political opinions or religious beliefs.

The provisions of this Article do not constitute an obstacle to the extradition, in pursuance of extradition treaties concluded before the outbreak of hostilities, of protected persons accused of offences against ordinary criminal law.

Section III. Occupied Territories

Article 47

Protected persons who are in occupied territory shall not be deprived, in any case or in any manner whatsoever, of the benefits of the present Convention by any change introduced, as the result of the occupation of a territory, into the institutions or government of the said territory, nor by any agreement concluded between the authorities of the occupied territories and the Occupying Power, nor by any annexation by the latter of the whole or part of the occupied territory.

Article 48

Protected persons who are not nationals of the Power whose territory is occupied may avail themselves of the right to leave the territory subject to the provisions of Article 35, and decisions thereon shall be taken according to the procedure which the Occupying Power shall establish in accordance with the said article.

Article 49

Individual or mass forcible transfers, as well as deportations of protected persons from occupied territory to the territory of the Occupying Power or to that of any other country, occupied or not, are prohibited, regardless of their motive.

Nevertheless, the Occupying Power may undertake total or partial evacuation of a given area if the security of the population or imperative military reasons so demand. Such evacuations may not involve the displacement of protected persons outside the bounds of the occupied territory except when for material reasons it is impossible to avoid such displacement. Persons thus evacuated shall be transferred back to their homes as soon as hostilities in the area in question have ceased.

The Occupying Power undertaking such transfers of evacuations shall ensure, to the greatest practicable extent, that proper accommodation is provided to receive the protected persons, that the removals are effected in satisfactory conditions of hygiene, health, safety and nutrition, and that members of the same family are not separated.

The Protecting Power shall be informed of any transfers and evacuations as soon as they have taken place.

The Occupying Power shall not detain protected persons in an area particularly exposed to the dangers of war unless the security of the population or imperative military reasons so demand.

The Occupying Power shall not deport or transfer parts of its own civilian population into the territory it occupies.

Article 50

The Occupying Power shall, with the cooperation of the national and local authorities, facilitate the proper working of all institutions devoted to the care and education of children.

The Occupying Power shall take all necessary steps to facilitate the identification of children and the registration of their parentage. It may not, in any case, change their personal status, nor enlist them in formations or organizations subordinate to it....

Article 53

Any destruction by the Occupying Power of real or personal property ... is prohibited, except where such destruction is rendered absolutely necessary by military operations.

Article 54

The Occupying Power may not alter the status of public officials or judges in the occupied territories, or in any way apply sanctions to or take any measures of coercion or discrimination against them, should they abstain from fulfilling their functions for reasons of conscience.

This prohibition does not prejudice the application of the second paragraph of Article 51. It does not affect the right of the Occupying Power to remove public officials from their posts.

Article 55

To the fullest extent of the means available to it, the Occupying Power has the duty of ensuring the food and medical supplies of the population; it should, in particular, bring in the necessary foodstuffs, medical stores and other articles if the resources of the occupied territory are inadequate ... [and may] requisition ... [such for its forces and administrative personnel] only if the requirements of the civilian population have been taken into account....

Article 56

To the fullest extent of the means available to it, the Occupying Power has the duty of ensuring and maintaining, with the cooperation of national and local authorities, the medical and hospital establishments and services, public health and hygiene in the occupied territory, with particular reference to the adoption and application of the prophylactic and preventive measures necessary to combat the spread of contagious diseases and epidemics. Medical personnel of all categories shall be allowed to carry out their duties....

Article 58

The Occupying Power shall permit ministers of religion to give spiritual assistance to the members of their religious communities.

The Occupying Power shall also accept consignments of books and articles required for religious needs and shall facilitate their distribution in occupied territory.

Article 59

If the whole or part of the population of an occupied territory is inadequately supplied, the Occupying Power shall agree to relief schemes on behalf of the said population, and shall facilitate them by all the means at its disposal.

Such schemes, which may be undertaken either by States or by impartial humanitarian organizations such as the International Committee of the Red Cross, shall consist, in particular, of the provision of consignments of foodstuffs, medical supplies and clothing.

All Contracting Parties shall permit the free passage of these consignments and shall guarantee their protection.

A Power granting free passage ... shall, however, have the right to search the consignments, to regulate their passage according to prescribed times and routes, and to be reasonably satisfied ... that these consignments are to be used for the relief of the needy population and are not to be used for the benefit of the Occupying Power.

Article 60

Relief consignments shall in no way relieve the Occupying Power of any of its responsibilities under Articles 55, 56 and 59. The Occupying Power shall in no way whatsoever divert relief consignments from the purpose for which they are intended, except in cases of urgent necessity, in the interests of the population....

Article 64

The penal laws of the occupied territory shall remain in force, with the exception that they may be repealed or suspended by the Occupying Power in cases where they constitute a threat to its security or an obstacle to the application of the present Convention. Subject to the latter consideration and to the necessity for ensuring the effective administration of justice, the tribunals of the occupied territory shall continue to function in respect of all offences covered by the said laws.

The Occupying Power may, however, subject the population of the occupied territory to provisions which are essential to enable the Occupying power to fulfil its obligations under the present Convention, to maintain the orderly government of the territory, and to ensure the security of the Occupying Power, of the members and property of the occupying forces or administration, and likewise of the establishments and lines of communication used by them.

Article 65

The penal provisions enacted by the Occupying Power shall not come into force before they have been published and brought to the knowledge of the inhabitants in their own language. The effect of these penal provisions shall not be retroactive.

Article 66

In case of a breach of the penal provisions promulgated by it by virtue of the second paragraph of Article 64, the Occupying Power may hand over the accused to its properly constituted, non-political military courts, on condition that the said courts sit in the occupied country. Courts of appeal shall preferably sit in the occupied country.

Article 67

The courts shall apply only those provisions of law which were applicable prior to the offence, and which are in accordance with general principles of law, in particular the principle that the penalty shall be proportionate to the offence. They shall take into consideration the fact that the accused is not a national of the Occupying Power.

Article 68

Protected persons who commit an offence which is solely intended to harm the Occupying Power, but which does not constitute an attempt on the life or limb of members of the occupying forces or administration, nor a grave collective danger, nor seriously damage the property of the occupying forces or administration or the installations used by them, shall be liable to internment or simple imprisonment, provided the duration of such internment or imprisonment is proportionate to the offence committed. Furthermore, internment or imprisonment shall, for such offences, be the only measure adopted for depriving protected persons of liberty. The courts provided for under Article 66 of the present Convention may at their discretion convert a sentence of imprisonment to one of internment for the same period.

The penal provisions promulgated by the Occupying Power in accordance with Articles 64 and 65 may impose the death penalty on a protected person only in cases where the person is guilty of espionage, of serious acts of sabotage against the military installations of the Occupying Power or of intentional offences which have caused the death of one or more persons, provided that such offences were punishable by death under the law of the occupied territory in force before the occupation began.

The death penalty may not be pronounced against a protected person unless the attention of the court has been particularly called to the fact that since the accused is not a national of the Occupying Power, he is not bound to it by any duty of allegiance.

In any case, the death penalty may not be pronounced against a protected person who was under eighteen years of age at the time of the offence.

Article 69

In all cases, the duration of the period during which a protected person accused of an offence is under arrest awaiting trial or punishment shall be deducted from any period of imprisonment awarded.

Article 70

Protected persons shall not be arrested, prosecuted or convicted by the Occupying Power for acts committed or for opinions expressed before the occupation, or during a temporary interruption thereof, with the exception of breaches of the laws and customs of war.

Nationals of the Occupying Power who, before the outbreak of hostilities, have sought refuge in the territory of the occupied State, shall not be arrested, prosecuted, convicted or deported from the occupied territory, except for offences committed after the outbreak of hostilities, or for offence under common law committed before the outbreak of hostilities which, according to the law of the occupied State, would have justified extradition in time of peace.

Article 71

No sentence shall be pronounced by the competent courts of the Occupying Power except after a regular trial.

Accused persons who are prosecuted by the Occupying Power shall be promptly informed, in writing, in a language which they understand, of the particulars of the charges preferred against them, and shall be brought to trial as rapidly as possible. The Protecting Power shall be informed of all proceedings instituted by the Occupying Power against protected persons in respect of charges involving the death penalty or imprisonment for two years or more; it shall be enabled, at any time, to obtain information regarding the state of such proceedings. Furthermore, the Protecting Power shall be entitled, on request, to be furnished with all particulars of these and of any other proceedings instituted by the Occupying Power against protected persons.

The notification to the Protecting Power, as provided for in the second paragraph above, shall be sent immediately, and shall in any case reach the Protecting Power three weeks before the date of the first hearing. Unless, at the opening of the trial, evidence is submitted that the provisions of the article are fully complied with, the trial shall not proceed. The notification shall include the following particulars:

(a) description of the accused;

(b) place of residence or detention;

(c) specification of the charge or charges (with mention of the penal provisions under which it is brought);

(d) designation of the court which will hear the case;

(e) place and date of the first hearing.

Article 72

Accused persons shall have the right to present evidence necessary to their defence and may, in particular, call witnesses. They shall have the right to be assisted by a qualified advocate or counsel of their own choice, who shall be able to visit them freely and shall enjoy the necessary facilities for preparing the defence.

Failing a choice by the accused, the Protecting Power may provide him with an advocate or counsel. When an accused person has to meet a serious charge and the Protecting Power is not functioning, the Occupying Power, subject to the consent of the accused, shall provide an advocate or counsel.

Accused persons shall, unless they freely waive such assistance, be aided by an interpreter, both during preliminary investigation and during the hearing in court. They shall have the right at any time to object to the interpreter and to ask for his replacement.

Article 73

A convicted person shall have the right of appeal provided for by the laws applied by the court. He shall be fully informed of his right to appeal or petition and of the time limit within which he may do so.

The penal procedure provided in the present Section shall apply, as far as it is applicable, to appeals. Where the laws applied by the Court make no provision for appeals, the convicted person shall have the right to petition against the finding and sentence to the competent authority of the Occupying Power.

Article 74

Representatives of the Protecting Power shall have the right to attend the trial of any protected person, unless the hearing has, as an exceptional measure, to be held *in camera* in the interests of the security of the Occupying Power, which shall then notify the Protecting Power. A notification in respect of the date and place of trial shall be sent to the Protecting Power.

Any judgment involving a sentence of death, or imprisonment for two years or more, shall be communicated, with the relevant grounds, as rapidly as possible to the Protecting Power. The notification shall contain a reference to the notification made under Article 71, and, in the case of sentences of imprisonment, the name of the place where the sentence is to be served. A record of judgments other than those referred to above shall be kept by the court and shall be open to inspection by representatives of Protecting Power. Any period allowed for appeal in the case of sentences involving the death penalty, or imprisonment of two years or more, shall not run until notification of judgment has been received by the Protecting Power.

Article 75

In no case shall persons condemned to death be deprived of the right of petition for pardon or reprieve.

No death sentence shall be carried out before the expiration of a period of at least six months from the date of receipt by the Protecting Power of the notification of the final judgment confirming such death sentence, or of an order denying pardon or reprieve.

The six months period of suspension of the death sentence herein prescribed may be reduced in individual cases in circumstances of grave emergency involving an organized threat to the security of the Occupying Power or its forces, provided always that the Protecting Power is notified of such reduction and is given reasonable time and opportunity to make representations to the competent occupying authorities in respect of such death sentences.

Article 76

Protected persons accused of offences shall be detained in the occupied country, and if convicted they shall serve their sentences therein. They shall, if possible, be separated from other detainees and shall enjoy conditions of food and hygiene which will be sufficient to keep them in good health, and which will be at least equal to those obtaining in prisons in the occupied country.

They shall receive the medical attention required by their state of health.

They shall also have the right to receive any spiritual assistance which they may require.

Women shall be confined in separate quarters and shall be under the direct supervision of women.

Proper regard shall be paid to the special treatment due to minors.

Protected persons who are detained shall have the right to be visited by delegates of the Protecting Power and of the International Committee of the Red Cross, in accordance with the provisions of Article 143.

Such persons shall have the right to receive at least one relief parcel monthly.

Article 77

Protected persons who have been accused of offences or convicted by the courts in occupied territory, shall be handed over at the close of occupation, with the relevant records, to the authorities of the liberated territory.

Article 78

If the Occupying Power considers it necessary, for imperative reasons of security, to take safety measures concerning protected persons, it may, at the most, subject them to assigned residence or to internment.

Decisions regarding such assigned residence or internment shall be made according to a regular procedure to be prescribed by the Occupying Power in accordance with the provisions of the present Convention. This procedure shall include the right of appeal for the parties concerned. Appeals shall be decided with the least possible delay....

Section IV. Regulations for the Treatment of Internees

Chapter I. General Provisions.

Article 79

The Parties to the conflict shall not intern protected persons, except in accordance with the provisions of Articles 41, 42, 43, 68 and 78.

Article 80

Internees shall retain their full civil capacity and shall exercise such attendant rights as may be compatible with their status....

Chapter VIII. Relations with the Exterior ...

Article 106

As soon as he is interned, or at the least not more than one week after his arrival in a place of internment, and likewise in cases of sickness or transfer to another place of internment or to a hospital, every internee shall be enabled to send direct to his family, on the one hand, and to the Central Agency, provided for by Article 140, on the other, an internment card similar, if possible, to the model annexed to the present Convention, informing his relatives of his detention, address and state of health. The said cards shall be forwarded as rapidly as possible and may not be delayed in any way.

Article 107

Internees shall be allowed to send and receive letters and cards....

Chapter XII. Release, Repatriation, and Accommodation in Neutral Countries.

Article132

Each interned person shall be released by the Detaining Power as soon as the reasons which necessitated his internment no longer exist ...

Article 133

Internment shall cease as soon as possible after the close of hostilities ...

Article 134

The High Contracting Parties shall endeavour, upon the close of hostilities or occupation, to ensure the return of all internees to their last place of residence, or to facilitate their repatriation ...

Part IV. Execution of the Convention.

Section I. General Provisions ...

Article 143

Representatives or delegates of the Protecting Powers shall have permission to go to all places where protected persons are, particularly to places of internment, detention and work.

They shall have access to all premises occupied by protected persons and shall be able to interview the latter without witnesses, personally or through an interpreter.

Such visits may not be prohibited except for reasons of imperative military necessity, and then only as an exceptional and temporary measure. Their duration and frequency shall not be restricted....

The delegates of the International Committee of the Red Cross shall also enjoy the above prerogatives....

Article 144

The High Contracting Parties undertake, in time of peace as in time or war, to disseminate the text of the present Convention as widely as possible in their respective countries, and in particular, to include the study thereof in their programmes of military and, if possible, civil instruction, so that the principles thereof may become known to the entire population.

Any civilian, military, police or other authorities, who in time of war assume responsibilities in respect of protected persons, must possess the text of the Conventions and be specially instructed as to its provisions.

Article 145

The High Contracting Parties shall communicate to one another through the Swiss Federal Council and, during hostilities, through the Protecting Powers, the official translations of the present Convention, as well as the laws and regulations which they may adopt to ensure the application thereof.

Article 146

The High Contracting Parties undertake to enact any legislation necessary to provide effective penal sanctions for persons committing, or ordering to be committed, any of the grave breaches of the present Convention defined in the following article.

Each High Contracting Party shall be under the obligation to search for persons alleged to have committed, or to have ordered to be committed, such grave breaches, and shall bring such persons, regardless of their nationality, before its own courts. It may also, if it prefers, and in accordance with the provisions of its own legislation, hand such persons over for trial to another High Contracting Party concerned, provided such High Contracting Party has made out a *prima facie* case.

Each High Contracting Party shall take measures necessary for the suppression of all acts contrary to the provisions of the present Convention other than the grave breaches defined in the following article.

In all circumstances, the accused persons shall benefit by safeguards of proper trial and defence, which shall not be less favourable than those provided by Article 105 and those following of the Geneva Convention relative to the Treatment of Prisoners of War of August 12, 1949.

Article 147

Grave breaches to which the preceding article relates shall be those involving any of the following acts, if committed against persons or property protected by the present Convention: wilful killing, torture or inhuman treatment, including biological experiments, wilfully causing great suffering or serious injury to body or health, unlawful deportation or transfer or unlawful confinement of a protected person, compelling a protected person to serve in the forces of a hostile Power or wilfully depriving a protected person of the rights of fair and regular trial prescribed in the present Convention, taking of hostages and extensive destruction and appropriation of property, not justified by military necessity and carried out unlawfully and wantonly.

Article 148

No High Contracting Party shall be allowed to absolve itself or any other High Contracting Part of any liability incurred by itself or by another High Contracting Party in respect of breaches referred to in the preceding article.

Article 149

At the request of a Party to the conflict, an enquiry shall be instituted, in a manner to be decided between the interested Parties, concerning any alleged violation of the Convention.

If agreement has not been reached concerning the procedure for the enquiry, the Parties should agree on the choice of an umpire who will decide upon the procedure to be followed.

Once the violation has been established, the Parties to the conflict shall put an end to it and shall repress it with the least possible delay....

Protocol Additional to the Geneva Conventions of 12 August 1949, and Relating to the Protection of Victims of International Armed Conflicts (Protocol I)

1125 U.N.T.S. 3 (8 June 1977)

PREAMBLE

The High Contracting Parties, Proclaiming their earnest wish to see peace prevail among peoples,

Recalling that every State has the duty, in conformity with the Charter of the United Nations, to refrain in its international relations from the threat or use of force against the sovereignty, territorial integrity or political independence of any State, or in any other manner inconsistent with the purposes of the United Nations,

Believing it necessary nevertheless to reaffirm and develop the provisions protecting the victims of armed conflicts and to supplement measures intended to reinforce their application,

Expressing their conviction that nothing in this Protocol or in the Geneva Conventions of 12 August 1949 can be construed as legitimizing or authorizing any act of aggression or any other use of force inconsistent with the Charter of the United Nations,

Reaffirming further that the provisions of the Geneva Conventions of 12 August 1949 and of this Protocol must be fully applied in all circumstances to all persons who are protected by those instruments, without any adverse distinction based on the nature or origin of the armed conflict or on the causes espoused by or attributed to the Parties to the conflict,

Have agreed on the following:

PART I. GENERAL PROVISIONS

Article 1
General principles and scope of application

1. The High Contracting Parties undertake to respect and to ensure respect for this Protocol in all circumstances.

2. In cases not covered by this Protocol or by other international agreements, civilians and combatants remain under the protection and authority of the principles of international law derived from established custom, from the principles of humanity and from the dictates of public conscience.

3. This Protocol, which supplements the Geneva Conventions of 12 August 1949 for the protection of war victims, shall apply in the situations referred to in Article 2 common to those Conventions.

4. The situations referred to in the preceding paragraph include armed conflicts in which peoples are fighting against colonial domination and alien occupation and against racist regimes in the exercise of their right of self-determination, as enshrined in the Charter of the United Nations and the Declaration on Principles of International Law concerning Friendly Relations and Co-operation among States in accordance with the Charter of the United Nations....

Article 3
Beginning and end of application

Without prejudice to the provisions which are applicable at all times:

(a) the Conventions and this Protocol shall apply from the beginning of any situation referred to in Article 1 of this Protocol;

(b) the application of the Conventions and of this Protocol shall cease, in the territory of Parties to the conflict, on the general close of military operations and, in the case of occupied territories, on the termination of the occupation, except, in either circumstance, for those persons whose final release, repatriation or re-establishment takes place thereafter. These persons shall continue to benefit from the relevant provisions of the Conventions and of this Protocol until their final release, repatriation or re-establishment.

Article 4
Legal status of the Parties to the conflict

The application of the Conventions and of this Protocol, as well as the conclusion of the agreements provided for therein, shall not affect the legal status of the Parties to the conflict. Neither the occupation of a territory nor the application of the Conventions and this Protocol shall affect the legal status of the territory in question.

Part II. Wounded, Sick and Shipwrecked

Section I. General Protection

Article 10
Protection and care

1. All the wounded, sick and shipwrecked, to whichever Party they belong, shall be respected and protected.

2. In all circumstances they shall be treated humanely and shall receive, to the fullest extent practicable and with the least possible delay, the medical care and attention required by their condition. There shall be no distinction among them founded on any grounds other than medical ones.

Article 11
Protection of persons

1. The physical or mental health and integrity of persons who are in the power of the adverse Party or who are interned, detained or otherwise deprived of liberty as a result of a situation referred to in Article 1 shall not be endangered by any unjustified act or omission. Accordingly, it is prohibited to subject the persons described in this article to any medical procedure which is not indicated by the state of health of the person concerned and which is not consistent with generally accepted medical standards which would be applied under similar medical circumstances to persons who are nationals of the Party conducting the procedure and who are in no way deprived of their liberty.

2. It is, in particular, prohibited to carry out on such persons, even with their consent:

(a) physical mutilations;

(b) medical or scientific experiments;

(c) removal of tissue or organs for transplantation, except where these acts are justified in conformity with the conditions provided for in paragraph 1....

4. Any wilful act or omission which seriously endangers the physical or mental health or integrity of any person who is in the power of a Party other than the one on which he depends and which either violates any of the prohibitions in paragraphs 1 and 2 or fails to comply with the requirements of paragraph 3 shall be a grave breach of this Protocol....

Part III. Methods and Means of Warfare, Combatant and Prisoner-of-War Status

Section I. Methods and Means of Warfare

Article 35
Basic rules

1. In any armed conflict, the right of the Parties to the conflict to choose methods and means of warfare is not unlimited.

2. It is prohibited to employ weapons, projectiles and material and methods of warfare of a nature to cause superfluous injury or unnecessary suffering.

3. It is prohibited to employ methods or means of warfare which are intended, or may be expected, to cause widespread, long-term and severe damage to the natural environment.

Article 36
New weapons

In the study, development, acquisition or adoption of a new weapon, means or method of warfare, a High Contracting Party is under an obligation to determine whether its employment would, in some or all circumstances, be prohibited by this Protocol or by any other rule of international law applicable to the High Contracting Party.

Article 37
Prohibition of perfidy

1. It is prohibited to kill, injure or capture an adversary by resort to perfidy. Acts inviting the confidence of an adversary to lead him to believe that he is entitled to, or is obligated to accord, protection under the rules of international law applicable in armed conflict, with intent to betray that confidence, shall constitute perfidy. The following acts are examples of perfidy:

(a) the feigning of an intent to negotiate under a flag of truce or of a surrender;

(b) the feigning of an incapacitation by wounds or sickness;

(c) the feigning of civilian, non-combatant status; and

(d) the feigning of protected status by the use of signs, emblems or uniforms of the United Nations or of neutral or other States not Parties to the conflict.

2. Ruses of war are not prohibited. Such ruses are acts which are intended to mislead an adversary or to induce him to act recklessly but which infringe no rule of international law applicable in armed conflict and which are not perfidious because they do not invite the confidence of an adversary with respect to protection under that law. The following are examples of such ruses: the use of camouflage, decoys, mock operations and misinformation.

Article 40
Quarter

It is prohibited to order that there shall be no survivors, to threaten an adversary therewith or to conduct hostilities on this bases....

Section II

Combatant and Prisoner-of-War Status

Article 43
Armed Forces

1. The armed forces of a Party to a conflict consist of all organized armed forces, groups and units which are under a command responsible to the Party for the conduct of its sub-

ordinates, even if the Party is represented by a government or an authority not recognized by an adverse Party. Such armed forces shall be subject to an internal disciplinary system which, inter alia, shall enforce compliance with the rules of international law applicable to armed conflict.

2. Members of the armed forces of a Party to a conflict (other than medical personnel and chaplains covered by Article 33 of the Third Convention) are combatants, that is to say, they have the right to participate directly in hostilities.

3. Whenever a Party to a conflict incorporates a paramilitary or armed law enforcement agency into its armed forces it shall notify the other Parties to the conflict.

Article 44
Combatants and Prisoners of War

1. Any combatant, as defined in Article 43, who falls into the power of an adverse Party shall be a prisoner of war.

2. While all combatants are obliged to comply with the rules of international law applicable to armed conflict, violations of these rules shall not deprive a combatant of his right to be a combatant or, if he falls into the power of an adverse Party, of his right to be a prisoner of war, except as provided in paragraphs 3 and 4.

3. In order to promote the protection of the civilian population from the effects of hostilities, combatants are obliged to distinguish themselves from the civilian population while they are engaged in an attack or in a military operation preparatory to an attack. Recognizing, however, that there are situations in armed conflicts where, owing to the nature of the hostilities an armed combatant cannot so distinguish himself, he shall retain his status as a combatant, provided that, in such situations, he carries his arms openly:

(a) during each military engagement, and

(b) during such time as he is visible to the adversary while he is engaged in a military deployment preceding the launching of an attack in which he is to participate.

Acts which comply with the requirements of this paragraph shall not be considered as perfidious within the meaning of Article 37, paragraph 1(c).

4. A combatant who falls into the power of an adverse Party while failing to meet the requirements set forth in the second sentence of paragraph 3 shall forfeit his right to be a prisoner of war, but he shall, nevertheless, be given protections equivalent in all respects to those accorded to prisoners of war by the Third Convention and by this Protocol. This protection includes protections equivalent to those accorded to prisoners of war by the Third Convention in the case where such a person is tried and punished for any offences he has committed.

5. Any combatant who falls into the power of an adverse Party while not engaged in an attack or in a military operation preparatory to an attack shall not forfeit his rights to be a combatant and a prisoner of war by virtue of his prior activities.

6. This Article is without prejudice to the right of any person to be a prisoner of war pursuant to Article 4 of the Third Convention.

7. This Article is not intended to change the generally accepted practice of States with respect to the wearing of the uniform by combatants assigned to the regular, uniformed armed units of a Party to the conflict.

8. In addition to the categories of persons mentioned in Article 13 of the First and Second Conventions, all members of the armed forces of a Party to the conflict, as defined

in Article 43 of this Protocol, shall be entitled to protection under those Conventions if they are wounded or sick or, in the case of the Second Convention, shipwrecked at sea or in other waters.

Article 45
Protection of Persons Who Have Taken Part in Hostilities

1. A person who takes part in hostilities and falls into the power of an adverse Party shall be presumed to be a prisoner of war....

2. If a person who has fallen into the power of an adverse Party is not held as a prisoner of war and is to be tried by the Party for an offence arising out of the hostilities, he shall have the right to assert his entitlement to prisoner of war statue before a judicial tribunal and to have that question adjudicated....

Part IV. Civilian Population

Section I. General Protection Against Effects of Hostilities

Chapter I. Basic Rule and Field of Application

Article 48
Basic rule

In order to ensure respect for and protection of the civilian population and civilian objects, the Parties to the conflict shall at all times distinguish between the civilian population and combatants and between civilian objects and military objectives and accordingly shall direct their operations only against military objectives.

Article 49
Definition of attacks and scope of application

1. "Attacks" means acts of violence against the adversary, whether in offence or in defence.

2. The provisions of this Protocol with respect to attacks apply to all attacks in whatever territory conducted, including the national territory belonging to a Party to the conflict but under the control of an adverse Party.

3. The provisions of this section apply to any land, air or sea warfare which may affect the civilian population, individual civilians or civilian objects on land. They further apply to all attacks from the sea or from the air against objectives on land but do not otherwise affect the ruled of international law applicable in armed conflict at sea or in the air.

4. The provisions of this section are additional to the rules concerning humanitarian protection contained in the Fourth Convention, particularly in part II thereof, and in other international agreements binding upon the High Contracting Parties, as well as to other rules of international law relating to the protection of civilians and civilian objects on land, at sea or in the air against the effects of hostilities.

Chapter II. Civilians and Civilian Population

Article 50
Definition of civilians and civilian population

1. A civilian is any person who does not belong to one of the categories of persons referred to in Article 4 (A) (1), (2), (3) and (6) of the Third Convention [GPW] and in Article 43 of this Protocol. In case of doubt whether a person is a civilian, that person shall be considered to be a civilian.

2. The civilian population comprises all persons who are civilians.

3. The presence within the civilian population of individuals who do not come within the definition of civilians does not deprive the population of its civilian character.

Article 51
Protection of the civilian population

1. The civilian population and individual civilians shall enjoy general protection against dangers arising from military operations. To give effect to this protection, the following rules, which are additional to other applicable rules of international law, shall be observed in all circumstances.

2. The civilian population as such, as well as individual civilians, shall not be the object of attack. Acts or threats of violence the primary purpose of which is to spread terror among the civilian population are prohibited.

3. Civilians shall enjoy the protection afforded by this section, unless and for such time as they take a direct part in hostilities.

4. Indiscriminate attacks are prohibited. Indiscriminate attacks are:

(a) those which are not directed at a specific military objective;

(b) those which employ a method or means of combat which cannot be directed at a specific military objective; or

(c) those which employ a method or means of combat the effects of which cannot be limited as required by this Protocol;

and consequently, in each such case, are of a nature to strike military objectives and civilians or civilian objects without distinction.

5. Among others, the following types of attacks are to be considered as indiscriminate:

(a) an attack by bombardment by any methods or means which treats as a single military objective a number of clearly separated and distinct military objectives located in a city, town, village or other area containing a similar concentration of civilians or civilian objects; and

(b) an attack which may be expected to cause incidental loss of civilian life, injury to civilians, damage to civilian objects, or a combination thereof, which would be excessive in relation to the concrete and direct military advantage anticipated.

6. Attacks against the civilian population or civilians by way of reprisals are prohibited.

7. The presence or movements of the civilian population or individual civilians shall not be used to render certain points or areas immune from military operations, in particular in attempts to shield military objectives from attacks or to shield, favor or impede military operations. The Parties to the conflict shall not direct the movement of the civilian population or individual civilians in order to attempt to shield military objectives from attacks or to shield military operations.

8. Any violation of these prohibitions shall not release the Parties to the conflict from their legal obligations with respect to the civilian population and civilians, including the obligation to take the precautionary measures provided for in Article 57.

Chapter III. Civilian Objects

Article 52
General protection of civilian objects

1. Civilian objects shall not be the object of attack or of reprisal. Civilian objects are all objects which are not military objectives as defined in paragraph 2.

2. Attacks shall be limited strictly to military objectives. In so far as objets are concerned, military objectives are limited to those objects which by their nature, location, purpose or use make an effective contribution to military action and whose total or partial destruction, capture or neutralization, in the circumstances ruling at the time, offers a definite military advantage.

3. In case of doubt whether an object which is normally dedicated to civilian purposes, such as a place of worship, a house or other dwelling or a school, is being used to make an effective contribution to military action, it shall be presumed not to be so used.

Article 53
Protection of cultural objects and of places of worship

Without prejudice to the provisions of the Hague Convention for the Protection of Cultural Property in the Event of Armed Conflict of 14 May 1954, and of other relevant international instruments, it is prohibited:

(a) to commit any acts of hostility directed against the historic monuments, works of art or places of worship which constitute the cultural or spiritual heritage of peoples;

(b) to use such objects in support of the military effort;

(c) to make such objects the object of reprisals.

Article 54
Protection of objects indispensable to the survival of the civilian population

1. Starvation of civilians as a method of warfare is prohibited.

2. It is prohibited to attack, destroy, remove or render useless objects indispensable to the survival of the civilian population, such as food-stuffs, agricultural areas for the production of food-stuffs, crops, livestock, drinking water installations and supplies and irrigation works, for the specific purpose of denying them for their sustenance value to the civilian population or to the adverse Party, whatever the motive, whether in order to starve out civilians, to cause them to move away, or for any other motive.

3. The prohibitions in paragraph 2 shall not apply to such of the objects covered by it as are used by an adverse Party:

(a) as sustenance solely for the members of its armed forces; or

(b) if not as sustenance, then in direct support of military action, provided, however, that in no event shall actions against these objects be taken which may be expected to leave the civilian population with such inadequate food or water as to cause its starvation or force its movement.

4. These objects shall not be made the object of reprisals.

5. In recognition of the vital requirements of any Party to the conflict in the defence of its national territory against invasion, derogation from the prohibitions contained in paragraph 2 may be made by a Party to the conflict within such territory under its own control where required by imperative military necessity.

Article 55
Protection of the natural environment

1. Care shall be taken in warfare to protect the natural environment against widespread, long-term and severe damage. This prohibition includes a prohibition of the use of methods or means of warfare which are intended or may be expected to cause such damage to the natural environment and thereby to prejudice the health or survival of the population.

2. Attacks against the natural environment by way of reprisals are prohibited.

Article 56
Protection of works and installations containing dangerous forces

1. Works or installations containing dangerous forces, namely dams, dykes and nuclear electrical generating stations, shall not be made the object of attack, even where these objects are military objectives, if such attack may cause the release of dangerous forces and consequent severe losses among the civilian population. Other military objectives located at or in the vicinity of these works or installations shall not be made the object of attack if such attack may cause the release of dangerous forces from the works or installations and consequent severe losses among the civilian population.

2. The special protection against attack provided in paragraph 1 shall cease:

(a) for a dam or a dyke if it is used for other than its normal function and in regular, significant and direct support of military operations and if such attack is the only feasible way to terminate such support;

(b) for a nuclear electrical generating station only if it provides electric power in regular, significant and direct support of military operations and if such attack is the only feasible way to terminate such support;

(c) for other military objectives located at or in the vicinity of these works or installations only if they are used in regular, significant and direct support of military operations and if such attack is the only feasible way to terminate such support....

Chapter IV. Precautionary Measures

Article 57
Precautions in attack

1. In the conduct of military operations, constant care shall be taken to spare the civilian population, civilians and civilian objects.

2. With respect to attacks, the following shall be taken:

(a) those who plan or decide upon an attack shall:

(i) do everything feasible to verify that the objectives to be attacked are neither civilians nor civilian objects and are not subject to special protection but are military objectives within the meaning of paragraph 2 of Article 52 and that it is not prohibited by the provisions of this Protocol to attack them;

(ii) take all feasible precautions in the choice of means and methods of attack with a view to avoiding, and in any event to minimizing, incidental loss of civilian life, injury to civilians and damage to civilian objects;

(iii) refrain from deciding to launch an attack which may be expected to cause incidental loss of civilian life, injury to civilians, damage to civilian objects, or a combination thereof, which would be excessive in relation to the concrete and direct military advantage anticipated....

Section III. Treatment of Persons in the Power of a Party to the Conflict

Chapter I. Field of Application and Protection of Persons and Objects

Article 72
Field of application

The provisions of this Section are additional to the rules concerning humanitarian protection of civilians and civilian objects in the power of a Party to the conflict contained in the Fourth Convention [GC], particularly Parts I and III thereof, as well as to other applicable rules of international law relating to protection of fundamental human rights during international armed conflict.

Article 73
Refugees and stateless persons

Persons who, before the beginning of hostilities, were considered as stateless persons or refugees under the relevant international instruments accepted by the Parties concerned or under the national legislation of the State of refuge or State of residence shall be protected persons within the meaning of Parts I and III of the Fourth Convention, in all circumstances and without any adverse distinction.

Article 74
Reunion of dispersed families

The High Contracting Parties and the Parties to the conflict shall facilitate in every possible way the reunion of families dispersed as a result of armed conflicts and shall encourage in particular the work of the humanitarian organizations engaged in this task in accordance with the provisions of the Conventions and of this Protocol and in conformity with their respective security regulations.

Article 75
Fundamental guarantees

1. In so far as they are affected by a situation referred to in Article 1 of this Protocol, persons who are in the power of a Party to the conflict and who do not benefit from more favourable treatment under the Conventions or under this Protocol shall be treated humanely in all circumstances and shall enjoy, as a minimum, the protection provided by this article without any adverse distinction based upon race, colour, sex, language, religion or belief, political or other opinion, national or social origin, wealth, birth or other status, or on any other similar criteria. Each Party shall respect the person, honour, convictions and religious practices of all such persons.

2. The following acts are and shall remain prohibited at any time and in any place whatsoever, whether committed by civilian or by military agents:

(a) violence to the life, health, or physical or mental well-being of persons, in particular:

(i) murder;

(ii) torture of all kinds, whether physical or mental;

(iii) corporal punishment; and

(iv) mutilation;

(b) outrages upon personal dignity, in particular humiliating and degrading treatment, enforced prostitution and any form of indecent assault;

(c) the taking of hostages;

(d) collective punishments; and

(e) threats to commit any of the foregoing acts.

3. Any person arrested, detained or interned for actions related to the armed conflict shall be informed promptly, in a language he understands, of the reasons why these measures have been taken. Except in cases of arrest or detention for penal offences,

such persons shall be released with the minimum delay possible and in any event as soon as the circumstances justifying the arrest, detention or internment have ceased to exist.

4. No sentence may be passed and no penalty may be executed on a person found guilty of a penal offence related to the armed conflict except pursuant to a conviction pronounced by an impartial and regularly constituted court respecting the generally recognized principles of regular judicial procedure, which include the following:

(a) the procedure shall provide for an accused to be informed without delay of the particulars of the offence alleged against him and shall afford the accused before and during his trial all necessary rights and means of defence;

(b) no one shall be convicted of an offence except on the basis of individual penal responsibility;

(c) no one shall be accused or convicted of a criminal offence on account of any act or omission which did not constitute a criminal offence under the national or international law to which he was subject at the time when it was committed; nor shall any heavier penalty be imposed than that which was applicable at the time when the criminal offence was committed; if, after the commission of the offence, provision is made by law for the imposition of a lighter penalty, the offender shall benefit thereby;

(d) anyone charged with an offence is presumed innocent until proved guilty according to law;

(e) anyone charged with an offence shall have the right to be tried in his presence;

(f) no one shall be compelled to testify against himself or to confess guilt;

(g) anyone charged with an offence shall have the right to examine, or have examined, the witnesses against him and to obtain the attendance and examination of witnesses on his behalf under the same conditions as witnesses against him;

(h) no one shall be prosecuted or punished by the same Party for an offence in respect of which a final judgment acquitting or convicting that person has been previously pronounced under the same law and judicial procedure;

(i) anyone prosecuted for an offence shall have the right to have the judgment pronounced publicly; and

(j) a convicted person shall be advised on conviction of his judicial and other remedies and of the time-limits within which they may be exercised.

5. Women whose liberty has been restricted for reasons related to the armed conflict shall be held in quarters separated from men's quarters. They shall be under the immediate supervision of women. Nevertheless, in cases where families are detained or interned, they shall, whenever possible, be held in the same place and accommodated as family units.

6. Persons arrested, detained or interned for reasons related to the armed conflict shall enjoy the protection provided by this article until their final release, repatriation or reestablishment, even after the end of the armed conflict.

7. In order to avoid any doubt concerning the prosecution and trial of persons accused of war crimes or crimes against humanity, the following principles shall apply:

(a) persons who are accused of such crimes should be submitted for the purpose of prosecution and trial in accordance with the applicable rules of international law; and

(b) any such persons who do not benefit from more favourable treatment under the Conventions or this Protocol shall be accorded the treatment provided by this article, whether or not the crimes of which they are accused constitute grave breaches of the Conventions or of this Protocol.

8. No provision of this article may be construed as limiting or infringing any other more favourable provision granting greater protection, under any applicable rules of international law, to persons covered by paragraph 1.

Chapter II. Measures in Favor of Women and Children

Article 76
Protection of Women

1. Women shall be the object of special respect and shall be protected in particular against rape, forced prostitution and any other form of indecent assault.

2. Pregnant women and mothers having dependent infants who are arrested, detained or interned for reasons related to the armed conflict, shall have their cases considered with the utmost priority.

3. To the maximum extent feasible, the Parties to the conflict shall endeavour to avoid the pronouncement of the death penalty on pregnant women or mothers having dependent infants, for an offence related to the armed conflict. The death penalty for such offences shall not be executed on such women.

Article 77
Protection of Children

1. Children shall be the object of special respect and shall be protected against any form of indecent assault. The Parties to the conflict shall provide them with the care and aid they require, whether because of their age or for any other reason.

2. The Parties to the conflict shall take all feasible measures in order that children who have not attained the age of fifteen years do not take a direct part in hostilities and, in particular, they shall refrain from recruiting them into their armed forces....

Part V. Execution of the Conventions and of this Protocol

Section I. General Provisions

Article 82
Legal advisers in armed forces

The High Contracting Parties at all times, and the Parties to the conflict in time of armed conflict, shall ensure that legal advisers are available, when necessary, to advise military commanders at the appropriate level on the application of the Conventions and this Protocol and on the appropriate instruction to be given to the armed forces on this subject.

Section II. Repression of Breaches of the Conventions and of this Protocol

Article 85
Repression of breaches of this Protocol

1. The provisions of the Conventions relating to the repression of breaches and grave breaches, supplemented by this Section, shall apply to the repression of breaches and grave breaches of this Protocol.

2. Acts described as grave breaches in the Conventions are grave breaches of this Protocol if committed against persons in the power of an adverse Party protected by Articles

44, 45 and 73 of this Protocol, or against the wounded, sick and shipwrecked of the adverse Party who are protected by this Protocol, or against those medical or religious personnel, medical units or medical transports which are under the control of the adverse Party and are protected by this Protocol.

3. In addition to the grave breaches defined in article 11, the following acts shall be regarded as grave breaches of this Protocol, when committed wilfully, in violation of the relevant provisions of this Protocol, and causing death or serious injury to body or health:

(a) making the civilian population or individual civilians the object of attack;

(b) launching an indiscriminate attack affecting the civilian population or civilian objects in the knowledge that such attack will cause excessive loss of life, injury to civilians or damage to civilian objects, as defined in Article 57, paragraph 2(a)(iii);

(c) launching an attack against works or installations containing dangerous forces in the knowledge that such attack will cause excessive loss of life, injury to civilians or damage to civilian objects, as defined in Article 57, paragraph 2(a)(iii);

(d) making non-defended localities and demilitarized zones the object of attack;

(e) making a person the object of attack in the knowledge that he is *hors de combat*;

(f) the perfidious use, in violation of Article 37, of the distinctive emblem of the red cross, red crescent or red lion and sun or of other protective signs recognized by the Convention or this Protocol.

4. In addition to the grave breaches defined in the preceding paragraphs and in the Conventions, the following shall be regarded as grave breaches of this Protocol, when committed wilfully and in violation of the Conventions or the Protocol:

(a) the transfer by the occupying Power of parts of its own civilian population into the territory it occupies, or the deportation or transfer of all or parts of the population of the occupied territory within or outside this territory, in violation of Article 49 of the Fourth Convention;

(b) unjustifiable delay in the repatriation of prisoners of war or civilians;

(c) practices of apartheid and other inhuman and degrading practices involving outrages upon personal dignity, based on racial discrimination;

(d) making the clearly-recognized historic monuments, works of art or places of worship which constitute the cultural or spiritual heritage of peoples and to which special protection has been given by special arrangement, for example, within the framework of a competent international organization, the object of attack, causing as a result extensive destruction thereof, where there is no evidence of the violation by the adverse Party of Article 53, subparagraph (b), and when such historic monuments, works of art and places of worship are not located in the immediate proximity of military objectives;

(e) depriving a person protected by the Conventions or referred to in paragraph 2 of this article of the rights of fair and regular trial.

5. Without prejudice to the application of the Conventions and of this Protocol, grave breaches of these instruments shall be regarded as war crimes.

Article 86
Failure to act

1. The High Contracting Parties and the Parties to the conflict shall repress grave breaches, and take measures necessary to suppress all other breaches, of the Conventions or of this Protocol which result from a failure to act when under a duty to do so.

2. The fact that a breach of the Conventions or of this Protocol was committed by a subordinate does not absolve his superiors from penal disciplinary responsibility, as the case may be, if they knew, or had information which should have enabled them to conclude in the circumstances at the time, that he was committing or was going to commit such a breach and if they did not take all feasible measures within their power to prevent or repress the breach.

Article 87
Duty of commanders

1. The High Contracting Parties and the Parties to the conflict shall require military commanders, with respect to members of the armed forces under their command and other persons under their control, to prevent and, where necessary, to suppress and to report to competent authorities breaches of the Conventions and of this Protocol.

2. In order to prevent and suppress breaches, High Contracting Parties and Parties to the conflict shall require that, commensurate with their level of responsibility, commanders ensure that members of the armed forces under their command are aware of their obligations under the Conventions and this Protocol.

3. The High Contracting Parties and Parties to the conflict shall require any commander who is aware that subordinates or other persons under his control are going to commit or have committed a breach of the Conventions or of this Protocol, to initiate such steps as are necessary to prevent such violations of the Conventions or this Protocol, and, where appropriate, to initiate disciplinary or penal action against violators thereof.

Article 88
Mutual assistance in criminal matters

1. The High Contracting Parties shall afford one another the greatest measure of assistance in connection with criminal proceedings brought in respect of grave breaches of the Convention or of this Protocol.

2. Subject to the rights and obligations established in the Conventions and in Article 85, paragraph 1 of this Protocol, and when circumstances permit, the High Contracting Parties shall co-operate in the matter of extradition. They shall give due consideration to the request of the State in whose territory the alleged offence has occurred.

3. The law of the High Contracting Party requested shall apply in all cases. the provisions of the preceding paragraphs shall not, however, affect the obligations arising from the provisions of any other treaty of a bilateral or multilateral nature which governs or will govern the whole or part of the subject of mutual assistance in criminal matters.

Article 89
Co-operation

In situations of serious violation of the Conventions or of this Protocol, the High Contracting Parties undertake to act jointly or individually, in co-operation with the United Nations and in conformity with the United Nations Charter.

Article 90
International Fact-Finding Commission

1. (a) An International Fact-Finding Commission ... consisting of 15 members of high moral standing and acknowledged impartiality shall be established;

(b) When not less than 20 High Contracting Parties have agreed to accept the competence of the Commission....

Article 91
Responsibility

A Party to the conflict which violates the provisions of the Conventions or this Protocol shall, if the case demands, be liable to pay compensation. It shall be responsible for all acts committed by persons forming part of its armed forces.

Protocol Additional to the Geneva Conventions of 12 August 1949, and Relating to the Protection of Victims of Non-International Armed Conflicts (Protocol II)

1125 U.N.T.S. 609 (8 June 1977)

PREAMBLE

The High Contracting Parties,

Recalling that the humanitarian principles enshrined in Article 3 common to the Geneva Conventions of 12 August 1949, constitute the foundation of respect for the human person in cases of armed conflict not of an international character,

Recalling furthermore that international instruments relating to human rights offer a basic protection to the human person,

Emphasizing the need to ensure a better protection for the victims of those armed conflicts,

Recalling that, in cases not covered by the law in force, the human person remains under the protection of the principles of humanity and the dictates of the public conscience,

Have agreed on the following:

Part I. Scope of this Protocol

Article 1 — Material field of application

1. This Protocol, which develops and supplements Article 3 common to the Geneva Conventions of 12 August 1949 without modifying its existing conditions of application, shall apply to all armed conflicts which are not covered by Article 1 of ... Protocol I and which take place in the territory of a High Contracting Party between its armed forces and dissident armed forces or other organized armed groups which, under responsible command, exercise such control over a part of its territory as to enable them to carry out sustained and concerted military operations and to implement this Protocol.

2. This Protocol shall not apply to situations of internal disturbances and tensions, such as riots, isolated and sporadic acts of violence and other acts of a similar nature, as not being armed conflicts.

Article 2 — Personal field of application

1. This Protocol shall be applied without any adverse distinction founded on race, colour, sex, language, religion or belief, political or other opinion, national or social origin, wealth, birth or other status, or on any other similar criteria (hereinafter referred to as "adverse distinction") to all persons affected by an armed conflict as defined in Article 1.

2. At the end of the armed conflict, all the persons who have been deprived of their liberty or whose liberty has been restricted for reasons related to such conflict, as well as those deprived of their liberty or whose liberty is restricted after the conflict for the same

reasons, shall enjoy the protection of Articles 5 and 6 until the end of such deprivation or restriction of liberty.

Article 3 — Non-intervention

1. Nothing in this Protocol shall be invoked for the purpose of affecting the sovereignty of a State or the responsibility of the government, by all legitimate means, to maintain or re-establish law and order in the State or to defend the national unity and territorial integrity of the State.

2. Nothing in this Protocol shall be invoked as a justification for intervening, directly or indirectly, for any reason whatsoever, in the armed conflict or in the internal or external affairs of the High Contracting Party in the territory of which that conflict occurs.

Part II. Human Treatment

Article 4 — Fundamental guarantees

1. All persons who do not take a direct part or who have ceased to take part in hostilities, whether or not their liberty has been restricted, are entitled to respect for their person, honour and convictions and religious practices. They shall in all circumstances be treated humanely, without any adverse distinction. It is prohibited to order that there shall be no survivors.

2. Without prejudice to the generality of the foregoing, the following acts against the persons referred to in paragraph 1 are and shall remain prohibited at any time and in any place whatsoever:

(a) violence to the life, health and physical or mental well-being of persons, in particular murder as well as cruel treatment such as torture, mutilation or any form of corporal punishment;

(b) collective punishments;

(c) taking of hostages;

(d) acts of terrorism;

(e) outrages upon personal dignity, in particular humiliating and degrading treatment, rape, enforced prostitution and any form of indecent assault;

(f) slavery and the slave trade in all their forms;

(g) pillage;

(h) threats to commit any of the foregoing acts.

3. Children shall be provided with the care and aid they require, and in particular:

(a) they shall receive an education, including religious and moral education, in keeping with the wishes of their parents, or in the absence of parents, of those responsible for their care;

(b) all appropriate steps shall be taken to facilitate the reunion of families temporarily separated;

(c) children who have not attained the age of fifteen years shall neither be recruited in the armed forces or groups nor allowed to take part in hostilities;

(d) the special protection provided by this article to children who have not attained the age of fifteen years shall remain applicable to them if they take a direct part in hostilities despite the provisions of subparagraph (c) and are captured;

(e) measures shall be taken, if necessary, and whenever possible with the consent of their parents or persons who by law or custom are primarily responsible for their care, to remove children temporarily from the area in which hostilities are taking place to a safer area within the country and ensure that they are accompanied by persons responsible for their safety and well-being.

Article 5 — Persons whose liberty has been restricted

1. In addition to the provisions of Article 4 the following provisions shall be respected as a minimum with regard to persons deprived of their liberty for reasons related to the armed conflict, whether they are interned or detained:

(a) the wounded and the sick shall be treated in accordance with Article 7;

(b) the persons referred to in this paragraph shall, to the same extent as the local civilian population, be provided with food and drinking water and be afforded safeguards as regards health and hygiene and protection against the rigours of the climate and the dangers of the armed conflict;

(c) they shall be allowed to receive individual or collective relief;

(d) they shall be allowed to practise their religion and, if requested and appropriate, to receive spiritual assistance from persons, such as chaplains, performing religious functions;

(e) they shall, if made to work, have the benefit of working conditions and safeguards similar to those enjoyed by the local civilian population.

2. Those who are responsible for the internment or detention of the persons referred to in paragraph 1 shall also, within the limits of their capabilities, respect the following provisions relating to such persons:

(a) except when men and women of a family are accommodated together, women shall be held in quarters separated from those of men and shall be under the immediate supervision of women;

(b) they shall be allowed to send and receive letters and cards, the number of which may be limited by competent authority if it deems necessary;

(c) places of internment and detention shall not be located close to the combat zone. The persons referred to in paragraph 1 shall be evacuated when the places where they are interned or detained become particularly exposed to danger arising out of the armed conflict, if their evacuation can be carried out under adequate conditions of safety;

(d) they shall have the benefit of medical examinations;

(e) their physical or mental health and integrity shall not be endangered by any unjustified act or omission. Accordingly, it is prohibited to subject the persons described in this article to any medical procedure which is not indicated by the state of health of the person concerned, and which is not consistent with the generally accepted medical standards applied to free persons under similar medical circumstances.

3. Persons who are not covered by paragraph 1 but whose liberty has been restricted in any way whatsoever for reasons related to the armed conflict shall be treated humanely in accordance with Article 4 and with paragraph 1 (a), (c) and (d), and 2 (b) of this article.

4. If it is decided to release persons deprived of their liberty, necessary measures to ensure their safety shall be taken by those so deciding.

Article 6 — Penal prosecutions

1. This article applies to the prosecution and punishment of criminal offences related to the armed conflict.

2. No sentence shall be passed and no penalty executed on a person found guilty of an offence except pursuant to a conviction pronounced by a court offering the essential guarantees of independence and impartiality. In particular:

(a) the procedure shall provide for an accused to be informed without delay of the particulars of the offence alleged against him and shall afford the accused before and during his trial all necessary rights and means of defence;

(b) no one shall be convicted of an offence except on the basis of individual penal responsibility;

(c) no one shall be held guilty of any criminal offence on account of any act or omission which did not constitute a criminal offence, under the law, at the time when it was committed; nor shall a heavier penalty be imposed than that which was applicable at the time when the criminal offence was committed; if, after the commission of the offence, provision is made by law for the imposition of a lighter penalty, the offender shall benefit thereby;

(d) anyone charged with an offence is presumed innocent until proved guilty according to law;

(e) anyone charged with an offence shall have the right to be tried in his presence;

(f) no one shall be compelled to testify against himself or confess guilt.

3. A convicted person shall be advised on conviction of his judicial and other remedies and of the time-limits within which they maybe exercised.

4. The death penalty shall not be pronounced on persons who were under the age of eighteen years at the time of the offence and shall not be carried out on pregnant women or mothers of young children.

5. At the end of hostilities, the authorities in power shall endeavour to grant the broadest possible amnesty to persons who have participated in the armed conflict, or those deprived of their liberty for reasons related to the armed conflict, weather they are interned or detained.

Part III. Wounded, Sick and Shipwrecked

Article 7 — Protection and care

1. All the wounded, sick and shipwrecked, whether or not they have taken part in the armed conflict, shall be respected and protected.

2. In all circumstances they shall be treated humanely and shall receive to the fullest extent practicable and with the least possible delay, the medical care and attention required by their condition. There shall be no distinction among them founded on any grounds other than medical ones.

Article 8 — Search

Whenever circumstances permit and particularly after an engagement, all possible measures shall be taken, without delay, to search for and collect the wounded, sick and shipwrecked, to protect them against pillage and ill-treatment, to ensure their adequate care, and to search for the dead, prevent their being despoiled, and decently dispose of them.

Article 9 — Protection of medical and religious personnel

1. Medical and religious personnel shall be respected and protected and shall be granted all available help for the performance of their duties. They shall not be compelled to carry out tasks which are not compatible with their humanitarian mission.

2. In the performance of their duties medical personnel may not be required to give priority to any person except on medical grounds.

Article 10 — General protection of medical duties

1. Under no circumstances shall any person be punished for having carried out medical activities compatible with medical ethics, regardless of the person benefitting therefrom.

2. Persons engaged in medical activities shall neither be compelled to perform acts or to carry out work contrary to, nor be compelled to refrain from acts required by, the rules of medical ethics or other rules designed for the benefit of the wounded and sick, or this Protocol.

3. The professional obligations of persons engaged in medical activities regarding information which they may acquire concerning the wounded and sick under their care shall, subject to national law, be respected.

4. Subject to national law, no person engaged in medical activities may be penalized in any way for refusing or failing to give information concerning the wounded and sick who are, or who have been, under his care.

Article 11 — Protection of medical units and transports

1. Medical unites and transports shall be respected and protected at all times and shall not be the object of attack.

2. The protection to which medical units and transport are entitled shall not cease unless they are used to commit hostile acts, outside their humanitarian function. Protection may, however, cease only after a warning has been given setting, whenever appropriate, a reasonable time-limit, and after such warning has remained unheeded.

Article 12 — The distinctive emblem

Under the direction of the competent authority concerned, the distinctive emblem of the red cross, red crescent or red lion and sun on a white ground shall be displayed by medical and religious personnel and medical units, and on medical transports. It shall be respected in all circumstances. It shall not be used improperly.

Part IV. Civilian Population

Article 13 — Protection of the civilian population

1. The civilian population and individual civilians shall enjoy general protection against the dangers arising from military operations. To give effect to this protection, the following rules shall be observed in all circumstances.

2. The civilian population as such, as well as individual civilians, shall not be the object of attack. Acts or threats of violence the primary purpose of which is to spread terror among the civilian population are prohibited.

3. Civilians shall enjoy the protection afforded by this part, unless and for such time as they take a direct part in hostilities.

Article 14 — Protection of objects indispensable to the survival of the civilian population

Starvation of civilians as a method of combat is prohibited. It is therefore prohibited to attack, destroy, remove or render useless, for that purpose, objects indispensable to the survival of the civilian population such as food-stuffs, agricultural areas for the production of food-stuffs, crops, livestock, drinking water installations and supplies and irrigation works.

Article 15 — Protection of works and installations containing dangerous forces

Works or installations containing dangerous forces, namely dams, dykes and nuclear electrical generating stations, shall not be made the object of attack, even where these objects are military objectives, if such attack may cause the release of dangerous forces and consequent severe losses among the civilian population.

Article 16 — Protection of cultural objects

Without prejudice to the provisions of the Hague Convention for the Protection of Cultural Property in the Event of Armed Conflict of 14 May 1954, it is prohibited to commit any acts of hostility directed against historic monuments, works of art or places of worship which constitute the cultural or spiritual heritage of peoples, and to use them in support of the military effort.

Article 17 — Prohibition of forced movement of civilians

1. The displacement of the civilian population shall not be ordered for reasons related to the conflict unless the security of the civilians involved or imperative military reasons so demand. Should such displacements have to be carried out, all possible measures shall be taken in order that the civilian population may be received under satisfactory conditions of shelter, hygiene, health, safety and nutrition.

2. Civilians shall not be compelled to leave their own territory for reasons connected with the conflict.

Article 18 — Relief societies and relief actions

1. Relief societies located in the territory of the High Contracting Party such as Red Cross (Red Crescent, Red Lion and Sun) organizations may offer their services for the performance of their traditional functions in relation to the victims of the armed conflict. The civilian population may, even on its own initiative, offer to collect and care for the wounded, sick and shipwrecked.

2. If the civilian population is suffering undue hardship owing to a lack of the supplies essential for its survival, such as food-stuffs and medical supplies, relief actions for the civilian population which are of an exclusively humanitarian and impartial nature and which are conducted without any adverse distinction shall be undertaken subject to the consent of the High Contracting Party concerned.

Part V. Final Provisions

Article 19 — Dissemination

This Protocol shall be disseminated as widely as possible.

Article 20 — Signature

This Protocol shall be open for signature by the Parties to the Conventions six months after the signing of the Final Act and will remain open for a period of twelve months.

Article 21 — Ratification

This Protocol shall be ratified as soon as possible. The instruments of ratification shall be deposited with the Swiss Federal Council, depository of the Conventions.

Article 22 — Accession

This Protocol shall be open for accession by any Party to the Conventions which has not signed it. The instruments of accession shall be deposited with the depositary.

Article 28 — Authentic texts

The original of this Protocol, of which the Arabic, Chinese, English, French, Russian and Spanish texts are equally authentic shall be deposited with the depository, which shall transmit certified true copies thereof to all the Parties to the Conventions.

Optional Protocol to the Convention on the Rights of the Child on the Involvement of Children in Armed Conflicts
U.N. G.A. Res. 54/263, Annex I, U.N. Doc. A/54/49 (2000)

Article 1

States Parties shall take all feasible measures to ensure that members of their armed forces who have not attained the age of 18 years do not take a direct part in hostilities.

Article 2

States Parties shall ensure that persons who have not attained the age of 18 years are not compulsorily recruited into their armed forces....

Article 4

1. Armed groups that are distinct from the armed forces of a State should not, under any circumstances, recruit or use in hostilities persons under the age of 18.

2. States Parties shall take all feasible measures to prevent such recruitment and use, including the adoption of legal measures necessary to prohibit and criminalize such practices.

3. The application of the present article under this Protocol shall not affect the legal status of any party to an armed conflict.

Article 5

Nothing in the present Protocol shall be construed as precluding provisions in the law of a State Party or in international instruments and international humanitarian law that are more conducive to the realization of the rights of the child....

Charter of the International Military Tribunal at Nuremberg
Annex to the London Agreement (8 Aug. 1945), 82 U.N.T.S. 279

I. Constitution of the International Military Tribunal

Article 1

In pursuance of the Agreement signed on the 8th day of August 1945 by the Government of the United States of America, the Provisional Government of the French Republic, the Government of the United Kingdom of Great Britain and Northern Ireland and the Government of the Union of Soviet Socialist Republics, there shall be established an International Military Tribunal (hereinafter called "the Tribunal") for the just and prompt trial and punishment of the major war criminals of the European Axis.

Article 2

The Tribunal shall consist of four members, each with an alternate. One member and one alternate shall be appointed by each of the Signatories. The alternates shall, so far as they are able, be present at all sessions of the Tribunal. In case of illness of any member of the Tribunal or his incapacity for some other reason to fulfill his functions, his alternate shall take his place.

Article 3

Neither the Tribunal, its members nor their alternates can be challenged by the prosecution, or by the Defendants or their Counsel. Each Signatory may replace its member of the Tribunal or his alternate for reasons of health or for other good reasons, except that no replacement may take place during a Trial, other than by an alternate.

Article 4

(a) The presence of all four members of the Tribunal or the alternate for any absent member shall be necessary to constitute the quorum.

(b) The members of the Tribunal shall, before any trial begins, agree among themselves upon the selection from their number of a President, and the President shall hold office during that trial, or as may otherwise be agreed by a vote of not less than three members. The principle of rotation or presidency for successive trials is agreed. If, however, a session of the Tribunal takes place on the territory of one of the four Signatories, the representative of that Signatory on the Tribunal shall preside.

(c) Save as aforesaid the Tribunal shall take decisions by a majority vote and in case the votes are evenly divided, the vote of the President shall be decisive: provided always that convictions and sentences shall only be imposed by affirmative votes of at least three members of the Tribunal.

Article 5

In case of need and depending on the number of the matters to be tried, other Tribunals may be set up; and the establishment, functions, and procedure of each Tribunal shall be identical, and shall be governed by this Charter.

II. Jurisdiction and General Principles

Article 6

The Tribunal established by the Agreement referred to in Article 1 hereof for the trial and punishment of the major war criminals of the European Axis countries shall have the power to try and punish persons who, acting in the interests of the European Axis countries, whether as individuals or as members of organizations, committed any of the following crimes.

The following acts, or any of them, are crimes coming within the jurisdiction of the Tribunal for which there shall be individual responsibility:

(a) *Crimes against peace*: namely, planning, preparation, initiation or waging of a war of aggression, or a war in violation of international treaties, agreements or assurances, or participation in a common plan or conspiracy for the accomplishment of any of the foregoing;

(b) *War crimes*: namely, violations of the laws or customs of war. Such violations shall include, but not be limited to, murder, ill-treatment or deportation to slave labour or for any other purpose of civilian population of or in occupied territory, murder or ill-treatment of prisoners of war or persons on the seas, killing of hostages, plunder of public or private property, wanton destruction of cities, towns or villages, or devastation not justified by military necessity;

(c) *Crimes against humanity*: namely, murder, extermination, enslavement, deportation, and other inhumane acts committed against any civilian population, before or during the war; or persecutions on political, racial or religious grounds in execution of or in connection with any crime within the jurisdiction of the Tribunal, whether or not in violation of the domestic law of the country where perpetrated.

Leaders, organizers, instigators and accomplices participating in the formulation or execution of a common plan or conspiracy to commit any of the foregoing crimes are responsible for all acts performed by any persons in execution of such plan.

Article 7

The official position of defendants, whether as Heads of State or responsible officials in Government Departments, shall not be considered as freeing them from responsibility or mitigating punishment.

Article 8

The fact that the Defendant acted pursuant to order of his Government or of a superior shall not free him from responsibility, but may be considered in mitigation of punishment if the Tribunal determines that justice so requires.

Article 9

At the trial of any individual member of any group or organization the Tribunal may declare (in connection with any act of which the individual may be convicted) that the group or organization of which the individual was a member was a criminal organization.

After receipt of the Indictment the Tribunal shall give notice as it thinks fit that the prosecution intends to ask the Tribunal to make such declaration and any member of the organization will be entitled to apply to the Tribunal for leave to be heard by the Tribunal upon the question of the criminal character of the organization. The Tribunal shall have the power to allow or reject the application. If the application is allowed, the Tribunal may direct in what manner the applicants shall be represented and heard.

Article 10

In cases where a group or organization is declared criminal by the Tribunal, the competent national authority of any Signatory shall have the right to bring individuals to trial for membership therein before national, military or occupation courts. In any such case the criminal nature of the group or organization is considered proved and shall not be questioned.

Article 11

Any person convicted by the Tribunal may be charged before a national, military or occupation court, referred to in Article 10 of this Charter, with a crime other than of membership in a criminal group or organization and such court may, after convicting him, impose upon him punishment independent of and additional to the punishment imposed by the Tribunal for participation in the criminal activities of such group or organization.

Article 12

The Tribunal shall have the right to take proceedings against a person charged with crimes set out in Article 6 of this Charter in his absence, if he has not been found or if the Tribunal, for any reason, finds it necessary, in the interests of justice, to conduct the hearing in his absence.

Article 13

The Tribunal shall draw up rules for its procedure. These rules shall not be inconsistent with the provisions of this Charter.

Article 14

Each Signatory shall appoint a Chief Prosecutor for the investigation of charges against and the prosecution of major war criminals.

The Chief Prosecutors shall act as a committee for the following purposes:

(a) to agree upon a plan of the individual work of each of the Chief Prosecutors and his staff,

(b) to settle the final designation of major war criminals to be tried by the Tribunal,

(c) to approve the Indictment and the documents to be submitted therewith,

(d) to lodge the Indictment and the accompanying documents with the Tribunal,

(e) to draw up and recommend to the Tribunal for its approval draft rules of procedure, contemplated by Article 13 of this Charter. The Tribunal shall have the power to accept, with or without amendments, or to reject, the rules so recommended.

The Committee shall act in all the above matters by a majority vote and shall appoint a Chairman as may be convenient and in accordance with the principle of rotation: provided that if there is an equal division of vote concerning the designation of a Defendant to be tried by the Tribunal, or the crimes with which he shall be charged, that proposal will be adopted which was made by the party which proposed that the particular Defendant be tried, or the particular charges be preferred against him.

Article 15

The Chief Prosecutors shall, individually, and acting in collaboration with one another, also undertake the following duties:

(a) investigation, collection and production before or at the Trial of all necessary evidence,

(b) the preparation of the Indictment for approval by the Committee in accordance with paragraph (c) of Article 14 hereof,

(c) the preliminary examination of all necessary witnesses and of the Defendants,

(d) to act as prosecutor at the Trial,

(e) to appoint representatives to carry out such duties as may be assigned to them,

(f) to undertake such other matters as may appear necessary to them for the purposes of the preparation for and conduct of the Trial.

It is understood that no witness or Defendant detained in any Signatory shall be taken out of the possession of that Signatory without its assent.

IV. Fair Trial for Defendants

Article 16

In order to ensure fair trial for the Defendants, the following procedures shall be followed:

(a) The Indictment shall include full particulars specifying in detail the charges against the Defendants. A copy of the Indictment and of all the documents lodged with the Indictment, translated into a language which he understands, shall be furnished to the Defendant as a reasonable time before the Trial.

(b) During any preliminary examination or trial of a Defendant he shall have the right to give any explanation relevant to the charges made against him.

(c) A preliminary examination of a Defendant and his Trial shall be conducted in, or translated into, a language which the Defendant understands.

(d) A defendant shall have the right to conduct his own defense before the Tribunal or to have the assistance of Counsel.

(e) A defendant shall have the right through himself or through his Counsel to present evidence at the Trial in support of his defense, and to cross-examine any witness called by the Prosecution.

V. Powers of the Tribunal and Conduct of the Trial

Article 17

The Tribunal shall have the power:

(a) to summon witnesses to the Trial and to require their attendance and testimony and to put questions to them,

(b) to interrogate any Defendant,

(c) to require the production of documents and other evidentiary material,

(d) to administer oaths to witnesses,

(e) to appoint officers for the carrying out of any task designated by the Tribunal including the power to have evidence taken on commission.

Article 18

The Tribunal shall:

(a) confine Trial strictly to an expeditious hearing of the issues raised by the charges,

(b) take strict measures to prevent any action which will cause unreasonable delay, and rule out irrelevant issues and statements of any kind whatsoever,

(c) deal summarily with any contumacy, imposing appropriate punishment, including exclusion of any Defendant or his Counsel from some or all further proceedings, but without prejudice to the determination of the charges.

Article 19

The Tribunal shall not be bound by technical rules of evidence. It shall adopt and apply to the greatest possible extent expeditious and non-technical procedure, and shall admit any evidence which it deems to have probative value.

Article 20

The Tribunal may require to be informed of the nature of any evidence before it is offered so that it may rule upon the relevance thereof.

Article 21

The Tribunal shall not require proof of facts of common knowledge but shall take judicial notice thereof. It shall also take judicial notice of official governmental documents and reports of the United Nations, including the acts and documents of the committees set up in the various Allied countries for the investigation of war crimes, and the records and findings of military or other Tribunals of any of the United Nations.

Article 22

The permanent seat of the Tribunal shall be in Berlin. The first meetings of the members of the Tribunal and of the Chief Prosecutors shall be held at Berlin in a place to be designated by the Control Council for Germany. The first trial shall be held at Nuremberg, and any subsequent trials shall be held at such places as the Tribunal may decide.

Article 23

One or more of the Chief Prosecutors may take part in the prosecution at each Trial. The function of any Chief Prosecutor may be discharged by him personally, or by any person or persons authorised by him.

The function of ... [Counsel] for a Defendant may be discharged at the Defendant's request by any Counsel professionally qualified to conduct cases before the Courts of his own country, or by any other person who may be specially authorised thereto by the Tribunal.

Article 24

The proceedings at the Trial shall take the following course:

(a) The Indictment shall be read in court.

(b) The Tribunal shall ask each Defendant whether he pleads "guilty" or "not guilty".

(c) The Prosecution shall make an opening statement.

(d) The Tribunal shall ask the Prosecution and the Defence what evidence (if any) they wish to submit to the Tribunal, and the Tribunal shall rule upon the admissibility of any such evidence.

(e) The witnesses for the Prosecution shall be examined and after that the witnesses for the Defence. Thereafter such rebutting evidence as may be held by the Tribunal to be admissible shall be called by either the Prosecution or the Defence.

(f) The Tribunal may put any question to any witness and to any Defendant, at any time.

(g) The Prosecution and the Defence shall interrogate and may cross-examine any witness and any Defendant who gives testimony.

(h) Defence shall address the court.

(i) The Prosecution shall address the court.

(j) Each Defendant may make a statement to the Tribunal.

(k) The Tribunal shall deliver judgment and pronounce sentence.

Article 25

All official documents shall be produced, and all court proceedings conducted, in English, French and Russian, and in the language of the Defendant. So much of the record and of the proceedings may also be translated into the language of any country in which the Tribunal is sitting, as the Tribunal considers desirable in the interests of justice and public opinion.

VI. Judgment and Sentence

Article 26

The judgment of the Tribunal as to the guilt or the innocence of any Defendant shall give the reasons on which it is based, and shall be final and not subject to review.

Article 27

The Tribunal shall have the right to impose upon a Defendant, on conviction, death or such other punishment as shall be determined by it to be just.

Article 28

In addition to any punishment imposed by it, the Tribunal shall have the right to deprive the convicted person of any stolen property and order its delivery to the Control Council for Germany.

Article 29

In case of guilt, sentences shall be carried out in accordance with the orders of the Control Council for Germany, which may at any time reduce or otherwise alter the sentences, but may not increase the severity thereof. If the Control Council for Germany, after any defendant has been convicted and sentenced, discovers fresh evidence which, in its opinion, would found a fresh charge against him, the Council shall report accordingly to the Committee established under Article 14 hereof for such action as they may consider proper, having regard to the interests of justice.

VII. Expenses

Article 30

The expenses of the Tribunal and of the Trials shall be charged by the Signatories against the funds allotted for maintenance of the Control Council for Germany.

Tokyo Charter for the International Military Tribunal for the Far East (1946)

as amended by General Orders No. 20 (26 April 1946), T.I.A.S. No. 1589

Section I. Constitution of Tribunal

Article 1

Tribunal Established. The International Tribunal for the Far East is hereby established for the just and prompt trial and punishment of the major war criminals in the Far East. The permanent seat of the Tribunal is in Tokyo.

Article 2

Members. The Tribunal shall consist of not less than five nor more than nine Members, appointed by the Supreme Commander for the Allied Powers from the names submitted by the Signatories to the Instrument of Surrender, India, and the Commonwealth of the Philippines.

Article 3

Offices and Secretariat.

a. *President.* The Supreme Commander for the Allied Powers shall appoint a Member to be President of the Tribunal.

b. *Secretariat.*

(1) The Secretariat of the Tribunal shall be composed of a General Secretary to be appointed by the Supreme Commander for the Allied Powers and such assistant secretaries, clerks, interpreters, and other personnel as may be necessary.

(2) The General Secretary shall organize and direct the work of the Secretariat.

(3) The Secretariat shall receive all documents addressed to the Tribunal, maintain the records of the Tribunal, provide necessary clerical services to the Tribunal and its members, and perform such other duties as may be designated by the Tribunal.

Article 4

Convening and Quorum, Voting, and Absence.

a. *Convening and Quorum.* When as many as six members of the Tribunal are present, they may convene the Tribunal in formal session. The presence of a majority of all members shall be necessary to constitute a quorum.

b. *Voting.* All decisions and judgments of this Tribunal, including convictions and sentences, shall be by a majority vote of those members of the Tribunal present. In case the votes are evenly divided, the vote of the President shall be decisive.

c. *Absence.* If a member at any time is absent and afterwards is able to be present, he shall take part in all subsequent proceedings; unless he declares in open court that he is disqualified by reason of insufficient familiarity with the proceedings which took place in his absence.

Section II. Jurisdiction and General Provisions

Article 5

Jurisdiction Over Persons and Offenses. The Tribunal shall have the power to try and punish Far Eastern war criminals who as individuals or as members of organizations are charged with offenses which include Crimes against Peace. The following acts, or any of them, are crimes coming within the jurisdiction of the Tribunal for which there shall be individual responsibility:

a. *Crimes against Peace*: Namely, the planning, preparation, initiation or waging of a declared or undeclared war of aggression, or a war in violation of international law, treaties, agreements or assurances, or participation in a common plan or conspiracy for the accomplishment of any of the foregoing;

b. *Conventional War Crimes*: Namely, violations of the laws or customs of war;

c. *Crimes against Humanity*: Namely, murder, extermination, enslavement, deportation, and other inhumane acts committed before or during the war, or persecutions on political or racial grounds in execution of or in connection with any crime within the jurisdiction of the Tribunal, whether or not in violation of the domestic law of the country where perpetrated.

Leaders, organizers, instigators and accomplices participating in the formulation or execution of a common plan or conspiracy to commit any of the foregoing crimes are responsible for all acts performed by any person in execution of such plan.

Article 6

Responsibility of Accused. Neither the official position, at any time, of an accused, nor the fact that an accused acted pursuant to order of his government or of a superior shall, of itself, be sufficient to free such accused from responsibility for any crime with which he is charged, but such circumstances may be considered in mitigation of punishment if the Tribunal determines that justice so requires.

Article 7

Rules of Procedure. The Tribunal may draft and amend rules of procedure consistent with the fundamental provisions of this Charter.

Article 8

Counsel.

a. *Chief Counsel.* The Chief of Counsel designated by the Supreme Commander for the Allied Powers is responsible for the investigation and prosecution of charges against war criminals within the jurisdiction of this Tribunal and will render such legal assistance to the Supreme Commander as is appropriate.

b. *Associate Counsel.* Any United Nation with which Japan has been at war may appoint an Associate Counsel to assist the Chief of Counsel.

Section III. Fair Trial for Accused

Article 9

Procedure for Fair Trial. In order to insure fair trial for the accused, the following procedure shall be followed:

a. *Indictment.* The indictment shall consist of a plain, concise and adequate statement of each offense charged. Each accused shall be furnished in adequate time for defense a copy of the indictment, including any amendment, and of this Charter, in a language understood by the accused.

b. *Language.* The trial and related proceedings shall be conducted in English and in the language of the accused. Translations of documents and other papers shall be provided as needed and requested.

c. *Counsel for Accused.* Each accused shall have the right to be represented by counsel of his own selection, subject to the disapproval of such counsel at any time by the Tribunal. The accused shall file with the General Secretary of the Tribunal the name of his counsel. If an accused is not represented by counsel and in open court requests the appointment of counsel, the Tribunal shall designate counsel for him. In the absence of such request the Tribunal may appoint counsel for an accused if in its judgment such appointment is necessary to provide a fair trial.

d. *Evidence for Defense.* An accused shall have the right, through himself or through his counsel (but not through both), to conduct his defense, including the right to examine any witness, subject to reasonable restrictions as the Tribunal may determine.

e. *Production of Evidence for the Defense.* An accused may apply in writing to the Tribunal for the production of witnesses or of documents. The application shall state where the witness or document is thought to be located. It shall also state the facts proposed to be proved by the witness or the document and the relevancy of such facts to the defense. If the Tribunal grants the application the Tribunal shall be given such aid in obtaining production of the evidence as the circumstances require.

Article 10

Applications and Motions before Trial. All motions, applications, or other requests addressed to the Tribunal prior to the commencement of trial shall be made in writing and filed with the General Secretary of the Tribunal for action by the Tribunal.

Section IV. Powers of Tribunal and Conduct of Trial

Article 11

Powers. The Tribunal shall have the power:

a. To summon witnesses to the trial, to require them to attend and testify, and to question them.

b. To interrogate each accused and to permit comment on his refusal to answer any question.

c. To require the production of documents and other evidentiary material.

d. To require of each witness an oath, affirmation, or such declaration as is customary in the country of the witness, and to administer oaths.

e. To appoint officers for the carrying out of any task designated by the Tribunal, including the power to have evidence taken on commission.

Article 12

Conduct of Trial. The Tribunal shall:

a. Confine the trial strictly to an expeditious hearing of the issues raised by the charges.

b. Take strict measures to prevent any action which would cause any unreasonable delay and rule out irrelevant issues and statements of any kind whatsoever.

c. Provide for the maintenance of order at the trial and deal summarily with any contumacy, imposing appropriate punishment, including exclusion of any accused or his counsel from some or all further proceedings, but without prejudice to the determination of the charges.

d. Determine the mental and physical capacity of any accused to proceed to trial.

Article 13

Evidence.

a. *Admissibility.* The Tribunal shall not be bound by technical rules of evidence. It shall adopt and apply to the greatest possible extent expeditious and non-technical procedure, and shall admit any evidence which it deems to have probative value. All purported admissions or statements of the accused are admissible.

b. *Relevance.* The Tribunal may require to be informed of the nature of any evidence before it is offered in order to rule upon the relevance.

c. *Specific evidence admissible.* In particular, and without limiting in any way the scope of the foregoing general rules, the following evidence may be admitted:

(1) A document, regardless of its security classification and without proof of its issuance or signature, which appears to the Tribunal to have been signed or

issued by any officer, department, agency or member of the armed forces of any government.

(2) A report which appears to the Tribunal to have been signed or issued by the International Red Cross or a member thereof, or by a doctor of medicine or any medical service personnel, or by an investigator or intelligence officer, of by any other person who appears to the Tribunal to have personal knowledge of the matters contained in the report.

(3) An affidavit, deposition or other signed statement.

(4) A diary, letter or other document, including sworn or unsworn statements, which appear to the Tribunal to contain information relating to the charge.

(5) A copy of a document or other secondary evidence of its contents, if the original is not immediately available.

d. *Judicial Notice.* The Tribunal shall neither require proof of facts of common knowledge, nor of the authenticity of official government documents and reports of any nation or of the proceedings, records, and findings of military or other agencies of any of the United Nations.

e. *Records, Exhibits, and Documents.* The transcript of the proceedings, and exhibits and documents submitted to the Tribunal, will be filed with the General Secretary of the Tribunal and will constitute part of the Record.

Article 14

Place of Trial. The first trial will be held in Tokyo, and any subsequent trials will be held at such places as the Tribunal decides.

Article 15

Course of Trial Proceedings. The proceedings of the Trial will take the following course:

a. The indictment will be read in court unless reading is waived by all accused.

b. The Tribunal will ask each accused whether he pleads "guilty" or "not guilty."

c. The prosecution and each accused (by counsel only, if represented) may make a concise opening statement.

d. The prosecution and defense may offer evidence, and the admissibility of the same shall be determined by the Tribunal.

e. The prosecution and each accused (by counsel only, if represented) may examine each witness and each accused who gives testimony.

f. Accused (by counsel only, if represented) may address the Tribunal.

g. The prosecution may address the Tribunal.

h. The Tribunal will deliver judgment and pronounce sentence.

Section V. Judgment and Sentence

Article 16

Penalty. The Tribunal shall have the power to impose upon an accused, on conviction, death, or such other punishment as shall be determined by it to be just.

Article 17

Judgment and Review. The judgment will be announced in open court and will give the reasons on which it is based. The record of the trial will be transmitted directly to the

Supreme Commander for the Allied Powers for his action. Sentence will be carried out in accordance with the Order of the Supreme Commander for the Allied Powers, who may at any time reduce or otherwise alter the sentence, except to increase its severity.

Allied Control Council Law No. 10 (20 Dec. 1945)

Control Council for Germany, Official Gazette 50 (Jan. 31, 1946)
Punishment of Persons Guilty of War Crimes, Crimes
Against Peace, and Crimes Against Humanity

In order to give effect to the terms of the Moscow Declaration of 30 October 1943 and the London Agreement of 8 August 1945, and the Charter issued pursuant thereto and in order to establish a uniform legal basis in Germany for the prosecution of war criminals and other similar offenders, other than those dealt with by the International Military Tribunal, the Control Council enacts as follows:

Article I

The Moscow Declaration of 30 October 1943 "Concerning Responsibility of Hitlerites for Committed Atrocities" and the London Agreement of 8 August 1945 "Concerning Prosecution and Punishment of Major War Criminals of the European Axis" are made integral parts of this Law. Adherence to the provisions of the London Agreement by any of the United Nations, as provided for in Article V of that Agreement, shall not entitle such Nation to participate or interfere in the operation of this Law within the Control Council area of authority in Germany.

Article II

1. Each of the following acts is recognized as a crime:

a) *Crimes against Peace.* Initiation of invasions of other countries and wars of aggression in violation of international laws and treaties, including but not limited to planning, preparation, initiation or waging a war of aggression, or a war ... [in] violation of international treaties, agreements or assurances, or participation in a common plan or conspiracy for the accomplishment of any of the foregoing

(b) *War Crimes.* Atrocities or offenses against persons or property constituting violations of the laws or customs of war, including, but not limited to, murder, ill treatment or deportation to slave labour or for any other purpose, of civilian population from occupied territory, murder or ill treatment of prisoners of war or persons on the seas, killing of hostages, plunder of public or private property, wanton destruction of cities, towns or villages, or devastation not justified by military necessity.

(c) *Crimes against Humanity.* Atrocities and offenses, including but not limited to murder, extermination, enslavement, deportation, imprisonment, torture, rape, or other inhumane acts committed against any civilian population, or persecutions on political, racial or religious grounds whether or not in violation of the domestic laws of the country where perpetrated.

(d) Membership in categories of a criminal group or organization declared criminal by the International Military Tribunal.

2. Any person without regard to nationality or the capacity in which he acted, is deemed to have committed a crime as defined in paragraph 1 of this article, if he was (a) a principal or (b) was an accessory to the commission of any such crime or ordered or abetted the same or (c) took a consenting part therein or (d) was connected with plans or enter-

prises involving its commission or (e) was a member of any organization or group connected with the commission of any such crime or (f) with reference to paragraph 1 (a) if he held a high political, civil or military (including General Staff) position in Germany or in one of its Allies, co-belligerents or satellites or held high position in financial, industrial or economic life of any such country.

3. Any person found guilty of any of the crimes above mentioned may upon conviction be punished as shall be determined by the tribunal to be just. Such punishment may consist of one or more of the following:

(a) Death.

(b) Imprisonment for life or a term of years, with or without hard labour.

(c) Fine, and imprisonment with or without hard labour, in lieu thereof.

(d) Forfeiture of property.

(e) Restitution of property wrongfully acquired.

(f) Deprivation of some or all civil rights.

Any property declared to be forfeited or the restitution of which is ordered by the Tribunal shall be delivered to the Control Council for Germany, which shall decide on its disposal.

4. (a) The official position of any person, whether as Head of State or as a responsible official in a Government Department, does not free him from responsibility for a crime or entitle him to mitigation of punishment.

(b) The fact that any person acted pursuant to the order of his Government or of a superior does not relieve him from responsibility for a crime, but may be considered in mitigation.

5. In any trial or prosecution for a crime herein referred to, the accused shall not be entitled to the benefits of any statute of limitation in respect of the period from 30 January 1933 to 1 July 1945, nor shall any immunity, pardon or amnesty granted under the Nazi regime be admitted as a bar to trial or punishment.

Article III

1. Each occupying authority, within its Zone of occupation,

(a) shall have the right to cause persons within such Zone suspected of having committed a crime, including those charged with crime by one of the United Nations, to be arrested and shall take under control the property, real and personal, owned or controlled by the said persons, pending decisions as to its eventual disposition.

(b) shall report to the Legal Directorate the names of all suspected criminals, the reasons for and the places of their detention, if they are detained, and the names and location of witnesses.

(c) shall take appropriate measures to see that witnesses and evidence will be available when required.

(d) shall have the right to cause all persons so arrested and charged, and not delivered to another authority as herein provided, or released, to be brought to trial before an appropriate tribunal. Such tribunal may, in the case of crimes committed by persons of German citizenship or nationality against other persons of German citizenship or nationality, or stateless persons, be a German Court, if authorized by the occupying authorities.

2. The tribunal by which persons charged with offenses hereunder shall be tried and the rules and procedure thereof shall be determined or designated by each Zone Commander for his respective Zone. Nothing herein is intended to, or shall impair or limit the jurisdiction or power of any court or tribunal now or hereafter established in any Zone by the Commander thereof, or of the International Military Tribunal established by the London Agreement of 8 August 1945.

3. Persons wanted for trial by an International Military Tribunal will not be tried without the consent of the Committee of Chief Prosecutors. Each Zone Commander will deliver such persons who are within his Zone to that committee upon request and will make witnesses and evidence available to it.

4. Persons known to be wanted for trial in another Zone or outside Germany will not be tried prior to decision under Article IV unless the fact of their apprehension has been reported in accordance with Section 1(b) of this Article, three months have elapsed thereafter, and no request for delivery of the type contemplated by Article IV has been received by the Zone Commander concerned.

5. The execution of death sentences may be deferred by not to exceed one month after the sentence has become final when the Zone Commander concerned has reason to believe that the testimony of those under sentence would be of value in the investigation and trial of crimes within or without his Zone.

6. Each Zone Commander will cause such effect to be given to the judgments of courts of competent jurisdiction, with respect to the property taken under his control pursuant thereto, as he may deem proper in the interest of justice.

Article IV

1. When any person in a Zone in Germany is alleged to have committed a crime, as defined in Article II, in a country other than Germany or in another Zone, the government of that nation or the Commander of the latter Zone, as the case may be, may request the Commander of the Zone in which the person is located for his arrest and delivery for trial to the country or Zone in which the crime was committed. Such request for delivery shall be granted by the Commander receiving it unless he believes such person is wanted for trial or as a witness by an International Military Tribunal, or in Germany, or in a nation other than the one making the request, or the Commander is not satisfied that delivery should be made, in any of which cases he shall have the right to forward the said request to the Legal Directorate of the Allied Control Authority. A similar procedure shall apply to witnesses, material exhibits and other forms of evidence.

2. The Legal Directorate shall consider all requests referred to it, and shall determine the same in accordance with the following principles, its determination to be communicated to the Zone Commander.

(a) A person wanted for trial or as witness by an International Military Tribunal shall not be delivered for trial or required to give evidence outside Germany, as the case may be, except upon approval by the Committee of Chief Prosecutors acting under the London Agreement of 8 August 1945.

(b) A person wanted for trial by several authorities (other than an International Military Tribunal) shall be disposed of in accordance with the following priorities:

(1) If wanted for trial in the Zone in which he is, he should not be delivered unless arrangements are made for his return after trial elsewhere;

(2) If wanted for trial in a Zone other than that in which he is, he should be delivered to that Zone in preference to delivery outside Germany unless arrangements are made for his return to that Zone after trial elsewhere;

(3) If wanted for trial outside Germany by two or more of the United Nations, of one of which he is a citizen, that one should have priority;

(4) If wanted for trial outside Germany by several countries, not all of which are United Nations, United Nations should have priority;

(5) If wanted for trial outside Germany by two or more of the United Nations, then, subject to Article IV 2 (b) (3) above, that which has the most serious charges against him, which are moreover supported by evidence, should have priority.

Article V

The delivery, under Article IV of this Law, of persons for trial shall be made on demands of the Governments or Zone Commanders in such a manner that the delivery of criminals to one jurisdiction will not become the means of defeating or unnecessarily delaying the carrying out of justice in another place. If within six months the delivered person has not been convicted by the Court of the zone or country to which he has been delivered, then such person shall be returned upon demand of the Commander of the Zone where the person was located prior to delivery.

Done at Berlin, 20 December 1945.

Principles of the Nuremberg Charter and Judgment

Formulated by the International Law Commission, 5 U.N. GAOR, Supp. No. 12, at 11–14, para. 99, U.N. Doc. A/1316 (1950)

I. Any person who commits an act which constitutes a crime under international law is responsible therefor and liable to punishment.

II. The fact that internal law does not impose a penalty for an act which constitutes a crime under international law does not relieve the person who committed the act from responsibility under international law.

III. The fact that a person who committed an act which constitutes a crime under international law acted as Head of State or responsible Government official does not relieve him from responsibility under international law.

IV. The fact that a person acted pursuant to order of his Government or of a superior does not relieve him from responsibility under international law, provided a moral choice was in fact possible to him.

V. Any person charge with a crime under international law has the right to a fair trial on the facts and law.

VI. The crimes hereinafter set out are punishable as crimes under international law:

a. Crimes against peace:

(i) Planning, preparation, initiation or waging of a war of aggression, or a war in violation of international treaties, agreements or assurances;

(ii) Participation in a common plan or conspiracy for the accomplishment of any of the acts mentioned under (i).

b. War crimes: Violation of the laws and customs of war which include, but are not limited to, murder, ill-treatment of prisoners of war or of persons on the seas, killing of hostages, plunder of public or private property, wanton destruction of cities, towns, or villages, or devastation not justified by military necessity.

c. Crimes against humanity: Murder, extermination, enslavement, deportation and other inhuman acts done against any civilian population, or persecution on political, racial or religious grounds, when such acts are done or such persecutions are carried on in execution of or in connection with any crime against peace or any war crime.

VII. Complicity in the commission of a crime against peace, a war crime, or a crime against humanity as set forth in Principle VI is a crime under international law.

U.N. Supplemental Rules of Criminal Procedure for Military Commissions of the United Nations Command, Korea
(Revised thru 17 March 1953)

SECTION I. *SCOPE, PURPOSE, AND CONSTRUCTION*

RULE 1. SCOPE OF RULES. These rules shall govern all Military Commissions of the United Nations Command conducting trials of prisoners of war charged with postcapture offenses, all reviews of such trials, and the submission and action upon all petitions for New Trial.

RULE 2. PURPOSE AND CONSTRUCTION OF RULES. These rules are intended to provide for the just determination of all proceedings; they shall be construed to secure simplicity in procedure, fairness in administration, and the elimination of unjustifiable delay.

SECTION II. *THE COMMISSIONS*

RULE 3. TYPES. There shall be two types of Military Commissions for the trial of prisoners of war for postcapture offenses: Special Military Commissions and General Military Commissions.

RULE 4. JURISDICTION OVER PERSONS. These Commissions shall have jurisdiction over all prisoners of war who are in the custody of the convening authority at the commencement of the trial and during the arraignment.

RULE 5. JURISDICTION OVER OFFENSES. These Commissions shall have jurisdiction over all postcapture offenses, including but not limited to, all violations of the laws and customs of war, all violations of the laws of the Republic of Korea, all violations of rules, regulations, or orders, applicable to prisoners of war, promulgated by the Commander-in-Chief, United Nations Command, or his authorized representatives, all violations of rules, regulations, or orders of prisoner of war camp commanders or their authorized representatives, and all other acts to the prejudice of good order and discipline among prisoners of war.

RULE 6. MEMBERSHIP OF COMMISSIONS.

a. *Appointment.* The members of each Military Commission will be appointed by the Commander-in-Chief, United Nations Command, or under authority delegated by him. Unless specifically provided in the delegation of authority, a commander to whom the authority to convene such commissions is delegated will not further delegate such authority.

b. *Number.*

(1) Each General Military Commission shall consist of not less than five members.

(2) Each Special Military Commission shall consist of one or more members but not more than three members.

c. *Designation.*

(1) The order appointing a General Military Commission shall designate a President and a Law Member. The same individual may be designated both President and Law Member.

(2) The order appointing a Special Military Commission shall designate a President.

d. *Eligibility.*

(1) Any commissioned officer of the armed forces of the United Nations Command, including any commissioned officer of the armed forces of the Republic of Korea, shall be eligible for membership on a Commission.

(2) The convening authority may, in his discretion, appoint as a member of a Commission any civilian who is a citizen of any nation of the United Nations, including any citizen of the Republic of Korea.

e. *Representation.* Where an offense involves victims of more than one nation, each such nation, in the discretion of the convening authority, may be represented on the Commissions.

f. *Vacancies.* Any vacancy occurring among the members may be filled, or any additions to a Commission may be made, by the convening authority, but the substance of all proceedings had and evidence taken in the case then on trial shall be made known to the new member. The fact that the substance of all proceedings had and evidence taken in the case has been made known to the new member will be announced by the President of a Commission in open court.

RULE 7. QUALIFICATIONS OF MEMBERS OF COMMISSION.

a. *General.* The convening authority shall appoint to a Commission only persons competent to perform the duties involved and not disqualified by personal interest or prejudice; provided that no person shall sit as a member of a Commission in any case in which he is the accuser or investigator or in which he may be required as a witness for the prosecution....

RULE 14. POWERS OF THE COMMISSIONS.

a. *General.* The Commissions shall have power to impound money and property, compel the attendance and detention of witnesses, require witnesses to produce documents and property, punish for contempt, debar from practice before the Commission any Counsel for cause subject to review by the convening authority, administer oaths and affirmations, and issue search warrants and warrants of arrest.

b. *Contempts.*

(1) A General Military Commission shall have the power to punish for contempt by imprisonment not exceeding six months, or by fine not exceeding $500.00, or by both fine and imprisonment, any disobedience of its mandates or any contempt.

(2) A Special Military Commission shall have the power to punish for contempt by imprisonment for one month or by fine not exceeding $50.00, or by both fine and imprisonment, any disobedience of its mandates or any contempt.

c. *Rules and Forms.* A Commission shall have the power to adopt supplementary rules and forms to govern its procedure, not inconsistent with the provisions hereof.

RULE 15. AUTHORIZED PUNISHMENT.

a. *General Military Commission.* A General Military Commission may sentence an accused, upon conviction, to death, to confinement at hard labor for life or for any lesser term, or such other punishment as the Commission shall determine to be proper, consistent with the customs of war in like cases in the armed forces of the nation of the convening authority.

b. *Special Military Commission.* A Special Military Commission may not sentence an accused, upon conviction to confinement at hard labor for more than six months, but may sentence the accused to confinement at hard labor for six months or for any lesser term, as the Commission shall determine to be proper, consistent with the customs of war in like cases in the armed forces of the nation of the convening authority.

c. *General.* The Table of Maximum Punishments or its equivalent, in effect in the armed forces of the nation of the convening authority, shall be used as a guide in determining proper punishment....

SECTION III. *TRIAL*

RULE 17. CONDUCT OF TRIAL. The Commissions shall confine each proceeding strictly to a fair, expeditious trial of the issues raised, excluding irrelevant issues or evidence and preventing any unnecessary delay or interference; hold public sessions except when otherwise required by the dictates of military necessity; hold each session at such time and place as it shall determine, or as may be directed by the convening authority.

RULE 18. TRIAL PROCEDURE. The order of proceedings of trial shall conform generally to that prescribed for general courts-martial, or its equivalent, in the armed forces of the nation of the convening authority. A suggested guide for procedure before Military Commissions is attached as Annex A.

RULE 19. JOINT AND COMMON TRIALS. Two or more persons may be tried together wherever jointly charged in any specification. Common trials may be held if two or more accused are alleged to have participated in the same act or acts, or in related acts, or in the same series of acts, constituting an offense or offenses.

RULE 20. PRESENCE OF LAW MEMBER. A General Military Commission shall not receive evidence upon any matter, nor shall it vote upon its findings or sentence, in the absence of the Law Member. When the Law Member is absent at any time during the trial, the Commission will adjourn until the Law Member is present or a New Law Member is appointed.

RULE 21. PROSECUTIONS AND PROCESS. All prosecutions before the Commissions shall be conducted, and all process returnable to such Commissions shall issue, under the authority of the United Nations.

RULE 22. CHARGES AND SPECIFICATIONS.

a. *Nature and Contents.* Charges and specifications shall be based on personal knowledge, or information and belief, and signed under oath by a member of the armed forces of the United Nations Command. Each charge and specification shall consist of a plain, concise, and clear statement of the essential facts constituting the offense charged.

b. *Surplusage.* A Commission may strike surplusage from the charges and specifications, and should do so when such action is plainly indicated.

c. *Amendments.* A Commission may permit the charges and specifications to be amended at any time before the findings, if no additional offense is charged and if the substantial rights of the accused are not prejudiced thereby.

d. *Bill of Particulars.* A Commission may direct in its discretion that the prosecution file a Bill of Particulars. A Bill of Particulars may be amended at any time subject to such conditions as justice requires....

RULE 24. PRESENCE OF THE ACCUSED. The accused shall be present at all times during the trial, except during any period of escape from custody after arraignment. The accused's presence shall not be required upon any review of his case, nor upon consideration of any petition for a New Trial.

RULE 25. SPECIFIC RIGHTS OF THE ACCUSED.

a. *Service of Charges.* Upon reference for trial, the accused shall furnished a copy of the charges and specifications against him. If the charges and specifications are stated in a language other than one which the accused understands, they shall be made known to him in a language understood by him.

b. *As a Witness.*

(1) The accused shall be entitled to remain silent, or, at his own request but not otherwise, to be sworn to testify as a witness in his own behalf, or to make an oral unsworn statement to the Commission.

(2) The Law Member of a General Military Commission or the President of a Special Military Commission may, at the request of the accused, permit him to testify as a witness for a limited purpose only, excepting therefrom all testimony relative to the issue of his guilt or innocence.

(3) The accused shall be entitled to testify as a witness in his own behalf with respect to less than all the offenses charged against him, in which case he may not be questioned about any offenses concerning which he does not testify.

c. *Representation by Counsel.*

(1) The accused shall be entitled, if he so desires, to assistance by one of his prisoner comrades in the conduct of his defense, and to be represented prior to and during trial by Counsel appointed by the convening authority, or by available Counsel of his own choice.

(2) The accused shall be entitled to reasonable opportunity to consult with his Counsel before and during the trial.

(3) The accused shall be entitled to representation by Counsel until completion of all appellate review on his case or until the expiration of the time during which he may submit a petition for a New Trial, whichever is later.

d. *Defense Witnesses.* An accused shall be entitled to call witnesses to testify in his behalf and to have all reasonable facilities in this regard extended to him.

e. *Cross Examination.* The accused shall be entitled to cross examine, personally or through Counsel, each adverse witness who personally appears before the Commission.

f. *Challenges.*

(1) Each accused shall be entitled, except as otherwise provided herein, to challenge any member of the Commission for cause, and to present evidence relative to such challenge.

(2) Each accused shall, except as otherwise provided herein, be entitled to one peremptory challenge.

g. *Interpretation for Accused.* The accused shall be entitled to have the substance of the proceedings and any documentary evidence translated when he is unable otherwise to understand them, and, in addition, the accused shall be entitled, if he deems it necessary, to the services of a competent interpreter.

RULE 26. PRIVILEGES AND FACILITIES AFFORDED DEFENSE COUNSEL. Advocate or Counsel conducting the defense on behalf of the accused, upon trial, review, and consideration of a petition for a New Trial, shall have at his disposal the reasonably necessary facilities to prepare the defense of the accused. He may, in particular, freely visit the accused and interview him in private. He may also confer with any witnesses for the defense, including prisoners of war.

RULE 27. TIME OF TRIAL.

a. *Limitation on Commencement of Proceedings.* Trial shall not commence until the expiration of a period of at least three weeks from the date of the receipt by the accredited Delegate of the International Committee of the Red Cross, the Prisoners' representative, and the accused of the notice required by Rule 53, below.

b. *Preparation of Defense.* No trial shall commence until the Advocate or Counsel conducting the defense on behalf of the accused shall have had at his disposal a period of at least two weeks to prepare the defense of the accused.

c. *Timely Selection of Individual Defense Counsel.* An accused shall be afforded reasonable opportunity before trial to secure Counsel of his own choice, but no court shall be prevented from proceeding because of the inability of an accused to secure Counsel of his own choosing.

RULE 28. PRELIMINARY MOTIONS. Prior to trial, both prosecution and defense will furnish opposing Counsel copies of any preliminary motions to be made to the Commission....

RULE 30. CHALLENGES.

a. *For Cause.* No challenges for cause may be asserted in the case of trial by a Special Military Commission consisting of only one member.

b. *Peremptory.* No peremptory challenge may be asserted against the Law Member of a General Military Commission, nor in the case of trial by a Special Military Commission, consisting of only one member.

RULE 31. RELIEF FROM PREJUDICIAL JOINDER. For good cause shown, a Commission may, in its discretion, grant a severance in the case of a joint or common trial, or provide whatever other relief justice requires.

RULE 32. PRESUMPTION OF INNOCENCE AND BURDEN OF PROOF. The accused shall be presumed innocent until his guilt is established by legal and competent evidence beyond a reasonable doubt. If there is a reasonable doubt as to the guilt of the accused, the doubt shall be resolved in the accused's favor and he shall be acquitted. If there is a reasonable doubt as to the guilt of the accused of the specific offense charged but the evidence supports a finding of guilty of an offense reasonably included therein, then the finding should be as to the latter only. The burden of proof to establish the guilt of the accused beyond a reasonable doubt is upon the prosecution.

RULE 33. EVIDENCE. These commissions will follow the rules of evidence prescribed in the Manual for Courts-Martial, United States, 1951....

RULE 37. VOTING.

    a. *Findings and Sentence.*

        (1) All voting on the findings and sentence shall be by secret written ballot.

        (2) The concurrence of at least two-thirds of the members of the commission present at the time the vote is taken shall, except as provided herein, be necessary for conviction and for sentence.

        (3) The concurrence of at least three-fourths of the members of the Commission present at the time the vote is taken shall be required for any sentence to life imprisonment or confinement in excess of ten years.

        (4) The concurrence of all the members of the Commission present at the time the vote is taken shall be required for any death sentence....

SECTION VI. *MISCELLANEOUS*

RULE 46. DOUBLE JEOPARDY. No accused shall be punished more than once for the same act or on the same charge pursuant to United Nations authority.

RULE 47. EX POST FACTO OFFENSES. No person shall be tried pursuant to these Rules for an act which was not forbidden by recognized law in effect at the time the said act was committed.

RULE 48. OFFICIAL POSITION AND SUPERIOR ORDERS. The official position of the accused shall not absolve him from responsibility, nor be considered in mitigation of punishment. Action pursuant to the order of the accused's superior, or of his government, shall not constitute a defense, but may be considered in mitigation of punishment if a Commission determines that justice so requires.

RULE 49. PRINCIPALS AND ACCESSORIES. Anyone who commits any of the offenses defined in Rule 5, or who aids, abets, counsels, commands, permits, induces, or procures its commission, is a principal; and anyone who causes an act to be done, which, if directly performed by him, would be an offense under Rule 5, is also a principal and punishable as such....

RULE 53. NOTICE OF TRIAL.

    a. *Persons Upon Whom Served.* Where an accredited Delegate of the International Committee of the Red Cross has been accepted by the United Nations Command, such Delegate shall be notified at the address previously indicated by him to the convening authority, as soon as possible and at least three weeks prior to trial, that judicial proceedings will be instituted against the accused. The prisoner's representative and the accused shall be similarly notified.

    b. *Contents of Notice.* The notice required by Rule 53a, above, shall contain the following information: (1) surname and first name of the accused, his rank, his army, regimental, personal, or serial number, his date of birth, and his profession or trade, if any; (2) place of internment or confinement; (3) specification of the charge or charges on which the accused is to be arraigned, giving the legal provisions applicable; (4) designation of the Commission which will try the case, likewise the date and place fixed for the opening of the trial.

    c. *Affidavit of Prosecutor.* The Prosecutor shall execute an affidavit certifying that the duties prescribed in subparagraph a of this Rule have been performed. Such affidavit shall be incorporated into the record as one of the allied papers of the case.

RULE 54. PARTICIPATION OF INTERNATIONAL COMMITTEE OF THE RED CROSS.

a. *Presence at Trial.*

(1) Where an accredited Delegate of the International Committee of the Red Cross has been accepted by the United Nations Command, such Delegate, if present, shall be entitled to attend all trials held pursuant to these Rules unless the proceedings are held in camera for purposes of state or military security. (No proceedings in camera will be held, however, without the concurrence of the Commander-in-Chief, United Nations Command, or his successor.)

(2) Where such Delegate has requested permission to attend proceedings to be held in camera, this request will be communicated immediately to Headquarters, United Nations Command. Attention: Command Judge Advocate.

b. *Selection of Counsel.*

(1) Where an accredited Delegate of the International Committee of the Red Cross has been accepted by the United Nations Command, the convening authority shall furnish such Delegate, on request, a list of available persons qualified to present the defense.

(2) Failing a choice of Counsel by the accused, the Delegate of the International Committee of the Red Cross, if requested, may select available Counsel for him and shall have at his disposal at least one week for such purpose.

(3) In the event that both the accused and International Committee of the Red Cross Delegate fail to select Counsel, the accused shall be represented by the Defense Counsel designated in the order appointing the Commission.

(4) Where the accused or the International Committee of the Red Cross Delegate retains individual Counsel to represent the accused, the Defense Counsel named in the order appointing the Commission may be excused from the proceedings or retained as advisory, associate, or assistant Defense Counsel, at the option of the accused.

Bangladesh International Crimes (Tribunals) Act of July 19, 1973

Dacca, the 20th July, 1973

The following Act of Parliament received the assent of the President on the 19th July, 1973, and is hereby published for general information:—

Act No. XIX of 1973

An Act to provide for the detention, prosecution and punishment of persons for genocide, crimes against humanity, war crimes and other crimes under international law.

WHEREAS it is expedient to provide for the detention, prosecution and punishment of persons for genocide, crimes against humanity, war crimes and other crimes under international law, and for matters connected therewith;

It is hereby enacted as follows:—

1. Short title, extent and commencement.—

(1) This Act may be called the International Crimes (Tribunals) Act 1973.

(2) It extends to the whole of Bangladesh.

(3) It shall come into force at once.

2. Definitions.—

In this Act, unless there is anything repugnant in the subject or context,

(a) "auxiliary forces" includes forces placed under the control of the Armed forces for operational, administrative, static and other purposes;

(b) "Government" means the Government of the People's Republic of Bangladesh;

(c) "Republic" means the People's Republic of Bangladesh;

(d) "service law" means the Army Act, 1952 (XXXIX of 1952), the Air Force Act, 1953 (VI of 1953), or the Navy Ordinance, 1961 (XXXV of 1961) and includes the rules and regulations made under any of them;

(e) "territory of Bangladesh" means the territory of the Republic as defined in article 2 of the Constitution of the People's Republic of Bangladesh;

(f) "Tribunal" means a Tribunal set up under this Act.

3. Jurisdiction of Tribunal and Crimes.—

(1) A Tribunal shall have the power to try and punish any person irrespective of this nationality who, being a member of any armed, defence or auxiliary forces commits or has committed, in the territory of Bangladesh, whether before or after the commencement of this Act, any of the following crimes.

(2) The following acts or any of them are crimes within the jurisdiction of a Tribunal for which there shall be individual responsibility, namely:—

(a) Crimes against Humanity: namely, murder, extermination, enslavement, deportation, imprisonment, abduction, confinement, torture, rape or other inhumane acts committed against any civilian population or persecutions on political, racial, ethnic or religious grounds, whether or not in violation of the domestic law of the country where perpetrated;

(b) Crimes against Peace: namely, planning, preparation, initiation or waging of a war of aggression or a war in violation of international treaties, agreements or assurances;

(c) Genocide: meaning and including any of the following acts committed with intent to destroy, in whole or in part, a national, ethnic, racial, religious or political group, such as:

(i) killing members of the group;

(ii) causing serious bodily or mental harm to members of the group;

(iii) deliberately inflicting on the group conditions of life calculated to bring about its physical destruction in whole or in part;

(iv) imposing measures intended to prevent births within the group;

(v) forcibly transferring children of the group to another group;

(d) War Crimes: namely, violation of laws or customs of war which include but are not limited to murder, ill-treatment or deportation to slave labour or for any other purpose of [the] civilian population in the territory of Bangladesh; murder or ill-treatment of prisoners of war or persons on the seas, killing of hostages and detainees, plunder of public or private property, wanton destruction of cities, towns or villages, or devastation not justified by military necessity;

(e) violation of any humanitarian rules applicable in armed conflicts laid down in the Geneva Conventions of 1949;

(f) any other crimes under international law;

(g) attempt, abetment or conspiracy to commit any such crimes;

(h) complicity in or failure to prevent commission of any such crimes.

4. Liability for Crimes.—

(1) When any crime as specified in section 3 is committed by several persons, each such person is liable for that crime in the same manner as if it were done by him alone.

(2) Any commander or superior officer who orders, permits, acquiesces or participates in the commission of any of the crimes specified in section 3 or is connected with any plans and activities involving the commission of such crimes or who fails or omits to discharge his duty to maintain discipline, or to control or supervise the actions of the persons under his command or his subordinates, whereby such persons or subordinates or any of them commit any such crimes, or who fails to take necessary measures to prevent the commission of such crimes, is guilty of such crimes.

5. Official position, etc. not to free an accused from responsibility for any crime.—

(1) The official position, at any time, of an accused shall not be considered freeing him from responsibility or mitigating punishment.

(2) The fact that the accused acted pursuant to his domestic law or to order of his Government or of a superior shall not free him from responsibility, but may be considered in mitigation of punishment if the Tribunal deems that justice so requires.

6. Tribunal.—

(1) For the purpose of section 3, the Government may, by notification in the *official Gazette*, set up one or more Tribunals, each consisting of a Chairman and not less than two and not more than four other members.

(2) Any person who is or is qualified to be a Judge of the Supreme Court of Bangladesh or has been a Judge of any High Court or Supreme Court which at any time was in existence in the territory of Bangladesh or who is qualified to be a member of General Court

Martial under any service law of Bangladesh may be appointed as a Chairman or member of a Tribunal.

(3) The permanent seat of a Tribunal shall be in Dacca:

Provided that a Tribunal may hold its sittings at such other place or places as it deems fit.

(4) If any member of a Tribunal dies or is, due to illness or any other reason, unable to continue to perform his functions, the Government may, by notification in the *official Gazette*, declare the office of such member to be vacant and appoint thereto another person qualified to hold the office.

(5) If, in the course of a trial, any one of the members of a Tribunal is, for any reason, unable to attend any sitting thereof, the trial may continue before the other members.

(6) A Tribunal shall not, merely by reason of any change in its membership or the absence of any member thereof from any sitting, be bound to recall and re-hear any witness who has already given any evidence and may act on the evidence already given or produced before it.

(7) If, upon any matter requiring the decision of a Tribunal, there is a difference of opinion among its members, the opinion of the majority shall prevail and the decision of the Tribunal shall be expressed in terms of the views of the majority.

(8) Neither the constitution of a Tribunal nor the appointment of its Chairman or members shall be challenged by the prosecution or by the accused persons or their counsel.

7. Prosecutors. —

(1) The Government may appoint one or more persons to conduct the prosecution before a Tribunal on such terms and conditions as may be determined by the Government; and every such person shall be deemed to be a Prosecutor for the purposes of this Act.

(2) The Government may designate one of such persons as the Chief Prosecutor.

8. Investigation. —

(1) The Government may establish an Agency for the purposes of investigation into crimes specified in section 3; and any officer belonging to the Agency shall have the right to assist the prosecution during the trial.

(2) Any person appointed as a Prosecutor is competent to act as an Investigation Officer and the provisions relating to investigation shall apply to such Prosecutor.

(3) Any Investigation Officer making an investigation under this Act may, by order in writing, require the attendance before himself of any person who appears to be acquainted with the circumstances of the case; and such person shall attend as so required.

(4) Any Investigation Officer making an investigation under this Act may examine orally any person who appears to be acquainted with the facts and circumstances of the case.

(5) Such person shall be bound to answer all questions put to him by an Investigation Officer and shall not be excused from answering any question on the ground that the answer to such question will criminate, or may tend directly or indirectly to criminate, such person:

Provided that no such answer, which a person shall be compelled to give, shall subject him to any arrest or prosecution, or be proved against him in any criminal proceeding.

(6) The Investigation Officer may reduce into writing any statement made to him in the course of examination under this section.

(7) Any person who fails to appear before an Investigation Officer for the purpose of examination or refuses to answer the questions put to him by such Investigation Officer shall be punished with simple imprisonment which may extend to six months, or with fine which may extend to Taka two thousand, or with both.

(8) Any Magistrate of the first class may take cognizance of an offence punishable under sub-section (7) upon a complaint in writing by an Investigation Officer.

(9) Any investigation done into the crimes specified in section 3 shall be deemed to have been done under the provisions of this Act.

9. Commencement of the Proceedings. —

(1) The proceedings before a Tribunal shall commence upon the submission by the Chief Prosecutor, or a prosecutor authorised by the Chief Prosecutor in this [sic] behalf, of formal charges of crimes alleged to have been committed by each of the accused persons.

(2) The Tribunal shall thereafter fix a date for the trial of such accused person.

(3) The Chief Prosecutor shall, at least three weeks before the commencement of the trial, furnish to the Tribunal a list of witnesses intended to be produced along with the recorded statement of such witnesses or copies thereof and copies of documents which the prosecution intends to rely upon in support of such charges.

(4) The submission of a list of witnesses and documents under sub-section (3) shall not preclude the prosecution from calling, with the permission of the Tribunal, additional witnesses or tendering any further evidence at any stage of the trial:

Provided that notice shall be given to the defence of the additional witnesses intended to be called or additional evidence sought to be tendered by the prosecution.

(5) A list of witnesses for the defence, if any, along with the documents or copies thereof, which the defence intends to rely upon, shall be furnished to the Tribunal and the prosecution at the time of the commencement of the trial.

10. Procedure of trial. —

(1) The following procedure shall be followed at a trial before a Tribunal, namely: —

(a) the charge shall be read out;

(b) the Tribunal shall ask each accused person whether he pleads guilty or not-guilty;

(c) if the accused person pleads guilty, the Tribunal shall record the plea, and may, in its discretion, convict him thereon;

(d) the prosecution shall make an opening statement;

(e) the witnesses for the prosecution shall be examined, the defence may cross-examine such witnesses and the prosecution may re-examine them;

(f) the witnesses for the defence, if any, shall be examined, the prosecution may cross-examine such witnesses and the defence may re-examine them;

(g) the Tribunal may, in its discretion, permit the party which calls a witness to put any question to him which might be put in cross-examination by the adverse party;

(h) the Tribunal may, in order to discover or obtain proof of relevant facts, ask any witness any question it pleases, in any form and at any time about any fact; and may order production of any document or thing or summon any witness, and neither the prosecution nor the defence shall be entitled either to make any objection to any such question or order or, without the leave of the Tribunal, to cross-examine any witness upon any answer given in reply to any such question;

(i) the prosecution shall first sum up its case, and thereafter the defence shall sum up its case:

Provided that if any witness is examined by the defence, the prosecution shall have the right to sum up its case after the defence has done so;

(j) the Tribunal shall deliver its judgment and pronounce its verdict.

(2) All proceedings before the Tribunal shall be in English.

(3) Any accused person or witness who is unable to express himself in, or does not understand, English may be provided the assistance of an interpreter.

(4) The proceedings of the Tribunal shall be in public:

Provided that the Tribunal may, if it thinks fit, take proceedings in camera.

(5) No oath shall be administered to any accused person.

11. Powers of Tribunal. —

(1) A Tribunal shall have power —

(a) to summon witnesses to the trial and to require their attendance and testimony and to put questions to them;

(b) to administer oaths to witnesses;

(c) to require the production of document and other evidentiary material;

(d) to appoint persons for carrying out any task designated by the Tribunal.

(2) For the purpose of enabling any accused person to explain circumstances appearing in the evidence against him, a Tribunal may, at any stage of the trial without previously warning the accused person, put such questions to him as the Tribunal considers necessary:

Provided that the accused person shall not render himself liable to punishment by refusing to answer such questions or by giving false answers to them; but the Tribunal may draw such inference from such refusal or answers as it thinks just;

(3) A Tribunal shall —

(a) confine the trial to an expeditious hearing of the issues raised by the charges;

(b) take measures to prevent any action which may cause unreasonable delay, and rule out irrelevant issues and statements.

(4) A Tribunal may punish any person, who obstructs or abuses its process or disobeys any of its orders or directions, or does anything which tends to prejudice the case of a party before it, or tends to bring it or any of its members into hatred or contempt, or does anything which constitutes contempt of the Tribunal, with simple imprisonment which may extend to one year, or with fine which may extend to Taka five thousand, or with both.

(5) Any member of a Tribunal shall have power to direct, or issue a warrant for, the arrest of, and to commit to custody, and to authorise the continued detention in custody of, any person charged with any crime specified in section 3.

(6) The Chairman of a Tribunal may make such administrative arrangements as he considers necessary for the performance of the functions of the Tribunal under this Act.

12. Provision for defence counsel. — Where an accused person in not represented by counsel, the Tribunal may, at any stage of the case, direct that a counsel shall be engaged at the expense of the Government to defend the accused person and may also determine the fees to be paid to such counsel.

13. Restriction of adjournment. — No trial before a Tribunal shall be adjourned for any purpose unless the Tribunal is of the opinion that the adjournment is in the interest of justice.

14. Statement or confession of accused persons. —

(1) Any Magistrate of the first class may record any statement or confession made to him by an accused person at any time in the course of investigation or at any time before the commencement of the trial.

(2) The Magistrate shall, before recording any such confession, explain to the accused person making it that he is not bound to make a confession and that if he does so it may be used as evidence against him and no Magistrate shall record any such confession unless, upon questioning the accused making it, he has reason to believe that it was made voluntarily.

15. Pardon of an approver. —

(1) At any stage of the trial, a Tribunal may with a view to obtaining the evidence of any person supposed to have been directly or indirectly concerned in, or privy to, any of the crimes specified in section 3, tender a pardon to such person on condition of his making a full and true disclosure of the whole of the circumstances within his knowledge relative to the crime and to every other person concerned, whether as principal or abettor, in the commission thereof.

(2) Every person accepting the tender under this section shall be examined as a witness in the trial.

(3) Such person shall be detained in custody until the termination of the trial.

16. Charge, etc. —

(1) Every charge against an accused person shall state —

    (a) the name and particulars of the accused person;

    (b) the crime of which the accused person is charged;

    (c) such particulars of the alleged crime as are reasonably sufficient to give the accused person notice of the matter with which he is charged.

(2) A copy of the formal charge and a copy of each of the documents lodged with the formal charge shall be furnished to the accused person at a reasonable time before the trial; and in case of any difficulty in furnishing copies of the documents, reasonable opportunity for inspection shall be given to the accused person in such manner as the Tribunal may decide.

17. Right of accused person during trial. —

(1) During trial of an accused person he shall have the right to give any explanation relevant to the charge made against him.

(2) An accused person shall have the right to conduct his own defence before the Tribunal or to have the assistance of counsel.

(3) An accused person shall have the right to present evidence at the trial in support of his defence, and to cross-examine any witness called by the prosecution.

18. No excuse from answering any question. — A witness shall not be excused from answering any question put to him on the ground that the answer to such question will criminate or may tend directly of indirectly to criminate such witness, or that it will expose or tend directly or indirectly to expose such witness to a penalty or forfeiture of any kind:

Provided that no such answer which a witness shall be compelled to give shall subject him to any arrest or prosecution or be proved against him in any criminal proceeding, except a prosecution for giving false evidence.

19. Rules of evidence. —

(1) A Tribunal shall not be bound by technical rules of evidence; and it shall adopt and apply to the greatest possible extent expeditious and non-technical procedure, and may admit any evidence, including reports and photographs published in newspapers, periodicals and magazines, films and tape-recordings and other materials as may be tendered before it, which it deems to have

probative value.

(2) A Tribunal may receive in evidence any statement recorded by a Magistrate or an Investigation Officer being a statement made by any person who, at the time of the trial, is dead or whose attendance cannot be procured without an amount of delay or expense which the Tribunal considers unreasonable.

(3) A Tribunal shall not require proof of facts of common knowledge but shall take judicial notice thereof.

(4) A Tribunal shall take judicial notice of official governmental documents and reports of the United Nations and its subsidiary agencies or other international bodies including non-governmental organisations.

20. Judgement and sentence. —

(1) The Judgement of a Tribunal as to the guilt or the innocence of any accused person shall give the reasons on which it is based:

Provided that each member of the Tribunal shall be competent to deliver a judgement of his own.

(2) Upon conviction of an accused person, the Tribunal shall award sentence of death or such other punishment proportionate to the gravity of the crime as appears to the Tribunal to be just and proper.

(3) The sentence awarded under this Act shall be carried out in accordance with the orders of the Government.

21. Right of appeal. — A person convicted of any crime specified in section 3 and sentenced by a Tribunal shall have the right of appeal to the Appellate Division of the Supreme Court of Bangladesh against such conviction and sentence:

Provided that such appeal may be proffered within sixty days of the date of order of conviction and sentence.

22. Rules of procedure. — Subject to the provision of this Act, a Tribunal may regulate its own procedure.

23. Certain laws not to apply. — The provisions of the Criminal Procedure Code, 1898 (V of 1898), and the Evidence Act, 1872 (I of 1872), shall not apply in any proceedings under this Act.

24. Bar of Jurisdiction. — No order, judgment or sentence of a Tribunal shall be called in question in any manner whatsoever in or before any Court or other authority in any legal proceedings whatsoever except in the manner provided in section 21.

25. Indemnity. — No suit, prosecution or other legal proceeding shall lie against the Government or any person for anything, in good faith, done or purporting to have been done under this Act.

26. Provisions of the Act over-riding all other laws. — The provisions of this Act shall have effect notwithstanding anything inconsistent therewith contained in any other law for the time being in force.

Iraqi High Criminal Court Law
Resolution No. (10)
No. 4006, Ramadan 14, 1426 Hijri, 47th year, Oct. 18, 2005

In the Name of the people

The presidency Council

Pursuant to what has been approved by the National Assembly and in accordance with Article No. (33) Paragraphs A and B and Article No. (30) of the Law of Administration for the State of Iraq for the Transitional Period.

The presidency Council decided in the session of October 9, 2005 to promulgate the following resolution:

Law No. (10) 2005
Law of
The Iraqi Higher Criminal Court

SECTION ONE
The Establishment and Organization
Of the Court

PART ONE
Establishment

Article 1

First: A court is hereby established and shall be known as The Iraqi Higher Criminal Court (the "Court"). The Court shall be fully independent.

Second: The Court shall have jurisdiction over every natural person whether Iraqi or non-Iraqi resident of Iraq and accused of one of the crimes listed in Articles 11 to 14 below, committed during the period from July 17, 1968 and until May 1, 2003, in the Republic of Iraq or elsewhere, including the following crimes:

A. The crime of genocide;

B. Crimes against humanity;

C. War crimes

D. Violations of certain Iraqi laws listed in Article 14 below.

Article 2

The Court shall have its main office in the city of Baghdad and may hold its sessions in any governorate, on the basis of a proposal by the Council of Ministers pursuant to a proposal from the President of the Court.

PART TWO
Organizational Structure of the Court

Article 3

The court shall consist of:

First:

    A. A Cassation Panel, which shall specialize in reviewing the provisions and decisions issued by one of the criminal or investigative courts.

    B. One or more criminal courts.

    C. Investigative judges.

Second: Public Prosecution.

Third: An administration, which shall provide administrative and financial services to the Court and the Public Prosecution.

Fourth:

    A. The Cassation Panel shall be composed of nine judges who shall elect a president for amongst them. The president of the Cassation Panel shall be the senior president of the court and shall supervise its administrative and financial affairs.

    B. The felony court shall be composed of five judges who shall elect a president from amongst them to supervise their work.

Fifth:

The Council of Ministers may, if deemed necessary, based upon a proposal by a President of the Court, appoint non-Iraqi judges who have experience in conducting criminal trials stipulated in this law, and who are of very high moral character, honest and virtuous to work in the Court, in the event that a State is one of the parties in a complaint, and the judges shall be commissioned with the help of the International Community and the United Nations.

PART THREE
Selection of Judges, Public Prosecutors and their retirement

Article 4

First: Judges and public prosecutors shall be of high moral character, integrity and uprightness. They shall possess experience in criminal law and shall fulfill the appointment requirements stipulated in the Judicial Organization Law No. 160 of 1979 and the Public Prosecution law No. 159 of 1979.

Second: As an exception to the provisions of paragraph (First) of this Article the candidates for the positions of judges at the Cassation Panel, the Criminal Court, the investigative judges and public prosecutors do not have to be active judges and public prosecutors. Retired judges and members of public prosecution may be nominated, without restrictions age requirement and Iraqi lawyers who possess a high level of experience, competence and efficiency and of absolute competence, in accordance with the Legal Profession Code No. 173 of 1965 and have served in judicial, legal and the legal profession fields for no less than (15) years.

Third:

    A. The Supreme Juridical Council shall nominate all judges and public prosecutors to this Court. The Council of Ministers after approving their nomination shall issue their appointment order from the Presidency Council and will be classified as class (A) judges, in an exception to the provisions of the Judicial Organization Law and the Public Prosecution Law. Their salaries and rewards shall be specified by guidelines issued by the Council of Ministers.

    B. The judges, public prosecutors and the employees appointed in accordance with the provisions of law before this legislation shall be deemed legally approved starting from the date of their appointment according to the provisions of paragraph (Third/A) of Article (4) taking into account the provisions of Article (33) of this law.

Fourth: The Presidency Council in accordance with a proposal from the Council of Ministers shall have the right to transfer Judges and Public Prosecutors from the Court to the Higher Judicial Council for any reason.

Fifth:

The term of service of a judge or a public prosecutor covered by the provisions of this law shall end for one of the following reasons:

1. If he is convicted of a non-political felony.

2. If he presents false information.

3. If he fails to perform his duties without a legitimate reason.

Article 6

First: A committee comprised of five members elected from among the Judges and public prosecutors shall be established in the Court under the supervision of the Cassation panel of the Court and they shall select a President for a term of one year. This committee shall be called "Judges and Public Prosecutors Affairs Committee". The Committee shall enjoy the authorities stipulated in the Judicial Organization Law and Public Prosecution Law. It shall consider disciplinary matters and the service of Judges and the members of the public prosecution. Its decisions shall be appealable before the extended panel of the Federal Court of Cassation if it decides to terminate the service of the judge or a member of the public prosecution.

Second: The committee shall submit a recommendations, after the appeal before the extended panel of the Federal Court of Cassation is denied, to the Council of Ministers to pass a resolution from the Presidency Council terminating the service of a judge or a public prosecutor, including the chief justice in case the provisions of Article (6) of this Law are met.

Third: At the end of the Court's work, the judges and the Public Prosecutors shall be reassigned to the Higher Judicial Council to work in the Federal Courts. Those reaching the legal age for retirement shall be retired in accordance with the Law.

PART FOUR
Presidency of the Court

Article 7

First: The president of the court shall:

A. Chair the proceedings of the Cassation Panel.

B. Name the original and alternate judges of the Criminal Courts.

C. Name any of the judges to the Criminal Court in case of absence.

D. Accomplish the Court's administrative work.

E. Appoint and end the service of the Administrative Director, security director, public relations director and archive and documents keeping director in the court.

F. Name the official spokesman for the Court from among the judges or public prosecutors.

Second: The President of the Court shall have the right to appoint non-Iraqi experts to act in an advisory capacity for the Criminal Court and the Cassation Panel. The role of the non-Iraqi nationals shall be to provide assistance with respect to international law and the experience of similar Courts (whether international or otherwise). The paneling of these experts is to be done with the help from the International Community, including the United Nations.

Third: The non-Iraqi experts referred to in paragraph (Second) of this Article shall also be persons of high moral character, uprightness and integrity. It would be preferable that such non-Iraqi expert should have worked in either a judicial or prosecutorial capacity in his or her respective country or at the International War Crimes Court.

PART FIVE
Investigative Judges

Article 8

First: Sufficient number of Investigative Judges shall be appointed.

Second: The Court's Investigative Judges shall undertake the investigation with those accused of crimes stipulated in paragraph (Second) Article (1) of this law.

Third: The Investigative Judges shall elect a Chief and his deputy from amongst them.

Fourth: The Chief shall refer cases under investigation to investigative judges individually.

Fifth: Each of the Investigative Judges' Offices shall be composed of an investigative Judge and qualified staff as may be required for the work of the investigative judge.

Sixth: An Investigative Judge shall collect evidence from any source he deems appropriate and question all relevant parties directly.

Seventh: An Investigative Judge shall act independently in the court since he is considered as a separate entity from the court. He shall not fall under nor receive requests or orders from any Government Department, or any other party.

Eight: The decisions of the Investigative Judge can be appealed in cassation before the Cassation Panel within fifteen days from the date of receipt of notification or from the date notification is considered received pursuant to law.

Ninth: The Chief Investigative Judge, after consulting with the President of the Court, have the right to appoint non-Iraqi nationals experts to assist the Investigative Judges in the investigation of cases covered by this law, whether international or otherwise. The Chief Investigative Judge can commission these experts with help from the International Community, including the United Nations.

Tenth: The non-Iraqi experts and observers referred to in paragraph (Ninth) of this Article are required to be persons of high moral character, honest and virtuous; it is preferred that the non-Iraqi expert and observer had worked in either a judicial or prosecutorial capacity in his or her respective country or in the International War Crimes Court.

PART SIX
The Public Prosecution

Article 9

First: Sufficient number of prosecutors shall be appointed.

Second: The Public Prosecution shall be composed of a number of public prosecutors who shall be responsible for the prosecution of persons accused of crimes that fall within the jurisdiction of the Court.

Third: Public prosecutors shall elect a Chief and his Deputy from amongst them.

Fourth: Each office of public prosecution shall be composed of a prosecutor and such other qualified staff as may be required for the work of the Public Prosecutor.

Fifth: Each prosecutor shall act with complete independence since he is considered as a separate entity from the Court. He shall not fall under, nor receive instructions from, any government department or from any other party.

Sixth: The chief prosecutor shall assign individual cases to a prosecutor to investigate and to try in court based on the authority granted to the public prosecutors pursuant to the law.

Seventh: The Chief Public Prosecutor, in consultation with the President of the Court, shall have the right to appoint non-Iraqi nationals to act as experts helping the public prosecutors in the investigation and prosecution of cases covered by this law whether in an international context or otherwise. The Chief Prosecutor can commission these experts with the help of the international community, including the United Nations.

Eighth: The non-Iraqi experts, referred to in Paragraph (Seventh) of this Article are required to be persons of high moral character, honest and virtuous. It is preferred that such non-Iraqi experts had worked in a prosecutorial capacity in his respective country or in the International War Crimes Court.

PART SEVEN
The Administration Department

Article 10

First: The Administration Department shall be managed by an officer with the title of Department Director who holds a bachelor degree in law and have judicial and administrative experience. He shall be assisted by a number of employees in managing the affairs of the department.

Second: The Administration Department is responsible for the administrative, financial and service affairs of the court and the Public Prosecution.

SECTION TWO
The Court Jurisdictions

PART ONE
The Crime of Genocide

Article 11

First: For the purposes of this law and in accordance with the International Convention on the Prevention and Punishment of the Crime of Genocide dated December 9, 1948 as ratified by Iraq on January 20, 1959, "genocide" means any of the following acts committed with the intent to abolish, in whole or in part, a national, ethnic, racial or religious group as such:

    A. Killing members of the group.

    B. Causing serious bodily or mental harm to members of the group.

    C. Deliberately inflicting on the group living conditions calculated to bring about its physical destruction in whole or in part.

    D. Imposing measures intended to prevent births within the group.

    E. Forcibly transferring children of the group to another group.

Second: The following acts shall be punishable

    A. Genocide.

B. Conspiracy to commit genocide.

C. Direct and public incitement to commit genocide.

D. Attempt to commit genocide.

E. Complicity in genocide.

PART TWO
Crimes against Humanity

Article 13

First: For the purposes of this Law, "crimes against humanity" means any of the following acts when committed as part of a widespread or systematic attack directed against any civilian population, with knowledge of the attack:

A. Willful murder;

B. Extermination;

C. Enslavement;

D. Deportation or forcible transfer of population;

E. Imprisonment or other severe deprivation of physical liberty in violation of fundamental norms of international law;

F. Torture;

G. Rape, sexual slavery, forcible prostitution, forced pregnancy, or any other form of sexual violence of comparable gravity;

H. Persecution against any specific party or group of the population on political, racial, national, ethnic, cultural, religious, gender or other grounds that are impermissible under international law, in connection with any act referred to as a form of sexual violence of comparable gravity.

I. Enforced disappearance of persons.

J. Other inhumane acts of a similar character intentionally causing great suffering, or serious injury to the body or to the mental or physical health.

Second: For the purposes of implementing the provisions of paragraph (First) of this Article, the below listed terms shall mean the stated definitions:

A. "Attack directed against any civilian population" means a course of conduct involving the multiple panel of acts referred to in the above paragraph

B. "First" against any civilian population, pursuant to or in furtherance of a state or organizational policy to commit such attack;

C. "Extermination" means the intentional infliction of living conditions, such as the deprivation of access to food and medicine, with the intent to bring about the destruction of part of the population;

D. "Enslavement" means the exercise of any or all of the powers attached to the right of ownership over a person and includes the exercise of such power in the course of human trafficking, in particular women and children;

E. "Deportation or forcible transfer of population" means forced displacement of the concerned persons concerned by expulsion or other coercive acts from the area in which they are lawfully present, without grounds permitted under international law;

F. "Persecution" means the intentional and severe deprivation of fundamental rights contrary to international law by reason of the identity of the group or collectivity; and

G. "Enforced disappearance of persons" means the arrest, detention or abduction of persons by, or with the authorization, support or acquiescence of, the State or a political organization, followed by a refusal to acknowledge that deprivation of freedom or to give information on the fate or whereabouts of those persons, with the intention of removing them from the protection of the law for a prolonged period of time.

PART THREE
War Crimes

Article 13

For the purposes of this Law, "war crimes" means:

First: Grave breaches of the Geneva Conventions of 12 August 1949, namely, any of the following acts against persons or property protected under the provisions of the relevant Geneva Convention:

A. Willful killing;

B. Torture or inhuman treatment, including biological experiments;

C. Willfully causing great suffering, or serious injury to body or health;

D. Extensive destruction and appropriation of property not justified by military necessity and carried out unlawfully and wantonly;

E. Compelling a prisoner of war or other protected person to serve in the forces of a hostile power;

F. Willfully denying the right of a fair trial to a prisoner of war or other protected person;

G. Unlawful confinement;

H. Unlawful deportation or transfer; and

I. Taking of hostages.

Second: Other serious violations of the laws and customs applicable in international armed conflicts, within the established framework of international law, namely, any of the following acts:

A. Intentionally directing attacks against the civilian population as such or against individual civilians not taking direct part in hostilities;

B. Intentionally directing attacks against civilian objects, that is, objects which are not military objectives;

C. Intentionally directing attacks against personnel, installations, material, units or vehicles used in a peacekeeping missions in accordance with the Charter of the United Nations or in a humanitarian assistance missions, as long as they are entitled to the protection given to civilians or civilian objects under the international law of armed conflicts;

D. Intentionally launching an attack in the knowledge that such attack will cause incidental loss of life or injury to civilians or damage to civilian objects which would be clearly excessive in relation to the concrete and direct overall military advantages anticipated;

E. Intentionally launching an attack in the knowledge that such attack will cause widespread, long-term and severe damage to the natural environment, which would be clearly excessive in relation to the concrete and direct overall military advantage anticipated;

F. Attacking or bombarding, by whatever means, towns, villages, dwellings or buildings which are undefended and which are not military objectives;

G. Killing or wounding a combatant who, having laid down his arms or having no longer means of defense, has surrendered at discretion;

H. Making improper use of a flag of truce, of the flag or of the military insignia and uniform of the enemy or of the United Nations, as well as of the distinctive emblems of the Geneva Conventions, resulting in death or serious personal injury;

I. The transfer, directly or indirectly, by the Government of Iraq or any of its instrumentalities (which includes for clarification any of the instruments of the Arab Ba'ath Socialist Party)), of parts of its own civilian population into any territory it occupies, or the deportation or transfer of all or parts of the population of the occupied territory within or outside this territory;

J. Intentionally directing attacks against buildings that are dedicated to religion, education, art, science or charitable purposes, historic monuments, hospitals and places where the sick and wounded are collected, provided they are not military objectives;

K. Subjecting persons of another nation to physical mutilation or to medical or scientific experiments of any kind that are neither justified by the medical, dental or hospital treatment of the person concerned nor carried out in his or her interest, and which cause death to or seriously endanger the health of such person or persons;

L. Killing or wounding treacherously individuals belonging to the hostile nation or army;

M. Declaring that no one remained alive;

N. Destroying or seizing the property of an adverse party unless such destruction or seizure be imperatively demanded by the necessities of war;

O. Declaring abolished, suspended or inadmissible in a court of law, or otherwise depriving, the rights and actions of the nationals of the hostile party;

P. Compelling the nationals of the hostile party to take part in the operations of war directed against their own country, even if they were in the belligerent's service before the commencement of the war;

Q. Pillaging a town or place, even when it is taken by force;

R. Using poison or poisoned weapons;

S. Using asphyxiating, poisonous or other gases, and all analogous liquids, materials or devices;

T. Using bullets, which expand or flatten easily in the human body, such as bullets with a hard envelope, which does not entirely cover the core or is pierced with incisions;

U. Committing outrages upon personal dignity, in particular humiliating and degrading treatment;

V.   Committing rape, sexual slavery, enforced prostitution, forced pregnancy, or any other form of sexual violence of comparable gravity;

W.   Utilizing the presence of a civilian or other protected person to render certain points, areas or military forces immune from military operations;

X.   Intentionally directing attacks against buildings, material and medical units, transport, and personnel using the distinctive emblems of the Geneva Conventions in conformity with international law;

Y.   Intentionally using starvation of civilians as a method of warfare by depriving them of objects indispensable to their survival, including willfully impeding relief supplies as provided for under international law; and

Z.   Conscripting or enlisting children under the age of fifteen years into the national armed forces or using them to participate actively in hostilities.

Third: In the case of an armed conflict, any of the following acts committed against persons taking no active part in the hostilities, including members of armed forces who have laid down their arms and those placed *hors de combat* by sickness, wounds, detention or any other cause:

A.   Use of violence against life and persons, in particular murder of all kinds, mutilation, cruel treatment and torture;

B.   Committing outrages upon personal dignity, in particular humiliating and degrading treatment;

C.   Taking of hostages;

D.   The passing of sentences and the carrying out of executions without previous judgment pronounced by a regularly constituted court, affording all judicial guarantees which are generally recognized as indispensable.

Fourth: Other serious violations of the laws and customs of war applicable in armed conflict not of an international character, within the established framework of international law, namely, any of the following acts:

A.   Intentionally directing attacks against the civilian population as such or against civilian individuals not taking direct part in hostilities;

B.   Intentionally directing attacks against buildings, materials, medical transportation units and means, and personnel using the distinctive emblems of the Geneva Conventions in conformity with international law;

C.   Intentionally directing attacks against personnel, installations, materials, units, or vehicles used in humanitarian assistance and peacekeeping missions in accordance with the Charter of the United Nations, as long as they are entitled to the protection given to civilians or civilian targets under the international law of armed conflict;

D.   Intentionally directing attacks against buildings that are dedicated to religious, educational, artistic, scientific or charitable purposes, and historic monuments, hospitals and places where the sick and wounded are collected, provided they are not military objectives;

E.   Pillaging any town or place, even when taken over by assault;

F.   Committing rape, sexual slavery, forced prostitution, forced pregnancy, or any other form of sexual violence of comparable gravity;

G. Conscripting or listing children under the age of fifteen years into armed forces or groups or using them to participate actively in hostilities;

H. Ordering the displacement of the civilian population for reasons related to the conflict, unless the security of the civilians involved or imperative military reasons so demand;

I. Killing or wounding treacherously a combatant adversary;

J. Declaring that no person is still alive;

K. Subjugation persons who are under the power of another party of the conflict to physical mutilation or to medical or scientific experiments of any kind that are neither justified by the medical, dental or hospital treatment of the person concerned nor carried out in his or her interest, causing death to such person or persons, or seriously endangering their health; and

L. Destroying or seizing the property of an adversary, unless such destruction or seizure is imperatively demanded by the necessities of the conflict.

PART FOUR
Violations of Iraqi Laws

Article 14

The Court shall have the power to prosecute persons who have committed the following crimes:

First: Intervention in the judiciary or the attempt to influence the functions of the judiciary.

Second: The wastage and squander of national resources, pursuant to, item G of Article 2 of the Law punishing those who conspire against the security of the homeland and corrupt the regime No. 7 of 1958.

Third: The abuse of position and the pursuit of policies that were about to lead to the threat of war or the use of the armed forces of Iraq against an Arab country, in accordance with Article 1 of Law Number 7 of 1958.

Fourth: If the court finds a default in the elements of any of the crimes stipulated in Articles 11, 12, 13 of this law, and it is proved to the Court that the act constitutes a crime punishable by the penal law or any other criminal law at the time of its commitment, then the court shall have jurisdiction to adjudicate this case.

SECTION THREE
Individual Criminal Responsibility

Article 15

First: A person who commits a crime within the jurisdiction of this Court shall be personally responsible and liable for punishment in accordance with this Law.

Second: In accordance with this Law, and the provisions of Iraqi criminal law, a person shall be criminally responsible if that person:

A. Commits such a crime, whether as an individual, jointly with another or through another person, regardless of whether that this person is criminally responsible or not;

B. Orders, solicits or induces the commission of such a crime, which in fact occurs or is attempted;

C. For the purpose of facilitating the commission of such a crime, aids, abets or by any other means assists in its commission or its attempted commission, including providing the means for its commission;

D. Participating by any other way with a group of persons, with a common criminal intention to commit or attempt to commit such a crime, such participation shall be intentional and shall either:

   1. Be made for the aim of consolidating the criminal activity or criminal purpose of the group, where such activity or purpose involves the commission of a crime within the jurisdiction of the Court; or

   2. Be made with the knowledge of the intention of the group to commit the crime;

E. In respect of the crime of genocide, directly and publicly incites others to commit genocide;

F. Attempts to commit such a crime by taking action that commences its execution, but the crime does not occur because of circumstances independent of the person's intentions. However, a person who abandons the effort to commit the crime or otherwise prevents the completion of the crime shall not be liable for punishment under this Law for the attempt to commit that crime if that person completely and voluntarily gave up the criminal purpose.

Third: The official position of any accused person, whether as president, chairman or a member of the Revolution Command Council, prime minister, member of the counsel of ministers, a member of the Ba'ath Party Command, shall not relieve such person of criminal penal, nor mitigate punishment. No person is entitled to any immunity with respect to any of the crimes stipulated in Articles 11, 12, 13, and 14 of this law.

Fourth: The crimes that were committed by a subordinate do not relieve his superior of criminal responsibility if he knew or had reason to know that the subordinate was about to commit such acts or had done so, and the superior failed to take the necessary and appropriate measures to prevent such acts or to submit the matter to the competent authorities for investigation and prosecution.

Fifth: The fact that an accused person acted pursuant to an order of the Government or of his superior, shall not relieve him of criminal responsibility, but may be considered in mitigation of punishment if the Court determines that justice so requires.

Sixth: Pardons issued prior to this law coming into force, do not apply to the accused in any of the crimes stipulated in it.

SECTION FOUR
Rules of Procedure and Evidence

Article 16

The Court shall apply the Criminal Procedure Law No. 23 of 1971, and the Rules of Procedure and Evidence appended to this law, which is an indivisible and integral part of the law.

SECTION FIVE
General Principles of Criminal Law

Article 17

First: In case a stipulation is not found in this Law and the rules made there under, the general provisions of criminal law shall be applied in connection with the accusation and prosecution of any accused person shall be those contained in:

A. The Baghdadi Penal Law of 1919, for the period starting from July 17, 1968, till Dec. 14, 1969.

B. The Penal law no.111 of 1969, which was in force in1985 (third version), for the period starting from Dec.15, 1969, till May, 1, 2003.

C. The Military Penal Law no.13 of 1940, and the military procedure law no.44 of 1941.

Second: To interpret Articles 11, 12, 13 of this law, the Cassation Court and Panel may resort to the relevant decisions of the international criminal courts.

Third: Grounds for exclusion of criminal responsibility under the Panel Law shall be interpreted in a manner consistent with this Law and with international legal obligations concerning the crimes within the jurisdiction of the Court.

Fourth: The crimes stipulated in Articles 11, 12, 13, and 14 shall not be subject to limitations that terminate the criminal case or punishment.

SECTION SIX
Investigations and Indictment

Article 18

First: The Investigative Judge shall initiate investigations *ex-officio* or on the basis of information obtained from any source, particularly from the police, or governmental and nongovernmental organizations. The Investigative Judge shall assess the information received and decide whether there is sufficient basis to proceed.

Second: The Court Investigative Judge shall have the power to question suspects, victims and witnesses, or their relatives to collect evidence and to conduct on-site investigations. In carrying out his task the Court Investigative Judge may, as appropriate, request the assistance of the relevant governmental authorities concerned, who shall be required to provide full co-operation with the request.

Third: Upon a determination that a *prima facie* case exists, the Investigative Judge shall prepare an indictment containing a concise statement of the facts of the crime with which the accused is charged under the Statute and shall refer the case to the criminal court.

PART ONE
Guarantees of the Accused

Article 19

First: All persons shall be equal before the Court.

Second: The accused shall be presumed innocent until proven guilty before the Court in accordance with this law.

Third: Every accused shall be entitled to a public hearing, in pursuance with the provisions of this law and the Rules issued according to it.

Fourth: In directing any charge against the accused pursuant to the present Law, the accused shall be entitled to a just fair trial in accordance with the following minimum guarantees:

A. To be informed promptly and in detail of the content nature and cause and of the charge against him;

B. To have adequate time and facilities for the preparation of his defense and to communicate freely with counsel of his own choosing and to meet with him privately. The accused is entitled to have non-Iraqi legal representation, so long as the principal lawyer of such accused is Iraqi;

C. To be tried without undue delay;

D. To be tried in his presence, and to use a lawyer of his own choosing, and to be informed of his right assistance of his own choosing; to be informed, if he does not have legal assistance, of this right; and to have legal assistance and to have the right to request such aid to appoint a lawyer without paying the fees, case if he does not have sufficient means to pay for it; if he does not have the financial ability to do so.

E. The accused shall have the right to request the defense witnesses, the witnesses for the prosecution, and to discuss with them any evidence that support his defense in accordance with the law.

F. The defendant shall not be forced to confess and shall have the right to remain silent and not provide any testimony and that silent shall not be interpreted as evidence of convection or innocence.

SECTION SEVEN
Trial Proceedings

Article 20

First: A person against whom an indictment has been issued shall, pursuant to an order or an arrest warrant of the Investigative Judge, be taken into custody, immediately informed of the charges against him and transferred to the Court.

Second: The Criminal Court shall ensure that a trial is fair and expeditious and that proceedings are conducted in accordance with this Statute and the Rules of Procedure and Evidence annexed to this Law, with full respect for the rights of the accused and due regard for the protection of the victims, their relatives and the witnesses.

Third: The Criminal Court shall read the indictment, satisfy itself that the rights of the accused are respected and guaranteed, insure that the accused understands the indictment, with charges directed against him and instruct the accused to enter a plea.

Fourth: The hearings shall be public unless the Criminal Court decides to close the proceedings in accordance with the Rules of Procedure and Evidence annexed to this Statue, and no decision shall be adopted under the session secrecy unless for extreme limited reasons.

Article 21

The Criminal Court shall, in its Rules of Procedure and Evidence annexed to this Statue, provide the protection for victims or their relatives and witnesses and also for the secrecy of their identity.

Article 22

Families of victims and Iraqi persons harmed may file a civil suit before this court against the accused for the harm they suffered through their actions constituting crimes according to the provisions of this Statue. The court shall have the power to adjudicate these claims in accordance with the Iraqi Criminal procedure Code No. 23 for the year 1971, and other relevant laws.

Article 23

First: The Criminal Court shall pronounce judgments and impose sentences and penalties on persons convicted of crimes within the jurisdiction of the Court.

Second: The judgment shall be issued by a majority of the judges of the Criminal Court, and shall announce it in public. The judgment shall not be issued except pursuant to the indictment decision. The opinion of the dissenting Judges can be appended.

Article 24

First: The penalties that shall be imposed by the Court shall be those prescribed by the Iraqi Penal Code No (111) of 1969, except for sentences of life imprisonment that means the remaining natural life of the person. With considering the provisions of Article (17) of this Statute.

Second: It shall be applied against the crimes stipulated in article (14) of this Statute the sentences provided under the Iraqi Penal Code and other punishable laws.

Third: The penalty for crimes under Articles 11, 12, 13 shall be determined by the Criminal Court, taking into account the provisions contained in paragraphs fourth and fifth.

Fourth: A person convicted of sentences stipulated under Iraqi Penal Code shall be punished if:

A.   He committed an offence of murder or rape as defined under Iraqi Penal Code.

B.   He participated in committing an offence of murder or rape.

Fifth: The penalty for any crimes under Articles 11, 12, 13 which do not have a counterpart under Iraqi law shall be determined by the Court taking into account such factors like the gravity of the crime, the individual circumstances of the convicted person, guided by judicial precedents and relevant sentences issued by the international criminal courts.

Sixth: The Criminal Court may order the forfeiture of proceeds, property or assets derived directly or indirectly from a crime, without prejudice to the rights of the *bona fide* third parties.

Seventh: In accordance with Article 307 of the Iraqi Criminal Procedure Code, the Criminal Court shall have the right to confiscate any material or goods prohibited by law regardless of whether the case has been discharged for any lawful reason.

SECTION EIGHT
Appeals Proceedings

PART ONE
Cassation

Article 25

First: The convicted pr the public prosecutor has the right to contest the judgments and decisions before the Cassation Panel for any of the following reasons:

1.   If a judgment issued is in contradiction with the law or there is an error in interrupting it.

2.   An error in procedures.

3.   Material error in the facts which has led to violation of justice.

Second: The Cassation Panel may affirm, reverse or revise the decisions taken by the Criminal Court or the decisions of the Investigative Judge.

Third: When the Cassation Panel issues its verdict to revoke the judgment of acquittal or release issued by the Criminal Court or the Investigative Judge, the case shall be referred back to the Court for retrial of the accused or for the Investigative Judge to implement the decision.

Fourth: The period of appeal shall be in accordance with the provisions of the Iraqi Criminal procedure Code No. 23 for the year 1971 that is in effect, in case there is no specific provision in that regard.

PART TWO
Retrial

Article 26

First: Where a new findings or facts have been discovered which were not known at the time of the proceedings before the Criminal Court or the Cassation Panel and which could have been a decisive factor in reaching the decision, the convicted person or the Prosecution may submit to the Court an application for a retrial.

Second: The Court shall reject the application if it considers it to be unfounded. If it determines that the application has merit, and for the purpose of reaching a modification of the court decision after hearing the parties in the case, may:

1. Send case back to the original Criminal Court that issued the ruling; or

2. Send case back to another Criminal Court; or

3. The Cassation Panel takes jurisdiction over the matter.

SECTION NINE
Enforcement of Sentences

Article 27

First: Sentences shall be carried out in accordance with the Iraqi legal system and its laws.

Second: No authority, including the President of the Republic, may grant a pardon or mitigate the punishment issued by the Court. The punishment must be executed within 30 days of the date when the judgment becomes final and non-appealable.

SECTION TEN
General and Final Provisions

Article 28

Investigative judges, Judge of the criminal courts, members of the public prosecution committee, the director of the administrative department and the court's staff must be Iraqi nationals with due considerations given to the provisions of Article 4 (Third) of this statute.

Article 29

First: The Court and the national courts shall have concurrent jurisdiction to prosecute persons for those offences stipulated in Article 14 of this statute.

Second: The Court shall have primacy over all other Iraqi courts with respect to the crimes stipulated in Articles 11, 12, and 13 of this statute.

Third: At any stage of the proceedings, the Court may demand of any other Iraqi court to transfer any case being tried by it involving any crimes stipulated in Articles 11, 12, 13, and 14 of this statue, and such court shall be required to transfer such case upon demand.

Fourth: At any stage of the proceedings, the Court may demand of any other Iraqi court to transfer any case being tried by it involving any crimes stipulated in Articles 13, 14, 15, 16 of this statue, and such court shall be required to transfer such case upon demand.

Article 30

First: No person shall be tried before any other Iraqi court for acts for which the Court, in accordance with Articles 300 and 301 of the Iraqi Criminal Procedure Code, has already tried him or her.

Second: A person, who has been tried by any Iraqi court for acts constituting crimes within the jurisdiction of the Court, may not be subsequently tried by the Court except if the Court determines that the previous court proceedings were not impartial or independent, or were designed to shield the accused from criminal responsibility. When decisions are made for a retrial, one of the conditions contained in Article 196 of the Iraqi Civil Procedure Code and Article (303) of the Iraqi Criminal Procedure Code must be met.

Third: In determining the penalty to be imposed on a person convicted of a crime under the present Statute, the Court shall take into account the time served of any penalty imposed by an Iraqi court on the same person for the same crime.

Article 31

First: The President of the Court, the Judges, the Court's Investigative Judges, the Public Prosecutors, the Director of the Administration Department and their staffs shall have immunity from civil suits in respect to their official functions.

Second: Other persons, including the accused, required at the seat of the Court shall be accorded such treatment as is necessary for the proper functioning of the Court.

Article 32

Arabic shall be the official language of the Court.

Article 33

No person who was previously a member of the disbanded Ba'ath Party shall be appointed as a judge, investigative judge, public prosecutor, an employee or any of the personnel of the Court.

Article 34

The expenses of the Court shall be borne by the State's general budget.

Article 35

The President of the Court shall prepare and submit an annual report on the Court activities to the Council of Ministers.

Article 36

The provisions of the civil service law No. (24) of 1960, Personnel law No. (25) of 1960, government and socialist sector employees disciplinary law No (14) of 1991 and civil pension law No.(33) of 1966 shall apply to the court's employees other than the judges and members of public prosecution.

Article 37

Law No. 1 for the year 2003 the Iraqi Special Tribunal and the Rules of Procedure and Evidence issued in accordance with the provisions of Article (16) thereof are revoked from the date this statute comes into force.

Article 38

All decisions and Orders of Procedure issued under law No. 1 for the year 2003 are correct and conform to the law.

Article 39

The Council of Ministers in coordination with the President of the Court shall issue instructions to facilitate the implementation of this statute.

Article 40

This law shall come into force on the date of its publication in the Official Gazette.

Jalal Talabani
President of the Republic

Adil Abdul-Mahdi
Vice-President

Ghazi Ajil Al-Yawir
Vice-President

Justifying Reasons

In order to expose the crimes committed in Iraq from July 17, 1968 until May 1, 2005 against the Iraqi people and the peoples of the region and the subsequent savage massacres, and for laying down the rules and punishments to condemn after a fair trial the perpetrators of such crimes for waging wars, mass extermination and crimes against humanity, and for the purpose of forming an Iraqi national high criminal court from among Iraqi judges with high experience, competence and integrity to specialize in trying these criminals.

And in order to reveal the truth and the agonies and injustice caused by the perpetrators of such crimes, and for protecting the rights of many Iraqis and alleviating injustice and for demonstrating heaven's justice as envisaged by the Almighty God....

This law has been legislated.

Statute of the International Criminal Tribunal for Former Yugoslavia
U.N. S.C. Res. 827 (1993)

Article 1
Competence of the International Tribunal

The International Tribunal shall have the power to prosecute persons responsible for serious violations of international humanitarian law committed in the territory of the former Yugoslavia since 1991 in accordance with the provisions of the present Statute.

Article 2
Grave breaches of the Geneva Conventions of 1949

The International Tribunal shall have the power to prosecute persons committing or ordering to be committed grave breaches of the Geneva Conventions of 12 August 1949, namely the following acts against persons or property protected under the provisions of the relevant Geneva Convention:

(a) wilful killing;

(b) torture or inhuman treatment, including biological experiments;

(c) wilfully causing great suffering or serious injury to body or health;

(d) extensive destruction and appropriation of property, not justified by military necessity and carried out unlawfully and wantonly;

(e) compelling a prisoner of war or a civilian to serve in the forces of a hostile power;

(f) wilfully depriving a prisoner of war or a civilian of the rights of fair and regular trial;

(g) unlawful deportation or transfer or unlawful confinement of a civilian;

(h) taking civilians as hostages.

Article 3
Violations of the laws or customs of war

The International Tribunal shall have the power to prosecute persons violating the laws or customs of war. Such violations shall include, but not be limited to:

(a) employment of poisonous weapons or other weapons calculated to cause unnecessary suffering;

(b) wanton destruction of cities, towns or villages, or devastation not justified by military necessity;

(c) attack, or bombardment, by whatever means, of undefended towns, villages, dwellings, or buildings;

(d) seizure of, destruction or wilful damage done to institutions dedicated to religion, charity and education, the arts and sciences, historic monuments and works of art and science;

(e) plunder of public or private property.

Article 4
Genocide

1. The International Tribunal shall have the power to prosecute persons committing genocide as defined in paragraph 2 of this article or of committing any of the other acts enumerated in paragraph 3 of this article.

2. Genocide means any of the following acts committed with intent to destroy, in whole or in part, a national, ethnical, racial or religious group, as such:

(a) killing members of the group;

(b) causing serious bodily or mental harm to members of the group;

(c) deliberately inflicting on the group conditions of life calculated to bring about its physical destruction in whole or in part;

(d) imposing measures intended to prevent births within the group;

(e) forcibly transferring children of the group to another group.

3. The following acts shall be punishable:

(a) genocide;

(b) conspiracy to commit genocide;

(c) direct and public incitement to commit genocide;

(d) attempt to commit genocide;

(e) complicity in genocide.

Article 5
Crimes against humanity

The International Tribunal shall have the power to prosecute persons responsible for the following crimes when committed in armed conflict, whether international or internal in character, and directed against any civilian population:

(a) murder;

(b) extermination;

    (c) enslavement;

    (d) deportation;

    (e) imprisonment;

    (f) torture;

    (g) rape;

    (h) persecutions on political, racial and religious grounds;

    (i) other inhumane acts.

Article 6
Personal jurisdiction

The International Tribunal shall have jurisdiction over natural persons pursuant to the provisions of the present Statute.

Article 7
Individual criminal responsibility

1. A person who planned, instigated, ordered, committed or otherwise aided and abetted in the planning, preparation or execution of a crime referred to in articles 2 to 5 of the present Statute, shall be individually responsible for the crime.

2. The official position of any accused person, whether as Head of State or Government or as a responsible Government official, shall not relieve such person of criminal responsibility nor mitigate punishment.

3. The fact that any of the acts referred to in articles 2 to 5 of the present Statute was committed by a subordinate does not relieve his superior of criminal responsibility if he knew or had reason to know that the subordinate was about to commit such acts or had done so and the superior failed to take the necessary and reasonable measures to prevent such acts or to punish the perpetrators thereof.

4. The fact that an accused person acted pursuant to an order of a Government or of a superior shall not relieve him of criminal responsibility, but may be considered in mitigation of punishment if the International Tribunal determines that justice so requires.

Article 8
Territorial and temporal jurisdiction

The territorial jurisdiction of the International Tribunal shall extend to the territory of the former Socialist Federal Republic of Yugoslavia, including its land surface, airspace and territorial waters. The temporal jurisdiction of the International Tribunal shall extend to a period beginning on 1 January 1991.

Article 9
Concurrent jurisdiction

1. The International Tribunal and national courts shall have concurrent jurisdiction to prosecute persons for serious violations of international humanitarian law committed in the territory of the former Yugoslavia since 1 January 1991.

2. The International Tribunal shall have primacy over national courts. At any stage of the procedure, the International Tribunal may formally request national courts to defer to the competence of the International Tribunal in accordance with the present Statute and the Rules of Procedure and Evidence of the International Tribunal.

Article 10
Non-bis-in-idem

1. No person shall be tried before a national court for acts constituting serious violations of international humanitarian law under the present Statute, for which he or she has already been tried by the International Tribunal.

2. A person who has been tried by a national court for acts constituting serious violations of international humanitarian law may be subsequently tried by the International Tribunal only if:

(a) the act for which he or she was tried was characterized as an ordinary crime; or

(b) the national court proceedings were not impartial or independent, were designed to shield the accused from international criminal responsibility, or the case was not diligently prosecuted.

3. In considering the penalty to be imposed on a person convicted of a crime under the present Statute, the International Tribunal shall take into account the extent to which any penalty imposed by a national court on the same person for the same act has already been served.

Article 11
Organization of the International Tribunal

The International Tribunal shall consist of the following organs:

(a) The Chambers, comprising two Trial Chambers and an Appeals Chamber;

(b) The Prosecutor, and

(c) A Registry, servicing both the Chambers and the Prosecutor.

Article 12
Composition of the Chambers

The Chambers shall be composed of eleven independent judges, no two of whom may be nationals of the same State, who shall serve as follows:

(a) Three judges shall serve in each of the Trial Chambers;

(b) Five judges shall serve in the Appeals Chamber.

Article 13
Qualifications and election of judges

1. The judges shall be persons of high moral character, impartiality and integrity who possess the qualifications required in their respective countries for appointment to the highest judicial offices. In the overall composition of the Chambers due account shall be taken of the experience of the judges in criminal law, international law, including international humanitarian law and human rights law.

2. The judges of the International Tribunal shall be elected by the General Assembly from a list submitted by the Security Council, in the following manner:

(a) The Secretary-General shall invite nominations for judges of the International Tribunal from States Members of the United Nations and non-member States maintaining permanent observer missions at United Nations Headquarters;

(b) Within sixty days of the date of the invitation of the Secretary-General, each State may nominate up to two candidates meeting the qualifications set out in paragraph 1 above, no two of whom shall be of the same nationality;

(c) The Secretary-General shall forward the nominations received to the Security Council. From the nominations received the Security Council shall establish a list of not less than twenty-two and not more than thirty-three candidates, taking due account of the adequate representation of the principal legal systems of the world;

(d) The President of the Security Council shall transmit the list of candidates to the President of the General Assembly. From that list the General Assembly shall elect the eleven judges of the International Tribunal. The candidates who receive an absolute majority of the votes of the States Members of the United Nations and of the non-Member States maintaining permanent observer missions at United Nations Headquarters, shall be declared elected. Should two candidates of the same nationality obtain the required majority vote, the one who received the higher number of votes shall be considered elected.

3. In the event of a vacancy in the Chambers, after consultation with the Presidents of the Security Council and of the General Assembly, the Secretary-General shall appoint a person meeting the qualifications of paragraph 1 above, for the remainder of the term of office concerned.

4. The judges shall be elected for a term of four years. The terms and conditions of service shall be those of the judges of the International Court of Justice. They shall be eligible for re-election.

Article 14
Officers and members of the Chambers

1. The judges of the International Tribunal shall elect a President.

2. The President of the International Tribunal shall be a member of the Appeals Chamber and shall preside over its proceedings.

3. After consultation with the judges of the International Tribunal, the President shall assign the judges to the Appeals Chamber and to the Trial Chambers. A judge shall serve only in the Chamber to which he or she was assigned.

4. The judges of each Trial Chamber shall elect a Presiding Judge, who shall conduct all of the proceedings of the Trial Chamber as a whole.

Article 15
Rules of procedure and evidence

The judges of the International Tribunal shall adopt rules of procedure and evidence for the conduct of the pre-trial phase of the proceedings, trials and appeals, the admission of evidence, the protection of victims and witnesses and other appropriate matters.

Article 16
The Prosecutor

1. The Prosecutor shall be responsible for the investigation and prosecution of persons responsible for serious violations of international humanitarian law committed in the territory of the former Yugoslavia since 1 January 1991.

2. The Prosecutor shall act independently as a separate organ of the International Tribunal. He or she shall not seek or receive instructions from any Government or from any other source.

3. The Office of the Prosecutor shall be composed of a Prosecutor and such other qualified staff as may be required.

4. The Prosecutor shall be appointed by the Security Council on nomination by the Secretary-General. He or she shall be of high moral character and possess the highest level of competence and experience in the conduct of investigations and prosecutions of criminal cases. The Prosecutor shall serve for a four-year term and be eligible for reappointment. The terms and conditions of service of the Prosecutor shall be those of an Under-Secretary-General of the United Nations.

5. The staff of the Office of the Prosecutor shall be appointed by the Secretary-General on the recommendation of the Prosecutor.

Article 17
The Registry

1. The Registry shall be responsible for the administration and servicing of the International Tribunal.

2. The Registry shall consist of a Registrar and such other staff as may be required.

3. The Registrar shall be appointed by the Secretary-General after consultation with the President of the International Tribunal. He or she shall serve for a four-year term and be eligible for reappointment. The terms and conditions of service of the Registrar shall be those of an Assistant Secretary-General of the United Nations.

4. The staff of the Registry shall be appointed by the Secretary-General on the recommendation of the Registrar.

Article 18
Investigation and preparation of indictment

1. The Prosecutor shall initiate investigations ex-officio or on the basis of information obtained from any source, particularly from Governments, United Nations organs, intergovernmental and non-governmental organizations. The Prosecutor shall assess the information received or obtained and decide whether there is sufficient basis to proceed.

2. The Prosecutor shall have the power to question suspects, victims and witnesses, to collect evidence and to conduct on-site investigations. In carrying out these tasks, the Prosecutor may, as appropriate, seek the assistance of the State authorities concerned.

3. If questioned, the suspect shall be entitled to be assisted by counsel of his own choice, including the right to have legal assistance assigned to him without payment by him in any such case if he does not have sufficient means to pay for it, as well as to necessary translation into and from a language he speaks and understands.

4. Upon a determination that a prima facie case exists, the Prosecutor shall prepare an indictment containing a concise statement of the facts and the crime or crimes with which the accused is charged under the Statute. The indictment shall be transmitted to a judge of the Trial Chamber.

Article 19
Review of the indictment

1. The judge of the Trial Chamber to whom the indictment has been transmitted shall review it. If satisfied that a prima facie case has been established by the Prosecutor, he shall confirm the indictment. If not so satisfied, the indictment shall be dismissed.

2. Upon confirmation of an indictment, the judge may, at the request of the Prosecutor, issue such orders and warrants for the arrest, detention, surrender or transfer of persons, and any other orders as may be required for the conduct of the trial.

Article 20
Commencement and conduct of trial proceedings

1. The Trial Chambers shall ensure that a trial is fair and expeditious and that proceedings are conducted in accordance with the rules of procedure and evidence, with full respect for the rights of the accused and due regard for the protection of victims and witnesses.

2. A person against whom an indictment has been confirmed shall, pursuant to an order or an arrest warrant of the International Tribunal, be taken into custody, immediately informed of the charges against him and transferred to the International Tribunal.

3. The Trial Chamber shall read the indictment, satisfy itself that the rights of the accused are respected, confirm that the accused understands the indictment, and instruct the accused to enter a plea. The Trial Chamber shall then set the date for trial.

4. The hearings shall be public unless the Trial Chamber decides to close the proceedings in accordance with its rules of procedure and evidence.

Article 21
Rights of the accused

1. All persons shall be equal before the International Tribunal.

2. In the determination of charges against him, the accused shall be entitled to a fair and public hearing, subject to article 22 of the Statute.

3. The accused shall be presumed innocent until proved guilty according to the provisions of the present Statute.

4. In the determination of any charge against the accused pursuant to the present Statute, the accused shall be entitled to the following minimum guarantees, in full equality:

 (a) to be informed promptly and in detail in a language which he understands of the nature and cause of the charge against him;

 (b) to have adequate time and facilities for the preparation of his defence and to communicate with counsel of his own choosing;

 (c) to be tried without undue delay;

 (d) to be tried in his presence, and to defend himself in person or through legal assistance of his own choosing; to be informed, if he does not have legal assistance, of this right; and to have legal assistance assigned to him, in any case where the interests of justice so require, and without payment by him in any such case if he does not have sufficient means to pay for it;

 (e) to examine, or have examined, the witnesses against him and to obtain the attendance and examination of witnesses on his behalf under the same conditions as witnesses against him;

 (f) to have the free assistance of an interpreter if he cannot understand or speak the language used in the International Tribunal;

 (g) not to be compelled to testify against himself or to confess guilt.

Article 22
Protection of victims and witnesses

The International Tribunal shall provide in its rules of procedure and evidence for the protection of victims and witnesses. Such protection measures shall include, but shall not be limited to, the conduct of in camera proceedings and the protection of the victim's identity.

Article 23
Judgement

1. The Trial Chambers shall pronounce judgements and impose sentences and penalties on persons convicted of serious violations of international humanitarian law.

2. The judgement shall be rendered by a majority of the judges of the Trial Chamber, and shall be delivered by the Trial Chamber in public. It shall be accompanied by a reasoned opinion in writing, to which separate or dissenting opinions may be appended.

Article 24
Penalties

1. The penalty imposed by the Trial Chamber shall be limited to imprisonment. In determining the terms of imprisonment, the Trial Chambers shall have recourse to the general practice regarding prison sentences in the courts of the former Yugoslavia.

2. In imposing the sentences, the Trial Chambers should take into account such factors as the gravity of the offence and the individual circumstances of the convicted person.

3. In addition to imprisonment, the Trial Chambers may order the return of any property and proceeds acquired by criminal conduct, including by means of duress, to their rightful owners.

Article 25
Appellate proceedings

1. The Appeals Chamber shall hear appeals from persons convicted by the Trial Chambers or from the Prosecutor on the following grounds:

(a) an error on a question of law invalidating the decision; or

(b) an error of fact which has occasioned a miscarriage of justice.

2. The Appeals Chamber may affirm, reverse or revise the decisions taken by the Trial Chambers.

Article 26
Review proceedings

Where a new fact has been discovered which was not known at the time of the proceedings before the Trial Chambers or the Appeals Chamber and which could have been a decisive factor in reaching the decision, the convicted person or the Prosecutor may submit to the International Tribunal an application for review of the judgement.

Article 27
Enforcement of sentences

Imprisonment shall be served in a State designated by the International Tribunal from a list of States which have indicated to the Security Council their willingness to accept convicted persons. Such imprisonment shall be in accordance with the applicable law of the State concerned, subject to the supervision of the International Tribunal.

Article 28
Pardon or commutation of sentences

If, pursuant to the applicable law of the State in which the convicted person is imprisoned, he or she is eligible for pardon or commutation of sentence, the State concerned shall notify the International Tribunal accordingly. The President of the International Tribunal, in consultation with the judges, shall decide the matter on the basis of the interests of justice and the general principles of law.

Article 29
Cooperation and judicial assistance

1. States shall cooperate with the International Tribunal in the investigation and prosecution of persons accused of committing serious violations of international humanitarian law.

2. States shall comply without undue delay with any request for assistance or an order issued by a Trial Chamber, including, but not limited to:

   (a) the identification and location of persons;

   (b) the taking of testimony and the production of evidence;

   (c) the service of documents;

   (d) the arrest or detention of persons;

   (e) the surrender or the transfer of the accused to the International Tribunal.

Article 30
The status, privileges and immunities of the International Tribunal

1. The Convention on the Privileges and Immunities of the United Nations of 13 February 1946 shall apply to the International Tribunal, the judges, the Prosecutor and his staff, and the Registrar and his staff.

2. The judges, the Prosecutor and the Registrar shall enjoy the privileges and immunities, exemptions and facilities accorded to diplomatic envoys, in accordance with international law.

3. The staff of the Prosecutor and of the Registrar shall enjoy the privileges and immunities accorded to officials of the United Nations under articles V and VII of the Convention referred to in paragraph 1 of this article.

4. Other persons, including the accused, required at the seat of the International Tribunal shall be accorded such treatment as is necessary for the proper functioning of the International Tribunal.

Article 31
Seat of the International Tribunal

The International Tribunal shall have its seat at The Hague.

Article 32
Expenses of the International Tribunal

The expenses of the International Tribunal shall be borne by the regular budget of the United Nations in accordance with Article 17 of the Charter of the United Nations.

Article 33
Working languages

The working languages of the International Tribunal shall be English and French.

Article 34
Annual report

The President of the International Tribunal shall submit an annual report of the International Tribunal to the Security Council and to the General Assembly.

ICTY Rules of Procedure and Evidence

(1994, revised as of 23 Nov. 2005) (excerpts)

Part Four
INVESTIGATIONS AND RIGHTS OF SUSPECTS

Rule 39
Conduct of Investigations

In the conduct of an investigation, the Prosecutor may:

(i) summon and question suspects, victims and witnesses and record their statements, collect evidence and conduct on-site investigations;

(ii) undertake such other matters as may appear necessary for completing the investigation and the preparation and conduct of the prosecution at the trial, including the taking of special measures to provide for the safety of potential witnesses and informants;

(iii) seek, to that end, the assistance of any State authority concerned, as well as of any relevant international body including the International Criminal Police Organization (INTERPOL); and

(iv) request such orders as may be necessary from a Trial Chamber or a Judge.

Rule 40
Provisional Measures

In case of urgency, the Prosecutor may request any State:

(i) to arrest a suspect or an accused provisionally;

(ii) to seise physical evidence;

(iii) to take all necessary measures to prevent the escape of a suspect or an accused, injury to or intimidation of a victim or witness, or the destruction of evidence.

The State concerned shall comply forthwith, in accordance with Article 29 of the Statute.

Rule 40 *bis*
Transfer and Provisional Detention of Suspects

(A) In the conduct of an investigation, the Prosecutor may transmit to the Registrar, for an order by a Judge assigned pursuant to Rule 28, a request for the transfer to and provisional detention of a suspect in the premises of the detention unit of the Tribunal. This request shall indicate the grounds upon which the request is made and, unless the Prosecutor wishes only to question the suspect, shall include a provisional charge and a summary of the material upon which the Prosecutor relies.

(B) The Judge shall order the transfer and provisional detention of the suspect if the following conditions are met:

(i) the Prosecutor has requested a State to arrest the suspect provisionally, in accordance Rule 40, or the suspect is otherwise detained by State authorities;

(ii) after hearing the Prosecutor, the Judge considers that there is a reliable and consistent body of material which tends to show that the suspect may have committed a crime over which the Tribunal has jurisdiction; and

(iii) the Judge considers provisional detention to be a necessary measure to prevent the escape of the suspect, injury to or intimidation of a victim or witness or the destruction of evidence, or to be otherwise necessary for the conduct of the investigation.

(C) The order for the transfer and provisional detention of the suspect shall be signed by the Judge and bear the seal of the Tribunal. The order shall set forth the basis of the application made by the Prosecutor under paragraph (A), including the provisional charge, and shall state the Judge's grounds for making the order, having regard to paragraph (B). The order shall also specify the initial time-limit for the provisional detention of the suspect, and be accompanied by a statement of the rights of a suspect, as specified in this Rule and in Rules 42 and 43.

(D) The provisional detention of a suspect shall be ordered for the period not exceeding thirty days from the date of the transfer of the suspect to the seat of the Tribunal. At the end of that period, at the Prosecutor's request, the Judge who made the order, or another permanent Judge of the same Trial Chamber, may decide, subsequent to an inter partes hearing of the Prosecutor and the suspect assisted by counsel, to extend the detention for a period not exceeding thirty days, if warranted by the needs of the investigation. At the end of that extension, at the Prosecutor's request, the Judge who made the order, or another permanent Judge of the same Trial Chamber, may decide, subsequent to an inter partes hearing of the Prosecutor and the suspect assisted by counsel, to extend the detention for a further period not exceeding thirty days, if warranted by special circumstances. The total period of detention shall in no case exceed ninety days, at the end of which, in the event the indictment has not been confirmed and an arrest warrant signed, the suspect shall be released or, if appropriate, be delivered to the authorities of the requested State.

(E) The provisions in Rules 55 (B) to 59 *bis* shall apply mutatis mutandis to the execution of the transfer order and the provisional detention order relative to a suspect.

(F) After being transferred to the seat of the Tribunal, the suspect, assisted by counsel, shall be brought, without delay, before the Judge who made the order, or another permanent Judge of the same Trial Chamber, who shall ensure that the rights of the suspect are respected.

(G) During detention, the Prosecutor and the suspect or the suspect's counsel may submit to the Trial Chamber of which the Judge who made the order is a member, all applications relative to the propriety of provisional detention or to the suspect's release.

(H) Without prejudice to paragraph (D), the Rules relating to the detention on remand of accused persons shall apply mutatis mutandis to the provisional detention of persons under this Rule.

Rule 41
Retention of Information

Subject to Rule 81, the Prosecutor shall be responsible for the retention, storage and security of information and physical material obtained in the course of the Prosecutor's investigations until formally tendered into evidence.

Rule 42
Rights of Suspects During Investigation

(A) A suspect who is to be questioned by the Prosecutor shall have the following rights, of which the Prosecutor shall inform the suspect prior to questioning, in a language the suspect understands:

(i) the right to be assisted by counsel of the suspect's choice or to be assigned legal assistance without payment if the suspect does not have sufficient means to pay for it;

(ii) the right to have the free assistance of an interpreter if the suspect cannot understand or speak the language to be used for questioning; and

(iii) the right to remain silent, and to be cautioned that any statement the suspect makes shall be recorded and may be used in evidence.

(B) Questioning of a suspect shall not proceed without the presence of counsel unless the suspect has voluntarily waived the right to counsel. In case of waiver, if the suspect subsequently expresses a desire to have counsel, questioning shall thereupon cease, and shall only resume when the suspect has obtained or has been assigned counsel.

Rule 43

Recording Questioning of Suspects

Whenever the Prosecutor questions a suspect, the questioning shall be audio-recorded or video-recorded, in accordance with the following procedure:

(i) the suspect shall be informed in a language the suspect understands that the questioning is being audio-recorded or video-recorded;

(ii) in the event of a break in the course of the questioning, the fact and the time of the break shall be recorded before audio-recording or video-recording ends and the time of resumption of the questioning shall also be recorded;

(iii) at the conclusion of the questioning the suspect shall be offered the opportunity to clarify anything the suspect has said, and to add anything the suspect may wish, and the time of conclusion shall be recorded;

(iv) a copy of the recorded tape will be supplied to the suspect or, if multiple recording apparatus was used, one of the original recorded tapes;

(v) after a copy has been made, if necessary, of the recorded tape, the original recorded tape or one of the original tapes shall be sealed in the presence of the suspect under the signature of the Prosecutor and the suspect; and

(vi) the tape shall be transcribed if the suspect becomes an accused.

Section 2: Of Counsel

Rule 44

Appointment, Qualifications and Duties of Counsel

(A) Counsel engaged by a suspect or an accused shall file a power of attorney with the Registrar at the earliest opportunity. Subject to any determination by a Chamber pursuant to Rule 46 or 77, a counsel shall be considered qualified to represent a suspect or accused if the counsel satisfies the Registrar that he or she:

(i) is admitted to the practice of law in a State, or is a university professor of law;

(ii) has written and oral proficiency in one of the two working languages of the Tribunal, unless the Registrar deems it is in the interests of justice to waive this requirement, as provided for in paragraph (B);

(iii) is a member in good standing of an association of counsel practicing at the Tribunal recognised by the Registrar;

(iv) has not been found guilty or otherwise disciplined in relevant disciplinary proceedings against him in a national or international forum, including proceedings pursuant to the Code of Professional Conduct for Defence Counsel Appearing Before the International Tribunal, unless the Registrar deems that, in the circumstances, it would be disproportionate to exclude such counsel;

(v) has not been found guilty in relevant criminal proceedings;

(vi) has not engaged in conduct whether in pursuit of his or her profession or otherwise which is dishonest or otherwise discreditable to a counsel, prejudicial to the administration of justice, or likely to diminish public confidence in the International Tribunal or the administration of justice, or otherwise bring the International Tribunal in to disrepute; and

(vii) has not provided false or misleading information in relation to his or her qualifications and fitness to practice or failed to provide relevant information.

(B) At he request of the suspect or accused and where the interests of justice so demand, the Registrar may admit a counsel who does not speak either of the two working languages of the Tribunal but who speaks the native language of the suspect or accused. The Registrar may impose such conditions as deemed appropriate, including the requirement that the counsel or accused undertake to meet all translations and interpretation costs not usually met by the Tribunal, and counsel undertakes not to request any extensions of time as a result of the fact that he does not speak one of the working languages. A suspect or accused may seek the President's review of the Registrar's decision.

(C) In the performance of their duties counsel shall be subject to the relevant provisions of the Statute, the Rules, the Rules of Detention and any other rules or regulations adopted by the Tribunal, the Host Country Agreement, the Code of Professional Conduct for Defence Counsel Appearing Before the International Tribunal and the codes of practice and ethics governing their profession and, if applicable, the Directive on the Assignment of Defence Counsel adopted by the Registrar and approved by the permanent Judges.

(D) An Advisory Panel shall be established to assist the President and the Registrar in all matters relating to defence counsel. The Panel members shall be selected from representatives of professional associations and from counsel who have appeared before the Tribunal. They shall have recognised professional legal experience. The composition of the Advisory Panel shall be representative of the different legal systems. A directive of the Registrar shall set out the structure and areas of responsibility of the Advisory Panel.

Rule 45
Assignment of Counsel

(A) Whenever the interests of justice so demand, counsel shall be assigned to suspects or accused who lack the means to remunerate such counsel. Such assignments shall be treated in accordance with the procedure established in a Directive set out by the Registrar and approved by the permanent Judges.

(B) For this purpose, the Registrar shall maintain a list of counsel who:

(i) fulfil all the requirements of Rule 44, although the language requirement of Rule 44(A)(ii) may be waived by the Registrar as provided for in the Directive;

(ii) possess established competence in criminal law and/or international criminal law/international humanitarian law/international human rights law;

(iii) possess at least seven years of relevant experience, whether as a judge, prosecutor, attorney or in some other capacity, in criminal proceedings; and

(iv) have indicated their availability and willingness to be assigned by the Tribunal to any person, detained under the authority of the Tribunal lacking the means to remunerate counsel, under the terms set out in the Directive.

(C) The Registrar shall maintain a separate list of counsel who, in addition to fulfilling the qualification requirements set out in paragraph (B), are readily available, as "duty counsel" for assignment to an accused for the purposes of the initial appearance, in accordance with Rule 62.

(D) The Registrar shall, in consultation with the permanent Judges, establish the criteria for the payment of fees to assigned counsel.

(E) Where a person is assigned counsel and is subsequently found not to be lacking the means to remunerate counsel, the Chamber may, on application by the Registrar, make an order of contribution to recover the cost of providing counsel.

(F) A suspect or an accused electing to conduct his or her own defence shall so notify the Registrar in writing at the first opportunity.

Rule 45 *bis*
Detained Persons

Rules 44 and 45 shall apply to any person detained under the authority of the Tribunal.

Rule 46
Misconduct of Counsel

(A) If a Judge or a Chamber finds that the conduct of a counsel is offensive, abusive or otherwise obstructs the proper conduct of the proceedings, or that a counsel is negligent or otherwise fails to meet the standard of professional competence and ethics in the performance of his duties, the Chamber may, after giving counsel due warning:

> (i) refuse audience to that counsel; and/or

> (ii) determine, after giving counsel an opportunity to be heard, that counsel is no longer eligible to represent a suspect or an accused before the Tribunal pursuant to Rule 44 and 45.

(B) A Judge or a Chamber may also, with the approval of the President, communicate any misconduct of counsel to the professional body regulating the conduct of counsel in the counsel's State of admission or, if a university professor of law and not otherwise admitted to the profession, to the governing body of that counsel's University.

(C) Under the supervision of the President, the Registrar shall publish and oversee the implementation of a Code of Professional Conduct for defence counsel.

Part Five
PRE-TRIAL PROCEEDINGS

Section 1: Indictments

Rule 47
Submission of Indictment by the Prosecutor

(A) An indictment, submitted in accordance with the following procedure, shall be reviewed by a Judge designated in accordance with Rule 28 for this purpose.

(B) The Prosecutor, if satisfied in the course of an investigation that there is sufficient evidence to provide reasonable grounds for believing that a suspect has committed a crime within the jurisdiction of the Tribunal, shall prepare and forward to the Registrar an indictment for confirmation by a Judge, together with supporting material.

(C) The indictment shall set forth the name and particulars of the suspect, and a concise statement of the facts of the case and of the crime with which the suspect is charged.

(D) The Registrar shall forward the indictment and accompanying material to the designated Judge, who will inform the Prosecutor of the date fixed for review of the indictment.

(E) The reviewing Judge shall examine each of the counts in the indictment, and any supporting materials the Prosecutor may provide, to determine, applying the standard set forth in Article 19, paragraph 1, of the Statute, whether a case exists against the suspect.

(F) The reviewing Judge may:

(i) request the Prosecutor to present additional material in support of any or all counts;

(ii) confirm each count;

(iii) dismiss each count; or

(iv) adjourn the review so as to give the Prosecutor the opportunity to modify the indictment.

(G) The indictment as confirmed by the Judge shall be retained by the Registrar, who shall prepare certified copies bearing the seal of the Tribunal. If the accused does not understand either of the official languages of the Tribunal and if the language understood is known to the Registrar, a translation of the indictment in that language shall also be prepared, and shall be included as part of each certified copy of the indictment.

(H) Upon confirmation of any or all counts in the indictment,

(i) the Judge may issue an arrest warrant, in accordance with Rule 55 (A), and any orders as provided in Article 19 of the Statute, and

(ii) the suspect shall have the status of an accused.

(I) The dismissal of an count in an indictment shall not preclude the Prosecutor from subsequently bringing an amended indictment based on the acts underlying that count if supported by additional evidence.

Rule 48
Joinder of Accused

Persons accused of the same or different crimes committed in the course of the same transaction may be jointly charged and tried.

Rule 49
Joinder of Crimes

Two or more crimes may be joined in one indictment if the series of acts committed together form the same transaction, and the said crimes were committed by the same accused.

Rule 50
Amendment of Indictment

(A) (i) The Prosecutor may amend an indictment:

(a) at any time before its confirmation, without leave;

(b) between its confirmation and the assignment of the case to a Trial Chamber, with the leave of the Judge who confirmed the indictment, or a Judge assigned by the President; and

(c) after the assignment of the case to a Trial Chamber, with the leave of that Trial Chamber or a Judge of that Chamber, after having heard the parties.

(ii) Independently of any other factors relevant to the exercise of the discretion, leave to amend an indictment shall not be granted unless the Trial Chamber or Judge is satisfied there is evidence which satisfies the standard set forth in Article 19, paragraph 1, of the Statute to support the proposed amendment.

(iii) Further confirmation is not required where an indictment is amended by leave.

(iv) Rule 47(G) and Rule 53 *bis* apply mutatis mutandis to the amended indictment.

(B) If the amended indictment includes new charges and the accused has already appeared before a Trial Chamber in accordance with Rule 62, a further appearance shall be held as soon as practicable to enable the accused to enter a plea on the new charges.

(C) The accused shall have a further period of thirty days in which to file preliminary motions pursuant to Rule 72 in respect of the new charges and, where necessary, the date for trial may be postponed to ensure adequate time for the preparation of the defence.

Rule 51
Withdrawal of Indictment

(A) The Prosecutor may withdraw an indictment:

(i) at any time before its confirmation, without leave;

(ii) between its confirmation and the assignment of the case to a Trial Chamber, with the leave of the Judge who confirmed the indictment, or a Judge assigned by the President; and

(iii) after the assignment of the case to a Trial Chamber, by motion before that Trial Chamber pursuant to Rule 73.

(B) The withdrawal of the indictment shall be promptly notified to the suspect or the accused and to the counsel of the suspect or accused.

Rule 52
Public Character of Indictment

Subject to Rule 53, upon confirmation by a Judge of a Trial Chamber, the indictment shall be made public.

Rule 53
Non-disclosure

(A) In exceptional circumstances, a Judge or a Trial Chamber may, in the interests of justice, order the non-disclosure to the public of any documents or information until further order.

(B) When confirming an indictment the Judge may, in consultation with the Prosecutor, order that there be no public disclosure of the indictment until it is served on the accused, or, in the case of joint accused, on all the accused.

(C) A Judge or Trial Chamber may, in consultation with the Prosecutor, also order that there be no disclosure of an indictment, or part thereof, or of all or any part of any particular document or information, if satisfied that the making of such an order is required to give effect to a provision of the Rules, to protect confidential information obtained by the Prosecutor, or is otherwise in the interests of justice.

(D) Notwithstanding paragraphs (A), (B) and (C), the Prosecutor may disclose an indictment or part thereof to the authorities of a State or an appropriate authority or international body where the Prosecutor deems it necessary to prevent an opportunity for securing the possible arrest of an accused from being lost.

Rule 53 *bis*
Service of Indictment

(A) Service of the indictment shall be effected personally on the accused at the time the accused is taken into custody or as soon as reasonably practicable thereafter.

(B) Personal service of an indictment on the accused is effected by giving the accused a copy of the indictment certified in accordance with Rule 47 (G).

Section 2: Orders and Warrants

Rule 54
General Rule

At the request of either party or *propio motu*, a Judge or a Trial Chamber may issue such orders, summonses, subpoenas, warrants and transfer orders as may be necessary for the purposes of an investigation or for the preparation or conduct of the trial.

Rule 54 *bis*
Orders Directed to States for the Production of Documents

(A) A party requesting an order under Rule 54 that a State produce documents or information shall apply in writing to the relevant Judge or Trial Chamber and shall:

(i) identify as far as possible the documents or information to which the application relates;

(ii) indicate how they are relevant to any matter in issue before the Judge or Trial Chamber and necessary for a fair determination of that matter; and

(iii) explain the steps that have been taken by the applicant to secure the State's assistance.

(B) The Judge or Trial Chamber may reject an application under paragraph (A) in limine if satisfied that:

(i) the documents or information are not relevant to any matter in issue in the proceedings before them or are not necessary for a fair determination of any such matter; or

(ii) no reasonable steps have been taken by the applicant to obtain the documents or information from the State.

(C) (i) A decision by a Judge or a Trial Chamber under paragraph (B) or (E) shall be subject to:

(a) review under Rule 108 *bis*; or

(b) appeal.

(ii) An appeal under paragraph (i) shall be filed within seven days of filing of the impugned decision. Where such decision is rendered orally, this time-limit shall run from the date of the oral decision, unless

(a) the party challenging the decision was not present or represented when the decision was pronounced, in which case the time-limit shall run from the date on which the challenging party is notified of the oral decision; or

(b) the Trial Chamber has indicated that a written decision will follow, in which case the time-limit shall run from filing of the written decision.

(D) (i) Except in cases where a decision has been taken pursuant to paragraph (B) or paragraph (E), the State concerned shall be given notice of the application, and not less than fifteen days' notice of the hearing of the application, at which the State shall have an opportunity to be heard.

(ii) Except in cases where the Judge or Trial Chamber determines otherwise, only the party making the application and the State concerned shall have the right to be heard.

(E) If, having regard to all circumstances, the Judge or Trial Chamber has good reasons for so doing, the Judge or Trial Chamber may make an order to which this Rule applies without giving the State concerned notice or the opportunity to be heard under paragraph (D), and the following provisions shall apply to such an order:

(i) the order shall be served on the State concerned;

(ii) subject to paragraph (iv), the order shall not have effect until fifteen days after such service;

(iii) a State may, within fifteen days of service of the order, apply by notice to the Judge or Trial Chamber to have the order set aside, on the grounds that disclosure would prejudice national security interests. Paragraph (F) shall apply to such a notice as it does to a notice of objection

(iv) where notice is given under paragraph (iii), the order shall thereupon be stayed until the decision on the application;

(v) paragraphs (F) and (G) shall apply to the determination of an application made pursuant to paragraph (iii) as they do to the determination of an application of which notice is given pursuant to paragraph (D)

(vi) the State and the party who applied for the order shall, subject to any special measures made pursuant to a request under paragraphs (F) or (G), have an opportunity to be heard at the hearing of an application made pursuant to paragraph (E)(iii) of this Rule.

(F) The State, if it raises an objection pursuant to paragraph (D), on the grounds that disclosure would prejudice its national security interests, shall file a notice of objection not less than five days before the date fixed for the hearing, specifying the grounds of objection. In its notice of objection the State:

(i) shall identify, as far as possible, the basis upon which it claims that its national security interests will be prejudiced; and

(ii) may request the Judge or Trial Chamber to direct that appropriate protective measures be made for the hearing of the objection, including in particular:

(a) hearing the objection in camera and ex parte;

(b) allowing documents to be submitted in redacted form, accompanied by an affidavit signed by a senior State official explaining the reasons for the redaction;

(c) ordering that no transcripts be made of the hearing and that documents not further required by the Tribunal be returned directly to the State without being filed with the Registry or otherwise retained.

(G) With regard to the procedure under paragraph (F) above, the Judge or Trial Chamber may order the following protective measures for the hearing of the objection:

(i) the designation of a single Judge from a Chamber to examine the documents or hear submissions; and/or

(ii) that the State be allowed to provide its own interpreters for the hearing and its own translations of sensitive documents.

(H) Rejection of an application made under this Rule shall not preclude a subsequent application by the requesting party in respect of the same documents or information if new circumstances arise.

(I) An order under this Rule may provide for the documents or information in question to be produced by the State under appropriate arrangements to protect its interests, which may include those arrangements specified in paragraphs (F)(ii) or (G).

Rule 55
Execution of Arrest Warrants

(A) A warrant of arrest shall be signed by a permanent Judge. It shall include an order for the prompt transfer of the accused to the Tribunal upon the arrest of the accused.

(B) The original warrant shall be retained by the Registrar, who shall prepare certified copies bearing the seal of the Tribunal.

(C) Each certified copy shall be accompanied by a copy of the indictment certified in accordance with Rule 47(G) and a statement of the rights of the accused set forth in Article 21 of the Statute, and in Rules 42 and 43 mutatis mutandis. If the accused does not understand either of the official languages of the Tribunal and if the language understood by the accused is known to the Registrar, each certified copy of the warrant of arrest shall also be accompanied by a translation of the statement of the rights of the accused in that language.

(D) Subject to any order of a Judge or Chamber, the Registrar may transmit a certified copy of a warrant of arrest to the person or authorities to which it is addressed, including the national authorities of a State in whose territory or under whose jurisdiction the accused resides, or was last known to be, or is believed by the Registrar to be likely to be found.

(E) The Registrar shall instruct the person or authorities to which a warrant is transmitted that at the time of arrest the indictment and the statement of the rights of the accused be read to the accused in a language that he or she understands and that the accused be cautioned in that language that the accused has the right to remain silent, and that any statement he or she makes shall be recorded and may be used in evidence.

(F) Notwithstanding paragraph (E), if at the time of arrest the accused is served with, or with a translation of, the indictment and the statement of rights of the accused in a language that the accused understands and is able to read, these need not be read to the accused at the time of arrest.

(G) When an arrest warrant issued by the Tribunal is executed by the authorities of a State, or an appropriate authority or international body, a member of the Office of the Prosecutor may be present as from the time of the arrest.

Rule 56
Cooperation of States

The State to which a warrant of arrest or a transfer order for a witness is transmitted shall act promptly and with all due diligence to ensure proper and effective execution thereof, in accordance with Article 29 of the Statute.

Rule 57
Procedure after Arrest

Upon arrest, the accused shall be detained by the State concerned which shall promptly notify the Registrar. The transfer of the accused to the seat of the Tribunal shall be arranged between the State authorities concerned, the authorities of the host country and the Registrar.

Rule 58
National Extradition Provisions

The obligations laid down in Article 29 of the Statute shall prevail over any legal impediment to the surrender or transfer of the accused or of a witness to the Tribunal which may exist under the national law or extradition treaties of the State concerned.

Rule 59
Failure to Execute a Warrant or Transfer Order

(A) Where the State to which a warrant of arrest or transfer order has been transmitted has been unable to execute the warrant, it shall report forthwith its inability to the Registrar, and the reasons therefor.

(B) If, within a reasonable time after the warrant of arrest or transfer order has been transmitted to the State, no report is made on action taken, this shall be deemed a failure to execute the warrant of arrest or transfer order and the Tribunal, through the President, may notify the Security Council accordingly.

Rule 59 *bis*
Transmission of Arrest Warrants

(A) Notwithstanding Rules 55 to 59, on the order of a permanent Judge, the Registrar shall transmit to an appropriate authority or international body or the Prosecutor a copy of a warrant for the arrest of an accused, on such terms as the Judge may determine, together with an order for the prompt transfer of the accused to the Tribunal in the event that the accused be taken into custody by that authority or international body or the Prosecutor.

(B) At the time of being taken into custody an accused shall be informed immediately, in a language the accused understands, of the charges against him or her and of the fact that he or she is being transferred to the Tribunal. Upon such transfer, the indictment and a statement of the rights of the accused shall be read to the accused and the accused shall be cautioned in such a language.

(C) Notwithstanding paragraph (B), the indictment and statement of rights of the accused need not be read to the accused if the accused is served with these, or with a translation of these, in a language the accused understands and is able to read.

Rule 60
Advertisement of Indictment

At the request of the Prosecutor, a form of advertisement shall be transmitted by the Registrar to the national authorities of any State or States, for publication in newspapers or for broadcast via radio and television, notifying publicly the existence of an indictment and calling upon the accused to surrender to the Tribunal and inviting any person with information as to the whereabouts of the accused to communicate that information to the Tribunal.

Rule 61
Procedure in Case of Failure to Execute a Warrant

(A) If, within a reasonable time, a warrant of arrest has not been executed, and personal service of the indictment has consequently not been effected, the Judge who confirmed the indictment shall invite the Prosecutor to report on the measures taken. When the Judge is satisfied that:

(i) the Registrar and the Prosecutor have taken all reasonable steps to secure the arrest of the accused, including recourse to the appropriate authorities of the State in whose territory or under whose jurisdiction and control the person to be served resides or was last known to them to be; and

(ii) if the whereabouts of the accused are unknown, the Prosecutor and the Registrar have taken all reasonable steps to ascertain those whereabouts, including by seeking publication of advertisements pursuant to Rule 60, the Judge shall order that the indictment be submitted by the Prosecutor to the Trial Chamber of which the Judge is a member.

(B) Upon obtaining such an order the Prosecutor shall submit the indictment to the Trial Chamber in open court, together with all the evidence that was before the Judge who initially confirmed the indictment. The Prosecutor may also call before the Trial Chamber and examine any witness whose statement has been submitted to the confirming Judge. In addition, the Trial Chamber may request the Prosecutor to call any other witness whose statement has been submitted to the confirming Judge.

(C) If the Trial Chamber is satisfied on that evidence, together with such additional evidence as the Prosecutor may tender, that there are reasonable grounds for believing that the accused has committed all or any of the crimes charged in the indictment, it shall so determine. The Trial Chamber shall have the relevant parts of the indictment read out by the Prosecutor together with an account of the efforts to effect service referred to in paragraph (A) above.

(D) The Trial Chamber shall also issue an international arrest warrant in respect of the accused which shall be transmitted to all States. Upon request by the Prosecutor or *proprio motu*, after having heard the Prosecutor, the Trial Chamber may order a State or States to adopt provisional measures to freeze the assets of the accused, without prejudice to the rights of third parties.

(E) If the Prosecutor satisfies the Trial Chamber that the failure to effect personal service was due in whole or in part to a failure or refusal of a State to cooperate with the Tribunal in accordance with Article 29 of the Statute, the Trial Chamber shall so certify. After consulting the Presiding Judges of the Chambers, the President shall notify the Security Council thereof in such manner as the President thinks fit.

Section 3: Preliminary Proceedings

Rule 62
Initial Appearance of Accused

(A) Upon transfer of an accused to the seat of the Tribunal, the President shall forthwith assign the case to a Trial Chamber. The accused shall be brought before that Trial Chamber or a Judge thereof without delay, and shall be formally charged. The Trial Chamber or the Judge shall:

(i) satisfy itself, himself or herself that the right of the accused to counsel is respected;

(ii) read or have the indictment read to the accused in a language the accused understands, and satisfy itself, himself or herself that the accused understands the indictment;

(iii) inform the accused that, within thirty days of the initial appearance, he or she will be called upon to enter a plea of guilty or not guilty on each count but that, should the accused so request, he or she may immediately enter a plea of guilty or not guilty on one or more count;

(iv) if the accused fails to enter a plea at the initial or any further appearance, enter a plea of not guilty on the accused's behalf;

(v) in case of a plea of not guilty, instruct the Registrar to set a date for trial;

(vi) in case of a plea of guilty:

(a) if before the Trial Chamber, act in accordance with Rule 62 *bis*, or

(b) if before a Judge, refer the plea to the Trial Chamber so that it may act in accordance with Rule 62 *bis*;

(vii) instruct the Registrar to set such other dates as appropriate.

(B) Where the interests of justice so require, the Registrar may assign a duty counsel as within Rule 45(ii) to represent the accused at the initial appearance. Such assignments shall be treated in accordance with the relevant provisions of the Directive referred to in Rule 45(A).

Rule 62 *bis*
Guilty Pleas

If an accused pleads guilty in accordance with Rule 62 (vi), or requests to change his or her plea to guilty and the Trial Chamber is satisfied that:

(i) the guilty plea has been made voluntarily;

(ii) the guilty plea is informed;

(iii) the guilty plea is not equivocal; and

(iv) there is a sufficient factual basis for the crime and the accused's participation in it, either on the basis of independent indicia or on lack of any material disagreement between the parties about the facts of the case, the Trial Chamber may enter a finding of guilt and instruct the Registrar to set a date for the sentencing hearing.

Rule 62 *ter*
Plea Agreement Procedure

(A) The Prosecutor and the defence may agree that, upon the accused entering a plea of guilty to the indictment or to one or more counts of the indictment, the Prosecutor shall do one or more of the following before the Trial Chamber:

(i) apply to amend the indictment accordingly;

(ii) submit that a specific sentence or sentencing range is appropriate;

(iii) not oppose a request by the accused for a particular sentence or sentencing range.

(B) The Trial Chamber shall not be bound by any agreement specified in paragraph (A).

(C) If a plea agreement has been reached by the parties, the Trial Chamber shall require the disclosure of the agreement in open session or, on showing of good cause, in closed session, at the time the accused pleads guilty in accordance with Rule 62 (vi), or requests to change his or her plea to guilty.

Rule 63
Questioning of Accused

(A) Questioning by the Prosecutor of an accused, including after the initial appearance, shall not proceed without the presence of counsel unless the accused has voluntarily and expressly agreed to proceed without counsel present. If the accused subsequently expresses a desire to have counsel, questioning shall thereupon cease, and shall only resume when the accused's counsel is present.

(B) The questioning, including any waiver of the right to counsel, shall be audio-recorded or video-recorded in accordance with the procedure provided for in Rule 43. The Prosecutor shall at the beginning of the questioning caution the accused in accordance with Rule 42(A)(iii).

Rule 64
Detention on Remand

Upon being transferred to the seat of the Tribunal, the accused shall be detained in facilities provided by the host country, or by another country. In exceptional circumstances, the accused may be held in facilities outside of the host country. The President may, on the application of a party, request modification of the conditions of detention of an accused.

Rule 65
Provisional Release

(A) Once detained, an accused may not be released except upon an order of a Chamber.

(B) Release may be ordered by a Trial Chamber only after giving the host country and the State to which the accused seeks to be released the opportunity to be heard and only if it is satisfied that the accused will appear for trial and, if released, will not pose a danger to any victim, witness or other person.

(C) The Trial Chamber may impose such conditions upon the release of the accused as it may determine appropriate, including the execution of a bail bond and the observance of such conditions as are necessary to ensure the presence of the accused for trial and the protection of others.

(D) Any decision rendered under this Rule by a Trial Chamber shall be subject to appeal. Subject to paragraph (F) below, an appeal shall be filed within seven days of filing of the impugned decision. Where such decision is rendered orally, the appeal shall be filed within seven days of the oral decision, unless

(i) the party challenging the decision was not present or represented when the decision was pronounced, in which case the time-limit shall run from the date on which the challenging party is notified of the oral decision; or

(ii) the Trial Chamber has indicated that a written decision will follow, in which case, the time-limit shall run from filing of the written decision.

(E) The Prosecutor may apply for a stay of a decision by the Trial Chamber to release an accused on the basis that the Prosecutor intends to appeal the decision, and shall make such an application at the time of filing his or her response to the initial application for provisional release by the accused.

(F) Where the Trial Chamber grants a stay of its decision to release an accused, the Prosecutor shall file his or her appeal not later than one day from the rendering of that decision.

(G) Where the Trial Chamber orders a stay of its decision to release the accused pending an appeal by the Prosecutor, the accused shall not be released until either:

(i) the time-limit for filing of an appeal by the Prosecutor has expired, and no such appeal is filed;

(ii) the Appeals Chamber dismisses the appeal; or

(iii) the Appeals Chamber otherwise orders.

(H) If necessary, the Trial Chamber may issue a warrant of arrest to secure the presence of an accused who has been released or is for any other reason at liberty. The provisions of Section 2 of Part Five shall apply mutatis mutandis.

(I) Without prejudice to the provisions of Rule 107, the Appeals Chamber may grant provisional release to convicted persons pending an appeal or for a fixed period if it is satisfied that:

(i) the appellant, if released, will either appear at the hearing of the appeal or will surrender into detention at the conclusion of the fixed period, as the case may be;

(ii) the appellant, if released, will not pose a danger to any victim, witness or other person, and

(iii) special circumstances exist warranting such release.

The provisions of paragraphs (C) and (H) shall apply mutatis mutandis.

Rule 65 *bis*
Status Conferences

(A) A Trial Chamber or a Trial Chamber Judge shall convene a status conference within one hundred and twenty days of the initial appearance of the accused and thereafter within one hundred and twenty days after the last status conference:

(i) to organize exchanges between the parties so as to ensure expeditious preparation for trial;

(ii) to review the status of his or her case and to allow the accused the opportunity to raise issues in relation thereto, including the mental and physical condition of the accused.

(B) The Appeals Chamber or an Appeals Chamber Judge shall convene a status conference, within one hundred and twenty days of the filing of a notice of appeal and thereafter within one hundred and twenty days after the last status conference, to allow any person in custody pending appeal the opportunity to raise issues in relation thereto, including the mental and physical condition of that person.

(C) With the written consent of the accused, given after receiving advice from his counsel, a status conference under this Rule may be conducted

(i) in his presence, but with his counsel participating either via tele-conference or video-conference; or

(ii) in Chambers in his absence, but with his participation via tele-conference if he so wishes and/or participation of his counsel via tele-conference or video-conference.

Rule 65 *ter*
Pre-Trial Judge

(A) The Presiding Judge of the Trial Chamber shall, no later than seven days after the initial appearance of the accused, designate from among its members a Judge responsible for the pre-trial proceedings (hereinafter "pre-trial Judge").

(B) The pre-trial Judge shall, under the authority and supervision of the Trial Chamber seised of the case, coordinate communication between the parties during the pre-trial phase. The pre-rail Judge shall ensure that the proceedings are not unduly delayed and shall take any measure necessary to prepare the case for a fair and expeditious trial.

(C) The pre-trial Judge shall be entrusted with all of the pre-trial functions set forth in Rule 66, Rule 67, Rule 73 *bis* and Rule 73 *ter*, and with all or part of the functions set forth in Rule 73.

(D) (i) The pre-trial Judge may be assisted in the performance of his or her duties by one of the Senior Legal Officers assigned to Chambers.

(ii) The pre-trial Judge shall establish a work plan indicating, in general terms, the obligations that the parties are required to meet pursuant to this Rule and the dates by which these obligations must be fulfilled.

(iii) Acting under the supervision of the pre-trial Judge, the Senior Legal Officer shall oversee the implementation of the work plan and shall keep the pre-trial Judge informed of the progress of the discussions between and with the parties and, in particular, of any potential difficulty. He or she shall present the pre-trial Judge with reports as appropriate and shall communicate to the parties, without delay, any observations and decisions made by the pre-trial Judge.

(iv) The pre-trial Judge shall order the parties to meet to discuss issues related to the preparation of the case, in particular, so that the Prosecutor can meet his or her obligations pursuant to paragraphs (E) (i) to (iii) of this Rule and for the defence to meet its obligations pursuant to paragraph (G) of this Rule and of Rule 73 *ter*.

(v) Such meetings are held inter partes or, at his or her request, with the Senior Legal Officer and one or more of the parties. The Senior Legal Officer ensures that the obligations set out in paragraphs (E) (i) to (iii) of this Rule and, at the appropriate time, that the obligations in paragraph (G) and Rule 73 ter, are satisfied in accordance with the work plan set by the pre-trial Judge.

(vi) The presence of the accused is not necessary for meetings convened by the Senior Legal Officer.

(vii) The Senior Legal Officer may be assisted by a representative of the Registry in the performance of his or her duties pursuant to this Rule and may require a transcript to be made.

(E) Once any existing preliminary motions filed within the time-limit provided by Rule 72 are disposed of, the pre-trial Judge shall order the Prosecutor, upon the report of the Senior Legal Officer, and within a time-limit set by the pre-trial Judge and not less than six weeks before the Pre-Trial Conference required by Rule 73 *bis*, to file the following:

(i) the final version of the Prosecutor's pre-trial brief including, for each count, a summary of the evidence which the Prosecutor intends to bring regarding the commission of the alleged crime and the form of responsibility incurred by the accused; this brief shall include any admissions by the parties and a statement of matters which are not in dispute; as well as a statement of contested matters of fact and law;

(ii) the list of witnesses the Prosecutor intends to call with:

(a) the name or pseudonym of each witness;

(b) a summary of the facts on which each witness will testify;

(c) the points in the indictment as to which each witness will testify, including specific references to counts and relevant paragraphs in the indictment;

(d) the total number of witnesses and the number of witnesses who will testify against each accused and on each count;

(e) an indication of whether the witness will testify in person or pursuant to Rule 92 *bis* by way of written statement or use of a transcript of testimony from other proceedings before the Tribunal; and

(f) the estimated length of time required for each witness and the total time estimated for presentation of the Prosecutor's case.

(iii) the list of exhibits the Prosecutor intends to offer stating where possible whether the defence has any objection as to authenticity. The Prosecutor shall serve on the defence copies of the exhibits so listed.

(F) After the submission by the Prosecutor of the items mentioned in paragraph (E), the pre-trial Judge shall order the defence, within a time-limit set by the pre-trial Judge, and not later than three weeks before the Pre-Trial Conference, to file a pre-trial brief addressing the factual and legal issues, and including a written statement setting out:

(i) in general terms, the nature of the accused's defence;

(ii) the matters with which the accused takes issue in the Prosecutor's pre-trial brief; and

(iii) in the case of each such matter, the reason why the accused takes issue with it.

(G) After the close of the Prosecutor's case and before the commencement of the defence case, the pre-trial Judge shall order the defence to file the following:

(i) a list of witnesses the defence intends to call with:

(a) the name or pseudonym of each witness;

(b) a summary of the facts on which each witness will testify;

(c) the points in the indictment as to which each witness will testify;

(d) the total number of witnesses and the number of witnesses who will testify for each accused and on each count;

(e) an indication of whether the witness will testify in person or pursuant to Rule 92 *bis* by way of written statement or use of a transcript of testimony from other proceedings before the Tribunal; and

(f) the estimated length of time required for each witness and the total time estimated for presentation of the defence case; and

(ii) a list of exhibits the defence intends to offer in its case, stating where possible whether the Prosecutor has any objection as to authenticity. The defence shall serve on the Prosecutor copies of the exhibits so listed.

(H) The pre-trial Judge shall record the points of agreement and disagreement on matters of law and fact. In this connection, he or she may order the parties to file written submissions with either the pre-trial Judge or the Trial Chamber.

(I) In order to perform his or her functions, the pre-trial Judge may *proprio motu*, where appropriate, hear the parties without the accused being present. The pre-trial Judge may hear the parties in his or her private room, in which case minutes of the meeting shall be taken by a representative of the Registry.

(J) The pre-trial Judge shall keep the Trial Chamber regularly informed, particularly where issues are in dispute and may refer such disputes to the Trial Chamber.

(K) The pre-trial Judge may set a time for the making of pre-trial motions and, if required, any hearing thereon. A motion made before trial shall be determined before trial unless the Judge, for good cause, orders that it be deferred for determination at trial. Failure by a party to raise objections or to make requests which can be made prior to trial at the time set by the Judge shall constitute waiver thereof, but the Judge for cause may grant relief from the waiver.

(L) (i) After the filings by the Prosecutor pursuant to paragraph (E), the pre-trial Judge shall submit to the Trial Chamber a complete file consisting of all the filings of the parties, transcripts of status conferences and minutes of meetings held in the performance of his or her functions pursuant to this Rule.

(ii) The pre-trial Judge shall submit a second file to the Trial Chamber after the defence filings pursuant to paragraph (G).

(M) The Trial Chamber may *proprio motu* exercise any of the functions of the pre-trial Judge.

(N) Upon a report of the pre-trial Judge, the Trial Chamber shall decide, should the case arise, on sanctions to be imposed on a party which fails to perform its obligations pursuant to the present Rule. Such sanctions may include the exclusion of testimonial or documentary evidence.

Section 4: Production of Evidence

Rule 66
Disclosure by the Prosecutor

(A) Subject to the provisions of Rules 53 and 69, the Prosecutor shall make available to the defence in a language which the accused understands

(i) within thirty days of the initial appearance of the accused, copies of the supporting material which accompanied the indictment when confirmation was sought as well as all prior statements obtained by the Prosecutor from the accused; and

(ii) within the time-limit prescribed by the Trial Chamber or by the pre-trial Judge appointed pursuant to Rule 65 *ter*, copies of the statements of all witnesses whom the Prosecutor intends to call to testify at trial, and copies of all written statements taken in accordance with Rule 92 *bis*; copies of the statements of additional prosecution witnesses shall be made available to the defence when a decision is made to call those witnesses.

(B) The Prosecutor shall, on request, permit the defence to inspect any books, documents, photographs and tangible objects in the Prosecutor's custody or control, which are material to the preparation of the defence, or are intended for use by the Prosecutor as evidence at trial or were obtained from or belonged to the accused.

(C) Where information is in the possession of the Prosecutor, the disclosure of which may prejudice further or ongoing investigations, or for any other reasons may be contrary to the public interest or affect the security interests of any State, the Prosecutor may apply to the Trial Chamber sitting in camera to be relieved from an obligation under the Rules to disclose that information. When making such application the Prosecutor shall provide the Trial Chamber (but only the Trial Chamber) with the information that is sought to be kept confidential.

Rule 67
Additional Disclosure

(A) Within the time-limit prescribed by the Trial Chamber or by the pre-trial Judge appointed pursuant to Rule 65 *ter*:

(i) the defence shall notify the Prosecutor of its intent to offer:

(a) the defence of alibi; in which case the notification shall specify the place or places at which the accused claims to have been present at the time of the alleged crime and the names and addresses of witnesses and any other evidence upon which the accused intends to rely to establish the alibi;

(b) any special defence, including that of diminished or lack of mental responsibility; in which case the notification shall specify the names and addresses of witnesses and any other evidence upon which the accused intends to rely to establish the special defence; and

(ii) the Prosecutor shall notify the defence of the names of the witnesses that the Prosecutor intends to call in rebuttal of any defence plea of which the Prosecutor has received notice in accordance with paragraph (i) above.

(B) Failure of the defence to provide notice under this Rule shall not limit the right of the accused to testify on the above defences.

(C) If either party discovers additional evidence or material which should have been disclosed earlier pursuant to the Rules, that party shall immediately disclose that evidence or material to the other party and the Trial Chamber.

Rule 68
Disclosure of Exculpatory and Other Relevant Material

Subject to the provisions of Rule 70,

(i) the Prosecutor shall, as soon as practicable, disclose to the Defence any material which in the actual knowledge of the Prosecutor may suggest the innocence or mitigate the guilt of the accused or affect the credibility of Prosecution evidence.

(ii) without prejudice to paragraph (i), the Prosecutor shall make available to the defence, in electronic form, collections of relevant material held by the Prosecutor, together with appropriate computer software with which the defence can search such collections electronically.

(iii) the Prosecutor shall take reasonable steps, if confidential information is provided to the Prosecutor by a person or entity under Rule 70 (B) and contains material referred to in paragraph (i) above, to obtain the consent of the provider to disclosure of that material, or the fact of its existence, to the accused.

(iv) the Prosecutor shall apply to the Chamber sitting in camera to be relieved from an obligation under paragraph (i) to disclose information in the possession of the Prosecutor, if its disclosure may prejudice further or ongoing investigations, or for any other reason may be contrary to the public interest or affect the security interests of any State, and when making such application, the Prosecutor shall provide the Trial Chamber (but only the Trial Chamber) with the information that is sought to be kept confidential.

(v) notwithstanding the completion of the trial and any subsequent appeal, the Prosecutor shall disclose to the other party any material referred to in paragraph (i) above.

Rule 68 *bis*
Failure to Comply with Disclosure Obligations

The pre-trial Judge or the Trial Chamber may decide *proprio motu*, or at the request of either party, on sanctions to be imposed on a party which fails to perform its disclosure obligations pursuant to the Rules.

Rule 69
Protection of Victims and Witnesses

(A) In exceptional circumstances, the Prosecutor may apply to a Judge or Trial Chamber to order the non-disclosure of the identity of a victim or witness who may be in danger or at risk until such person is brought under the protection of the Tribunal.

(B) In the determination of protective measures for victims and witnesses, the Judge or Trial Chamber may consult the Victims and Witnesses Section.

(C) Subject to Rule 75, the identity of the victim or witness shall be disclosed in sufficient time prior to the trial to allow adequate time for preparation of the defence.

Rule 70
Matters not Subject to Disclosure

(A) Notwithstanding the provisions of Rules 66 and 67, reports, memoranda, or other internal documents prepared by a party, its assistants or representatives in connection with the investigation or preparation of the case, are not subject to disclosure or notification under those Rules.

(B) If the Prosecutor is in possession of information which has been provided to the Prosecutor on a confidential basis and which has been used solely for the purpose of generating new evidence, that initial information and its origin shall not be disclosed by the Prosecutor without the consent of the person or entity providing the initial information and shall in any event not be given in evidence without prior disclosure to the accused.

(C) If, after obtaining the consent of the person or entity providing information under this Rule, the Prosecutor elects to present as evidence any testimony, document or other material so provided, the Trial Chamber, notwithstanding Rule 98, may not order either party to produce additional evidence received from the person or entity providing the initial information, nor may the Trial Chamber for the purpose of obtaining such additional evidence itself summon that person or a representative of that entity as a witness or order their attendance. A Trial Chamber may not use its power to order the attendance of witnesses or to require production of documents in order to compel the production of such additional evidence.

(D) If the Prosecutor calls a witness to introduce in evidence any information provided under this Rule, the Trial Chamber may not compel that witness to answer any question relating to the information or its origin, if the witness declines to answer on grounds of confidentiality.

(E) The right of the accused to challenge the evidence presented by the Prosecution shall remain unaffected subject only to the limitations contained in paragraphs (C) and (D).

(F) The Trial Chamber may order upon an application by the accused or defence counsel that, in the interests of justice, the provisions of this Rule shall apply mutatis mutandis to specific information in the possession of the accused.

(G) Nothing in paragraph (C) or (D) above shall affect a Trial Chamber's power under Rule 89 (D) to exclude evidence if its probative value is substantially outweighed by the need to ensure a fair trial.

Section 5: Depositions

Rule 71
Depositions

(A) Where it is in the interests of justice to do so, a Trial Chamber may order, *proprio motu* or at the request of a party, that a deposition be taken for use at trial, whether or not the person whose deposition is sought is able physically to appear before the Tribunal to give evidence. The Trial Chamber shall appoint a Presiding Officer for that purpose.

(B) The motion for the taking of a deposition shall indicate the name and whereabouts of the person whose deposition is sought, the date and place at which the deposition is to be taken, a statement of the matters on which the person is to be examined, and of the circumstances justifying the taking of the deposition.

(C) If the motion is granted, the party at whose request the deposition is to be taken shall give reasonable notice to the other party, who shall have the right to attend the taking of the deposition and cross-examine the person whose deposition is being taken.

(D) Deposition evidence may be taken either at or away from the seat of the Tribunal, and it may also be given by means of a video-conference.

(E) The Presiding Officer shall ensure that the deposition is taken in accordance with the Rules and that a record is made of the deposition, including cross-examination and objections raised by either party for decision by the Trial Chamber. The Presiding Officer shall transmit the record to the Trial Chamber.

Rule 71 *bis*
Testimony by Video-Conference Link

At the request of either party, a Trial Chamber may, in the interests of justice, order that testimony be received via video-conference link.

Section 6: Motions

Rule 72
Preliminary Motions

(A) Preliminary motions, being motions which

(i) challenge jurisdiction;

(ii) allege defects in the form of the indictment;

(iii) seek the severance of counts joined in one indictment under Rule 49 or seek separate trials under Rule 82 (B); or

(iv) raise objections based on the refusal of a request for assignment of counsel made under Rule 45 (C)

shall be in writing and be brought not later than thirty days after disclosure by the Prosecutor to the defence of all material and statements referred to in Rule 66 (A)(i) and shall be disposed of not later than sixty days after they were filed and before the commencement of the opening statements provided for in Rule 84.

(B) Decisions on preliminary motions are without interlocutory appeal save

(i) in the case of motions challenging jurisdiction

(ii) in other cases where certification has been granted by the Trial Chamber, which may grant such certification if the decision involves an issue that would significantly affect the fair and expeditious conduct of the proceedings or the outcome of the trial, and for which, in the opinion of the Trial Chamber, an immediate resolution by the Appeals Chamber may materially advance the proceedings.

(C) Appeals under paragraph (B)(i) shall be filed within fifteen days and requests for certification under paragraph (B)(ii) shall be filed within seven days of filing of the impugned decision. Where such decision is rendered orally, this time-limit shall run from the date of the oral decision, unless

(i) the party challenging the decision was not present or represented when the decision was pronounced, in which case the time-limit shall run from the date on which the challenging party is notified of the oral decision; or

(ii) the Trial Chamber has indicated that a written decision will follow, in which case, the time-limit shall run from filing of the written decision.

If certification is given, a party shall appeal to the Appeals Chamber within seven days of the filing of the decision to certify.

(D) For the purpose of paragraphs (A)(i) and (B)(i), a motion challenging jurisdiction refers exclusively to a motion which challenges an indictment on the ground that it does not relate to:

(i) any of the persons indicated in Articles 1, 6, 7 and 9 of the Statute;

(ii) the territories indicated in Articles 1, 8 and 9 of the Statute;

(iii) the period indicated in Articles 1, 8 and 9 of the Statute;

(iv) any of the violations indicated in Articles 2, 3, 4, 5 and 7 of the Statute.

Rule 73
Other Motions

(A) After a case is assigned to a Trial Chamber, either party may at any time move before the Chamber by way of motion, not being a preliminary motion, for appropriate ruling or relief. Such motions may be written or oral, at the discretion of the Trial Chamber.

(B) Decisions on all motions are without interlocutory appeal save with certification by the Trial Chamber, which may grant such certification if the decision involves an issue that would significantly affect the fair and expeditious conduct of the proceedings or the outcome of the trial, and for which, in the opinion of the Trial Chamber, an immediate resolution by the Appeals Chamber may materially advance the proceedings.

(C) Requests for certification shall be filed within seven days of the filing of the impugned decision. Where such decision is rendered orally, this time-limit shall run from the date of the oral decision, unless

(i) the party challenging the decision was not present or represented when the decision was pronounced, in which case the time-limit shall run from the date on which the challenging party is notified of the oral decision; or

(ii) the Trial Chamber has indicated that a written decision will follow, in which case the time-limit shall run from filing of the written decision.

If certification is given, a party shall appeal to the Appeals Chamber within seven days of the filing of the decision to certify.

(D) Irrespective of any sanctions which may be imposed under Rule 46 (A), when a Chamber finds that a motion is frivolous or is an abuse of process, the Registrar shall withhold payment of fees associated with the production of that motion and/ or costs thereof.

Section 7: Conferences

Rule 73 *bis*
Pre-Trial Conference

(A) Prior to the commencement of the trial, the Trial Chamber shall hold a Pre-Trial Conference.

(B) In the light of the file submitted to the Trial Chamber by the pre-trial Judge pursuant to Rule 65 *ter* (L)(i), the Trial Chamber may call upon the Prosecutor to shorten the estimated length of the examination-in-chief for some witnesses.

(C) In the light of the file submitted to the Trial Chamber by the pre-trial Judge pursuant to Rule 65 *ter* (L)(i), the Trial Chamber, after having heard the Prosecutor, shall determine

(i) the number of witnesses the Prosecutor may call; and

(ii) the time available to the Prosecutor for presenting evidence.

(D) After having heard the Prosecutor, the Trial Chamber may fix a number of crime sites or incidents comprised in one or more of the charges in respect of which evidence may be presented by the Prosecutor which, having regard to all the relevant circumstances, including the crimes charged in the indictment, their classification and nature, the places where they are alleged to have been committed, their scale and the victims of the crimes, are reasonably representative of the crimes charged.

(E) After commencement of the trial, the Prosecutor may file a motion to vary the decision as to the number of crime sites or incidents in respect of which evidence may be presented or the number of witnesses that are to be called or for additional time to present evidence and the Trial Chamber may grant the Prosecutor's request if satisfied that this is in the interests of justice.

Rule 73 *ter*
Pre-Defence Conference

(A) Prior to the commencement by the defence of its case the Trial Chamber may hold a Conference.

(B) In the light of the file submitted to the Trial Chamber by the pre-trial Judge pursuant to Rule 65 *ter* (L)(ii), the Trial Chamber may call upon the defence to shorten the estimated length of the examination-in-chief for some witnesses.

(C) In th light of the file submitted to the Trial Chamber by the pre-trial Judge pursuant to Rule 65 *ter* (L)(ii), the trial Chamber, after having heard the defence, shall set the number of witnesses the defence may call.

(D) After commencement of the defence case, the defence may, if it considers it to be in the interests of justice, file a motion to reinstate the list of witnesses or to vary the decision as to which witnesses are to be called.

(E) After having heard the defence, the Trial Chamber shall determine the time available to the defence for presenting evidence.

(F) During a trial, the Trial Chamber may grant a defence request for additional time to present evidence if this is in the interests of justice.

Part Six
PROCEEDINGS BEFORE TRIAL CHAMBERS

Section 1: General Provisions

Rule 74
Amicus Curiae

A Chamber may, if it considers it desirable for the proper determination of the case, invite or grant leave to a State, organization or person to appear before it and make submissions on any issue specified by the Chamber.

Rule 74 *bis*
Medical Examination of the Accused

A Trial Chamber may, *proprio motu* or at the request of a party, order a medical, psychiatric or psychological examination of the accused. In such a case, unless the Trial Chamber otherwise orders, the Registrar shall entrust this task to one or several experts whose names appear on a list previously drawn up by the Registry and approved by the Bureau.

Rule 75
Measures for the Protection of Victims and Witnesses

(A) A Judge or a Chamber may, *proprio motu* or at the request of either party, or of the victim or witness concerned, or of the Victims and Witnesses Section, order appropriate measures for the privacy and protection of victims and witnesses, provided that the measures are consistent with the rights of the accused.

(B) A Chamber may hold an in camera proceeding to determine whether to order:

(i) measures to prevent disclosure to the public or the media of the identity or whereabouts of a victim or a witness, or of persons related to or associated with a victim or witness by such means as:

(a) expunging names and identifying information from the Tribunal's public records;

(b) non-disclosure to the public of any records identifying the victim;

(c) giving of testimony through image- or voice-altering devices or closed circuit television; and

(d) assignment of a pseudonym;

(ii) closed sessions, in accordance with Rule 79;

(iii) appropriate measures to facilitate the testimony of vulnerable victims and witnesses, such as one-way closed circuit television.

(C) The Victims and Witnesses Section shall ensure that the witness has been informed before giving evidence that his or her testimony and his or her identity may be disclosed at a later date in another case, pursuant to Rule 75 (F).

(D) A Chamber shall, whenever necessary, control the manner of questioning to avoid any harassment or intimidation.

(E) When making an order under paragraph (A) above, a Judge or Chamber shall wherever appropriate state in the order whether the transcript of those proceedings relating to the evidence of the witness to whom the measures relate shall be made available for use in other proceedings before the Tribunal.

(F) Once protective measures have been ordered in respect of a victim or witness in any proceedings before the Tribunal (the "first proceedings"), such protective measures:

(i) shall continue to have effect mutatis mutandis in any other proceedings before

the Tribunal (the "second proceedings") unless and until they are rescinded, varied or augmented in accordance with the procedure set out in this Rule; but

(ii) shall not prevent the Prosecutor from discharging any disclosure obligation under the Rules in the second proceedings, provided that the Prosecutor notifies the Defence to whom the disclosure is being made of the nature of the protective measures ordered in the first proceedings.

(G) A party to the second proceedings seeking to rescind, vary or augment protective measures ordered in the first proceedings must apply:

(i) to any Chamber, however constituted, remaining seised of the first proceedings; or

(ii) if no Chamber remains seised of the first proceedings, to the Chamber seised of the second proceedings.

(H) Before determining an application under paragraph (G)(ii) above, the Chamber seised of the second proceedings shall obtain all relevant information from the first proceedings, and shall consult with any Judge who ordered the protective measures in the first proceedings, if that Judge remains a Judge of the Tribunal.

(I) An application to a Chamber to rescind, vary or augment protective measures in respect of a victim or witness may be dealt with either by the Chamber or by a Judge of that Chamber, and any reference in this Rule to "a Chamber" shall include a reference to "a Judge of that Chamber".

Rule 76
Solemn Declaration by Interpreters and Translators

Before performing any duties, an interpreter or a translator shall solemnly declare to do so faithfully, independently, impartially and with full respect for the duty of confidentiality.

Rule 77
Contempt of the Tribunal

(A) The Tribunal in the exercise of its inherent power may hold in contempt those who knowingly and wilfully interfere with its administration of justice, including any person who

(i) being a witness before a Chamber, contumaciously refuses or fails to answer a question;

(ii) discloses information relating to those proceedings in knowing violation of an order of a Chamber;

(iii) without just excuse fails to comply with an order to attend before or produce documents before a Chamber;

(iv) threatens, intimidates, causes any injury or offers a bribe to, or otherwise interferes with, a witness who is giving, has give, or is about to give evidence in proceedings

before a Chamber, or a potential witness; or

(v) threatens, intimidates, offers a bribe to, or otherwise seeks to coerce any other person, with the intention of preventing that other person from complying with an obligation under an order of a Judge or Chamber.

(B) Any incitement or attempt to commit any of the acts punishable under paragraph (A) is punishable as contempt of the Tribunal with the same penalties.

(C) When a Chamber has reason to believe that a person may be in contempt of the Tribunal, it may:

(i) direct the Prosecutor to investigate the matter with a view to the preparation

and submission of an indictment for contempt;

(ii) where the Prosecutor, in the view of the Chamber, has a conflict of interest with respect to the relevant conduct, direct the Registrar to appoint an *amicus curiae* to investigate the matter and report back to the Chamber as to whether there are sufficient grounds for instigating contempt proceedings; or

(iii) initiate proceedings itself.

(D) If the Chamber considers that there are sufficient grounds to proceed against a person for contempt, the Chamber may:

(i) in circumstances described in paragraph (C)(i), direct the Prosecutor to prosecute the matter; or

(ii) in circumstances described in paragraph (C)(ii) or (iii), issue an order in lieu of an indictment and either direct *amicus curiae* to prosecute the matter or prosecute the matter itself.

(E) The rules of procedure and evidence in Parts Four to Eight shall apply mutatis mutandis to proceedings under this Rule.

(F) Any person indicted for or charged with contempt shall, if that person satisfies the criteria for determination of indigence established by the Registrar, be assigned counsel in accordance with Rule 45.

(G) The maximum penalty that may be imposed on a person found to be in contempt of the Tribunal shall be a term of imprisonment not exceeding seven years, or a fine not exceeding 100,000 Euros, or both.

(H) Payment of a fine shall be made to the Registrar to be held in a separate account.

(I) If a counsel is found guilty of contempt of the Tribunal pursuant to this Rule, the Chamber making such finding may also determine that counsel is no longer eligible to represent a suspect or accused before the Tribunal or that such conduct amounts to misconduct of counsel pursuant to Rule 46, or both.

(J) Any decision rendered by a Trial Chamber under this Rule shall be subject to appeal. Notice of appeal shall be filed within fifteen days of filing of the impugned decision. Where such decision is rendered orally, the notice shall be filed within fifteen days of the oral decision, unless

(i) the party challenging the decision was not present or represented when the decision was pronounced, in which case the time-limit shall run from the date on which the challenging party is notified of the oral decision; or

(ii) the Trial Chamber has indicated that a written decision will follow, in which case the time-limit shall run from filing of the written decision.

(K) In the case of decisions under this Rule by the Appeals Chamber sitting as a Chamber of first instance, an appeal may be submitted in writing to the President within fifteen days of the filing of the impugned decision. Such appeal shall be decided by five different Judges as assigned by the President. Where the impugned decision is rendered orally, the appeal shall be filed within fifteen days of the oral decision, unless

(i) the party challenging the decision was not present or represented when the decision was pronounced, in which case the time-limit shall run from the date on which the challenging party is notified of the oral decision; or

(ii) the Appeals Chamber has indicated that a written decision will follow, in which case the time-limit shall run from filing of the written decision.

Rule 77 *bis*
Payment of Fines

(A) In imposing a fine under Rule 77 or Rule 91, a Chamber shall specify the time for its payment.

(B) Where a fine imposed under Rule 77 or Rule 91 is not paid within the time specified, the Chamber imposing the fine may issue an order requiring the person on whom the fine is imposed to appear before, or to respond in writing to, the Tribunal to explain why the fine has not been paid.

(C) After affording the person on whom the fine is imposed an opportunity to be heard, the Chamber may make a decision that appropriate measures be taken, including:

(i) extending the time for payment of the fine;

(ii) requiring the payment of the fine to be made in instalments;

(iii) in consultation with the Registrar, requiring that the moneys owed be deducted from any outstanding fees owing to the person by the Tribunal where the person is a counsel retained by the Tribunal pursuant to the Directive on the Assignment of Defence Counsel;

(iv) converting the whole or part of the fine to a term of imprisonment not exceeding twelve months.

(D) In addition to a decision under paragraph (C), the Chamber may find the person in contempt of the Tribunal and impose a new penalty applying Rule 77 (G), if that person was able to pay the fine within the specified time and has wilfully failed to do so. This penalty for contempt of the Tribunal shall be additional to the original fine imposed.

(E) The Chamber may, if necessary, issue an arrest warrant to secure the person's presence where he or she fails to appear before or respond in writing pursuant to an order under paragraph (B). A State or authority to whom such a warrant is addressed, in accordance with Article 29 of the Statute, shall act promptly and with all due diligence to ensure proper and effective execution thereof. Where an arrest warrant is issued under this Sub-rule, the provisions of Rules 45, 57, 58, 59, 59 *bis*, and 60 shall apply mutatis mutandis. Following the transfer of the person concerned to the Tribunal, the provisions of Rules 64, 65 and 99 shall apply mutatis mutandis.

(F) Where under this Rule a penalty of imprisonment is imposed, or a fine is converted to a term of imprisonment, the provisions of Rules 102, 103 and 104 and Part Nine shall apply mutatis mutandis.

(G) Any finding of contempt or penalty imposed under this Rule shall be subject to appeal as allowed for in Rule 77 (J).

Rule 78
Open Sessions

All proceedings before a Trial Chamber, other than deliberations of the Chamber, shall be held in public, unless otherwise provided.

Rule 79
Closed Sessions

(A) The Trial Chamber may order that the press and the public be excluded from all or part of the proceedings for reasons of:

(i) public order or morality;

(ii) safety, security or non-disclosure of the identity of a victim or witness as provided in

Rule 75; or

(iii) the protection of the interests of justice.

(B) The Trial Chamber shall make public the reasons for its order.

Rule 80
Control of Proceedings

(A) The Trial Chamber may exclude a person from the courtroom in order to protect the right of the accused to a fair and public trial, or to maintain the dignity and decorum of the proceedings.

(B) The Trial Chamber may order the removal of an accused from the courtroom and continue the proceedings in the absence of the accused if the accused has persisted in disruptive conduct following a warning that such conduct may warrant the removal of the accused from the courtroom.

Rule 81
Records of Proceedings and Evidence

(A) The Registrar shall cause to be made and preserve a full and accurate record of all proceedings, including audio recordings, transcripts and, when deemed necessary by the Trial Chamber, video recordings.

(B) The Trial Chamber, after giving due consideration to any matters relating to witness protection, may order the disclosure of all or part of the record of closed proceedings when the reasons for ordering its non-disclosure no longer exist.

(C) The Registrar shall retain and preserve all physical evidence offered during the proceedings subject to any Practice Direction or any order which a Chamber may at any time make with respect to the control or disposition of physical evidence offered during proceedings before that Chamber.

(D) Photography, video-recording or audio-recording of the trial, otherwise than by the Registrar, may be authorised at the discretion of the Trial Chamber.

Section 2. Case Presentation

Rule 82
Joint and Separate Trials

(A) In joint trials, each accused shall be accorded the same rights as if such accused were being tried separately.

(B) The Trial Chamber may order that persons accused jointly under Rule 48 be tried separately if it considers it necessary in order to avoid a conflict of interests that might cause serious prejudice to an accused, or to protect the interests of justice.

Rule 83
Instruments of Restraint

Instruments of restraint, such as handcuffs, shall be used only on the order of the Registrar as a precaution against escape during transfer or in order to prevent an accused from self-injury, injury to others or to prevent serious damage to property. Instruments of restraint shall be removed when the accused appears before a Chamber or a Judge.

Rule 84
Opening Statements

Before presentation of evidence by the Prosecutor, each party may make an opening statement. The defence may, however, elect to make its statement after the conclusion of the Prosecutor's presentation of evidence and before the presentation of evidence for the defence.

Rule 84 *bis*
Statement of the Accused

(A) After the opening statements of the parties or, if the defence elects to defer its opening statement pursuant to Rule 84, after the opening statement of the Prosecutor, if any, the accused may, if he or she so wishes, and the Trial Chamber so decides, make a statement under the control of the Trial Chamber. The accused shall not be compelled to make a solemn declaration and shall not be examined about the content of the statement.

(B) The Trial Chamber shall decide on the probative value, if any, of the statement.

Rule 85
Presentation of Evidence

(A) Each party is entitled to call witnesses and present evidence. Unless otherwise directed by the Trial Chamber in the interests of justice, evidence at the trial shall be presented in the following sequence:

(i) evidence for the prosecution;

(ii) evidence for the defence;

(iii) prosecution evidence in rebuttal;

(iv) defence evidence in rejoinder;

(v) evidence ordered by the Trial Chamber pursuant to Rule 98; and

(vi) any relevant information that may assist the Trial Chamber in determining an appropriate sentence if the accused is found guilty on one or more of the charges in the indictment.

(B) Examination-in-chief, cross-examination and re-examination shall be allowed in each case. It shall be for the party calling a witness to examine such witness in chief, but a Judge may at any stage put any question to the witness.

(C) If the accused so desires, the accused may appear as a witness in his or her own defence.

Rule 86
Closing Arguments

(A) After the presentation of all the evidence, the Prosecutor may present a closing argument; whether or not the Prosecutor does so, the defence may make a closing argument. The Prosecutor may present a rebuttal argument to which the defence may present a rejoinder.

(B) Not later than five days prior to presenting a closing argument, a party shall file a final trial brief.

(C) The parties shall also address matters of sentencing in closing Arguments.

Rule 87
Deliberations

(A) When both parties have completed their presentation of the case, the Presiding Judge shall declare the hearing closed, and the Trial Chamber shall deliberate in private. A finding of guilt may be reached only when a majority of the Trial Chamber is satisfied that guilt has been proved beyond reasonable doubt.

(B) The Trial Chamber shall vote separately on each charge contained in the indictment. If two or more accused are tried together under Rule 48, separate findings shall be made as to each accused.

(C) If the Trial Chamber finds the accused guilty on one or more of the charges contained in the indictment, it shall impose a sentence in respect of each finding of guilt and indicate whether such sentences shall be served consecutively or concurrently, unless it decides to exercise its power to impose a single sentence reflecting the totality of the criminal conduct of the accused.

Rule 88
[Deleted 1998]

Rule 88 bis
[Deleted 1998]

Section 3: Rules of Evidence

Rule 89
General Provisions

(A) A Chamber shall apply the rules of evidence set forth in this Section, and shall not be bound by national rules of evidence.

(B) In cases not otherwise provided for in this Section, a Chamber shall apply rules of evidence which will best favour a fair determination of the matter before it and are consonant with the spirit of the Statute and the general principles of law.

(C) A Chamber may admit any relevant evidence which it deems to have probative value.

(D) A Chamber may exclude evidence if its probative value is substantially outweighed by the need to ensure a fair trial.

(E) A Chamber may request verification of the authenticity of evidence obtained out of court.

(F) A Chamber may receive the evidence of a witness orally or, where the interests of justice allow, in written form.

Rule 90
Testimony of Witnesses

(A) Every witness shall, before giving evidence, make the following solemn declaration: "I solemnly declare that I will speak the truth, the whole truth and nothing but the truth".

(B) A child who, in the opinion of the Chamber, does not understand the nature of a solemn declaration, may be permitted to testify without that formality, if the Chamber is of the opinion that the child is sufficiently mature to be able to report the facts of which the child had knowledge and understands the duty to tell the truth. A judgement, however, cannot be based on such testimony alone.

(C) A witness, other than an expert, who has not yet testified not be present when the testimony of another witness is given. However, a witness who has heard the testimony of another witness shall not for that reason alone be disqualified from testifying.

(D) Notwithstanding paragraph (C), upon order of the Chamber, an investigator in charge of a party's investigation shall not be precluded from being called as a witness on the ground that he or she has been present in the courtroom during the proceedings.

(E) A witness may object to making any statement which might tend to incriminate the witness. The Chamber may, however, compel the witness to answer the question. Testimony compelled in this way shall not be used as evidence in a subsequent prosecution against the witness for any offence other than false testimony.

(F) The Trial Chamber shall exercise control over the mode and order of interrogating witnesses and presenting evidence so as to

(i) make the interrogation and presentation effective for the ascertainment of the truth; and

(ii) avoid needless consumption of time.

(G) The Trial Chamber may refuse to hear a witness whose name does not appear on the list of witnesses compiled pursuant to Rules 73 *bis* (C) and 73 *ter* (C).

(H) (i) Cross-examination shall be limited to the subject-matter of the evidence-in-chief and matters affecting the credibility of the witness and, where the witness is able to give evidence relevant to the case for the cross-examining party, to the subject-matter of that case.

(ii) In the cross-examination of a witness who is able to give evidence relevant to the case for the cross-examining party, counsel shall put to that witness the nature of the case of the party for whom that counsel appears which is in contradiction of the evidence given by the witness.

(iii) The Trial Chamber may, in the exercise of its discretion, permit enquiry into additional matters.

Rule 90 *bis*
Transfer of a Detained Witness

(A) Any detained person whose personal appearance as a witness has been requested by the Tribunal shall be transferred temporarily to the detention unit of the Tribunal, conditional on the person's return within the period decided by the Tribunal.

(B) The transfer order shall be issued by a permanent Judge or Trial Chamber only after prior verification that the following conditions have been met:

(i) the presence of the detained witness is not required for any criminal proceedings in progress in the territory of the requested State during the period the witness is required by the Tribunal;

(ii) transfer of the witness does not extend the period of detention as foreseen by the requested State.

(C) The Registrar shall transmit the order of transfer to the national authorities of the State on whose territory, or under whose jurisdiction or control, the witness is detained. Transfer shall be arranged by the national authorities concerned in liaison with the host country and the Registrar.

(D) The Registrar shall ensure the proper conduct of the transfer, including the supervision of the witness in the detention unit of the Tribunal; the Registrar shall remain abreast of any changes which might occur regarding the conditions of detention provided for by the requested State and which may possibly affect the length of the detention of the witness in the detention unit and, as promptly as possible, shall inform the relevant Judge or Chamber.

(E) On expiration of the period decided by the Tribunal for the temporary transfer, the detained witness shall be remanded to the authorities of the requested State, unless the State, within that period, has transmitted an order of release of the witness, which shall take effect immediately.

(F) If, by the end of the period decided by the Tribunal, the presence of the detained witness continues to be necessary, a permanent Judge or Chamber may extend the period on the same conditions as stated in paragraph (B).

Rule 91
False Testimony under Solemn Declaration

(A) A Chamber, *proprio motu* or at the request of a party, may warn a witness of the duty to tell the truth and the consequences that may result from a failure to do so.

(B) If a Chamber has strong grounds for believing that a witness has knowingly and wilfully given false testimony, it may:

    (i) direct the Prosecutor to investigate the matter with a view to the preparation and submission of an indictment for false testimony; or

    (ii) where the Prosecutor, in the view of the Chamber, has a conflict of interest with respect to the relevant conduct, direct the Registrar to appoint an *amicus curiae* to investigate the matter and report back to the Chamber as to whether there are sufficient grounds for instigating proceedings for false testimony.

(C) If the Chamber considers that there are sufficient grounds to proceed against a person for giving false testimony, the Chamber may:

    (i) in circumstances described in paragraph (B)(i), direct the Prosecutor to prosecute the matter; or

    (ii) in circumstances described in paragraph (B)(ii), issue an order in lieu of an indictment and direct *amicus curiae* to prosecute the matter.

(D) The rules of procedure and evidence in Parts Four to Eight shall apply mutatis mutandis to proceedings under this Rule.

(E) Any person indicted for or charged with false testimony shall, if that person satisfies the criteria for determination of indigence established by the Registrar, be assigned counsel in accordance with Rule 45.

(F) No Judge who sat as a member of the Trial Chamber before which the witness appeared shall sit for the trial of the witness for false testimony.

(G) The maximum penalty for false testimony under solemn declaration shall be a fine of 100,000 Euros or a term of imprisonment of seven years, or both. The payment of any fine imposed shall be paid to the Registrar to be held in the account referred to in Rule 77(H).

(H) Paragraphs (B) to (G) apply mutatis mutandis to a person who knowingly and willingly makes a false statement in a written statement taken in accordance with Rule 92 *bis* which the person knows or has reason to know may be used as evidence in proceedings before the Tribunal.

(I) Any decision rendered by a Trial Chamber under this Rule shall be subject to appeal. Notice of appeal shall be filed within fifteen days of filing of the impugned decision. Where such decision is rendered orally, the notice shall be filed within fifteen days of the oral decision, unless

    (i) the party challenging the decision was not present or represented when the decision was pronounced, in which case the time-limit shall run from the date on which the challenging

    party is notified of the oral decision; or

    (ii) the Trial Chamber has indicated that a written decision will follow, in which case the time-limit shall run from filing of the written decision.

Rule 92

Confessions

A confession by the accused given during questioning by the Prosecutor shall, provided the requirements of Rule 63 were strictly complied with, be presumed to have been free and voluntary unless the contrary is proved.

Rule 92 *bis*
Proof of Facts other than by Oral Evidence

(A) A Trial Chamber may admit, in whole or in part, the evidence of a witness in the form of a written statement in lieu of oral testimony which goes to proof of a matter other than the acts and conduct of the accused as charged in the indictment.

(i) Factors in favour of admitting evidence in the form of a written statement include but are not limited to circumstances in which the evidence in question:

(a) is of a cumulative nature, in that other witnesses will give or have given oral testimony of similar facts;

(b) relates to relevant historical, political or military background;

(c) consists of a general or statistical analysis of the ethnic composition of the population in the places to which the indictment relates;

(d) concerns the impact of crimes upon victims;

(e) relates to issues of the character of the accused; or

(f) relates to factors to be taken into account in determining sentence.

(ii) Factors against admitting evidence in the form of a written statement include whether:

(a) there is an overriding public interest in the evidence in question being presented orally;

(b) a party objecting can demonstrate that its nature and source renders it unreliable, or that its prejudicial effect outweighs its probative value; or

(c) there are any other factors which make it appropriate for the witness to attend for cross-examination.

(B) A written statement under this Rule shall be admissible if it attaches a declaration by the person making the written statement that the contents of the statement are true and correct to the best of that person's knowledge and belief and

(i) the declaration is witnessed by:

(a) a person authorised to witness such a declaration in accordance with the law and procedure of a State; or

(b) a Presiding Officer appointed by the Registrar of the Tribunal for that purpose; and

(ii) the person witnessing the declaration verifies in writing:

(a) that the person making the statement is the person identified in the said statement;

(b) that the person making the statement stated that the contents of the written statement are, to the best of that person's knowledge and belief, true and correct;

(c) that the person making the statement was informed that if the content

of the written statement is not true then he or she may be subject to proceedings for giving false testimony; and

(d) the date and place of the declaration.

The declaration shall be attached to the written statement presented to the Trial Chamber.

(C) A written statement not in the form prescribed by paragraph (B) may nevertheless be admissible if made by a person who has subsequently died, or by a person who can no longer with reasonable diligence be traced, or by a person who is by reason of bodily or mental condition unable to testify orally, if the Trial Chamber:

    (i) is so satisfied on a balance of probabilities; and

    (ii) finds from the circumstances in which the statement was made and recorded that there are satisfactory indicia of its reliability.

(D) A Chamber may admit a transcript of evidence given by a witness in proceedings before the Tribunal which goes to proof of a matter other than the acts and conduct of the accused.

(E) Subject to Rule 127 or any order to the contrary, a party seeking to adduce a written statement or transcript shall give fourteen days notice to the opposing party, who may within seven days object. The Trial Chamber shall decide, after hearing the parties, whether to admit the statement or transcript in whole or in part and whether to require the witness to appear for cross-examination.

Rule 93
Evidence of Consistent Pattern of Conduct

(A) Evidence of a consistent pattern of conduct relevant to serious violations of international humanitarian law under the Statute may be admissible in the interests of justice.

(B) Acts tending to show such a pattern of conduct shall be disclosed by the Prosecutor to the defence pursuant to Rule 66.

Rule 94
Judicial Notice

(A) A Trial Chamber shall not require proof of facts of common knowledge but shall take judicial notice thereof.

(B) At the request of a party or *proprio motu*, a Trial Chamber, after hearing the parties, may decide to take judicial notice of adjudicated facts or documentary evidence from other proceedings of the Tribunal relating to matters at issue in the current proceedings.

Rule 94 *bis*
Testimony of Expert Witnesses

(A) The full statement of any expert witness to be called by a party shall be disclosed within the time-limit prescribed by the Trial Chamber or by the pre-trial Judge.

(B) Within thirty days of disclosure of the statement of the expert witness, or such other time prescribed by the Trial Chamber or pre-trial Judge, the opposing party shall file a notice indicating whether:

    (i) it accepts the expert witness statement; or

    (ii) it wishes to cross-examine the expert witness; and

    (iii) it challenges the qualifications of the witness as an expert or the relevance of all or parts of the report and, if so, which parts

(C) If the opposing party accepts the statement of the expert witness, the statement may be admitted into evidence by the Trial Chamber without calling the witness to testify in person.

Rule 94 *ter*
[Deleted 2000]

Rule 95
Exclusion of Certain Evidence

No evidence shall be admissible if obtained by methods which cast substantial doubt on its reliability or if its admission is antithetical to, and would seriously damage, the integrity of the proceedings.

Rule 96
Evidence in Cases of Sexual Assault

In cases of sexual assault:

(i) no corroboration of the victim's testimony shall be required;

(ii) consent shall not be allowed as a defence if the victim

(a) has been subjected to or threatened with or has had reason to fear violence, duress, detention or psychological oppression, or

(b) reasonably believed that if the victim did not submit, another might be so subjected, threatened or put in fear;

(iii) before evidence of the victim's consent is admitted, the accused shall satisfy the Trial Chamber in camera that the evidence is relevant and credible;

(iv) prior sexual conduct of the victim shall not be admitted in evidence.

Rule 97
Lawyer-Client Privilege

All communications between lawyer and client shall be regarded as privileged, and consequently not subject to disclosure at trial, unless:

(i) the client consents to such disclosure; or

(ii) the client has voluntarily disclosed the content of the communication to a third party, and that third party then gives evidence of that disclosure.

Rule 98
Power of Chambers to Order Production of Additional Evidence

A Trial Chamber may order either party to produce additional evidence. It may *proprio motu* summon witnesses and order their attendance.

Section 4: Judgement

Rule 98 *bis*
Judgement of Acquittal

At the close of the Prosecutor's case, the Trial Chamber shall, by oral decision and after hearing the oral submissions of the parties, enter a judgement of acquittal on any count if there is no evidence capable of supporting a conviction.

Rule 98 *ter*
Judgement

(A) The judgement shall be pronounced in public, on a date of which notice shall have been given to the parties and counsel and at which they shall be entitled to be present, subject to the provisions of Rule 102 (B).

(B) If the Trial Chamber finds the accused guilty of a crime and concludes from the evidence that unlawful taking of property by the accused was associated with it, it shall make a specific finding to that effect in its judgement. The Trial Chamber may order restitution as provided in Rule 105.

(C) The judgement shall be rendered by a majority of the Judges. It shall be accompanied or followed as soon as possible by a reasoned opinion in writing, to which separate or dissenting opinions may be appended.

(D) A copy of the judgement and of the Judges' opinions in a language which the accused understands shall as soon as possible be served on the accused if in custody. Copies thereof in that language and in the language in which they were delivered shall also as soon as possible be provided to counsel for the accused.

Rule 99
Status of the Acquitted Person

(A) Subject to paragraph (B), in the case of an acquittal or the upholding of a challenge to jurisdiction, the accused shall be released immediately.

(B) If, at the time the judgement is pronounced, the Prosecutor advises the Trial Chamber in open court of the Prosecutor's intention to file notice of appeal pursuant to Rule 108, the Trial Chamber may, on application in that behalf by the Prosecutor and upon hearing the parties, in its discretion, issue an order for the continued detention of the accused, pending the determination of the appeal.

Section 5: Sentencing and Penalties

Rule 100
Sentencing Procedure on a Guilty Plea

(A) If the Trial Chamber convicts the accused on a guilty plea, the Prosecutor and the defence may submit any relevant information that may assist the Trial Chamber in determining an appropriate sentence.

(B) The sentence shall be pronounced in a judgement in public and in the presence of the convicted person, subject to Rule 102 (B).

Rule 101
Penalties

(A) A convicted person may be sentenced to imprisonment for a term up to and including the remainder of the convicted person's life.

(B) In determining the sentence, the Trial Chamber shall take into account the factors mentioned in Article 24, paragraph 2, of the Statute, as well as such factors as:

(i) any aggravating circumstances;

(ii) any mitigating circumstances including the substantial cooperation with the Prosecutor by the convicted person before or after conviction;

(iii) the general practice regarding prison sentences in the courts of the former Yugoslavia;

(iv) the extent to which any penalty imposed by a court of any State on the convicted person for the same act has already been served, as referred to in Article 10, paragraph 3, of the Statute.

(C) Credit shall be given to the convicted person for the period, if any, during which the convicted person was detained in custody pending surrender to the Tribunal or pending trial or appeal.

Rule 102
Status of the Convicted Person

(A) The sentence shall begin to run from the day it is pronounced. However, as soon as notice of appeal is given, the enforcement of the judgement shall thereupon be stayed until the decision on the appeal has been delivered, the convicted person meanwhile remaining in detention, as provided in Rule 64.

(B) If, by a previous decision of the Trial Chamber, the convicted person has been released, or is for any other reason at liberty, and is not present when the judgement is pronounced, the Trial Chamber shall issue a warrant for the convicted person's arrest. On arrest, the convicted person shall be notified of the conviction and sentence, and the procedure provided in Rule 103 shall be followed.

Rule 103
Place of Imprisonment

(A) Imprisonment shall be served in a State designated by the President of the Tribunal from a list of States which have indicated their willingness to accept convicted persons.

(B) Transfer of the convicted person to that State shall be effected as soon as possible after the time-limit for appeal has elapsed.

(C) Pending the finalisation of arrangements for his or her transfer to the State where his or her sentence will be served, the convicted person shall remain in the custody of the Tribunal.

Rule 104
Supervision of Imprisonment

All sentences of imprisonment shall be supervised by the Tribunal or a body designated by it.

Rule 105
Restitution of Property

(A) After a judgement of conviction containing a specific finding as provided in Rule 98 *ter* (B), the Trial Chamber shall, at the request of the Prosecutor, or may, *proprio motu*, hold a special hearing to determine the matter of the restitution of the property or the proceeds thereof, and may in the meantime order such provisional measures for the preservation and protection of the property or proceeds as it considers appropriate.

(B) The determination may extend to such property or its proceeds, even in the hands of third parties not otherwise connected with the crime of which the convicted person has been found guilty.

(C) Such third parties shall be summoned before the Trial Chamber and be given an opportunity to justify their claim to the property or its proceeds.

(D) Should the Trial Chamber be able to determine the rightful owner on the balance of probabilities, it shall order the restitution either of the property or the proceeds or make such other order as it may deem appropriate.

(E) Should the Trial Chamber not be able to determine ownership, it shall notify the competent national authorities and request them so to determine.

(F) Upon notice from the national authorities that an affirmative determination has been made, the Trial Chamber shall order the restitution either of the property or the proceeds or make such other order as it may deem appropriate.

(G) The Registrar shall transmit to the competent national authorities any summonses, orders and requests issued by a Trial Chamber pursuant to paragraphs (C), (D), (E) and (F).

Rule 106
Compensation to Victims

(A) The Registrar shall transmit to the competent authorities of the States concerned the judgement finding the accused guilty of a crime which has caused injury to a victim.

(B) Pursuant to the relevant national legislation, a victim or persons claiming through the victim may bring an action in a national court or other competent body to obtain compensation.

(C) For the purposes of a claim made under paragraph (B) the judgement of the Tribunal shall be final and binding as to the criminal responsibility of the convicted person for such injury.

Part Seven
APPELLATE PROCEEDINGS

Rule 107
General Provision

The rules of procedure and evidence that govern proceedings in the Trial Chambers shall apply mutatis mutandis to proceedings in the Appeals Chamber.

Rule 108
Notice of Appeal

A party seeking to appeal a judgement shall, not more than thirty days from the date on which the judgement was pronounced, file a notice of appeal, setting forth the grounds. The Appellant should also identify the order, decision or ruling challenged with specific reference to the date of its filing, and/or the transcript page, and indicate the substance of the alleged errors and the relief sought. The Appeals Chamber may, on good cause being shown by motion, authorise a variation of the grounds of appeal.

Rule 108 *bis*
State Request for Review

(A) A State directly affected by an interlocutory decision of a Trial Chamber may, within fifteen days from the date of the decision, file a request for review of the decision by the Appeals Chamber if that decision concerns issues of general importance relating to the powers of the Tribunal.

(B) The party upon whose motion the Trial Chamber issued the impugned decision shall be heard by the Appeals Chamber. The other party may be heard if the Appeals Chamber considers that the interests of justice so require.

(C) The Appeals Chamber may at any stage suspend the execution of the impugned decision.

(D) Rule 116 *bis* shall apply mutatis mutandis.

Rule 109
Record on Appeal

The record on appeal shall consist of the trial record, as certified by the Registrar.

Rule 110
Copies of Record

The Registrar shall make a sufficient number of copies of the record on appeal for the use of the Judges of the Appeals Chamber and of the parties.

Rule 111
Appellant's Brief

An Appellant's brief setting out all the arguments and authorities shall be filed within seventy-five days of filing of the notice of appeal pursuant to Rule 108. Where limited to sentencing, an Appellant's brief shall be filed within thirty days of filing of the notice of appeal pursuant to Rule 108.

Where the Prosecutor is the Appellant, the Prosecutor shall make a declaration in the Appellant's brief that disclosure has been completed with respect to the material available to the Prosecutor at the time of filing the brief.

Rule 112
Respondent's Brief

A Respondent's brief of argument and authorities shall be filed within forty days of the filing of the Appellant's brief. Where limited to sentencing, a Respondent's brief shall be filed within thirty days of filing of the Appellant's brief.

Where the Prosecutor is the Respondent, the Prosecutor shall make a declaration in the Respondent's brief that disclosure had been completed with respect to the material available to the Prosecutor at the time of filing the brief.

Rule 113
Brief in Reply

An Appellant may file a brief in reply within fifteen days of filing of the Respondent's brief. Where limited to sentencing, a brief in reply shall be filed within ten days of filing of the Respondent's brief.

Rule 114
Date of Hearing

After the expiry of the time-limits for filing the briefs provided for in Rules 111, 112 and 113, the Appeals Chamber shall set the date for the hearing and the Registrar shall notify the parties.

Rule 115
Additional Evidence

(A) A party may apply by motion to present additional evidence before the Appeals Chamber. Such motion shall clearly identify with precision the specific finding of fact made by the Trial Chamber to which the additional evidence is directed, and must be served on the other party and filed with the Registrar not later than thirty days from the date for filing the brief in reply, unless good cause or, after the appeal hearing, cogent reasons are shown for a delay. Rebuttal material may be presented by any party affected by the motion. Parties are permitted to file supplemental briefs on the impact of the additional evidence within fifteen days of the expiry of the time limit set for the filing of rebuttal material, if no such material is filed, or if rebuttal material is filed, within fifteen days of the decision on the admissibility of that material.

(B) If the Appeals Chamber finds that the additional evidence was not available at trial and is relevant and credible, it will determine if it could have been a decisive factor in reaching the decision at trial. If it could have been such a factor, the Appeals Chamber will consider the additional evidence and any rebuttal material along with that already on the record to arrive at a final judgement in accordance with Rule 117.

(C) The Appeals Chamber may decide the motion prior to the appeal, or at the time of the hearing on appeal. It may decide the motion with or without an oral hearing.

(D) If several defendants are parties to the appeal, the additional evidence admitted on behalf of any one of them will be considered with respect to all of them, where relevant.

Rule 116
[Deleted 1997]

Rule 116 *bis*
Expedited Appeals Procedure

(A) An appeal under Rule 72 or Rule 73 or appeal from a decision rendered under Rule 11 *bis*, 54 *bis*, Rule 65, Rule 77 or Rule 91 shall be heard expeditiously on the basis of the original record of the Trial Chamber. Appeals may be determined entirely on the basis of written briefs.

(B) Rules 109 to 114 shall not apply to such appeals.

(C) The Presiding Judge, after consulting the members of the Appeals Chamber, may decide not to apply Rule 117 (D).

Rule 117
Judgement on Appeal

(A) The Appeals Chamber shall pronounce judgement on the basis of the record on appeal together with such additional evidence as has been presented to it.

(B) The judgement shall be rendered by a majority of the Judges. It shall be accompanied or followed as soon as possible by a reasoned opinion in writing, to which separate or dissenting opinions may be appended.

(C) In appropriate circumstances the Appeals Chamber may order that the accused be retried according to law.

(D) The judgement shall be pronounced in public, on a date of which notice shall have been given to the parties and counsel and at which they shall be entitled to be present.

Rule 118
Status of the Accused following Appeal

(A) A sentence pronounced by the Appeals Chamber shall be enforced immediately.

(B) Where the accused is not present when the judgement is due to be delivered, either as having been acquitted on all charges or as a result of an order issued pursuant to Rule 65, or for any other reason, the Appeals Chamber may deliver its judgement in the absence of the accused and shall, unless it pronounces an acquittal, order the arrest or surrender of the accused to the Tribunal.

Part Eight
REVIEW PROCEEDINGS

Rule 119
Request for Review

(A) Where a new fact has been discovered which was not known to the moving party at the time of the proceedings before a Trial Chamber or the Appeals Chamber, and could not have been discovered through the exercise of due diligence, the defence or, within one year after the final judgement has been pronounced, the Prosecutor, may make a motion to that Chamber for review of the judgement. If, at the time of the request for review, any of the Judges who constituted the original Chamber are no longer Judges of the Tribunal, the President shall appoint a Judge or Judges in their place.

(B) Any brief in response to a request for review shall be filed within forty days of the filing of the request.

(C) Any brief in reply shall be filed within fifteen days after the filing of the response.

Rule 120
Preliminary Examination

If a majority of Judges of the Chamber constituted pursuant to Rule 119 agree that the new fact, if proved, could have been a decisive factor in reaching a decision, the Chamber shall review the judgement, and pronounce a further judgement after hearing the parties.

Rule 121
Appeals

The judgement of a Trial Chamber on review may be appealed in accordance with the provisions of Part Seven.

Rule 122
Return of Case to Trial Chamber

If the judgement to be reviewed is under appeal at the time the motion for review is filed, the Appeals Chamber may return the case to the Trial Chamber for disposition of the motion.

Part Nine
PARDON AND COMMUTATION OF SENTENCE

Rule 123
Notification by States

If, according to the law of the State of imprisonment, a convicted person is eligible for pardon or commutation of sentence, the State shall, in accordance with Article 28 of the Statute, notify the Tribunal of such eligibility.

Rule 124
Determination by the President

The President shall, upon such notice, determine, in consultation with the members of the Bureau and any permanent Judges of the sentencing Chamber who remain Judges of the Tribunal, whether pardon or commutation is appropriate.

Rule 125
General Standards for Granting Pardon or Commutation

In determining whether pardon or commutation is appropriate, the President shall take into account, *inter alia*, the gravity of the crime or crimes for which the prisoner was convicted, the treatment of similarly-situated prisoners, the prisoner's demonstration of rehabilitation, as well as any substantial cooperation of the prisoner with the Prosecutor.

PART TEN
TIME

Rule 126
General Provisions

A. Where the time prescribed by or under these Rules for the doing of any act is to run as from the occurrence of an event, that time shall begin to run as from the date of the event.

B. Should the last day of a time prescribed by a Rule or directed by a Chamber fall upon a day when the Registry of the Tribunal does not accept documents for filing it shall be considered as falling on the first day thereafter when the Registry does accept documents for filing.

Rule 126 bis
Time for Filing Responses to Motions

Unless otherwise ordered by a Chamber either generally or in the particular case, a response, if any, to a motion filed by a party shall be filed within fourteen days of the filing of the motion. A reply to the response, if any, shall be filed within seven days of the filing of the response, with the leave of the relevant Chamber.

Rule 127
Variation of Time-limits

A. Save as provided by paragraph (C), a Trial Chamber or Pre-Trial Judge may, on good cause being shown by motion,

    1. enlarge or reduce any time prescribed by or under these Rules;

    2. recognize as validly done any act done after the expiration of a time so prescribed on such terms, if any, as is thought just and whether or not that time has already expired.

B. In relation to any step falling to be taken in connection with an appeal, the Appeals Chamber or Pre-Appeal Judge may exercise the like power as is conferred by paragraph (A) and in like manner and subject to the same conditions as are therein set out.

C. The Rule shall not apply to the times prescribed in Rules 40 *bis* and 90 *bis*.

Statute of the International Criminal Tribunal for Rwanda
U.N.S.C. Res. 955 (8 Nov. 1994)

The Security Council,

Reaffirming all its previous resolutions on the situation in Rwanda,

Having considered the reports of the Secretary-General pursuant to paragraph 3 of resolution 935 (1994) 1 July 1994 (S/1994/879 and S/1994/906), and having taken note of the reports of the Special Rapporteur for Rwanda of the United Nations Commission on Human Rights (S/1994/1157, annex I and annex II),

Expressing appreciation for the work of the Commission of Experts established pursuant to resolution 935 (1994), in particular its preliminary report on violations of international humanitarian law in Rwanda transmitted by the Secretary-General's letter of 1 October 1994 (S/1994/1125),

Expressing once again its grave concern at the reports indicating that genocide and other systematic, widespread and flagrant violations of international humanitarian law have been committed in Rwanda,

Determining that this situation continues to constitute a threat to international peace and security,

Determined to put an end to such crimes and to take effective measures to bring to justice the persons who are responsible for them,

Convinced that in the particular circumstances of Rwanda, the prosecution of persons responsible for serious violations of international humanitarian law would enable this aim to be achieved and would contribute to the process of national reconciliation and to the restoration and maintenance of peace,

Believing that the establishment of an international tribunal for the prosecution of persons responsible for genocide and the other above-mentioned violations of international humanitarian law will contribute to ensuring that such violations are halted and effectively redressed,

Stressing also the need for international cooperation to strengthen the courts and judicial system of Rwanda, having regard in particular to the necessity for those courts to deal with large numbers of suspects,

Considering that the Commission of Experts established pursuant to resolution 935 (1994) should continue on an urgent basis the collection of information relating to evidence of grave violations of international humanitarian law committed in the territory of Rwanda and should submit its final report to the Secretary-General by 30 November 1994,

Acting under Chapter VII of the Charter of the United Nations,

1. *Decides* hereby, having received the request of the Government of Rwanda (S/1994/1115), to establish an international tribunal for the sole purpose of prosecuting persons responsible for genocide and other serious violations of international humanitarian law committed in the territory of Rwanda and Rwandan citizens responsible for genocide and other such violations committed in the territory of neighbouring states, between 1 January 1994 and 31 December 1994 and to this end to adopt the Statute of the International Criminal Tribunal for Rwanda annexed hereto;

2. *Decides* that all States shall cooperate fully with the International Tribunal and its organs in accordance with the present resolution and the Statute of the International Tribunal and that consequently all States shall take any measures necessary under their domestic law to implement the provisions of the present resolution and the Statute, including the obligation of States to comply with requests for assistance or orders issued by a Trial Chamber under Article 28 of the Statute, and requests States to keep the Secretary-General informed of such measures;

3. *Considers* that the Government of Rwanda should be notified prior to the taking of decisions under articles 26 and 27 of the Statute;

4. *Urges* States and intergovernmental and non-governmental organisations to contribute funds, equipment and services to the International Tribunal, including the offer of expert personnel;

5. *Requests* the Secretary-General to implement this resolution urgently and in particular to make practical arrangements for the effective functioning of the International Tribunal, including recommendations to the Council as to possible locations for the seat of the International Tribunal at the earliest time to report periodically to the Council;

6. *Decides* that the seat of the International Tribunal shall be determined by the Council having regard to considerations of justice and fairness as well as administrative efficiency, including access to witnesses, and economy, and subject to the conclusion of appropri-

ate arrangements between the United Nations and the State of the seat, acceptable to the Council, having regard to the fact that the International Tribunal may meet away from its seat when it considers necessary for the efficient exercise of its functions; and decides that an office will be established and proceedings will be conducted in Rwanda, where feasible and appropriate, subject to the conclusion of similar appropriate arrangements;

7. *Decides* to consider increasing the number of judges and Trial Chambers of the International Tribunal if it becomes necessary;

8. *Decides* to remain actively seized of the matter.

Annex
Statute of the International Tribunal for Rwanda

Having been established by the Security Council acting under Chapter VII of the Charter of the United Nations, the International Criminal Tribunal for the Prosecution of Persons Responsible for Genocide and Other Serious Violations of International Humanitarian Law Committed in the Territory of Rwanda and Rwandan Citizens responsible for genocide and other such violations committed in the territory of neighbouring States, between 1 January 1994 and 31 December 1994 (hereinafter referred to as "The International Tribunal for Rwanda") shall function in accordance with the provisions of the present Statute.

Article 1. Competence of the International Tribunal for Rwanda

The International Tribunal for Rwanda shall have the power to prosecute persons responsible for serious violations of international humanitarian law committed in the territory of Rwanda and Rwandan citizens responsible for such violations committed in the territory of neighbouring States between 1 January 1994 and 31 December 1994, in accordance with the provisions of the present Statute.

Article 2. Genocide

1. The International Tribunal for Rwanda shall have the power to prosecute persons committing genocide as defined in paragraph 2 of this article or of committing any of the other acts enumerated in paragraph 3 of this article.

2. Genocide means any of the following acts committed with intent to destroy, in whole or in part, a national, ethnical, racial or religious group, as such:

(a) Killing members of the group;

(b) Causing serious bodily or mental harm to members of the group;

(c) Deliberately inflicting on the group conditions of life calculated to bring about its physical destruction in whole or in part;

(d) Imposing measures intended to prevent births within the group;

(e) Forcibly transferring children of the group to another group.

3. The following acts shall be punishable:

(a) Genocide;

(b) Conspiracy to commit genocide;

(c) Direct and public incitement to commit genocide;

(d) Attempt to commit genocide;

(e) Complicity in genocide.

Article 3. Crimes against Humanity

The International Tribunal for Rwanda shall have the power to prosecute persons responsible for the following crimes when committed as part of a widespread or systematic attack against any civilian population on national, political, ethnic, racial or religious grounds:

(a) Murder;

(b) Extermination;

(c) Enslavement;

(d) Deportation;

(e) Imprisonment;

(f) Torture;

(g) Rape;

(h) Persecutions on political, racial and religious grounds;

(i) Other inhumane acts.

Article 4. Violations of Article 3 common to the Geneva Conventions and of Additional Protocol II

The International Tribunal for Rwanda shall have the power to prosecute persons committing or ordering to be committed serious violations of Article 3 common to the Geneva Conventions of 12 August 1949 for the Protection of War Victims, and of Additional Protocol II thereto of 8 June 1977. These violations shall include, but shall not be limited to:

(a) Violence to life, health and physical or mental well-being of persons, in particular murder as well as cruel treatment such as torture, mutilation or any form of corporal punishment;

(b) Collective punishments;

(c) Taking of hostages;

(d) Acts of terrorism;

(e) Outrages upon personal dignity, in particular humiliating and degrading treatment, rape, enforced prostitution and any form of indecent assault;

(f) Pillage;

(g) The passing of sentences and the carrying out of executions without previous judgement pronounced by a regularly constituted court, affording all the judicial guarantees which are recognised as indispensable by civilised peoples;

(h) Threats to commit any of the foregoing acts.

Article 5. Personal jurisdiction

The International Tribunal for Rwanda shall have jurisdiction over natural persons pursuant to the provisions of the present Statute.

Article 6. Individual Criminal Responsibility

1. A person who planned, instigated, ordered, committed or otherwise aided and abetted in the planning, preparation or execution of a crime referred to in Articles 2 to 4 of the present Statute, shall be individually responsible for the crime.

2. The official position of any accused person, whether as Head of State or Government or as a responsible Government official, shall not relieve such person of criminal responsibility nor mitigate punishment.

3. The fact that any of the acts referred to in Articles 2 to 4 of the present Statute was committed by a subordinate does not relieve his or her superior of criminal responsibility if he or she knew or had reason to know that the subordinate was about to commit such acts or had done so and the superior failed to take the necessary and reasonable measures to prevent such acts or to punish the perpetrators thereof.

4. The fact that an accused person acted pursuant to an order of a Government or of a superior shall not relieve him or her of criminal responsibility, but may be considered in mitigation of punishment if the International Tribunal for Rwanda determines that justice so requires.

Article 7. Territorial and temporal jurisdiction

The territorial jurisdiction of the International Tribunal for Rwanda shall extend to the territory of Rwanda including its land surface and airspace as well as to the territory of neighbouring States in respect of serious violations of international humanitarian law committed by Rwandan citizens. The temporal jurisdiction of the International Tribunal for Rwanda shall extend to a period beginning on 1 January 1994 and ending on 31 December 1994.

Article 8. Concurrent jurisdiction

1. The International Tribunal for Rwanda and national courts shall have concurrent jurisdiction to prosecute persons for serious violations of international humanitarian law committed in the territory of Rwanda and Rwandan citizens for such violations committed in the territory of the neighbouring States, between 1 January 1994 and 31 December 1994.

2. The International Tribunal for Rwanda shall have the primacy over the national courts of all States. At any stage of the procedure, the International Tribunal for Rwanda may formally request national courts to defer to its competence in accordance with the present Statute and the Rules of Procedure and Evidence of the International Tribunal for Rwanda.

Article 9. *Non bis in idem*

1. No person shall be tried before a national court for acts constituting serious violations of international humanitarian law under the present Statute, for which he or she has already been tried by the International Tribunal for Rwanda.

2. A person who has been tried before a national court for acts constituting serious violations of international humanitarian law may be subsequently tried by the International Tribunal for Rwanda only if:

(a) The act for which he or she was tried was characterised as an ordinary crime; or

(b) The national court proceedings were not impartial or independent, were designed to shield the accused from international criminal responsibility, or the case was not diligently prosecuted.

3. In considering the penalty to be imposed on a person convicted of a crime under the present Statute, the International Tribunal for Rwanda shall take into account the extent to which any penalty imposed by a national court on the same person for the same act has already been served.

Article 10. Organisation of the International Tribunal for Rwanda

The International Tribunal for Rwanda shall consist of the following organs:

(a) The Chambers, comprising three Trial Chambers and an Appeals Chamber;

(b) The Prosecutor;

(c) A registry.

Article 11. Composition of the Chambers

The Chambers shall be composed of fourteen independent judges, no two of whom may be nationals of the same State, who shall serve as follows:

(a) Three judges shall serve in each of the Trial Chambers;

(b) Five judges shall serve in the Appeals Chamber.

Article 12. Qualification and election of judges

1. The judges shall be persons of high moral character, impartiality and integrity who possess the qualifications required in their respective countries for appointment to the highest judicial offices. In the overall composition of the Chambers due account shall be taken of the experience of the judges in criminal law, international law, including international humanitarian law and human rights law.

2. The members of the Appeals Chamber of the International Tribunal for the Prosecution of Persons Responsible for Serious Violations of International Humanitarian Law Committed in the Territory of the former Yugoslavia since 1991 (hereinafter referred to as "the International Tribunal for the former Yugoslavia") shall also serve as the members of the Appeals Chamber of the International Tribunal for Rwanda.

3. The judges of the Trial Chambers of the International Tribunal for Rwanda shall be elected by the General Assembly from a list submitted by the Security Council, in the following manner:

(a) The Secretary-General shall invite nominations for judges of the Trial Chambers from States Members of the United Nations and non-member States maintaining permanent observer missions at the United Nations Headquarters;

(b) Within thirty days of the date of the invitation of the Secretary-General, each State may nominate up to two candidates meeting the qualifications set out in paragraph 1 above, no two of whom shall be of the same nationality and neither of whom shall be one of the same nationality as any judge on the Appeals Chamber;

(c) The Secretary-General shall forward the nominations received to the Security Council. From the nominations received the Security Council shall establish a list of not less that eighteen and not more that twenty-seven candidates, taking due account of adequate representation on the International Tribunal for Rwanda of the principal legal systems of the world;

(d) The President of the Security Council shall transmit the list of candidates to the President of the General Assembly. From that list the General Assembly shall elect the nine judges of the Trial Chambers. The candidates who receive an absolute majority of the votes of the States Members of the United Nations and of the non-member States maintaining permanent observer missions at United Nations headquarters, shall be declared elected. Should two candidates of the same nationality obtain the required majority vote, the one who received the higher number of votes shall be considered elected.

4. In the event of a vacancy in the Trial Chambers, after consultation with the Presidents of the Security Council and of the General Assembly, the Secretary-General shall appoint a person meeting the qualifications of paragraph 1 above, for the remainder of the term of office concerned.

5. The judges of the Trial Chambers shall be elected for a term of four years. The terms and conditions of service shall be those of the judges of the International Tribunal for the former Yugoslavia. They shall be eligible for re-election.

Article 13. Officers and members of the Chambers

1. The judges of the International Tribunal for Rwanda shall elect a President.

2. After consultation with the judges of the International Tribunal for Rwanda, the President shall assign the judges to the Trial Chambers. A judge shall serve only in the Chamber to which he or she was assigned.

3. The judges of each Trial Chamber shall elect a Presiding Judge, who shall conduct all of the proceedings of that Trial Chamber as a whole.

Article 14. Rules of procedure and evidence

The judges of the International Tribunal for Rwanda shall adopt, for the purpose of proceedings before the International Tribunal for Rwanda, the rules of procedure and evidence for the conduct of the pre-trial phase of the proceedings, trials and appeals, the admission of evidence, the protection of victims and witnesses and other appropriate matters of the International Tribunal for the former Yugoslavia with such changes as they deem necessary.

Article 15. The Prosecutor

1. The Prosecutor shall be responsible for the investigation and prosecution of persons responsible for serious violations of international humanitarian law committed in the territory of Rwanda and Rwandan citizens responsible for such violations committed in the territory of neighbouring States, between 1 January 1994 and 31 December 1994.

2. The Prosecutor shall act independently as a separate organ of the International Tribunal for Rwanda. He or she shall not seek or receive instructions from any Government or from any other source.

3. The Prosecutor of the International Tribunal for the Former Yugoslavia shall also serve as the Prosecutor of the International Tribunal for Rwanda. He or she shall have additional staff, including an additional Deputy Prosecutor, to assist with prosecutions before the International Tribunal for Rwanda. Such staff shall be appointed by the Secretary-General on the recommendation of the Prosecutor.

Article 16. The Registry

1. The Registry shall be responsible for the administration and servicing of the International Tribunal for Rwanda.

2. The Registry shall consist of a Registrar and such other staff as may be required.

3. The Registrar shall be appointed by the Secretary-General after consultation with the President of the International Tribunal for Rwanda. He or she shall serve for a four-year term and be eligible for re-appointment. The terms and conditions of service of the Registrar shall be those of an Assistant Secretary-General of the United Nations.

4. The Staff of the Registry shall be appointed by the Secretary-General on the recommendation of the Registrar.

Article 17. Investigation and preparation of indictment

1. The Prosecutor shall initiate investigations ex-officio or on the basis of information obtained from any source, particularly from Governments, United Nations organs, intergovernmental and non-governmental organisations. The Prosecutor shall assess the information received or obtained and decide whether there is sufficient basis to proceed.

2. The Prosecutor shall have the power to question suspects, victims and witnesses, to collect evidence and to conduct on-site investigations. In carrying out these tasks, the Prosecutor may, as appropriate, seek the assistance of the State authorities concerned.

3. If questioned, the suspect shall be entitled to be assisted by counsel of his or her own choice, including the right to have legal assistance assigned to the suspect without payment by him or her in any such case if he or she does not have sufficient means to pay for it, as well as necessary translation into and from a language he or she speaks and understands.

4. Upon a determination that a *prima facie* case exists, the Prosecutor shall prepare an indictment containing a concise statement of the facts and the crime or crimes with which the accused is charged under the Statute. The indictment shall be transmitted to a judge of the Trial Chamber.

Article 18. Review of the Indictment

1. The judge of the Trial Chamber to whom the indictment has been transmitted shall review it. If satisfied that a *prima facie* case has been established by the Prosecutor, he or she shall confirm the indictment. If not so satisfied, the indictment shall be dismissed.

2. Upon confirmation of an indictment, the judge may, at the request of the Prosecutor, issue such orders and warrants for the arrest, detention, surrender or transfer of persons, and any other orders as may be required for the conduct of the trial.

Article 19. Commencement and conduct of trial proceedings

1. The Trial Chambers shall ensure that a trial is fair and expeditious and that proceedings are conducted in accordance with the rules of procedure and evidence, with full respect for the rights of the accused with due regard for the protection of victims and witnesses.

2. A person against whom an indictment has been confirmed shall, pursuant to an order or an arrest warrant of the International Tribunal for Rwanda, be taken into custody, immediately informed of the charges against him or her and transferred to the International Tribunal for Rwanda.

3. The Trial Chamber shall read the indictment, satisfy itself that the rights of the accused are respected, confirm that the accused understands the indictment, and instruct the accused to enter a plea. The Trial Chamber shall then set the date for trial.

4. The hearings shall be public unless the Trial Chamber decides to close the proceedings in accordance with its rules of procedure and evidence.

Article 20. Rights of the Accused

1. All persons shall be equal before the International Tribunal for Rwanda.

2. In the determination of charges against him or her, the accused shall be entitled to a fair and public hearing, subject to Article 21 of the Statute.

3. The accused shall be presumed innocent until proven guilty according to the provisions of the present Statute.

4. In determination of any charge against the accused pursuant to the present Statute, the accused shall be entitled to the following minimum guarantees, in full equality:

(a) To be informed promptly and in detail in a language which he or she understands of the nature and cause of the charge against him or her;

(b) To have adequate time and facilities for the preparation of his or her defence and to communicate with counsel of his or her own choosing;

(c) To be tried without undue delay;

(d) To be tried in his or her presence, and to defend himself or herself in person or through legal assistance of his or her own choosing; to be informed, if he or she does not have legal assistance, of this right; and to have legal assistance assigned to him or her, in any case where the interest of justice so require, and without payment by him or her in any such case if he or she does not have sufficient means to pay for it;

(e) To examine, or have examined, the witnesses against him or her and to obtain the attendance and examination of witnesses on his or her behalf under the same conditions as witnesses against him or her;

(f) To have the free assistance of an interpreter if her or she cannot understand or speak the language used in the International Tribunal for Rwanda;

(g) Not to be compelled to testify against himself or herself or to confess guilt.

Article 21. Protection of victims and witnesses

The International Tribunal for Rwanda shall provide in its rules of procedure and evidence for the protection of victims and witnesses. Such protection measures shall include, but shall not be limited to, the conduct of in camera proceedings and the protection of the victim's identity.

Article 22. Judgement

1. The Trial Chambers shall pronounce judgements and impose sentences and penalties on persons convicted of serious violations of international humanitarian law.

2. The judgement shall be rendered by a majority of the judges of the Trial Chamber, and shall be delivered by the Trial Chamber in public. It shall be accompanied by a reasoned opinion in writing, to which separate or dissenting opinions may be appended.

Article 23. Penalties

1. The penalty imposed by the Trial Chamber shall be limited to imprisonment. In determining the terms of imprisonment, the Trial Chambers shall have recourse to the general practice regarding prison sentences in the courts of Rwanda.

2. In imposing the sentences, the Trial Chambers should take into account such factors as the gravity of the offence and the individual circumstances of the convicted person.

3. In addition to imprisonment, the Trial Chambers may order the return of any property and proceeds acquired by criminal conduct, including by means of duress, to their rightful owners.

Article 24. Appellate Proceedings

1. The Appeals Chamber shall hear appeals from persons convicted by the Trial Chambers or from the Prosecutor on the following grounds:

(a) An error on a question of law invalidating the decision; or

(b) An error of fact which has occasioned a miscarriage of justice.

2. The Appeals Chamber may affirm, reverse or revise the decisions taken by the Trial Chambers.

Article 25. Review Proceedings

Where a new fact has been discovered which was not known at the time of the proceedings before the Trial Chambers or the Appeals Chamber and which could have been a decisive factor in reaching the decision, the convicted person or the Prosecutor may submit to the International Tribunal for Rwanda an application for review of the judgement.

Article 26. Enforcement of Sentences

Imprisonment shall be served in Rwanda or any of the States on a list of States which have indicated to the Security Council their willingness to accept convicted persons, as designated by the International Tribunal for Rwanda. Such imprisonment shall be in accordance with the applicable law of the State concerned, subject to the supervision of the International Tribunal for Rwanda.

Article 27. Pardon or commutation of sentences

If, pursuant to the applicable law of the State in which the convicted person is imprisoned, he or she is eligible for pardon or commutation of sentence, the State concerned shall notify the International Tribunal for Rwanda accordingly. There shall only be pardon or commutation of sentence if the President of the International Tribunal for Rwanda, in consultation with the judges, so decides on the basis of the interests of justice and the general principles of law.

Article 28. Cooperation and judicial assistance

1. States shall cooperate with the International Tribunal for Rwanda in the investigation and prosecution of persons accused of committing serious violations of international humanitarian law.

2. States shall comply without undue delay with any request for assistance or an order issued by a Trial Chamber, including but not limited to:

(a) The identification and location of persons;

(b) The taking of testimony and the production of evidence;

(c) The service of documents;

(d) The arrest or detention of persons;

(e) The surrender or the transfer of the accused to the International Tribunal for Rwanda.

Article 29. The status, privileges and immunities of the International Tribunal for Rwanda

1. The Convention on the Privileges and Immunities of the United Nations of 13 February 1946 shall apply to the Registrar and his or her staff.

2. The judges, the Prosecutor and the Registrar shall enjoy the privileges and immunities, exemptions and facilities accorded to diplomatic envoys, in accordance with international law.

3. The staff of the Prosecutor and of the Registrar shall enjoy the privileges and immunities accorded to officials of the United Nations under Articles V and VII of the Convention referred to in paragraph 1 of this article.

4. Other persons, including the accused, required at the seat or meeting place of the International Tribunal for Rwanda shall be accorded such treatment as is necessary for the proper functioning of the International Tribunal for Rwanda.

Article 30. Expenses of the International Tribunal for Rwanda

The expenses of the International Tribunal for Rwanda shall be expenses of the Organisation in accordance with Article 17 of the Charter of the United Nations.

Article 31. Working languages

The working languages of the International Tribunal for Rwanda shall be English and French.

Article 32. Annual Report

The President of the International Tribunal for Rwanda shall submit an annual report of the International Tribunal for Rwanda to the Security Council and to the General Assembly.

Rome Statute of the International Criminal Court (ICC)
Adopted by the U.N. Diplomatic Conference, July 17, 1998
2187 U.N.T.S. 90

Preamble

Conscious that all peoples are united by common bonds, their cultures pieced together in a shared heritage, and concerned that this delicate mosaic may be shattered at any time,

Mindful that during this century millions of children, women and men have been victims of unimaginable atrocities that deeply shock the conscience of humanity,

Recognizing that such grave crimes threaten the peace, security and well-being of the world,

Affirming that the most serious crimes of concern to the international community as a whole must not go unpunished and that their effective prosecution must be ensured by taking measures at the national level and by enhancing international cooperation,

Determined to put an end to impunity for the perpetrators of these crimes and thus to contribute to the prevention of such crimes,

Recalling that it is the duty of every State to exercise its criminal jurisdiction over those responsible for international crimes,

Reaffirming the Purposes and Principles of the Charter of the United Nations, and in particular that all States shall refrain from the threat or use of force against the territorial integrity or political independence of any State, or in any other manner inconsistent with the Purposes of the United Nations,

Emphasizing in this connection that nothing in this Statute shall be taken as authorizing any State Party to intervene in an armed conflict in the internal affairs of any State,

Determined to these ends and for the sake of present and future generations, to establish an independent permanent International Criminal Court in relationship with the United Nations system, with jurisdiction over the most serious crimes of concern to the international community as a whole,

Emphasizing that the International Criminal Court established under this Statute shall be complementary to national criminal jurisdictions,

Resolved to guarantee lasting respect for the enforcement of international justice,

Have agreed as follows:

Part 1. Establishment of the Court

Article 1. The Court

An International Criminal Court ("the Court") is hereby established. It shall be a permanent institution and shall have the power to exercise its jurisdiction over persons for the most serious crimes of international concern, as referred to in this Statute, and shall be complementary to national criminal jurisdictions. The jurisdiction and functioning of the Court shall be governed by the provisions of this Statute.

Article 2. Relationship of the Court with the United Nations

The Court shall be brought into relationship with the United Nations through an agreement to be approved by the Assembly of States Parties to this Statute and thereafter concluded by the President of the Court on its behalf.

Article 3. Seat of the Court

1. The seat of the Court shall be established at The Hague in the Netherlands ("the host State").

2. The Court shall enter into a headquarters agreement with the host State, to be approved by the Assembly of States Parties and thereafter concluded by the President of the Court on its behalf.

3. The Court may sit elsewhere, whenever it considers it desirable, as provided in this Statute.

Article 4. Legal status and powers of the Court

1. The Court shall have international legal personality. It shall also have such legal capacity as may be necessary for the exercise of its functions and the fulfilment of its purposes.

2. The Court may exercise its functions and powers, as provided in this Statute, on the territory of any State Party and, by special agreement, on the territory of any other State.

Part 2. Jurisdiction, Admissibility and Applicable Law

Article 5. Crimes within the jurisdiction of the Court

1. The jurisdiction of the Court shall be limited to the most serious crimes of concern to the international community as a whole. The Court has jurisdiction in accordance with this Statute with respect to the following crimes:

   (a) The crime of genocide;

   (b) Crimes against humanity;

   (c) War crimes;

   (d) The crime of aggression.

2. The Court shall exercise jurisdiction over the crime of aggression once a provision is adopted in accordance with Articles 121 and 123 defining the crime and setting out the conditions under which the Court shall exercise jurisdiction with respect to this crime. Such a provision shall be consistent with the relevant provisions of the Charter of the United Nations.

Article 6. Genocide

For the purpose of this Statute, "genocide" means any of the following acts committed with intent to destroy, in whole or in part, a national, ethnical, racial or religious group, as such:

(a) Killing members of the group;

(b) Causing serious bodily or mental harm to members of the group;

(c) Deliberately inflicting on the group conditions of life calculated to bring about its physical destruction in whole or in part;

(d) Imposing measures intended to prevent births within the group;

(e) Forcibly transferring children of the group to another group.

Article 7. Crimes against humanity

1. For the purpose of this Statute, "crime against humanity" means any of the following acts when committed as part of a widespread or systematic attack directed against any civilian population, with knowledge of the attack:

(a) Murder;

(b) Extermination;

(c) Enslavement;

(d) Deportation or forcible transfer of population;

(e) Imprisonment or other severe deprivation of physical liberty in violation of fundamental rules of international law;

(f) Torture;

(g) Rape, sexual slavery, enforced prostitution, forced pregnancy, enforced sterilization, or any other form of sexual violence of comparable gravity;

(h) Persecution against any identifiable group or collectivity on political, racial, national, ethnic, cultural, religious, gender as defined in paragraph 3, or other grounds that are universally recognised as impermissible under international law, in connection with any act referred to in this paragraph or any crime within the jurisdiction of the Court;

(i) Enforced disappearance of persons;

(j) The crime of apartheid;

(k) Other inhumane acts of a similar character intentionally causing great suffering, or serious injury to body or to mental or physical health.

2. For the purpose of paragraph 1:

(a) "Attack directed against any civilian population" means a course of conduct involving the multiple commission of acts referred to in paragraph 1 against any civilian population, pursuant to or in furtherance of a State or organizational policy to commit such attack;

(b) "Extermination" includes the intentional infliction of conditions of life, *inter alia* the deprivation of access to food and medicine, calculated to bring about the destruction of part of a population;

(c) "Enslavement" means the exercise of any or all of the powers attaching to the right of ownership over a person and includes the exercise of such power in the course of trafficking in persons, in particular women and children;

(d) "Deportation or forcible transfer of population" means forced displacement of the persons concerned by expulsion or other coercive acts from the area in which they are lawfully present, without grounds permitted under international law;

(e) "Torture" means the intentional infliction of severe pain or suffering, whether physical or mental, upon a person in the custody or under the control of the accused; except that torture shall not include pain or suffering arising only from, inherent in or incidental to, lawful sanctions;

(f) "Forced pregnancy" means the unlawful confinement, of a woman forcibly made pregnant, with the intent of affecting the ethnic composition of any population or carrying out other grave violations of international law. This definition shall not in any way be interpreted as affecting national laws relating to pregnancy;

(g) "Persecution" means the intentional and severe deprivation of fundamental rights contrary to international law by reason of the identity of the group or collectivity;

(h) "The crime of apartheid" means inhumane acts of a character similar to those referred to in paragraph 1, committed in the context of an institutionalized regime of systematic oppression and domination by one racial group over any other racial group or groups and committed with the intention of maintaining that regime;

(i) "Enforced disappearance of persons" means the arrest, detention or abduction of persons by, or with the authorization, support or acquiescence of, a State or a political organization, followed by a refusal to acknowledge that deprivation of freedom or to give information on the fate or whereabouts of those persons, with the intention of removing them from the protection of the law for a prolonged period of time.

3. For the purpose of this Statute, it is understood that the term "gender" refers to the two sexes, male and female, within the context of society. The term "gender" does not indicate any meaning different from the above.

Article 8. War Crimes

1. The Court shall have jurisdiction in respect of war crimes in particular when committed as a part of a plan or policy or as part of a large-scale commission of such crimes.

2. For the purpose of this Statute, "war crimes" means:

(a) Grave breaches of the Geneva Conventions of 12 August 1949, namely, any of the following acts against persons or property protected under the provisions of the relevant Geneva Convention:

(i) Wilful killing;

(ii) Torture or inhuman treatment, including biological experiments;

(iii) Wilfully causing great suffering, or serious injury to body or health;

(iv) Extensive destruction and appropriation of property, not justified by military necessity and carried out unlawfully and wantonly;

(v) Compelling a prisoner of war or other protected person to serve in the forces of a hostile Power;

(vi) Wilfully depriving a prisoner of war or other protected person of the rights of fair and regular trial;

(vii) Unlawful deportation or transfer or unlawful confinement;

(viii) Taking of hostages.

(b) Other serious violations of the laws and customs applicable in international armed conflict, within the established framework of international law, namely, any of the following acts:

(i) Intentionally directing attacks against the civilian population as such or against individual civilians not taking direct part in hostilities;

(ii) Intentionally directing attacks against civilian objects, that is, objects which are not military objectives;

(iii) Intentionally directing attacks against personnel, installations, material, units or vehicles involved in a humanitarian assistance or peacekeeping mission in accordance with the Charter of the United Nations, as long as they are entitled to the protection given to civilians or civilian objects under the international law of armed conflict;

(iv) Intentionally launching an attack in the knowledge that such attack will cause incidental loss of life or injury to civilians or damage to civilian objects or widespread, long-term and severe damage to the natural environment which would be clearly excessive in relation to the concrete and direct overall military advantage anticipated;

(v) Attacking or bombarding, by whatever means, towns, villages, dwellings or buildings which are undefended and which are not military objectives;

(vi) Killing or wounding a combatant who, having laid down his arms or having no longer means of defence, has surrendered at discretion;

(vii) Making improper use of a flag of truce, of the flag or of the military insignia and uniform of the enemy or of the United Nations, as well as of the distinctive emblems of the Geneva Conventions, resulting in death or serious personal injury;

(viii) The transfer, directly or indirectly, by the Occupying Power of parts of its own civilian population into the territory it occupies, or the deportation or transfer of all or parts of the population of the occupied territory within or outside this territory;

(ix) Intentionally directing attacks against buildings dedicated to religion, education, art, science or charitable purposes, historic monuments, hospitals and places where the sick and wounded are collected, provided they are not military objectives;

(x) Subjecting persons who are in the power of an adverse party to physical mutilation or to medical or scientific experiments of any kind which are neither justified by the medical, dental or hospital treatment of the person concerned nor carried out in his or her interest, and which cause death to or seriously endanger the health of such person or persons;

(xi) Killing or wounding treacherously individuals belonging to the hostile nation or army;

(xii) Declaring that no quarter will be given;

(xiii) Destroying or seizing the enemy's property unless such destruction or seizure be imperatively demanded by the necessities of war;

(xiv) Declaring abolished, suspended or inadmissible in a court of law the rights and actions of the nationals of the hostile party;

(xv) Compelling the nationals of the hostile party to take part in the operations of war directed against their own country, even if they were in the belligerent's service before the commencement of the war;

(xvi) Pillaging a town or place, even when taken by assault;

(xvii) Employing poison or poisoned weapons;

(xviii) Employing asphyxiating, poisonous or other gases, and all analogous liquids, materials or devices;

(xix) Employing bullets which expand or flatten easily in the human body, such as bullets with a hard envelope which does not entirely cover the core or is pierced with incisions;

(xx) Employing weapons, projectiles and material and methods of warfare which are of a nature to cause superfluous injury or unnecessary suffering or which are inherently indiscriminate in violation of the international law of armed conflict, provided that such weapons, projectiles and material and methods of warfare are the subject of a comprehensive prohibition and are included in an annex to this Statute, by an amendment in accordance with the relevant provisions set forth in Articles 121 and 123;

(xxi) Committing outrages upon personal dignity, in particular humiliating and degrading treatment;

(xxii) Committing rape, sexual slavery, enforced prostitution, forced pregnancy, as defined in Article 7, paragraph 2 (f), enforced sterilization, or any other form of sexual violence also constituting a grave breach of the Geneva Conventions;

(xxiii) Utilizing the presence of a civilian or other protected person to render certain points, areas or military forces immune from military operations;

(xxiv) Intentionally directing attacks against buildings, material, medical units and transport, and personnel using the distinctive emblems of the Geneva Conventions in conformity with international law;

(xxv) Intentionally using starvation of civilians as a method of warfare by depriving them of objects indispensable to their survival, including wilfully impeding relief supplies as provided for under the Geneva Conventions;

(xxvi) Conscripting or enlisting children under the age of fifteen years into the national armed forces or using them to participate actively in hostilities.

(c) In the case of an armed conflict not of an international character, serious violations of Article 3 common to the four Geneva Conventions of 12 August 1949, namely, any of the following acts committed against persons taking no active part in the hostilities, including members of armed forces who have laid down their arms and those placed *hors de combat* by sickness, wounds, detention or any other cause:

(i) Violence to life and person, in particular murder of all kinds, mutilation, cruel treatment and torture;

(ii) Committing outrages upon personal dignity, in particular humiliating and degrading treatment;

(iii) Taking of hostages;

(iv) The passing of sentences and the carrying out of executions without previous judgement pronounced by a regularly constituted court, affording all judicial guarantees which are generally recognized as indispensable.

(d) Paragraph 2 (c) applies to armed conflicts not of an international character and thus does not apply to situations of internal disturbances and tensions, such as riots, isolated and sporadic acts of violence or other acts of a similar nature.

(e) Other serious violations of the laws and customs applicable in armed conflicts not of an international character, within the established framework of international law, namely, any of the following acts:

(i) Intentionally directing attacks against the civilian population as such or against individual civilians not taking direct part in hostilities;

(ii) Intentionally directing attacks against buildings, material, medical units and transport, and personnel using the distinctive emblems of the Geneva Conventions in conformity with international law;

(iii) Intentionally directing attacks against personnel, installations, material, units or vehicles involved in a humanitarian assistance or peacekeeping mission in accordance with the Charter of the United Nations, as long as they are entitled to the protection given to civilians or civilian objects under the law of armed conflict;

(iv) Intentionally directing attacks against buildings dedicated to religion, education, art, science or charitable purposes, historic monuments, hospitals and places where the sick and wounded are collected, provided they are not military objectives;

(v) Pillaging a town or place, even when taken by assault;

(vi) Committing rape, sexual slavery, enforced prostitution, forced pregnancy, as defined in Article 7, paragraph 2 (f), enforced sterilization, and any other form of sexual violence also constituting a serious violation of Article 3 common to the four Geneva Conventions;

(vii) Conscripting or enlisting children under the age of fifteen years into armed forces or groups or using them to participate actively in hostilities;

(viii) Ordering the displacement of the civilian population for reasons related to the conflict, unless the security of the civilians involved or imperative military reasons so demand;

(ix) Killing or wounding treacherously a combatant adversary;

(x) Declaring that no quarter will be given;

(xi) Subjecting persons who are in the power of another party to the conflict to physical mutilation or to medical or scientific experiments of any kind which are neither justified by the medical, dental or hospital treatment of the person concerned nor carried out in his or her interest, and which cause death to or seriously endanger the health of such person or persons;

(xii) Destroying or seizing the property of an adversary unless such destruction or seizure be imperatively demanded by the necessities of the conflict;

(f) Paragraph 2 (e) applies to armed conflicts not of an international character and thus does not apply to situations of internal disturbances and tensions, such as riots, isolated and sporadic acts of violence or other acts of a similar nature. It applies to armed conflicts that take place in the territory of a State when there is protracted armed conflict between governmental authorities and organized armed groups or between such groups.

3. Nothing in paragraphs 2 (c) and (d) shall affect the responsibility of a Government to maintain or reestablish law and order in the State or to defend the unity and territorial integrity of the State, by all legitimate means.

Article 9

1. Elements of Crimes shall assist the Court in the interpretation and application of Articles 6, 7 and 8. They shall be adopted by a two-thirds majority of the members of the Assembly of States Parties.

2. Amendments to the Elements of Crimes may be proposed by:

(a) Any State Party;

(b) The judges acting by an absolute majority;

(c) The Prosecutor.

Such amendments shall be adopted by a two-thirds majority of the members of the Assembly of States Parties.

3. The Elements of Crimes and amendments thereto shall be consistent with this Statute.

Article 10

Nothing in this Part shall be interpreted as limiting or prejudicing in any way existing or developing rules of international law for purposes other than this Statute.

Article 11

1. The Court has jurisdiction only with respect to crimes committed after the entry into force of this Statute.

2. If a State becomes a Party to this Statute after its entry into force, the Court may exercise its jurisdiction only with respect to crimes committed after the entry into force of this Statute for that State, unless that State has made a declaration under Article 12, paragraph 3.

Article 12. Preconditions to the exercise of jurisdiction

1. A State which becomes a Party to this Statute thereby accepts the jurisdiction of the Court with respect to the crimes referred to in Article 5.

2. In the case of Article 13, paragraph (a) or (c), the Court may exercise its jurisdiction if one or more of the following States are Parties to this Statute or have accepted the jurisdiction of the Court in accordance with paragraph 3:

(a) The State on the territory of which the conduct in question occurred or, if the crime was committed on board a vessel or aircraft, the State of registration of that vessel or aircraft;

(b) The State of which the person accused of the crime is a national.

3. If the acceptance of a State which is not a Party to this Statute is required under paragraph 2, that State may, by declaration lodged with the Registrar, accept the exercise of jurisdiction by the Court with respect to the crime in question. The accepting State shall cooperate with the Court without any delay or exception in accordance with Part 9.

Article 13. Exercise of jurisdiction

The Court may exercise its jurisdiction with respect to a crime referred to in Article 5 in accordance with the provisions of this Statute if:

(a) A situation in which one or more of such crimes appears to have been committed is referred to the Prosecutor by a State Party in accordance with Article 14;

(b) A situation in which one or more of such crimes appears to have been committed is referred to the Prosecutor by the Security Council acting under Chapter VII of the United Nations; or

(c) The Prosecutor has initiated an investigation in respect of such a crime in accordance with Article 15.

Article 14. Referral of a situation by a State Party

1. A State Party may refer to the Prosecutor a situation in which one or more crimes within the jurisdiction of the Court appear to have been committed requesting the Prosecutor to investigate the situation for the purpose of determining whether one or more specific persons should be charged with the commission of such crimes.

2. As far as possible, a referral shall specify the relevant circumstances and be accompanied by such supporting documentation as is available to the State referring the situation.

Article 15. Prosecutor

1. The Prosecutor may initiate investigations *proprio motu* on the basis of information on crimes within the jurisdiction of the Court.

2. The Prosecutor shall analyse the seriousness of the information received. For this purpose, he or she may seek additional information from States, organs of the United Nations, intergovernmental or non-governmental organizations, or other reliable sources that he or she deems appropriate, and may receive written or oral testimony at the seat of the Court.

3. If the Prosecutor concludes that there is a reasonable basis to proceed with an investigation, he or she shall submit to the Pre-Trial Chamber a request for authorization of an investigation, together with any supporting material collected. Victims may make representations to the Pre-Trial Chamber, in accordance with the Rules of Procedure and Evidence.

4. If the Pre-Trial Chamber, upon examination of the request and the supporting material, considers that there is a reasonable basis to proceed with an investigation, and that the case appears to fall within the jurisdiction of the Court, it shall authorize the commencement of the investigation, without prejudice to subsequent determinations by the Court with regard to the jurisdiction and admissibility of a case.

5. The refusal of the Pre-Trial Chamber to authorize the investigation shall not preclude the presentation of a subsequent request by the Prosecutor based on new facts or evidence regarding the same situation.

6. If, after the preliminary examination referred to in paragraphs 1 and 2, the Prosecutor concludes that the information provided does not constitute a reasonable basis for an investigation, he or she shall inform those who provided the information. This shall not preclude the Prosecutor from considering further information submitted to him or her regarding the same situation in the light of new facts or evidence.

Article 16. Deferral of investigation or prosecution

No investigation or prosecution may be commenced or proceeded with under this Statute for a period of 12 months after the Security Council, in a resolution adopted under Chapter VII of the Charter of the United Nations, has requested the Court to that effect; that request may be renewed by the Council under the same conditions.

Article 17. Issues of admissibility

1. Having regard to paragraph 10 of the Preamble and Article 1, the Court shall determine that a case is inadmissible where:

(a) The case is being investigated or prosecuted by a State which has jurisdiction over it, unless the State is unwilling or unable genuinely to carry out the investigation or prosecution;

(b) The case has been investigated by a State which has jurisdiction over it and the State has decided not to prosecute the person concerned, unless the decision resulted from the unwillingness or inability of the State genuinely to prosecute;

(c) The person concerned has already been tried for conduct which is the subject of the complaint, and a trial by the Court is not permitted under Article 20, paragraph 3;

(d) The case is not of sufficient gravity to justify further action by the Court.

2. In order to determine unwillingness in a particular case, the Court shall consider, having regard to the principles of due process recognized by international law, whether one or more of the following exist, as applicable:

(a) The proceedings were or are being undertaken or the national decision was made for the purpose of shielding the person concerned from criminal responsibility for crimes within the jurisdiction of the Court referred to in Article 5;

(b) There has been an unjustified delay in the proceedings which in the circumstances is inconsistent with an intent to bring the person concerned to justice;

(c) The proceedings were not or are not being conducted independently or impartially, and they were or are being conducted in a manner which, in the circumstances, is inconsistent with an intent to bring the person concerned to justice.

3. In order to determine inability in a particular case, the Court shall consider whether, due to a total or substantial collapse or unavailability of its national judicial system, the State is unable to obtain the accused or the necessary evidence and testimony or otherwise unable to carry out its proceedings.

Article 18. Preliminary rulings regarding admissibility

1. When a situation has been referred to the Court pursuant to Article 13 (a) and the Prosecutor has determined that there would be a reasonable basis to commence an investigation, or the Prosecutor initiates an investigation pursuant to Articles 13 (c) and 15, the Prosecutor shall notify all States Parties and those States which, taking into account the information available, would normally exercise jurisdiction over the crimes concerned. The Prosecutor may notify such States on a confidential basis and, where the Prosecutor believes it necessary to protect persons, prevent destruction of evidence or prevent the absconding of persons, may limit the scope of the information provided to States.

2. Within one month of receipt of that notice, a State may inform the Court that it is investigating or has investigated its nationals or others within its jurisdiction with respect to criminal acts which may constitute crimes referred to in Article 5 and which relate to the information provided in the notification to States. At the request of that State, the Prosecutor shall defer to the State's investigation of those persons unless the Pre-Trial Chamber, on the application of the Prosecutor, decides to authorize the investigation.

3. The Prosecutor's deferral to a State's investigation shall be open to review by the Prosecutor six months after the date of deferral or at any time when there has been a significant change of circumstances based on the State's unwillingness or inability genuinely to carry out the investigation.

4. The State concerned or the Prosecutor may appeal to the Appeals Chamber against a ruling of the Pre-Trial Chamber, in accordance with Article 82, paragraph 2. The appeal may be heard on an expedited basis.

5. When the Prosecutor has deferred an investigation in accordance with paragraph 2, the Prosecutor may request that the State concerned periodically inform the Prosecutor of the progress of its investigations and any subsequent prosecutions. States Parties shall respond to such requests without undue delay.

6. Pending a ruling by the Pre-Trial Chamber, or at any time when the Prosecutor has deferred an investigation under this article, the Prosecutor may, on an exceptional basis, seek authority from the Pre-Trial Chamber to pursue necessary investigative steps for the purpose of preserving evidence where there is a unique opportunity to obtain important evidence or there is a significant risk that such evidence may not be subsequently available.

7. A State which has challenged a ruling of the Pre-Trial Chamber under this article may challenge the admissibility of a case under Article 19 on the grounds of additional significant facts or significant change of circumstances.

Article 19. Challenges to the jurisdiction of the Court or the admissibility of a case

1. The Court shall satisfy itself that it has jurisdiction in any case brought before it. The Court may, on its own motion, determine the admissibility of a case in accordance with Article 17.

2. Challenges to the admissibility of a case on the grounds referred to in Article 17 or challenges to the jurisdiction of the Court may be made by:

(a) An accused or a person for whom a warrant of arrest or a summons to appear has been issued under Article 58;

(b) A State which has jurisdiction over a case, on the ground that it is investigating or prosecuting the case or has investigated or prosecuted; or

(c) A State from which acceptance of jurisdiction is required under Article 12.

3. The Prosecutor may seek a ruling from the Court regarding a question of jurisdiction or admissibility. In proceedings with respect to jurisdiction or admissibility, those who have referred the situation under Article 13, as well as victims, may also submit observations to the Court.

4. The admissibility of a case or the jurisdiction of the Court may be challenged only once by any person or State referred to in paragraph 2. The challenge shall take place prior to or at the commencement of the trial. In exceptional circumstances, the Court may grant leave for a challenge to be brought more than once or at a time later than the commencement of the trial. Challenges to the admissibility of a case, at the commencement of a trial, or subsequently with the leave of the Court, may be based only on Article 17, paragraph 1 (c).

5. A State referred to in paragraph 2 (b) and (c) shall make a challenge at the earliest opportunity.

6. Prior to the confirmation of the charges, challenges to the admissibility of a case or challenges to the jurisdiction of the Court shall be referred to the Pre-Trial Chamber.

After confirmation of the charges, they shall be referred to the Trial Chamber. Decisions with respect to jurisdiction or admissibility may be appealed to the Appeals Chamber in accordance with Article 82.

7. If a challenge is made by a State referred to in paragraph 2 (b) or (c), the Prosecutor shall suspend the investigation until such time as the Court makes a determination in accordance with Article 17.

8. Pending a ruling by the Court, the Prosecutor may seek authority from the Court:

(a) To pursue necessary investigative steps of the kind referred to in Article 18, paragraph 6;

(b) To take a statement or testimony from a witness or complete the collection and examination of evidence which had begun prior to the making of the challenge; and

(c) In cooperation with the relevant States, to prevent the absconding of persons in respect of whom the Prosecutor has already requested a warrant of arrest under Article 58.

9. The making of challenge shall not affect the validity of any act performed by the Prosecutor or any order or warrant issued by the Court prior to the making of the challenge.

10. If the Court has decided that a case is inadmissible under Article 17, the Prosecutor may submit a request for a review of the decision when he or she is fully satisfied that new facts have arisen which negate the basis on which the case had previously been found inadmissible under Article 17.

11. If the Prosecutor, having regard to the matters referred to in Article 17, defers an investigation, the Prosecutor may request that the relevant State make available to the Prosecutor information on the proceedings. That information shall, at the request of the State concerned, be confidential. If the Prosecutor thereafter decides to proceed with an investigation, he or she shall notify the State in respect of the proceedings of which deferral has taken place.

Article 20. *Ne bis in idem*

1. Except as provided in this Statute, no person shall be tried before the Court with respect to conduct which formed the basis of crimes for which the person has been convicted or acquitted by the Court.

2. No person shall be tried before another court for a crime referred to in Article 5 for which that person has already been convicted or acquitted by the Court.

3. No person who has been tried by another court for conduct also proscribed under Articles 6, 7 or 8 shall be tried by the Court with respect to the same conduct unless the proceedings in the other court:

(a) Were for the purpose of shielding the person concerned from criminal responsibility for crimes within the jurisdiction of the Court; or

(b) Otherwise were not conducted independently or impartially in accordance with the norms of due process recognized by international law and were conducted in a manner which, in the circumstances, was inconsistent with an intent to bring the person concerned to justice.

Article 21. Applicable law

1. The Court shall apply:

(a) In the first place, this Statute, Elements of Crimes and its Rules of Procedure and Evidence;

(b) In the second place, where appropriate, applicable treaties and the principles and rules of international law, including the established principles of the international law of armed conflict;

(c) Failing that, general principles of law derived by the Court from national laws and legal systems of the world....

2. The Court may apply principles and rules of law as interpreted in its previous decisions.

3. The application and interpretation of law pursuant to this article must be consistent with internationally recognized human rights, and be without any adverse distinction founded on grounds such as gender, as defined in Article 7, paragraph 3, age, race, colour, language, religion or belief, political or other opinion, national, ethnic or social origin, wealth, birth or other status.

Part 3. General Principles of Criminal Law

Article 22. *Nullum crimen sine lege*

1. A person shall not be criminally responsible under this Statute unless the conduct in question constitutes, at the time it takes place, a crime within the jurisdiction of this Court.

2. The definition of a crime shall be strictly construed and shall not be extended by analogy. In case of ambiguity, the definition shall be interpreted in favour of the person being investigated, prosecuted or convicted.

3. This article shall not affect the characterization of any conduct as criminal under international law independently of this Statute.

Article 23. *Nulla poena sine lege*

A person convicted by the Court may be punished only in accordance with this Statute.

Article 24. Non-retroactivity *ratione personae*

1. No person shall be criminally responsible under this Statute for conduct prior to entry into force of the Statute.

2. In the event of a change in the law applicable to a given case prior to a final judgment, the law more favourable to the person being investigated, prosecuted or convicted shall apply.

Article 25. Individual criminal responsibility

1. The Court shall have jurisdiction over natural persons pursuant to this Statute.

2. A person who commits a crime within the jurisdiction of the Court shall be individually responsible and liable for punishment in accordance with this Statute.

3. In accordance with this Statute, a person shall be criminally responsible and liable for punishment for a crime within the jurisdiction of the Court if that person:

(a) Commits such a crime, whether as an individual, jointly with another or through another person, regardless of whether that other person is criminally responsible;

(b) Orders, solicits or induces the commission of such a crime which in fact occurs or is attempted;

(c) For the purpose of facilitating the commission of such a crime, aids, abets or otherwise assists in its commission or its attempted commission, including providing the means for its commission;

(d) In any other way contributes to the commission or attempted commission of such a crime by a group of persons acting with a common purpose. Such contribution shall be intentional and shall either:

(i) Be made with the aim of furthering the criminal activity or criminal purpose of the group, where such activity or purpose involves the commission of a crime within the jurisdiction of the Court; or

(ii) Be made in the knowledge of the intention of the group to commit the crime;

(e) In respect of the crime of genocide, directly and publicly incites others to commit genocide;

(f) Attempts to commit such a crime by taking action that commences its execution by means of a substantial step, but the crime does not occur because of circumstances independent of the person's intentions. However, a person who abandons the effort to commit the crime or otherwise prevents the completion of the crime shall not be liable for punishment under this Statute for the attempt to commit that crime if that person completely and voluntarily gave up the criminal purpose.

4. No provision in this Statute relating to individual criminal responsibility shall affect the responsibility of States under international law.

Article 26. Exclusion of jurisdiction over persons under eighteen

The Court shall have no jurisdiction over any person who was under the age of 18 at the time of the alleged commission of a crime.

Article 27. Irrelevance of official capacity

1. This Statute shall apply equally to all persons without any distinction based on official capacity. In particular, official capacity as a Head of State or Government, a member of a Government or parliament, an elected representative or a government official shall in no case exempt a person from criminal responsibility under this Statute, nor shall it, in and of itself, constitute a ground for reduction of sentence.

2. Immunities or special procedural rules which may attach to the official capacity of a person, whether under national or international law, shall not bar the Court from exercising its jurisdiction over such a person.

Article 28. Responsibility of commanders and other superiors

In addition to other grounds of criminal responsibility under this Statute for crimes within the jurisdiction of the Court:

1. A military commander or person effectively acting as a military commander shall be criminally responsible for crimes within the jurisdiction of the Court committed by forces under his or her effective command and control, or effective authority and control as the case may be, as a result of his or her failure to exercise control properly over such forces, where:

(a) That military commander or person either knew or, owing to the circumstances at the time, should have known that the forces were committing or about to commit such crimes; and

(b) That military commander or person failed to take all necessary and reasonable measures within his or her power to prevent or repress their commission or to submit the matter to the competent authorities for investigation and prosecution.

2. With respect to superior and subordinate relationships not described in paragraph 1, a superior shall be criminally responsible for crimes within the jurisdiction of the Court committed by subordinates under his or her effective authority and control, as a result of his or her failure to exercise control properly over such subordinates, where:

(a) The superior either knew, or consciously disregarded information which clearly indicated, that the subordinates were committing or about to commit such crimes;

(b) The crimes concerned activities that were within the effective responsibility and control of the superior; and

(c) The superior failed to take all necessary and reasonable measures within his or her power to prevent or repress their commission or to submit the matter to the competent authorities for investigation and prosecution.

Article 29. Non-applicability of statute of limitations

The crimes within the jurisdiction of the Court shall not be subject to any statute of limitations.

Article 30. Mental Element

1. Unless otherwise provided, a person shall be criminally responsible and liable for punishment for a crime within the jurisdiction of the Court only if the material elements are committed with intent and knowledge.

2. For the purposes of this article, a person has intent where:

(a) In relation to conduct, that person means to engage in the conduct;

(b) In relation to a consequence, that person means to cause that consequence or is aware that it will occur in the ordinary course of events.

3. For the purposes of this article, "knowledge" means awareness that a circumstance exists or a consequence will occur in the ordinary course of events. "Know" and "knowingly" shall be construed accordingly.

Article 31. Grounds for excluding criminal responsibility

1. In addition to other grounds for excluding criminal responsibility provided for in this Section, a person shall not be criminally responsible if, at the time of that person's conduct:

(a) The person suffers from a mental disease or defect that destroys that person's capacity to appreciate the unlawfulness or nature of his or her conduct, or capacity to control his or her conduct to conform to the requirements of law;

(b) The person is in a state of intoxication that destroys that person's capacity to appreciate the unlawfulness or nature of his or her conduct, or capacity to control his or her conduct to conform to the requirements of law, unless the person has become voluntarily intoxicated under such circumstances that the person knew, or disregarded the risk, that, as a result of the intoxication, he or she was likely to engage in conduct constituting a crime within the jurisdiction of the Court;

(c) The person acts reasonably to defend himself or herself or another person or, in the case of war crimes, property which is essential for the survival of the person or another person or property which is essential for accomplishing a military mission, against an imminent and unlawful use of force in a manner proportionate to the degree of danger to the person or the other person or property protected. The fact that the person was involved in a defensive operation conducted by forces shall not in itself constitute a ground for excluding criminal responsibility under this subparagraph;

(d) The conduct which is alleged to constitute a crime within the jurisdiction of the Court has been caused by duress resulting from a threat of imminent death or of continuing or imminent serious bodily harm against that person or another person, and the person acts necessarily and reasonably to avoid this threat, provided that the person does not intend to cause a greater harm than the one sought to be avoided. Such a threat may either be:

(i) Made by other persons; or

(ii) Constituted by other circumstances beyond that person's control.

2. The Court shall determine the applicability of the grounds for excluding criminal responsibility provided for in this Statute to the case before it.

3. At trial, the Court may consider a ground for excluding criminal responsibility other than those referred to in paragraph 1 where such a ground is derived from applicable law as set forth in Article 21. The procedure relating to the consideration of such a ground shall be provided for in the Rules of Procedure and Evidence.

Article 32. Mistake of fact or mistake of law

1. A mistake of fact shall be a ground for excluding criminal responsibility only if it negates the mental element required by the crime.

2. A mistake of law as to whether a particular type of conduct is a crime within the jurisdiction of the Court shall not be a ground for excluding criminal responsibility. A mistake of law may, however, be a ground for excluding criminal responsibility if it negates the mental element required by such a crime, or as provided for in Article 33.

Article 33. Superior orders and prescription of law

1. The fact that a crime within the jurisdiction of the Court has been committed by a person pursuant to an order of a Government or of a superior, whether military or civilian, shall not relieve that person of criminal responsibility unless:

(a) The person was under a legal obligation to obey orders of the Government or the superior in question;

(b) The person did not know that the order was unlawful; and

(c) The order was not manifestly unlawful.

2. For the purposes of this article, orders to commit genocide or crimes against humanity are manifestly unlawful.

Part 4. Composition and Administration of the Court

Article 34. Organs of the Court

The Court shall be composed of the following organs:

(a) The Presidency;

(b) An Appeals Division, a Trial Division and a Pre-Trial Division;

(c) The Office of the Prosecutor;

(d) The Registry.

Article 35. Service of judges

1. All judges shall be elected as full-time members of the Court and shall be available to serve on that basis from the commencement of their terms of office.

2. The judges composing the Presidency shall serve on a full-time basis as soon as they are elected.

3. The Presidency may, on the basis of the workload of the Court and in consultation with its members, decide from time to time to what extent the remaining judges shall be required to serve on a full-time basis. Any such arrangement shall be without prejudice to the provisions of Article 40.

4. The financial arrangements for judges not required to serve on a full-time basis shall be made in accordance with Article 49.

Article 36. Qualifications, nomination and election of judges

1. Subject to the provisions of paragraph 2, there shall be 18 judges of the Court.

2. (a) The Presidency, acting on behalf of the Court, may propose an increase in the number of judges specified in paragraph 1, indicating the reasons why this is considered necessary and appropriate. The Registrar shall promptly circulate any such proposal to all States Parties.

(b) Any such proposal shall then be considered at a meeting of the Assembly of States Parties to be convened in accordance with Article 112. The proposal shall be considered adopted if approved at the meeting by a vote of two-thirds of the members of the Assembly of States Parties and shall enter into force at such time as decided by the Assembly of States Parties.

(c) (i) Once a proposal for an increase in the number of judges has been adopted under subparagraph (b), the election of the additional judges shall take place at the next session of the Assembly of States Parties in accordance with paragraphs 3 to 8 inclusive, and Article 37, paragraph 2;

(ii) Once a proposal for an increase in the number of judges has been adopted and brought into effect under subparagraphs (b) and (c) (i), it shall be open to the Presidency at any time thereafter, if the workload of the Court justifies it, to propose a reduction in the number of judges, provided that the number of judges shall not be reduced below that specified in paragraph 1. The proposal shall be dealt with in accordance with the procedure laid down in subparagraphs (a) and (b). In the event that the proposal is adopted, the number of judges shall be progressively decreased as the terms of office of serving judges expire, until the necessary number has been reached.

3. (a) The judges shall be chosen from among persons of high moral character, impartiality and integrity who possess the qualifications required in their respective States for appointment to the highest judicial offices.

(b) Every candidate for election to the Court shall:

(i) Have established competence in criminal law and procedure, and the necessary relevant experience, whether as judge, prosecutor, advocate or in other similar capacity, in criminal proceedings; or

(ii) Have established competence in relevant areas of international law such as international humanitarian law and the law of human rights, and extensive experience in a professional legal capacity which is of relevance to the judicial work of the Court;

(c) Every candidate for election to the Court shall have an excellent knowledge of and be fluent in at least one of the working languages of the Court.

4. (a) Nominations of candidates for election to the Court may be made by any State Party to this Statute, and shall be made either:

(i) By the procedure for the nomination of candidates for appointment to the highest judicial offices in the State in question; or

(ii) By the procedure provided for the nomination of candidates for the International Court of Justice in the Statute of that Court. Nominations shall be accompanied by a statement in the necessary detail specifying how the candidate fulfils the requirements of paragraph 3.

(b) Each State Party may put forward one candidate for any given election who need not necessarily be a national of that State Party but shall in any case be a national of a State Party.

(c) The Assembly of States Parties may decide to establish, if appropriate, an Advisory Committee on nominations. In that event, the Committee's composition and mandate shall be established by the Assembly of States Parties.

5. For the purposes of the election, there shall be two lists of candidates:

List A containing the names of candidates with the qualifications specified in paragraph 3 (b) (i); and

List B containing the names of candidates with the qualifications specified in paragraph 3 (b) (ii).

A candidate with sufficient qualifications for both lists may choose on which list to appear. At the first election to the Court, at least nine judges shall be elected from list A and at least five judges from list B. Subsequent elections shall be so organized as to maintain the equivalent proportion on the Court of judges qualified on the two lists.

6. (a) The judges shall be elected by secret ballot at a meeting of the Assembly of States Parties convened for that purpose under Article 112. Subject to paragraph 7, the persons elected to the Court shall be the 18 candidates who obtain the highest number of votes and a two-thirds majority of the States Parties present and voting.

(b) In the event that a sufficient number of judges is not elected on the first ballot, successive ballots shall be held in accordance with the procedures laid down in subparagraph (a) until the remaining places have been filled.

7. No two judges may be nationals of the same State. A person who, for the purposes of membership in the Court, could be regarded as a national of more than one State shall be deemed to be a national of the State in which that person ordinarily exercises civil and political rights.

8. (a) The States Parties shall, in the selection of judges, take into account the need, within the membership of the Court, for:

(i) The representation of the principal legal systems of the world;

(ii) Equitable geographical representation; and

(iii) A fair representation of female and male judges.

(b) States Parties shall also take into account the need to include judges with legal expertise on specific issues, including, but not limited to, violence against women or children.

9. (a) Subject to subparagraph (b), judges shall hold office for a term of nine years and, subject to subparagraph (c) and to Article 37, paragraph 2, shall not be eligible for re-election.

(b) At the first election, one third of the judges elected shall be selected by lot to serve for a term of three years; one third of the judges elected shall be selected by lot to serve for a term of six years; and the remainder shall serve for a term of nine years.

(c) A judge who is selected to serve for a term of three years under subparagraph (b) shall be eligible for re-election for a full term.

10. Notwithstanding paragraph 9, a judge assigned to a Trial or Appeals Chamber in accordance with Article 39 shall continue in office to complete any trial or appeal the hearing of which has already commenced before that Chamber.

Article 37. Judicial Vacancies

1. In the event of a vacancy, an election shall be held in accordance with Article 36 to fill the vacancy.

2. A judge elected to fill a vacancy shall serve for the remainder of the predecessor's term and, if that period is three years or less, shall be eligible for re-election for a full term under Article 36.

Article 38. The Presidency

1. The President and the First and Second Vice-Presidents shall be elected by an absolute majority of the judges. They shall each serve for a term of three years or until the end of their respective terms of office as judges, whichever expires earlier. They shall be eligible for re-election once.

2. The First Vice-President shall act in place of the President in the event that the President is unavailable or disqualified. The Second Vice-President shall act in place of the President in the event that both the President and the First Vice-President are unavailable or disqualified.

3. The President, together with the First and Second Vice-Presidents, shall constitute the Presidency, which shall be responsible for:

(a) The proper administration of the Court, with the exception of the Office of the Prosecutor; and

(b) The other functions conferred upon it in accordance with this Statute.

4. In discharging its responsibility under paragraph 3 (a), the Presidency shall coordinate with and seek the concurrence of the Prosecutor on all matters of mutual concern.

Article 39. Chambers

1. As soon as possible after the election of the judges, the Court shall organize itself into the divisions specified in Article 34, paragraph (b). The Appeals Division shall be composed of the President and four other judges, the Trial Division of not less than six judges and the Pre-Trial Division of not less than six judges. The assignment of judges to divisions shall be based on the nature of the functions to be performed by each division and the qualifications and experience of the judges elected to the Court, in such a way that each division shall contain an appropriate combination of expertise in criminal law and procedure and in international law. The Trial and Pre-Trial Divisions shall be composed predominantly of judges with criminal trial experience.

2. (a) The judicial functions of the Court shall be carried out in each division by Chambers.

(b) (i) The Appeals Chamber shall be composed of all the judges of the Appeals Division;

(ii) The functions of the Trial Chamber shall be carried out by three judges of the Trial Division;

(iii) The functions of the Pre-Trial Chamber shall be carried out either by three judges of the Pre-Trial Division or by a single judge of that division in accordance with this Statute and the Rules of Procedure and Evidence;

(c) Nothing in this paragraph shall preclude the simultaneous constitution of more than one Trial Chamber or Pre-Trial Chamber when the efficient management of the Court's workload so requires.

3. (a) Judges assigned to the Trial and Pre-Trial Divisions shall serve in those divisions for a period of three years, and thereafter until the completion of any case the hearing of which has already commenced in the division concerned.

(b) Judges assigned to the Appeals Division shall serve in that division for their entire term of office.

4. Judges assigned to the Appeals Division shall serve only in that division. Nothing in this article shall, however, preclude the temporary attachment of judges from the Trial Division to the Pre-Trial Division or vice versa, if the Presidency considers that the efficient management of the Court's workload so requires, provided that under no circumstances shall a judge who has participated in the pre-trial phase of a case be eligible to sit on the Trial Chamber hearing that case.

Article 40. Independence of the judges

1. The judges shall be independent in the performance of their functions.

2. Judges shall not engage in any activity which is likely to interfere with their judicial functions or to affect confidence in their independence.

3. Judges required to serve on a full-time basis at the seat of the Court shall not engage in any other occupation of a professional nature.

4. Any question regarding the application of paragraphs 2 and 3 shall be decided by an absolute majority of the judges. Where any such question concerns an individual judge, that judge shall not take part in the decision.

Article 41. Excusing and disqualification of judges

1. The Presidency may, at the request of a judge, excuse that judge from the exercise of a function under this Statute, in accordance with the Rules of Procedure and Evidence.

2. (a) A judge shall not participate in any case in which his or her impartiality might reasonably be doubted on any ground. A judge shall be disqualified from a case in accordance with this paragraph if, *inter alia*, that judge has previously been involved in any capacity in that case before the Court or in a related criminal case at the national level involving the person being investigated or prosecuted. A judge shall also be disqualified on such other grounds as may be provided for in the Rules of Procedure and Evidence.

(b) The Prosecutor or the person being investigated or prosecuted may request the disqualification of a judge under this paragraph.

(c) Any question as to the disqualification of a judge shall be decided by an absolute majority of the judges. The challenged judge shall be entitled to present his or her comments on the matter, but shall not take part in the decision.

Article 42. The Office of the Prosecutor

1. The Office of the Prosecutor shall act independently as a separate organ of the Court. It shall be responsible for receiving referrals and any substantiated information on crimes within the jurisdiction of the Court, for examining them and for conducting investigations and prosecutions before the Court. A member of the Office shall not seek or act on instructions from any external source.

2. The Office shall be headed by the Prosecutor. The Prosecutor shall have full authority over the management and administration of the Office, including the staff, facilities and other resources thereof. The Prosecutor shall be assisted by one or more Deputy Prosecutors, who shall be entitled to carry out any of the acts required of the Prosecutor under this Statute. The Prosecutor and the Deputy Prosecutors shall be of different nationalities. They shall serve on a full-time basis.

3. The Prosecutor and the Deputy Prosecutors shall be persons of high moral character, be highly competent in and have extensive practical experience in the prosecution or trial of criminal cases. They shall have an excellent knowledge of and be fluent in at least one of the working languages of the Court.

4. The Prosecutor shall be elected by secret ballot by an absolute majority of the members of the Assembly of States Parties. The Deputy Prosecutors shall be elected in the same way from a list of candidates provided by the Prosecutor. The Prosecutor shall nominate three candidates for each position of Deputy Prosecutor to be filled. Unless a shorter term is decided upon at the time of their election, the Prosecutor and the Deputy Prosecutors shall hold office for a term of nine years and shall not be eligible for re-election.

5. Neither the Prosecutor nor a Deputy Prosecutor shall engage in any activity which is likely to interfere with his or her prosecutorial functions or to affect confidence in his or her independence. They shall not engage in any other occupation of a professional nature.

6. The Presidency may excuse the Prosecutor or a Deputy Prosecutor, at his or her request, from acting in a particular case.

7. Neither the Prosecutor nor a Deputy Prosecutor shall participate in any matter in which their impartiality might reasonably be doubted on any ground. They shall be disqualified from a case in accordance with this paragraph if, *inter alia*, they have previously been involved in any capacity in that case before the Court or in a related criminal case at the national level involving the person being investigated or prosecuted.

8. Any question as to the disqualification of the Prosecutor or a Deputy Prosecutor shall be decided by the Appeals Chamber.

(a) The person being investigated or prosecuted may at any time request the disqualification of the Prosecutor or a Deputy Prosecutor on the grounds set out in this article.

(b) The Prosecutor or the Deputy Prosecutor, as appropriate, shall be entitled to present his or her comments on the matter.

9. The Prosecutor shall appoint advisers with legal expertise on specific issues, including, but not limited to, sexual and gender violence and violence against children.

Article 43. The Registry

1. The Registry shall be responsible for the non-judicial aspects of the administration and servicing of the Court, without prejudice to the functions and powers of the Prosecutor in accordance with Article 42.

2. The Registry shall be headed by the Registrar, who shall be the principal administrative officer of the Court. The Registrar shall exercise his or her functions under the authority of the President of the Court.

3. The Registrar and the Deputy Registrar shall be persons of high moral character, be highly competent and have an excellent knowledge of and be fluent in at least one of the working languages of the Court.

4. The judges shall elect the Registrar by an absolute majority by secret ballot, taking into account any recommendation by the Assembly of States Parties. If the need arises and upon the recommendation of the Registrar, the judges shall elect, in the same manner, a Deputy Registrar.

5. The Registrar shall hold office for a term of five years, shall be eligible for re-election once and shall serve on a full-time basis. The Deputy Registrar shall hold office for a term of five years or such shorter term as may be decided upon by an absolute majority of the judges, and may be elected on the basis that the Deputy Registrar shall be called upon to serve as required.

6. The Registrar shall set up a Victims and Witnesses Unit within the Registry. This Unit shall provide, in consultation with the Office of the Prosecutor, protective measures and security arrangements, counselling and other appropriate assistance for witnesses, victims who appear before the Court and others who are at risk on account of testimony given by such witnesses. The Unit shall include staff with expertise in trauma, including trauma related to crimes of sexual violence.

Article 44. Staff

1. The Prosecutor and the Registrar shall appoint such qualified staff as may be required to their respective offices. In the case of the Prosecutor, this shall include the appointment of investigators.

2. In the employment of staff, the Prosecutor and the Registrar shall ensure the highest standards of efficiency, competency and integrity, and shall have regard, mutatis mutandis, to the criteria set forth in Article 36, paragraph 8.

3. The Registrar, with the agreement of the Presidency and the Prosecutor, shall propose Staff Regulations which include the terms and conditions upon which the staff of the Court shall be appointed, remunerated and dismissed. The Staff Regulations shall be approved by the Assembly of States Parties.

4. The Court may, in exceptional circumstances, employ the expertise of gratis personnel offered by States Parties, intergovernmental organizations or non-governmental organizations to assist with the work of any of the organs of the Court. The Prosecutor may accept any such offer on behalf of the Office of the Prosecutor. Such gratis personnel shall be employed in accordance with guidelines to be established by the Assembly of States Parties.

Article 45. Solemn undertaking

Before taking up their respective duties under this Statute, the judges, the Prosecutor, the Deputy Prosecutors, the Registrar and the Deputy Registrar shall each make a solemn undertaking in open court to exercise his or her respective functions impartially and conscientiously.

Article 46. Removal from office

1. A judge, the Prosecutor, a Deputy Prosecutor, the Registrar or the Deputy Registrar shall be removed from office if a decision to this effect is made in accordance with paragraph 2, in cases where that person:

(a) Is found to have committed serious misconduct or a serious breach of his or her duties under this Statute, as provided for in the Rules of Procedure and Evidence; or

(b) Is unable to exercise the functions required by this Statute.

2. A decision as to the removal from office of a judge, the Prosecutor or a Deputy Prosecutor under paragraph 1 shall be made by the Assembly of States Parties, by secret ballot:

(a) In the case of a judge, by a two-thirds majority of the States Parties upon a recommendation adopted by a two-thirds majority of the other judges;

(b) In the case of the Prosecutor, by an absolute majority of the States Parties;

(c) In the case of a Deputy Prosecutor, by an absolute majority of the States Parties upon the recommendation of the Prosecutor.

3. A decision as to the removal from office of the Registrar or Deputy Registrar shall be made by an absolute majority of the judges.

4. A judge, Prosecutor, Deputy Prosecutor, Registrar or Deputy Registrar whose conduct or ability to exercise the functions of the office as required by this Statute is challenged under this article shall have full opportunity to present and receive evidence and to make submissions in accordance with the Rules of Procedure and Evidence. The person in question shall not otherwise participate in the consideration of the matter.

Article 47. Disciplinary measures

A judge, Prosecutor, Deputy Prosecutor, Registrar or Deputy Registrar who has committed misconduct of a less serious nature than that set out in Article 46, paragraph 1, shall be subject to disciplinary measures, in accordance with the Rules of Procedure and Evidence.

Article 48. Privileges and immunities

1. The Court shall enjoy in the territory of each State Party such privileges and immunities as are necessary for the fulfilment of its purposes.

2. The judges, the Prosecutor, the Deputy Prosecutors and the Registrar shall, when engaged on or with respect to the business of the Court, enjoy the same privileges and immunities as are accorded to heads of diplomatic missions and shall, after the expiry of their terms of office, continue to be accorded immunity from legal process of every kind in respect of words spoken or written and acts performed by them in their official capacity.

3. The Deputy Registrar, the staff of the Office of the Prosecutor and the staff of the Registry shall enjoy the privileges and immunities and facilities necessary for the performance of their functions, in accordance with the agreement on the privileges and immunities of the Court.

4. Counsel, experts, witnesses or any other person required to be present at the seat of the Court shall be accorded such treatment as is necessary for the proper functioning of the Court, in accordance with the agreement on the privileges and immunities of the Court.

5. The privileges and immunities of:

(a) A judge or the Prosecutor may be waived by an absolute majority of the judges;

(b) The Registrar may be waived by the Presidency;

(c) The Deputy Prosecutors and staff of the Office of the Prosecutor may be waived by the Prosecutor;

(d) The Deputy Registrar and staff of the Registry may be waived by the Registrar.

Article 49. Salaries, allowances and expenses

The judges, the Prosecutor, the Deputy Prosecutors, the Registrar and the Deputy Registrar shall receive such salaries, allowances and expenses as may be decided upon by the Assembly of States Parties. These salaries and allowances shall not be reduced during their terms of office.

Article 50. Official and working languages

1. The official languages of the Court shall be Arabic, Chinese, English, French, Russian and Spanish. The judgements of the Court, as well as other decisions resolving fundamental issues before the Court, shall be published in the official languages. The Presidency shall, in accordance with the criteria established by the Rules of Procedure and Evidence, determine which decisions may be considered as resolving fundamental issues for the purposes of this paragraph.

2. The working languages of the Court shall be English and French. The Rules of Procedure and Evidence shall determine the cases in which other official languages may be used as working languages.

3. At the request of any party to a proceeding or a State allowed to intervene in a proceeding, the Court shall authorize a language other than English or French to be used by such a party or State, provided that the Court considers such authorization to be adequately justified.

Article 51. Rules of Procedure and Evidence

1. The Rules of Procedure and Evidence shall enter into force upon adoption by a two-thirds majority of the members of the Assembly of States Parties.

2. Amendments to the Rules of Procedure and Evidence may be proposed by:

(a) Any State Party;

(b) The judges acting by an absolute majority; or

(c) The Prosecutor.

Such amendments shall enter into force upon adoption by a two-thirds majority of the members of the Assembly of States Parties.

3. After the adoption of the Rules of Procedure and Evidence, in urgent cases where the Rules do not provide for a specific situation before the Court, the judges may, by a two-thirds majority, draw up provisional Rules to be applied until adopted, amended or rejected at the next ordinary or special session of the Assembly of States Parties.

4. The Rules of Procedure and Evidence, amendments thereto and any provisional Rule shall be consistent with this Statute. Amendments to the Rules of Procedure and Evidence as well as provisional Rules shall not be applied retroactively to the detriment of the person who is being investigated or prosecuted or who has been convicted.

5. In the event of conflict between the Statute and the Rules of Procedure and Evidence, the Statute shall prevail.

Article 52. Regulations of the Court

1. The judges shall, in accordance with this Statute and the Rules of Procedure and Evidence, adopt, by an absolute majority, the Regulations of the Court necessary for its routine functioning.

2. The Prosecutor and the Registrar shall be consulted in the elaboration of the Regulations and any amendments thereto.

3. The Regulations and any amendments thereto shall take effect upon adoption unless otherwise decided by the judges. Immediately upon adoption, they shall be circulated to States Parties for comments. If within six months there are no objections from a majority of States Parties, they shall remain in force.

PART 5. INVESTIGATION AND PROSECUTION

Article 53. Initiation of an investigation

1. The Prosecutor shall, having evaluated the information made available to him or her, initiate an investigation unless he or she determines that there is no reasonable basis to proceed under this Statute. In deciding whether to initiate an investigation, the Prosecutor shall consider whether:

(a) The information available to the Prosecutor provides a reasonable basis to believe that a crime within the jurisdiction of the Court has been or is being committed;

(b) The case is or would be admissible under Article 17; and

(c) Taking into account the gravity of the crime and the interests of victims, there are nonetheless substantial reasons to believe that an investigation would not serve the interests of justice.

If the Prosecutor determines that there is no reasonable basis to proceed and his or her determination is based solely on subparagraph (c) above, he or she shall inform the Pre-Trial Chamber.

2. If, upon investigation, the Prosecutor concludes that there is not a sufficient basis for a prosecution because:

(a) There is not a sufficient legal or factual basis to seek a warrant or summons under Article 58;

(b) The case is inadmissible under Article 17; or

(c) A prosecution is not in the interests of justice, taking into account all the circumstances, including the gravity of the crime, the interests of victims and the age or infirmity of the alleged perpetrator, and his or her role in the alleged crime;

The Prosecutor shall inform the Pre-Trial Chamber and the State making a referral under Article 14 or the Security Council in a case under Article 13, paragraph (b), of his or her conclusion and the reasons for the conclusion.

3. (a) At the request of the State making a referral under Article 14 or the Security Council under Article 13, paragraph (b), the Pre-Trial Chamber may review a decision of the Prosecutor under paragraph 1 or 2 not to proceed and may request the Prosecutor to reconsider that decision.

(b) In addition, the Pre-Trial Chamber may, on its own initiative, review a decision of the Prosecutor not to proceed if it is based solely on paragraph 1(c) or 2(c). In such a case, the decision of the Prosecutor shall be effective only if confirmed by the Pre-Trial Chamber.

4. The Prosecutor may, at any time, reconsider a decision whether to initiate an investigation prosecution based on new facts or information.

Article 54. Duties and powers of the Prosecutor with respect to investigations

1. The Prosecutor shall:

(a) In order to establish the truth, extend the investigation to cover all facts and evidence relevant to an assessment of whether there is criminal responsibility under this Statute, and, in doing so, investigate incriminating and exonerating circumstances equally;

(b) Take appropriate measures to ensure the effective investigation and prosecution of crimes within the jurisdiction of the Court, and in doing so, respect the interests and personal circumstances of victims and witnesses, including age, gender as defined in Article 7, paragraph 3, and health, and take into account the nature of the crime, in particular where it involves sexual violence, gender violence or violence against children; and

(c) Fully respect the rights of persons arising under this Statute.

2. The Prosecutor may conduct investigations on the territory of a State:

(a) In accordance with the provisions of Part 9; or

(b) As authorized by the Pre-Trial Chamber under Article 57, paragraph 3 (d).

3. The Prosecutor may:

(a) Collect and examine evidence;

(b) Request the presence of and question persons being investigated, victims and witnesses;

(c) Seek the cooperation of any State or intergovernmental organization or arrangement in accordance with its respective competence and/or mandate;

(d) Enter into such arrangements or agreements, not inconsistent with this Statute, as may be necessary to facilitate the cooperation of a State, intergovernmental organization or person;

(e) Agree not to disclose, at any stage of the proceedings, documents or information that the Prosecutor obtains on the condition of confidentiality and solely for the purpose of generating new evidence, unless the provider of the information consents; and

(f) Take necessary measures, or request that necessary measures be taken, to ensure the confidentiality of information, the protection of any person or the preservation of evidence.

Article 55. Rights of persons during an investigation

1. In respect of an investigation under this Statute, a person:

(a) Shall not be compelled to incriminate himself or herself or to confess guilt;

(b) Shall not be subjected to any form of coercion, duress or threat, to torture or to any other form of cruel, inhuman or degrading treatment or punishment; and

(c) Shall, if questioned in a language other than a language the person fully understands and speaks, have, free of any cost, the assistance of a competent interpreter and such translations as are necessary to meet the requirements of fairness;

(d) Shall not be subjected to arbitrary arrest or detention; and shall not be deprived of his or her liberty except on such grounds and in accordance with such procedures as are established in the Statute.

2. Where there are grounds to believe that a person has committed a crime within the jurisdiction of the Court and that person is about to be questioned either by the Prosecutor, or by national authorities pursuant to a request made under Part 9 of this Statute, that person shall also have the following rights of which he or she shall be informed prior to being questioned:

(a) To be informed, prior to being questioned, that there are grounds to believe that he or she has committed a crime within the jurisdiction of the Court;

(b) To remain silent, without such silence being a consideration in the determination of guilt or innocence;

(c) To have legal assistance of the person's choosing, or, if the person does not have legal assistance, to have legal assistance assigned to him or her, in any case where the interests of justice so require, and without payment by the person in any such case if the person does not have sufficient means to pay for it;

(d) To be questioned in the presence of counsel unless the person has voluntarily waived his or her right to counsel.

Article 56. Role of the Pre-Trial Chamber in relation to a unique investigative opportunity

1. (a) Where the Prosecutor considers an investigation to present a unique opportunity to take testimony or a statement from a witness or to examine, collect or test evidence, which may not be available subsequently for the purposes of a trial, the Prosecutor shall so inform the Pre-Trial Chamber.

(b) In that case, the Pre-Trial Chamber may, upon request of the Prosecutor, take such measures as may be necessary to ensure the efficiency and integrity of the proceedings and, in particular, to protect the rights of the defence.

(c) Unless the Pre-Trial Chamber orders otherwise, the Prosecutor shall provide the relevant information to the person who has been arrested or appeared in response to a summons in connection with the investigation referred to in subparagraph (a), in order that he or she may be heard on the matter.

2. The measures referred to in paragraph 1(b) may include:

(a) Making recommendations or orders regarding procedures to be followed;

(b) Directing that a record be made of the proceedings;

(c) Appointing an expert to assist;

(d) Authorizing counsel for a person who has been arrested, or appeared before the Court in response to a summons, to participate, or where there has not yet been such an arrest or appearance or counsel has not been designated, appointing another counsel to attend and represent the interests of the defence;

(e) Naming one of its members or, if necessary, another available judge of the Pre-Trial or Trial Division to observe and make recommendations or orders regarding the collection and preservation of evidence and the questioning of persons;

(f) Taking such other action as may be necessary to collect or preserve evidence.

3. (a) Where the Prosecutor has not sought measures pursuant to this article but the Pre-Trial Chamber considers that such measures are required to preserve evidence that it

deems would be essential for the defence at trial, it shall consult with the Prosecutor as to whether there is good reason for the Prosecutor's failure to request the measures. If upon consultation, the Pre-Trial Chamber concludes that the Prosecutor's failure to request such measures is unjustified, the Pre-Trial Chamber may take such measures on its own initiative.

(b) A decision of the Pre-Trial Chamber to act on its own initiative under this paragraph may be appealed by the Prosecutor. The appeal shall be heard on an expedited basis.

4. The admissibility of evidence preserved or collected for trial pursuant to this article, or the record thereof, shall be governed at trial by Article 69, and given such weight as determined by the Trial Chamber.

Article 57. Functions and powers of the Pre-Trial Chamber

1. Unless otherwise provided for in this Statute, the Pre-Trial Chamber shall exercise its functions in accordance with the provisions of this article.

2. (a) Orders or rulings of the Pre-Trial Chamber issued under Articles 15, 18, 19, 54, paragraph 2, 61, paragraph 7, and 72 must be concurred in by a majority of its judges.

(b) In all other cases, a single judge of the Pre-Trial Chamber may exercise the functions provided for in this Statute, unless otherwise provided for in the Rules of Procedure and Evidence or by a majority of the Pre-Trial Chamber.

3. In addition to its other functions under this Statute, the Pre-Trial Chamber may:

(a) At the request of the Prosecutor, issue such orders and warrants as may be required for the purposes of an investigation;

(b) Upon the request of a person who has been arrested or has appeared pursuant to a summons under Article 58, issue such orders, including measures such as those described in Article 56, or seek such cooperation pursuant to Part 9 as may be necessary to assist the person in the preparation of his or her defence;

(c) Where necessary, provide for the protection and privacy of victims and witnesses, the preservation of evidence, the protection of persons who have been arrested or appeared in response to a summons, and the protection of national security information;

(d) Authorize the Prosecutor to take specific investigative steps within the territory of a State Party without having secured the cooperation of that State under Part 9 if, whenever possible having regard to the views of the State concerned, the Pre-Trial Chamber has determined in that case that the State is clearly unable to execute a request for cooperation due to the unavailability of any authority or any component of its judicial system competent to execute the request for cooperation under Part 9.

(e) Where a warrant of arrest or a summons has been issued under Article 58, and having due regard to the strength of the evidence and the rights of the parties concerned, as provided for in this Statute and the Rules of Procedure and Evidence, seek the cooperation of States pursuant to Article 93, paragraph 1(j), to take protective measures for the purpose of forfeiture in particular for the ultimate benefit of victims.

Article 58. Issuance by the Pre-Trial Chamber of a warrant of arrest or a summons to appear

1. At any time after the initiation of an investigation, the Pre-Trial Chamber shall, on the application of the Prosecutor, issue a warrant of arrest of a person if, having exam-

ined the application and the evidence or other information submitted by the Prosecutor, it is satisfied that:

(a) There are reasonable grounds to believe that the person has committed a crime within the jurisdiction of the Court; and

(b) The arrest of the person appears necessary:

(i) To ensure the person's appearance at trial.

(ii) To ensure that the person does not obstruct or endanger the investigation or the court proceedings, or

(iii) Where applicable, to prevent the person from continuing with the commission of that crime or a related crime which is within the jurisdiction of the Court and which arises out of the same circumstances.

2. The application of the Prosecutor shall contain:

(a) The name of the person and any other relevant identifying information;

(b) A specific reference to the crimes within the jurisdiction of the Court which the person is alleged to have committed;

(c) A concise statement of the facts which are alleged to constitute those crimes;

(d) A summary of the evidence and any other information which establish reasonable grounds to believe that the person committed those crimes; and

(e) The reason why the Prosecutor believes that the arrest of the person is necessary.

3. The warrant of arrest shall contain:

(a) The name of the person and any other relevant identifying information;

(b) A specific reference to the crimes within the jurisdiction of the Court for which the person's arrest is sought; and

(c) A concise statement of the facts which are alleged to constitute those crimes.

4. The warrant of arrest shall remain in effect until otherwise ordered by the Court.

5. On the basis of the warrant of arrest, the Court may request the provisional arrest or the arrest and surrender of the person under Part 9.

6. The Prosecutor may request the Pre-Trial Chamber to amend the warrant of arrest by modifying or adding to the crimes specified therein. The Pre-Trial Chamber shall so amend the warrant if it is satisfied that there are reasonable grounds to believe that the person committed the modified or additional crimes.

7. As an alternative to seeking a warrant of arrest, the Prosecutor may submit an application requesting that the Pre-Trial Chamber issue a summons for the person to appear. If the Pre-Trial Chamber is satisfied that there are reasonable grounds to believe that the person committed the crime alleged and that a summons is sufficient to ensure the person's appearance, it shall issue the summons, with or without conditions restricting liberty (other than detention) if provided for by national law, for the person to appear. The summons shall contain:

(a) The name of the person and any other relevant identifying information;

(b) The specified date on which the person is to appear;

(c) A specific reference to the crimes within the jurisdiction of the Court which the person is alleged to have committed; and

(d) A concise statement of the facts which are alleged to constitute the crime.

The summons shall be served on the person.

Article 59. Arrest proceedings in the custodial State

1. A State Party which has received a request for provisional arrest or for arrest and surrender shall immediately take steps to arrest the person in question in accordance with its laws and the provisions of Part 9.

2. A person arrested shall be brought promptly before the competent judicial authority in the custodial State which shall determine, in accordance with the law of that State, that:

   (a) The warrant applies to that person;

   (b) The person has been arrested in accordance with the proper process; and

   (c) The person's rights have been respected.

3. The person arrested shall have the right to apply to the competent authority in the custodial State for interim release pending surrender.

4. In reaching a decision on any such application, the competent authority in the custodial State shall consider whether, given the gravity of the alleged crimes, there are urgent and exceptional circumstances to justify interim release and whether necessary safeguards exist to ensure that the custodial State can fulfil its duty to surrender the person to the Court. It shall not be open to the competent authority of the custodial State to consider whether the warrant of arrest was properly issued in accordance with Article 58, paragraph 1(a) and (b).

5. The Pre-Trial Chamber shall be notified of any request for interim release and shall make recommendations to the competent authority in the custodial State. The competent authority in the custodial State shall give full consideration to such recommendations, including any recommendations on measures to prevent the escape of the person, before rendering its decision.

6. If the person is granted interim release, the Pre-Trial Chamber may request periodic reports on the status of the interim release.

7. Once ordered to be surrendered by the custodial State, the person shall be delivered to the Court as soon as possible.

Article 60. Initial proceedings before the Court

1. Upon the surrender of the person to the Court, or the person's appearance before the Court voluntarily or pursuant to a summons, the Pre-Trial Chamber shall satisfy itself that the person has been informed of the crimes which he or she is alleged to have committed, and of his or her rights under this Statute, including the right to apply for interim release pending trial.

2. A person subject to a warrant of arrest may apply for interim release pending trial. If the Pre-Trial Chamber is satisfied that the conditions set forth in Article 58, paragraph 1, are met, the person shall continue to be detained. If it is not so satisfied, the Pre-Trial Chamber shall release the person, with or without conditions.

3. The Pre-Trial Chamber shall periodically review its ruling on the release or detention of the person, and may do so at any time on the request of the Prosecutor or the person. Upon such review, it may modify its ruling as to detention, release or conditions of release, if it is satisfied that changed circumstances so require.

4. The Pre-Trial Chamber shall ensure that a person is not detained for an unreasonable period prior to trial due to inexcusable delay by the Prosecutor. If such delay occurs, the Court shall consider releasing the person, with or without conditions.

5. If necessary, the Pre-Trial Chamber may issue a warrant of arrest to secure the presence of a person who has been released.

Article 61. Confirmation of the charges before trial

1. Subject to the provisions of paragraph 2, within a reasonable time after the person's surrender or voluntary appearance before the Court, the Pre-Trial Chamber shall hold a hearing to confirm the charges on which the Prosecutor intends to seek trial. The hearing shall be held in the presence of the Prosecutor and the person charged, as well as his or her counsel.

2. The Pre-Trial Chamber may, upon request of the Prosecutor or on its own motion, hold a hearing in the absence of the person charged to confirm the charges on which the Prosecutor intends to seek trial when the person has:

(a) Waived his or her right to be present; or

(b) Fled or cannot be found and all reasonable steps have been taken to secure his or her appearance before the Court and to inform the person of the charges and that a hearing to confirm those charges will be held.

In that case, the person shall be represented by counsel where the Pre-Trial Chamber determines that it is in the interests of justice.

3. Within a reasonable time before the hearing, the person shall:

(a) Be provided with a copy of the document containing the charges on which the Prosecutor intends to bring the person to trial; and

(b) Be informed of the evidence on which the Prosecutor intends to rely at the hearing.

The Pre-Trial Chamber may issue orders regarding the disclosure of information for the purposes of the hearing.

4. Before the hearing, the Prosecutor may continue the investigation and may amend or withdraw any charges. The person shall be given reasonable notice before the hearing of any amendment to or withdrawal of charges. In case of a withdrawal of charges, the Prosecutor shall notify the Pre-Trial Chamber of the reasons for the withdrawal.

5. At the hearing, the Prosecutor shall support each charge with sufficient evidence to establish substantial grounds to believe that the person committed the crime charged. The Prosecutor may rely on documentary or summary evidence and need not call the witnesses expected to testify at the trial.

6. At the hearing, the person may:

(a) Object to the charges;

(b) Challenge the evidence presented by the Prosecutor; and

(c) Present evidence.

7. The Pre-Trial Chamber shall, on the basis of the hearing, determine whether there is sufficient evidence to establish substantial grounds to believe that the person committed each of the crimes charged. Based on its determination, the Pre-Trial Chamber shall:

(a) Confirm those charges in relation to which it has determined that there is sufficient evidence; and commit the person to a Trial Chamber for trial on the charges as confirmed;

(b) Decline to confirm those charges in relation to which it has determined that there is insufficient evidence;

(c) Adjourn the hearing and request the Prosecutor to consider;

 (i) Providing further evidence or conducting further investigation with respect to a particular charge; or

 (ii) Amending a charge because the evidence submitted appears to establish a different crime within the jurisdiction of the Court.

8. Where the Pre-Trial Chamber declines to confirm a charge, the Prosecutor shall not be precluded from subsequently requesting its confirmation if the request is supported by additional evidence.

9. After the charges are confirmed and before the trial has begun, the Prosecutor may, with the permission of the Pre-Trial Chamber and after notice to the accused, amend the charges. If the Prosecutor seeks to add additional charges or to substitute more serious charges, a hearing under this article to confirm those charges must be held. After commencement of the trial, the Prosecutor may, with the permission of the Trial Chamber, withdraw the charges.

10. Any warrant previously issued shall cease to have effect with respect to any charges which have not been confirmed by the Pre-Trial Chamber or which have been withdrawn by the Prosecutor.

11. Once the charges have been confirmed in accordance with this article, the Presidency shall constitute a Trial Chamber which, subject to paragraph 8 and to Article 64, paragraph 4, shall be responsible for the conduct of subsequent proceedings and may exercise any function of the Pre-Trial Chamber that is relevant and capable of application in those proceedings.

PART 6. THE TRIAL

Article 62. Place of trial

Unless otherwise decided, the place of the trial shall be the seat of the Court.

Article 63. Trial in the presence of the accused

1. The accused shall be present during the trial.

2. If the accused, being present before the Court, continues to disrupt the trial, the Trial Chamber may remove the accused and shall make provision for him or her to observe the trial and instruct counsel from outside the courtroom, through the use of communications technology, if required. Such measures shall be taken only in exceptional circumstances after other reasonable alternatives have proved inadequate, and only for such duration as is strictly required.

Article 64. Functions and powers of the Trial Chamber

1. The functions and powers of the Trial Chamber set out in this article shall be exercised in accordance with this Statute and the Rules of Procedure and Evidence.

2. The Trial Chamber shall ensure that a trial is fair and expeditious and is conducted with full respect for the rights of the accused and due regard for the protection of victims and witnesses.

3. Upon assignment of a case for trial in accordance with this Statute, the Trial Chamber assigned to deal with the case shall:

 (a) Confer with the parties and adopt such procedures as are necessary to facilitate the fair and expeditious conduct of the proceedings;

 (b) Determine the language or languages to be used at trial; and

(c) Subject to any other relevant provisions of this Statute, provide for disclosure of documents or information not previously disclosed, sufficiently in advance of the commencement of the trial to enable adequate preparation for trial.

4. The Trial Chamber may, if necessary for its effective and fair functioning, refer preliminary issues to the Pre-Trial Chamber or, if necessary, to another available judge of the Pre-Trial Division.

5. Upon notice to the parties, the Trial Chamber may, as appropriate, direct that there be joinder or severance in respect of charges against more than one accused.

6. In performing its functions prior to trial or during the course of a trial, the Trial Chamber may, as necessary:

(a) Exercise any functions of the Pre-Trial Chamber referred to in Article 61,paragraph 11;

(b) Require the attendance and testimony of witnesses and production of documents and other evidence by obtaining, if necessary, the assistance of States as provided in this Statute;

(c) Provide for the protection of confidential information;

(d) Order the production of evidence in addition to that already collected prior to the trial or presented during the trial by the parties;

(e) Provide for the protection of the accused, witnesses and victims; and

(f) Rule on any other relevant matters.

7. The trial shall be held in public. The Trial Chamber may, however, determine that special circumstances require that certain proceedings be in closed session for the purposes set forth in Article 68, or to protect confidential or sensitive information to be given in evidence.

8. (a) At the commencement of the trial, the Trial Chamber shall have read to the accused the charges previously confirmed by the Pre-Trial Chamber. The Trial Chamber shall satisfy itself that the accused understands the nature of the charges. It shall afford him or her the opportunity to make an admission of guilt in accordance with Article 65 or to plead not guilty.

(b) At the trial, the presiding judge may give directions for the conduct of proceedings, including to ensure that they are conducted in a fair and impartial manner. Subject to any directions of the presiding judge, the parties may submit evidence in accordance with the provisions of this Statute.

9. The Trial Chamber shall have, *inter alia*, the power on application of a party or on its own motion to:

(a) Rule on the admissibility or relevance of evidence; and

(b) Take all necessary steps to maintain order in the course of a hearing.

10. The Trial Chamber shall ensure that a complete record of the trial, which accurately reflects the proceedings, is made and that it is maintained and preserved by the Registrar.

Article 65. Proceedings on an admission of guilt

1. Where the accused makes an admission of guilt pursuant to Article 64, paragraph 8 (a), the Trial Chamber shall determine whether:

(a) The accused understands the nature and consequences of the admission of guilt;

(b) The admission is voluntarily made by the accused after sufficient consultation with defence counsel; and

(c) The admission of guilt is supported by the facts of the case that are contained in:

(i) The charges brought by the Prosecutor and admitted by the accused;

(ii) Any materials presented by the Prosecutor which supplement the charges and which the accused accepts; and

(iii) Any other evidence, such as the testimony of witnesses, presented by the Prosecutor or the accused.

2. Where the Trial Chamber is satisfied that the matters referred to in paragraph 1 are established, it shall consider the admission of guilt, together with any additional evidence presented, as establishing all the essential facts that are required to prove the crime to which the admission of guilt relates, and may convict the accused of that crime.

3. Where the Trial Chamber is not satisfied that the matters referred to in paragraph 1 are established, it shall consider the admission of guilt as not having been made, in which case it shall order that the trial be continued under the ordinary trial procedures provided by this Statute and may remit the case to another Trial Chamber.

4. Where the Trial Chamber is of the opinion that a more complete presentation of the facts of the case is required in the interests of justice, in particular the interests of the victims, the Trial Chamber may:

(a) Request the Prosecutor to present additional evidence, including the testimony of witnesses; or

(b) Order that the trial be continued under the ordinary trial procedures provided by this Statute, in which case it shall consider the admission of guilt as not having been made and may remit the case to another Trial Chamber.

5. Any discussions between the Prosecutor and the defence regarding modification of the charges, the admission of guilt or the penalty to be imposed shall not be binding on the Court.

Article 66. Presumption of innocence

1. Everyone shall be presumed innocent until proved guilty before the Court in accordance with the applicable law.

2. The onus is on the Prosecutor to prove the guilt of the accused.

3. In order to convict the accused, the Court must be convinced of the guilt of the accused beyond reasonable doubt.

Article 67. Rights of the accused

1. In the determination of any charge, the accused shall be entitled to a public hearing, having regard to the provisions of this Statute, to a fair hearing conducted impartially, and to the following minimum guarantees, in full equality:

(a) To be informed promptly and in detail of the nature, cause and content of the charge, in a language which the accused fully understands and speaks;

(b) To have adequate time and facilities for the preparation of the defence and to communicate freely with counsel of the accused's choosing in confidence;

(c) To be tried without undue delay;

(d) Subject to Article 63, paragraph 2, to be present at the trial, to conduct the defence in person or through legal assistance of the accused's choosing, to be informed, if the accused does not have legal assistance, of this right and to have legal assistance assigned by the Court in any case where the interests of justice so require, and without payment if the accused lacks sufficient means to pay for it;

(e) To examine, or have examined, the witnesses against him or her and to obtain the attendance and examination of witnesses on his or her behalf under the same conditions as witnesses against him or her. The accused shall also be entitled to raise defences and to present other evidence admissible under this Statute;

(f) To have, free of any cost, the assistance of a competent interpreter and such translations as are necessary to meet the requirements of fairness, if any of the proceedings of or documents presented to the Court are not in a language which the accused fully understands and speaks;

(g) Not to be compelled to testify or to confess guilt and to remain silent, without such silence being a consideration in the determination of guilt or innocence;

(h) To make an unsworn oral or written statement in his or her defence; and

(i) Not to have imposed on him or her any reversal of the burden of proof or any onus of rebuttal.

2. In addition to any other disclosure provided for in this Statute, the Prosecutor shall, as soon as practicable, disclose to the defence evidence in the Prosecutor's possession or control which he or she believes shows or tends to show the innocence of the accused, or to mitigate the guilt of the accused, or which may affect the credibility of prosecution evidence. In case of doubt as to the application of this paragraph, the Court shall decide.

Article 68. Protection of the victims and witnesses and their participation in the proceedings

1. The Court shall take appropriate measures to protect the safety, physical and psychological well-being, dignity and privacy of victims and witnesses. In so doing, the Court shall have regard to all relevant factors, including age, gender as defined in Article 2, paragraph 3, and health, and the nature of the crime, in particular, but not limited to, where the crime involves sexual or gender violence or violence against children. The Prosecutor shall take such measures particularly during the investigation and prosecution of such crimes. These measures shall not be prejudicial to or inconsistent with the rights of the accused and a fair and impartial trial.

2. As an exception to the principle of public hearings provided for in Article 67, the Chambers of the Court may, to protect victims and witnesses or an accused, conduct any part of the proceedings in camera or allow the presentation of evidence by electronic or other special means. In particular, such measures shall be implemented in the case of a victim of sexual violence or a child who is a victim or a witness, unless otherwise ordered by the Court, having regard to all the circumstances, particularly the views of the victim or witness.

3. Where the personal interests of the victims are affected, the Court shall permit their views and concerns to be presented and considered at stages of the proceedings determined to be appropriate by the Court and in a manner which is not prejudicial to or inconsistent with the rights of the accused and a fair and impartial trial. Such views and concerns may be presented by the legal representatives of the victims where the Court considers it appropriate, in accordance with the Rules of Procedure and Evidence.

4. The Victims and Witnesses Unit may advise the Prosecutor and the Court on appropriate protective measures, security arrangements, counselling and assistance as referred to in Article 43, paragraph 6.

5. Where the disclosure of evidence or information pursuant to this Statute may lead to the grave endangerment of the security of a witness or his or her family, the Prosecutor may, for the purposes of any proceedings conducted prior to the commencement of the trial, withhold such evidence or information and instead submit a summary thereof. Such measures shall be exercised in a manner which is not prejudicial to or inconsistent with the rights of the accused and a fair and impartial trial.

6. A State may make an application for necessary measures to be taken in respect of the protection of its servants or agents and the protection of confidential or sensitive information.

Article 69. Evidence

1. Before testifying, each witness shall, in accordance with the Rules of Procedure and Evidence, give an undertaking as to the truthfulness of the evidence to be given by that witness.

2. The testimony of a witness at trial shall be given in person, except to the extent provided by the measures set forth in Article 68 or in the Rules of Procedure and Evidence. The Court may also permit the giving of *viva voce* (oral) or recorded testimony of a witness by means of video or audio technology, as well as the introduction of documents or written transcripts, subject to this Statute and in accordance with the Rules of Procedure and Evidence. These measures shall not be prejudicial to or inconsistent with the rights of the accused.

3. The parties may submit evidence relevant to the case, in accordance with Article 64. The Court shall have the authority to request the submission of all evidence that it considers necessary for the determination of the truth.

4. The Court may rule on the relevance or admissibility of any evidence, taking into account, *inter alia*, the probative value of the evidence and any prejudice that such evidence may cause to a fair trial or to a fair evaluation of the testimony of a witness, in accordance with the Rules of Procedure and Evidence.

5. The Court shall respect and observe privileges on confidentiality as provided for in the Rules of Procedure and Evidence.

6. The Court shall not require proof of facts of common knowledge but may take judicial notice of them.

7. Evidence obtained by means of a violation of this Statute or internationally recognized human rights shall not be admissible if:

(a) The violation casts substantial doubt on the reliability of the evidence; or

(b) The admission of the evidence would be antithetical to and would seriously damage the integrity of the proceedings.

8. When deciding on the relevance or admissibility of evidence collected by a State, the Court shall not rule on the application of the State's national law.

Article 70. Offences against the administration of justice

1. The Court shall have jurisdiction over the following offences against its administration of justice when committed intentionally:

(a) Giving false testimony when under an obligation pursuant to Article 69, paragraph 1, to tell the truth;

(b) Presenting evidence that the party knows is false or forged;

(c) Corruptly influencing a witness, obstructing or interfering with the attendance or testimony of a witness, retaliating against a witness for giving testimony or destroying, tampering with or interfering with the collection of evidence;

(d) Impeding, intimidating or corruptly influencing an official of the Court for the purpose of forging or persuading the official not to perform, or to perform improperly, his or her duties;

(e) Retaliating against an official of the Court on account of duties performed by that or another official;

(f) Soliciting or accepting a bribe as an official of the Court in conjunction with his or her official duties.

2. The principles and procedures governing the Court's exercise of jurisdiction over offences under this articles shall be those provided for in the Rules of Procedure and Evidence. The conditions for providing international cooperation to the Court with respect to its proceedings under this article shall be governed by the domestic laws of the requested State.

3. In the event of conviction, the Court may impose a term of imprisonment not exceeding five years, or a fine in accordance with the Rules of Procedure and Evidence, or both.

4. (a) Each State Party shall extend its criminal laws penalizing offences against the integrity of its own investigative or judicial process to offences against the administration of justice referred to in this article, committed on its territory, or by one of its nationals;

(b) Upon request by the Court, whenever it deems it proper, the State Party shall submit the case to its competent authorities for the purpose of prosecution. Those authorities shall treat such cases with diligence and devote sufficient resources to enable them to be conducted effectively.

Article 71. Sanctions for misconduct before the Court

1. The Court may sanction persons present before it who commit misconduct, including disruption of its proceedings or deliberate refusal to comply with its directions, by administrative measures other than imprisonment, such as temporary or permanent removal from the courtroom, a fine or other similar measures provided for in the Rules of Procedure and Evidence.

2. The procedures governing the imposition of the measures set forth in paragraph 1 shall be those provided for in the Rules of Procedure and Evidence.

Article 72. Protection of national security information

1. This article applies in any case where the disclosure of the information or documents of a State would, in the opinion of that State, prejudice its national security interests. Such cases include those falling within the scope of Article 56, paragraphs 2 and 3, Article 61, paragraph 3, Article 64, paragraph 3, Article 67, paragraph 2, Article 68, paragraph 6, Article 87, paragraph 6 and Article 93, as well as cases arising at any other stage of the proceedings where such disclosure may be at issue.

2. This article shall also apply when a person who has been requested to give information or evidence has refused to do so or has referred the matter to the State on the ground that disclosure would prejudice the national security interests of a State and the State concerned confirms that it is of the opinion that disclosure would prejudice its national security interests.

3. Nothing in this article shall prejudice the requirements of confidentiality applicable under Article 54, paragraph 3(e) and (f), or the application of Article 73.

4. If a State learns that information or documents of the State are being, or are likely to be, disclosed at any stage of the proceedings, and it is of the opinion that disclosure would prejudice its national security interests, that State shall have the right to intervene in order to obtain resolution of the issue in accordance with this article.

5. If, in the opinion of a State, disclosure of information would prejudice its national security interests, all reasonable steps will be taken by the State, acting in conjunction with the Prosecutor, the Defence or the Pre-Trial Chamber or Trial Chamber, as the case may be, to seek to resolve the matter by cooperative means. Such steps may include:

(a) Modification or clarification of the request;

(b) A determination by the Court regarding the relevance of the information or evidence sought, or a determination as to whether the evidence, though relevant, could be or has been obtained from a source other than the requested State;

(c) Obtaining the information or evidence from a different source or in a different form; or

(d) Agreement on conditions under which the assistance could be provided including, among other things, providing summaries or redactions, limitations on disclosure, use of in camera or *ex parte* proceedings, or other protective measures permissible under the Statute and the Rules.

6. Once all reasonable steps have been taken to resolve the matter through cooperative means, and if the State considers that there are no means or conditions under which the information or documents could be provided or disclosed without prejudice to its national security interests, it shall so notify the Prosecutor or the Court of the specific reasons for its decision, unless a specific description of the reasons would itself necessarily result in such prejudice to the State's national security interests.

7. Thereafter, if the Court determines that the evidence is relevant and necessary for the establishment of the guilt or innocence of the accused, the Court may undertake the following actions:

(a) Where disclosure of the information or document is sought pursuant to a request for cooperation under Part 9 or the circumstances described in paragraph 2, and the State has invoked the ground for refusal referred to in Article 93, paragraph 4:

(i) The Court may, before making any conclusion referred to in subparagraph 7 (a)(ii), request further consultations for the purpose of considering the State's representations, which may include, as appropriate, hearings in camera and *ex parte*;

(ii) If the Court concludes that, by invoking the ground for refusal under Article 93, paragraph 4, in the circumstances of the case, the requested State is not acting in accordance with its obligations under the Statute, the Court may refer the matter in accordance with Article 87, paragraph 7, specifying the reasons for its conclusion; and

(iii) The Court may make such inference in the trial of the accused as to the existence or non-existence of a fact, as may be appropriate in the circumstances; or

(b) In all other circumstances:

(i) Order disclosure; or

(ii) To the extent it does not order disclosure, make such inference in the trial of the accused as to the existence or non-existence of a fact, as may be appropriate in the circumstances.

Article 73. Third-party information or documents

If a State Party is requested by the Court to provide a document or information in its custody, possession or control, which was disclosed to it in confidence by a State, inter-governmental organization or international organization, it shall seek the consent of the originator to disclose that document or information. If the originator is a State Party, it shall either consent to disclosure of the information or document or undertake to resolve the issue of disclosure with the Court, subject to the provisions of Article 72. If the originator is not a State Party and refuses consent to disclosure, the requested State shall inform the Court that it is unable to provide the document or information because of a pre-existing obligation of confidentiality to the originator.

Article 74. Requirements for the decision

1. All the judges of the Trial Chamber shall be present at each stage of the trial and throughout their deliberations. The Presidency may, on a case-by-case basis, designate, as available, one or more alternate judges to be present at each stage of the trial and to replace a member of the Trial Chamber if that member is unable to continue attending.

2. The Trial Chamber's decision shall be based on its evaluation of the evidence and the entire proceedings. The decision shall not exceed the facts and circumstances described in the charges and any amendments to the charges. The Court may base its decision only on evidence submitted and discussed before it at the trial.

3. The judges shall attempt to achieve unanimity in their decision, failing which the decision shall be taken by a majority of the judges.

4. The deliberations of the Trial Chamber shall remain secret.

5. The decision shall be in writing and shall contain a full and reasoned statement of the Trial Chamber's findings on the evidence and conclusions. The Trial Chamber shall issue one decision. When there is no unanimity, the Trial Chamber's decision shall contain the views of the majority and the minority. The decision or a summary thereof shall be delivered in open court.

Article 75. Reparations to victims

1. The Court shall establish principles relating to reparations to, or in respect of, victims, including restitution, compensation and rehabilitation. On this basis, in its decision the Court may, either upon request or on its own motion in exceptional circumstances, determine the scope and extent of any damage, loss and injury to, or in respect of, victims and will state the principles on which it is acting.

2. The Court may make an order directly against a convicted person specifying appropriate reparations to, or in respect of, victims, including restitution, compensation and rehabilitation. Where appropriate, the Court may order that the award for reparations be made through the Trust Fund provided for in Article 79.

3. Before making an order under this article, the Court may invite and shall take account of representations from or on behalf of the convicted person, victims, other interested persons or interested States.

4. In exercising its power under this article, the Court may, after a person is convicted of a crime within the jurisdiction of the Court, determine whether, in order to give effect to an order which it may make under this article, it is necessary to seek measures under Article 93, paragraph 1.

5. A State Party shall give effect to a decision under this article as if the provisions of Article 109 were applicable to this article.

6. Nothing in this article shall be interpreted as prejudicing the rights of victims under national or international law.

Article 76. Sentencing

1. In the event of a conviction, the Trial Chamber shall consider the appropriate sentence to be imposed and shall take into account the evidence presented and submissions made during the trial that are relevant to the sentence.

2. Except where Article 65 applies and before the completion of the trial, the Trial Chamber may on its own motion and shall, at the request of the Prosecutor or the accused, hold a further hearing to hear any additional evidence or submissions relevant to the sentence, in accordance with the Rules of Procedure and Evidence.

3. Where paragraph 2 applies, any representations under Article 75 shall be heard during the further hearing referred to in paragraph 2 and, if necessary, during any additional hearing.

4. The sentence shall be pronounced in public and, wherever possible, in the presence of the accused.

PART 7. PENALTIES

Article 77. Applicable penalties

1. Subject to Article 110, the Court may impose one of the following penalties on a person convicted of a crime under Article 5 of this Statute:

(a) Imprisonment for a specified number of years, which may not exceed a maximum of 30 years; or

(b) A term of life imprisonment when justified by the extreme gravity of the crime and the individual circumstances of the convicted person.

2. In addition to imprisonment, the Court may order:

(a) A fine under the criteria provided for in the Rules of Procedure and Evidence;

(b) A forfeiture of proceeds, property and assets derived directly or indirectly from that crime, without prejudice to the rights of bona fide third parties.

Article 78. Determination of the sentence

1. In determining the sentence, the Court shall, in accordance with the Rules of Procedure and Evidence, take into account such factors as the gravity of the crime and the individual circumstances of the convicted person.

2. In imposing a sentence of imprisonment, the Court shall deduct the time, if any, previously spent in detention in accordance with an order of the Court. The Court may deduct any time otherwise spent in detention in connection with conduct underlying the crime.

3. When a person has been convicted of more than one crime, the Court shall pronounce a sentence for each crime and a joint sentence specifying the total period of imprisonment.

This period shall be no less than the highest individual sentence pronounced and shall not exceed 30 years imprisonment or a sentence of life imprisonment in conformity with Article 77, paragraph 1(b).

Article 79. Trust Fund

1. A Trust Fund shall be established by decision of the Assembly of States Parties for the benefit of victims of crimes within the jurisdiction of the Court, and of the families of such victims.

2. The Court may order money and other property collected through fines or forfeiture to be transferred, by order of the Court, to the Trust Fund.

3. The Trust Fund shall be managed according to criteria to be determined by the Assembly of States Parties.

Article 80. Non-prejudice to national application of penalties and national laws

Nothing in this Part of the Statute affects the application by States of penalties prescribed by their national law, nor the law of States which do not provide for penalties prescribed in this Part.

PART 8. APPEAL AND REVISION

Article 81. Appeal against decision of acquittal or conviction or against sentence

1. A decision under Article 74 may be appealed in accordance with the Rules of Procedure and Evidence as follows:

(a) The Prosecutor may make an appeal on any of the following grounds:

(i) Procedural error,

(ii) Error of fact, or

(iii) Error of law;

(b) The convicted person or the Prosecutor on that person's behalf may make an appeal on any of the following grounds:

(i) Procedural error,

(ii) Error of fact,

(iii) Error of law, or

(iv) Any other ground that affects the fairness or reliability of the proceedings or decision.

2. (a) A sentence may be appealed, in accordance with the Rules of Procedure and Evidence, by the Prosecutor or the convicted person on the ground of disproportion between the crime and the sentence;

(b) If on an appeal against sentence the Court considers that there are grounds on which the conviction might be set aside, wholly or in part, it may invite the Prosecutor and the convicted person to submit grounds under Article 81, paragraph 1(a) or (b), and may render a decision on conviction in accordance with Article 83;

(c) The same procedure applies when the Court, on an appeal against conviction only, considers that there are grounds to reduce the sentence under paragraph 2 (a).

3. (a) Unless the Trial Chamber orders otherwise, a convicted person shall remain in custody pending an appeal;

(b) When a convicted person's time in custody exceeds the sentence of imprisonment imposed, that person shall be released, except that if the Prosecutor is also appealing, the release may be subject to the conditions under subparagraph (c) below;

(c) In case of an acquittal, the accused shall be released immediately, subject to the following:

(i) Under exceptional circumstances, and having regard, *inter alia*, to the concrete risk of flight, the seriousness of the offence charged and the probability of success on appeal, the Trial Chamber, at the request of the Prosecutor, may maintain the detention of the person pending appeal;

(ii) A decision by the Trial Chamber under subparagraph (c)(i) may be appealed in accordance with the Rules of Procedure and Evidence.

4. Subject to the provisions of paragraph 3(a) and (b), execution of the decision or sentence shall be suspended during the period allowed for appeal and for the duration of the appeal proceedings.

Article 82. Appeal against other decisions

1. Either party may appeal any of the following decisions in accordance with the Rules of Procedure and Evidence:

(a) A decision with respect to jurisdiction or admissibility;

(b) A decision granting or denying release of the person being investigated or prosecuted;

(c) A decision of the Pre-Trial Chamber to act on its own initiative under Article 56, paragraph 3;

(d) A decision that involves an issue that would significantly affect the fair and expeditious conduct of the proceedings or the outcome of the trial, and for which, in the opinion of the Pre-Trial or Trial Chamber, an immediate resolution by the Appeals Chamber may materially advance the proceedings.

2. A decision of the Pre-Trial Chamber under Article 57, paragraph 3(d), may be appealed against by the State concerned or by the Prosecutor, with the leave of the Pre-Trial Chamber. The appeal shall be heard on an expedited basis.

3. An appeal shall not of itself have suspensive effect unless the Appeals Chamber so orders, upon request, in accordance with the Rules of Procedure and Evidence.

4. A legal representative of the victims, the convicted person or a bona fide owner of property adversely affected by an order under Article 73 may appeal against the order for reparations, as provided in the Rules of Procedure and Evidence.

Article 83. Proceedings on appeal

1. For the purposes of proceedings under Article 81 and this article, the Appeals Chamber shall have all the powers of the Trial Chamber.

2. If the Appeals Chamber finds that the proceedings appealed from were unfair in a way that affected the reliability of the decision or sentence, or that the decision or sentence appealed from was materially affected by error of fact or law or procedural error, it may:

(a) Reverse or amend the decision or sentence; or

(b) Order a new trial before a different Trial Chamber.

For these purposes, the Appeals Chamber may remand a factual issue to the original Trial Chamber for it to determine the issue and to report back accordingly, or may itself call evidence to determine the issue. When the decision or sentence has been appealed only by the person convicted, or the Prosecutor on that person's behalf, it cannot be amended to his or her detriment.

3. If in an appeal against sentence the Appeals Chamber finds that the sentence is disproportionate to the crime, it may vary the sentence in accordance with Part 7.

4. The judgement of the Appeals Chamber shall be taken by a majority of the judges and shall be delivered in open court. The judgement shall state the reasons on which it is based. When there is no unanimity, the judgement of the Appeals Chamber shall contain the views of the majority and the minority, but a judge may deliver a separate or dissenting opinion on a question of law.

5. The Appeals Chamber may deliver its judgement in the absence of the person acquitted or convicted.

Article 84. Revision of conviction or sentence

1. The convicted person or, after death, spouses, children, parents or one person alive at the time of the accused's death who has been given express written instructions from the accused to bring such a claim, or the Prosecutor on the person's behalf, may apply to the Appeals Chamber to revise the final judgement of conviction or sentence on the grounds that:

(a) New evidence has been discovered that:

(i) Was not available at the time of trial, and such unavailability was not wholly or partially attributable to the party making application; and

(ii) Is sufficiently important that had it been proved at trial it would have been likely to have resulted in a different verdict;

(b) It has been newly discovered that decisive evidence, taken into account at trial and upon which the conviction depends, was false, forged or falsified;

(c) One or more of the judges who participated in conviction or confirmation of the charges has committed, in that case, an act of serious misconduct or serious breach of duty of sufficient gravity to justify the removal of that judge or those judges from office under Article 46.

2. The Appeals Chamber shall reject the application if it considers it to be unfounded. If it determines that the application is meritorious, it may, as appropriate:

(a) Reconvene the original Trial Chamber;

(b) Constitute a new Trial Chamber; or

(c) Retain jurisdiction over the matter, with a view to, after hearing the parties in the manner set forth in the Rules of Procedure and Evidence, arriving at a determination on whether the judgement should be revised.

Article 85. Compensation to an arrested or convicted person

1. Anyone who has been the victim of unlawful arrest or detention shall have an enforceable right to compensation.

2. When a person has by a final decision been convicted of a criminal offence, and when subsequently his or her conviction has been reversed on the ground that a new or newly discovered fact shows conclusively that there has been a miscarriage of justice, the

person who has suffered punishment as a result of such conviction shall be compensated according to law, unless it is proved that the non-disclosure of the unknown fact in time is wholly or partly attributable to him or her.

3. In exceptional circumstances, where the Court finds conclusive facts showing that there has been a grave and manifest miscarriage of justice, it may in its discretion award compensation, according to the criteria provided in the Rules of Procedure and Evidence, to a person who has been released from detention following a final decision of acquittal or a termination of the proceedings for that reason.

PART 9. INTERNATIONAL COOPERATION AND JUDICIAL ASSISTANCE

Article 86. General obligation to cooperate

States Parties shall, in accordance with the provisions of this Statute, cooperate fully with the Court in its investigation and prosecution of crimes within the jurisdiction of the Court.

Article 87. Requests for cooperation: general provisions

1. (a) The Court shall have the authority to make requests to States Parties for cooperation. The requests shall be transmitted through the diplomatic channel or any other appropriate channel as may be designated by each State Party upon ratification, acceptance, approval or accession. Subsequent changes to the designation shall be made by each State Party in accordance with the Rules of Procedure and Evidence.

(b) When appropriate, without prejudice to the provisions of subparagraph (a), requests may also be transmitted through the International Criminal Police Organization or any appropriate regional organization.

2. Requests for cooperation and any documents supporting the request shall either be in or be accompanied by a translation into an official language of the requested State or in one of the working languages of the Court, in accordance with the choice made by that State upon ratification, acceptance, approval or accession.

Subsequent changes to this choice shall be made in accordance with the Rules of Procedure and Evidence.

3. The requested State shall keep confidential a request for cooperation and any documents supporting the request, except to the extent that the disclosure is necessary for execution of the request.

4. In relation to any request for assistance presented under Part 9, the Court may take such measures, including measures related to the protection of information, as may be necessary to ensure the safety or physical or psychological well-being of any victims, potential witnesses and their families. The Court may request that any information that is made available under Part 9 shall be provided and handled in a manner that protects the safety and physical or psychological well-being of any victims, potential witnesses and their families.

5. The Court may invite any State not party to this Statute to provide assistance under this Part on the basis of an ad hoc arrangement, an agreement with such State or any other appropriate basis. Where a State not party to this Statute, which has entered into an ad hoc arrangement or an agreement with the Court, fails to cooperate with requests pursuant to any such arrangement or agreement, the Court may so inform the Assembly of States Parties or, where the Security Council referred the matter to the Court, the Security Council.

6. The Court may ask any intergovernmental organization to provide information or documents. The Court may also ask for other forms of cooperation and assistance which

may be agreed upon with such an organization and which are in accordance with its competence or mandate.

7. Where a State Party fails to comply with a request to cooperate by the Court contrary to the provisions of this Statute, thereby preventing the Court from exercising its functions and powers under this Statute, the Court may make a finding to that effect and refer the matter to the Assembly of States Parties or, where the Security Council referred the matter to the Court, to the Security Council.

Article 88. Availability of procedures under national law

States Parties shall ensure that there are procedures available under their national law for all of the forms of cooperation which are specified under this Part.

Article 89. Surrender of persons to the Court

1. The Court may transmit a request for the arrest and surrender of a person, together with the material supporting the request outlined in Article 91, to any State on the territory of which that person may be found and shall request the cooperation of that State in the arrest and surrender of such a person. States Parties shall, in accordance with the provisions of this Part and the procedure under their national law, comply with requests for arrest and surrender.

2. Where the person sought for surrender brings a challenge before a national court on the basis of the principle of *ne bis in idem* as provided in Article 20, the requested State shall immediately consult with the Court to determine if there has been a relevant ruling on admissibility. If the case is admissible, the requested State shall proceed with the execution of the request. If an admissibility ruling is pending, the requested State may postpone the execution of the request for surrender of the person until the Court makes a determination on admissibility.

3. (a) A State Party shall authorize, in accordance with its national procedural law, transportation through its territory of a person being surrendered to the Court by another State, except where transit through that State would impede or delay the surrender.

(b) A request by the Court for transit shall be transmitted in accordance with Article 87. The request for transit shall contain:

(i) A description of the person being transported;

(ii) A brief statement of the facts of the case and their legal characterization; and

(iii) The warrant for arrest and surrender;

(c) A person being transported shall be detained in custody during the period of transit;

(d) No authorization is required if the person is transported by air and no landing is scheduled on the territory of the transit State;

(e) If an unscheduled landing occurs on the territory of the transit State, that State may require a request for transit from the Court as provided for in subparagraph (b). The transit State shall detain the person being transported until the request for transit is received and the transit is effected; provided that detention for purposes of this subparagraph may not be extended beyond 96 hours from the unscheduled landing unless the request is received within that time.

4. If the person sought is being proceeded against or is serving a sentence in the requested State for a crime different from that for which surrender to the Court is sought, the requested State, after making its decision to grant the request, shall consult with the Court.

Article 90. Competing requests

1. A State Party which receives a request from the Court for the surrender of a person under Article 89 shall, if it also receives a request from any other State for the extradition of the same person for the same conduct which forms the basis of the crime for which the Court seeks the person's surrender, notify the Court and the requesting State of that fact.

2. Where the requesting State is a State Party, the requested State shall give priority to the request from the Court if:

(a) The Court has, pursuant to Articles 18 and 19, made a determination that the case in respect of which surrender is sought is admissible and that determination takes into account the investigation or prosecution conducted by the requesting State in respect of its request for extradition; or

(b) The Court makes the determination described in subparagraph (a) pursuant to the requested State's notification under paragraph 1.

3. Where a determination under paragraph 2 (a) has not been made, the requested State may, at its discretion, pending the determination of the Court under paragraph 2 (b), proceed to deal with the request for extradition from the requesting State but shall not extradite the person until the Court has determined that the case is inadmissible. The Court's determination shall be made on an expedited basis.

4. If the requesting State is a State not Party to this Statute the requested State, if it is not under an international obligation to extradite the person to the requesting State, shall give priority to the request for surrender from the Court, if the Court has determined that the case is admissible.

5. Where a case under paragraph 4 has not been determined to be admissible by the Court, the requested State may, at its discretion, proceed to deal with the request for extradition from the requesting State.

6. In cases where paragraph 4 applies except that the requested State is under an existing international obligation to extradite the person to the requesting State not Party to this Statute, the requested State shall determine whether to surrender the person to the Court or extradite the person to the requesting State. In making its decision, the requested State shall consider all the relevant factors, including but not limited to:

(a) The respective dates of the requests;

(b) The interests of the requesting State including, where relevant, whether the crime was committed in its territory and the nationality of the victims and of the person sought; and

(c) The possibility of subsequent surrender between the Court and the requesting State.

7. Where a State Party which receives a request from the Court for the surrender of a person also receives a request from any State for the extradition of the same person for conduct other than that which constitutes the crime for which the Court seeks the person's surrender:

(a) The requested State shall, if it is not under an existing international obligation to extradite the person to the requesting State, give priority to the request from the Court;

(b) The requested State shall, if it is under an existing international obligation to extradite the person to the requesting State, determine whether to surrender the person to the Court or extradite the person to the requesting State. In making its decision, the requested State shall consider all the relevant factors, including but not limited to those set out in paragraph 6, but shall give special consideration to the relative nature and gravity of the conduct in question.

8. Where pursuant to a notification under this article, the Court has determined a case to be inadmissible, and subsequently extradition to the requesting State is refused, the requested State shall notify the Court of this decision.

Article 91. Contents of request for arrest and surrender

1. A request for arrest and surrender shall be made in writing. In urgent cases, a request may be made by any medium capable of delivering a written record, provided that the request shall be confirmed through the channel provided for in Article 87, paragraph 1 (a).

2. In the case of a request for the arrest and surrender of a person for whom a warrant of arrest has been issued by the Pre-Trial Chamber under Article 58, the request shall contain or be supported by:

(a) Information describing the person sought, sufficient to identify the person, and information as to that person's probable location;

(b) A copy of the warrant of arrest; and

(c) Such documents, statements or information as may be necessary to meet the requirements for the surrender process in the requested State, except that those requirements should not be more burdensome than those applicable to requests for extradition pursuant to treaties or arrangements between the requested State and other States and should, if possible, be less burdensome, taking into account the distinct nature of the Court.

3. In the case of a request for the arrest and surrender of a person already convicted, the request shall contain or be supported by:

(a) A copy of any warrant of arrest for that person;

(b) A copy of the judgement of conviction;

(c) Information to demonstrate that the person sought is the one referred to in the judgement of conviction; and

(d) If the person sought has been sentenced, a copy of the sentence imposed and, in the case of a sentence for imprisonment, a statement of any time already served and the time remaining to be served.

4. Upon the request of the Court, a State Party shall consult with the Court, either generally or with respect to a specific matter, regarding any requirements under its national law that may apply under paragraph 2 (c). During the consultations, the State Party shall advise the Court of the specific requirements of its national law.

Article 92. Provisional arrest

1. In urgent cases, the Court may request the provisional arrest of the person sought, pending presentation of the request for surrender and the documents supporting the request as specified in Article 91.

2. The request for provisional arrest shall be made by any medium capable of delivering a written record and shall contain:

(a) Information describing the person sought, sufficient to identify the person, and information as to that person's probable location;

(b) A concise statement of the crimes for which the person's arrest is sought and of the facts which are alleged to constitute those crimes, including, where possible, the date and location of the crime;

(c) A statement of the existence of a warrant of arrest or a judgement of conviction against the person sought; and

(d) A statement that a request for surrender of the person sought will follow.

3. A person who is provisionally arrested may be released from custody if the requested State has not received the request for surrender and the documents supporting the request as specified in Article 91 within the time limits specified in the Rules of Procedure and Evidence. However, the person may consent to surrender before the expiration of this period if permitted by the law of the requested State. In such a case, the requested State shall proceed to surrender the person to the Court as soon as possible.

4. The fact that the person sought has been released from custody pursuant to paragraph 3 shall not prejudice the subsequent arrest and surrender of that person if the request for surrender and the documents supporting the request are delivered at a later date.

Article 93. Other forms of cooperation

1. States Parties shall, in accordance with the provisions of this Part and under procedures of national law, comply with requests by the Court to provide the following assistance in relation to investigations or prosecutions:

(a) The identification and whereabouts of persons or the location of items;

(b) The taking of evidence, including testimony under oath, and the production of evidence, including expert opinions and reports necessary to the Court;

(c) The questioning of any person being investigated or prosecuted;

(d) The service of documents, including judicial documents;

(e) Facilitating the voluntary appearance of persons as witnesses or experts before the Court;

(f) The temporary transfer of persons as provided in paragraph 7;

(g) The examination of places or sites, including the exhumation and examination of grave sites;

(h) The execution of searches and seizures;

(i) The provision of records and documents, including official records and documents;

(j) The protection of victims and witnesses and the preservation of evidence;

(k) The identification, tracing and freezing or seizure of proceeds, property and assets and instrumentalities of crimes for the purpose of eventual forfeiture, without prejudice to the rights of bona fide third parties; and

(l) Any other type of assistance which is not prohibited by the law of the requested State, with a view to facilitating the investigation and prosecution of crimes within the jurisdiction of the Court.

2. The Court shall have the authority to provide an assurance to a witness or an expert appearing before the Court that he or she will not be prosecuted, detained or subjected to any restriction of personal freedom by the Court in respect of any act or omission that preceded the departure of that person from the requested State.

3. Where execution of a particular measure of assistance detailed in a request presented under paragraph 1, is prohibited in the requested State on the basis of an existing fundamental legal principle of general application, the requested State shall promptly consult with the Court to try to resolve the matter. In the consultations, consideration should be given to whether the assistance can be rendered in another manner or subject to conditions. If after consultations the matter cannot be resolved, the Court shall modify the request as necessary.

4. In accordance with Article 72, a State Party may deny a request for assistance, in whole or in part, only if the request concerns the production of any documents or disclosure of evidence which relates to its national security.

5. Before denying a request for assistance under paragraph 1 (1), the requested State shall consider whether the assistance can be provided subject to specified conditions, or whether the assistance can be provided at a later date or in an alternative manner, provided that if the Court or the Prosecutor accepts the assistance subject to conditions, the Court of the Prosecutor shall abide by them.

6. If a request for assistance is denied, the requested State Party shall promptly inform the Court or the Prosecutor of the reasons for such denial.

7. (a) The Court may request the temporary transfer of a person in custody for purposes of identification or for obtaining testimony or other assistance. The person may be transferred if the following conditions are fulfilled:

(i) The person freely gives his or her informed consent to the transfer; and

(ii) The requested State agrees to the transfer, subject to such conditions as that State and the Court may agree.

(b) The person being transferred shall remain in custody. When the purposes of the transfer have been fulfilled, the Court shall return the person without delay to the requested State.

8. (a) The Court shall ensure the confidentiality of documents and information, except as required for the investigation and proceedings described in the request.

(b) The requested State may, when necessary, transmit documents or information to the Prosecutor on a confidential basis. The Prosecutor may then use them solely for the purpose of generating new evidence;

(c) The requested State may, on its own motion or at the request of the Prosecutor, subsequently consent to the disclosure of such documents or information. They may then be used as evidence pursuant to the provisions of Parts 5 and 6 and in accordance with the Rules of Procedure and Evidence.

9. (a) (i) In the event that a State Party receives competing requests, other than for surrender or extradition, from the Court and from another State pursuant to an international obligation, the State Party shall endeavour, in consultation with the Court and the other State, to meet both requests, if necessary by postponing or attaching conditions to one or the other request.

(ii) Failing that, competing requests shall be resolved in accordance with the principles established in Article 90.

(b) Where, however, the request from the Court concerns information, property or persons which are subject to the control of a third State or an international organization by virtue of an international agreement, the requested States shall so inform the Court and the Court shall direct its request to the third State or international organization.

10. (a) The Court may, upon request, cooperate with and provide assistance to a State Party conducting an investigation into or trial in respect of conduct which constitutes a crime within the jurisdiction of the Court or which constitutes a serious crime under the national law of the requesting State.

(b) (i) The assistance provided under subparagraph (a) shall include, *inter alia*:

(1) The transmission of statements, documents or other types of evidence obtained in the course of an investigation or a trial conducted by the Court; and

(2) The questioning of any person detained by order of the Court;

(ii) In the case of assistance under subparagraph (b)(i)(1):

(1) If the documents or other types of evidence have been obtained with the assistance of a State, such transmission shall require the consent of that State;

(2) If the statements, documents or other types of evidence have been provided by a witness or expert, such transmission shall be subject to the provisions of Article 68.

(c) The Court may, under the conditions set out in this paragraph, grant a request for assistance under this paragraph from a State which is not a Party to the Statute.

Article 94. Postponement of execution of a request in respect of ongoing investigation or prosecution

1. If the immediate execution of a request would interfere with an ongoing investigation or prosecution of a case different from that to which the request relates, the requested State may postpone the execution of the request for a period of time agreed upon with the Court. However, the postponement shall be no longer than is necessary to complete the relevant investigation or prosecution in the requested State. Before making a decision to postpone, the requested State should consider whether the assistance may be immediately provided subject to certain conditions.

2. If a decision to postpone is taken pursuant to paragraph 1, the Prosecutor may, however, seek measures to preserve evidence, pursuant to Article 93, paragraph 1(j).

Article 95. Postponement of execution of a request in respect of an admissibility challenge

Without prejudice to Article 53, paragraph 2, where there is an admissibility challenge under consideration by the Court pursuant to Articles 18 or 19, the requested State may postpone the execution of a request under this Part pending a determination by the Court, unless the Court has specifically ordered that the Prosecutor may pursue the collection of such evidence pursuant to Articles 18 or 19.

Article 96. Contents of request for other forms of assistance under Article 93

Upon the request for other forms of assistance referred to in Article 93 shall be made in writing. In urgent cases, a request may be made by any medium capable of delivering a written record, provided that the request shall be confirmed through the channel provided for in Article 87, paragraph 1 (a).

2. The request shall, as applicable, contain or be supported by the following:

(a) A concise statement of the purpose of the request and the assistance sought, including the legal basis and the grounds for the request;

(b) As much detailed information as possible about the location or identification of any person or place that must be found or identified in order for the assistance sought to be provided;

(c) A concise statement of the essential facts underlying the request;

(d) The reasons for and details of any procedure or requirement to be followed;

(e) Such information as may be required under the law of the requested State in order to execute the request; and

(f) Any other information relevant in order for the assistance sought to be provided.

3. Upon the request of the Court, a State Party shall consult with the Court, either generally or with respect to a specific matter, regarding any requirements under its national law that may apply under paragraph 2 (e). During the consultations, the State Party shall advise the Court of the specific requirements of its national law.

4. The provisions of this article shall, where applicable, also apply in respect of a request for assistance made to the Court.

Article 97. Consultations

Where a State Party receives a request under this Part in relation to which it identifies problems which may impede or prevent the execution of the request, that State shall consult with the Court without delay in order to resolve the matter. Such problems may include, *inter alia*:

(a) Insufficient information to execute the request;

(b) In the case of a request for surrender, the fact that despite best efforts, the person sought cannot be located or that the investigation conducted has determined that the person in the custodial State is clearly not the person named in the warrant; or

(c) The fact that execution of the request in its current form would require the requested State to breach a pre-existing treaty obligation undertaken with respect to another State.

Article 98. Cooperation with respect to waiver of immunity and consent to surrender

1. The Court may not proceed with a request for surrender or assistance which would require the requested State to act inconsistently with its obligations under international law with respect to the State or diplomatic immunity of a person or property of a third State, unless the Court can first obtain the cooperation of that third State for the waiver of the immunity.

2. The Court may not proceed with a request for surrender which would require the requested State to act inconsistently with its obligations under international agreements pursuant to which the consent of a sending State is required to surrender a person of that State to the Court, unless the Court can first obtain the cooperation of the sending State for the giving of consent for the surrender.

Article 99. Execution of requests under Articles 93 and 96

1. Requests for assistance shall be executed in accordance with the relevant procedure under the law of the requested State and, unless prohibited by such law, in the manner specified in the request, including following any procedure outlined therein or permitting persons specified in the request to be present at and assist in the execution process.

2. In the case of an urgent request, the documents or evidence produced in response shall, at the request of the Court, be sent urgently.

3. Replies from the requested State shall be transmitted in their original language and form.

4. Without prejudice to other articles in this Part, where it is necessary for the successful execution of a request which can be executed without any compulsory measures, including specifically the interview of or taking evidence from a person on a voluntary basis, including doing so without the presence of the authorities of the requested State Party if it is essential for the request to be executed, and the examination without modification of a public site or other public place, the Prosecutor may execute such request directly on the territory of a State as follows:

(a) When the State Party requested is a State on the territory of which the crime is alleged to have been committed, and there has been a determination of admissibility pursuant to Articles 18 or 19, the Prosecutor may directly execute such request following all possible consultations with the requested State Party;

(b) In other cases, the Prosecutor may execute such request following consultations with the requested State Party and subject to any reasonable conditions or concerns raised by that State Party. Where the requested State Party identifies problems with the execution of a request pursuant to this subparagraph it shall, without delay, consult with the Court to resolve the matter.

5. Provisions allowing a person heard or examined by the Court under Article 72 to invoke restrictions designed to prevent disclosure of confidential information connected with national defence or security shall also apply to the execution of requests for assistance under this article.

Article 100. Costs

1. The ordinary costs for execution of requests in the territory of the requested State shall be borne by that State, except for the following, which shall be borne by the Court:

(a) Costs associated with the travel and security of witnesses and experts or the transfer under Article 93 of persons in custody;

(b) Costs of translation, interpretation and transcription;

(c) Travel and subsistence costs of the judges, the Prosecutor, the Deputy Prosecutors, the Registrar, the Deputy Registrar and staff of any organ of the Court;

(d) Costs of any expert opinion or report requested by the Court;

(e) Costs associated with the transport of a person being surrendered to the Court by a custodial State; and

(f) Following consultations, any extraordinary costs that may result from the execution of a request.

2. The provisions of paragraph 1 shall, as appropriate, apply to requests from States Parties to the Court. In that case, the Court shall bear the ordinary costs of execution.

Article 101. Rule of speciality

1. A person surrendered to the Court under this Statute shall not be proceeded against, punished or detained for any conduct committed prior to surrender, other than the conduct or course of conduct which forms the basis of the crimes for which that person has been surrendered.

2. The Court may request a waiver of the requirements of paragraph 1 from the State which surrendered the person to the Court and, if necessary, the Court shall provide additional information in accordance with Article 91. States Parties shall have the authority to provide a waiver to the Court and should endeavour to do so.

Article 102. Use of terms

For the purposes of this Statute:

(a) "surrender" means the delivering up of a person by a State to the Court, pursuant to this Statute.

(b) "extradition" means the delivering up of a person by one State to another as provided by treaty, convention or national legislation.

PART 10. ENFORCEMENT

Article 103. Role of States in enforcement of sentences of imprisonment

1. (a) A sentence of imprisonment shall be served in a State designated by the Court from a list of States which have indicated to the Court their willingness to accept sentenced persons.

(b) At the time of declaring its willingness to accept sentenced persons, a State may attach conditions to its acceptance as agreed by the Court and in accordance with this Part.

(c) A State designated in a particular case shall promptly inform the Court whether it accepts the Court's designation.

2. (a) The State of enforcement shall notify the Court of any circumstances, including the exercise of any conditions agreed under paragraph 1, which could materially affect the terms or extent of the imprisonment. The Court shall be given at least 45 days' notice of any such known or foreseeable circumstances. During this period, the State of enforcement shall take no action that might prejudice its obligations under Article 110.

(b) Where the Court cannot agree to the circumstances referred to in subparagraph (a), it shall notify the State of enforcement and proceed in accordance with Article 104, paragraph 1.

3. In exercising its discretion to make a designation under paragraph 1, the Court shall take into account the following:

(a) The principle that States Parties should share the responsibility for enforcing sentences of imprisonment, in accordance with principles of equitable distribution, as provided in the Rules of Procedure and Evidence;

(b) The application of widely accepted international treaty standards governing the treatment of prisoners;

(c) The views of the sentenced person; and

(d) The nationality of the sentenced person;

(e) Such other factors regarding the circumstances of the crime or the person sentenced, or the effective enforcement of the sentence, as may be appropriate in designating the State of enforcement.

4. If no State is designated under paragraph 1, the sentence of imprisonment shall be served in a prison facility made available by the host State, in accordance with the conditions set out in the headquarters agreement referred to in Article 3, paragraph 2. In such a case, the costs arising out of the enforcement of a sentence of imprisonment shall be borne by the Court.

Article 104. Change in designation of State of enforcement

1. The Court may, at any time, decide to transfer a sentenced person to a prison of another State.

2. A sentenced person may, at any time, apply to the Court to be transferred from the State of enforcement.

Article 105. Enforcement of the sentence

1. Subject to conditions which a State may have specified in accordance with Article 103, paragraph 1 (b), the sentence of imprisonment shall be binding on the States Parties, which shall in no case modify it.

2. The Court alone shall have the right to decide any application for appeal and revision. The State of enforcement shall not impede the making of any such application by a sentenced person.

Article 106. Supervision of enforcement of sentences and conditions of imprisonment

1. The enforcement of a sentence of imprisonment shall be subject to the supervision of the Court and shall be consistent with widely accepted international treaty standards governing treatment of prisoners.

2. The conditions of imprisonment shall be governed by the law of the State of enforcement and shall be consistent with widely accepted international treaty standards governing treatment of prisoners; in no case shall such conditions be more or less favourable than those available to prisoners convicted of similar offences in the State of enforcement.

3. Communications between a sentenced person and the Court shall be unimpeded and confidential.

Article 107. Transfer of the person upon completion of sentence

1. Following completion of the sentence, a person who is not a national of the State of enforcement may, in accordance with the law of the State of enforcement, be transferred to a State which is obliged to receive him or her, or to another State which agrees to receive him or her, taking into account any wishes of the person to be transferred to that State, unless the State of enforcement authorizes the person to remain in its territory.

2. If no State bears the costs arising out of transferring the person to another State pursuant to paragraph 1, such costs shall be borne by the Court.

3. Subject to the provisions of Article 108, the State of enforcement may also, in accordance with its national law, extradite or otherwise surrender the person to the State which has requested the extradition or surrender of the person for purposes of trial or enforcement of a sentence.

Article 108. Limitation on the prosecution or punishment of other offences

1. A sentenced person in the custody of the State of enforcement shall not be subject to prosecution or punishment or to extradition to a third State for any conduct engaged in prior to that person's delivery to the State of enforcement, unless such prosecution, punishment or extradition has been approved by the Court at the request of the State of enforcement.

2. The Court shall decide the matter after having heard the views of the sentenced person.

3. Paragraph 1 shall cease to apply if the sentenced person remains voluntarily for more than 30 days in the territory of the State of enforcement after having served the full sentence imposed by the Court, or returns to the territory of that State after having left it.

Article 109. Enforcement of fines and forfeiture measures

1. States Parties shall give effect to fines or forfeitures ordered by the Court under Part 7, without prejudice to the rights of bona fide third parties, and in accordance with the procedure of their national law.

2. If a State Party is unable to give effect to an order for forfeiture, it shall take measures to recover the value of the proceeds, property or assets ordered by the Court to be forfeited, without prejudice to the rights of bona fide third parties.

3. Property, or the proceeds of the sale of real property or, where appropriate, the sale of other property, which is obtained by a State Party as a result of its enforcement of a judgement of the Court shall be transferred to the Court.

Article 110. Review by the Court concerning reduction of sentence

1. The State of enforcement shall not release the person before expiry of the sentence pronounced by the Court.

2. The Court alone shall have the right to decide any reduction of sentence, and shall rule on the matter after having heard the person.

3. When the person has served two thirds of the sentence, or 25 years in the case of life imprisonment, the Court shall review the sentence to determine whether it should be reduced. Such a review shall not be conducted before that time.

4. In its review under paragraph 3, the Court may reduce the sentence if it finds that one or more of the following factors are present:

(a) The early and continuing willingness of the person to cooperate with the Court in its investigations and prosecutions;

(b) The voluntary assistance of the person in enabling the enforcement of the judgements and orders of the Court in other cases, and in particular providing assistance in locating assets subject to orders of fine, forfeiture or reparation which may be used for the benefit of victims; or

(c) Other factors establishing a clear and significant change of circumstances sufficient to justify the reduction of sentence, as provided in the Rules of Procedure and Evidence.

5. If the Court determines in its initial review under paragraph 3 that it is not appropriate to reduce the sentence, it shall thereafter review the question of reduction of sentence at such intervals and applying such criteria as provided for in the Rules of Procedure and Evidence.

Article 111. Escape

If a convicted person escapes from custody and flees the State of enforcement, that State may, after consultation with the Court, request the person's surrender from the State in which the person is located pursuant to existing bilateral or multilateral arrangements, or may request that the Court seek the person's surrender. It may direct that the person be delivered to the State in which he or she was serving the sentence or to another State designated by the Court.

PART 11. ASSEMBLY OF STATES PARTIES

Article 112. Assembly of States Parties

1. An Assembly of States Parties to this Statute is hereby established. Each State Party shall have one representative in the Assembly who may be accompanied by alternates and

advisers. Other States which have signed the Statute or the Final Act may be observers in the Assembly.

2. The Assembly shall:

(a) Consider and adopt, as appropriate, recommendations of the Preparatory Commission;

(b) Provide management oversight to the Presidency, the Prosecutor and the Registrar regarding the administration of the Court;

(c) Consider the reports and activities of the Bureau established under paragraph 3 and take appropriate action in regard thereto;

(d) Consider and decide the budget for the Court;

(e) Decide whether to alter, in accordance with Article 36, the number of judges;

(f) Consider pursuant to Article 87, paragraphs 5 and 7, any question relating to non-cooperation;

(g) Perform any other function consistent with this Statute or the Rules of Procedure and Evidence.

3. (a) The Assembly shall have a Bureau consisting of a President, two Vice-Presidents and 18 members elected by the Assembly for three-year terms.

(b) The Bureau shall have a representative character, taking into account, in particular, equitable geographical distribution and the adequate representation of the principal legal systems of the world.

(c) The Bureau shall meet as often as necessary, but at least once a year. It shall assist the Assembly in the discharge of its responsibilities.

4. The Assembly may establish such subsidiary bodies as may be necessary, including an independent oversight mechanism for inspection, evaluation and investigation of the Court, in order to enhance its efficiency and economy.

5. The President of the Court, the Prosecutor and the Registrar or their representatives may participate, as appropriate, in meetings of the Assembly and of the Bureau.

6. The Assembly shall meet at the seat of the Court or at the Headquarters of the United Nations once a year and, when circumstances so require, hold special sessions. Except as otherwise specified in this Statute, special sessions shall be convened by the Bureau on its own initiative or at the request of one third of the States Parties.

7. Each State Party shall have one vote. Every effort shall be made to reach decisions by consensus in the Assembly and in the Bureau. If consensus cannot be reached, except as otherwise provided in the Statute:

(a) Decisions on matters of substance must be approved by a two-thirds majority of those present and voting provided that an absolute majority of States Parties constitutes the quorum for voting;

(b) Decisions on matters of procedure shall be taken by a simple majority of States Parties present and voting.

8. A State Party which is in arrears in the payment of its financial contributions towards the costs of the Court shall have no vote in the Assembly and in the Bureau if the amount of its arrears equals or exceeds the amount of the contributions due from it for the preceding two full years. The Assembly may, nevertheless, permit such a State Party to vote in the Assembly and in the Bureau if it is satisfied that the failure to pay is due to conditions beyond the control of the State Party.

9. The Assembly shall adopt its own rules of procedure.

10. The official and working languages of the Assembly shall be those of the General Assembly of the United Nations.

PART 12. FINANCING

Article 113. Financial Regulations

Except as otherwise specifically provided, all financial matters related to the Court and the meetings of the Assembly of States Parties, including its Bureau and subsidiary bodies, shall be governed by this Statute and the Financial Regulations and Rules adopted by the Assembly of States Parties.

Article 114. Payment of expenses

Expenses of the Court and the Assembly of States Parties, including its Bureau and subsidiary bodies, shall be paid from the funds of the Court.

Article 115. Funds of the Court and of the Assembly of States Parties

The expenses of the Court and the Assembly of States Parties, including its Bureau and subsidiary bodies, as provided for in the budget decided by the Assembly of States Parties, shall be provided by the following sources:

(a) Assessed contributions made by States Parties;

(b) Funds provided by the United Nations, subject to the approval of the General Assembly, in particular in relation to the expenses incurred due to referrals by the Security Council.

Article 116. Voluntary contributions

Without prejudice to Article 115, the Court may receive and utilize, as additional funds, voluntary contributions from Governments, international organizations, individuals, corporations and other entities, in accordance with relevant criteria adopted by the Assembly of States Parties.

Article 117. Assessment of contributions

The contributions of States Parties shall be assessed in accordance with an agreed scale of assessment, based on the scale adopted by the United Nations for its regular budget and adjusted in accordance with the principles on which that scale is based.

Article 118. Annual audit

The records, books and accounts of the Court, including its annual financial statements, shall be audited annually by an independent auditor.

PART 13. FINAL CLAUSES

Article 119. Settlement of disputes

1. Any dispute concerning the judicial functions of the Court shall be settled by the decision of the Court.

2. Any other dispute between two or more States Parties relating to the interpretation or application of this Statute which is not settled through negotiations within three months of their commencement shall be referred to the Assembly of States Parties. The Assembly may itself seek to settle the dispute or make recommendations on further means of settlement of the dispute, including referral to the International Court of Justice in conformity with the Statute of that Court.

Article 120. Reservations

No reservations may be made to this Statute.

Article 121. Amendments

1. After the expiry of seven years from the entry into force of this Statute, any State Party may propose amendments thereto. The text of any proposed amendment shall be submitted to the Secretary-General of the United Nations, who shall promptly circulate it to all States Parties.

2. No sooner than three months from the date of notification, the next Assembly of States Parties shall, by a majority of those present and voting, decide whether to take up the proposal. The Assembly may deal with the proposal directly or convene a Review Conference if the issue involved so warrants.

3. The adoption of an amendment at a meeting of the Assembly of States Parties or at a Review Conference on which consensus cannot be reached shall require a two-thirds majority of States Parties.

4. Except as provided in paragraph 5, an amendment shall enter into force for all States Parties one year after instruments of ratification or acceptance have been deposited with the Secretary-General of the United Nations by seven-eighths of them.

5. Any amendment to Article 5 of this Statute shall enter into force for those States Parties which have accepted the amendment one year after the deposit of their instruments of ratification or acceptance. In respect of a State Party which has not accepted the amendment, the Court shall not exercise its jurisdiction regarding a crime covered by the amendment when committed by that State Party's nationals or on its territory.

6. If an amendment has been accepted by seven-eighths of States Parties in accordance with paragraph 4, any State Party which has not accepted the amendment may withdraw from the Statute with immediate effect, notwithstanding paragraph 1 of Article 127, but subject to paragraph 2 of Article 127, by giving notice no later than one year after the entry into force of such amendment.

7. The Secretary-General of the United Nations shall circulate to all States Parties any amendment adopted at a meeting of the Assembly of States Parties or at a Review Conference.

Article 122. Amendments to provisions of an institutional nature

1. Amendments to provisions of the Statute which are of an exclusively institutional nature, namely, Article 35, Article 36, paragraphs 8 and 9 Article 37, Article 38, Article 39, paragraphs 1 (first two sentences), 2 and 4, Article 42, paragraphs 4 to 9, Article 43, paragraphs 2 and 3, and Articles 44, 46, 47 and 49, may be proposed at any time, notwithstanding Article 121, paragraph 1, by any State Party. The text of any proposed amendment shall be submitted to the Secretary-General of the United Nations or such other person designated by the Assembly of States Parties who shall promptly circulate it to all States Parties and to others participating in the Assembly.

2. Amendments under this article on which consensus cannot be reached shall be adopted by the Assembly of States Parties or by a Review Conference, by a two-thirds majority of States Parties. Such amendments shall enter into force for all States Parties six months after their adoption by the Assembly or, as the case may be, by the Conference.

Article 123. Review of the Statute

1. Seven years after the entry into force of this Statute the Secretary-General of the United Nations shall convene a Review Conference to consider any amendments to this

Statute. Such review may include, but is not limited to, the list of crimes contained in Article 5. The Conference shall be open to those participating in the Assembly of States Parties and on the same conditions.

2. At any time thereafter, at the request of a State Party and for the purposes set out in paragraph 1, the Secretary-General of the United Nations shall, upon approval by a majority of States Parties, convene a Review Conference.

3. The provisions of Article 121, paragraphs 3 to 7, shall apply to the adoption and entry into force of any amendment to the Statute considered at a Review Conference.

Article 124. Transitional Provision

Notwithstanding Article 12, paragraph 1, a State, on becoming a party to this Statute, may declare that, for a period of seven years after the entry into force of this Statute for the State concerned, it does not accept the jurisdiction of the Court with respect to the category of crimes referred to in Article 8 when a crime is alleged to have been committed by its nationals or on its territory. A declaration under this article may be withdrawn at any time. The provisions of this article shall be reviewed at the Review Conference convened in accordance with Article 123, paragraph 1.

Article 125. Signature, ratification, acceptance, approval or accession

1. This Statute shall be open for signature by all States in Rome, at the headquarters of the Food and Agriculture Organization of the United Nations, on 17 July 1998. Thereafter, it shall remain open for signature in Rome at the Ministry of Foreign Affairs of Italy until 17 October 1998. After that date, the Statute shall remain open for signature in New York, at United Nations Headquarters, until 31 December 2000.

2. This Statute is subject to ratification, acceptance or approval by signatory States. Instruments of ratification, acceptance or approval shall be deposited with the Secretary-General of the United Nations.

3. This Statute shall be open to accession by all States. Instruments of accession shall be deposited with the Secretary-General of the United Nations.

Article 126. Entry into force

1. This Statute shall enter into force on the first day of the month after the 60th day following the date of the deposit of the 60th instrument of ratification, acceptance, approval or accession with the Secretary-General of the United Nations.

2. For each State ratifying, accepting, approving or acceding to the Statute after the deposit of the 60th instrument of ratification, acceptance, approval or accession, the Statute shall enter into force on the first day of the month after the 60th day following the deposit by such State of its instrument of ratification, acceptance, approval or accession.

Article 127. Withdrawal

1. A State Party may, by written notification addressed to the Secretary-General of the United Nations, withdraw from this Statute. The withdrawal shall take effect one year after the date of receipt of the notification, unless the notification specifies a later date.

2. A State shall not be discharged, by reason of its withdrawal, from the obligations arising from this Statute while it was a Party to the Statute, including any financial obligations which may have accrued. Its withdrawal shall not affect any cooperation with the Court in connection with criminal investigations and proceedings in relation to which the withdrawing State had a duty to cooperate and which were commenced prior to the date on which the withdrawal became effective, nor shall it prejudice in any way the con-

tinued consideration of any matter which was already under consideration by the Court prior to the date on which the withdrawal became effective.

Article 128. Authentic texts

The original of this Statute, of which the Arabic, Chinese, English, French, Russian and Spanish texts are equally authentic, shall be deposited with the Secretary-General of the United Nations, who shall send certified copies thereof to all States.

IN WITNESS WHEREOF, the undersigned, being duly authorized thereto by their respective Governments, have signed this Statute.

DONE at Rome, this 17th day of July 1998.

International Criminal Court, Elements of Crimes
U.N. Doc. PCNICC/2000/1/Add.2 (2000)

General Introduction

1. Pursuant to article 9, the following Elements of Crimes shall assist the Court in the interpretation and application of articles 6, 7 and 8, consistent with the Statute. The provisions of the Statute, including article 21 and the general principles set out in Part 3, are applicable to the Elements of Crimes.

2. As stated in article 30, unless otherwise provided, a person shall be criminally responsible and liable for punishment for a crime within the jurisdiction of the Court only if the material elements are committed with intent and knowledge. Where no reference is made in the Elements of Crimes to a mental element for any particular conduct, consequence or circumstance listed, it is understood that the relevant mental element, i.e., intent, knowledge or both, set out in article 30 applies. Exceptions to the article 30 standard, based on the Statute, including applicable law under its relevant provisions, are indicated below.

3. Existence of intent and knowledge can be inferred from relevant facts and circumstances.

4. With respect to mental elements associated with elements involving value judgement, such as those using the terms "inhumane" or "severe", it is not necessary that the perpetrator personally completed a particular value judgement, unless otherwise indicated.

5. Grounds for excluding criminal responsibility or the absence thereof are generally not specified in the elements of crimes listed under each crime.[1]

6. The requirement of "unlawfulness" found in the Statute or in other parts of international law, in particular international humanitarian law, is generally not specified in the elements of crimes.

7. The elements of crimes are generally structured in accordance with the following principles:

— As the elements of crimes focus on the conduct, consequences and circumstances associated with each crime, they are generally listed in that order;

— When required, a particular mental element is listed after the affected conduct, consequence or circumstance;

— Contextual circumstances are listed last.

8. As used in the Elements of Crimes, the term "perpetrator" is neutral as to guilt or innocence. The elements, including the appropriate mental elements, apply, mutatis mu-

tandis, to all those whose criminal responsibility may fall under articles 25 and 28 of the Statute.

9. A particular conduct may constitute one or more crimes.

10. The use of short titles for the crimes has no legal effect.

Article 6
Genocide

Introduction

—The term "in the context of" would include the initial acts in an emerging pattern;

—The term "manifest" is an objective qualification;

—Notwithstanding the normal requirement for a mental element provided for in article 30, and recognizing that knowledge of the circumstances will usually be addressed in proving genocidal intent, the appropriate requirement, if any, for a mental element regarding this circumstance will need to be decided by the Court on a case-by-case basis.

Article 6 (a)
Genocide by killing

Elements

1. The perpetrator killed[2] one or more persons.

2. Such person or persons belonged to a particular national, ethnical, racial or religious group.

3. The perpetrator intended to destroy, in whole or in part, that national, ethnical, racial or religious group, as such.

4. The conduct took place in the context of a manifest pattern of similar conduct directed against that group or was conduct that could itself effect such destruction.

Article 6 (b)
Genocide by causing serious bodily or mental harm

Elements

1. The perpetrator caused serious bodily or mental harm to one or more persons.[3]

2. Such person or persons belonged to a particular national, ethnical, racial or religious group.

3. The perpetrator intended to destroy, in whole or in part, that national, ethnical, racial or religious group, as such.

4. The conduct took place in the context of a manifest pattern of similar conduct directed against that group or was conduct that could itself effect such destruction.

Article 6 (c)
Genocide by deliberately inflicting conditions of life
calculated to bring about physical destruction

Elements

1. The perpetrator inflicted certain conditions of life upon one or more persons.

2. Such person or persons belonged to a particular national, ethnical, racial or religious group.

3. The perpetrator intended to destroy, in whole or in part, that national, ethnical, racial or religious group, as such.

4. The conditions of life were calculated to bring about the physical destruction of that group, in whole or in part.[4]

5. The conduct took place in the context of a manifest pattern of similar conduct directed against that group or was conduct that could itself effect such destruction.

Article 6 (d)
Genocide by imposing measures intended to prevent births

Elements

1. The perpetrator imposed certain measures upon one or more persons.

2. Such person or persons belonged to a particular national, ethnical, racial or religious group.

3. The perpetrator intended to destroy, in whole or in part, that national, ethnical, racial or religious group, as such.

4. The measures imposed were intended to prevent births within that group.

5. The conduct took place in the context of a manifest pattern of similar conduct directed against that group or was conduct that could itself effect such destruction.

Article 6 (e)
Genocide by forcibly transferring children

Elements

1. The perpetrator forcibly transferred one or more persons.[5]

2. Such person or persons belonged to a particular national, ethnical, racial or religious group.

3. The perpetrator intended to destroy, in whole or in part, that national, ethnical, racial or religious group, as such.

4. The transfer was from that group to another group.

5. The person or persons were under the age of 18 years.

6. The perpetrator knew, or should have known, that the person or persons were under the age of 18 years.

7. The conduct took place in the context of a manifest pattern of similar conduct directed against that group or was conduct that could itself effect such destruction.

Article 7
Crimes against humanity

Introduction

1. Since article 7 pertains to international criminal law, its provisions, consistent with article 22, must be strictly construed, taking into account that crimes against humanity as defined in article 7 are among the most serious crimes of concern to the international community as a whole, warrant and entail individual criminal responsibility, and require conduct which is impermissible under generally applicable international law, as recognized by the principal legal systems of the world.

2. The last two elements for each crime against humanity describe the context in which the conduct must take place. These elements clarify the requisite participation in and

knowledge of a widespread or systematic attack against a civilian population. However, the last element should not be interpreted as requiring proof that the perpetrator had knowledge of all characteristics of the attack or the precise details of the plan or policy of the State or organization. In the case of an emerging widespread or systematic attack against a civilian population, the intent clause of the last element indicates that this mental element is satisfied if the perpetrator intended to further such an attack.

3. "Attack directed against a civilian population" in these context elements is understood to mean a course of conduct involving the multiple commission of acts referred to in article 7, paragraph 1, of the Statute against any civilian population, pursuant to or in furtherance of a State or organizational policy to commit such attack. The acts need not constitute a military attack. It is understood that "policy to commit such attack" requires that the State or organization actively promote or encourage such an attack against a civilian population.[6]

Article 7 (1) (a)
Crime against humanity of murder

Elements

1. The perpetrator killed[7] one or more persons.

2. The conduct was committed as part of a widespread or systematic attack directed against a civilian population.

3. The perpetrator knew that the conduct was part of or intended the conduct to be part of a widespread or systematic attack against a civilian population.

Article 7 (1) (b)
Crime against humanity of extermination

Elements

Article 7 (1) (c)
Crime against humanity of enslavement

Elements

1. The perpetrator exercised any or all of the powers attaching to the right of ownership over one or more persons, such as by purchasing, selling, lending or bartering such a person or persons, or by imposing on them a similar deprivation of liberty.[11]

2. The conduct was committed as part of a widespread or systematic attack directed against a civilian population.

3. The perpetrator knew that the conduct was part of or intended the conduct to be part of a widespread or systematic attack directed against a civilian population.

Article 7 (1) (d)
Crime against humanity of deportation or forcible transfer of population

Elements

Article 7 (1) (e)
Crime against humanity of imprisonment or other severe deprivation of physical liberty

Elements

1. The perpetrator imprisoned one or more persons or otherwise severely deprived one or more persons of physical liberty.

2. The gravity of the conduct was such that it was in violation of fundamental rules of international law.

3. The perpetrator was aware of the factual circumstances that established the gravity of the conduct.

4. The conduct was committed as part of a widespread or systematic attack directed against a civilian population.

5. The perpetrator knew that the conduct was part of or intended the conduct to be part of a widespread or systematic attack directed against a civilian population.

Article 7 (1) (f)
Crime against humanity of torture[14]

Elements

Article 7 (1) (g)-1
Crime against humanity of rape

Elements

Article 7 (1) (g)-2
Crime against humanity of sexual slavery[17]

Elements

Article 7 (1) (g)-3
Crime against humanity of enforced prostitution

Elements

Article 7 (1) (g)-4
Crime against humanity of forced pregnancy

Elements

Article 7 (1) (g)-5
Crime against humanity of enforced sterilization

Elements

Article 7 (1) (g)-6
Crime against humanity of sexual violence

Elements

Article 7 (1) (h)
Crime against humanity of persecution

Elements

1. The perpetrator severely deprived, contrary to international law,[21] one or more persons of fundamental rights.

2. The perpetrator targeted such person or persons by reason of the identity of a group or collectivity or targeted the group or collectivity as such.

3. Such targeting was based on political, racial, national, ethnic, cultural, religious, gender as defined in article 7, paragraph 3, of the Statute, or other grounds that are universally recognized as impermissible under international law.

4. The conduct was committed in connection with any act referred to in article 7, paragraph 1, of the Statute or any crime within the jurisdiction of the Court.[22]

5. The conduct was committed as part of a widespread or systematic attack directed against a civilian population.

6. The perpetrator knew that the conduct was part of or intended the conduct to be part of a widespread or systematic attack directed against a civilian population.

Article 7 (1) (i)
Crime against humanity of enforced disappearance of persons[23] [24]

Elements

1. The perpetrator:

(a) Arrested, detained[25] [26] or abducted one or more persons; or

(b) Refused to acknowledge the arrest, detention or abduction, or to give information on the fate or whereabouts of such person or persons.

2. (a) Such arrest, detention or abduction was followed or accompanied by a refusal to acknowledge that deprivation of freedom or to give information on the fate or whereabouts of such person or persons; or

(b) Such refusal was preceded or accompanied by that deprivation of freedom.

3. The perpetrator was aware that:[27]

(a) Such arrest, detention or abduction would be followed in the ordinary course of events by a refusal to acknowledge that deprivation of freedom or to give information on the fate or whereabouts of such person or persons;[28] or

(b) Such refusal was preceded or accompanied by that deprivation of freedom.

4. Such arrest, detention or abduction was carried out by, or with the authorization, support or acquiescence of, a State or a political organization.

5. Such refusal to acknowledge that deprivation of freedom or to give information on the fate or whereabouts of such person or persons was carried out by, or with the authorization or support of, such State or political organization.

6. The perpetrator intended to remove such person or persons from the protection of the law for a prolonged period of time.

7. The conduct was committed as part of a widespread or systematic attack directed against a civilian population.

8. The perpetrator knew that the conduct was part of or intended the conduct to be part of a widespread or systematic attack directed against a civilian population.

Article 7 (1) (j)
Crime against humanity of apartheid

Elements

Article 7 (1) (k)
Crime against humanity of other inhumane acts

Elements

1. The perpetrator inflicted great suffering, or serious injury to body or to mental or physical health, by means of an inhumane act.

2. Such act was of a character similar to any other act referred to in article 7, paragraph 1, of the Statute.[30]

3. The perpetrator was aware of the factual circumstances that established the character of the act.

4. The conduct was committed as part of a widespread or systematic attack directed against a civilian population.

5. The perpetrator knew that the conduct was part of or intended the conduct to be part of a widespread or systematic attack directed against a civilian population.

Article 8
War crimes

Introduction

The elements for war crimes under article 8, paragraph 2 (c) and (e), are subject to the limitations addressed in article 8, paragraph 2 (d) and (f), which are not elements of crimes.

The elements for war crimes under article 8, paragraph 2, of the Statute shall be interpreted within the established framework of the international law of armed conflict including, as appropriate, the international law of armed conflict applicable to armed conflict at sea.

With respect to the last two elements listed for each crime:

  • There is no requirement for a legal evaluation by the perpetrator as to the existence of an armed conflict or its character as international or non-international;

  • In that context there is no requirement for awareness by the perpetrator of the facts that established the character of the conflict as international or non-international;

  • There is only a requirement for the awareness of the factual circumstances that established the existence of an armed conflict that is implicit in the terms "took place in the context of and was associated with".

Article 8 (2) (a)

Article 8 (2) (a) (i)
War crime of wilful killing

Elements

1. The perpetrator killed one or more persons.[31]

2. Such person or persons were protected under one or more of the Geneva Conventions of 1949.

3. The perpetrator was aware of the factual circumstances that established that protected status.[32] [33]

4. The conduct took place in the context of and was associated with an international armed conflict.[34]

5. The perpetrator was aware of factual circumstances that established the existence of an armed conflict.

Article 8 (2) (a) (ii)-1
War crime of torture

Elements[35]

Article 8 (2) (a) (ii)-2
War crime of inhuman treatment

Elements

1. The perpetrator inflicted severe physical or mental pain or suffering upon one or more persons.

2. Such person or persons were protected under one or more of the Geneva Conventions of 1949.

3. The perpetrator was aware of the factual circumstances that established that protected status.

4. The conduct took place in the context of and was associated with an international armed conflict.

5. The perpetrator was aware of factual circumstances that established the existence of an armed conflict.

Article 8 (2) (a) (ii)-3
War crime of biological experiments

Elements

1. The perpetrator subjected one or more persons to a particular biological experiment.

2. The experiment seriously endangered the physical or mental health or integrity of such person or persons.

3. The intent of the experiment was non-therapeutic and it was neither justified by medical reasons nor carried out in such person's or persons' interest.

4. Such person or persons were protected under one or more of the Geneva Conventions of 1949.

5. The perpetrator was aware of the factual circumstances that established that protected status.

6. The conduct took place in the context of and was associated with an international armed conflict.

7. The perpetrator was aware of factual circumstances that established the existence of an armed conflict.

Article 8 (2) (a) (iii)
War crime of wilfully causing great suffering

Elements

1. The perpetrator caused great physical or mental pain or suffering to, or serious injury to body or health of, one or more persons.

2. Such person or persons were protected under one or more of the Geneva Conventions of 1949.

3. The perpetrator was aware of the factual circumstances that established that protected status.

4. The conduct took place in the context of and was associated with an international armed conflict.

5. The perpetrator was aware of factual circumstances that established the existence of an armed conflict.

Article 8 (2) (a) (iv)
War crime of destruction and appropriation of property

Elements

1. The perpetrator destroyed or appropriated certain property.

2. The destruction or appropriation was not justified by military necessity.

3. The destruction or appropriation was extensive and carried out wantonly.

4. Such property was protected under one or more of the Geneva Conventions of 1949.

5. The perpetrator was aware of the factual circumstances that established that protected status.

6. The conduct took place in the context of and was associated with an international armed conflict.

7. The perpetrator was aware of factual circumstances that established the existence of an armed conflict.

Article 8 (2) (a) (v)
War crime of compelling service in hostile forces

Elements

Article 8 (2) (a) (vi)
War crime of denying a fair trial

Elements

1. The perpetrator deprived one or more persons of a fair and regular trial by denying judicial guarantees as defined, in particular, in the third and the fourth Geneva Conventions of 1949.

2. Such person or persons were protected under one or more of the Geneva Conventions of 1949.

3. The perpetrator was aware of the factual circumstances that established that protected status.

4. The conduct took place in the context of and was associated with an international armed conflict.

5. The perpetrator was aware of factual circumstances that established the existence of an armed conflict.

Article 8 (2) (a) (vii)-1
War crime of unlawful deportation and transfer

Elements

1. The perpetrator deported or transferred one or more persons to another State or to another location.

2. Such person or persons were protected under one or more of the Geneva Conventions of 1949.

3. The perpetrator was aware of the factual circumstances that established that protected status.

4. The conduct took place in the context of and was associated with an international armed conflict.

5. The perpetrator was aware of factual circumstances that established the existence of an armed conflict.

Article 8 (2) (a) (vii)-2
War crime of unlawful confinement

Elements

1. The perpetrator confined or continued to confine one or more persons to a certain location.

2. Such person or persons were protected under one or more of the Geneva Conventions of 1949.

3. The perpetrator was aware of the factual circumstances that established that protected status.

4. The conduct took place in the context of and was associated with an international armed conflict.

5. The perpetrator was aware of factual circumstances that established the existence of an armed conflict.

Article 8 (2) (a) (viii)
War crime of taking hostages

Elements

1. The perpetrator seized, detained or otherwise held hostage one or more persons.

2. The perpetrator threatened to kill, injure or continue to detain such person or persons.

3. The perpetrator intended to compel a State, an international organization, a natural or legal person or a group of persons to act or refrain from acting as an explicit or implicit condition for the safety or the release of such person or persons.

4. Such person or persons were protected under one or more of the Geneva Conventions of 1949.

5. The perpetrator was aware of the factual circumstances that established that protected status.

6. The conduct took place in the context of and was associated with an international armed conflict.

7. The perpetrator was aware of factual circumstances that established the existence of an armed conflict.

Article 8 (2) (b)

Article 8 (2) (b) (i)
War crime of attacking civilians

Elements

Article 8 (2) (b) (ii)
War crime of attacking civilian objects

Elements

1. The perpetrator directed an attack.

2. The object of the attack was civilian objects, that is, objects which are not military objectives.

3. The perpetrator intended such civilian objects to be the object of the attack.

4. The conduct took place in the context of and was associated with an international armed conflict.

5. The perpetrator was aware of factual circumstances that established the existence of an armed conflict.

Article 8 (2) (b) (iii)
War crime of attacking personnel or objects involved in a humanitarian assistance or peacekeeping mission

Elements

Article 8 (2) (b) (iv)
War crime of excessive incidental death, injury, or damage

Elements

1. The perpetrator launched an attack.

2. The attack was such that it would cause incidental death or injury to civilians or damage to civilian objects or widespread, long-term and severe damage to the natural environment and that such death, injury or damage would be of such an extent as to be clearly excessive in relation to the concrete and direct overall military advantage anticipated.[36]

3. The perpetrator knew that the attack would cause incidental death or injury to civilians or damage to civilian objects or widespread, long-term and severe damage to the natural environment and that such death, injury or damage would be of such an extent as to be clearly excessive in relation to the concrete and direct overall military advantage anticipated.[37]

4. The conduct took place in the context of and was associated with an international armed conflict.

5. The perpetrator was aware of factual circumstances that established the existence of an armed conflict.

Article 8 (2) (b) (v)
War crime of attacking undefended places[38]

Elements

1. The perpetrator attacked one or more towns, villages, dwellings or buildings.

2. Such towns, villages, dwellings or buildings were open for unresisted occupation.

3. Such towns, villages, dwellings or buildings did not constitute military objectives.

4. The conduct took place in the context of and was associated with an international armed conflict.

5. The perpetrator was aware of factual circumstances that established the existence of an armed conflict.

Article 8 (2) (b) (vi)
War crime of killing or wounding a person hors de combat

Elements

1. The perpetrator killed or injured one or more persons.

2. Such person or persons were hors de combat.

3. The perpetrator was aware of the factual circumstances that established this status.

4. The conduct took place in the context of and was associated with an international armed conflict.

5. The perpetrator was aware of factual circumstances that established the existence of an armed conflict.

Article 8 (2) (b) (vii)-1
War crime of improper use of a flag of truce

Elements

Article 8 (2) (b) (vii)-2
War crime of improper use of a flag, insignia or uniform of the hostile party

Elements

1. The perpetrator used a flag, insignia or uniform of the hostile party.

2. The perpetrator made such use in a manner prohibited under the international law of armed conflict while engaged in an attack.

3. The perpetrator knew or should have known of the prohibited nature of such use.[40]

4. The conduct resulted in death or serious personal injury.

5. The perpetrator knew that the conduct could result in death or serious personal injury.

6. The conduct took place in the context of and was associated with an international armed conflict.

7. The perpetrator was aware of factual circumstances that established the existence of an armed conflict.

Article 8 (2) (b) (vii)-3
War crime of improper use of a flag, insignia or uniform of the United Nations

Elements

1. The perpetrator used a flag, insignia or uniform of the United Nations.

2. The perpetrator made such use in a manner prohibited under the international law of armed conflict.

3. The perpetrator knew of the prohibited nature of such use.[41]

4. The conduct resulted in death or serious personal injury.

5. The perpetrator knew that the conduct could result in death or serious personal injury.

6. The conduct took place in the context of and was associated with an international armed conflict.

7. The perpetrator was aware of factual circumstances that established the existence of an armed conflict.

Article 8 (2) (b) (vii)-4
War crime of improper use of the distinctive emblems of the Geneva Conventions

Elements

1. The perpetrator used the distinctive emblems of the Geneva Conventions.

2. The perpetrator made such use for combatant purposes[42] in a manner prohibited under the international law of armed conflict.

3. The perpetrator knew or should have known of the prohibited nature of such use.[43]

4. The conduct resulted in death or serious personal injury.

5. The perpetrator knew that the conduct could result in death or serious personal injury.

6. The conduct took place in the context of and was associated with an international armed conflict.

7. The perpetrator was aware of factual circumstances that established the existence of an armed conflict.

Article 8 (2) (b) (viii)
The transfer, directly or indirectly, by the Occupying Power of parts of
its own civilian population into the territory it occupies, or the deportation
or transfer of all or parts of the population of the occupied
territory within or outside this territory

Elements

1. The perpetrator:

  (a) Transferred,[44] directly or indirectly, parts of its own population into the territory it occupies; or

  (b) Deported or transferred all or parts of the population of the occupied territory within or outside this territory.

2. The conduct took place in the context of and was associated with an international armed conflict.

3. The perpetrator was aware of factual circumstances that established the existence of an armed conflict.

Article 8 (2) (b) (ix)
War crime of attacking protected objects[45]

Elements

1. The perpetrator directed an attack.

2. The object of the attack was one or more buildings dedicated to religion, education, art, science or charitable purposes, historic monuments, hospitals or places where the sick and wounded are collected, which were not military objectives.

3. The perpetrator intended such building or buildings dedicated to religion, education, art, science or charitable purposes, historic monuments, hospitals or places where the sick and wounded are collected, which were not military objectives, to be the object of the attack.

4. The conduct took place in the context of and was associated with an international armed conflict.

5. The perpetrator was aware of factual circumstances that established the existence of an armed conflict.

Article 8 (2) (b) (x)-1
War crime of mutilation

Elements

Article 8 (2) (b) (x)-2
War crime of medical or scientific experiments

Elements

1. The perpetrator subjected one or more persons to a medical or scientific experiment.

2. The experiment caused death or seriously endangered the physical or mental health or integrity of such person or persons.

3. The conduct was neither justified by the medical, dental or hospital treatment of such person or persons concerned nor carried out in such person's or persons' interest.

4. Such person or persons were in the power of an adverse party.

5. The conduct took place in the context of and was associated with an international armed conflict.

6. The perpetrator was aware of factual circumstances that established the existence of an armed conflict.

Article 8 (2) (b) (xi)
War crime of treacherously killing or wounding

Elements

1. The perpetrator invited the confidence or belief of one or more persons that they were entitled to, or were obliged to accord, protection under rules of international law applicable in armed conflict.

2. The perpetrator intended to betray that confidence or belief.

3. The perpetrator killed or injured such person or persons.

4. The perpetrator made use of that confidence or belief in killing or injuring such person or persons.

5. Such person or persons belonged to an adverse party.

6. The conduct took place in the context of and was associated with an international armed conflict.

7. The perpetrator was aware of factual circumstances that established the existence of an armed conflict.

Article 8 (2) (b) (xii)
War crime of denying quarter

Elements

1. The perpetrator declared or ordered that there shall be no survivors.

2. Such declaration or order was given in order to threaten an adversary or to conduct hostilities on the basis that there shall be no survivors.

3. The perpetrator was in a position of effective command or control over the subordinate forces to which the declaration or order was directed.

4. The conduct took place in the context of and was associated with an international armed conflict.

5. The perpetrator was aware of factual circumstances that established the existence of an armed conflict.

Article 8 (2) (b) (xiii)
War crime of destroying or seizing the enemy's property

Elements

1. The perpetrator destroyed or seized certain property.

2. Such property was property of a hostile party.

3. Such property was protected from that destruction or seizure under the international law of armed conflict.

4. The perpetrator was aware of the factual circumstances that established the status of the property.

5. The destruction or seizure was not justified by military necessity.

6. The conduct took place in the context of and was associated with an international armed conflict.

7. The perpetrator was aware of factual circumstances that established the existence of an armed conflict.

Article 8 (2) (b) (xiv)
War crime of depriving the nationals of the hostile power of rights or actions

Elements

1. The perpetrator effected the abolition, suspension or termination of admissibility in a court of law of certain rights or actions.

2. The abolition, suspension or termination was directed at the nationals of a hostile party.

3. The perpetrator intended the abolition, suspension or termination to be directed at the nationals of a hostile party.

4. The conduct took place in the context of and was associated with an international armed conflict.

5. The perpetrator was aware of factual circumstances that established the existence of an armed conflict.

Article 8 (2) (b) (xv)
War crime of compelling participation in military operations

Elements

1. The perpetrator coerced one or more persons by act or threat to take part in military operations against that person's own country or forces.

2. Such person or persons were nationals of a hostile party.

3. The conduct took place in the context of and was associated with an international armed conflict.

4. The perpetrator was aware of factual circumstances that established the existence of an armed conflict.

Article 8 (2) (b) (xvi)
War crime of pillaging

Elements

1. The perpetrator appropriated certain property.

2. The perpetrator intended to deprive the owner of the property and to appropriate it for private or personal use.[47]

3. The appropriation was without the consent of the owner.

4. The conduct took place in the context of and was associated with an international armed conflict.

5. The perpetrator was aware of factual circumstances that established the existence of an armed conflict.

Article 8 (2) (b) (xvii)
War crime of employing poison or poisoned weapons

Elements

Article 8 (2) (b) (xviii)
War crime of employing prohibited gases, liquids, materials or devices

Elements

1. The perpetrator employed a gas or other analogous substance or device.

2. The gas, substance or device was such that it causes death or serious damage to health in the ordinary course of events, through its asphyxiating or toxic properties.[48]

3. The conduct took place in the context of and was associated with an international armed conflict.

4. The perpetrator was aware of factual circumstances that established the existence of an armed conflict.

Article 8 (2) (b) (xix)
War crime of employing prohibited bullets

Elements

Article 8 (2) (b) (xx)
War crime of employing weapons, projectiles or materials or methods of warfare listed in the Annex to the Statute

Elements

[Elements will have to be drafted once weapons, projectiles or material or methods of warfare have been included in an annex to the Statute.]

Article 8 (2) (b) (xxi)
War crime of outrages upon personal dignity

Elements

1. The perpetrator humiliated, degraded or otherwise violated the dignity of one or more persons.[49]

2. The severity of the humiliation, degradation or other violation was of such degree as to be generally recognized as an outrage upon personal dignity.

3. The conduct took place in the context of and was associated with an international armed conflict.

4. The perpetrator was aware of factual circumstances that established the existence of an armed conflict.

Article 8 (2) (b) (xxii)-1
War crime of rape

Elements

Article 8 (2) (b) (xxii)-2
War crime of sexual slavery[52]

Elements

1. The perpetrator exercised any or all of the powers attaching to the right of ownership over one or more persons, such as by purchasing, selling, lending or bartering such a person or persons, or by imposing on them a similar deprivation of liberty.[53]

2. The perpetrator caused such person or persons to engage in one or more acts of a sexual nature.

3. The conduct took place in the context of and was associated with an international armed conflict.

4. The perpetrator was aware of factual circumstances that established the existence of an armed conflict.

Article 8 (2) (b) (xxii)-3
War crime of enforced prostitution

Elements

Article 8 (2) (b) (xxii)-4
War crime of forced pregnancy

Elements

Article 8 (2) (b) (xxii)-5
War crime of enforced sterilization

Elements

1. The perpetrator deprived one or more persons of biological reproductive capacity.[54]

2. The conduct was neither justified by the medical or hospital treatment of the person or persons concerned nor carried out with their genuine consent.[55]

3. The conduct took place in the context of and was associated with an international armed conflict.

4. The perpetrator was aware of factual circumstances that established the existence of an armed conflict.

Article 8 (2) (b) (xxii)-6
War crime of sexual violence

Elements

1. The perpetrator committed an act of a sexual nature against one or more persons or caused such person or persons to engage in an act of a sexual nature by force, or by threat of force or coercion, such as that caused by fear of violence, duress, detention, psychological oppression or abuse of power, against such person or persons or another person, or by taking advantage of a coercive environment or such person's or persons' incapacity to give genuine consent.

2. The conduct was of a gravity comparable to that of a grave breach of the Geneva Conventions.

3. The perpetrator was aware of the factual circumstances that established the gravity of the conduct.

4. The conduct took place in the context of and was associated with an international armed conflict.

5. The perpetrator was aware of factual circumstances that established the existence of an armed conflict.

Article 8 (2) (b) (xxiii)
War crime of using protected persons as shields

Elements

1. The perpetrator moved or otherwise took advantage of the location of one or more civilians or other persons protected under the international law of armed conflict.

2. The perpetrator intended to shield a military objective from attack or shield, favour or impede military operations.

3. The conduct took place in the context of and was associated with an international armed conflict.

4. The perpetrator was aware of factual circumstances that established the existence of an armed conflict.

Article 8 (2) (b) (xxiv)
War crime of attacking objects or persons using the distinctive emblems of the Geneva Conventions

Elements

1. The perpetrator attacked one or more persons, buildings, medical units or transports or other objects using, in conformity with international law, a distinctive emblem or other method of identification indicating protection under the Geneva Conventions.

2. The perpetrator intended such persons, buildings, units or transports or other objects so using such identification to be the object of the attack.

3. The conduct took place in the context of and was associated with an international armed conflict.

4. The perpetrator was aware of factual circumstances that established the existence of an armed conflict.

Article 8 (2) (b) (xxv)

War crime of starvation as a method of warfare

Elements

1. The perpetrator deprived civilians of objects indispensable to their survival.

2. The perpetrator intended to starve civilians as a method of warfare.

3. The conduct took place in the context of and was associated with an international armed conflict.

4. The perpetrator was aware of factual circumstances that established the existence of an armed conflict.

Article 8 (2) (b) (xxvi)
War crime of using, conscripting or enlisting children

Elements

1. The perpetrator conscripted or enlisted one or more persons into the national armed forces or used one or more persons to participate actively in hostilities.

2. Such person or persons were under the age of 15 years.

3. The perpetrator knew or should have known that such person or persons were under the age of 15 years.

4. The conduct took place in the context of and was associated with an international armed conflict.

5. The perpetrator was aware of factual circumstances that established the existence of an armed conflict.

Article 8 (2) (c)

Article 8 (2) (c) (i)-1
War crime of murder

Elements

1. The perpetrator killed one or more persons.

2. Such person or persons were either hors de combat, or were civilians, medical personnel, or religious personnel[56] taking no active part in the hostilities.

3. The perpetrator was aware of the factual circumstances that established this status.

4. The conduct took place in the context of and was associated with an armed conflict not of an international character.

5. The perpetrator was aware of factual circumstances that established the existence of an armed conflict.

Article 8 (2) (c) (i)-2
War crime of mutilation

Elements

1. The perpetrator subjected one or more persons to mutilation, in particular by permanently disfiguring the person or persons, or by permanently disabling or removing an organ or appendage.

2. The conduct was neither justified by the medical, dental or hospital treatment of the person or persons concerned nor carried out in such person's or persons' interests.

3. Such person or persons were either hors de combat, or were civilians, medical personnel or religious personnel taking no active part in the hostilities.

4. The perpetrator was aware of the factual circumstances that established this status.

5. The conduct took place in the context of and was associated with an armed conflict not of an international character.

6. The perpetrator was aware of factual circumstances that established the existence of an armed conflict.

Article 8 (2) (c) (i)-3
War crime of cruel treatment

Elements

1. The perpetrator inflicted severe physical or mental pain or suffering upon one or more persons.

2. Such person or persons were either hors de combat, or were civilians, medical personnel, or religious personnel taking no active part in the hostilities.

3. The perpetrator was aware of the factual circumstances that established this status.

4. The conduct took place in the context of and was associated with an armed conflict not of an international character.

5. The perpetrator was aware of factual circumstances that established the existence of an armed conflict.

Article 8 (2) (c) (i)-4
War crime of torture

Elements

1. The perpetrator inflicted severe physical or mental pain or suffering upon one or more persons.

2. The perpetrator inflicted the pain or suffering for such purposes as: obtaining information or a confession, punishment, intimidation or coercion or for any reason based on discrimination of any kind.

3. Such person or persons were either hors de combat, or were civilians, medical personnel or religious personnel taking no active part in the hostilities.

4. The perpetrator was aware of the factual circumstances that established this status.

5. The conduct took place in the context of and was associated with an armed conflict not of an international character.

6. The perpetrator was aware of factual circumstances that established the existence of an armed conflict.

Article 8 (2) (c) (ii)
War crime of outrages upon personal dignity

Elements

1. The perpetrator humiliated, degraded or otherwise violated the dignity of one or more persons.[57]

2. The severity of the humiliation, degradation or other violation was of such degree as to be generally recognized as an outrage upon personal dignity.

3. Such person or persons were either hors de combat, or were civilians, medical personnel or religious personnel taking no active part in the hostilities.

4. The perpetrator was aware of the factual circumstances that established this status.

5. The conduct took place in the context of and was associated with an armed conflict not of an international character.

6. The perpetrator was aware of factual circumstances that established the existence of an armed conflict.

Article 8 (2) (c) (iii)
War crime of taking hostages

Elements

1. The perpetrator seized, detained or otherwise held hostage one or more persons.

2. The perpetrator threatened to kill, injure or continue to detain such person or persons.

3. The perpetrator intended to compel a State, an international organization, a natural or legal person or a group of persons to act or refrain from acting as an explicit or implicit condition for the safety or the release of such person or persons.

4. Such person or persons were either hors de combat, or were civilians, medical personnel or religious personnel taking no active part in the hostilities.

5. The perpetrator was aware of the factual circumstances that established this status.

6. The conduct took place in the context of and was associated with an armed conflict not of an international character.

7. The perpetrator was aware of factual circumstances that established the existence of an armed conflict.

Article 8 (2) (c) (iv)
War crime of sentencing or execution without due process

Elements

1. The perpetrator passed sentence or executed one or more persons.[58]

2. Such person or persons were either hors de combat, or were civilians, medical personnel or religious personnel taking no active part in the hostilities.

3. The perpetrator was aware of the factual circumstances that established this status.

4. There was no previous judgement pronounced by a court, or the court that rendered judgement was not "regularly constituted", that is, it did not afford the essential guarantees of independence and impartiality, or the court that rendered judgement did not afford all other judicial guarantees generally recognized as indispensable under international law.[59]

5. The perpetrator was aware of the absence of a previous judgement or of the denial of relevant guarantees and the fact that they are essential or indispensable to a fair trial.

6. The conduct took place in the context of and was associated with an armed conflict not of an international character.

7. The perpetrator was aware of factual circumstances that established the existence of an armed conflict.

Article 8 (2) (e)

Article 8 (2) (e) (i)
War crime of attacking civilians

Elements

1. The perpetrator directed an attack.

2. The object of the attack was a civilian population as such or individual civilians not taking direct part in hostilities.

3. The perpetrator intended the civilian population as such or individual civilians not taking direct part in hostilities to be the object of the attack.

4. The conduct took place in the context of and was associated with an armed conflict not of an international character.

5. The perpetrator was aware of factual circumstances that established the existence of an armed conflict.

Article 8 (2) (e) (ii)
War crime of attacking objects or persons using the distinctive emblems of the Geneva Conventions

Elements

1. The perpetrator attacked one or more persons, buildings, medical units or transports or other objects using, in conformity with international law, a distinctive emblem or other method of identification indicating protection under the Geneva Conventions.

2. The perpetrator intended such persons, buildings, units or transports or other objects so using such identification to be the object of the attack.

3. The conduct took place in the context of and was associated with an armed conflict not of an international character.

4. The perpetrator was aware of factual circumstances that established the existence of an armed conflict.

Article 8 (2) (e) (iii)
War crime of attacking personnel or objects involved in a humanitarian assistance or peacekeeping mission

Elements

Article 8 (2) (e) (iv)
War crime of attacking protected objects[60]

Elements

1. The perpetrator directed an attack.

2. The object of the attack was one or more buildings dedicated to religion, education, art, science or charitable purposes, historic monuments, hospitals or places where the sick and wounded are collected, which were not military objectives.

3. The perpetrator intended such building or buildings dedicated to religion, education, art, science or charitable purposes, historic monuments, hospitals or places where the sick and wounded are collected, which were not military objectives, to be the object of the attack.

4. The conduct took place in the context of and was associated with an armed conflict not of an international character.

5. The perpetrator was aware of factual circumstances that established the existence of an armed conflict.

Article 8 (2) (e) (v)
War crime of pillaging

Elements

1. The perpetrator appropriated certain property.

2. The perpetrator intended to deprive the owner of the property and to appropriate it for private or personal use.[61]

3. The appropriation was without the consent of the owner.

4. The conduct took place in the context of and was associated with an armed conflict not of an international character.

5. The perpetrator was aware of factual circumstances that established the existence of an armed conflict.

Article 8 (2) (e) (vi)-1
War crime of rape

Elements

1. The perpetrator invaded[62] the body of a person by conduct resulting in penetration, however slight, of any part of the body of the victim or of the perpetrator with a sexual organ, or of the anal or genital opening of the victim with any object or any other part of the body.

2. The invasion was committed by force, or by threat of force or coercion, such as that caused by fear of violence, duress, detention, psychological oppression or abuse of power, against such person or another person, or by taking advantage of a coercive environment, or the invasion was committed against a person incapable of giving genuine consent.[63]

3. The conduct took place in the context of and was associated with an armed conflict not of an international character.

4. The perpetrator was aware of factual circumstances that established the existence of an armed conflict.

Article 8 (2) (e) (vi)-2
War crime of sexual slavery[64]

Elements

Article 8 (2) (e) (vi)-3
War crime of enforced prostitution

Elements

1. The perpetrator caused one or more persons to engage in one or more acts of a sexual nature by force, or by threat of force or coercion, such as that caused by fear of violence, duress, detention, psychological oppression or abuse of power, against such person or persons or another person, or by taking advantage of a coercive environment or such person's or persons' incapacity to give genuine consent.

2. The perpetrator or another person obtained or expected to obtain pecuniary or other advantage in exchange for or in connection with the acts of a sexual nature.

3. The conduct took place in the context of and was associated with an armed conflict not of an international character.

4. The perpetrator was aware of factual circumstances that established the existence of an armed conflict.

Article 8 (2) (e) (vi)-4
War crime of forced pregnancy

Elements

1. The perpetrator confined one or more women forcibly made pregnant, with the intent of affecting the ethnic composition of any population or carrying out other grave violations of international law.

2. The conduct took place in the context of and was associated with an armed conflict not of an international character.

3. The perpetrator was aware of factual circumstances that established the existence of an armed conflict.

Article 8 (2) (e) (vi)-5
War crime of enforced sterilization

Elements

1. The perpetrator deprived one or more persons of biological reproductive capacity.[66]

2. The conduct was neither justified by the medical or hospital treatment of the person or persons concerned nor carried out with their genuine consent.[67]

3. The conduct took place in the context of and was associated with an armed conflict not of an international character.

4. The perpetrator was aware of factual circumstances that established the existence of an armed conflict.

Article 8 (2) (e) (vi)-6
War crime of sexual violence

Elements

1. The perpetrator committed an act of a sexual nature against one or more persons or caused such person or persons to engage in an act of a sexual nature by force, or by threat of force or coercion, such as that caused by fear of violence, duress, detention, psychological oppression or abuse of power, against such person or persons or another person, or by taking advantage of a coercive environment or such person's or persons' incapacity to give genuine consent.

2. The conduct was of a gravity comparable to that of a serious violation of article 3 common to the four Geneva Conventions.

3. The perpetrator was aware of the factual circumstances that established the gravity of the conduct.

4. The conduct took place in the context of and was associated with an armed conflict not of an international character.

5. The perpetrator was aware of factual circumstances that established the existence of an armed conflict.

Article 8 (2) (e) (vii)
War crime of using, conscripting and enlisting children

Elements

Article 8 (2) (e) (viii)
War crime of displacing civilians

Elements

1. The perpetrator ordered a displacement of a civilian population.

2. Such order was not justified by the security of the civilians involved or by military necessity.

3. The perpetrator was in a position to effect such displacement by giving such order.

4. The conduct took place in the context of and was associated with an armed conflict not of an international character.

5. The perpetrator was aware of factual circumstances that established the existence of an armed conflict.

Article 8 (2) (e) (ix)
War crime of treacherously killing or wounding

Elements

1. The perpetrator invited the confidence or belief of one or more combatant adversaries that they were entitled to, or were obliged to accord, protection under rules of international law applicable in armed conflict.

2. The perpetrator intended to betray that confidence or belief.

3. The perpetrator killed or injured such person or persons.

4. The perpetrator made use of that confidence or belief in killing or injuring such person or persons.

5. Such person or persons belonged to an adverse party.

6. The conduct took place in the context of and was associated with an armed conflict not of an international character.

7. The perpetrator was aware of factual circumstances that established the existence of an armed conflict.

Article 8 (2) (e) (x)
War crime of denying quarter

Elements

1. The perpetrator declared or ordered that there shall be no survivors.

2. Such declaration or order was given in order to threaten an adversary or to conduct hostilities on the basis that there shall be no survivors.

3. The perpetrator was in a position of effective command or control over the subordinate forces to which the declaration or order was directed.

4. The conduct took place in the context of and was associated with an armed conflict not of an international character.

5. The perpetrator was aware of factual circumstances that established the existence of an armed conflict.

Article 8 (2) (e) (xi)-1
War crime of mutilation

Elements

1. The perpetrator subjected one or more persons to mutilation, in particular by permanently disfiguring the person or persons, or by permanently disabling or removing an organ or appendage.

2. The conduct caused death or seriously endangered the physical or mental health of such person or persons.

3. The conduct was neither justified by the medical, dental or hospital treatment of the person or persons concerned nor carried out in such person's or persons' interest.[68]

4. Such person or persons were in the power of another party to the conflict.

5. The conduct took place in the context of and was associated with an armed conflict not of an international character.

6. The perpetrator was aware of factual circumstances that established the existence of an armed conflict.

Article 8 (2) (e) (xi)-2
War crime of medical or scientific experiments

Elements

1. The perpetrator subjected one or more persons to a medical or scientific experiment.

2. The experiment caused the death or seriously endangered the physical or mental health or integrity of such person or persons.

3. The conduct was neither justified by the medical, dental or hospital treatment of such person or persons concerned nor carried out in such person's or persons' interest.

4. Such person or persons were in the power of another party to the conflict.

5. The conduct took place in the context of and was associated with an armed conflict not of an international character.

6. The perpetrator was aware of factual circumstances that established the existence of an armed conflict.

Article 8 (2) (e) (xii)
War crime of destroying or seizing the enemy's property

Elements

1. The perpetrator destroyed or seized certain property.

2. Such property was property of an adversary.

3. Such property was protected from that destruction or seizure under the international law of armed conflict.

4. The perpetrator was aware of the factual circumstances that established the status of the property.

5. The destruction or seizure was not required by military necessity.

6. The conduct took place in the context of and was associated with an armed conflict not of an international character.

7. The perpetrator was aware of factual circumstances that established the existence of an armed conflict.

Endnotes:

[1] This paragraph is without prejudice to the obligation of the Prosecutor under article 54, paragraph 1, of the Statute.

[2] The term "killed" is interchangeable with the term "caused death".

[3] This conduct may include, but is not necessarily restricted to, acts of torture, rape, sexual violence or inhuman or degrading treatment.

[4] The term "conditions of life" may include, but is not necessarily restricted to, deliberate deprivation of resources indispensable for survival, such as food or medical services, or systematic expulsion from homes.

[5] The term "forcibly" is not restricted to physical force, but may include threat of force or coercion, such as that caused by fear of violence, duress, detention, psycholog-

ical oppression or abuse of power, against such person or persons or another person, or by taking advantage of a coercive environment.

[6] A policy which has a civilian population as the object of the attack would be implemented by State or organizational action. Such a policy may, in exceptional circumstances, be implemented by a deliberate failure to take action, which is consciously aimed at encouraging such attack. The existence of such a policy cannot be inferred solely from the absence of governmental or organizational action.

[7] The term "killed" is interchangeable with the term "caused death". This footnote applies to all elements which use either of these concepts.

[8] The conduct could be committed by different methods of killing, either directly or indirectly.

[9] The infliction of such conditions could include the deprivation of access to food and medicine.

[10] The term "as part of" would include the initial conduct in a mass killing.

[11] It is understood that such deprivation of liberty may, in some circumstances, include exacting forced labour or otherwise reducing a person to a servile status as defined in the Supplementary Convention on the Abolition of Slavery, the Slave Trade, and Institutions and Practices Similar to Slavery of 1956. It is also understood that the conduct described in this element includes trafficking in persons, in particular women and children.

[12] The term "forcibly" is not restricted to physical force, but may include threat of force or coercion, such as that caused by fear of violence, duress, detention, psychological oppression or abuse of power against such person or persons or another person, or by taking advantage of a coercive environment.

[13] "Deported or forcibly transferred" is interchangeable with "forcibly displaced".

[14] It is understood that no specific purpose need be proved for this crime.

[15] The concept of "invasion" is intended to be broad enough to be gender-neutral.

[16] It is understood that a person may be incapable of giving genuine consent if affected by natural, induced or age-related incapacity. This footnote also applies to the corresponding elements of article 7 (1) (g)-3, 5 and 6.

[17] Given the complex nature of this crime, it is recognized that its commission could involve more than one perpetrator as a part of a common criminal purpose.

[18] It is understood that such deprivation of liberty may, in some circumstances, include exacting forced labour or otherwise reducing a person to a servile status as defined in the Supplementary Convention on the Abolition of Slavery, the Slave Trade, and Institutions and Practices Similar to Slavery of 1956. It is also understood that the conduct described in this element includes trafficking in persons, in particular women and children.

[19] The deprivation is not intended to include birth-control measures which have a non-permanent effect in practice.

[20] It is understood that "genuine consent" does not include consent obtained through deception.

[21] This requirement is without prejudice to paragraph 6 of the General Introduction to the Elements of Crimes.

[22] It is understood that no additional mental element is necessary for this element other than that inherent in element 6.

[23] Given the complex nature of this crime, it is recognized that its commission will normally involve more than one perpetrator as a part of a common criminal purpose.

[24] This crime falls under the jurisdiction of the Court only if the attack referred to in elements 7 and 8 occurs after the entry into force of the Statute.

[25] The word "detained" would include a perpetrator who maintained an existing detention.

[26] It is understood that under certain circumstances an arrest or detention may have been lawful.

[27] This element, inserted because of the complexity of this crime, is without prejudice to the General Introduction to the Elements of Crimes.

[28] It is understood that, in the case of a perpetrator who maintained an existing detention, this element would be satisfied if the perpetrator was aware that such a refusal had already taken place.

[29] It is understood that "character" refers to the nature and gravity of the act.

[30] It is understood that "character" refers to the nature and gravity of the act.

[31] The term "killed" is interchangeable with the term "caused death". This footnote applies to all elements which use either of these concepts.

[32] This mental element recognizes the interplay between articles 30 and 32. This footnote also applies to the corresponding element in each crime under article 8 (2) (a), and to the element in other crimes in article 8 (2) concerning the awareness of factual circumstances that establish the status of persons or property protected under the relevant international law of armed conflict.

[33] With respect to nationality, it is understood that the perpetrator needs only to know that the victim belonged to an adverse party to the conflict. This footnote also applies to the corresponding element in each crime under article 8 (2) (a).

[34] The term "international armed conflict" includes military occupation. This footnote also applies to the corresponding element in each crime under article 8 (2) (a).

[35] As element 3 requires that all victims must be "protected persons" under one or more of the Geneva Conventions of 1949, these elements do not include the custody or control requirement found in the elements of article 7 (1) (e).

[36] The expression "concrete and direct overall military advantage" refers to a military advantage that is foreseeable by the perpetrator at the relevant time. Such advantage may or may not be temporally or geographically related to the object of the attack. The fact that this crime admits the possibility of lawful incidental injury and collateral damage does not in any way justify any violation of the law applicable in armed conflict. It does not address justifications for war or other rules related to jus ad bellum. It reflects the proportionality requirement inherent in determining the legality of any military activity undertaken in the context of an armed conflict.

[37] As opposed to the general rule set forth in paragraph 4 of the General Introduction, this knowledge element requires that the perpetrator make the value judgement as described therein. An evaluation of that value judgement must be based on the requisite information available to the perpetrator at the time.

[38] The presence in the locality of persons specially protected under the Geneva Conventions of 1949 or of police forces retained for the sole purpose of maintaining law and order does not by itself render the locality a military objective.

[39] This mental element recognizes the interplay between article 30 and article 32. The term "prohibited nature" denotes illegality.

[40] This mental element recognizes the interplay between article 30 and article 32. The term "prohibited nature" denotes illegality.

[41] This mental element recognizes the interplay between article 30 and article 32. The "should have known" test required in the other offences found in article 8 (2) (b) (vii) is not applicable here because of the variable and regulatory nature of the relevant prohibitions.

[42] "Combatant purposes" in these circumstances means purposes directly related to hostilities and not including medical, religious or similar activities.

[43] This mental element recognizes the interplay between article 30 and article 32. The term "prohibited nature" denotes illegality.

[44] The term "transfer" needs to be interpreted in accordance with the relevant provisions of international humanitarian law.

[45] The presence in the locality of persons specially protected under the Geneva Conventions of 1949 or of police forces retained for the sole purpose of maintaining law and order does not by itself render the locality a military objective.

[46] Consent is not a defence to this crime. The crime prohibits any medical procedure which is not indicated by the state of health of the person concerned and which is not consistent with generally accepted medical standards which would be applied under similar medical circumstances to persons who are nationals of the party conducting the procedure and who are in no way deprived of liberty. This footnote also applies to the same element for article 8 (2) (b) (x) 2.

[47] As indicated by the use of the term "private or personal use", appropriations justified by military necessity cannot constitute the crime of pillaging.

[48] Nothing in this element shall be interpreted as limiting or prejudicing in any way existing or developing rules of international law with respect to the development, production, stockpiling and use of chemical weapons.

[49] For this crime, "persons" can include dead persons. It is understood that the victim need not personally be aware of the existence of the humiliation or degradation or other violation. This element takes into account relevant aspects of the cultural background of the victim.

[50] The concept of "invasion" is intended to be broad enough to be gender-neutral.

[51] It is understood that a person may be incapable of giving genuine consent if affected by natural, induced or age-related incapacity. This footnote also applies to the corresponding elements of article 8 (2) (b) (xxii)-3, 5 and 6.

[52] Given the complex nature of this crime, it is recognized that its commission could involve more than one perpetrator as a part of a common criminal purpose.

[53] It is understood that such deprivation of liberty may, in some circumstances, include exacting forced labour or otherwise reducing a person to servile status as defined in the Supplementary Convention on the Abolition of Slavery, the Slave Trade, and Institutions and Practices Similar to Slavery of 1956. It is also understood that the conduct described in this element includes trafficking in persons, in particular women and children.

[54] The deprivation is not intended to include birth-control measures which have a non-permanent effect in practice.

[55] It is understood that "genuine consent" does not include consent obtained through deception.

[56] The term "religious personnel" includes those non-confessional non-combatant military personnel carrying out a similar function.

[57] For this crime, "persons" can include dead persons. It is understood that the victim need not personally be aware of the existence of the humiliation or degradation or other violation. This element takes into account relevant aspects of the cultural background of the victim.

[58] The elements laid down in these documents do not address the different forms of individual criminal responsibility, as enunciated in articles 25 and 28 of the Statute.

[59] With respect to elements 4 and 5, the Court should consider whether, in the light of all relevant circumstances, the cumulative effect of factors with respect to guarantees deprived the person or persons of a fair trial.

[60] The presence in the locality of persons specially protected under the Geneva Conventions of 1949 or of police forces retained for the sole purpose of maintaining law and order does not by itself render the locality a military objective.

[61] As indicated by the use of the term "private or personal use", appropriations justified by military necessity cannot constitute the crime of pillaging.

[62] The concept of "invasion" is intended to be broad enough to be gender-neutral.

[63] It is understood that a person may be incapable of giving genuine consent if affected by natural, induced or age-related incapacity. This footnote also applies to the corresponding elements in article 8 (2) (e) (vi)-3, 5 and 6.

[64] Given the complex nature of this crime, it is recognized that its commission could involve more than one perpetrator as a part of a common criminal purpose.

[65] It is understood that such deprivation of liberty may, in some circumstances, include exacting forced labour or otherwise reducing a person to servile status as defined in the Supplementary Convention on the Abolition of Slavery, the Slave Trade, and Institutions and Practices Similar to Slavery of 1956. It is also understood that the conduct described in this element includes trafficking in persons, in particular women and children.

[66] The deprivation is not intended to include birth-control measures which have a non-permanent effect in practice.

[67] It is understood that "genuine consent" does not include consent obtained through deception.

[68] Consent is not a defence to this crime. The crime prohibits any medical procedure which is not indicated by the state of health of the person concerned and which is not consistent with generally accepted medical standards which would be applied under similar medical circumstances to persons who are nationals of the party conducting the procedure and who are in no way deprived of liberty. This footnote also applies to the similar element in article 8 (2) (e).

ICC Definition of Aggression

Resolution RC/Res.6*

Adopted at the 13th plenary meeting, on 11 June 2010, by consensus

RC/Res.6

The crime of aggression

The Review Conference,

---

* See Depository Notification C.N.651.2010 Treaties-8, dated 29 November 2010, available at http://treaties.un.org.

Recalling paragraph 1 of article 12 of the Rome Statute,

Recalling paragraph 2 of article 5 of the Rome Statute,

Recalling also paragraph 7 of resolution F, adopted by the United Nations Diplomatic Conference of Plenipotentiaries on the Establishment of an International Criminal Court on 17 July 1998,

Recalling further resolution ICC-ASP/1/Res.1 on the continuity of work in respect of the crime of aggression, and *expressing its appreciation* to the Special Working Group on the Crime of Aggression for having elaborated proposals on a provision on the crime of aggression,

Taking note of resolution ICC-ASP/8/Res.6, by which the Assembly of States Parties forwarded proposals on a provision on the crime of aggression to the Review Conference for its consideration, *Resolved* to activate the Court's jurisdiction over the crime of aggression as early as possible,

1. *Decides* to adopt, in accordance with article 5, paragraph 2, of the Rome Statute of the International Criminal Court (hereinafter: "the Statute") the amendments to the Statute contained in annex I of the present resolution, which are subject to ratification or acceptance and shall enter into force in accordance with article 121, paragraph 5; and *notes* that any State Party may lodge a declaration referred to in article 15 *bis* prior to ratification or acceptance;

2. *Also decides* to adopt the amendments to the Elements of Crimes contained in annex II of the present resolution;

3. *Also decides* to adopt the understandings regarding the interpretation of the abovementioned amendments contained in annex III of the present resolution;

4. *Further decides* to review the amendments on the crime of aggression seven years after the beginning of the Court's exercise of jurisdiction;

5. *Calls upon* all States Parties to ratify or accept the amendments contained in annex I.

Annex I
Amendments to the Rome Statute of the International
Criminal Court on the crime of aggression

1. Article 5, paragraph 2, of the Statute is deleted.

2. The following text is inserted after article 8 of the Statute:

Article 8 *bis*
Crime of aggression

1. For the purpose of this Statute, "crime of aggression" means the planning, preparation, initiation or execution, by a person in a position effectively to exercise control over or to direct the political or military action of a State, of an act of aggression which, by its character, gravity and scale, constitutes a manifest violation of the Charter of the United Nations.

2. For the purpose of paragraph 1, "act of aggression" means the use of armed force by a State against the sovereignty, territorial integrity or political independence of another State, or in any other manner inconsistent with the Charter of the United Nations. Any of the following acts, regardless of a declaration of war, shall, in accordance with United Nations General Assembly resolution 3314 (XXIX) of 14 December 1974, qualify as an act of aggression:

(a) The invasion or attack by the armed forces of a State of the territory of another State, or any military occupation, however temporary, resulting from such invasion or attack, or any annexation by the use of force of the territory of another State or part thereof;

(b) Bombardment by the armed forces of a State against the territory of another State or the use of any weapons by a State against the territory of another State;

(c) The blockade of the ports or coasts of a State by the armed forces of another State;

(d) An attack by the armed forces of a State on the land, sea or air forces, or marine and air fleets of another State;

(e) The use of armed forces of one State which are within the territory of another State with the agreement of the receiving State, in contravention of the conditions provided for in the agreement or any extension of their presence in such territory beyond the termination of the agreement;

(f) The action of a State in allowing its territory, which it has placed at the disposal of another State, to be used by that other State for perpetrating an act of aggression against a third State;

(g) The sending by or on behalf of a State of armed bands, groups, irregulars or mercenaries, which carry out acts of armed force against another State of such gravity as to amount to the acts listed above, or its substantial involvement therein.

3. The following text is inserted after article 15 of the Statute:

Article 15 *bis*
Exercise of jurisdiction over the crime of aggression
(State referral, *proprio motu*)

1. The Court may exercise jurisdiction over the crime of aggression in accordance with article 13, paragraphs (a) and (c), subject to the provisions of this article.

2. The Court may exercise jurisdiction only with respect to crimes of aggression committed one year after the ratification or acceptance of the amendments by thirty States Parties.

3. The Court shall exercise jurisdiction over the crime of aggression in accordance with this article, subject to a decision to be taken after 1 January 2017 by the same majority of States Parties as is required for the adoption of an amendment to the Statute.

4. The Court may, in accordance with article 12, exercise jurisdiction over a crime of aggression, arising from an act of aggression committed by a State Party, unless that State Party has previously declared that it does not accept such jurisdiction by lodging a declaration with the Registrar. The withdrawal of such a declaration may be effected at any time and shall be considered by the State Party within three years.

5. In respect of a State that is not a party to this Statute, the Court shall not exercise its jurisdiction over the crime of aggression when committed by that State's nationals or on its territory.

6. Where the Prosecutor concludes that there is a reasonable basis to proceed with an investigation in respect of a crime of aggression, he or she shall first ascertain whether the Security Council has made a determination of an act of aggression committed by the State concerned. The Prosecutor shall notify the Secretary-General of the United Nations of the situation before the Court, including any relevant information and documents.

7. Where the Security Council has made such a determination, the Prosecutor may proceed with the investigation in respect of a crime of aggression.

8. Where no such determination is made within six months after the date of notification, the Prosecutor may proceed with the investigation in respect of a crime of aggression, provided that the Pre-Trial Division has authorized the commencement of the investigation in respect of a crime of aggression in accordance with the procedure contained in article 15, and the Security Council has not decided otherwise in accordance with article 16.

9. A determination of an act of aggression by an organ outside the Court shall be without prejudice to the Court's own findings under this Statute.

10. This article is without prejudice to the provisions relating to the exercise of jurisdiction with respect to other crimes referred to in article 5.

4. The following text is inserted after article 15 bis of the Statute:

Article 15 *ter*
Exercise of jurisdiction over the crime of aggression
(Security Council referral)

1. The Court may exercise jurisdiction over the crime of aggression in accordance with article 13, paragraph (b), subject to the provisions of this article.

2. The Court may exercise jurisdiction only with respect to crimes of aggression committed one year after the ratification or acceptance of the amendments by thirty States Parties.

3. The Court shall exercise jurisdiction over the crime of aggression in accordance with this article, subject to a decision to be taken after 1 January 2017 by the same majority of States Parties as is required for the adoption of an amendment to the Statute.

4. A determination of an act of aggression by an organ outside the Court shall be without prejudice to the Court's own findings under this Statute.

5. This article is without prejudice to the provisions relating to the exercise of jurisdiction with respect to other crimes referred to in article 5.

5. The following text is inserted after article 25, paragraph 3, of the Statute: 3 bis. In respect of the crime of aggression, the provisions of this article shall apply only to persons in a position effectively to exercise control over or to direct the political or military action of a State.

6. The first sentence of article 9, paragraph 1, of the Statute is replaced by the following sentence:

1. Elements of Crimes shall assist the Court in the interpretation and application of articles 6, 7, 8 and 8 *bis*.

7. The chapeau of article 20, paragraph 3, of the Statute is replaced by the following paragraph; the rest of the paragraph remains unchanged:

3. No person who has been tried by another court for conduct also proscribed under article 6, 7, 8 or 8 *bis* shall be tried by the Court with respect to the same conduct unless the proceedings in the other court:

Annex II
Amendments to the Elements of Crimes

Article 8 *bis*
Crime of aggression

Introduction

1. It is understood that any of the acts referred to in article 8 *bis*, paragraph 2, qualify as an act of aggression.

2. There is no requirement to prove that the perpetrator has made a legal evaluation as to whether the use of armed force was inconsistent with the Charter of the United Nations.

3. The term "manifest" is an objective qualification.

4. There is no requirement to prove that the perpetrator has made a legal evaluation as to the "manifest" nature of the violation of the Charter of the United Nations.

Elements

1. The perpetrator planned, prepared, initiated or executed an act of aggression.

2. The perpetrator was a person[1] in a position effectively to exercise control over or to direct the political or military action of the State which committed the act of aggression.

3. The act of aggression—the use of armed force by a State against the sovereignty, territorial integrity or political independence of another State, or in any other manner inconsistent with the Charter of the United Nations—was committed.

4. The perpetrator was aware of the factual circumstances that established that such a use of armed force was inconsistent with the Charter of the United Nations.

5. The act of aggression, by its character, gravity and scale, constituted a manifest violation of the Charter of the United Nations.

6. The perpetrator was aware of the factual circumstances that established such a manifest violation of the Charter of the United Nations.

Annex III
Understandings regarding the amendments to the Rome Statute of the International Criminal Court on the crime of aggression

Referrals by the Security Council

1. It is understood that the Court may exercise jurisdiction on the basis of a Security Council referral in accordance with article 13, paragraph (b), of the Statute only with respect to crimes of aggression committed after a decision in accordance with article 15 *ter*, paragraph 3, is taken, and one year after the ratification or acceptance of the amendments by thirty States Parties, whichever is later.

2. It is understood that the Court shall exercise jurisdiction over the crime of aggression on the basis of a Security Council referral in accordance with article 13, paragraph (b), of the Statute irrespective of whether the State concerned has accepted the Court's jurisdiction in this regard.

Jurisdiction *ratione temporis*

3. It is understood that in case of article 13, paragraph (a) or (c), the Court may exercise its jurisdiction only with respect to crimes of aggression committed after a decision in accordance with article 15 *bis*, paragraph 3, is taken, and one year after the ratification or acceptance of the amendments by thirty States Parties, whichever is later.

Domestic jurisdiction over the crime of aggression

4. It is understood that the amendments that address the definition of the act of aggression and the crime of aggression do so for the purpose of this Statute only. The amend-

---

1. With respect to an act of aggression, more than one person may be in a position that meets these criteria.

ments shall, in accordance with article 10 of the Rome Statute, not be interpreted as limiting or prejudicing in any way existing or developing rules of international law for purposes other than this Statute.

5. It is understood that the amendments shall not be interpreted as creating the right or obligation to exercise domestic jurisdiction with respect to an act of aggression committed by another State.

Other understandings

6. It is understood that aggression is the most serious and dangerous form of the illegal use of force; and that a determination whether an act of aggression has been committed requires consideration of all the circumstances of each particular case, including the gravity of the acts concerned and their consequences, in accordance with the Charter of the United Nations.

7. It is understood that in establishing whether an act of aggression constitutes a manifest violation of the Charter of the United Nations, the three components of character, gravity and scale must be sufficient to justify a "manifest" determination. No one component can be significant enough to satisfy the manifest standard by itself.

Convention on the Prevention and Punishment of the Crime of Genocide
78 U.N.T.S. 277 (1948)

The Contracting Parties,

Having considered the declaration made by the General Assembly of the United Nations in its resolution 96(I) dated 11 December 1946 that genocide is a crime under international law, contrary to the spirit and aims of the United Nations and condemned by the civilized world;

Recognizing that at all periods of history genocide has inflicted great losses on humanity; and

Being convinced that, in order to liberate mankind from such an odious scourge, international co-operation is required;

Hereby agree as hereinafter provided.

Article I

The Contracting Parties confirm that genocide, whether committed in time of peace or in time of war, is a crime under international law which they undertake to prevent and to punish.

Article II

In the present Convention, genocide means any of the following acts committed with intent to destroy, in whole or in part, a national, ethnical, racial or religious group as such:

(a) Killing members of the group;

(b) Causing serious bodily or mental harm to members of the group;

(c) Deliberately inflicting on the group conditions of life calculated to bring about its physical destruction in whole or in part;

(d) Imposing measures intended to prevent births within the group;

(e) Forcibly transferring children of the group to another group.

Article III

The following acts shall be punishable:

(a) Genocide;

(b) Conspiracy to commit genocide;

(c) Direct and public incitement to commit genocide;

(d) Attempt to commit genocide;

(e) Complicity in genocide.

Article IV

Persons committing genocide or any of the other acts enumerated in Article III shall be punished, whether they are constitutionally responsible rulers, public officials or private individuals.

Article V

The Contracting Parties undertake to enact, in accordance with their respective Constitutions, the necessary legislation to give effect to the provisions of the present Convention and, in particular, to provide effective penalties for persons guilty of genocide or any of the other acts enumerated in Article III.

Article VI

Persons charged with genocide or any of the other acts enumerated in Article III shall be tried by a competent tribunal of the State in the territory of which the act was committed, or by such international penal tribunal as may have jurisdiction with respect to those Contracting Parties which shall have accepted its jurisdiction.

Article VII

Genocide and the other acts enumerated in Article III shall not be considered as political crimes for the purpose of extradition.

The Contracting Parties pledge themselves in such cases to grant extradition in accordance with their laws and treaties in force.

Article VIII

Any Contracting Party may call upon the competent organs of the United Nations to take such action under the Charter of the United Nations as they consider appropriate for the prevention and suppression of acts of genocide or any of the other acts enumerated in Article III.

Article IX

Disputes between the Contracting Parties relating to the interpretation, application or fulfilment of the present Convention, including those relating to the responsibility of a State for genocide or any of the other acts enumerated in Article II, shall be submitted to the International Court of Justice at the request of any of the parties to the dispute.

Article X

The present Convention, of which the Chinese, English, French, Russian and Spanish texts are equally authentic, shall bear the date of 9 December 1948....

International Convention on the Suppression and Punishment of the Crime of "Apartheid"
done in New York, Nov. 30, 1973, 1015 U.N.T.S. 243

Article I

(1) The States Parties to the present Convention declare that apartheid is a crime against humanity and that inhuman acts resulting from the policies and practices of apartheid and similar policies and practices of racial segregation and discrimination, as defined in Article II of the Convention, are crimes violating the principles of international law, in particular the purposes and principles of the Charter of the United Nations, and constituting a serious threat to international peace and security.

(2) States Parties to the present Convention declare criminal those organizations, institutions and individuals committing the crime of apartheid.

Article II

For the purpose of the present Convention, the term "the crime of apartheid" which shall include similar policies and practices of racial segregation and discrimination as practiced in southern Africa, shall apply to the following inhuman acts committed for the purpose of establishing and maintaining domination by one racial group of persons over any other racial group of persons and systematically oppressing them:

(a) Denial to a member or members of a racial group or groups of the right to life and liberty of person:

(i) By murder of members of a racial group or groups;

(ii) By the infliction upon the members of a racial group or groups of serious bodily or mental harm by the infringement of their freedom or dignity, or by subjecting them to torture or to cruel, inhuman or degrading treatment or punishment;

(iii) By arbitrary arrest and illegal imprisonment of the members of a racial group or groups;

(b) Deliberate imposition on a racial group or groups of living conditions calculated to cause its or their physical destruction in whole or in part;

(c) Any legislative measures and other measures calculated to prevent a racial group or groups from participation in the political, social, economic and cultural life of the country and the deliberate creation of conditions preventing the full development of such a group or groups, in particular by denying to members of a racial group or groups basic human rights and freedoms, including the right to work, the right to form recognized trade unions, the right to education, the right to leave and to return to their country, the right to freedom of opinion and expression, and the right to freedom of peaceful assembly and association;

(d) Any measures, including legislative measures, designed to divide the population along racial lines by the creation of separate reserves and ghettos for the members of a racial group or groups, the prohibition of mixed marriages among members of various racial groups, the expropriation of landed property belonging to a racial group or groups or to members thereof;

(e) Exploitation of the labour of the members of a racial group or groups, in particular by submitting them to forced labour;

(f) Persecution of organizations and persons, by depriving them of fundamental rights and freedoms, because they oppose apartheid.

Article III

International criminal responsibility shall apply, irrespective of the motive involved, to individuals, members of organizations and institutions and representatives of the State, whether residing in the territory of the State in which the acts are perpetrated or in some other State, whenever they:

(a) Commit, participate in, directly incite or conspire in the commission of the acts mentioned in Article II of the present Convention;

(b) Directly abet, encourage or co-operate in the commission of the crime of *apartheid.*

Article IV

The States Parties to the present Convention undertake:

(a) To adopt any legislative or other measure necessary to suppress as well as to prevent any encouragement of the crime of apartheid and similar segregationist policies or their manifestations and to punish persons guilty of that crime;

(b) To adopt legislative, judicial and administrative measures to prosecute, bring to trial and punish in accordance with their jurisdiction persons responsible for, or accused of, the acts defined in Article II of the present Convention, whether or not such persons reside in the territory of the State in which the acts are committed or are nationals of that State or of some other State or are stateless persons.

Article V

Persons charged with the acts enumerated in Article II of the present Convention may be tried by a competent tribunal of any State Party to the Convention which may acquire jurisdiction with respect to those State Parties which shall have accepted its jurisdiction.

Article VI

The States Parties to the present Convention undertake to accept and carry out in accordance with the Charter of the United Nations the decisions taken by the Security Council aimed at the prevention, suppression and punishment of the crime of apartheid, and to co-operate in the implementation of decisions adopted by other competent organs of the United Nations with a view to achieving the purposes of the Convention.

Article XI

(1) Acts enumerated in Article II of the present Convention shall not be considered political crimes for the purpose of extradition.

(2) The States Parties to the present Convention undertake in such cases to grant extradition with their legislation and with the treaties in force.

International Convention on the Elimination of All Forms of Racial Discrimination

660 U.N.T.S. 195 (opened for signature Mar. 7, 1966)

Part I

Article 1

1. In this Convention, the term "racial discrimination" shall mean any distinction, exclusion, restriction or preference based on race, colour, descent, or national or ethnic origin which has the purpose or effect of nullifying or impairing the recognition, enjoyment or exercise, on an equal footing, of human rights and fundamental freedoms in the political, economic, social, cultural or any other field of public life.

2. This Convention shall not apply to distinctions, exclusions, restrictions or preferences made by a State Party to this Convention between citizens and non-citizens.

3. Nothing in this Convention may be interpreted as affecting in any way the legal provisions of States Parties concerning nationality, citizenship or naturalization, provided that such provisions do not discriminate against any particular nationality.

4. Special measures taken for the sole purpose of securing adequate advancement of certain racial or ethnic groups or individuals requiring such protection as may be necessary in order to ensure such groups or individuals equal enjoyment or exercise of human rights and fundamental freedoms shall not be deemed racial discrimination, provided, however, that such measures do not, as a consequence, lead to the maintenance of separate rights for different racial groups and that they shall not be continued after the objectives for which they were taken have been achieved.

Article 2

1. States Parties condemn racial discrimination and undertake to pursue by all appropriate means and without delay a policy of eliminating racial discrimination in all its forms and promoting understanding among all races, and, to this end:

(a) Each State Party undertakes to engage in no act or practice of racial discrimination against persons, groups of persons or institutions and to ensure that all public authorities and public institutions, national and local, shall act in conformity with this obligation;

(b) Each State Party undertakes not to sponsor, defend or support racial discrimination by any persons or organizations;

(c) Each State Party shall take effective measures to review governmental, national and local policies, and to amend, rescind or nullify any laws and regulations which have the effect of creating or perpetuating racial discrimination wherever it exists;

(d) Each State Party shall prohibit and bring to an end, by all appropriate means, including legislation as required by circumstances, racial discrimination by any persons, group or organization;

(e) Each State Party undertakes to encourage, where appropriate, integrationist multi-racial organizations and movements and other means of eliminating barriers between races, and to discourage anything which tends to strengthen racial division.

2. States Parties shall, when the circumstances so warrant, take, in the social, economic, cultural and other fields, special and concrete measures to ensure the adequate development and protection of certain racial groups or individuals belonging to them, for

the purpose of guaranteeing them the full and equal enjoyment of human rights and fundamental freedoms. These measures shall in no case entail as a consequence the maintenance or unequal or separate rights for different racial groups after the objectives for which they were taken have been achieved.

Article 3

States Parties particularly condemn racial segregation and apartheid and undertake to prevent, prohibit and eradicate all practices of this nature in territories under their jurisdiction.

Article 4

States Parties condemn all propaganda and all organizations which are based on ideas or theories of superiority of one race or group of persons of one colour or ethnic origin, or which attempt to justify or promote racial hatred and discrimination in any form, and undertake to adopt immediate and positive measures designed to eradicate all incitement to, or acts of, such discrimination and, to this end, with due regard to the principles embodied in the Universal Declaration of Human Rights and the rights expressly set forth in Article 5 of this Convention, inter alia:

(a) Shall declare an offence punishable by law all dissemination of ideas based on racial superiority or hatred, incitement to racial discrimination, as well as all acts of violence or incitement to such acts against any race or group of persons of another colour or ethnic origin, and also the provision of any assistance to racist activities, including the financing thereof;

(b) Shall declare illegal and prohibit organizations, and also organized and all other propaganda activities, which promote and incite racial discrimination, and shall recognize participation in such organizations or activities as an offence punishable by law;

(c) Shall not permit public authorities or public institutions, national or local, to promote or incite racial discrimination.

Article 5

In compliance with the fundamental obligations laid down in Article 2 of this Convention, States Parties undertake to prohibit and to eliminate racial discrimination in all its forms and to guarantee the right of everyone, without distinction as to race, colour, or national or ethnic origin, to equality before the law, notably in the enjoyment of the following rights:

(a) The right to equal treatment before the tribunals and all other organs administering justice;

(b) The right to security of person and protection by the State against violence or bodily harm, whether inflicted by government officials or by any individual, group or institution;

(c) Political rights, in particular the rights to participate in elections—to vote and to stand for election—on the basis of universal and equal suffrage, to take part in the Government as well as in the conduct of public affairs at any level and to have equal access to public service;

(d) Other civil rights, in particular:

(i) The right to freedom of movement and residence within the border of the State;

(ii) The right to leave any country, including one's own, and to return to one's country;

(iii) The right to nationality;

(iv) The right to marriage and choice of spouse;

(v) The right to own property alone as well as in association with others;

(vi) The right to inherit;

(vii) The right to freedom of thought, conscience and religion;

(viii) The right to freedom of opinion and expression;

(ix) The right to freedom of peaceful assembly and association;

(e) Economic, social and cultural rights, in particular:

(i) The rights to work, to free choice of employment, to just and favourable conditions of work, to protection against unemployment, to equal pay for equal work, to just and favourable remuneration;

(ii) The right to form and join trade unions;

(iii) The right to housing;

(iv) The right to public health, medical care, social security and social services;

(v) The right to education and training;

(vi) The right to equal participation in cultural activities;

(f) The right of access to any place or service intended for use by the general public, such as transport, hotels, restaurants, cafes, theatres and parks.

Article 6

States Parties shall assure to everyone within their jurisdiction effective protection and remedies, through the competent national tribunals and other State institutions, against any acts of racial discrimination which violate his human rights and fundamental freedoms contrary to this Convention, as well as the right to seek from such tribunals just and adequate reparation or satisfaction for any damage suffered as a result of such discrimination.

Article 7

States Parties undertake to adopt immediate and effective measures, particularly in the fields of teaching, education, culture and information, with a view to combating prejudices which lead to racial discrimination and to promoting understanding, tolerance and friendship among nations and racial or ethnical groups, as well as to propagating the purposes and principles of the Charter of the United Nations, the Universal Declaration of Human Rights, the United Nations Declaration on the Elimination of All Forms of Racial Discrimination, and this Convention.

Part II

Article 8

1. There shall be established a Committee on the Elimination of Racial Discrimination (hereinafter referred to as the Committee) consisting of eighteen experts of high moral standing and acknowledged impartiality elected by States Parties from among their nationals, who shall serve in their personal capacity, consideration being given to equitable geographical distribution and to the representation of the different forms of civilization as well as of the principal legal systems.

2. The members of the Committee shall be elected by secret ballot from a list of persons nominated by the States Parties. Each State Party may nominate one person from among its own nationals.

3. The initial election shall be held six months after the date of the entry into force of this Convention. At least three months before the date of each election the Secretary-General of the United Nations shall address a letter to the States Parties inviting them to submit their nominations within two months. The Secretary-General shall prepare a list in alphabetical order of all persons thus nominated, indicating the States Parties which have nominated them, and shall submit it to the States Parties.

4. Elections of the members of the Committee shall be held at a meeting of States Parties convened by the Secretary-General at United Nations Headquarters. At that meeting, for which two-thirds of the States Parties shall constitute a quorum, the persons elected to the Committee shall be those nominees who obtain the largest number of votes and an absolute majority of the votes of the representatives of States Parties present and voting.

5. (a) The members of the Committee shall be elected for a term of four years. However, the terms of nine of the members elected at the first election shall expire at the end of two years; immediately after the first election the names of these nine members shall be chosen by lot by the Chairman of the Committee.

(b) For the filling of casual vacancies, the State Party whose expert has ceased to function as a member of the Committee shall appoint another expert from among its nationals, subject to the approval of the Committee.

6. States Parties shall be responsible for the expenses of the members of the Committee while they are in performance of Committee duties.

Article 9

1. States Parties undertake to submit to the Secretary-General of the United Nations, for consideration by the Committee, a report on the legislative, judicial, administrative or other measures which they have adopted and which give effect to the provisions of this Convention:

(a) within one year after the entry into force of the Convention for the State concerned; and

(b) thereafter every two years and whenever the Committee so requests. The Committee may request further information from the States Parties.

2. The Committee shall report annually, through the Secretary-General, to the General Assembly of the United Nations on its activities and may make suggestions and general recommendations based on the examination of the reports and information received from the States Parties. Such suggestions and general recommendations shall be reported to the General Assembly together with comments, if any, from States Parties.

Article 10

1. The Committee shall adopt its own rules of procedure.

2. The Committee shall elect its officers for a term of two years.

3. The secretariat of the Committee shall be provided by the Secretary-General of the United Nations.

4. The meetings of the Committee shall normally be held at United Nations Headquarters.

Article 11

1. If a State Party considers that another State Party is not giving effect to the provisions of this Convention, it may bring the matter to the attention of the Committee. The Committee shall then transmit the communication to the State Party concerned. Within three months, the receiving State shall submit to the Committee written explanations or statements clarifying the matter and the remedy, if any, that may have been taken by that State.

2. If the matter is not adjusted to the satisfaction of both parties, either by bilateral negotiations or by any other procedure open to them, within six months after the receipt by the receiving State of the initial communication, either State shall have the right to refer the matter again to the Committee by notifying the Committee and also the other State.

3. The Committee shall deal with a matter referred to it in accordance with paragraph 2 of this article after it has ascertained that all available domestic remedies have been invoked and exhausted in the case, in conformity with the generally recognized principles of international law. This shall not be the rule where the application of the remedies is unreasonably prolonged.

4. In any matter referred to it, the Committee may call upon the States Parties concerned to supply any other relevant information.

5. When any matter arising out of this article is being considered by the Committee, the States Parties concerned shall be entitled to send a representative to take part in the proceedings of the Committee, without voting rights, while the matter is under consideration.

Article 12

1. (a) After the Committee has obtained and collated all the information it deems necessary, the Chairman shall appoint an ad hoc Conciliation Commission (hereinafter referred to as the Commission) comprising five persons who may or may not be members of the Committee. The members of the Commission shall be appointed with the unanimous consent of the parties to the dispute, and its good offices shall be made available to the States concerned with a view to an amicable solution of the matter on the basis or respect for this Convention.

   (b) If the States Parties to the dispute fail to reach agreement within three months on all or part of the composition of the Commission, the members of the Commission not agreed upon by the States parties to the dispute shall be elected by secret ballot by a two-thirds majority vote of the Committee from among its own members.

2. The members of the Commission shall serve in their personal capacity. They shall not be nationals of the States parties to the dispute or of a State not Party to this Convention.

3. The Commission shall elect its own Chairman and adopt its own rules of procedure.

4. The meetings of the Commission shall normally be held at United Nations Headquarters or at any other convenient place as determined by the Commission.

5. The secretariat provided in accordance with Article 10, paragraph 3, of this Convention shall also service the Commission whenever a dispute among States Parties brings the Commission into being.

6. The States parties to the dispute shall share equally all the expenses of the members of the Commission in accordance with estimates to be provided by the Secretary-General of the United Nations.

7. The Secretary-General shall be empowered to pay the expenses of the members of the Commission, if necessary, before reimbursement by the States parties to the dispute in accordance with paragraph 6 of this article.

8. The information obtained and collated by the Committee shall be made available to the Commission, and the Commission may call upon the States concerned to supply any other relevant information.

Article 13

1. When the Commission has fully considered the matter, it shall prepare and submit to the Chairman of the Committee a report embodying its findings on all questions of fact relevant to the issue between the parties and containing such recommendations as it may think proper for the amicable solution of the dispute.

2. The Chairman of the Committee shall communicate the report of the Commission to each of the States Parties to the dispute. These States shall, within three months, inform the Chairman of the Committee whether or not they accept the recommendations contained in the report of the Commission.

3. After the period provided for in paragraph 2 of Chairman of the Committee shall communicate the report of the Commission and the declarations of the States Parties concerned to the other States Parties to this Convention.

Article 14

1. A State Party may at any time declare that it recognizes the competence of the Committee to receive and consider communications from individuals or groups of individuals within its jurisdiction claiming to be victims of a violation by that State Party of any of the rights set forth in this Convention. No communication shall be received by the Committee if it concerns a State Party which has not made such a declaration.

2. Any State Party which makes a declaration as provided for in paragraph 1 of this article may establish or indicate a body within its national legal order which shall be competent to receive and consider petitions from individuals and groups of individuals within its jurisdiction who claim to be victims of a violation of any of the rights set forth in this Convention and who have exhausted other available local remedies.

3. A declaration made in accordance with paragraph 1 of this article and the name of any body established or indicated in accordance with paragraph 2 of this article shall be deposited by the State Party concerned with the Secretary-General of the United Nations, who shall transmit copies thereof to the other States Parties. A declaration may be withdrawn at any time by notification to the Secretary-General, but such a withdrawal shall not affect communications pending before the Committee.

4. A register of petitions shall be kept by the body established or indicated in accordance with paragraph 2 of this article, and certified copies of the register shall be filed annually through appropriate channels with the Secretary-General on the understanding that the contents shall not be publicly disclosed.

5. In the event of failure to obtain satisfaction from the body established or indicated in accordance with paragraph 2 of this article, the petitioner shall have the right to communicate the matter to the Committee within six months.

6. (a) The Committee shall confidentially bring any communication referred to it to the attention of the State Party alleged to be violating any provision of this Convention, but the identity of the individual or groups of individuals concerned shall not be revealed without his or their express consent. The Committee shall not receive anonymous communications.

(b) Within three months, the receiving State shall submit to the Committee written explanations or statements clarifying the matter and the remedy, if any, that may have been taken by that State.

7. (a) The Committee shall consider communications in the light of all information made available to it by the State Party concerned and by the petitioner. The Committee shall not consider any communication from a petitioner unless it has ascertained that the petitioner has exhausted all available domestic remedies. However, this shall not be the rule where the application of the remedies is unreasonably prolonged.

(b) The Committee shall forward its suggestions and recommendations, if any, to the State Party concerned and to the petitioner.

8. The Committee shall include in its annual report a summary of such communications and, where appropriate, a summary of the explanations and statements of the States Parties concerned and of its own suggestions and recommendations.

9. The Committee shall be competent to exercise the functions provided for in this article only when at least ten States Parties to this Convention are bound by declarations in accordance with paragraph 1 of this article.

Article 20

1. The Secretary-General of the United Nations shall receive and circulate to all States which are or may become Parties to this Convention reservations made by States at the time of ratification or accession. Any State which objects to the reservation shall, within a period of ninety days from the date of the said communication, notify the Secretary-General that it does not accept it.

2. A reservation incompatible with the object and purpose of this Convention shall not be permitted, nor shall a reservation the effect of which would inhibit the operation of any of the bodies established by this Convention be allowed. A reservation shall be considered incompatible or inhibitive if at least two-thirds of the States Parties to this Convention object to it.

3. Reservations may be withdrawn at any time by notification to this effect addressed to the Secretary-General. Such notification shall take effect on the date on which it is received.

Article 22

Any dispute between two or more States Parties with respect to the interpretation or application of this Convention, which is not settled by negotiation or by the procedures expressly provided for in this Convention, shall, at the request of any of the parties to the dispute, be referred to the International Court of Justice for decision, unless the disputants agree to another mode of settlement.

International Convention Against the Taking of Hostages
1316 U.N.T.S. 205 (1979)

The States Parties to this Convention,

Having in mind the purposes and principles of the Charter of the United Nations concerning the maintenance of international peace and security and the promotion of friendly relations and co-operation among States,

Recognizing in particular that everyone has the right to life, liberty and security of person, as set out in the Universal Declaration of Human Rights and the International Covenant on Civil and Political Rights,

Reaffirming the principle of equal rights and self-determination of peoples as enshrined in the Charter of the United Nations and the Declaration on Principles of International Law concerning Friendly Relations and Co-operation among States in accordance with the Charter of the United Nations, as well as in other relevant resolutions of the General Assembly,

Considering that the taking of hostages is an offence of grave concern to the international community and that, in accordance with the provisions of this Convention, any person committing an act of hostage taking shall either be prosecuted or extradited,

Being convinced that it is urgently necessary to develop international co-operation between States in devising and adopting effective measures for the prevention, prosecution and punishment of all acts of taking of hostages as manifestations of international terrorism,

Have agreed as follows:

Article 1

1. Any person who seizes or detains and threatens to kill, to injure or to continue to detain another person (hereinafter referred to as the "hostage") in order to compel a third party, namely, a State, an international intergovernmental organization, a natural or juridical person, or a group of persons, to do or abstain from doing any act as an explicit or implicit condition for the release of the hostage commits the offence of taking of hostages ("hostage-taking") within the meaning of this Convention.

2. Any person who:

(a) attempts to commit an act of hostage-taking, or

(b) participates as an accomplice of anyone who commits or attempts to commit an act of hostage-taking likewise commits an offence for the purposes of this Convention.

Article 2

Each State Party shall make the offences set forth in Article 1 punishable by appropriate penalties which take into account the grave nature of those offences.

Article 3

1. The State Party in the territory of which the hostage is held by the offender shall take all measures it considers appropriate to ease the situation of the hostage, in particular, to secure his release and, after his release, to facilitate, when relevant, his departure.

2. If any object which the offender has obtained as a result of the taking of hostages comes into the custody of a State Party, that State Party shall return it as soon as possible to the hostage or the third party referred to in Article 1, as the case may be, or to the appropriate authorities thereof.

Article 4

States Parties shall co-operate in the prevention of the offences set forth in Article 1, particularly by:

(a) taking all practicable measures to prevent preparations in their respective territories for the commission of those offences within or outside their territories, including measures to prohibit in their territories illegal activities of persons, groups and organizations that encourage, instigate, organize or engage in the perpetration of acts of taking of hostages;

(b) exchanging information and co-ordinating the taking of administrative and other measures as appropriate to prevent the commission of those offences.

Article 5

1. Each State Party shall take such measures as may be necessary to establish its jurisdiction over any of the offences set forth in Article 1 which are committed:

(a) in its territory or on board a ship or aircraft registered in that State;

(b) by any of its nationals or, if that State considers it appropriate, by those stateless persons who have their habitual residence in its territory;

(c) in order to compel that State to do or abstain from doing any act; or

(d) with respect to a hostage who is a national of that State, if that State considers it appropriate.

2. Each State Party shall likewise take such measures as may be necessary to establish its jurisdiction over the offences set forth in Article 1 in cases where the alleged offender is present in its territory and it does not extradite him to any of the States mentioned in paragraph 1 of this article.

3. This Convention does not exclude any criminal jurisdiction exercised in accordance with internal law.

Article 6

1. Upon being satisfied that the circumstances so warrant, any State Party in the territory of which the alleged offender is present shall, in accordance with its laws, take him into custody or take other measures to ensure his presence for such time as is necessary to enable any criminal or extradition proceedings to be instituted. That State Party shall immediately make a preliminary inquiry into the facts.

2. The custody or other measures referred to in paragraph 1 of this article shall be notified without delay directly or through the Secretary-General of the United Nations to:

(a) the State where the offence was committed;

(b) the State against which compulsion has been directed or attempted;

(c) the State of which the natural or juridical person against whom compulsion has been directed or attempted is a national;

(d) the State of which the hostage is a national or in the territory of which he has his habitual residence;

(e) the State of which the alleged offender is a national or, if he is a stateless person, in the territory of which he has his habitual residence;

(f) the international intergovernmental organization against which compulsion has been directed or attempted;

(g) all other States concerned.

3. Any person regarding whom the measures referred to in paragraph 1 of this article are being taken shall be entitled:

(a) to communicate without delay with the nearest appropriate representative of the State of which he is a national or which is otherwise entitled to establish such communication or, if he is a stateless person, the State in the territory of which he has his habitual residence;

(b) to be visited by a representative of that State.

4. The rights referred to in paragraph 3 of this article shall be exercised in conformity with the laws and regulations of the State in the territory of which the alleged offender is present subject to the proviso, however, that the said laws and regulations must enable full effect to be given to the purposes for which the rights accorded under paragraph 3 of this article are intended.

5. The provisions of paragraphs 3 and 4 of this article shall be without prejudice to the right of any State Party having a claim to jurisdiction in accordance with paragraph 1(b) of Article 5 to invite the International Committee of the Red Cross to communicate with and visit the alleged offender.

6. The State which makes the preliminary inquiry contemplated in paragraph 1 of this article shall promptly report its findings to the States or organization referred to in paragraph 2 of this article and indicate whether it intends to exercise jurisdiction.

Article 7

The State Party where the alleged offender is prosecuted shall in accordance with its laws communicate the final outcome of the proceedings to the Secretary-General of the United Nations, who shall transmit the information to the other States concerned and the international intergovernmental organizations concerned.

Article 8

1. The State Party in the territory of which the alleged offender is found shall, if it does not extradite him, be obliged, without exception whatsoever and whether or not the offence was committed in its territory, to submit the case to its competent authorities for the purpose of prosecution, through proceedings in accordance with the laws of that State. Those authorities shall take their decision in the same manner as in the case of any ordinary offence of a grave nature under the law of that State.

2. Any person regarding whom proceedings are being carried out in connection with any of the offences set forth in Article 1 shall be guaranteed fair treatment at all stages of the proceedings, including enjoyment of all the rights and guarantees provided by the law of the State in the territory of which he is present.

Article 9

1. A request for the extradition of an alleged offender, pursuant to this Convention, shall not be granted if the requested State Party has substantial grounds for believing:

(a) that the request for extradition for an offence set forth in Article 1 has been made for the purpose of prosecuting or punishing a person on account of his race, religion, nationality, ethnic origin or political opinion; or

(b) that the person's position may be prejudiced:

(i) for any of the reasons mentioned in subparagraph (a) of this paragraph; or

(ii) for the reason that communication with him by the appropriate authorities of the State entitled to exercise rights of protection cannot be effected.

2. With respect to the offences as defined in this Convention the provisions of all extradition treaties and arrangements applicable between States Parties are modified as between States Parties to the extent that they are incompatible with this Convention.

Article 10

1. The offences set forth in Article 1 shall be deemed to be included as extraditable offences in any extradition treaty existing between States Parties. States Parties undertake

to include such offences as extraditable offences in every extradition treaty to be concluded between them.

2. If a State Party which makes extradition conditional on the existence of a treaty receives a request for extradition from another State Party with which it has no extradition treaty, the requested State may at its option consider this Convention as the legal basis for extradition in respect of the offences set forth in Article 1. Extradition shall be subject to the other conditions provided by the law of the requested State.

3. States Parties which do not make extradition conditional on the existence of a treaty shall recognize the offences set forth in Article 1 as extraditable offences between themselves subject to the conditions provided by the law of the requested State.

4. The offences set forth in Article 1 shall be treated, for the purpose of extradition between States Parties, as if they had been committed not only in the place in which they occurred but also in the territories of the States required to establish their jurisdiction in accordance with paragraph 1 of Article 5.

Article 11

1. States Parties shall afford one another the greatest measure of assistance in connection with criminal proceedings brought in respect of the offences set forth in Article 1, including the supply of all evidence at their disposal necessary for the proceedings.

2. The provisions of paragraph 1 of this article shall not affect obligations concerning mutual judicial assistance embodied in any other treaty.

Article 12

In so far as the Geneva Conventions of 1949 for the protection of war victims or the Additional Protocols to those Conventions are applicable to a particular act of hostage-taking, and in so far as States Parties to this Convention are bound under those conventions to prosecute or hand over the hostage-taker, the present Convention shall not apply to an act of hostage-taking committed in the course of armed conflicts as defined in the Geneva Conventions of 1949 and the Protocols thereto, including armed conflicts mentioned in Article 1, paragraph 4, of Additional Protocol I of 1977, in which peoples are fighting against colonial domination and alien occupation and against racist regimes in the exercise of their right of self-determination, as enshrined in the Charter of the United Nations and the Declaration on Principles of International Law concerning Friendly Relations and Co-operation among States in accordance with the Charter of the United Nations.

Article 13

This Convention shall not apply where the offence is committed within a single State, the hostage and the alleged offender are nationals of that State and the alleged offender is found in the territory of that State.

Article 14

Nothing in this Convention shall be construed as justifying the violation of the territorial integrity or political independence of a State in contravention of the Charter of the United Nations.

Article 15

The provisions of this Convention shall not affect the application of the Treaties on Asylum, in force at the date of the adoption of this Convention, as between the States which are parties to those Treaties; but a State Party to this Convention may not invoke those Treaties with respect to another State Party to this Convention which is not a party to those treaties....

Convention Against Torture and Other Cruel, Inhuman or Degrading Treatment or Punishment
1465 U.N.T.S. 85 (Dec. 10, 1984)

The States Parties to this Convention,

Considering that, in accordance with the principles proclaimed in the Charter of the United Nations, recognition of the equal and inalienable rights of all members of the human family is the foundation of freedom, justice and peace in the world,

Recognizing that those rights derive from the inherent dignity of the human person,

Considering the obligation of States under the Charter, in particular Article 55, to promote universal respect for, and observance of, human rights and fundamental freedoms,

Having regard to Article 5 of the Universal Declaration of Human Rights and Article 7 of the International Covenant on Civil and Political Rights, both of which provide that no one may be subjected to torture or to cruel, inhuman or degrading treatment or punishment,

Having regard also to the Declaration on the Protection of All Persons from Being Subjected to Torture and Other Cruel, Inhuman or Degrading Treatment or Punishment, adopted by the General Assembly on 9 December 1975 (resolution 3452 (XXX)),

Desiring to make more effective the struggle against torture and other cruel, inhuman or degrading treatment or punishment throughout the world,

Have agreed as follows:

Part I

Article 1

1. For the purposes of this Convention, torture means any act by which severe pain or suffering, whether physical or mental, is intentionally inflicted on a person for such purposes as obtaining from him or a third person information or a confession, punishing him for an act he or a third person has committed or is suspected of having committed, or intimidating or coercing him or a third person, or for any reason based on discrimination of any kind, when such pain or suffering is inflicted by or at the instigation of or with the consent or acquiescence of a public official or other person acting in an official capacity. It does not include pain or suffering arising only from, inherent in or incidental to lawful sanctions.

2. This article is without prejudice to any international instrument or national legislation which does or may contain provisions of wider application.

Article 2

1. Each State Party shall take effective legislative, administrative, judicial or other measures to prevent acts of torture in any territory under its jurisdiction.

2. No exceptional circumstances whatsoever, whether a state of war or a threat of war, internal political instability or any other public emergency, may be invoked as a justification of torture.

3. An order from a superior officer or a public authority may not be invoked as a justification of torture.

Article 3

1. No State Party shall expel, return (*"refouler"*) or extradite a person to another State where there are substantial grounds for believing that he would be in danger of being subjected to torture.

2. For the purpose of determining whether there are such grounds, the competent authorities shall take into account all relevant considerations including, where applicable, the existence in the State concerned of a consistent pattern of gross, flagrant or mass violations of human rights.

Article 4

1. Each State Party shall ensure that all acts of torture are offences under its criminal law. The same shall apply to an attempt to commit torture and to an act by any person which constitutes complicity or participation in torture.

2. Each State Party shall make these offences punishable by appropriate penalties which take into account their grave nature.

Article 5

1. Each State Party shall take such measures as may be necessary to establish its jurisdiction over the offences referred to in Article 4 in the following cases:

(a) When the offences are committed in any territory under its jurisdiction or on board a ship or aircraft registered in that State;

(b) When the alleged offender is a national of that State;

(c) When the victim is a national of that State if that State considers it appropriate.

2. Each State Party shall likewise take such measures as may be necessary to establish its jurisdiction over such offences in cases where the alleged offender is present in any territory under its jurisdiction and it does not extradite him pursuant to Article 8 to any of the States mentioned in paragraph 1 of this article.

3. This Convention does not exclude any criminal jurisdiction exercised in accordance with internal law.

Article 6

1. Upon being satisfied, after an examination of information available to it, that the circumstances so warrant, any State Party in whose territory a person alleged to have committed any offence referred to in Article 4 is present, shall take him into custody or take other legal measures to ensure his presence. The custody and other legal measures shall be as provided in the law of that State but may be continued only for such time as is necessary to enable any criminal or extradition proceedings to be instituted.

2. Such State shall immediately make a preliminary inquiry into the facts.

3. Any person in custody pursuant to paragraph 1 of this article shall be assisted in communicating immediately with the nearest appropriate representative of the State of which he is a national, or, if he is a stateless person, to the representative of the State where he usually resides.

4. When a State, pursuant to this article, has taken a person into custody, it shall immediately notify the States referred to in Article 5, paragraph 1, of the fact that such person in is custody and of the circumstances which warrant his detention. The State

which makes the preliminary inquiry contemplated in paragraph 2 of this article shall promptly report its findings to the said States and shall indicate whether it intends to exercise jurisdiction.

Article 7

1. The State Party in territory under whose jurisdiction a person alleged to have committed any offence referred to in Article 4 is found, shall in the cases contemplated in Article 5, if it does not extradite him, submit the case to its competent authorities for the purpose of prosecution.

2. These authorities shall take their decision in the same manner as in the case of any ordinary offence of a serious nature under the law of that State. In the cases referred to in Article 5, paragraph 2, the standards of evidence required for prosecution and conviction shall in no way be less stringent than those which apply in the cases referred to in Article 5, paragraph 1.

3. Any person regarding whom proceedings are brought in connection with any of the offenses referred to in Article 4 shall be guaranteed fair treatment at all stages of the proceedings.

Article 8

1. The offenses referred to in Article 4 shall be deemed to be included as extraditable offenses in any extradition treaty existing between States Parties. States Parties undertake to include such offenses as extraditable offenses in every extradition treaty to be concluded between them.

2. If a State Party which makes extradition conditional on the existence of a treaty receives a request for extradition from another State Party with which it has no extradition treaty, it may consider this Convention as the legal basis for extradition in respect of such offenses. Extradition shall be subject to the other conditions provided by the law of the requested State.

3. States Parties which do not make extradition conditional on the existence of a treaty shall recognize such offenses as extraditable offenses between themselves subject to the conditions provided by the law of the requested State.

4. Such offenses shall be treated, for the purpose of extradition between States Parties, as if they had been committed not only in the place in which they occurred but also in the territories of the States required to establish their jurisdiction in accordance with Article 5, paragraph 1.

Article 9

1. States Parties shall afford one another the greatest measure of assistance in connection with criminal proceedings brought in respect of any of the offenses referred to in Article 4, including the supply of all evidence at their disposal necessary for the proceedings.

2. States Parties shall carry out their obligations under paragraph 1 of this article in conformity with any treaties on mutual judicial assistance that may exist between them.

Article 10

1. Each State Party shall ensure that education and information regarding the prohibition against torture are fully included in the training of law enforcement personnel,

civil or military, medical personnel, public officials and other persons who may be involved in the custody, interrogation or treatment of any individual subjected to any form of arrest, detention or imprisonment.

2. Each State Party shall include this prohibition in the rules or instructions issued in regard to the duties and functions of any such persons.

Article 11

Each State Party shall keep under systematic review interrogation rules, instructions, methods and practices as well as arrangements for the custody and treatment of persons subjected to any form of arrest, detention or imprisonment in any territory under its jurisdiction, with a view to preventing any cases of torture.

Article 12

Each State Party shall ensure that its competent authorities proceed to a prompt and impartial investigation, wherever there is reasonable ground to believe that an act of torture has been committed in any territory under its jurisdiction.

Article 13

Each State Party shall ensure that any individual who alleges he has been subjected to torture in any territory under its jurisdiction has the right to complain to and to have his case promptly and impartially examined by its competent authorities. Steps shall be taken to insure that the complainant and witnesses are protected against all ill-treatment or intimidation as a consequence of his complaint or any evidence given.

Article 14

1. Each State Party shall ensure in its legal system that the victim of an act of torture obtains redress and has an enforceable right to fair and adequate compensation including the means for as full rehabilitation as possible. In the event of the death of the victim as a result of an act of torture, his dependents shall be entitled to compensation.

2. Nothing in this article shall affect any right of the victim or other persons to compensation which may exist under national law.

Article 15

Each State Party shall ensure that any statement which is established to have been made as a result of torture shall not be invoked as evidence in any proceedings, except against a person accused of torture as evidence that the statement was made.

Article 16

1. Each State Party shall undertake to prevent in any territory under its jurisdiction other acts of cruel, inhuman or degrading treatment or punishment which do not amount to torture as defined in Article 1, when such acts are committed by or at the instigation of or with the consent or acquiescence of a public official or other person acting in an official capacity. In particular, the obligations contained in Articles 10, 11, 12 and 13 shall apply with the substitution for references to torture of references to other forms of cruel, inhuman or degrading treatment or punishment.

2. The provisions of this Convention are without prejudice to the provisions of any other international instrument or national law which prohibit cruel, inhuman or degrading treatment or punishment or which relate to extradition or expulsion....

International Convention for the Protection of All Persons from Enforced Disappearance

adopted by U.N. G.A. Res. 61/177 (20 Dec. 2006)

Preamble

The States Parties to this Convention,

Considering the obligation of States under the Charter of the United Nations to promote universal respect for, and observance of, human rights and fundamental freedoms,

Having regard to the Universal Declaration of Human Rights,

Recalling the International Covenant on Economic, Social and Cultural Rights, the International Covenant on Civil and Political Rights and the other relevant international instruments in the fields of human rights, humanitarian law and international criminal law,

Also recalling the Declaration on the Protection of All Persons from Enforced Disappearance adopted by the General Assembly of the United Nations in its resolution 47/133 of 18 December 1992,

Aware of the extreme seriousness of enforced disappearance, which constitutes a crime and, in certain circumstances defined in international law, a crime against humanity,

Determined to prevent enforced disappearances and to combat impunity for the crime of enforced disappearance,

Considering the right of any person not to be subjected to enforced disappearance, the right of victims to justice and to reparation,

Affirming the right of any victim to know the truth about the circumstances of an enforced disappearance and the fate of the disappeared person, and the right to freedom to seek, receive and impart information to this end,

Have agreed on the following articles:

Part I

Article 1

1. No one shall be subjected to enforced disappearance.

2. No exceptional circumstances whatsoever, whether a state of war or a threat of war, internal political instability or any other public emergency, may be invoked as a justification for enforced disappearance.

Article 2

For the purposes of this Convention, "enforced disappearance" is considered to be the arrest, detention, abduction or any other form of deprivation of liberty by agents of the State or by persons or groups of persons acting with the authorization, support or acquiescence of the State, followed by a refusal to acknowledge the deprivation of liberty or by concealment of the fate or whereabouts of the disappeared person, which place such a person outside the protection of the law.

Article 3

Each State Party shall take appropriate measures to investigate acts defined in article 2 committed by persons or groups of persons acting without the authorization, support or acquiescence of the State and to bring those responsible to justice.

Article 4

Each State Party shall take the necessary measures to ensure that enforced disappearance constitutes an offence under its criminal law.

Article 5

The widespread or systematic practice of enforced disappearance constitutes a crime against humanity as defined in applicable international law and shall attract the consequences provided for under such applicable international law.

Article 6

1. Each State Party shall take the necessary measures to hold criminally responsible at least:

(a) Any person who commits, orders, solicits or induces the commission of, attempts to commit, is an accomplice to or participates in an enforced disappearance;

(b) A superior who:

(i) Knew, or consciously disregarded information which clearly indicated, that subordinates under his or her effective authority and control were committing or about to commit a crime of enforced disappearance;

(ii) Exercised effective responsibility for and control over activities which were concerned with the crime of enforced disappearance; and

(iii) Failed to take all necessary and reasonable measures within his or her power to prevent or repress the commission of an enforced disappearance or to submit the matter to the competent authorities for investigation and prosecution;

(c) Subparagraph (b) above is without prejudice to the higher standards of responsibility applicable under relevant international law to a military commander or to a person effectively acting as a military commander.

2. No order or instruction from any public authority, civilian, military or other, may be invoked to justify an offence of enforced disappearance.

Article 7

1. Each State Party shall make the offence of enforced disappearance punishable by appropriate penalties which take into account its extreme seriousness.

2. Each State Party may establish:

(a) Mitigating circumstances, in particular for persons who, having been implicated in the commission of an enforced disappearance, effectively contribute to bringing the disappeared person forward alive or make it possible to clarify cases of enforced disappearance or to identify the perpetrators of an enforced disappearance;

(b) Without prejudice to other criminal procedures, aggravating circumstances, in particular in the event of the death of the disappeared person or the commission of an enforced disappearance in respect of pregnant women, minors, persons with disabilities or other particularly vulnerable persons.

Article 8

Without prejudice to article 5,

1. A State Party which applies a statute of limitations in respect of enforced disappearance shall take the necessary measures to ensure that the term of limitation for criminal proceedings:

(*a*) Is of long duration and is proportionate to the extreme seriousness of this offence;

(*b*) Commences from the moment when the offence of enforced disappearance ceases, taking into account its continuous nature.

2. Each State Party shall guarantee the right of victims of enforced disappearance to an effective remedy during the term of limitation.

Article 9

1. Each State Party shall take the necessary measures to establish its competence to exercise jurisdiction over the offence of enforced disappearance:

(*a*) When the offence is committed in any territory under its jurisdiction or on board a ship or aircraft registered in that State;

(*b*) When the alleged offender is one of its nationals;

(*c*) When the disappeared person is one of its nationals and the State Party considers it appropriate.

2. Each State Party shall likewise take such measures as may be necessary to establish its competence to exercise jurisdiction over the offence of enforced disappearance when the alleged offender is present in any territory under its jurisdiction, unless it extradites or surrenders him or her to another State in accordance with its international obligations or surrenders him or her to an international criminal tribunal whose jurisdiction it has recognized.

3. This Convention does not exclude any additional criminal jurisdiction exercised in accordance with national law.

Article 10

1. Upon being satisfied, after an examination of the information available to it, that the circumstances so warrant, any State Party in whose territory a person suspected of having committed an offence of enforced disappearance is present shall take him or her into custody or take such other legal measures as are necessary to ensure his or her presence. The custody and other legal measures shall be as provided for in the law of that State Party but may be maintained only for such time as is necessary to ensure the person's presence at criminal, surrender or extradition proceedings.

2. A State Party which has taken the measures referred to in paragraph 1 of this article shall immediately carry out a preliminary inquiry or investigations to establish the facts. It shall notify the States Parties referred to in article 9, paragraph 1, of the measures it has taken in pursuance of paragraph 1 of this article, including detention and the circumstances warranting detention, and of the findings of its preliminary inquiry or its investigations, indicating whether it intends to exercise its jurisdiction.

3. Any person in custody pursuant to paragraph 1 of this article may communicate immediately with the nearest appropriate representative of the State of which he or she is a national, or, if he or she is a stateless person, with the representative of the State where he or she usually resides.

Article 11

1. The State Party in the territory under whose jurisdiction a person alleged to have committed an offence of enforced disappearance is found shall, if it does not extradite that person or surrender him or her to another State in accordance with its international obligations or surrender him or her to an international criminal tribunal whose juris-

diction it has recognized, submit the case to its competent authorities for the purpose of prosecution.

2. These authorities shall take their decision in the same manner as in the case of any ordinary offence of a serious nature under the law of that State Party. In the cases referred to in article 9, paragraph 2, the standards of evidence required for prosecution and conviction shall in no way be less stringent than those which apply in the cases referred to in article 9, paragraph 1.

3. Any person against whom proceedings are brought in connection with an offence of enforced disappearance shall be guaranteed fair treatment at all stages of the proceedings. Any person tried for an offence of enforced disappearance shall benefit from a fair trial before a competent, independent and impartial court or tribunal established by law.

Article 12

1. Each State Party shall ensure that any individual who alleges that a person has been subjected to enforced disappearance has the right to report the facts to the competent authorities, which shall examine the allegation promptly and impartially and, where necessary, undertake without delay a thorough and impartial investigation. Appropriate steps shall be taken, where necessary, to ensure that the complainant, witnesses, relatives of the disappeared person and their defence counsel, as well as persons participating in the investigation, are protected against all ill-treatment or intimidation as a consequence of the complaint or any evidence given.

2. Where there are reasonable grounds for believing that a person has been subjected to enforced disappearance, the authorities referred to in paragraph 1 of this article shall undertake an investigation, even if there has been no formal complaint.

3. Each State Party shall ensure that the authorities referred to in paragraph 1 of this article:

(a) Have the necessary powers and resources to conduct the investigation effectively, including access to the documentation and other information relevant to their investigation;

(b) Have access, if necessary with the prior authorization of a judicial authority, which shall rule promptly on the matter, to any place of detention or any other place where there are reasonable grounds to believe that the disappeared person may be present.

4. Each State Party shall take the necessary measures to prevent and sanction acts that hinder the conduct of an investigation. It shall ensure in particular that persons suspected of having committed an offence of enforced disappearance are not in a position to influence the progress of an investigation by means of pressure or acts of intimidation or reprisal aimed at the complainant, witnesses, relatives of the disappeared person or their defence counsel, or at persons participating in the investigation.

Article 13

1. For the purposes of extradition between States Parties, the offence of enforced disappearance shall not be regarded as a political offence or as an offence connected with a political offence or as an offence inspired by political motives. Accordingly, a request for extradition based on such an offence may not be refused on these grounds alone.

2. The offence of enforced disappearance shall be deemed to be included as an extraditable offence in any extradition treaty existing between States Parties before the entry into force of this Convention.

3. States Parties undertake to include the offence of enforced disappearance as an extraditable offence in any extradition treaty subsequently to be concluded between them.

4. If a State Party which makes extradition conditional on the existence of a treaty receives a request for extradition from another State Party with which it has no extradition treaty, it may consider this Convention as the necessary legal basis for extradition in respect of the offence of enforced disappearance.

5. States Parties which do not make extradition conditional on the existence of a treaty shall recognize the offence of enforced disappearance as an extraditable offence between themselves.

6. Extradition shall, in all cases, be subject to the conditions provided for by the law of the requested State Party or by applicable extradition treaties, including, in particular, conditions relating to the minimum penalty requirement for extradition and the grounds upon which the requested State Party may refuse extradition or make it subject to certain conditions.

7. Nothing in this Convention shall be interpreted as imposing an obligation to extradite if the requested State Party has substantial grounds for believing that the request has been made for the purpose of prosecuting or punishing a person on account of that person's sex, race, religion, nationality, ethnic origin, political opinions or membership of a particular social group, or that compliance with the request would cause harm to that person for any one of these reasons.

Article 14

1. States Parties shall afford one another the greatest measure of mutual legal assistance in connection with criminal proceedings brought in respect of an offence of enforced disappearance, including the supply of all evidence at their disposal that is necessary for the proceedings.

2. Such mutual legal assistance shall be subject to the conditions provided for by the domestic law of the requested State Party or by applicable treaties on mutual legal assistance, including, in particular, the conditions in relation to the grounds upon which the requested State Party may refuse to grant mutual legal assistance or may make it subject to conditions.

Article 15

States Parties shall cooperate with each other and shall afford one another the greatest measure of mutual assistance with a view to assisting victims of enforced disappearance, and in searching for, locating and releasing disappeared persons and, in the event of death, in exhuming and identifying them and returning their remains.

Article 16

1. No State Party shall expel, return ("refouler"), surrender or extradite a person to another State where there are substantial grounds for believing that he or she would be in danger of being subjected to enforced disappearance.

2. For the purpose of determining whether there are such grounds, the competent authorities shall take into account all relevant considerations, including, where applicable, the existence in the State concerned of a consistent pattern of gross, flagrant or mass violations of human rights or of serious violations of international humanitarian law.

Article 17

1. No one shall be held in secret detention.

2. Without prejudice to other international obligations of the State Party with regard to the deprivation of liberty, each State Party shall, in its legislation:

(a) Establish the conditions under which orders of deprivation of liberty may be given;

(b) Indicate those authorities authorized to order the deprivation of liberty;

(c) Guarantee that any person deprived of liberty shall be held solely in officially recognized and supervised places of deprivation of liberty;

(d) Guarantee that any person deprived of liberty shall be authorized to communicate with and be visited by his or her family, counsel or any other person of his or her choice, subject only to the conditions established by law, or, if he or she is a foreigner, to communicate with his or her consular authorities, in accordance with applicable international law;

(e) Guarantee access by the competent and legally authorized authorities and institutions to the places where persons are deprived of liberty, if necessary with prior authorization from a judicial authority;

(f) Guarantee that any person deprived of liberty or, in the case of a suspected enforced disappearance, since the person deprived of liberty is not able to exercise this right, any persons with a legitimate interest, such as relatives of the person deprived of liberty, their representatives or their counsel, shall, in all circumstances, be entitled to take proceedings before a court, in order that the court may decide without delay on the lawfulness of the deprivation of liberty and order the person's release if such deprivation of liberty is not lawful.

3. Each State Party shall assure the compilation and maintenance of one or more up-to-date official registers and/or records of persons deprived of liberty, which shall be made promptly available, upon request, to any judicial or other competent authority or institution authorized for that purpose by the law of the State Party concerned or any relevant international legal instrument to which the State concerned is a party. The information contained therein shall include, as a minimum:

(a) The identity of the person deprived of liberty;

(b) The date, time and place where the person was deprived of liberty and the identity of the authority that deprived the person of liberty;

(c) The authority that ordered the deprivation of liberty and the grounds for the deprivation of liberty;

(d) The authority responsible for supervising the deprivation of liberty;

(e) The place of deprivation of liberty, the date and time of admission to the place of deprivation of liberty and the authority responsible for the place of deprivation of liberty;

(f) Elements relating to the state of health of the person deprived of liberty;

(g) In the event of death during the deprivation of liberty, the circumstances and cause of death and the destination of the remains;

(h) The date and time of release or transfer to another place of detention, the destination and the authority responsible for the transfer.

Article 18

1. Subject to articles 19 and 20, each State Party shall guarantee to any person with a legitimate interest in this information, such as relatives of the person deprived of liberty, their representatives or their counsel, access to at least the following information:

(a) The authority that ordered the deprivation of liberty;

(b) The date, time and place where the person was deprived of liberty and admitted to the place of deprivation of liberty;

(c) The authority responsible for supervising the deprivation of liberty;

(d) The whereabouts of the person deprived of liberty, including, in the event of a transfer to another place of deprivation of liberty, the destination and the authority responsible for the transfer;

(e) The date, time and place of release;

(f) Elements relating to the state of health of the person deprived of liberty;

(g) In the event of death during the deprivation of liberty, the circumstances and cause of death and the destination of the remains.

2. Appropriate measures shall be taken, where necessary, to protect the persons referred to in paragraph 1 of this article, as well as persons participating in the investigation, from any ill-treatment, intimidation or sanction as a result of the search for information concerning a person deprived of liberty.

Article 19

1. Personal information, including medical and genetic data, which is collected and/or transmitted within the framework of the search for a disappeared person shall not be used or made available for purposes other than the search for the disappeared person. This is without prejudice to the use of such information in criminal proceedings relating to an offence of enforced disappearance or the exercise of the right to obtain reparation.

2. The collection, processing, use and storage of personal information, including medical and genetic data, shall not infringe or have the effect of infringing the human rights, fundamental freedoms or human dignity of an individual.

Article 20

1. Only where a person is under the protection of the law and the deprivation of liberty is subject to judicial control may the right to information referred to in article 18 be restricted, on an exceptional basis, where strictly necessary and where provided for by law, and if the transmission of the information would adversely affect the privacy or safety of the person, hinder a criminal investigation, or for other equivalent reasons in accordance with the law, and in conformity with applicable international law and with the objectives of this Convention. In no case shall there be restrictions on the right to information referred to in article 18 that could constitute conduct defined in article 2 or be in violation of article 17, paragraph 1.

2. Without prejudice to consideration of the lawfulness of the deprivation of a person's liberty, States Parties shall guarantee to the persons referred to in article 18, paragraph 1, the right to a prompt and effective judicial remedy as a means of obtaining without delay the information referred to in article 18, paragraph 1. This right to a remedy may not be suspended or restricted in any circumstances.

Article 21

Each State Party shall take the necessary measures to ensure that persons deprived of liberty are released in a manner permitting reliable verification that they have actually been released. Each State Party shall also take the necessary measures to assure the physical integrity of such persons and their ability to exercise fully their rights at the time of release, without prejudice to any obligations to which such persons may be subject under national law.

Article 22

Without prejudice to article 6, each State Party shall take the necessary measures to prevent and impose sanctions for the following conduct:

(a) Delaying or obstructing the remedies referred to in article 17, paragraph 2 *(f)*, and article 20, paragraph 2;

(b) Failure to record the deprivation of liberty of any person, or the recording of any information which the official responsible for the official register knew or should have known to be inaccurate;

(c) Refusal to provide information on the deprivation of liberty of a person, or the provision of inaccurate information, even though the legal requirements for providing such information have been met.

Article 23

1. Each State Party shall ensure that the training of law enforcement personnel, civil or military, medical personnel, public officials and other persons who may be involved in the custody or treatment of any person deprived of liberty includes the necessary education and information regarding the relevant provisions of this Convention, in order to:

(a) Prevent the involvement of such officials in enforced disappearances;

(b) Emphasize the importance of prevention and investigations in relation to enforced disappearances;

(c) Ensure that the urgent need to resolve cases of enforced disappearance is recognized.

2. Each State Party shall ensure that orders or instructions prescribing, authorizing or encouraging enforced disappearance are prohibited. Each State Party shall guarantee that a person who refuses to obey such an order will not be punished.

3. Each State Party shall take the necessary measures to ensure that the persons referred to in paragraph 1 of this article who have reason to believe that an enforced disappearance has occurred or is planned report the matter to their superiors and, where necessary, to the appropriate authorities or bodies vested with powers of review or remedy.

Article 24

1. For the purposes of this Convention, "victim" means the disappeared person and any individual who has suffered harm as the direct result of an enforced disappearance.

2. Each victim has the right to know the truth regarding the circumstances of the enforced disappearance, the progress and results of the investigation and the fate of the disappeared person. Each State Party shall take appropriate measures in this regard.

3. Each State Party shall take all appropriate measures to search for, locate and release disappeared persons and, in the event of death, to locate, respect and return their remains.

4. Each State Party shall ensure in its legal system that the victims of enforced disappearance have the right to obtain reparation and prompt, fair and adequate compensation.

5. The right to obtain reparation referred to in paragraph 4 of this article covers material and moral damages and, where appropriate, other forms of reparation such as:

(a) Restitution;

(b) Rehabilitation;

(c) Satisfaction, including restoration of dignity and reputation;

(d) Guarantees of non-repetition.

6. Without prejudice to the obligation to continue the investigation until the fate of the disappeared person has been clarified, each State Party shall take the appropriate steps with regard to the legal situation of disappeared persons whose fate has not been clarified and that of their relatives, in fields such as social welfare, financial matters, family law and property rights.

7. Each State Party shall guarantee the right to form and participate freely in organizations and associations concerned with attempting to establish the circumstances of enforced disappearances and the fate of disappeared persons, and to assist victims of enforced disappearance.

Article 25

1. Each State Party shall take the necessary measures to prevent and punish under its criminal law:

(a) The wrongful removal of children who are subjected to enforced disappearance, children whose father, mother or legal guardian is subjected to enforced disappearance or children born during the captivity of a mother subjected to enforced disappearance;

(b) The falsification, concealment or destruction of documents attesting to the true identity of the children referred to in subparagraph (a) above.

2. Each State Party shall take the necessary measures to search for and identify the children referred to in paragraph 1 (a) of this article and to return them to their families of origin, in accordance with legal procedures and applicable international agreements.

3. States Parties shall assist one another in searching for, identifying and locating the children referred to in paragraph 1 (a) of this article.

4. Given the need to protect the best interests of the children referred to in paragraph 1 (a) of this article and their right to preserve, or to have re-established, their identity, including their nationality, name and family relations as recognized by law, States Parties which recognize a system of adoption or other form of placement of children shall have legal procedures in place to review the adoption or placement procedure, and, where appropriate, to annul any adoption or placement of children that originated in an enforced disappearance.

5. In all cases, and in particular in all matters relating to this article, the best interests of the child shall be a primary consideration, and a child who is capable of forming his or her own views shall have the right to express those views freely, the views of the child being given due weight in accordance with the age and maturity of the child.

Part II

Article 26

1. A Committee on Enforced Disappearances (hereinafter referred to as "the Committee") shall be established to carry out the functions provided for under this Conven-

tion. The Committee shall consist of ten experts of high moral character and recognized competence in the field of human rights, who shall serve in their personal capacity and be independent and impartial. The members of the Committee shall be elected by the States Parties according to equitable geographical distribution. Due account shall be taken of the usefulness of the participation in the work of the Committee of persons having relevant legal experience and of balanced gender representation.

2. The members of the Committee shall be elected by secret ballot from a list of persons nominated by States Parties from among their nationals, at biennial meetings of the States Parties convened by the Secretary-General of the United Nations for this purpose. At those meetings, for which two thirds of the States Parties shall constitute a quorum, the persons elected to the Committee shall be those who obtain the largest number of votes and an absolute majority of the votes of the representatives of States Parties present and voting.

3. The initial election shall be held no later than six months after the date of entry into force of this Convention. Four months before the date of each election, the Secretary-General of the United Nations shall address a letter to the States Parties inviting them to submit nominations within three months. The Secretary-General shall prepare a list in alphabetical order of all persons thus nominated, indicating the State Party which nominated each candidate, and shall submit this list to all States Parties.

4. The members of the Committee shall be elected for a term of four years. They shall be eligible for re-election once. However, the term of five of the members elected at the first election shall expire at the end of two years; immediately after the first election, the names of these five members shall be chosen by lot by the chairman of the meeting referred to in paragraph 2 of this article.

5. If a member of the Committee dies or resigns or for any other reason can no longer perform his or her Committee duties, the State Party which nominated him or her shall, in accordance with the criteria set out in paragraph 1 of this article, appoint another candidate from among its nationals to serve out his or her term, subject to the approval of the majority of the States Parties. Such approval shall be considered to have been obtained unless half or more of the States Parties respond negatively within six weeks of having been informed by the Secretary-General of the United Nations of the proposed appointment.

6. The Committee shall establish its own rules of procedure.

7. The Secretary-General of the United Nations shall provide the Committee with the necessary means, staff and facilities for the effective performance of its functions. The Secretary-General of the United Nations shall convene the initial meeting of the Committee.

8. The members of the Committee shall be entitled to the facilities, privileges and immunities of experts on mission for the United Nations, as laid down in the relevant sections of the Convention on the Privileges and Immunities of the United Nations.

9. Each State Party shall cooperate with the Committee and assist its members in the fulfilment of their mandate, to the extent of the Committee's functions that the State Party has accepted.

Article 27

A Conference of the States Parties will take place at the earliest four years and at the latest six years following the entry into force of this Convention to evaluate the functioning of the Committee and to decide, in accordance with the procedure described in article 44, paragraph 2, whether it is appropriate to transfer to another body—without excluding any possibility—the monitoring of this Convention, in accordance with the functions defined in articles 28 to 36.

Article 28

1. In the framework of the competencies granted by this Convention, the Committee shall cooperate with all relevant organs, offices and specialized agencies and funds of the United Nations, with the treaty bodies instituted by international instruments, with the special procedures of the United Nations and with the relevant regional intergovernmental organizations or bodies, as well as with all relevant State institutions, agencies or offices working towards the protection of all persons against enforced disappearances.

2. As it discharges its mandate, the Committee shall consult other treaty bodies instituted by relevant international human rights instruments, in particular the Human Rights Committee instituted by the International Covenant on Civil and Political Rights, with a view to ensuring the consistency of their respective observations and recommendations.

Article 29

1. Each State Party shall submit to the Committee, through the Secretary-General of the United Nations, a report on the measures taken to give effect to its obligations under this Convention, within two years after the entry into force of this Convention for the State Party concerned.

2. The Secretary-General of the United Nations shall make this report available to all States Parties.

3. Each report shall be considered by the Committee, which shall issue such comments, observations or recommendations as it may deem appropriate. The comments, observations or recommendations shall be communicated to the State Party concerned, which may respond to them, on its own initiative or at the request of the Committee.

4. The Committee may also request States Parties to provide additional information on the implementation of this Convention.

Article 30

1. A request that a disappeared person should be sought and found may be submitted to the Committee, as a matter of urgency, by relatives of the disappeared person or their legal representatives, their counsel or any person authorized by them, as well as by any other person having a legitimate interest.

2. If the Committee considers that a request for urgent action submitted in pursuance of paragraph 1 of this article:

(a) Is not manifestly unfounded;

(b) Does not constitute an abuse of the right of submission of such requests;

(c) Has already been duly presented to the competent bodies of the State Party concerned, such as those authorized to undertake investigations, where such a possibility exists;

(d) Is not incompatible with the provisions of this Convention; and

(e) The same matter is not being examined under another procedure of international investigation or settlement of the same nature;

it shall request the State Party concerned to provide it with information on the situation of the persons sought, within a time limit set by the Committee.

3. In the light of the information provided by the State Party concerned in accordance with paragraph 2 of this article, the Committee may transmit recommendations to the State Party, including a request that the State Party should take all the necessary measures, including interim measures, to locate and protect the person concerned in accordance with this Convention and to inform the Committee, within a specified period of time, of measures taken, taking into account the urgency of the situation. The Committee shall inform the person submitting the urgent action request of its recommendations and of the information provided to it by the State as it becomes available.

4. The Committee shall continue its efforts to work with the State Party concerned for as long as the fate of the person sought remains unresolved. The person presenting the request shall be kept informed.

Article 31

1. A State Party may at the time of ratification of this Convention or at any time afterwards declare that it recognizes the competence of the Committee to receive and consider communications from or on behalf of individuals subject to its jurisdiction claiming to be victims of a violation by this State Party of provisions of this Convention. The Committee shall not admit any communication concerning a State Party which has not made such a declaration.

2. The Committee shall consider a communication inadmissible where:

(a) The communication is anonymous;

(b) The communication constitutes an abuse of the right of submission of such communications or is incompatible with the provisions of this Convention;

(c) The same matter is being examined under another procedure of international investigation or settlement of the same nature; or where

(d) All effective available domestic remedies have not been exhausted. This rule shall not apply where the application of the remedies is unreasonably prolonged.

3. If the Committee considers that the communication meets the requirements set out in paragraph 2 of this article, it shall transmit the communication to the State Party concerned, requesting it to provide observations and comments within a time limit set by the Committee.

4. At any time after the receipt of a communication and before a determination on the merits has been reached, the Committee may transmit to the State Party concerned for its urgent consideration a request that the State Party will take such interim measures as may be necessary to avoid possible irreparable damage to the victims of the alleged violation. Where the Committee exercises its discretion, this does not imply a determination on admissibility or on the merits of the communication.

5. The Committee shall hold closed meetings when examining communications under the present article. It shall inform the author of a communication of the responses provided by the State Party concerned. When the Committee decides to finalize the procedure, it shall communicate its views to the State Party and to the author of the communication.

Article 32

A State Party to this Convention may at any time declare that it recognizes the competence of the Committee to receive and consider communications in which a State Party claims that another State Party is not fulfilling its obligations under this Convention. The

Committee shall not receive communications concerning a State Party which has not made such a declaration, nor communications from a State Party which has not made such a declaration.

Article 33

1. If the Committee receives reliable information indicating that a State Party is seriously violating the provisions of this Convention, it may, after consultation with the State Party concerned, request one or more of its members to undertake a visit and report back to it without delay.

2. The Committee shall notify the State Party concerned, in writing, of its intention to organize a visit, indicating the composition of the delegation and the purpose of the visit. The State Party shall answer the Committee within a reasonable time.

3. Upon a substantiated request by the State Party, the Committee may decide to postpone or cancel its visit.

4. If the State Party agrees to the visit, the Committee and the State Party concerned shall work together to define the modalities of the visit and the State Party shall provide the Committee with all the facilities needed for the successful completion of the visit.

5. Following its visit, the Committee shall communicate to the State Party concerned its observations and recommendations.

Article 34

If the Committee receives information which appears to it to contain well-founded indications that enforced disappearance is being practiced on a widespread or systematic basis in the territory under the jurisdiction of a State Party, it may, after seeking from the State Party concerned all relevant information on the situation, urgently bring the matter to the attention of the General Assembly of the United Nations, through the Secretary-General of the United Nations.

Article 35

1. The Committee shall have competence solely in respect of enforced disappearances which commenced after the entry into force of this Convention.

2. If a State becomes a party to this Convention after its entry into force, the obligations of that State vis-à-vis the Committee shall relate only to enforced disappearances which commenced after the entry into force of this Convention for the State concerned.

Article 36

1. The Committee shall submit an annual report on its activities under this Convention to the States Parties and to the General Assembly of the United Nations.

2. Before an observation on a State Party is published in the annual report, the State Party concerned shall be informed in advance and shall be given reasonable time to answer. This State Party may request the publication of its comments or observations in the report.

Part III

Article 37

Nothing in this Convention shall affect any provisions which are more conducive to the protection of all persons from enforced disappearance and which may be contained in:

(a) The law of a State Party;

(b) International law in force for that State.

Article 38

1. This Convention is open for signature by all Member States of the United Nations.

2. This Convention is subject to ratification by all Member States of the United Nations. Instruments of ratification shall be deposited with the Secretary-General of the United Nations.

3. This Convention is open to accession by all Member States of the United Nations. Accession shall be effected by the deposit of an instrument of accession with the Secretary-General.

Article 39

1. This Convention shall enter into force on the thirtieth day after the date of deposit with the Secretary-General of the United Nations of the twentieth instrument of ratification or accession.

2. For each State ratifying or acceding to this Convention after the deposit of the twentieth instrument of ratification or accession, this Convention shall enter into force on the thirtieth day after the date of the deposit of that State's instrument of ratification or accession.

Article 40

The Secretary-General of the United Nations shall notify all States Members of the United Nations and all States which have signed or acceded to this Convention of the following:

(*a*) Signatures, ratifications and accessions under article 38;

(*b*) The date of entry into force of this Convention under article 39.

Article 41

The provisions of this Convention shall apply to all parts of federal States without any limitations or exceptions.

Article 42

1. Any dispute between two or more States Parties concerning the interpretation or application of this Convention which cannot be settled through negotiation or by the procedures expressly provided for in this Convention shall, at the request of one of them, be submitted to arbitration. If within six months from the date of the request for arbitration the Parties are unable to agree on the organization of the arbitration, any one of those Parties may refer the dispute to the International Court of Justice by request in conformity with the Statute of the Court.

2. A State may, at the time of signature or ratification of this Convention or accession thereto, declare that it does not consider itself bound by paragraph 1 of this article. The other States Parties shall not be bound by paragraph 1 of this article with respect to any State Party having made such a declaration.

3. Any State Party having made a declaration in accordance with the provisions of paragraph 2 of this article may at any time withdraw this declaration by notification to the Secretary-General of the United Nations.

Article 43

This Convention is without prejudice to the provisions of international humanitarian law, including the obligations of the High Contracting Parties to the four Geneva Conventions of 12 August 1949 and the two Additional Protocols thereto of 8 June 1977, or to the opportunity available to any State Party to authorize the International Committee of the Red Cross to visit places of detention in situations not covered by international humanitarian law.

Article 44

1. Any State Party to this Convention may propose an amendment and file it with the Secretary-General of the United Nations. The Secretary-General shall thereupon communicate the proposed amendment to the States Parties to this Convention with a request that they indicate whether they favour a conference of States Parties for the purpose of considering and voting upon the proposal. In the event that within four months from the date of such communication at least one third of the States Parties favour such a conference, the Secretary-General shall convene the conference under the auspices of the United Nations.

2. Any amendment adopted by a majority of two thirds of the States Parties present and voting at the conference shall be submitted by the Secretary-General of the United Nations to all the States Parties for acceptance.

3. An amendment adopted in accordance with paragraph 1 of this article shall enter into force when two thirds of the States Parties to this Convention have accepted it in accordance with their respective constitutional processes.

4. When amendments enter into force, they shall be binding on those States Parties which have accepted them, other States Parties still being bound by the provisions of this Convention and any earlier amendment which they have accepted.

Article 45

1. This Convention, of which the Arabic, Chinese, English, French, Russian and Spanish texts are equally authentic, shall be deposited with the Secretary-General of the United Nations.

2. The Secretary-General of the United Nations shall transmit certified copies of this Convention to all States referred to in article 38.

Inter-American Convention on the Forced Disappearance of Persons
done in Belem do Para, Brazil, June 9, 1994

The Member States of the Organization of American States,

Disturbed by the persistence of the forced disappearance of persons;

Reaffirming that the true meaning of American solidarity and good neighborliness can be none other than that of consolidating in this Hemisphere, in the framework of democratic institutions, a system of individual freedom and social justice based on respect for essential human rights;

Considering that the forced disappearance of persons is an affront to the conscience of the Hemisphere and a grave and abominable offense against the inherent dignity of the human being, and one that contradicts the principles and purposes enshrined in the Charter of the Organization of American States;

Considering that the forced disappearance of persons violates numerous non-derogable and essential human rights enshrined in the American Convention on Human Rights, in the American Declaration of the Rights and Duties of Man, and in the Universal Declaration of Human Rights;

Recalling that the international protection of human rights is in the form of a convention reinforcing or complementing the protection provided by domestic law and is based upon the attributes of the human personality;

Reaffirming that the systematic practice of the forced disappearance of persons constitutes a crime against humanity;

Hoping that this Convention may help to prevent, punish, and eliminate the forced disappearance of persons in the Hemisphere and make a decisive contribution to the protection of human rights and the rule of law,

Resolve to adopt the following Inter-American Convention on the Forced Disappearance of Persons:

Article I

The States Parties to this Convention undertake:

(a) Not to practice, permit, or tolerate the forced disappearance of persons, even in states of emergency or suspension of individual guarantees;

(b) To punish within their jurisdictions those persons who commit or attempt to commit the crime of forced disappearance of persons and their accomplices and accessories;

(c) To cooperate with one another in helping to prevent, punish and eliminate the forced disappearance of persons;

(d) To take legislative, administrative, judicial, and any other measures necessary to comply with the commitments undertaken in this Convention.

Article II

For the purposes of this Convention, forced disappearance is considered to be the act of depriving a person or persons of his or their freedom, in whatever way, perpetrated by agents of the state or by persons or groups of persons acting with the authorization, support, or acquiescence of the state, followed by an absence of information or a refusal to acknowledge that deprivation of freedom or to give information on the whereabouts of that person, thereby impeding his or her recourse to the applicable legal remedies and procedural guarantees.

Article III

The States Parties undertake to adopt, in accordance with their constitutional procedures, the legislative measures that may be needed to define the forced disappearance of persons as an offense and to impose an appropriate punishment commensurate with its extreme gravity. This offense shall be deemed continuous or permanent as long as the fate or whereabouts of the victim has not been determined.

The States Parties may establish mitigating circumstances for persons who have participated in acts constituting forced disappearance when they help to cause the victim to reappear alive or provide information that sheds light on the forced disappearance of a person.

Article IV

The acts constituting the forced disappearance of persons shall be considered offenses in every State Party. Consequently, each State Party shall take measures to establish its jurisdiction over such cases in the following instances:

(a) When the forced disappearance of persons or any act constituting such offense was committed within its jurisdiction;

(b) When the accused is a national of that state;

(c) When the victim is a national of that state and that state sees fit to do so.

Every State Party shall, moreover, take the necessary measures to establish its jurisdiction over the crime described in this Convention when the alleged criminal is within its territory and it does not proceed to extradite him.

This Convention does not authorize any State Party to undertake, in the territory of another State Party, the exercise of jurisdiction or the performance of functions that are placed within the exclusive purview of the authorities of that other Party by its domestic law.

Article V

The forced disappearance of persons shall not be considered a political offense for purposes of extradition.

The forced disappearance of persons shall be deemed to be included among the extraditable offenses in every extradition treaty entered into between State Parties.

The States Parties undertake to include the offense of forced disappearance as one which is extraditable in every extradition treaty to be concluded between them in the future.

Every State Party that makes extradition conditional on the existence of a treaty and receives a request for extradition from another State Party with which it has no extradition treaty may consider this Convention as the necessary legal basis for extradition with respect to the offense of forced disappearance.

State Parties which do not make extradition conditional on the existence of a treaty shall recognize such offense as extraditable, subject to the conditions imposed by the law of the requested state.

Extradition shall be subject to the provisions set forth in the constitution and other laws of the requested state.

Article VI

When a State Party does not grant the extradition, the case shall be submitted to its competent authorities as if the offense had been committed within its jurisdiction, for the purposes of investigation and when appropriate, for criminal action, in accordance with its national law. Any decision adopted by these authorities shall be communicated to the state that has requested the extradition.

Article VII

Criminal prosecution for the forced disappearance of persons and the penalty judicially imposed on its perpetrator shall not be subject to statutes of limitations.

However, if there should be a norm of a fundamental character preventing application of the stipulation contained in the previous paragraph, the period of limitation shall be equal to that which applies to the gravest crime in the domestic laws of the corresponding State Party.

Article VIII

The defense of due obedience to superior orders or instructions that stipulate, authorize, or encourage forced disappearance shall not be admitted.

All persons who receive such orders have the right and duty not to obey them.

The States Parties shall ensure that the training of public law-enforcement personnel or officials includes the necessary education on the offense of forced disappearance of persons.

Article IX

Persons alleged to be responsible for the acts constituting the offense of forced disappearance of persons may be tried only in the competent jurisdictions of ordinary law in each state, to the exclusion of all other special jurisdictions, particularly military jurisdictions.

The acts constituting forced disappearance shall not be deemed to have been committed in the course of military duties.

Privileges, immunities, or special dispensations shall not be admitted in such trials, without prejudice to the provisions set forth in the Vienna Convention on Diplomatic Relations.

Article X

In no case may exceptional circumstances such as a state of war, the threat of war, internal political instability, or any other public emergency be invoked to justify the forced disappearance of persons. In such cases, the right to expeditious and effective judicial procedures and recourse shall be retained as a means of determining the whereabouts or state of health of a person who has been deprived of freedom, or of identifying the official who ordered or carried out such deprivation of freedom.

In pursuing such procedures or recourse, and in keeping with applicable domestic law, the competent judicial authorities shall have free and immediate access to all detention centers and to each of their units, and to all places where there is reason to believe the disappeared person might be found, including places that are subject to military jurisdiction.

Article XI

Every person deprived of liberty shall be held in an officially recognized place of detention and be brought before a competent judicial authority without delay, in accordance with applicable domestic law.

The States Parties shall establish and maintain official up-to-date registries of their detainees and, in accordance with their domestic law, shall make them available to relatives, judges, attorneys, any other person having a legitimate interest, and other authorities.

Article XII

The States Parties shall give each other mutual assistance in the search for, identification, location, and return of minors who have been removed to another state or detained therein as a consequence of the forced disappearance of their parents or guardians.

Article XIII

For the purposes of this Convention, the processing of petitions or communications presented to the Inter-American Commission on Human Rights alleging the forced disappearance of persons shall be subject to the procedures established in the American Convention on Human Rights and to the Statute and Regulations of the Inter-American Commission on Human Rights and to the Statute and Rules of Procedure of the Inter-American Court of Human Rights, including the provisions on precautionary measures.

Article XIV

Without prejudice to the provisions of the preceding article, when the Inter-American Commission on Human Rights receives a petition or communication regarding an alleged forced disappearance, its Executive Secretariat shall urgently and confidentially address the respective government and shall request that government to provide as soon as possible information as to the whereabouts of the allegedly disappeared person together with any other information it considers pertinent, and such request shall be without prejudice as to the admissibility of the petition.

Article XV

None of the provisions of this Convention shall be interpreted as limiting other bilateral or multilateral treaties or other agreements signed by the Parties.

This Convention shall not apply to the international armed conflicts governed by the 1949 Geneva Convention and its Protocol concerning protection of wounded, sick, and shipwrecked members of the armed forces; and prisoners of war and civilians in time of war.

Article XVI

This Convention is open for signature by the member states of the Organization of American States.

Article XVII

This Convention is subject to ratification. The instruments of ratification shall be deposited with the General Secretariat of the Organization of American States.

Article XVIII

This Convention shall be open to accession by any other state. The instruments of accession shall be deposited with the General Secretariat of the Organization of American States.

Article XIX

The states may make reservations with respect to this Convention when signing, ratifying or acceding to it, unless such reservations are incompatible with the object and purpose of the Convention and as long as they refer to one or more specific provisions.

Article XX

This Convention shall enter into force for the ratifying states on the thirtieth day from the date of deposit of the second instrument of ratification.

For each state ratifying or acceding to the Convention after the second instrument of ratification has been deposited, the Convention shall enter into force on the thirtieth day from the date on which that state deposited its instrument of ratification or accession.

Article XXI

This Convention shall remain in force indefinitely, but may be denounced by any State Party. The instrument of denunciation shall be deposited with the General Secretariat of the Organization of American States. The Convention shall cease to be in effect for the denouncing state and shall remain in force for the other State Parties one year from the date of deposit of the instrument of denunciation.

Article XXII

The original instrument of this Convention, the Spanish, English, Portuguese and French texts of which are equally authentic, shall be deposited with the General Secretariat of the Organization of American States, which shall forward certified copies thereof to the United Nations Secretariat, for registration and publication, in accordance with Article 102 of the Charter of the United Nations. The General Secretariat of the Organization of

American States shall notify member states of the Organization and states acceding to the Convention of the signatures and deposit of instruments of ratification, accession or denunciation, as well as of any reservations that may be expressed.

In Witness Whereof the undersigned Plenipotentiaries, being duly authorized thereto by their respective governments, have signed this Convention, which shall be called the "Inter-American Convention on the Forced Disappearance of Persons."

Convention on the Safety of United Nations and Associated Personnel
U.N. G.A. Res. 49/59 (9 Dec. 1994)

The General Assembly,

Considering that the codification and progressive development of international law contributes to the implementation of the purposes and principles set forth in Articles 1 and 2 of the Charter of the United Nations,

Gravely concerned at the increasing number of attacks on United Nations and associated personnel that have caused death or serious injury,

Bearing in mind that United Nations operations may be conducted in situations that entail risk to the safety of United Nations and associated personnel,

Recognizing the need to strengthen and to keep under review arrangements for the protection of United Nations and associated personnel,

Recalling its resolution 48/37 of 9 December 1993, by which it established the Ad Hoc Committee on the Elaboration of an International Convention Dealing with the Safety and Security of United Nations and Associated Personnel, with particular reference to responsibility for attacks on such personnel,

Taking into account the report of the Ad Hoc Committee, in particular the revised negotiating text resulting from the work of the Ad Hoc Committee,

Recalling its decision, in accordance with the recommendation of the Ad Hoc Committee, to re-establish, at its current session, a working group within the framework of the Sixth Committee to continue consideration of the revised negotiating text and of proposals relating thereto,

Having considered the text of the draft convention prepared by the working group and submitted to the Sixth Committee for consideration with a view to its adoption,

1. Adopts and opens for signature and ratification, acceptance or approval, or for accession, the Convention on the Safety of United Nations and Associated Personnel, the text of which is annexed to the present resolution;

2. Urges States to take all appropriate measures to ensure the safety and security of United Nations and associated personnel within their territory;

3. Recommends that the safety and security of United Nations and associated personnel be kept under continuing review by all relevant bodies of the Organization;

4. Underlines the importance it attaches to the speedy conclusion of a comprehensive review of arrangements for compensation for death, disability, injury or illness attributable to peace-keeping service, with a view to developing equitable and appropriate arrangements and to ensuring expeditious reimbursement.

Annex
Convention on the Safety of United Nations and Associated Personnel

The States Parties to this Convention,

Deeply concerned over the growing number of deaths and injuries resulting from deliberate attacks against United Nations and associated personnel,

Bearing in mind that attacks against, or other mistreatment of, personnel who act on behalf of the United Nations are unjustifiable and unacceptable, by whomsoever committed,

Recognizing that United Nations operations are conducted in the common interest of the international community and in accordance with the principles and purposes of the Charter of the United Nations,

Acknowledging the important contribution that United Nations and associated personnel make in respect of United Nations efforts in the fields of preventive diplomacy, peacemaking, peace-keeping, peace-building and humanitarian and other operations,

Conscious of the existing arrangements for ensuring the safety of United Nations and associated personnel, including the steps taken by the principal organs of the United Nations, in this regard,

Recognizing none the less that existing measures of protection for United Nations and associated personnel are inadequate,

Acknowledging that the effectiveness and safety of United Nations operations are enhanced where such operations are conducted with the consent and cooperation of the host State,

Appealing to all States in which United Nations and associated personnel are deployed and to all others on whom such personnel may rely, to provide comprehensive support aimed at facilitating the conduct and fulfilling the mandate of United Nations operations,

Convinced that there is an urgent need to adopt appropriate and effective measures for the prevention of attacks committed against United Nations and associated personnel and for the punishment of those who have committed such attacks,

Have agreed as follows:

Article 1. Definitions

For the purposes of this Convention:

(a) "United Nations personnel" means:

(i) Persons engaged or deployed by the Secretary-General of the United Nations as members of the military, police or civilian components of a United Nations operation;

(ii) Other officials and experts on mission of the United Nations or its specialized agencies or the International Atomic Energy Agency who are present in an official capacity in the area where a United Nations operation is being conducted;

(b) "Associated personnel" means:

(i) Persons assigned by a Government or an intergovernmental organization with the agreement of the competent organ of the United Nations;

(ii) Persons engaged by the Secretary-General of the United Nations or by a specialized agency or by the International Atomic Energy Agency;

(iii) Persons deployed by a humanitarian non-governmental organization or agency under an agreement with the Secretary-General of the United Nations or with a specialized agency or with the International Atomic Energy Agency, to carry out activities in support of the fulfilment of the mandate of a United Nations operation;

(c) "United Nations operation" means an operation established by the competent organ of the United Nations in accordance with the Charter of the United Nations and conducted under United Nations authority and control:

(i) Where the operation is for the purpose of maintaining or restoring international peace and security; or

(ii) Where the Security Council or the General Assembly has declared, for the purposes of this Convention, that there exists an exceptional risk to the safety of the personnel participating in the operation;

(d) "Host State" means a State in whose territory a United Nations operation is conducted;

(e) "Transit State" means a State, other than the host State, in whose territory United Nations and associated personnel or their equipment are in transit or temporarily present in connection with a United Nations operation.

Article 2. Scope of application

1. This Convention applies in respect of United Nations and associated personnel and United Nations operations, as defined in Article 1.

2. This Convention shall not apply to a United Nations operation authorized by the Security Council as an enforcement action under Chapter VII of the Charter of the United Nations in which any of the personnel are engaged as combatants against organized armed forces and to which the law of international armed conflict applies.

Article 3. Identification

1. The military and police components of a United Nations operation and their vehicles, vessels and aircraft shall bear distinctive identification. Other personnel, vehicles, vessels and aircraft involved in the United Nations operation shall be appropriately identified unless otherwise decided by the Secretary-General of the United Nations.

2. All United Nations and associated personnel shall carry appropriate identification documents.

Article 4. Agreements on the status of the operation

The host State and the United Nations shall conclude as soon as possible an agreement on the status of the United Nations operation and all personnel engaged in the operation including, *inter alia*, provisions on privileges and immunities for military and police components of the operation.

Article 5. Transit

A transit State shall facilitate the unimpeded transit of United Nations and associated personnel and their equipment to and from the host State.

Article 6. Respect for laws and regulations

1. Without prejudice to such privileges and immunities as they may enjoy or to the requirements of their duties, United Nations and associated personnel shall:

(a) Respect the laws and regulations of the host State and the transit State; and

(b) Refrain from any action or activity incompatible with the impartial and international nature of their duties.

2. The Secretary-General of the United Nations shall take all appropriate measures to ensure the observance of these obligations.

Article 7. Duty to ensure the safety and security of United Nations and associated personnel

1. United Nations and associated personnel, their equipment and premises shall not be made the object of attack or of any action that prevents them from discharging their mandate.

2. States Parties shall take all appropriate measures to ensure the safety and security of United Nations and associated personnel. In particular, States Parties shall take all appropriate steps to protect United Nations and associated personnel who are deployed in their territory from the crimes set out in Article 9.

3. States Parties shall cooperate with the United Nations and other States Parties, as appropriate, in the implementation of this Convention, particularly in any case where the host State is unable itself to take the required measures.

Article 8. Duty to release or return United Nations and associated personnel captured or detained

Except as otherwise provided in an applicable status-of-forces agreement, if United Nations or associated personnel are captured or detained in the course of the performance of their duties and their identification has been established, they shall not be subjected to interrogation and they shall be promptly released and returned to United Nations or other appropriate authorities. Pending their release such personnel shall be treated in accordance with universally recognized standards of human rights and the principles and spirit of the Geneva Conventions of 1949.

Article 9. Crimes against United Nations and associated personnel

1. The intentional commission of:

(a) A murder, kidnapping or other attack upon the person or liberty of any United Nations or associated personnel;

(b) A violent attack upon the official premises, the private accommodation or the means of transportation of any United Nations or associated personnel likely to endanger his or her person or liberty;

(c) A threat to commit any such attack with the objective of compelling a physical or juridical person to do or to refrain from doing any act;

(d) An attempt to commit any such attack; and

(e) An act constituting participation as an accomplice in any such attack, or in an attempt to commit such attack, or in organizing or ordering others to commit such attack, shall be made by each State Party a crime under its national law.

2. Each State Party shall make the crimes set out in paragraph 1 punishable by appropriate penalties which shall take into account their grave nature.

Article 10. Establishment of jurisdiction

1. Each State Party shall take such measures as may be necessary to establish its jurisdiction over the crimes set out in Article 9 in the following cases:

(a) When the crime is committed in the territory of that State or on board a ship or aircraft registered in that State;

(b) When the alleged offender is a national of that State.

2. A State Party may also establish its jurisdiction over any such crime when it is committed:

(a) By a stateless person whose habitual residence is in that State; or

(b) With respect to a national of that State; or

(c) In an attempt to compel that State to do or to abstain from doing any act.

3. Any State Party which has established jurisdiction as mentioned in paragraph 2 shall notify the Secretary-General of the United Nations. If such State Party subsequently rescinds that jurisdiction, it shall notify the Secretary-General of the United Nations.

4. Each State Party shall take such measures as may be necessary to establish its jurisdiction over the crimes set out in Article 9 in cases where the alleged offender is present in its territory and it does not extradite such person pursuant to Article 15 to any of the States Parties which have established their jurisdiction in accordance with paragraph 1 or 2.

5. This Convention does not exclude any criminal jurisdiction exercised in accordance with national law.

Article 11. Prevention of crimes against United Nations and associated personnel

States Parties shall cooperate in the prevention of the crimes set out in Article 9, particularly by:

(a) Taking all practicable measures to prevent preparations in their respective territories for the commission of those crimes within or outside their territories; and

(b) Exchanging information in accordance with their national law and coordinating the taking of administrative and other measures as appropriate to prevent the commission of those crimes.

Article 12. Communication of information

1. Under the conditions provided for in its national law, the State Party in whose territory a crime set out in Article 9 has been committed shall, if it has reason to believe that an alleged offender has fled from its territory, communicate to the Secretary-General of the United Nations and, directly or through the Secretary-General, to the State or States concerned all the pertinent facts regarding the crime committed and all available information regarding the identity of the alleged offender.

2. Whenever a crime set out in Article 9 has been committed, any State Party which has information concerning the victim and circumstances of the crime shall endeavour to transmit such information, under the conditions provided for in its national law, fully and promptly to the Secretary-General of the United Nations and the State or States concerned.

Article 13. Measures to ensure prosecution or extradition

1. Where the circumstances so warrant, the State Party in whose territory the alleged offender is present shall take the appropriate measures under its national law to ensure that person's presence for the purpose of prosecution or extradition.

2. Measures taken in accordance with paragraph 1 shall be notified, in conformity with national law and without delay, to the Secretary-General of the United Nations and, either directly or through the Secretary-General, to:

(a) The State where the crime was committed;

(b) The State or States of which the alleged offender is a national or, if such person is a stateless person, in whose territory that person has his or her habitual residence;

(c) The State or States of which the victim is a national; and

(d) Other interested States.

Article 14. Prosecution of alleged offenders

The State Party in whose territory the alleged offender is present shall, if it does not extradite that person, submit, without exception whatsoever and without undue delay, the case to its competent authorities for the purpose of prosecution, through proceedings in accordance with the law of that State. Those authorities shall take their decision in the same manner as in the case of an ordinary offence of a grave nature under the law of that State.

Article 15. Extradition of alleged offenders

1. To the extent that the crimes set out in Article 9 are not extraditable offences in any extradition treaty existing between States Parties, they shall be deemed to be included as such therein. States Parties undertake to include those crimes as extraditable offences in every extradition treaty to be concluded between them.

2. If a State Party which makes extradition conditional on the existence of a treaty receives a request for extradition from another State Party with which it has no extradition treaty, it may at its option consider this Convention as the legal basis for extradition in respect of those crimes. Extradition shall be subject to the conditions provided in the law of the requested State.

3. States Parties which do not make extradition conditional on the existence of a treaty shall recognize those crimes as extraditable offences between themselves subject to the conditions provided in the law of the requested State.

4. Each of those crimes shall be treated, for the purposes of extradition between States Parties, as if it had been committed not only in the place in which it occurred but also in the territories of the States Parties which have established their jurisdiction in accordance with paragraph 1 or 2 of Article 10.

Article 16. Mutual assistance in criminal matters

1. States Parties shall afford one another the greatest measure of assistance in connection with criminal proceedings brought in respect of the crimes set out in Article 9, including assistance in obtaining evidence at their disposal necessary for the proceedings. The law of the requested State shall apply in all cases.

2. The provisions of paragraph 1 shall not affect obligations concerning mutual assistance embodied in any other treaty.

Article 17. Fair treatment

1. Any person regarding whom investigations or proceedings are being carried out in connection with any of the crimes set out in Article 9 shall be guaranteed fair treatment, a fair trial and full protection of his or her rights at all stages of the investigations or proceedings.

2. Any alleged offender shall be entitled:

(a) To communicate without delay with the nearest appropriate representative of the State or States of which such person is a national or which is otherwise entitled to protect that person's rights or, if such person is a stateless person, of the State which, at that person's request, is willing to protect that person's rights; and

(b) To be visited by a representative of that State or those States.

Article 18. Notification of outcome of proceedings

The State Party where an alleged offender is prosecuted shall communicate the final outcome of the proceedings to the Secretary-General of the United Nations, who shall transmit the information to other States Parties.

Article 19. Dissemination

The States Parties undertake to disseminate this Convention as widely as possible and, in particular, to include the study thereof, as well as relevant provisions of international humanitarian law, in their programmes of military instruction.

Article 20. Savings clauses

Nothing in this Convention shall affect:

(a) The applicability of international humanitarian law and universally recognized standards of human rights as contained in international instruments in relation to the protection of United Nations operations and United Nations and associated personnel or the responsibility of such personnel to respect such law and standards;

(b) The rights and obligations of States, consistent with the Charter of the United Nations, regarding the consent to entry of persons into their territories;

(c) The obligation of United Nations and associated personnel to act in accordance with the terms of the mandate of a United Nations operation;

(d) The right of States which voluntarily contribute personnel to a United Nations operation to withdraw their personnel from participation in such operation; or

(e) The entitlement to appropriate compensation payable in the event of death, disability, injury or illness attributable to peace-keeping service by persons voluntarily contributed by States to United Nations operations.

Article 21. Right of self-defence

Nothing in this Convention shall be construed so as to derogate from the right to act in self-defence.

Article 22. Dispute settlement

1. Any dispute between two or more States Parties concerning the interpretation or application of this Convention which is not settled by negotiation shall, at the request of one of them, be submitted to arbitration. If within six months from the date of the request for arbitration the parties are unable to agree on the organization of the arbitration, any one of those parties may refer the dispute to the International Court of Justice by application in conformity with the Statute of the Court.

2. Each State Party may at the time of signature, ratification, acceptance or approval of this Convention or accession thereto declare that it does not consider itself bound by all or part of paragraph 1. The other States Parties shall not be bound by paragraph 1 or the relevant part thereof with respect to any State Party which has made such a reservation.

3. Any State Party which has made a reservation in accordance with paragraph 2 may at any time withdraw that reservation by notification to the Secretary-General of the United Nations.

Article 23. Review meetings

At the request of one or more States Parties, and if approved by a majority of States Parties, the Secretary-General of the United Nations shall convene a meeting of the States Parties to review the implementation of the Convention, and any problems encountered with regard to its application.

Article 24. Signature

This Convention shall be open for signature by all States, until 31 December 1995, at United Nations Headquarters in New York.

Article 25. Ratification, acceptance or approval

This Convention is subject to ratification, acceptance or approval. Instruments of ratification, acceptance or approval shall be deposited with the Secretary-General of the United Nations.

Article 26. Accession

This Convention shall be open for accession by any State. The instruments of accession shall be deposited with the Secretary-General of the United Nations.

Article 27. Entry into force

1. This Convention shall enter into force thirty days after twenty-two instruments of ratification, acceptance, approval or accession have been deposited with the Secretary-General of the United Nations.

2. For each State ratifying, accepting, approving or acceding to the Convention after the deposit of the twenty-second instrument of ratification, acceptance, approval or accession, the Convention shall enter into force on the thirtieth day after the deposit by such State of its instrument of ratification, acceptance, approval or accession.

Article 28. Denunciation

1. A State Party may denounce this Convention by written notification to the Secretary-General of the United Nations.

2. Denunciation shall take effect one year following the date on which notification is received by the Secretary-General of the United Nations.

Article 29. Authentic texts

The original of this Convention, of which the Arabic, Chinese, English, French, Russian and Spanish texts are equally authentic, shall be deposited with the Secretary-General of the United Nations, who shall send certified copies thereof to all States.

U.N. G.A. Resolution 46/51
U.N. Doc. A/46/654 (9 Dec. 1991)

The General Assembly, ...

Recalling moreover the existing international conventions relating to various aspects of the problem of international terrorism, *inter alia,* the Convention on Offenses and Certain Other Acts Committed on Board Aircraft, signed at Tokyo on 14 September 1963, the Convention for the Suppression of Unlawful Seizure of Aircraft, signed at The Hague on 16 December 1970, the Convention for the Suppression of Unlawful Acts against the Safety of Civil Aviation, concluded at Montreal on 23 September 1971, the Convention on the Prevention and Punishment of Crimes against Internationally Protected Persons, including Diplomatic Agents, adopted in New York on 14 December 1973, the International Convention against the Taking of Hostages, adopted in New York on 17 December 1979, the Convention on the Physical Protection of Nuclear Material, adopted at Vienna on 3 March 1980, the Protocol for the Suppression of Unlawful Acts of Violence at Airports Serving International Civil Aviation, supplementary to the Convention for the Suppression of Unlawful Acts against the Safety of Civil Aviation, signed at Montreal on 24 February 1988, the Convention for the Suppression of Unlawful Acts against the Safety of Maritime Navigation, done at Rome on 10 March 1988, the Protocol for the Suppression of Unlawful Acts against the Safety of Fixed Platforms located on the Continental Shelf, done at Rome on 10 March 1988, and the Convention on the Marking of Plastic Explosives for the Purpose of Detection, done at Montreal on 1 March 1991,

Convinced that a policy of firmness and effective measures should be taken in accordance with international law in order that all acts, methods and practices of international terrorism may be brought to an end,

Taking note of Security Council resolution 638 (1989) of 31 July 1989 on the taking of hostages,

Deeply disturbed by the world-wide persistence of acts of international terrorism in all its forms, including those in which States are directly or indirectly involved, which endanger or take innocent lives, have a deleterious effect on international relations and may jeopardize the territorial integrity and security of States,

Calling attention to the growing connection between terrorist groups and drug traffickers,

Convinced of the importance of the observance by States of their obligations under the relevant international conventions to ensure that appropriate law enforcement measures are taken in connection with the offenses addressed in those conventions,

Convinced also of the importance of expanding and improving international cooperation among States, on a bilateral, regional and multilateral basis, which will contribute to the elimination of acts of international terrorism and their underlying causes and to the prevention and elimination of this criminal scourge,

Convinced further that international cooperation in combating and preventing terrorism will contribute to the strengthening of confidence among States, reduce tensions and create a better climate among them,

Mindful of the need to enhance the role of the United Nations and the relevant specialized agencies in combating international terrorism,

Mindful also of the necessity of maintaining and protecting the basic rights of, and guarantees for, the individual in accordance with the relevant international human rights instruments and generally accepted international standards,

Reaffirming the principle of self-determination of peoples as enshrined in the Charter of the United Nations,

Reaffirming also the inalienable right to self-determination and independence of all peoples under colonial and racist regimes and other forms of alien domination and foreign occupation, and upholding the legitimacy of their struggle, in particular the struggle of national liberation movements, in accordance with the purposes and principles of the Charter and the Declaration on Principles of International Law concerning Friendly Relations and Cooperation among States in accordance with the Charter of the United Nations,

Recognizing that the effectiveness of the struggle against terrorism could be enhanced by the establishment of a generally agreed definition of international terrorism,

Taking note of the report of the Secretary-General,

1. *Once again unequivocally condemns,* as criminal and unjustifiable, all acts, methods and practices of terrorism wherever and by whomever committed, including those which jeopardize the friendly relations among States and their security;

2. *Deeply deplores* the loss of human lives which results from such acts of terrorism, as well as the pernicious impact of these acts on relations and cooperation among States;

3. *Calls upon* all States to fulfil their obligations under international law to refrain from organizing, instigating, assisting or participating in terrorist acts in other States, or acquiescing in or encouraging activities within their territory directed towards the commission of such acts;

4. *Urges* all States to fulfil their obligations under international law and take effective and resolute measures for the speedy and final elimination of international terrorism and to that end, in particular:

(a) To prevent the preparation and operations in their respective territories, for commission within or outside their territories, of terrorist and subversive acts directed against other States and their citizens;

(b) To ensure the apprehension and prosecution or extradition or perpetrators of terrorist acts;

(c) To endeavor to conclude special agreements to that effect on a bilateral, regional and multilateral basis;

(d) To cooperate with one another in exchanging relevant information concerning the prevention and combating of terrorism;

(e) To take promptly all steps necessary to implement the existing international conventions on this subject to which they are parties, including the harmonization of their domestic legislation with those conventions;

5. *Appeals* to all States that have not yet done so to consider becoming party to the international conventions relating to various aspects of international terrorism referred to in the preamble to the present resolution;

6. *Urges* all States, unilaterally and in cooperation with other States, as well as relevant United Nations organs, to contribute to the progressive elimination of the causes underlying international terrorism and to pay special attention to all situations, including colonialism, racism and situations involving mass and flagrant violations of human rights and fundamental freedoms and those involving alien domination and foreign occupation, that may give rise to international terrorism and may endanger international peace and security;

7. *Firmly calls* for the immediate and safe release of all hostages and abducted persons, wherever and by whomever they are being held;

8. *Calls upon* all States to use their political influence in accordance with the Charter of the United Nations and the principles of international law to secure the safe release of all hostages and abducted persons and to prevent the commission of acts of hostage-taking and abduction;

9. *Expresses concern* at the growing and dangerous links between terrorist groups, drug traffickers and their paramilitary gangs, which have resorted to all types of violence, thus endangering the constitutional order of States and violating basic human rights;

10. *Welcomes* the efforts undertaken by the International Civil Aviation Organization aimed at promoting universal acceptance of, and strict compliance with, international air security conventions, and welcomes the recent adoption of the Convention on the Marking of Plastic Explosives for the Purpose of Detection;

11. *Requests* the other relevant specialized agencies and intergovernmental organizations, in particular the International Maritime Organization, the Universal Postal Union, the World Tourism Organization, the International Atomic Energy Agency and the United Nations Educational, Scientific and Cultural Organization, within their respective spheres of competence, to consider what further measures can usefully be taken to combat and eliminate terrorism;

12. *Requests* the Secretary-General to continue seeking the views of Member States on international terrorism in all its aspects and on ways and means of combating it, including the convening at an appropriate time, under the auspices of the United Nations, of an international conference to deal with international terrorism in the light of the proposal referred to in the penultimate preambular paragraph of General Assembly resolution 44/29 [calling for an international conference to define terrorism]; ...

15. *Considers* that nothing in the present resolution could in any way prejudice the right to self-determination, freedom and independence, as derived from the Charter of the United Nations, of peoples forcibly deprived of that right referred to in the Declaration on Principles of International Law concerning Friendly Relations and Cooperation among States in accordance with the Charter of the United Nations, particularly peoples under colonial and racist regimes or other forms of alien domination, or the right of these peoples to struggle legitimately to this end and to seek and receive support in accordance with the principles of the Charter, the above-mentioned Declaration and the relevant General Assembly resolutions, including the present resolution.

Declaration on Measures to Eliminate International Terrorism
U.N. G.A. Res. 49/60 (9 Dec. 1994)

The General Assembly,

Recalling its resolution 46/51 of 9 December 1991 and its decision 48/411 of 9 December 1993,

Taking note of the report of the Secretary-General,

Having considered in depth the question of measures to eliminate international terrorism,

Convinced that the adoption of the declaration on measures to eliminate international terrorism should contribute to the enhancement of the struggle against international terrorism,

1. Approves the Declaration on Measures to Eliminate International Terrorism, the text of which is annexed to the present resolution;

2. Invites the Secretary-General to inform all States, the Security Council, the International Court of Justice and the relevant specialized agencies, organizations and organisms of the adoption of the Declaration;

3. Urges that every effort be made in order that the Declaration becomes generally known and is observed and implemented in full;

4. Urges States, in accordance with the provisions of the Declaration, to take all appropriate measures at the national and international levels to eliminate terrorism;....

ANNEX
Declaration on Measures to Eliminate International Terrorism

The General Assembly,

Guided by the purposes and principles of the Charter of the United Nations,

Recalling the Declaration on Principles of International Law concerning Friendly Relations and Cooperation among States in accordance with the Charter of the United Nations, the Declaration on the Strengthening of International Security, the Definition of Aggression, the Declaration on the Enhancement of the Effectiveness of the Principle of Refraining from the Threat or Use of Force in International Relations, the Vienna Declaration and Programme of Action, adopted by the World Conference on Human Rights, the International Covenant on Economic, Social and Cultural Rights and the International Covenant on Civil and Political Rights,

Deeply disturbed by the world-wide persistence of acts of international terrorism in all its forms and manifestations, including those in which States are directly or indirectly involved, which endanger or take innocent lives, have a deleterious effect on international relations and may jeopardize the security of States,

Deeply concerned by the increase, in many regions of the world, of acts of terrorism based on intolerance or extremism,

Concerned at the growing and dangerous links between terrorist groups and drug traffickers and their paramilitary gangs, which have resorted to all types of violence, thus endangering the constitutional order of States and violating basic human rights,

Convinced of the desirability for closer coordination and cooperation among States in combating crimes closely connected with terrorism, including drug trafficking, unlawful arms trade, money laundering and smuggling of nuclear and other potentially deadly materials, and bearing in mind the role that could be played by both the United Nations and regional organizations in this respect,

Firmly determined to eliminate international terrorism in all its forms and manifestations,

Convinced also that the suppression of acts of international terrorism, including those in which States are directly or indirectly involved, is an essential element for the maintenance of international peace and security,

Convinced further that those responsible for acts of international terrorism must be brought to justice,

Stressing the imperative need to further strengthen international cooperation between States in order to take and adopt practical and effective measures to prevent, combat and eliminate all forms of terrorism that affect the international community as a whole,

Conscious of the important role that might be played by the United Nations, the relevant specialized agencies and States in fostering widespread cooperation in preventing and combating international terrorism, inter alia, by increasing public awareness of the problem,

Recalling the existing international treaties relating to various aspects of the problem of international terrorism...,

Welcoming the conclusion of regional agreements and mutually agreed declarations to combat and eliminate terrorism in all its forms and manifestations,

Convinced of the desirability of keeping under review the scope of existing international legal provisions to combat terrorism in all its forms and manifestations, with the aim of ensuring a comprehensive legal framework for the prevention and elimination of terrorism,

Solemnly declares the following:

I

1. The States Members of the United Nations solemnly reaffirm their unequivocal condemnation of all acts, methods and practices of terrorism, as criminal and unjustifiable, wherever and by whomever committed, including those which jeopardize the friendly relations among States and peoples and threaten the territorial integrity and security of States;

2. Acts, methods and practices of terrorism constitute a grave violation of the purposes and principles of the United Nations, which may pose a threat to international peace and security, jeopardize friendly relations among States, hinder international cooperation and aim at the destruction of human rights, fundamental freedoms and the democratic bases of society;

3. Criminal acts intended or calculated to provoke a state of terror in the general public, a group of persons or particular persons for political purposes are in any circumstance unjustifiable, whatever the considerations of a political, philosophical, ideological, racial, ethnic, religious or any other nature that may be invoked to justify them;

II

4. States, guided by the purposes and principles of the Charter of the United Nations and other relevant rules of international law, must refrain from organizing, instigating, assisting or participating in terrorist acts inn territories of other States, or from acquiescing in or encouraging activities within their territories directed towards the commission of such acts;

5. States must also fulfil their obligations under the Charter of the United Nations and other provisions of international law with respect to combating international terrorism and are urged to take effective and resolute measures in accordance with the relevant provisions of international law and international standards of human rights for the speedy and final elimination of international terrorism, in particular:

(a) To refrain from organizing, instigating, facilitating, financing, encouraging or tolerating activities and to take appropriate practical measures to ensure that their respective territories are not used for terrorist installations or training camps, or for the preparation of organization of terrorist acts intended to be committed against other States or their citizens;

(b) To ensure the apprehension and prosecution or extradition of perpetrators of terrorist acts, in accordance with the relevant provisions of their national law;

(c) To endeavour to conclude special agreements to that effect on a bilateral, regional and multilateral basis, and to prepare, to that effect, model agreements on cooperation;

(d) To cooperate with one another in exchanging relevant information concerning the prevention and combating of terrorism;

(e) To take promptly all steps necessary to implement the existing international conventions on this subject to which they are parties, including the harmonization of their domestic legislation with those conventions;

(f) To take appropriate measures, before granting asylum, for the purpose of ensuring that the asylum seeker has not engaged in terrorist activities and, after granting asylum, for the purpose of ensuring that the refugee status is not used in a manner contrary to the provisions set out in subparagraph (a) above; ...

III

9. The United Nations, the relevant specialized agencies and intergovernmental organizations and other relevant bodies must make every effort with a view to promoting measures to combat and eliminate acts of terrorism and to strengthening their role in this field; ...

IV

11. All States are urged to promote and implement in good faith and effectively the provisions of the present Declaration in all its aspects;

12. Emphasis is placed on the need to pursue efforts aiming at eliminating definitively all acts of terrorism by the strengthening of international cooperation and progressive development of international law and its codification, as well as by enhancement of coordination between, and increase of the efficiency of, the United Nations and the relevant specialized agencies, organizations and bodies.

Protection of Human Rights and Fundamental Freedoms While Countering Terrorism
U.N. G.A. Res. 59/191 (20 Dec. 2004)

The General Assembly,

Reaffirming the purposes and principles of the Charter of the United Nations,

Reaffirming also the fundamental importance, including in response to terrorism and the fear of terrorism, of respecting all human rights and fundamental freedoms and the rule of law,

Recalling that States are under the obligation to protect all human rights and fundamental freedoms of all persons, and deploring violations of human rights and fundamental freedoms in the context of the fight against terrorism,

Recognizing that the respect for human rights, the respect for democracy and the respect for the rule of law are interrelated and mutually reinforcing,

Noting the declarations, statements and recommendations of a number of human rights treaty monitoring bodies and special procedures on the question of the compatibility of counter-terrorism measures with human rights obligations, ...

Reaffirming that acts, methods and practices of terrorism in all its forms and manifestations are activities aimed at the destruction of human rights, fundamental freedoms and democracy, threatening the territorial integrity and the security of States and destabilizing legitimately constituted Governments, and that the international community should take the necessary steps to enhance cooperation to prevent and combat terrorism, ...

Reaffirming its unequivocal condemnation of all acts, methods and practices of terrorism in all its forms and manifestations, wherever and by whomever committed, regardless of their motivation, as criminal and unjustifiable, and renewing its commitment to strengthen international cooperation to prevent and combat terrorism,

Deploring the suffering caused by terrorism to the victims and their families and expressing its profound solidarity with them,

Stressing that everyone is entitled to all the rights and freedoms recognized in the Universal Declaration of Human Rights without distinction of any kind, including on the grounds of race, colour, sex, language, religion, political or other opinion, national or social origin, property, birth or other status,

1. *Reaffirms* that States must ensure that any measure taken to combat terrorism complies with their obligations under international law, in particular international human rights, refugee and humanitarian law;

2. *Also reaffirms* the obligations of States, in accordance with article 4 of the International Covenant on Civil and Political Rights, to respect certain rights as non-derogable in any circumstances, recalls, in regard to all other Covenant rights, that any measures derogating from the provisions of the Covenant must be in accordance with that article in all cases, and underlines the exceptional and temporary nature of any such derogations;

3. *Calls upon* States to raise awareness about the importance of these obligations among national authorities involved in combating terrorism....

Human Rights and Terrorism
U.N. G.A. Res. 59/195 (20 Dec. 2004)

The General Assembly,

Guided by the Charter of the United Nations, the Universal Declaration of Human Rights, the Declaration on Principles of International Law concerning Friendly Relations and Cooperation among States in accordance with the Charter of the United Nations and the International Covenants on Human Rights, ...

Recalling previous resolutions of the Commission on Human Rights on the issue of human rights and terrorism, as well as on hostage-taking,

Bearing in mind all other relevant General Assembly resolutions,

Bearing in mind also relevant Security Council resolutions,

Aware that, at the dawn of the twenty-first century, the world is witness to historic and far-reaching transformations, in the course of which forces of aggressive nationalism and religious and ethnic extremism continue to produce fresh challenges,

Alarmed that acts of terrorism in all its forms and manifestations aimed at the destruction of human rights have continued despite national and international efforts,

Convinced that terrorism in all its forms and manifestations, wherever and by whomever committed, can never be justified in any instance, including as a means to promote and protect human rights, ...

Bearing in mind that the right to life is the basic human right, without which a human being can exercise no other right,

Bearing in mind also that terrorism creates an environment that destroys the right of people to live in freedom from fear,

Reiterating that all States have an obligation to promote and protect all human rights and fundamental freedoms and to ensure effective implementation of their obligations under international law,

Seriously concerned about the gross violations of human rights perpetuated by terrorist groups,

Expressing its deepest sympathy and condolences to all the victims of terrorism and their families,

Alarmed in particular at the possibility that terrorist groups may exploit new technologies to facilitate acts of terrorism, which may cause massive damage, including huge loss of life,

Emphasizing the need to intensify the fight against terrorism at the national level, to enhance effective international cooperation in combating terrorism in conformity with international law, including relevant State obligations under international human rights and international humanitarian law, and to strengthen the role of the United Nations in this respect,

Emphasizing also that States shall deny safe haven to those who finance, plan, support or commit terrorist acts or provide safe haven,

Reaffirming that all measures to counter terrorism must be in strict conformity with international law, including international human rights standards and obligations,

Mindful of the need to protect the human rights of and guarantees for the individual in accordance with the relevant human rights principles and instruments, in particular the right to life,

Noting the growing consciousness within the international community of the negative effects of terrorism in all its forms and manifestations on the full enjoyment of human rights and fundamental freedoms and on the establishment of the rule of law and democratic freedoms enshrined in the Charter of the United Nations and the International Covenants on Human Rights,

Concerned by the tendencies to link terrorism and violence with religion, ...

1. *Reiterates* its unequivocal condemnation of the acts, methods and practices of terrorism in all its forms and manifestations as activities aimed at the destruction of human rights, fundamental freedoms and democracy, threatening the territorial integrity and the security of States, destabilizing legitimately constituted Governments, undermining pluralistic civil society and having adverse consequences for the economic and social development of States;

2. *Strongly condemns* the violations of the right to life, liberty and security;

3. *Rejects* the identification of terrorism with any religion, nationality or culture;

4. *Profoundly deplores* the increasing number of innocent persons, including women, children and the elderly, killed, massacred and maimed by terrorists in indiscriminate and random acts of violence and terror, which cannot be justified in any circumstances;

5. *Expresses its solidarity* with the victims of terrorism;

6. *Reaffirms* the decision of the Heads of State and Government, as contained in the United Nations Millennium Declaration [res. 55/2], to take concerted action against international terrorism and to accede as soon as possible to all the relevant regional and international conventions;

7. *Urges* the international community to enhance cooperation at the regional and international levels in the fight against terrorism in all its forms and manifestations, in accordance with relevant international instruments, including those relating to human rights, with the aim of its eradication;

8. *Calls upon* States to take all necessary and effective measures, in accordance with relevant provisions of international law, including international human rights standards,

to prevent, combat and eliminate terrorism in all its forms and manifestations, wherever and by whomever it is committed, and also calls upon States to strengthen, where appropriate, their legislation to combat terrorism in all its forms and manifestations;

9. *Urges* all States to deny safe haven to terrorists;

10. *Calls upon* States to take appropriate measures, in conformity with relevant provisions of national and international law, including human rights standards, before granting refugee status, for the purpose of ensuring that an asylum-seeker has not planned, facilitated or participated in the commission of terrorist acts, including assassinations, and to ensure, in conformity with international law, that refugee status is not abused by the perpetrators, organizers or facilitators of terrorist acts and that claims of political motivation are not recognized as grounds for refusing requests for the extradition of alleged terrorists; ...

12. *Condemns* the incitement to ethnic hatred, violence and terrorism;

13. *Stresses* that every person, regardless of nationality, race, sex, religion or any other distinction, has a right to protection from terrorism and terrorist acts;

14. *Expresses concern* that the growing connection between terrorist groups and other criminal organizations engaged in the illegal traffic in arms and drugs at the national and international levels, as well as the consequent commission of serious crimes such as murder, extortion, kidnapping, assault, the taking of hostages and robbery, and requests the relevant United Nations bodies to continue to give special attention to this question;....

Lawfulness of Detentions by the United States in Guantanamo Bay

Parliamentary Assembly, Council of Europe,
Resolution 1433 (26 April 2005)

1. The Parliamentary Assembly recalls and restates its outrage and disgust at the terrorist attacks on the United States of America of 11 September 2001, the horror of which has not been dimmed by the passage of time. It shares the United States' determination to combat international terrorism and fully endorses the importance of detecting and preventing terrorist crimes, prosecuting and punishing terrorists and protecting human lives.

2. Whilst the Assembly therefore offers its full support to the United States in its efforts to fight terrorism, this must be on condition that all measures taken are fully respectful of human rights and the rule of law. Conformity with international human rights and humanitarian law is not a weakness in the fight against terrorism but a weapon, ensuring the widest international support for actions and avoiding situations which could provoke misplaced sympathy for terrorists or their causes.

3. The United States has long been a beacon of democracy and a champion of human rights throughout the world and its positive influence on European development in this respect since the Second World War is greatly appreciated. Nevertheless, the Assembly considers that the United States Government has betrayed its own highest principles in the zeal with which it has attempted to pursue the "war on terror". These errors have perhaps been most manifest in relation to Guantánamo Bay.

4. At no time have detentions at Guantánamo Bay been within a "legal black hole". International human rights law has at all times been fully applicable to all detainees. For those captured during the international armed conflict in Afghanistan, protection of certain rights may have been complemented by the provisions of international humanitarian law

(IHL) for the duration of that conflict. Since that international armed conflict ceased, however, international human rights standards have applied in the normal fashion.

5. The Assembly applauds and supports the work of the International Committee of the Red Cross (ICRC) and the various United Nations human rights protection mechanisms, along with that of non-governmental organisations including Human Rights First, the Center for Constitutional Rights and Amnesty International, in striving to improve detention conditions at Guantánamo Bay and ensure that detainees' rights are respected. It also thanks the European Commission for Democracy through Law (Venice Commission) for its opinion on the possible need for further development of the Geneva Conventions, produced in response to a request from the Assembly's Committee on Legal Affairs and Human Rights.

6. The Assembly recalls the evidence provided by Mr. Jamal Al Harith, former detainee, along with lawyers representing current and former detainees and other international experts, at the hearing held by its Committee on Legal Affairs and Human Rights in Paris on 17 December 2004.

7. On the basis of an extensive review of legal and factual material from these and other reliable sources, the Assembly concludes that the circumstances surrounding detentions by the United States at Guantánamo Bay show unlawfulness and inconsistency with the rule of law, on the following grounds:

i. many if not all detainees have been subjected to cruel, inhuman or degrading treatment occurring as a direct result of official policy, authorised at the very highest levels of government;

ii. many detainees have been subjected to ill-treatment amounting to torture which has occurred systematically and with the knowledge and complicity of the United States Government;

iii. the right of those detained in connection with the international armed conflict previously conducted by the United States in Afghanistan to be presumptively recognised as prisoners of war (POWs) and to have their status independently determined by a competent tribunal was not respected;

iv. there have been numerous violations of various aspects of all detainees' rights to liberty and security of the person, making their detention arbitrary;

v. there have been numerous violations of various aspects of all detainees' rights to fair trial, amounting to a flagrant denial of justice;

vi. the United States has engaged in the unlawful practice of secret detention;

vii. the United States has, by practising "rendition" (removal of persons to other countries, without judicial supervision, for purposes such as interrogation or detention), allowed detainees to be subjected to torture and to cruel, inhuman or degrading treatment, in violation of the prohibition on *non-refoulement*;

viii. the United States' proposals to return or transfer detainees to other countries, even where reliant on "diplomatic assurances" concerning the detainees' subsequent treatment, risk violating the prohibition on *non-refoulement*.

8. The Assembly therefore calls on the United States Government to ensure respect for the rule of law and human rights by remedying these situations and in particular:

i. to cease immediately all ill-treatment of Guantánamo Bay detainees;

ii. to investigate, prosecute and punish all instances of unlawful mistreatment of detainees, no matter what the status or office of the person responsible;

iii. to allow all detainees to challenge the lawfulness of their detention before a regularly constituted court competent to order their release if detention is not lawful;

iv. to release immediately all those detainees against whom there is not sufficient evidence to justify laying criminal charges;

v. to charge those suspected of criminal offences and bring them for trial before a competent, independent and impartial tribunal guaranteeing all the procedural safeguards required by international law, without delay, whilst excluding imposition of the death penalty against them;

vi. to respect its obligations under international law and the Constitution of the United States to exclude any statement established to have been made as a result of torture or other cruel, inhuman or degrading treatment or punishment from any proceedings, except against a person accused of such ill-treatment as evidence that the statement was made;

vii. to cease immediately the practice of secret detentions and to ensure full respect for the rights of any detainees currently held in secret, in particular the prohibition on torture and cruel, inhuman or degrading treatment and the right to have relatives informed of the fact of detention, to recognition as a person before the law, to judicial review of the lawfulness of detention and to release or trial without delay;

viii. to allow access to all detainees by family members, legal representatives, consular representatives and officials of international humanitarian and human rights organisations;

ix. to cease the practice of "rendition" in violation of the prohibition on *non-refoulement*;

x. not to return or transfer detainees in reliance on "diplomatic assurances" from countries known to engage in the systematic practice of torture and in all cases unless the absence of a risk of ill-treatment is firmly established;

xi. to comply fully and promptly with the recommendations of the ICRC and to avoid any actions that might have the effect of undermining its activities, reputation or standing.

9. Furthermore, the Assembly also calls on the United States Government to ensure that the "war on terror" is conducted in all respects in accordance with international law, particularly international human rights and humanitarian law.

10. In addition, the Assembly calls on member states of the Council of Europe:

i. to enhance their diplomatic and consular efforts to protect the rights and ensure the release of any of their citizens, nationals or former residents currently detained at Guantánamo Bay, whether legally obliged to do so or not;

ii. with respect to any of their citizens, nationals or former residents who have been returned or transferred from detention at Guantánamo Bay:

a. to treat such persons according to the usual provisions of criminal law, respecting the presumption in favour of immediate liberty on arrival;

b. to provide such persons with all necessary support and assistance, in particular legal aid to bring cases relating to detention at Guantánamo Bay;

c. to protect such persons from prejudice or discrimination and to ensure their mental and physical well-being during the process of reintegration;

d. to ensure that such persons do not suffer detriment to their rights or interests as a result of being held in unlawful detention at Guantánamo Bay, especially in relation to immigration status;

iii. not to permit their authorities to participate or assist in the interrogation of Guantánamo Bay detainees;

iv. to respect their obligations under international law to exclude any statement established to have been made as a result of torture or other cruel, inhuman or degrading treatment or punishment from any proceedings, except against a person accused of such ill-treatment as evidence that the statement was made;

v. to refuse to comply with United States' requests for extradition of terrorist suspects liable to detention at Guantánamo Bay;

vi. to refuse to comply with United States' requests for mutual legal assistance in relation to Guantánamo Bay detainees, other than by providing exculpatory evidence, or unless in connection with legal proceedings before a regularly constituted court;

vii. to ensure that their territory and facilities are not used in connection with practices of secret detention or rendition in possible violation of international human rights law;

viii. to respect the *erga omnes* nature of human rights by taking all possible measures to persuade the United States authorities to respect fully the rights under international law of all Guantánamo Bay detainees.

11. Finally, the Assembly resolves to pursue this issue further through bilateral dialogue with the United States Congress.

International Convention for the Suppression of Terrorist Bombings
adopted by U.N. G.A. Res. 52/164 (9 Jan. 1998) (15 Dec. 1997) 2149 U.N.T.S. 256

The States Parties to this Convention,

Having in mind the purposes and principles of the Charter of the United Nations concerning the maintenance of international peace and security and the promotion of good-neighbourliness and friendly relations and cooperation among States,

Deeply concerned about the worldwide escalation of acts of terrorism in all its forms and manifestations,

Recalling the Declaration on the Occasion of the Fiftieth Anniversary of the United Nations of 24 October 1995,

Recalling also the Declaration on Measures to Eliminate International Terrorism, annexed to General Assembly resolution 49/60 of 9 December 1994, in which, *inter alia,* "the States Members of the United Nations solemnly reaffirm their unequivocal condemnation of all acts, methods and practices of terrorism as criminal and unjustifiable, wherever and by whomever committed, including those which jeopardize the friendly relations among States and peoples and threaten the territorial integrity and security of States,"

Noting that the Declaration also encouraged States "to review urgently the scope of the existing international legal provisions on the prevention, repression and elimination of terrorism in all its forms and manifestations, with the aim of ensuring that there is a comprehensive legal framework covering all aspects of the matter,"

Recalling General Assembly resolution 51/210 of 17 December 1996 and the Declaration to Supplement the 1994 Declaration on Measures to Eliminate International Terrorism annexed thereto,

Noting that terrorist attacks by means of explosives or other lethal devices have become increasingly widespread,

Noting also that existing multilateral legal provisions do not adequately address these attacks,

Being convinced of the urgent need to enhance international cooperation between States in devising and adopting effective and practical measures for the prevention of such acts of terrorism and for the prosecution and punishment of their perpetrators,

Considering that the occurrence of such acts is a matter of grave concern to the international community as a whole,

Noting that the activities of military forces of States are governed by rules of international law outside the framework of this Convention and that the exclusion of certain actions from the coverage of this Convention does not condone or make lawful otherwise unlawful acts, or preclude prosecution under other laws,

Have agreed as follows:

Article 1

For the purposes of this Convention:

1. "State or government facility" includes any permanent or temporary facility or conveyance that is used or occupied by representatives of a State, members of Government, the legislature or the judiciary or by officials or employees of a State or any other public authority or entity or by employees or officials of an intergovernmental organization in connection with their official duties.

2. "Infrastructure facility" means any publicly or privately owned facility providing or distributing services for the benefit of the public, such as water, sewage, energy, fuel or communications.

3. "Explosive or other lethal device" means:

(a) An explosive or incendiary weapon or device that is designed, or has the capability, to cause death, serious bodily injury or substantial material damage; or

(b) A weapon or device that is designed, or has the capability, to cause death, serious bodily injury or substantial material damage through the release, dissemination or impact of toxic chemicals, biological agents or toxins or similar substances or radiation or radioactive material.

4. "Military forces of a State" means the armed forces of a State which are organized, trained and equipped under its internal law for the primary purpose of national defence or security and persons acting in support of those armed forces who are under their formal command, control and responsibility.

5. "Place of public use" means those parts of any building, land, street, waterway or other location that are accessible or open to members of the public, whether continuously, periodically or occasionally, and encompasses any commercial, business, cultural, historical, educational, religious, governmental, entertainment, recreational or similar place that is so accessible or open to the public.

6. "Public transportation system" means all facilities, conveyances and instrumentalities, whether publicly or privately owned, that are used in or for publicly available services for the transportation of persons or cargo.

Article 2

1. Any person commits an offence within the meaning of this Convention if that person unlawfully and intentionally delivers, places, discharges or detonates an explosive or other lethal device in, into or against a place of public use, a State or government facility, a public transportation system or an infrastructure facility:

(a) With the intent to cause death or serious bodily injury; or

(b) With the intent to cause extensive destruction of such a place, facility or system, where such destruction results in or is likely to result in major economic loss.

2. Any person also commits an offence if that person attempts to commit an offence as set forth in paragraph 1 of the present article.

3. Any person also commits an offence if that person:

(a) Participates as an accomplice in an offence as set forth in paragraph 1 or 2 of the present article; or

(b) Organizes or directs others to commit an offence as set forth in paragraph 1 or 2 of the present article; or

(c) In any other way contributes to the commission of one or more offences as set forth in paragraph 1 or 2 of the present article by a group of persons acting with a common purpose; such contribution shall be intentional and either be made with the aim of furthering the general criminal activity or purpose of the group or be made in the knowledge of the intention of the group to commit the offence or offences concerned.

Article 3

This Convention shall not apply where the offence is committed within a single State, the alleged offender and the victims are nationals of that State, the alleged offender is found in the territory of that State and no other State has a basis under Article 6, paragraph 1 or paragraph 2, of this Convention to exercise jurisdiction, except that the provisions of Articles 10 to 15 shall, as appropriate, apply in those cases.

Article 4

Each State Party shall adopt such measures as may be necessary:

(a) To establish as criminal offences under its domestic law the offences set forth in Article 2 of this Convention;

(b) To make those offences punishable by appropriate penalties which take into account the grave nature of those offences.

Article 5

Each State Party shall adopt such measures as may be necessary, including, where appropriate, domestic legislation, to ensure that criminal acts within the scope of this Convention, in particular where they are intended or calculated to provoke a state of terror in the general public or in a group of persons or particular persons, are under no circumstances justifiable by considerations of a political, philosophical, ideological, racial, ethnic, religious or other similar nature and are punished by penalties consistent with their grave nature.

Article 6

1. Each State Party shall take such measures as may be necessary to establish its jurisdiction over the offences set forth in Article 2 when:

(a) The offence is committed in the territory of that State; or

(b) The offence is committed on board a vessel flying the flag of that State or an aircraft which is registered under the laws of that State at the time the offence is committed; or

(c) The offence is committed by a national of that State.

2. A State Party may also establish its jurisdiction over any of that when:

(a) The offence is committed against a national of that State; or

(b) The offence is committed against a State or government facility of that State abroad, including an embassy or other diplomatic or consular premises of that State; or

(c) The offence is committed by a stateless person who has his or her habitual residence in the territory of that State; or

(d) The offence is committed in an attempt to compel that State to do or abstain from doing any act; or

(e) The offence is committed on board an aircraft which is operated by the Government of that State.

3. Upon ratifying, accepting, approving or acceding to this Convention, each State Party shall notify the Secretary-General of the United Nations of the jurisdiction it has established under its domestic law in accordance with paragraph 2 of the present article. Should any change take place, the State Party concerned shall immediately notify the Secretary-General.

4. Each State Party shall likewise take such measures as may be necessary to establish its jurisdiction over the offences set forth in Article 2 in cases where the alleged offender is present in its territory and it does not extradite that person to any of the States Parties which have established their jurisdiction in accordance with paragraph 1 or 2 of the present article.

5. This Convention does not exclude the exercise of any criminal jurisdiction established by a State Party in accordance with its domestic law.

Article 7

1. Upon receiving information that a person who has committed or who is alleged to have committed an offence as set forth in Article 2 may be present in its territory, the State Party concerned shall take such measures as may be necessary under its domestic law to investigate the facts contained in the information.

2. Upon being satisfied that the circumstances so warrant, the State Party in whose territory the offender or alleged offender is present shall take the appropriate measures under its domestic law so as to ensure that person's presence for the purpose of prosecution or extradition.

3. Any person regarding whom the measures referred to in paragraph 2 of the present article are being taken shall be entitled to:

(a) Communicate without delay with the nearest appropriate representative of the State of which that person is a national or which is otherwise entitled to protect that person's rights or, if that person is a stateless person, the State in the territory of which that person habitually resides;

(b) Be visited by a representative of that State;

(c) Be informed of that person's rights under subparagraphs (a) and (b).

4. The rights referred to in paragraph 3 of the present article shall be exercised in conformity with the laws and regulations of the State in he territory of which the offender or alleged offender is present, subject to the provision that the said laws and regulations must enable full effect to be given to the purposes for which the rights accorded under paragraph 3 are intended.

5. The provisions of paragraphs 3 and 4 of the present article shall be without prejudice to the right of any State Party having a claim to jurisdiction in accordance with Article 6, subparagraph 1 (c) or 2 (c),to invite the International Committee of the Red Cross to communicate with and visit the alleged offender.

6. When a State Party, pursuant to the present article, has taken a person into custody, it shall immediately notify, directly or through the Secretary-General of the United Nations, the States Parties which have established jurisdiction in accordance with Article 6, paragraphs 1 and 2, and, if it considers it advisable, any other interested States Parties, of the fact that that person is in custody and of he circumstances which warrant that person's detention. The State which makes the investigation contemplated in paragraph 1 of the present article shall promptly inform the said States Parties of its findings and shall indicate whether it intends to exercise jurisdiction.

Article 8

1. The State Party in the territory of which the alleged offender is present shall, in cases to which Article 6 applies, if it does not extradite that person, be obliged, without exception whatsoever and whether or not the offence was committed in its territory, to submit the case without undue delay to its competent authorities for the purpose of prosecution, through proceedings in accordance with the laws of that State. Those authorities shall take their decision in the same manner as in the case of any other offence of a grave nature under the law of that State.

2. Whenever a State Party is permitted under its domestic law to extradite or otherwise surrender one of its nationals only upon the condition that the person will be returned to that State to serve the sentence imposed as a result of the trial or proceeding for which the extradition or surrender of the person was sought, and this State and the State seeking the extradition of the person agree with this option and other terms they may deem appropriate, such a conditional extradition or surrender shall be sufficient to discharge the obligation set forth in paragraph 1 of the present article.

Article 9

1. The offences set forth in Article 2 shall be deemed to be included as extraditable offences in any extradition treaty existing between any of the States Parties before the entry into force of this Convention. States Parties undertake to include such offences as extraditable offences in every extradition treaty to be subsequently concluded between them.

2. When a State Party which makes extradition conditional on the existence of a treaty receives a request for extradition from another State Party with which it has no extradition treaty, the requested State Party may, at its option, consider this Convention as a legal basis for extradition in respect of the offences set forth in Article 2. Extradition shall be subject to the other conditions provided by the law of the requested State.

3. States Parties which do not make extradition conditional on the existence of a treaty shall recognize the offences set forth in Article 2 as extraditable offences between themselves, subject to the conditions provided by the law of the requested State.

4. If necessary, the offences set forth in Article 2 shall be treated, for the purposes of extradition between States Parties, as if they had been committed not only in the place in which they occurred but also in the territory of the States that have established jurisdiction in accordance with Article 6, paragraphs 1 and 2. The provisions of all extradition treaties and arrangements between States Parties with regard to offences set forth in Article 2 shall be deemed to be modified as between State Parties to the extent that they are incompatible with this Convention.

Article 10

1. States Parties shall afford one another the greatest measure of assistance in connection with investigations or criminal or extradition proceedings brought in respect of the offences set forth in Article 2,including assistance in obtaining evidence at their disposal necessary for the proceedings.

2. States Parties shall carry out their obligations under paragraph 1 of the present article in conformity with any treaties or other arrangements on mutual legal assistance that may exist between them. In the absence of such treaties or arrangements, States Parties shall afford one another assistance in accordance with their domestic law.

Article 11

None of the offences set forth in Article 2 shall be regarded, for the purposes of extradition or mutual legal assistance, as a political offence or as an offence connected with a political offence or as an offence inspired by political motives. Accordingly, a request for extradition or for mutual legal assistance based on such an offence may not be refused on the sole ground that it concerns a political offence or an offence connected with a political offence or an offence inspired by political motives.

Article 12

Nothing in this Convention shall be interpreted as imposing an obligation to extradite or to afford mutual legal assistance, if the requested State Party has substantial grounds for believing that the request for extradition for offences set forth in Article 2 or for mutual legal assistance with respect to such offences has been made for the purpose of prosecuting or punishing a person on account of that person's race, religion, nationality, ethnic origin or political opinion or that compliance with the request would cause prejudice to that person's position for any of these reasons.

Article 13

1. A person who is being detained or is serving a sentence in the territory of one State Party whose presence in another State Party is requested for purposes of testimony, identification or otherwise providing assistance in obtaining evidence for the investigation or prosecution of offences under this Convention may be transferred if the following conditions are met:

(a) The person freely gives his or her informed consent; and

(b) The competent authorities of both States agree, subject to such conditions as those States may deem appropriate.

2. For the purposes of the present article:

(a) The State to which the person is transferred shall have the authority and obligation to keep the person transferred in custody, unless otherwise requested or authorized by the State from which the person was transferred;

(b) The State to which the person is transferred shall without delay implement its obligation to return the person to the custody of the State from which the person was transferred as agreed beforehand, or as otherwise agreed, by the competent authorities of both States;

(c) The State to which the person is transferred shall not require the State from which the person was transferred to initiate extradition proceedings for the return of the person;

(d) The person transferred shall receive credit for service of the sentence being served in the State from which he was transferred for time spent in the custody of the State to which he was transferred. Unless the State Party from which a person is to be transferred in accordance with the present article so agrees, that person, whatever his or her nationality, shall not be prosecuted or detained or subjected to any other restriction of his or her personal liberty in the territory of the State to which that person is transferred in respect of acts or convictions anterior to his or her departure from the territory of the State from which such person was transferred.

Article 14

Any person who is taken into custody or regarding whom any other measures are taken or proceedings are carried out pursuant to this Convention shall be guaranteed fair treatment, including enjoyment of all rights and guarantees in conformity with the law of the State in the territory of which that person is present and applicable provisions of international law, including international law of human rights.

Article 15

States Parties shall cooperate in the prevention of the offences set forth in Article 2, particularly:

(a) By taking all practicable measures, including, if necessary, adapting their domestic legislation, to prevent and counter preparations in their respective territories for the commission of those offences within or outside their territories, including measures to prohibit in their territories illegal activities of persons, groups and organizations that encourage, instigate, organize, knowingly finance or engage in the perpetration of offences as set forth in Article 2;

(b) By exchanging accurate and verified information in accordance with their national law, and coordinating administrative and other measures taken as appropriate to prevent the commission of offences asset forth in Article 2;

(c) Where appropriate, through research and development regarding methods of detection of explosives and other harmful substances that can cause death or bodily injury, consultations on the development of standards for marking explosives in order to identify their origin in post-blast investigations, exchange of information on preventive measures, cooperation and transfer of technology, equipment and related materials.

Article 16

The State Party where the alleged offender is prosecuted shall, in accordance with its domestic law or applicable procedures, communicate the final outcome of the proceedings to the Secretary-General of the United Nations, who shall transmit the information to the other States Parties.

Article 17

The States Parties shall carry out their obligations under this Convention in a manner consistent with the principles of sovereign equality and territorial integrity of States and that of non-intervention in the domestic affairs of other States.

Article 18

Nothing in this Convention entitles a State Party to undertake in the territory of another State Party the exercise of jurisdiction and performance of functions which are exclusively reserved for the authorities of that other State Party by its domestic law.

Article 19

1. Nothing in this Convention shall affect other rights, obligations and responsibilities of States and individuals under international law, in particular the purposes and principles of the Charter of the United Nations and international humanitarian law.

2. The activities of armed forces during an armed conflict, as those terms are understood under international humanitarian law, which are governed by that law, are not governed by this Convention, and the activities undertaken by military forces of a State in the exercise of their official duties, inasmuch as they are governed by other rules of international law, are not governed by this Convention.

Article 20

1. Any dispute between two or more States Parties concerning the interpretation or application of this Convention which cannot be settled through negotiation within a reasonable time shall, at the request of one of them, be submitted to arbitration. If, within six months from the date of the request for arbitration, the parties are unable to agree on the organization of the arbitration, any one of those parties may refer the dispute to the International Court of Justice, by application, in conformity with the Statute of the Court.

2. Each State may at the time of signature, ratification, acceptance or approval of this Convention or accession thereto declare that it does not consider itself bound by paragraph 1 of the present article. The other States Parties shall not be bound by paragraph 1 with respect to any State Party which has made such a reservation.

3. Any State which has made a reservation in accordance with paragraph 2 of the present article may at any time withdraw that reservation by notification to the Secretary-General of the United Nations.

Article 21

1. This Convention shall be open for signature by all States from 12 January 1998 until 31 December 1999 at United Nations Headquarters in New York.

2. This Convention is subject to ratification, acceptance or approval. The instruments of ratification, acceptance or approval shall be deposited with the Secretary-General of the United Nations.

3. This Convention shall be open to accession by any State. The instruments of accession shall be deposited with the Secretary-General of the United Nations.

Article 22

1. This Convention shall enter into force on the thirtieth day following the date of the deposit of the twenty-second instrument of ratification, acceptance, approval or accession with the Secretary-General of the United Nations.

2. For each State ratifying, accepting, approving or acceding to the Convention after the deposit of the twenty-second instrument of ratification, acceptance, approval or accession, the Convention shall enter into force on the thirtieth day after deposit by such State of its instrument of ratification, acceptance, approval or accession.

Article 23

1. Any State Party may denounce this Convention by written notification to the Secretary-General of the United Nations.

2. Denunciation shall take effect one year following the date on which notification is received by the Secretary-General of the United Nations.

Article 24

The original of this Convention, of which the Arabic, Chinese, English, French, Russian and Spanish texts are equally authentic, shall be deposited with the Secretary-General of the United Nations, who shall send certified copies thereof to all States.

In Witness Whereof, the undersigned, being duly authorized thereto by their respective Governments, have signed this Convention, opened for signature at United Nations Headquarters in New York on 12 January 1998.

International Convention for the Suppression of the Financing of Terrorism
adopted by U.N. G.A. Res. 54/109 (9 December 1999)
2178 U.N.T.S. 197

Preamble

The States Parties to this Convention,

Bearing in mind the purposes and principles of the Charter of the United Nations concerning the maintenance of international peace and security and the promotion of good-neighbourliness and friendly relations and cooperation among States,

Deeply concerned about the worldwide escalation of acts of terrorism in all its forms and manifestations,

Recalling the Declaration on the Occasion of the Fiftieth Anniversary of the United Nations, contained in General Assembly resolution 50/6 of 24 October 1995,

Recalling also all the relevant General Assembly resolutions on the matter, including resolution 49/60 of 9 December 1994 and its annex on the Declaration on Measures to Eliminate International Terrorism, in which the States Members of the United Nations solemnly reaffirmed their unequivocal condemnation of all acts, methods and practices of terrorism as criminal and unjustifiable, wherever and by whomever committed, including those which jeopardize the friendly relations among States and peoples and threaten the territorial integrity and security of States,

Noting that the Declaration on Measures to Eliminate International Terrorism also encouraged States to review urgently the scope of the existing international legal provisions on the prevention, repression and elimination of terrorism in all its forms and manifestations, with the aim of ensuring that there is a comprehensive legal framework covering all aspects of the matter,

Recalling General Assembly resolution 51/210 of 17 December 1996, paragraph 3, subparagraph (f), in which the Assembly called upon all States to take steps to prevent and counteract, through appropriate domestic measures, the financing of terrorists and terrorist organizations, whether such financing is direct or indirect through organizations which also have or claim to have charitable, social or cultural goals or which are also engaged in unlawful activities such as illicit arms trafficking, drug dealing and racketeering, including the exploitation of persons for purposes of funding terrorist activities, and in particular to consider, where appropriate, adopting regulatory measures to prevent and counteract movements of funds suspected to be intended for terrorist purposes without impeding in any way the freedom of legitimate capital movements and to intensify the exchange of information concerning international movements of such funds,

Recalling also General Assembly resolution 52/165 of 15 December 1997, in which the Assembly called upon States to consider, in particular, the implementation of the measures set out in paragraphs 3 (a) to (f) of its resolution 51/210 of 17 December 1996,

Recalling further General Assembly resolution 53/108 of 8 December 1998, in which the Assembly decided that the Ad Hoc Committee established by General Assembly resolution 51/210 of 17 December 1996 should elaborate a draft international convention for the suppression of terrorist financing to supplement related existing international instruments,

Considering that the financing of terrorism is a matter of grave concern to the international community as a whole,

Noting that the number and seriousness of acts of international terrorism depend on the financing that terrorists may obtain,

Noting also that existing multilateral legal instruments do not expressly address such financing,

Being convinced of the urgent need to enhance international cooperation among States in devising and adopting effective measures for the prevention of the financing of terrorism, as well as for its suppression through the prosecution and punishment of its perpetrators,

Have agreed as follows:

Article 1

For the purposes of this Convention:

1. "Funds" means assets of every kind, whether tangible or intangible, movable or immovable, however acquired, and legal documents or instruments in any form, including electronic or digital, evidencing title to, or interest in, such assets, including, but not limited to, bank credits, travellers cheques, bank cheques, money orders, shares, securities, bonds, drafts, letters of credit.

2. "A State or governmental facility" means any permanent or temporary facility or conveyance that is used or occupied by representatives of a State, members of Government, the legislature or the judiciary or by officials or employees of a State or any other public authority or entity or by employees or officials of an intergovernmental organization in connection with their official duties.

3. "Proceeds" means any funds derived from or obtained, directly or indirectly, through the commission of an offence set forth in Article 2.

Article 2

1. Any person commits an offence within the meaning of this Convention if that person by any means, directly or indirectly, unlawfully and wilfully, provides or collects funds

with the intention that they should be used or in the knowledge that they are to be used, in full or in part, in order to carry out:

(a) An act which constitutes an offence within the scope of and as defined in one of the treaties listed in the annex; or

(b) Any other act intended to cause death or serious bodily injury to a civilian, or to any other person not taking an active part in the hostilities in a situation of armed conflict, when the purpose of such act, by its nature or context, is to intimidate a population, or to compel a government or an international organization to do or to abstain from doing any act.

2. (a) On depositing its instrument of ratification, acceptance, approval or accession, a State Party which is not a party to a treaty listed in the annex may declare that, in the application of this Convention to the State Party, the treaty shall be deemed not to be included in the annex referred to in paragraph 1, subparagraph (a). The declaration shall cease to have effect as soon as the treaty enters into force for the State Party, which shall notify the depositary of this fact;

(b) When a State Party ceases to be a party to a treaty listed in the annex, it may make a declaration as provided for in this article, with respect to that treaty.

3. For an act to constitute an offence set forth in paragraph 1, it shall not be necessary that the funds were actually used to carry out an offence referred to in paragraph 1, subparagraphs (a) or (b).

4. Any person also commits an offence if that person attempts to commit an offence as set forth in paragraph 1 of this article.

5. Any person also commits an offence if that person:

(a) Participates as an accomplice in an offence as set forth in paragraph 1 or 4 of this article;

(b) Organizes or directs others to commit an offence as set forth in paragraph 1 or 4 of this article;

(c) Contributes to the commission of one or more offences as set forth in paragraphs 1 or 4 of this article by a group of persons acting with a common purpose. Such contribution shall be intentional and shall either:

(i) Be made with the aim of furthering the criminal activity or criminal purpose of the group, where such activity or purpose involves the commission of an offence as set forth in paragraph 1 of this article; or

(ii) Be made in the knowledge of the intention of the group to commit an offence as set forth in paragraph 1 of this article.

Article 3

This Convention shall not apply where the offence is committed within a single State, the alleged offender is a national of that State and is present in the territory of that State and no other State has a basis under Article 7, paragraph 1, or Article 7, paragraph 2, to exercise jurisdiction, except that the provisions of Articles 12 to 18 shall, as appropriate, apply in those cases.

Article 4

Each State Party shall adopt such measures as may be necessary:

(a) To establish as criminal offences under its domestic law the offences set forth in Article 2;

(b) To make those offences punishable by appropriate penalties which take into account the grave nature of the offences.

Article 5

1. Each State Party, in accordance with its domestic legal principles, shall take the necessary measures to enable a legal entity located in its territory or organized under its laws to be held liable when a person responsible for the management or control of that legal entity has, in that capacity, committed an offence set forth in Article 2. Such liability may be criminal, civil or administrative.

2. Such liability is incurred without prejudice to the criminal liability of individuals having committed the offences.

3. Each State Party shall ensure, in particular, that legal entities liable in accordance with paragraph 1 above are subject to effective, proportionate and dissuasive criminal, civil or administrative sanctions. Such sanctions may include monetary sanctions.

Article 6

Each State Party shall adopt such measures as may be necessary, including, where appropriate, domestic legislation, to ensure that criminal acts within the scope of this Convention are under no circumstances justifiable by considerations of a political, philosophical, ideological, racial, ethnic, religious or other similar nature.

Article 7

1. Each State Party shall take such measures as may be necessary to establish its jurisdiction over the offences set forth in Article 2 when:

(a) The offence is committed in the territory of that State;

(b) The offence is committed on board a vessel flying the flag of that State or an aircraft registered under the laws of that State at the time the offence is committed;

(c) The offence is committed by a national of that State.

2. A State Party may also establish its jurisdiction over any such offence when:

(a) The offence was directed towards or resulted in the carrying out of an offence referred to in Article 2, paragraph 1, subparagraph (a) or (b), in the territory of or against a national of that State;

(b) The offence was directed towards or resulted in the carrying out of an offence referred to in Article 2, paragraph 1, subparagraph (a) or (b), against a State or government facility of that State abroad, including diplomatic or consular premises of that State;

(c) The offence was directed towards or resulted in an offence referred to in Article 2, paragraph 1, subparagraph (a) or (b), committed in an attempt to compel that State to do or abstain from doing any act;

(d) The offence is committed by a stateless person who has his or her habitual residence in the territory of that State;

(e) The offence is committed on board an aircraft which is operated by the Government of that State.

3. Upon ratifying, accepting, approving or acceding to this Convention, each State Party shall notify the Secretary-General of the United Nations of the jurisdiction it has established in accordance with paragraph 2. Should any change take place, the State Party concerned shall immediately notify the Secretary-General.

4. Each State Party shall likewise take such measures as may be necessary to establish its jurisdiction over the offences set forth in Article 2 in cases where the alleged offender is present in its territory and it does not extradite that person to any of the States Parties that have established their jurisdiction in accordance with paragraphs 1 or 2.

5. When more than one State Party claims jurisdiction over the offences set forth in Article 2, the relevant States Parties shall strive to coordinate their actions appropriately, in particular concerning the conditions for prosecution and the modalities for mutual legal assistance.

6. Without prejudice to the norms of general international law, this Convention does not exclude the exercise of any criminal jurisdiction established by a State Party in accordance with its domestic law.

Article 8

1. Each State Party shall take appropriate measures, in accordance with its domestic legal principles, for the identification, detection and freezing or seizure of any funds used or allocated for the purpose of committing the offences set forth in Article 2 as well as the proceeds derived from such offences, for purposes of possible forfeiture.

2. Each State Party shall take appropriate measures, in accordance with its domestic legal principles, for the forfeiture of funds used or allocated for the purpose of committing the offences set forth in Article 2 and the proceeds derived from such offences.

3. Each State Party concerned may give consideration to concluding agreements on the sharing with other States Parties, on a regular or case-by-case basis, of the funds derived from the forfeitures referred to in this article.

4. Each State Party shall consider establishing mechanisms whereby the funds derived from the forfeitures referred to in this article are utilized to compensate the victims of offences referred to in Article 2, paragraph 1, subparagraph (a) or (b), or their families.

5. The provisions of this article shall be implemented without prejudice to the rights of third parties acting in good faith.

Article 9

1. Upon receiving information that a person who has committed or who is alleged to have committed an offence set forth in Article 2 may be present in its territory, the State Party concerned shall take such measures as may be necessary under its domestic law to investigate the facts contained in the information.

2. Upon being satisfied that the circumstances so warrant, the State Party in whose territory the offender or alleged offender is present shall take the appropriate measures under its domestic law so as to ensure that person's presence for the purpose of prosecution or extradition.

3. Any person regarding whom the measures referred to in paragraph 2 are being taken shall be entitled to:

(a) Communicate without delay with the nearest appropriate representative of the State of which that person is a national or which is otherwise entitled to protect that person's rights or, if that person is a stateless person, the State in the territory of which that person habitually resides;

(b) Be visited by a representative of that State;

(c) Be informed of that person's rights under subparagraphs (a) and (b).

4. The rights referred to in paragraph 3 shall be exercised in conformity with the laws and regulations of the State in the territory of which the offender or alleged offender is present, subject to the provision that the said laws and regulations must enable full effect to be given to the purposes for which the rights accorded under paragraph 3 are intended.

5. The provisions of paragraphs 3 and 4 shall be without prejudice to the right of any State Party having a claim to jurisdiction in accordance with Article 7, paragraph 1, sub-paragraph (b), or paragraph 2, subparagraph (b), to invite the International Committee of the Red Cross to communicate with and visit the alleged offender.

6. When a State Party, pursuant to the present article, has taken a person into custody, it shall immediately notify, directly or through the Secretary-General of the United Nations, the States Parties which have established jurisdiction in accordance with Article 7, paragraph 1 or 2, and, if it considers it advisable, any other interested States Parties, of the fact that such person is in custody and of the circumstances which warrant that person's detention. The State which makes the investigation contemplated in paragraph 1 shall promptly inform the said States Parties of its findings and shall indicate whether it intends to exercise jurisdiction.

Article 10

1. The State Party in the territory of which the alleged offender is present shall, in cases to which Article 7 applies, if it does not extradite that person, be obliged, without exception whatsoever and whether or not the offence was committed in its territory, to submit the case without undue delay to its competent authorities for the purpose of prosecution, through proceedings in accordance with the laws of that State. Those authorities shall take their decision in the same manner as in the case of any other offence of a grave nature under the law of that State.

2. Whenever a State Party is permitted under its domestic law to extradite or otherwise surrender one of its nationals only upon the condition that the person will be returned to that State to serve the sentence imposed as a result of the trial or proceeding for which the extradition or surrender of the person was sought, and this State and the State seeking the extradition of the person agree with this option and other terms they may deem appropriate, such a conditional extradition or surrender shall be sufficient to discharge the obligation set forth in paragraph 1.

Article 11

1. The offences set forth in Article 2 shall be deemed to be included as extraditable offences in any extradition treaty existing between any of the States Parties before the entry into force of this Convention. States Parties undertake to include such offences as extraditable offences in every extradition treaty to be subsequently concluded between them.

2. When a State Party which makes extradition conditional on the existence of a treaty receives a request for extradition from another State Party with which it has no extradition treaty, the requested State Party may, at its option, consider this Convention as a legal basis for extradition in respect of the offences set forth in Article 2. Extradition shall be subject to the other conditions provided by the law of the requested State.

3. States Parties which do not make extradition conditional on the existence of a treaty shall recognize the offences set forth in Article 2 as extraditable offences between themselves, subject to the conditions provided by the law of the requested State.

4. If necessary, the offences set forth in Article 2 shall be treated, for the purposes of extradition between States Parties, as if they had been committed not only in the place

in which they occurred but also in the territory of the States that have established jurisdiction in accordance with Article 7, paragraphs 1 and 2.

5. The provisions of all extradition treaties and arrangements between States Parties with regard to offences set forth in Article 2 shall be deemed to be modified as between States Parties to the extent that they are incompatible with this Convention.

Article 12

1. States Parties shall afford one another the greatest measure of assistance in connection with criminal investigations or criminal or extradition proceedings in respect of the offences set forth in Article 2, including assistance in obtaining evidence in their possession necessary for the proceedings.

2. States Parties may not refuse a request for mutual legal assistance on the ground of bank secrecy.

3. The requesting Party shall not transmit nor use information or evidence furnished by the requested Party for investigations, prosecutions or proceedings other than those stated in the request without the prior consent of the requested Party.

4. Each State Party may give consideration to establishing mechanisms to share with other States Parties information or evidence needed to establish criminal, civil or administrative liability pursuant to Article 5.

5. States Parties shall carry out their obligations under paragraphs 1 and 2 in conformity with any treaties or other arrangements on mutual legal assistance or information exchange that may exist between them. In the absence of such treaties or arrangements, States Parties shall afford one another assistance in accordance with their domestic law.

Article 13

None of the offences set forth in Article 2 shall be regarded, for the purposes of extradition or mutual legal assistance, as a fiscal offence. Accordingly, States Parties may not refuse a request for extradition or for mutual legal assistance on the sole ground that it concerns a fiscal offence.

Article 14

None of the offences set forth in Article 2 shall be regarded for the purposes of extradition or mutual legal assistance as a political offence or as an offence connected with a political offence or as an offence inspired by political motives. Accordingly, a request for extradition or for mutual legal assistance based on such an offence may not be refused on the sole ground that it concerns a political offence or an offence connected with a political offence or an offence inspired by political motives.

Article 15

Nothing in this Convention shall be interpreted as imposing an obligation to extradite or to afford mutual legal assistance, if the requested State Party has substantial grounds for believing that the request for extradition for offences set forth in Article 2 or for mutual legal assistance with respect to such offences has been made for the purpose of prosecuting or punishing a person on account of that person's race, religion, nationality, ethnic origin or political opinion or that compliance with the request would cause prejudice to that person's position for any of these reasons.

Article 16

1. A person who is being detained or is serving a sentence in the territory of one State Party whose presence in another State Party is requested for purposes of identification,

testimony or otherwise providing assistance in obtaining evidence for the investigation or prosecution of offences set forth in Article 2 may be transferred if the following conditions are met:

(a) The person freely gives his or her informed consent;

(b) The competent authorities of both States agree, subject to such conditions as those States may deem appropriate.

2. For the purposes of the present article:

(a) The State to which the person is transferred shall have the authority and obligation to keep the person transferred in custody, unless otherwise requested or authorized by the State from which the person was transferred;

(b) The State to which the person is transferred shall without delay implement its obligation to return the person to the custody of the State from which the person was transferred as agreed beforehand, or as otherwise agreed, by the competent authorities of both States;

(c) The State to which the person is transferred shall not require the State from which the person was transferred to initiate extradition proceedings for the return of the person;

(d) The person transferred shall receive credit for service of the sentence being served in the State from which he or she was transferred for time spent in the custody of the State to which he or she was transferred.

3. Unless the State Party from which a person is to be transferred in accordance with the present article so agrees, that person, whatever his or her nationality, shall not be prosecuted or detained or subjected to any other restriction of his or her personal liberty in the territory of the State to which that person is transferred in respect of acts or convictions anterior to his or her departure from the territory of the State from which such person was transferred.

Article 17

Any person who is taken into custody or regarding whom any other measures are taken or proceedings are carried out pursuant to this Convention shall be guaranteed fair treatment, including enjoyment of all rights and guarantees in conformity with the law of the State in the territory of which that person is present and applicable provisions of international law, including international human rights law.

Article 18

1. States Parties shall cooperate in the prevention of the offences set forth in Article 2 by taking all practicable measures, inter alia, by adapting their domestic legislation, if necessary, to prevent and counter preparations in their respective territories for the commission of those offences within or outside their territories, including:

(a) Measures to prohibit in their territories illegal activities of persons and organizations that knowingly encourage, instigate, organize or engage in the commission of offences set forth in Article 2;

(b) Measures requiring financial institutions and other professions involved in financial transactions to utilize the most efficient measures available for the identification of their usual or occasional customers, as well as customers in whose interest accounts are opened, and to pay special attention to unusual or suspicious transactions and report transactions suspected of stemming from a criminal activity. For this purpose, States Parties shall consider:

(i) Adopting regulations prohibiting the opening of accounts the holders or beneficiaries of which are unidentified or unidentifiable, and measures to ensure that such institutions verify the identity of the real owners of such transactions;

(ii) With respect to the identification of legal entities, requiring financial institutions, when necessary, to take measures to verify the legal existence and the structure of the customer by obtaining, either from a public register or from the customer or both, proof of incorporation, including information concerning the customer's name, legal form, address, directors and provisions regulating the power to bind the entity;

(iii) Adopting regulations imposing on financial institutions the obligation to report promptly to the competent authorities all complex, unusual large transactions and unusual patterns of transactions, which have no apparent economic or obviously lawful purpose, without fear of assuming criminal or civil liability for breach of any restriction on disclosure of information if they report their suspicions in good faith;

(iv) Requiring financial institutions to maintain, for at least five years, all necessary records on transactions, both domestic or international.

2. States Parties shall further cooperate in the prevention of offences set forth in Article 2 by considering:

(a) Measures for the supervision, including, for example, the licensing, of all money-transmission agencies;

(b) Feasible measures to detect or monitor the physical cross-border transportation of cash and bearer negotiable instruments, subject to strict safeguards to ensure proper use of information and without impeding in any way the freedom of capital movements.

3. States Parties shall further cooperate in the prevention of the offences set forth in Article 2 by exchanging accurate and verified information in accordance with their domestic law and coordinating administrative and other measures taken, as appropriate, to prevent the commission of offences set forth in Article 2, in particular by:

(a) Establishing and maintaining channels of communication between their competent agencies and services to facilitate the secure and rapid exchange of information concerning all aspects of offences set forth in Article 2;

(b) Cooperating with one another in conducting inquiries, with respect to the offences set forth in Article 2, concerning:

(i) The identity, whereabouts and activities of persons in respect of whom reasonable suspicion exists that they are involved in such offences;

(ii) The movement of funds relating to the commission of such offences.

4. States Parties may exchange information through the International Criminal Police Organization (Interpol).

Article 19

The State Party where the alleged offender is prosecuted shall, in accordance with its domestic law or applicable procedures, communicate the final outcome of the proceedings to the Secretary-General of the United Nations, who shall transmit the information to the other States Parties.

Article 20

The States Parties shall carry out their obligations under this Convention in a manner consistent with the principles of sovereign equality and territorial integrity of States and that of non-intervention in the domestic affairs of other States.

Article 21

Nothing in this Convention shall affect other rights, obligations and responsibilities of States and individuals under international law, in particular the purposes of the Charter of the United Nations, international humanitarian law and other relevant conventions.

Article 22

Nothing in this Convention entitles a State Party to undertake in the territory of another State Party the exercise of jurisdiction or performance of functions which are exclusively reserved for the authorities of that other State Party by its domestic law.

Article 23

1. The annex may be amended by the addition of relevant treaties that:

   (a) Are open to the participation of all States;

   (b) Have entered into force;

   (c) Have been ratified, accepted, approved or acceded to by at least twenty-two States Parties to the present Convention.

2. After the entry into force of this Convention, any State Party may propose such an amendment. Any proposal for an amendment shall be communicated to the depositary in written form. The depositary shall notify proposals that meet the requirements of paragraph 1 to all States Parties and seek their views on whether the proposed amendment should be adopted.

3. The proposed amendment shall be deemed adopted unless one third of the States Parties object to it by a written notification not later than 180 days after its circulation.

4. The adopted amendment to the annex shall enter into force 30 days after the deposit of the twenty-second instrument of ratification, acceptance or approval of such amendment for all those States Parties having deposited such an instrument. For each State Party ratifying, accepting or approving the amendment after the deposit of the twenty-second instrument, the amendment shall enter into force on the thirtieth day after deposit by such State Party of its instrument of ratification, acceptance or approval.

Article 24

1. Any dispute between two or more States Parties concerning the interpretation or application of this Convention which cannot be settled through negotiation within a reasonable time shall, at the request of one of them, be submitted to arbitration. If, within six months from the date of the request for arbitration, the parties are unable to agree on the organization of the arbitration, any one of those parties may refer the dispute to the International Court of Justice, by application, in conformity with the Statute of the Court.

2. Each State may at the time of signature, ratification, acceptance or approval of this Convention or accession thereto declare that it does not consider itself bound by para-

graph 1. The other States Parties shall not be bound by paragraph 1 with respect to any State Party which has made such a reservation.

3. Any State which has made a reservation in accordance with paragraph 2 may at any time withdraw that reservation by notification to the Secretary-General of the United Nations.

Article 25

1. This Convention shall be open for signature by all States from 10 January 2000 to 31 December 2001 at United Nations Headquarters in New York.

2. This Convention is subject to ratification, acceptance or approval. The instruments of ratification, acceptance or approval shall be deposited with the Secretary-General of the United Nations.

3. This Convention shall be open to accession by any State. The instruments of accession shall be deposited with the Secretary-General of the United Nations.

Article 26

1. This Convention shall enter into force on the thirtieth day following the date of the deposit of the twenty-second instrument of ratification, acceptance, approval or accession with the Secretary-General of the United Nations.

2. For each State ratifying, accepting, approving or acceding to the Convention after the deposit of the twenty-second instrument of ratification, acceptance, approval or accession, the Convention shall enter into force on the thirtieth day after deposit by such State of its instrument of ratification, acceptance, approval or accession.

Article 27

1. Any State Party may denounce this Convention by written notification to the Secretary-General of the United Nations.

2. Denunciation shall take effect one year following the date on which notification is received by the Secretary-General of the United Nations.

Article 28

The original of this Convention, of which the Arabic, Chinese, English, French, Russian and Spanish texts are equally authentic, shall be deposited with the Secretary-General of the United Nations who shall send certified copies thereof to all States.

In Witness Whereof, the undersigned, being duly authorized thereto by their respective Governments, have signed this Convention, opened for signature at United Nations Headquarters in New York on 10 January 2000.

Annex

1. Convention for the Suppression of Unlawful Seizure of Aircraft, done at The Hague on 16 December 1970.

2. Convention for the Suppression of Unlawful Acts against the Safety of Civil Aviation, done at Montreal on 23 September 1971.

3. Convention on the Prevention and Punishment of Crimes against Internationally Protected Persons, including Diplomatic Agents, adopted by the General Assembly of the United Nations on 14 December 1973.

4. International Convention against the Taking of Hostages, adopted by the General Assembly of the United Nations on 17 December 1979.

5. Convention on the Physical Protection of Nuclear Material, adopted at Vienna on 3 March 1980.

6. Protocol for the Suppression of Unlawful Acts of Violence at Airports Serving International Civil Aviation, supplementary to the Convention for the Suppression of Unlawful Acts against the Safety of Civil Aviation, done at Montreal on 24 February 1988.

7. Convention for the Suppression of Unlawful Acts against the Safety of Maritime Navigation, done at Rome on 10 March 1988.

8. Protocol for the Suppression of Unlawful Acts against the Safety of Fixed Platforms located on the Continental Shelf, done at Rome on 10 March 1988.

9. International Convention for the Suppression of Terrorist Bombings, adopted by the General Assembly of the United Nations on 15 December 1997.

Protocol for the Suppression of Unlawful Acts of Violence at Airports Serving International Civil Aviation, Supplementary to the Convention for the Suppression of Unlawful Acts Against the Safety of Civil Aviation

International Civil Aviation Organization Doc. 9518
(signed at Montreal on 24 February 1988)

Article I

This Protocol supplements the Convention for the Suppression of Unlawful Acts against the Safety of Civil Aviation, done at Montreal on 23 September 1971 (hereinafter referred to as "the Convention"), and, as between the Parties to this Protocol, the Convention and the Protocol shall be read and interpreted together as one single instrument.

Article II

1. In Article 1 of the Convention, the following shall be added as new paragraph 1 *bis*:

"1 *bis*. Any person commits an offense if he unlawfully and intentionally using any device, substance or weapon:

(a) performs an act of violence against a person at an airport serving international civil aviation which causes or is likely to cause serious injury or death; or

(b) destroys or seriously damages the facilities of an airport serving international civil aviation or aircraft not in service located thereon or disrupts the services of the airport, if such an act endangers or is likely to endanger safety at that airport."

Article III

In Article 5 of the Convention, the following shall be added as paragraph 2 *bis*:

"2 *bis*. Each Contracting State shall likewise take such measures as may be necessary to establish its jurisdiction over the offenses mentioned in Article 1, paragraph 1 *bis*, and in Article 1, paragraph 2, in so far as that paragraph relates to these offenses, in the case where the alleged offender is present in its territory and it does not extradite him pursuant to Article 8 to the State mentioned in paragraph 1 (a) of this article."

Tokyo Convention on Offences and Certain Other Acts Committed on Board Aircraft

704 U.N.T.S. 219, 20 U.S.T. 2941, T.I.A.S. No. 6768 (1963)

The States Parties to this Convention

Have agreed as follows:

Chapter I — Scope of the Convention

Article 1

1. This Convention shall apply in respect of:

(a) offences against penal law;

(b) acts which, whether or not they are offences, may or do jeopardize the safety of the aircraft or of persons or property therein or which jeopardize good order and discipline on board.

2. Except as provided in Chapter III, this Convention shall apply in respect of offences committed or acts done by a person on board any aircraft registered in a Contracting State, while that aircraft is in flight or on the surface of the high seas or of any other area outside the territory of any State.

3. For the purposes of this Convention, an aircraft is considered to be in flight from the moment when power is applied for the purpose of take-off until the moment when the landing run ends.

4. This Convention shall not apply to aircraft used in military, customs or police services.

Article 2

Without prejudice to the provisions of Article 4 and except when the safety of the aircraft or of persons or property on board so requires, no provision of this Convention shall be interpreted as authorizing or requiring any action in respect of offences against penal laws of a political nature or those based on racial or religious discrimination.

Chapter II — Jurisdiction

Article 3

1. The State of registration of the aircraft is competent to exercise jurisdiction over offences and acts committed on board.

2. Each Contracting State shall take such measures as may be necessary to establish its jurisdiction as the State of registration over offences committed on board aircraft registered in such State.

3. This Convention does not exclude any criminal jurisdiction exercised in accordance with national law.

Article 4

A Contracting State which is not the State of registration may not interfere with an aircraft in flight in order to exercise its criminal jurisdiction over an offence committed on board except in the following cases:

(a) the offence has effect on the territory of such State;

(b) the offence has been committed by or against a national or permanent resident of such State;

(c) the offence is against the security of such State;

(d) the offence consists of a breach of any rules or regulations relating to the flight or manoeuvre of aircraft in force in such State;

(e) the exercise of jurisdiction is necessary to ensure the observance of any obligation of such State under a multilateral international agreement.

Chapter III — Powers of the aircraft commander

Article 5

1. The provisions of this Chapter shall not apply to offences and acts committed or about to be committed by a person on board an aircraft in flight in the airspace of the State of registration or over the high seas or any other area outside the territory of any State unless the last point of take-off or the next point of intended landing is situated in a State other than that of registration, or the aircraft subsequently flies in the airspace of a State other than that of registration with such person still on board.

2. Notwithstanding the provisions of Article 1, paragraph 3, an aircraft shall for the purposes of this Chapter, be considered to be in flight at any time from the moment when all its external doors are closed following embarkation until the moment when any such door is opened for disembarkation. In the case of a forced landing, the provisions of this Chapter shall continue to apply with respect to offences and acts committed on board until competent authorities of a State take over the responsibility for the aircraft and for the persons and property on board.

Article 6

1. The aircraft commander may, when he has reasonable grounds to believe that a person has committed, or is about to commit, on board the aircraft, an offence or act contemplated in Article 1, paragraph 1, impose upon such person reasonable measures including restraint which are necessary:

(a) to protect the safety of the air-craft, or of persons or property therein; or

(b) to maintain good order and discipline on board; or

(c) to enable him to deliver such person to competent authorities or to disembark him in accordance with the provisions of this Chapter.

2. The aircraft commander may require or authorize the assistance of other crew members and may request or authorize, but not require, the assistance of passengers to restrain any person whom he is entitled to restrain. Any crew member or passenger may also take reasonable preventive measures without such authorization when he has reasonable grounds to believe that such action is immediately necessary to protect the safety of the aircraft, or of persons or property therein.

Article 7

1. Measures of restraint imposed upon a person in accordance with Article 6 shall not be continued beyond any point at which the aircraft lands unless:

(a) such point is in the territory of a non-Contracting State and its authorities refuse to permit disembarkation of that person or those measures have been imposed in accordance with Article 6, paragraph 1 (c) in order to enable his delivery to competent authorities;

(b) the aircraft makes a forced landing and the aircraft commander is unable to deliver that person to competent authorities; or

(c) that person agrees to onward carriage under restraint.

2. The aircraft commander shall as soon as practicable, and if possible before landing in the territory of a State with a person on board who has been placed under restraint in accordance with the provisions of Article 6, notify the authorities of such State of the fact that a person on board is under restraint and of the reasons for such restraint.

Article 8

1. The aircraft commander may, in so far as it is necessary for the purpose of sub-paragraph (a) or (b) of paragraph 1 of Article 6, disembark in the territory of any State in which the aircraft lands any person who he has reasonable grounds to believe has committed, or is about to commit, on board the aircraft an act contemplated in Article 1, paragraph 1 (b).

2. The aircraft commander shall report to the authorities of the State in which he disembarks any person pursuant to this article, the fact of, and the reasons for, such disembarkation.

Article 9

1. The aircraft commander may deliver to the competent authorities of any Contracting State in the territory of which the aircraft lands any person who he has reasonable grounds to believe has committed on board the aircraft an act which, in his opinion, is a serious offence according to the penal law of the State of registration of the aircraft.

2. The aircraft commander shall as soon as practicable and if possible before landing in the territory of a Contracting State with a person on board whom the aircraft commander intends to deliver in accordance with the preceding paragraph, notify the authorities of such State of his intention to deliver such person and the reasons therefor.

3. The aircraft commander shall furnish the authorities to whom any suspected offender is delivered in accordance with the provisions of this article with evidence and information which, under the law of the State of registration of the aircraft, are lawfully in his possession.

Article 10

For actions taken in accordance with this Convention, neither the aircraft commander, any other member of the crew, any passenger, the owner or operator of the aircraft, nor the person on whose behalf the flight was performed shall be held responsible in any proceeding on account of the treatment undergone by the person against whom the actions were taken.

Chapter IV — Unlawful Seizure of Aircraft

Article 11

1. When a person on board has unlawfully committed by force or threat thereof an act of interference, seizure, or other wrongful exercise of control of an aircraft in flight or when such an act is about to be committed, Contracting States shall take all appropriate measures to restore control of the aircraft to its lawful commander or to preserve his control of the aircraft.

2. In the cases contemplated in the preceding paragraph, the Contracting State in which the aircraft lands shall permit its passengers and crew to continue their journey as soon as practicable, and shall return the aircraft and its cargo to the persons lawfully entitled to possession.

Chapter V — Powers and Duties of States

Article 12

Any Contracting State shall allow the commander of an aircraft registered in another Contracting State to disembark any person pursuant to Article 8, paragraph 1.

Article 13

1. Any Contracting State shall take delivery of any person whom the aircraft commander delivers pursuant to Article 9, paragraph 1.

2. Upon being satisfied that the circumstances so warrant, any Contracting State shall take custody or other measures to ensure the presence of any person suspected of an act contemplated in Article 11, paragraph 1 and of any person of whom it has taken delivery. The custody and other measures shall be as provided in the law of that State but may only be continued for such time as is reasonably necessary to enable any criminal or extradition proceedings to be instituted.

3. Any person in custody pursuant to the previous paragraph shall be assisted in communicating immediately with the nearest appropriate representative of the State of which he is a national.

4. Any Contracting State, to which a person is delivered pursuant to Article 9, paragraph 1, or in whose territory an aircraft lands following the commission of an act contemplated in Article 11, paragraph 1, shall immediately make a preliminary inquiry into the facts.

5. When a State, pursuant to this article, has taken a person into custody, it shall immediately notify the State of registration of the aircraft and the State of nationality of the detained person and, if it considers it advisable, any other interested State of the fact that such person is in custody and of the circumstances which warrant his detention. The State which makes the preliminary enquiry contemplated in paragraph 4 of this article shall promptly report its findings to the said States and shall indicate whether it intends to exercise jurisdiction.

Article 14

1. When any person has been disembarked in accordance with Article 8, paragraph 1, or delivered in accordance with Article 9, paragraph 1, or has disembarked after committing an act contemplated in Article 11, paragraph 1, and when such person cannot or does not desire to continue his journey and the State of landing refuses to admit him, that State may, if the person in question is not a national or permanent resident of that State, return him to the territory of the State of which he is a national or permanent resident or to the territory of the State in which he began his journey by air.

2. Neither disembarkation, nor delivery, nor the taking of custody or other measures contemplated in Article 13, paragraph 2, nor return of the person concerned, shall be considered as admission to the territory of the Contracting State concerned for the purpose of its law relating to entry or admission of persons and nothing in this Convention shall affect the law of a Contracting State relating to the expulsion of persons from its territory.

Article 15

1. Without prejudice to Article 14, any person who has been disembarked in accordance with Article 8, paragraph 1, or delivered in accordance with Article 9, paragraph 1, or has disembarked after committing an act contemplated in Article 11, paragraph 1, and

who desires to continue his journey shall be at liberty as soon as practicable to proceed to any destination of his choice unless his presence is required by the law of the State of landing for the purpose of extradition or criminal proceedings.

2. Without prejudice to its law as to entry and admission to, and extradition and expulsion from its territory, a Contracting State in whose territory a person has been disembarked in accordance with Article 8, paragraph 1, or delivered in accordance with Article 9, paragraph 1 or has disembarked and is suspected of having committed an act contemplated in Article 11, paragraph 1, shall accord to such person treatment which is no less favourable for his protection and security than that accorded to nationals of such Contracting State in like circumstances.

Chapter VI—Other Provisions

Article 16

1. Offences committed on aircraft registered in a Contracting State shall be treated, for the purpose of extradition, as if they had been committed not only in the place in which they have occurred but also in the territory of the State of registration of the aircraft.

2. Without prejudice to the provisions of the preceding paragraph, nothing in this Convention shall be deemed to create an obligation to grant extradition.

Article 17

In taking any measures for investigation or arrest or otherwise exercising jurisdiction in connection with any offence committed on board an aircraft the Contracting States shall pay due regard to the safety and other interests of air navigation and shall so act as to avoid unnecessary delay of the aircraft, passengers, crew or cargo.

Article 18

If Contracting States establish joint air transport operating organizations or international operating agencies, which operate aircraft not registered in any one State those States shall, according to the circumstances of the case, designate the State among them which, for the purposes of this Convention, shall be considered as the State of registration and shall give notice thereof to the International Civil Aviation Organization which shall communicate the notice to all States Parties to this Convention.

Chapter VII—Final Clauses

Article 19

Until the date on which this Convention comes into force in accordance with the provisions of Article 21, it shall remain open for signature on behalf of any State which at that date is a Member of the United Nations or of any of the Specialized Agencies.

Article 20

1. This Convention shall be subject to ratification by the signatory States in accordance with their constitutional procedures.

2. The instruments of ratification shall be deposited with the International Civil Aviation Organization.

Article 21

1. As soon as twelve of the signatory States have deposited their instruments of ratification of this Convention, it shall come into force between them on the ninetieth day after the date of the deposit of the twelfth instrument of ratification. It shall come into

force for each State ratifying thereafter on the ninetieth day after the deposit of its instrument of ratification.

2. As soon as this Convention comes into force, it shall be registered with the Secretary-General of the United Nations by the International Civil Aviation Organization.

Article 22

1. This Convention shall, after it has come into force, be open for accession by any State Member of the United Nations or of any of the Specialized Agencies.

2. The accession of a State shall be effected by the deposit of an instrument of accession with the International Civil Aviation Organization and shall take effect on the ninetieth day after the date of such deposit.

Article 23

1. Any Contracting State may denounce this Convention by notification addressed to the International Civil Aviation Organization.

2. Denunciation shall take effect six months after the date of receipt by the International Civil Aviation Organization of the notification of denunciation.

Article 24

1. Any dispute between two or more Contracting States concerning the interpretation or application of this Convention which cannot be settled through negotiation, shall, at the request of one of them, be submitted to arbitration. If within six months from the date of the request for arbitration the Parties are unable to agree on the organization of the arbitration, any one of those Parties may refer the dispute to the International Court of Justice by request in conformity with the Statute of the Court.

2. Each State may at the time of signature or ratification of this Convention or accession thereto, declare that it does not consider itself bound by the preceding paragraph. The other Contracting States shall not be bound by the preceding paragraph with respect to any Contracting State having made such a reservation.

3. Any Contracting State having made a reservation in accordance with the preceding paragraph may at any time withdraw this reservation by notification to the International Civil Aviation Organization.

Article 25

Except as provided in Article 24 no reservation may be made to this Convention.

Article 26

The International Civil Aviation Organization shall give notice to all States Members of the United Nations or of any of the Specialized Agencies:

(a) of any signature of this Convention and the date thereof;

(b) of the deposit of any instrument of ratification or accession and the date thereof;

(c) of the date on which this Convention comes into force in accordance with Article 21, paragraph 1;

(d) of the receipt of any notification of denunciation and the date thereof; and

(e) of the receipt of any declaration or notification made under Article 24 and the date thereof.

In Witness Whereof the undersigned Plenipotentiaries, having been duly authorized, have signed this Convention.

Done at Tokyo on the fourteenth day of September One Thousand Nine Hundred and Sixty-three in three authentic texts drawn up in the English, French and Spanish languages.

This Convention shall be deposited with the International Civil Aviation Organization with which, in accordance with Article 19, it shall remain open for signature and the said Organization shall send certified copies thereof to all States Members of the United Nations or of any Specialized Agency.

Hague Convention on the Suppression of Unlawful Seizure of Aircraft (Hijacking)
860 U.N.T.S. 105, 22 U.S.T. 1641, T.I.A.S. 7192 (1970)

Preamble

The States Parties to this Convention

Considering that unlawful acts of seizure or exercise of control of aircraft in flight jeopardize the safety of persons and property, seriously affect the operation of air services, and undermine the confidence of the peoples of the world in the safety of civil aviation;

Considering that the occurrence of such acts is a matter of grave concern;

Considering that, for the purpose of deterring such acts, there is an urgent need to provide appropriate measures for punishment of offenders;

Have agreed as follows:

Article 1

Any person who on board an aircraft in flight:

(a) unlawfully, by force or threat thereof, or by any other form of intimidation, seizes, or exercises control of, that aircraft, or attempts to perform any such act, or

(b) is an accomplice of a person who performs or attempts to perform any such act commits an offence (hereinafter referred to as the offence).

Article 2

Each Contracting State undertakes to make the offence punishable by severe penalties.

Article 3

1. For the purposes of this Convention, an aircraft is considered to be in flight at any time from the moment when all its external doors are closed following embarkation until the moment when any such door is opened for disembarkation. In the case of a forced landing, the flight shall be deemed to continue until the competent authorities take over the responsibility for the aircraft and for persons and property on board.

2. This Convention shall not apply to aircraft used in military, customs or police services.

3. This Convention shall apply only if the place of take-off or the place of actual landing of the aircraft on board which the offence is committed is situated outside the territory of the State of registration of that aircraft; it shall be immaterial whether the aircraft is engaged in an international or domestic flight.

4. In the cases mentioned in Article 5, this Convention shall not apply if the place of take-off and the place of actual landing of the aircraft on board which the offence is com-

mitted are situated within the territory of the same State where that State is one of those referred to in that Article.

5. Notwithstanding paragraphs 3 and 4 of this article, Articles 6, 7, 8 and 10 shall apply whatever the place of take-off or the place of actual landing of the aircraft, if the offender or the alleged offender is found in the territory of a State other than the State of registration of that aircraft.

Article 4

1. Each Contracting State shall take such measures as may be necessary to establish its jurisdiction over the offence and any other act of violence against passengers or crew committed by the alleged offender in connection with the offence, in the following cases:

(a) when the offence is committed on board an aircraft registered in that State;

(b) when the aircraft on board which the offence is committed lands in its territory with the alleged offender still on board;

(c) when the offence is committed on board an aircraft leased without crew to a lessee who has his principal place of business or, if the lessee has no such place of business, his permanent residence, in that State.

2. Each Contracting State shall likewise take such measures as may be necessary to establish its jurisdiction over the offence in the case where the alleged offender is present in its territory and it does not extradite him pursuant to Article 8 to any of the State mentioned in paragraph 1 of this article.

3. This Convention does not exclude any criminal jurisdiction exercised in accordance with national law.

Article 5

The Contracting States which establish joint air transport operating organizations or international operating agencies, which operate aircraft which are subject to joint or international registration shall, by appropriate means, designate for each aircraft the State among them which shall exercise the jurisdiction and have the attributes of the State of registration for the purpose of this Convention and shall give notice thereof to the International Civil Aviation Organization which shall communicate the notice to all States Parties to this Convention.

Article 6

1. Upon being satisfied that the circumstances so warrant, any Contracting State in the territory of which the offender or the alleged offender is present, shall take him into custody or take other measures to ensure his presence. The custody and other measures shall be as provided in the law of that State but may only be continued for such time as is necessary to enable any criminal or extradition proceedings to be instituted.

2. Such State shall immediately make a preliminary enquiry into the facts.

3. Any person in custody pursuant to paragraph 1 of this article shall be assisted in communicating immediately with the nearest appropriate representative of the State of which he is a national.

4. When a State, pursuant to this article, has taken a person into custody, it shall immediately notify the State of registration of the aircraft, the State mentioned in Article 4, paragraph 1(c), the State of nationality of the detained person and, if it considers it advisable, any other interested States of the fact that such person is in custody and of the

circumstances which warrant his detention. The State which makes the preliminary enquiry contemplated in paragraph 2 of this article shall promptly report its findings to the said States and shall indicate whether it intends to exercise jurisdiction.

Article 7

The Contracting State in the territory of which the alleged offender is found shall, if it does not extradite him, be obliged, without exception whatsoever and whether or not the offence was committed in its territory, to submit the case to its competent authorities for the purpose of prosecution. Those authorities shall take their decision in the same manner as in the case of any ordinary offence of a serious nature under the law of that State.

Article 8

1. The offence shall be deemed to be included as an extraditable offence in any extradition treaty existing between Contracting States. Contracting States undertake to include the offence as an extraditable offence in every extradition treaty to be concluded between them.

2. If a Contracting State which makes extradition conditional on the existence of a treaty receives a request for extradition from another Contracting State with which it has no extradition treaty, it may at its option consider this Convention as the legal basis for extradition in respect of the offence. Extradition shall be subject to the other conditions provided by the law of the requested State.

3. Contracting States which do not make extradition conditional on the existence of a treaty shall recognize the offence as an extraditable offence between themselves subject to the provided by the law to the requested State.

4. The offence shall be treated, for the purpose of extradition between Contracting States, as if it had been committed not only in the place in which it occurred but also in the territories of the States required to establish their jurisdiction in accordance with Article 4, paragraph 1.

Article 9

1. When any of the acts mentioned in Article 1(a) has occurred or is about to occur, Contracting States shall take all appropriate measures to restore control of the aircraft to its lawful commander or to preserve his control of the aircraft.

2. In the cases contemplated by the preceding paragraph, any Contracting State in which the aircraft or its passengers or crew are present shall facilitate the continuation of the journey of the passengers and crew as soon as practicable, and shall without delay return the aircraft and its cargo to the persons lawfully entitled to possession.

Article 10

1. Contracting States shall afford one another the greatest measure of assistance in connection with criminal proceedings brought in respect of the offence and other acts mentioned in Article 4. The law of the State requested shall apply in all cases.

2. The provisions of paragraph 1 of this article shall not affect obligations under any other treaty, bilateral or multilateral, which governs or will govern, in whole or in part, mutual assistance in criminal matters.

Article 11

Each Contracting State shall in accordance with its national law report to the Council of the International Civil Aviation Organization as promptly as possible any relevant information in its possession concerning:

(a) the circumstances of the offence;

(b) the action taken pursuant to Article 9;

(c) the measures taken in relation to the offender or the alleged offender, and, in particular, the results of any extradition proceedings or other legal proceedings.

Article 12

1. Any dispute between two or more Contracting States concerning the interpretation or application of this Convention which cannot be settled through negotiation, shall, at the request of one of them, be submitted to arbitration. If within six months from the date of the request for arbitration the Parties are unable to agree on the organization of the arbitration, any one of those Parties may refer the dispute to the International Court of Justice by request in conformity with the Statute of the Court.

2. Each State may at the time of signature or ratification of this Convention or accession thereto, declare that it does not consider itself bound by the preceding paragraph. The other Contracting States shall not be bound by the preceding paragraph with respect to any Contracting State having made such a reservation.

3. Any Contracting State having made a reservation in accordance with the preceding paragraph may at any time withdraw this reservation by notification to the Depositary Governments.

Article 13

1. This Convention shall be open for signature at The Hague on 16 December 1970, by States participating in the International Conference on Air Law held at The Hague from 1 to 16 December 1970 (hereinafter referred to as The Hague Conference). After 31 December 1970, the Convention shall be open to all States for signature in Moscow, London and Washington. Any State which does not sign this Convention before its entry into force in accordance with paragraph 3 of this article may accede to it at any time.

2. This Convention shall be subject to ratification by the signatory States. Instruments of ratification and instruments of accession shall be deposited with the Governments of the Union of Soviet Socialist Republics, the United Kingdom of Great Britain and Northern Ireland, and the United States of America, which are hereby designated the Depositary Governments.

3. This Convention shall enter into force thirty days following the date of the deposit of instruments of ratification by ten States signatory to this Convention which participated in The Hague Conference.

4. For other States, this Convention shall enter into force on the date of entry into force of this Convention in accordance with paragraph 3 of this article, or thirty days following the date of deposit of their instruments of ratification or accession, whichever is later.

5. The Depositary Governments shall promptly inform all signatory and acceding States of the date of each signature, the date of deposit of each instrument of ratification or accession, the date of entry into force of this Convention, and other notices.

6. As soon as this Convention comes into force, it shall be registered by the Depositary Governments pursuant to Article 102 of the Charter of the United Nations and pursuant to Article 83 of the Convention on International Civil Aviation (Chicago, 1944).

Article 14

1. Any Contracting State may denounce this Convention by written notification to the Depositary Governments.

2. Denunciation shall take effect six months following the date on which notification is received by the Depositary Governments.

In Witness Whereof the undersigned Plenipotentiaries, being duly authorised thereto by their Governments, have signed this Convention.

Done at The Hague, this sixteenth day of December, one thousand nine hundred and seventy, in three originals, each being drawn up in four authentic texts in the English, French, Russian and Spanish languages.

Montreal Convention for the Suppression of Unlawful Acts Against the Safety of Civil Aviation
974 U.N.T.S. 177, 24 U.S.T. 564, T.I.A.S. No. 7570 (1971)

Article 1

1. Any person commits an offence if he unlawfully and intentionally:

(a) performs an act of violence against a person on board an aircraft in flight if that act is likely to endanger the safety of that aircraft; or

(b) destroys an aircraft in service or causes damage to such aircraft which renders it incapable of flight or which is likely to endanger its safety in flight; or

(c) places or causes to be placed on an aircraft in service, by any means whatsoever, a device or substance which is likely to destroy that aircraft, or to cause damage to it which renders it incapable of flight, or to cause damage to it which is likely to endanger its safety in flight; or

(d) destroys or damages air navigation facilities or interferes with their operation, if any such act is likely to endanger the safety of aircraft in flight; or

(e) communicates information which he knows to be false, thereby endangering the safety of an aircraft in flight.

2. Any person also commits an offence if he:

(a) attempts to commit any of the offences mentioned in paragraph 1 of this article; or

(b) is an accomplice of a person who commits to attempts to commit any such offence.

Article 2

For the purposes of this Convention:

(a) an aircraft is considered to be in flight at any time from the moment when all its external doors are closed following embarkation until the moment when any such door is opened for disembarkation; in the case of a forced landing, the flight shall be deemed to continue until the competent authorities take over the responsibility for the aircraft and for the aircraft and for persons and property on board;

(b) an aircraft is considered to be in service from the beginning of the preflight preparation of the aircraft by ground personnel or by the crew for a specific flight until twenty-four hours after any landing; the period of service shall, in any event, extend for the entire period during which the aircraft is in flight as defined in paragraph (a) of this article.

Article 3

Each Contracting State undertakes to make the offences mentioned in Article 1 punishable by severe penalties.

Article 4

1. This Convention shall not apply to aircraft used in military, customs or police services.

2. In the cases contemplated in subparagraphs (a), (b), (c) and (e) of paragraph 1 of Article 1, this Convention shall apply, irrespective of whether the aircraft is engaged in an international or domestic flight, only if:

(a) the place of take-off or landing, actual or intended, of the aircraft is situated outside the territory of the State of registration of that aircraft; or

(b) the offence is committed in the territory of a State other than the State of registration of the aircraft.

3. Notwithstanding paragraph 2 of this article, in the cases contemplated in subparagraphs (a), (b), (c) and (e) of paragraph 1 of Article 1, this Convention shall also apply if the offender or the alleged offender is found in the territory of a State other than the State of registration of the aircraft.

4. With respect to the States mentioned in Article 9 and in the cases mentioned in subparagraphs (a), (b), (c) and (e) of paragraph 1 of Article 1, this Convention shall not apply if the places referred to in subparagraph (a) of paragraph 2 of this article are situated within the territory of the same State where that State is one of those referred to in Article 9, unless the offence is committed or the offender or alleged offender is found in the territory of a State other than that State.

5. In the cases contemplated in subparagraph (d) of paragraph 1 of Article 1, this Convention shall apply only if the air navigation facilities are used in international air navigation.

6. The provisions of paragraphs 2, 3, 4 and 5 of this article shall also apply in the cases contemplated in paragraph 2 of Article 1.

Article 5

1. Each Contracting State shall take such measures as may be necessary to establish its jurisdiction over the offences in the following cases:

(a) when the offence is committed in the territory of that State;

(b) when the offence is committed against or on board an aircraft registered in that State;

(c) when the aircraft on board which the offence is committed lands in its territory with the alleged offender still on board;

(d) when the offence is committed against or on board an aircraft leased without crew to a lessee who has his principal place of business or, if the lessee has no such place of business, his permanent residence, in that State.

2. Each Contracting State shall likewise take such measures as may be necessary to establish its jurisdiction over the offences mentioned in Article 1, paragraph 1 (a), (b) and (c), and in Article 1, paragraph 2, in so far as that paragraph relates to those offences, in the case where the alleged offender is present in its territory and it does not extradite him pursuant to Article 8 to any of the States mentioned in paragraph 1 of this article.

3. This Convention does not exclude any criminal jurisdiction exercised in accordance with national law.

Article 6

1. Upon being satisfied that the circumstances so warrant, any Contracting State in the territory of which the offender or the alleged offender is present, shall take him into custody or take other measures to ensure his presence. The custody and other measures shall be as provided in the law of that State but may only be continued for such time as is necessary to enable any criminal or extradition proceedings to be instituted.

2. Such State shall immediately make a preliminary enquiry into the facts.

3. Any person in custody pursuant to paragraph 1 of this article shall be assisted in communicating immediately with the nearest appropriate representative of the State of which he is a national.

4. When a State, pursuant to this article, has taken a person into custody, it shall immediately notify the States mentioned in Article 5, paragraph 1, the State of nationality of the detained person and, if it considers it advisable, any other interested States of the fact that such person is in custody and of the circumstances which warrant his detention. The State which makes the preliminary enquiry contemplated in paragraph 2 of this article shall promptly report its findings to the said States and shall indicate whether it intends to exercise jurisdiction.

Article 7

The Contracting State in the territory of which the alleged offender is found shall, if it does not extradite him, be obliged, without exception whatsoever and whether or not the offence was committed in its territory, to submit the case to its competent authorities for the purpose of prosecution. Those authorities shall take their decision in the same manner as in the case of any ordinary offence of a serious nature under the law of that State.

Article 8

1. The offences shall be deemed to be included as extraditable offences in any extradition treaty existing between Contracting States. Contracting States undertake to include the offences as extraditable offences in every extradition treaty to be concluded between them.

2. If a Contracting State which makes extradition conditional on the existence of a treaty receives a request for extradition from another Contracting State with which it has no extradition treaty, it may at its option consider this Convention as the legal basis for extradition in respect of the offences. Extradition shall be subject to the other conditions provided by the law of the requested State.

3. Contracting States which do not make extradition conditional on the existence of a treaty shall recognize the offences as extraditable offences between themselves subject to the conditions provided by the law of the requested State.

4. Each of the offences shall be treated, for the purpose of extradition between Contracting States, as if it had been committed not only in the place in which it occurred but also in the territories of the States required to establish their jurisdiction in accordance with Article 5, paragraph 1 (b), (c) and (d).

Article 9

The Contracting States which establish joint air transport operating organizations or international operating agencies, which operate aircraft which are subject to joint or international registration shall, by appropriate means, designate for each aircraft the State among them which shall exercise the jurisdiction and have the attributes of the State of registration for the purpose of this Convention and shall give notice thereof to the International Civil Aviation Organization which shall communicate the notice to all States Parties to this Convention.

Article 10

1. Contracting States shall, in accordance with international and national law, endeavour to take all practicable measures for the purpose of preventing the offences mentioned in Article 1.

2. When, due to the commission of one of the offences mentioned in Article 1, a flight has been delayed or interrupted, any Contracting State in whose territory the aircraft or passengers or crew are present shall facilitate the continuation of the journey of the passengers and crew as soon as practicable, and shall without delay return the aircraft and its cargo to the persons lawfully entitled to possession.

Article 11

1. Contracting States shall afford one another the greatest measure of assistance in connection with criminal proceedings brought in respect of the offences. The law of the State requested shall apply in all cases.

2. The Provisions of paragraph 1 of this article shall not affect obligations under any other treaty, bilateral or multilateral, which governs or will govern, in whole or in part, mutual assistance in criminal matters.

Article 12

Any Contracting State having reason to believe that one of the offences mentioned in Article 1 will be committed shall, in accordance with its national law, furnish any relevant information in its possession to those States which it believes would be the States mentioned in Article 5, paragraph 1.

Article 13

Each Contracting State shall in accordance with its national law report to the Council of the International Civil Aviation Organization as promptly as possible any relevant information in its possession concerning:

(a) the circumstances of the offence;

(b) the action taken pursuant to Article 10, paragraph 2;

(c) the measures taken in relation to the offender or the alleged offender and, in particular, the results of any extradition proceedings or other legal proceedings.

Article 14

1. Any dispute between two or more Contracting States concerning the interpretation or application of this Convention which cannot be settled through negotiation, shall, at the request of one of them, be submitted to arbitration. If within six months from the date of the request for arbitration the Parties are unable to agree on the organization of the arbitration, any of those Parties may refer the dispute to the International Court of Justice by request in conformity with the Statute of the Court.

2. Each State may at the time of signature or ratification of this Convention or accession thereto, declare that it does not consider itself bound by the preceding paragraph.

The other Contracting States shall not be bound by the preceding paragraph with respect to any Contracting State having made such a reservation.

3. Any Contracting State having made a reservation in accordance with the preceding paragraph may at any time withdraw this reservation by notification to the Depository Governments.

Article 15

1. This Convention shall be open for signature at Montreal on 23 September 1971, by States participating in the International Conference on Air Law held at Montreal from 8 to 23 September 1971 (hereinafter referred to as the Montreal Conference). After 10 October 1971, the Convention shall be open to all States for signature in Moscow, London and Washington. Any State which does not sign this Convention before its entry into force in accordance with paragraph 3 of this article may accede to it at any time.

2. This Convention shall be subject to ratification by the signatory States. Instruments of ratification and instruments of accession shall be deposited with the Governments of the Union of Soviet Socialist republics, the united Kingdom of Great Britain and Northern Ireland, and the United States of America, which are hereby designated by the Depository Governments.

3. This Convention shall enter into force thirty days following the date of the deposit of instruments of ratification by ten States signatory to this Convention which participated in the Montreal Conference.

4. For other States, this Convention shall enter into force on the date of entry into force of this Convention in accordance with paragraph 3 of this article, or thirty days following the date of deposit of their instruments of ratification or accession, whichever is later.

5. The Depository Governments shall promptly inform all signatory and acceding States of the date of each signature, the date of deposit of each instrument of ratification or accession, the date of entry into force of this Convention, and other notices.

6. As soon as this Convention comes into force, it shall be registered by the Depositary Governments pursuant to Article 102 of the Charter of the United Nations and pursuant to Article 83 of the Convention on International Civil Aviation (Chicago, 1944).

Article 16

1. Any Contracting State may denounce this Convention by written notification to the Depositary Governments.

2. Denunciation shall take effect six months following the date on which notification is received by the Depositary Governments.

In witness whereof the undersigned Plenipotentiaries, being duly authorized thereto by their Governments, have signed this Convention.

Done at Montreal, this twenty-third day of September, one thousand nine hundred and seventy-one, in three originals, each being drawn up in four authentic texts in the English, French, Russian and Spanish languages.

Convention for the Suppression of Unlawful Acts Against the Safety of Maritime Navigation

done at Rome on 10 March 1988, International Maritime Organization
Doc. SUA/CON/15/Rev.1, 1993 Can. T.S. No. 10

Article 3

1. Any person commits an offence if that person unlawfully and intentionally:

(a) seizes or exercises control over a ship by force or threat thereof or any other form of intimidation; or

(b) performs an act of violence against a person on board a ship if that act is likely to endanger the safe navigation of that ship; or

(c) destroys a ship or causes damage to a ship or to its cargo which is likely to endanger the safe navigation of that ship; or

(d) places or causes to be placed on a ship, by any means whatsoever, a device or substance which is likely to destroy that ship, or cause damage to that ship or its cargo which endangers or is likely to endanger the safe navigation of that ship; or

(e) destroys or seriously damages maritime navigational facilities or seriously interferes with their operation, if any such act is likely to endanger the safe navigation of a ship; or

(f) communicates information which he knows to be false, thereby endangering the safe navigation of a ship; or

(g) injures or kills any person, in connection with the commission or the attempted commission of any of the offenses set forth in subparagraphs (a) to (f).

2. Any person also commits an offence if that person:

(a) attempts to commit any of the offenses set forth in paragraph 1; or

(b) abets the commission of any of the offenses set forth in paragraph 1 perpetrated by any person or is otherwise an accomplice of a person who commits such an offence; or

(c) threatens, with or without a condition, as is provided for under national law, aimed at compelling a physical or juridical person to do or refrain from doing any act, to commit any of the offenses set forth in paragraph 1, subparagraphs (b), (c) and (e), if that threat is likely to endanger the safe navigation of the ship in question. . . .

Article 6

1. Each State Party shall take such measures as may be necessary to establish its jurisdiction over the offenses set forth in Article 3 when the offence is committed:

(a) against or on board a ship flying the flag of the State at the time the offence is committed; or

(b) in the territory of that State, including its territorial sea; or

(c) by a national of that State.

2. A State Party may also establish its jurisdiction over any such offence when:

(a) it is committed by a stateless person whose habitual residence is in that State; or

(b) during its commission a national of that State is seized, threatened, injured or killed; or

(c) it is committed in an attempt to compel that State to do or abstain from doing any act.

3. Any State Party which has established jurisdiction, mentioned in paragraph 2 shall notify the Secretary-General of the International Maritime Organization (hereinafter referred to as "the Secretary-General"). If such State Party subsequently rescinds that jurisdiction, it shall notify the Secretary-General.

4. Each State Party shall take such measures as may be necessary to establish its jurisdiction over the offenses set forth in Article 3 in cases where the alleged offender is present in its territory and its does not extradite him to any of the States Parties which have established their jurisdiction in accordance with paragraphs 1 and 2 of this article.

Protocol for the Suppression of Unlawful Acts Against the Safety of Fixed Platforms Located on the Continental Shelf

done at Rome on 10 March 1988, International Maritime Organization
Doc. SUA/CONF/15/Rev.1

Article 1

1. The provisions of Articles 5 and 7 and of Articles 10 to 16 of the Convention for the Suppression of Unlawful Acts against the Safety of Maritime Navigation (hereinafter referred to as "the Convention") shall also apply mutatis mutandis to the offenses set forth in Article 2 of this Protocol where such offenses are committed on board or against fixed platforms located on the continental shelf.

2. In cases where this Protocol does not apply pursuant to paragraph 1, it nevertheless applies when the offender or the alleged offender is found in the territory of a State Party other than the State in whose internal waters or territorial sea the fixed platform is located.

3. For the purposes of this Protocol, "fixed platform" means an artificial island, installation or structure permanently attached to the sea-bed for the purpose of exploration or exploitation of resources or for other economic purposes.

Article 2

1. Any person commits an offence if that person unlawfully and intentionally:

(a) seizes or exercises control over a fixed platform for force or threat thereof or any other form of intimidation; or

(b) performs an act of violence against a person on board a fixed platform if that act is likely to endanger its safety; or

(c) destroys a fixed platform or causes damage to it which is likely to endanger its safety; or

(d) places or causes to be placed on a fixed platform, by any means whatsoever, a device or substance which is likely to destroy that fixed platform or likely to endanger its safety; or

(e) injuries or kills any person in connection with the commission or the attempted commission of any of the offenses set forth in subparagraphs (a) to (d).

2. Any person also commits an offence if that person:

(a) attempts to commit any of the offenses set forth in paragraph 1; or

(b) abets the commission of any such offenses perpetrated by any person or is otherwise an accomplice of a person who commits such an offence; or

(c) threatens, with or without a condition, as is provided for under national law, aimed at compelling a physical or juridical person to do or refrain from doing any act, to commit any of the offenses set forth in paragraph 1, subparagraphs (b) and (c), if that threat is likely to endanger the safety of the fixed platform.

Convention on the Prevention and Punishment of Crimes Against Internationally Protected Persons, Including Diplomatic Agents
1035 U.N.T.S. 167, 28 U.S.T. 1975, T.I.A.S. No. 8532 (1973)

Article 1

For the purposes of this Convention:

1. "internationally protected person" means:

(a) a Head of State, including any member of a collegial body performing the functions of a Head of State under the constitution of the State concerned, a Head of Government or a Minister for Foreign Affairs, whenever any such person is in a foreign State, as well as members of his family who accompany him;

(b) any representative or official of a State or any official or other agent of an international organization of an intergovernmental character who, at the time when and in the place where a crime against him, his official premises, his private accommodation or his means of transport is committed, is entitled pursuant to international law to special protection from any attack on is person, freedom or dignity, as well as members of his family forming part of his household;

2. "alleged offender" means a person as to whom there is sufficient evidence to determine *prima facie* that he has committed or participated in one or more of the crimes set forth in Article 2.

Article 2

1. The intentional commission of:

(a) a murder, kidnapping or other attack upon the person or liberty of an internationally protected person;

(b) a violent attack upon the official premises, the private accommodation or the means of transport of an internationally protected person likely to endanger his person or liberty;

(c) a threat to commit any such attack;

(d) an attempt to commit any such attack; and

(e) an act constituting participation as an accomplice in any such attack shall be made by each State Party a crime under its internal law.

2. Each State Party shall make these crimes punishable by appropriate penalties which take into account their grave nature.

3. Paragraphs 1 and 2 of this article in no way derogate from the obligations of States Parties under international law to take all appropriate measure to prevent other attacks on the person, freedom or dignity of an internationally protect person.

Article 3

1. Each State Party shall take such measures as may be necessary to establish its jurisdiction over the crimes set forth in Article 2 in the following cases:

(a) when the crime is committed in the territory of that State or on board a ship or aircraft registered in that State;

(b) when the alleged offender is a national of that State;

(c) when the crime is committed against an internationally protected person as defined in Article 1 who enjoys his status as such by virtue of functions which he exercises on behalf of that State.

2. Each State Party shall likewise take such measures as may be necessary to establish its jurisdiction over these crimes in cases where the alleged offender is present in its territory and it does not extradite him pursuant to Article 8 to any of the States mentioned in paragraph 1 of this article.

3. This convention does not exclude any criminal jurisdiction exercised in accordance with internal law.

Convention for the Suppression of the Illicit Traffic in Dangerous Drugs, 1936

198 L.N.T.S. 299, 1939 Can. T.S. No. 12; 1946 Can. T.S. No. 50;
as amend. by Protocol (11 Dec. 1946), 12 U.N.T.S. 179,
T.I.A.S. No. 1671, 61 Stat. 2230

Article 1

1. In the present Convention, "narcotic drugs" shall be deemed to mean the drugs and substances to which the provisions of the Hague Convention of January 23rd, 1912, and the Geneva Conventions of February 19th, 1925, and July 13th, 1931, are now or hereafter may be applicable.

2. For the purposes of the present Convention, the word "extraction" connotes an operation whereby a narcotic drug is separated from the substance or compound of which it forms part, without involving any actual manufacture or conversion properly so called. This definition of the word "extraction" is not intended to include the processes whereby raw opium is obtained from the opium poppy, these being covered by the term "production".

Article 2

Each of the High Contracting Parties agrees to make the necessary provisions for severely punishing, particularly by imprisonment or other penalties of deprivation of liberty, the following acts—namely:

(a) The manufacture, conversion, extraction, preparation, possession, offering, offering for sale, distribution, purchase, sale, delivery on any terms whatsoever, brokerage, despatch, despatch in transit, transport, importation and exportation of narcotic drugs, contrary to the provisions of the said Conventions;

(b) Intentional participation in the offences specified in this article;

(c) Conspiracy to commit any of the above-mentioned offences;

(d) Attempts, and subject to the conditions prescribed by national law, preparatory acts.

Article 3

The High Contracting Parties who possess extra-territorial jurisdiction in the territory of another High Contracting Party undertake to enact the necessary legislative provisions for punishing such of their nationals as are guilty within that territory of any offence specified in Article 2 at least as severely as if the offence had been committed in their own territory.

Article 4

Each of the acts specified in Article 2 shall, if committed in different countries, be considered as a distinct offence.

Article 5

The High Contracting Parties, whose national law regulates cultivation, gathering and production with a view to obtaining narcotic drugs, shall likewise make severely punishable contraventions thereof.

Article 6

In countries where the principle of the international recognition of previous convictions is recognized, foreign convictions for the offences referred to in Article 2 shall, subject to the conditions prescribed by the domestic law, be recognized for the purpose of establishing habitual criminality.

Article 7

1. In countries where the principle of the extradition of nationals is not recognized, nationals who have returned to the territory of their own country, after the commission abroad of any of the offences referred to in Article 2, shall be prosecuted and punished in the same manner as if the offence had been committed in the said territory, even in a case where the offender has acquired his nationality after the commission of the offence.

2. This provision does not apply if, in a similar case, the extradition of a foreigner cannot be granted.

Article 8

Foreigners who are in the territory of a High Contracting Party and who have committed abroad any of the offences set out in Article 2 shall be prosecuted and punished as though the offence had been committed in that territory if the following conditions are realized — namely, that:

(a) Extradition has been requested and could not be granted for a reason independent of the offence itself;

(b) The law of the country of refuge considers prosecution for offences committed abroad by foreigners admissible as a general rule.

Article 9

1. The offences set out in Article 2 shall be deemed to be included as extradition crimes in any extradition treaty which has been or may hereafter be concluded between any of the High Contracting Parties.

2. The High Contracting Parties who do not make extradition conditional on the existence of a treaty or on reciprocity shall as between themselves recognize the offences referred to above as extradition crimes.

3. Extradition shall be granted in conformity with the law of the country to which application is made.

4. The High Contracting Party to whom application for extradition is made shall, in all cases, have the right to refuse to effect the arrest or to grant the extradition of a fugitive offender if his competent authorities consider that the offence of which the fugitive offender is accused or convicted is not sufficiently serious.

Article 10

Any narcotic drugs as well as any substances and instruments intended for the commission of any of the offences referred to in Article 2 shall be liable to seizure and confiscation.

Article 11

1. Each of the High Contracting Parties shall set up, within the framework of its domestic law, a central office for the supervision and co-ordination of all operations necessary to prevent the offences specified in Article 2, and for ensuring that steps are taken to prosecute persons guilty of such offences.

2. This central office:

(a) Shall be in close contact with other official institutions of bodies dealing with narcotic drugs;

(b) Shall centralize all information of a nature to facilitate the investigation and prevention of the offences specified in Article 2;

(c) Shall be in close contact with and may correspond direct with the central offices of other countries.

3. Where the Government of a High Contracting Party is federal in character, or where the executive authority of its Government is distributed between central and local Governments, the supervision and co-ordination specified in paragraph 1 and the execution of the functions specified in (a) and (b) of paragraph 2 shall be carried out in conformity with the constitutional or administrative system thereof.

4. Where the present convention has been applied to any territory by virtue of Article 18, the requirements of the present article may be carried out by means of a central office set up in or for that territory acting in conjunction, if necessary, with the central office in the metropolitan territory concerned.

5. The powers and the functions of the central office may be delegated to the special administration referred to in Article 15 of the Convention for Limiting the Manufacture and regulating the Distribution of Narcotic Drugs of 1931.

Article 12

1. The central office shall co-operate with the central offices of foreign countries to the greatest extent possible, in order to facilitate the prevention and punishment of the offences specified in Article 2.

2. The office shall, so far as it thinks expedient, communicate to the central office of any country which may be concerned:

(a) Particulars which would make it possible to carry out any investigations or operations relating to any transactions in progress or proposed;

(b) Any particulars which it has been able to secure regarding the identity and the description of traffickers with a view to supervising their movements;

(c) Discoveries of secret factories of narcotic drugs.

Article 13

1. The transmission of letters of request relating to the offences referred to in Article 2 shall be effected:

(a) Preferably by direct communication between the competent authorities of each country or through the central offices, or

(b) By direct correspondence between the Ministers of Justice of the two countries or by direct communication from another competent authority of the country making the request to the Minister of Justice of the country to which the request is made, or

(c) Through the diplomatic or consular representative of the country making the request in the country to which the request is made. For this purpose, the letters of request shall be sent by such representative to the authority designated by the country to which the request is made.

2. Each High Contracting Party may, by communication to the other High Contracting Parties, express its desire that letters of request to be executed within its territory should be sent to it through the diplomatic channel.

3. In case (c) of paragraph 1, a copy of the letter of request shall at the same time be sent by the diplomatic or consular representative of the country making the request to the Minister of Foreign Affairs of the country to which application is made.

4. Unless otherwise agreed, the letter of request shall be drawn up in the language of the authority to which request is made or in a language agreed upon by the two countries concerned.

5. Each High Contracting Party shall notify to each of the other High Contracting Parties the method, or methods, of transmission mentioned above which it will recognize for the letters of request of the latter High Contracting Party.

6. Until such notification is made by a High Contracting Party, its existing procedure in regard to letters of request shall remain in force.

7. The execution of letters of request shall not be subject to payment of taxes or expenses other than the expenses of experts.

8. Nothing in the present article shall be construed as an undertaking on the part of the High Contracting Parties to adopt in criminal matters any form or methods of proof contrary to their laws or to execute letters of request otherwise than within the limits of their laws.

Article 14

The participation of a High Contracting Party in the present Convention shall not be interpreted as affecting that Party's attitude on the general question of criminal jurisdiction as a question of international law.

Article 15

The present Convention does not affect the principle that the offences referred to in Articles 2 and 5 shall in each country be defined, prosecuted and punished in conformity with the general rules of its domestic law.

Article 16

The High Contracting Parties shall communicate to one another through the Secretary-General of the United Nations the laws and regulations promulgated in order to give effect to the present Convention, and also an annual report on the working of the Convention in their territories.

Article 17

If there should arise between the High Contracting Parties a dispute of any kind relating to the interpretation or application of the present Convention, and if such dispute cannot be satisfactorily settled by diplomacy, it shall be settled in accordance with any applicable agreements in force between the Parties providing for the settlement of international disputes.

In case there is no such agreement between the Parties, the dispute shall be referred to arbitration or judicial settlement. In the absence of agreement on the choice of another tribunal, the dispute shall, at the request of any one of the Parties, be referred to the International Court of Justice, if all the Parties to the dispute are Parties to the Statute, and, if any of the Parties to the dispute is not a Party to the Statute, to an arbitral tribunal constituted in accordance with the Hague Convention on 18 October 1907 for the Pacific Settlement of International Disputes.

Single Convention on Narcotic Drugs, 1961
520 U.N.T.S. 151, 1964 Can. T.S. No. 30, 18 U.S.T. 1407, T.I.A.S. No. 6298

The Parties,

Concerned with the health and welfare of mankind,

Recognizing that the medical use of narcotic drugs continues to be indispensable for the relief of pain and suffering and that adequate provision must be made to ensure the availability of narcotic drugs for such purposes,

Recognizing that addiction to narcotic drugs constitutes a serious evil for the individual and is fraught with social and economic danger to mankind,

Conscious of their duty to prevent and combat evil,

Considering that effective measures against abuse of narcotic drugs require co-ordinated and universal action,

Understanding that such universal action calls for international co-operation guided by the same principles and aimed at common objectives,

Acknowledging the competence of the United Nations in the field of narcotics control and desirous that the international organs concerned should be within the framework of that Organization,

Desiring to conclude a generally acceptable international convention replacing existing treaties on narcotic drugs, limiting such drugs to medical and scientific use, and providing for continuous international co-operation and control for the achievement of such aims and objectives,

Hereby agree as follows:

Article 1 — Definitions

1. Except where otherwise expressly indicated or where the context otherwise requires, the following definitions shall apply throughout the Convention: ...

   (l) "Illicit traffic" means cultivation or trafficking in drugs contrary to the provisions of this Convention.

(m) "Import" and "export" means in their respective connotations the physical transfer of drugs from one State to another State, or from one territory to another territory of the same State, ...

Article 4 — General Obligations

1. The Parties shall take such legislative and administrative measures as may be necessary:

(a) To give effect to and carry out the provisions of this Convention within their own territories;

(b) To co-operate with other States in the execution of the provisions of this Convention; and

(c) Subject to the provisions of this Convention, to limit exclusively to medical and scientific purposes the production, manufacture, export, import, distribution of, trade in, use and possession of drugs....

Article 35 — Action against the illicit traffic

Having due regard to their constitutional, legal and administrative systems, the Parties shall:

(a) Make arrangements at the national level for co-ordination of preventive and repressive action against the illicit traffic; to this end they may usefully designate an appropriate agency responsible for such co-ordination;

(b) Assist each other in the campaign against the illicit traffic in narcotic drugs;

(c) Co-operate closely with each other and with competent international organizations of which they are members with a view to maintaining a co-ordinated campaign against the illicit traffic;

(d) Ensure that international co-operation between the appropriate agencies be conducted in an expeditious manner; and

(e) Ensure that where legal papers are transmitted internationally for the purposes of a prosecution, the transmittal be effected in an expeditious manner to the bodies designated by the Parties; this requirement shall be without prejudice to the right of a Party to require that legal papers be sent to it through the diplomatic channel.

Article 36 — Penal Provisions

1. Subject to its constitutional limitations, each Party shall adopt such measures as will ensure that cultivation, production, manufacture, extraction, preparation, possession, offering, offering for sale, distribution, purchase, sale, delivery on any terms whatsoever, brokerage, dispatch, dispatch in transit, transport, importation and exportation of drugs contrary to the provisions of this Convention, and any other action which in the opinion of such Party may be contrary to the provisions of this Convention, shall be punishable offences when committed intentionally, and that serious offences shall be liable to adequate punishment particularly by imprisonment or other penalties of deprivation of liberty.

2. Subject to the constitutional limitations of a Party, its legal system and domestic law,

(a) (i) Each of the offences enumerated in paragraph 1, if committed in different countries, shall be considered as a distinct offence;

(ii) Intentional participation in, conspiracy to commit and attempts to commit, any of such offences, and preparatory acts and financial operations in connection with the offences referred to in this article, shall be punishable offences as provided in paragraph 1;

(iii) Foreign convictions for such offences shall be taken into account for the purpose of establishing recidivism; and

(iv) Serious offences heretofore referred to committed either by nationals or by foreigners shall be prosecuted by the Party in whose territory the offence was committed, or by the Party in whose territory the offender is found if extradition is not acceptable in conformity with the law of the Party to which application is made, and if such offender has not already been prosecuted and judgment given.

(b) It is desirable that the offences referred to in paragraph 1 and paragraph 2(a)(ii) be included as extradition crimes in any extradition treaty which has been or may hereafter be concluded between any of the Parties, and, as between any of the Parties which do not make extradition conditional on the existence of a treaty or on reciprocity, be recognized as extradition crimes; provided that extradition shall be granted in conformity with the law of the Party to which application is made, and that the Party shall have the right to refuse to effect the arrest or grant the extradition in cases where the competent authorities consider that the offence is not sufficiently serious.

3. The provisions of this article shall be subject to the provisions of the criminal law of the Party concerned on questions of jurisdiction.

4. Nothing contained in this article shall affect the principle that the offences to which it refers shall be defined, prosecuted and punished in conformity with the domestic law of a Party.

Article 37 — Seizure and confiscation

Any drugs, substances and equipment used in or intended for the commission of any of the offences, referred to in article 36, shall be liable to seizure and confiscation....

Geneva Protocol of 1972 Amending the Single Convention on Narcotic Drugs

1976 Can. T.S. No. 48

The Parties to the present Protocol,

Considering the provisions of the Single Convention on Narcotic Drugs, 1961, done at New York on 30 March 1961 (hereinafter called the Single Convention).

Desiring to amend the Single Convention,

Have agreed as follows: ...

Article 13

Amendment to article 35 of the Single Convention Article 35 of the Single Convention shall be amended to read as follows:

"Having due regard to their constitutional, legal and administrative systems, the Parties shall:

(a) Make arrangements at the national level for co-ordination of preventive and repressive action against the illicit traffic; to this end they may usefully designate an appropriate agency responsible for such co-ordination;

(b) Assist each other in the campaign against the illicit traffic in narcotic drugs;

(c) Co-operate closely with each other and with the competent international organizations of which they are members with a view to maintaining a co-ordinated campaign against the illicit traffic;

(d) Ensure that international co-operation between the appropriate agencies be conducted in an expeditious manner;

(e) Ensure that where legal papers are transmitted internationally for the purposes of a prosecution, the transmittal be effected in an expeditious manner to the bodies designated by the Parties; this requirement shall be without prejudice to the right of a Party to require that legal papers be sent to it through the diplomatic channel;

(f) Furnish, if they deem it appropriate, to the Board and the Commission through the Secretary-General, in addition to information required by article 18, information relating to illicit drug activity within their borders, including information on illicit cultivation, production, manufacture and use of, and on illicit trafficking, in drugs; and

(g) Furnish the information referred to in the preceding paragraph as far as possible in such manner and by such dates as the Board may request; if requested by a Party, the Board may offer its advice to it in furnishing the information and in endeavouring to reduce the illicit drug activity within the borders of that Party."

Article 14

Amendments to Article 36, paragraphs 1 and 2, of the Single Convention.

Article 36, paragraphs 1 and 2, of the Single Convention shall be amended to read as follows:

1. (a) Subject to its constitutional limitations, each Party shall adopt such measures as will ensure that cultivation, production, manufacture, extraction, preparation, possession, offering, offering for sale, distribution, purchase, sale, delivery on any terms whatsoever, brokerage, dispatch, dispatch in transit, transport, importation and exportation of drugs contrary to the provisions of this Convention, and any other action which in the opinion of such Party may be contrary to the provisions of this Convention, shall be punishable offences when committed intentionally, and that serious offences shall be liable to adequate punishment particularly by imprisonment or other penalties of deprivation of liberty.

(b) Notwithstanding the preceding sub-paragraph, when abusers of drugs have committed such offences, the Parties may provide, either as an alternative to conviction or punishment or in addition to conviction or punishment, that such abusers shall undergo measures of treatment, education, after-care, rehabilitation and social reintegration in conformity with paragraph 1 of Article 38.

2. Subject to the constitutional limitations of a Party, its legal system and domestic law,

(a) (i) Each of the offences enumerated in paragraph 1, if committed in different countries, shall be considered as a distinct offence;

(ii) Intentional participation in, conspiracy to commit and attempts to commit, any of such offences, and preparatory acts and financial operations in connection with the offences referred to in this article, shall be punishable offences as provided in paragraph 1;

(iii) Foreign convictions for such offences shall be taken into account for the purpose of establishing recidivism; and

(iv) Serious offences heretofore referred to committed either by nationals or by foreigners shall be prosecuted by the Party in whose territory the offence was committed, or by the Party in whose territory the offender is found if extradition is not acceptable in conformity with the law of the Party to which application is made, and if such offender has not already been prosecuted and judgment given.

(b) (i) Each of the offences enumerated in paragraphs 1 and 2(a)(ii) of this article shall be deemed to be included as an extraditable offence in any extradition treaty existing between Parties. Parties undertake to include such offences as extraditable offences in every extradition treaty to be concluded between them.

(ii) If a Party which makes extradition conditional on the existence of a treaty receives a request for extradition from another Party with which it has no extradition treaty, it may at its option consider this Convention as the legal basis for extradition in respect of the offences enumerated in paragraphs 1 and 2(a)(ii) of this article. Extradition shall be subject to the other conditions provided by the law of the requested Party.

(iii) Parties which do not make extradition conditional on the existence of a treaty shall recognize the offences enumerated in paragraphs 1 and 2(a)(ii) of this article as extraditable offences between themselves, subject to the conditions provided by the law of the requested Party.

(iv) Extradition shall be granted in conformity with the law of the Party to which application is made, and, notwithstanding sub-paragraphs (b)(i), (ii) and (iii) of this paragraph, the Party shall have the right to refuse to grant the extradition in cases where the competent authorities consider that the offence is not sufficiently serious.

United Nations Convention Against Illicit Traffic in Narcotic Drugs and Psychotropic Substances
1582 U.N.T.S. 164 (1988)

The Parties to this Convention,

Deeply concerned by the magnitude of and rising trend in the illicit production of, demand for and traffic in narcotic drugs and psychotropic substances, which pose a serious threat to the health and welfare of human beings and adversely affect the economic, cultural and political foundations of society,

Deeply concerned also by the steadily increasing inroads into various social groups made by illicit traffic in narcotic drugs and psychotropic substances, and particularly by the fact that children are used in many parts of the world as an illicit drug consumers market and for purposes of illicit production, distribution and trade in narcotic drugs and psychotropic substances, which entails a danger of incalculable gravity,

Recognizing the links between illicit traffic and other related organized criminal activities which undermine the legitimate economies and threaten the stability, security and sovereignty of States, ...

Aware that illicit traffic generates large financial profits and wealth enabling transnational criminal organizations to penetrate, contaminate and corrupt the structures of government, legitimate commercial and financial business, and society at all levels,

Determined to deprive persons engaged in illicit traffic of the proceeds of their criminal activities and thereby eliminate their main incentive for so doing, ...

Recognizing that eradication of illicit traffic is a collective responsibility of all States and that, to that end, co-ordinated action within the framework of international co-operation is necessary, ...

Hereby agree as follows:

Article 2 — Scope of the Convention

1. The purpose of this Convention is to promote co-operation among the Parties so that they may address more effectively the various aspects of illicit traffic in narcotic drugs and psychotropic substances having an international dimension. In carrying out their obligations under the Convention, the Parties shall take necessary measures, including legislative and administrative measures, in conformity with the fundamental provisions of their respective domestic legislative systems.

2. The Parties shall carry out their obligations under this Convention in a manner consistent with the principles of sovereign equality and territorial integrity of States and that of non-intervention in the domestic affairs of other States.

3. A Party shall not undertake in the territory of another Party the exercise of jurisdiction and performance of functions which are exclusively reserved for the authorities of that other Party by its domestic law.

Article 3 — Offences and Sanctions

1. Each party shall adopt such measures as may be necessary to establish criminal offences under its domestic law, when committed intentionally:

(a) (i) The production, manufacture, extraction, preparation, offering, offering for sale, distribution, sale, delivery on any terms whatsoever, brokerage, dispatch, dispatch in transit, transport, importation or exportation of any narcotic drug or psychotropic substance ... ;

(ii) The cultivation of opium poppy, coca bush or cannabis plant for the purpose of the production of narcotic drugs ... ;

(iii) The possession or purchase of any narcotic drug or psychotropic substance for the purpose of any of the activities enumerated in (i) above;

(iv) The manufacture, transport or distribution of equipment, materials or of substances listed in Table I and Table II, knowing that they are to be used in or for the illicit cultivation, production or manufacture of narcotic drugs or psychotropic substances;

(v) The organization, management or financing of any of the offences enumerated in (i), (ii), (iii) or (iv) above;

(b) (i) The conversion or transfer of property, knowing that such property is derived from any offence or offences established in accordance with subparagraph (a) of this paragraph, or from an act of participation in such offence or offences, for the purpose of concealing or disguising the illicit origin of the property or of assisting any person who is involved in the commission of such an offence or offences to evade the legal consequences of his actions;

(ii) The concealment or disguise of the true nature, source, location, disposition, movement, rights with respect to, or ownership of property, knowing that such property is derived from an offence....

(c) Subject to its constitutional principles and basic concepts of its legal system:

(i) The acquisition, possession or use of property, knowing, at the time of receipt, that such property was derived from an offence....

(ii) The possession of equipment or materials or substance listed in Table I and Table II, knowing that they are being or are about to be used in or for the illicit cultivation, production or manufacture of narcotic drugs or psychotropic substances;

(iii) Publicly inciting or inducing others, by any means, to commit any of the offences established in accordance with this article or to use narcotic drugs or psychotropic substances illicitly;

(iv) Participation in, association or conspiracy to commit, attempts to commit and aiding, abetting, facilitating and counselling the commission of any of the offences established in accordance with this article.

2. Subject to its constitutional principles and the basic concepts of its legal system, each Party shall adopt such measures as may be necessary to establish as a criminal offence under its domestic law, when committed intentionally, the possession, purchase or cultivation contrary of narcotic drugs or psychotropic substances for personal consumption....

5. The Parties shall ensure that their courts and other competent authorities having jurisdiction can take into account factual circumstances which make the commission of the offence established in accordance with paragraph 1 of this article particularly serious, such as:

(a) The involvement in the offence of an organized criminal group to which the offender belongs;

(b) The involvement of the offender in other international organized criminal activities;

(c) The involvement of the offender in other illegal activities facilitated by commission of the offence;

(d) The use of violence or arms by the offender;

(e) The fact that the offender holds a public office and that the offence is connected with the office in question;

(f) The victimization or use of minors;

(g) The fact that the offence is committed in a penal institution or in an educational institution or social service facility or in their immediate vicinity or in other places to which school children and students resort for educational, sports and social activities;

(h) Prior conviction, particularly for similar offences, whether foreign or domestic, to the extent permitted under the domestic law of a Party....

Article 4 — Jurisdiction

1. Each Party:

(a) Shall take such measures as may be necessary to establish its jurisdiction over the offences it has established in accordance with Article 3, paragraph 1, when:

(i) The offence is committed in its territory;

(ii) The offence is committed on board a vessel flying its flag or an aircraft which is registered under its laws at the time the offence is committed;

(b) May take such measures as may be necessary to establish its jurisdiction over the offences it has established in accordance with Article 3, paragraph 1, when:

(i) The offence is committed by one of its nationals or by a person who has his habitual residence in its territory; ...

2. Each Party:

(a) Shall also take such measures as may be necessary to establish its jurisdiction over the offences it has established in accordance with Article 3, paragraph 1, when the alleged offender is present in its territory and it does not extradite him to another Party on the ground:

(i) That the offence has been committed in its territory or on board a vessel flying its flag or an aircraft which was registered under its law at the time the offence was committed; or

(ii) That the offence has been committed by one of its nationals;

(b) May also take such measures as may be necessary to establish its jurisdiction over the offences it has established in accordance with Article 3, paragraph 1, when the alleged offender is present in its territory and its does not extradite him to another Party.

3. This Convention does not exclude the exercise of any criminal jurisdiction established by a Party in accordance with its domestic law.

Article 5 — Confiscation

1. Each Party shall adopt such measures as may be necessary to enable confiscation of:

(a) Proceeds derived from offences established in accordance with Article 3, paragraph 1, or property the value of which corresponds to that of such proceeds;

(b) Narcotic drugs and psychotropic substances, materials and equipment or other instrumentalities used in or intended for use in any manner in offences established in accordance with Article 3, paragraph 1.

2. Each Party shall also adopt such measures as may be necessary to enable its competent authorities to identify, trace, and freeze or seize proceeds, property, instrumentalities or other things referred to in paragraph 1 or this article, for the purpose of eventual confiscation.

3. In order to carry out the measures referred to in this article, each Party shall empower its courts or other competent authorities to order that bank, financial or commercial records be made available or be seized. A Party shall not decline to act under the provisions of this paragraph on the ground of bank secrecy....

Article 6 — Extradition

1. This article shall apply to the offences established by the Parties in accordance with Article 3, paragraph 1.

2. Each of the offences to which this article applies shall be deemed to be included as an extraditable offence in any extradition treaty existing between Parties. The Parties undertake to include such offences as extraditable offences in every extradition treaty to be concluded between them.

3. If a Party which makes extradition conditional on the existence of a treaty receives a request for extradition from another Party with which it has no extradition treaty, it may consider this Convention as the legal basis for extradition in respect of any offence to which this article applies. The Parties which require detailed legislation in order to use this Convention as a legal basis for extradition shall consider enacting such legislation as may be necessary.

4. The Parties which do not make extradition conditional on the existence of a treaty shall recognize offences to which this article applies as extraditable offences between themselves.

5. Extradition shall be subject to the conditions provided for by the law of the requested Party or by applicable extradition treaties, including the grounds upon which the requested Party may refuse extradition.

6. In considering requests pursuant to this article, the requested State may refuse to comply with such requests where there are substantial grounds leading its judicial or other

competent authorities to believe that compliance would facilitate the prosecution or punishment of any person on account of his race, religion, nationality or political opinions, or would cause prejudice for any of those reasons to any person affected by the request.

7. The Parties shall endeavour to expedite extradition procedures and to simplify evidentiary requirements relating thereto in respect of any offence to which this article applies....

9. Without prejudice to the exercise of any criminal jurisdiction established in accordance with its domestic law, a Party in whose territory an alleged offender is found shall:

(a) If it does not extradite him ... submit the case to its competent authorities for the purpose of prosecution....

10. If extradition, sought for the purposes of enforcing a sentence, is refused because the person sought is a national of the requested Party, the requested Party shall, if its law so permits and in conformity with the requirements of such law, upon application of the requesting Party, consider the enforcement of the sentence which has been imposed under the law of the requesting Party, or the remainder thereof....

Article 7 — Mutual Legal Assistance

1. The Parties shall afford one another, pursuant to this article, the widest measure of mutual legal assistance in investigations, prosecutions and judicial proceedings in relation to criminal offences established in accordance with Article 3, paragraph 1.

2. Mutual legal assistance to be afforded in accordance with this article may be requested for any of the following purposes:

(a) Taking of evidence or statements from persons;

(b) Effecting service of judicial documents;

(c) Executing searches or seizures:

(d) Examining objects and sites:

(e) Providing information and evidentiary items;

(f) Providing originals or certified copies of relevant documents and records, including bank, financial, corporate or business records;

(g) Identifying or tracing proceeds, property, instrumentalities or other things for evidentiary purposes....

12. A request shall be executed in accordance with the domestic law of the requested Party....

13. The requesting Party shall not transmit nor use information or evidence furnished by the requested Party for investigations, prosecutions or proceedings other than those stated in the request without the prior consent of the requested Party....

15. Mutual legal assistance may be refused:

(a) If the request is not made in conformity with the provisions of this article;

(b) If the requested Party considers that execution of the request is likely to prejudice its sovereignty, security, *ordre public* or other essential interests; ...

17. Mutual legal assistance may be postponed by the requested Party on the ground that it interferes with an ongoing investigation, prosecution or proceeding....

18. A witness, expert or other person who consents to give evidence in a proceeding or to assist in an investigation, prosecution or judicial proceeding in the territory of the

requesting Party, shall not be prosecuted, detained, punished or subjected to any other restriction of his personal liberty in that territory in respect of acts, omissions or convictions prior to his departure....

Article 8 — Transfer of proceedings

The Parties shall give consideration to the possibility of transferring to one another proceedings for criminal prosecution of offences established in accordance with Article 3, paragraph 1, in cases where such transfer is considered to be in the interests of a proper administration of justice.

Article 9 — Other forms of co-operation and training

1. The Parties shall co-operate closely with one another, consistent with their respective domestic legal and administrative systems, with a view to enhancing the effectiveness of law enforcement action to suppress the commission of offences established in accordance with Article 3, paragraph 1....

Article 10 — International co-operation and assistance for transit States

1. The Parties shall co-operate, directly or through competent international or regional organizations, to assist and support transit States and, in particular, developing countries....

Article 11 — Controlled delivery

1. If permitted by the basic principles of their respective domestic legal systems, the Parties shall take the necessary measures, within their possibilities, to allow for the appropriate use of controlled delivery at the international level, on the basis of agreements or arrangements mutually consented to, with a view to identifying persons involved in offences....

Article 12 — Substances frequently used in the illicit manufacture of narcotic drugs or psychotropic substances

1. The Parties shall take the measures they deem appropriate to prevent diversion of substances in Table I and Table II used for the purpose of illicit manufacture of narcotic drugs or psychotropic substances....

Article 13 — Materials and equipment

The Parties shall take such measures as they deem appropriate to prevent trade in and the diversion of materials and equipment for illicit production or manufacture of narcotic drugs and psychotropic substances and shall co-operate to this end.

Article 14 — Measures to eradicate illicit cultivation of narcotic plants and to eliminate illicit demand for narcotic drugs and psychotropic substances

... 2. Each Party shall take appropriate measures to prevent illicit cultivation of and to eradicate plants containing narcotic or psychotropic substances, such as opium poppy, coca bush and cannabis plants, cultivated illicitly in its territory. The measures adopted shall respect fundamental human rights and shall take due account of traditional licit uses, where there is historic evidence of such use, as well as the protection of the environment.

3. (a) The Parties may co-operate to increase the effectiveness of eradication efforts. Such co-operation may, *inter alia*, include support, when appropriate, for integrated rural development leading to economically viable alternatives to illicit cultivation....

4. The Parties shall adopt appropriate measures aimed at eliminating or reducing illicit demand for narcotic drugs and psychotropic substances, with a view to reducing human suffering and eliminating financial incentives for illicit traffic. . . .

Article 15 — Commercial carriers

1. The Parties shall take appropriate measures to ensure that means of transport operated by commercial carriers are not used in the commission of offences. . . .

Article 16 — Commercial documents and labelling of exports

1. Each Party shall require that lawful exports of narcotic drugs and psychotropic substances be properly documented. . . .

Article 17 — Illicit traffic by sea

1. The Parties shall co-operate to the fullest extent possible to suppress illicit traffic by sea, in conformity with the international law of the sea. . . .

Article 18 — Free Trade Zones and Free Ports

1. The Parties shall apply measures to suppress illicit traffic in narcotic drugs, psychotropic substances and substances in Table I and Table II in free trade zones and in free ports that are no less stringent than those applied in other parts of their territories. . . .

Article 19 — The Use of the Mails

1. In conformity with their obligations under the Conventions of the Universal Postal Union, and in accordance with the basic principles of their domestic legal systems, the Parties shall adopt measures to suppress the use of the mails for illicit traffic and shall co-operate with one another to that end. . . .

Article 20 — Information to be Furnished by the Parties

1. The Parties shall furnish, through the Secretary-General, information to the Commission on the working of this Convention in their territories and, in particular:

> . . . (b) Particulars of cases of illicit traffic within their jurisdiction which they consider important because of new trends disclosed, the quantities involved, the sources from which the substances are obtained, or the methods employed by persons so engaged. . . .

Article 21 — Functions of the Commission

The Commission is authorized to consider all matters pertaining to the aims of this Convention. . . .

Annex

Table I	Table II
Ephedrine	Acetic anhydride
Ergometrine	Acetone
Ergomatine	Anthranilic acid
Lysergic acid	Ethyl ether
1-phenyl-2-propanone	Phenylacetic acid
Pseudephedrine	Piperidine

The salts of the substances listed in this Table whenever the existence of such salts is possible.

General Act of the Conference of Berlin Concerning the Congo

(signed Feb. 26, 1885 by United States, Germany, Prussia,
Austria, Bohemia, Hungary, Belgium, Denmark, Spain, France,
United Kingdom, The Indies, Italy, the Netherlands, Luxembourg,
Portugal, Russia, Sweden and Norway, the Ottomans)

Declaration Concerning the Slave Trade

Article 9

Conformably to the principles of the law of nations, as they are recognized by the signatory Powers, the slave trade being interdicted, and as the operations which, by land or sea, furnish slaves to the trade ought to be equally considered as interdicted, the Powers who exercise or shall exercise rights of sovereignty or an influence in the territories forming the conventional basin of the Congo declare that these territories shall not serve either for a market or way of transit for the trade in slaves of any race whatever. Each of these Powers engages itself to employ all the means in its power to put an end to this commerce and to punish those who are occupied in it.

General Act Between the United States of America and Other Powers for the Repression of the African Slave Trade, etc.

(signed at Brussels, July 2, 1890 by United States, German Empire,
Austria, Belgium, Denmark, Spain, the Congo, France, United Kingdom,
Italy, the Netherlands, Persia, Portugal, Russia, Sweden and
Norway, the Ottomans, Zanzibar)

Preamble

Being equally actuated by the firm intention of putting an end to the crimes and devastations engendered by the traffic in African slaves, of efficiently protecting the aboriginal population of Africa, and the securing for that vast continent the benefits of peace and civilization....

Article V

The contracting powers pledge themselves, unless this has already been provided for by laws in accordance with the spirit of the present article, to enact or propose to their respective legislative bodies, in the course of one year at the latest from the date of the signing of the present general act, a law rendering applicable, on the one hand, the provisions of their penal laws concerning grave offenses against the person, to the organizers and abettors of slave-hunting, to those guilty of mutilating male adults and children, and to all persons taking part in the capture of slaves by violence; and, on the other hand, the provisions relating to offenses against individual liberty, to carriers and transporters of, and to dealers in, slaves.

The accessories and accomplices of the different categories of slave captors and dealers above specified shall be punished with penalties proportionate to those incurred by the principals.

Guilty persons who may have escaped from the jurisdiction of the authorities of the country where the crimes or offenses have been committed shall be arrested either on communication of the incriminating evidence by the authorities who have ascertained the violation of the law, or on production of any other proof of guilt by the power in whose territory they may have been discovered, and shall be kept, without other formality, at the disposal of the tribunals competent to try them.

The powers shall communicate to one another, with the least possible delay, the laws or decrees existing or promulgated in execution of the present article....

Article XIX

The penal arrangements provided for by Article V shall be applicable to all offences committed in the course of operations connected with the transportation of the traffic in slaves on land whenever such offences may be ascertained to have been committed.

Any person having incurred a penalty in consequence of an offence provided for by the present general act, shall incur the obligation of furnishing security before being able to engage in any commercial transaction in countries where the slave-trade is carried on.

Slavery Convention, 1926
60 L.N.T.S. 253, amended by Protocol, 1953, 7 U.S.T. 479; 182 U.N.T.S. 51

Article 1

For the purpose of the present Convention, the following definitions are agreed upon:

(1) Slavery is the status or condition of a person over whom any or all of the powers attaching to the right of ownership are exercised.

(2) The slave trade includes all acts involved in the capture, acquisition or disposal of a person with intent to reduce him to slavery; all acts involved in the acquisition of a slave with a view to selling or exchanging him; all acts of disposal by sale or exchange of a slave acquired with a view to being sold or exchanged, and, in general, every act of trade or transport in slaves.

Article 2

The High Contracting Parties undertake, each in respect of the territories placed under its sovereignty, jurisdiction, protection, suzerainty or tutelage, so far as they have not already taken the necessary steps:

(a) To prevent and suppress the slave trade;

(b) To bring about, progressively and as soon as possible, the complete abolition of slavery in all its forms.

Article 3

The High Contracting Parties undertake to adopt all appropriate measures with a view to preventing and suppressing the embarkation, disembarkation and transport of slaves in their territorial waters and upon all vessels flying their respective flags.

The High Contracting Parties undertake to negotiate as soon as possible a general Convention with regard to the slave trade which will give them rights and impose upon them duties of the same nature as those provided for in the Convention of 17 June, 1925, relative to the International Trade in Arms (Articles 12, 20, 21, 22, 23, 24, and paragraphs 3, 4 and 5 of Section II of Annex II), with the necessary adaptations, it being understood that this general Convention will not place the ships (even of small tonnage) of any High Contracting Parties in a position different from that of the other High Contracting Parties.

It is also understood that, before or after the coming into force of this general Convention, the High Contracting Parties are entirely free to conclude between themselves, without, however, derogating from the principles laid down in the preceding paragraph, such special agreements as, by reason of their peculiar situation, might appear to be suitable in order to bring about as soon as possible the complete disappearance of the slave trade.

Article 4

The High Contracting Parties shall give to one another every assistance with the object of securing the abolition of slavery and the slave trade.

Article 5

The High Contracting Parties recognize that recourse to compulsory or forced labour may have grave consequences and undertake, each in respect of the territories placed under its sovereignty, jurisdiction, protection, suzerainty or tutelage, to take all necessary measures to prevent compulsory or forced labour from developing into conditions analogous to slavery.

It is agreed that:

(1) Subject to the transitional provisions laid down in paragraph (2) below, compulsory or forced labour may only be exacted for public purposes.

(2) In territories in which compulsory or forced labour for other than public purposes still survives, the High Contracting Parties shall endeavour progressively and as soon as possible to put an end to the practice. So long as such forced or compulsory labour exists, this labour shall invariably be of an exceptional character, shall always receive adequate remuneration, and shall not involve the removal of the labourers from their usual place of residence.

(3) In all cases, the responsibility for any recourse to compulsory or forced labour shall rest with the competent central authorities of the territory concerned.

Article 6

Those of the High Contracting Parties whose laws do not at present make adequate provision for the punishment of infractions of laws and regulations enacted with a view to giving effect to the purposes of the present Convention undertake to adopt the necessary measures in order that severe penalties may be imposed in respect of such infractions.

Article 7

The High Contracting Parties undertake to communicate to each other and to the Secretary-General of the United Nations any laws and regulations which they may enact with a view to the application of the provisions of the present Convention.

Article 8

The High Contracting Parties agree that disputes arising between them relating to the interpretation or application of this Convention shall, if they cannot be settled by direct negotiation, be referred for decision to the International Court of Justice. In case either or both the States Parties to such a dispute should not be parties to the Statute of the International Court of Justice, the dispute shall be referred, at the choice of the Parties and in accordance with the constitutional procedure or each State, either to the International Court of Justice or to a court of arbitration constituted in accordance with the Convention of 18 October, 1907, for the Pacific Settlement of International Disputes, or to some other court of arbitration.

Article 9

At the time of signature or of ratification or of accession, any High Contracting Party may declare that its acceptance of the present Convention does not bind some or all of the territories placed under its sovereignty, jurisdiction, protection, suzerainty or tutelage in respect of all or any provisions of the Convention; it may subsequently accede separately on behalf of any one of them or in respect of any provision to which any one of them is not a party.

Article 10

In the event of a High Contracting Party wishing to denounce the present Convention, the denunciation shall be notified in writing to the Secretary-General of the United Nations, who will at once communicate a certified true copy of the notification to all the other High Contracting Parties, informing them of the date on which it was received.

The denunciation shall only have effect in regard to the notifying State, and one year after the notification has reached the Secretary-General of the United Nations.

Denunciation may also be made separately in respect of any territory placed under its sovereignty, jurisdiction, protection, suzerainty or tutelage.

Article 11

The present Convention, which will bear this day's date and of which the French and English texts are both authentic, will remain open for signature by the States members of the League of Nations until 1 April, 1927.

The present Convention shall be open to accession by all States, including States which are not members of the United Nations, to which the Secretary-General of the United Nations shall have communicated a certified copy of the Convention.

Accession shall be effected by the deposit of a formal instrument with the Secretary-General of the United Nations, who shall give notice thereof to all States Parties to the Convention and to all other States contemplated in the present article, informing them of the date on which each such instrument of accession was received in deposit.

Article 12

The present Convention will be ratified and the instruments of ratification shall be deposited in the office of the Secretary-General of the United Nations. The Secretary-General will inform all the High Contracting Parties of such deposit.

The Convention will come into operation for each State on the date of the deposit of its ratification or of its accession.

Protocol Amending the Slavery Convention

The States Parties to the present Protocol,

Considering that under the Slavery Convention signed at Geneva on 25 September, 1926 (hereinafter called "the Convention") the League of Nations was invested with certain duties and functions, and

Considering that it is expedient that these duties and functions should be continued by the United Nations,

Have agreed as follows:

Article I

The States Parties to the present Protocol undertake that as between themselves they will, in accordance with the provisions of the Protocol, attribute full legal force and effect to and duly apply the amendments to the Convention set forth in the annex to the Protocol.

Article II

1. The present Protocol shall be open for signature or acceptance by any of the States Parties to the Convention to which the Secretary-General has communicated for this purpose a copy of the Protocol.

2. States may become Parties to the present Protocol by:

(a) Signature without reservation as to acceptance;

(b) Signature with reservation as to acceptance, followed by acceptance;

(c) Acceptance.

3. Acceptance shall be effected by the deposit of a formal instrument with the Secretary-General of the United Nations.

Article III

1. The present Protocol shall come into force on the date on which two States shall have become Parties thereto, and shall thereafter come into force in respect of each State upon the date on which it becomes a Party to the Protocol.

2. The amendments set forth in the annex to the present Protocol shall come into force when twenty-three States shall have become Parties to the Protocol, and consequently any State becoming a party to the Convention, after the amendments thereto have come into force, shall become a party to the Convention as so amended....

Supplementary Convention on the Abolition of Slavery, The Slave Trade, and Institutions and Practices Similar to Slavery, 1956
266 U.N.T.S. 3; 18 U.S.T. 3201; T.I.A.S. 6418

Preamble

The States Parties to the present Convention,

Considering that freedom is the birthright of every human being;

Mindful that the peoples of the United Nations reaffirm in the Charter their faith in the dignity and worth of the human person;

Considering that the Universal Declaration of Human Rights, proclaimed by the General Assembly of the United Nations as a common standard of achievement for all peoples and all nations, states that no one shall be held in slavery or servitude and that slavery and the slave trade shall be prohibited in all their forms;

Recognizing that, since the conclusion of the Slavery Convention signed at Geneva on 25 September, 1926, which was designed to secure the abolition of slavery and of the slave trade, further progress has been made towards this end;

Having regard to the forced Labour Convention of 1930 and to subsequent action by the International Labour Organization in regard to forced or compulsory labour;

Being aware, however, that slavery, the slave trade and institutions and practices similar to slavery have not yet been eliminated in all parts of the world;

Having decided, therefore, that the Convention of 1926, which remains operative, should now be augmented by the conclusion of a supplementary convention designed to intensify national as well as international efforts towards the abolition of slavery, the slave trade and institutions and practices similar to slavery;

Have agreed as follows:

Section I. Institutions and Practices Similar to Slavery

Article 1

Each of the States Parties to this Convention shall take all practicable and necessary legislative and other measures to bring about progressively and as soon as possible the complete abolition or abandonment of the following institutions and practices, where they still exist and whether or not they are covered by the definition of slavery contained in Article 1 of the Slavery Convention signed at Geneva on 25 September, 1926:

(a) debt bondage, that is to say, the status or condition arising from a pledge by a debtor of his personal services or of those of a person under his control as security for a debt, if the value of those services as reasonably assessed is not applied towards the liquidation of the debt or the length and nature of those services are not respectively limited and defined;

(b) serfdom, that is to say, the condition or status of a tenant who is by law, custom or agreement bound to live and labour on land belonging to another person and to render some determinate service to such other person, whether for reward or not, and is not free to change his status;

(c) any institution or practice whereby:

(i) a woman, without the right to refuse, is promised or given in marriage on payment of a consideration in money or in kind to her parents, guardian, family or any other person or group; or

(ii) the husband of a woman, his family, or his clan, has the right to transfer her to another person for value received or otherwise; or

(iii) a woman on the death of her husband is liable to be inherited by another person;

(d) any institution or practice whereby a child or young person under the age of eighteen years is delivered by either or both of his natural parents or by his guardian to another person, whether for reward or not, with a view to the exploitation of the child or young person or of his labour.

Article 2

With a view to bringing to an end the institutions and practices mentioned in Article 1(c) of this Convention, the States Parties undertake to prescribe, where appropriate, suitable minimum ages of marriage, to encourage the use of facilities whereby the consent of both parties to a marriage may be freely expressed in the presence of a competent civil or religious authority, and to encourage the registration of marriages.

Section II. The Slave Trade

Article 3

1. The act of conveying or attempting to convey slaves from one country to another by whatever means of transport, or of being accessory thereto, shall be a criminal offence

under the laws of the States Parties to this Convention and persons convicted thereof shall be liable to very severe penalties.

2. (a) The States Parties shall take all effective measures to prevent ships and aircraft authorized to fly their flags from conveying slaves and to punish persons guilty of such acts or of using national flags for that purpose.

(b) The States Parties shall take all effective measures to ensure that their ports, airfields and coasts are not used for the conveyance of slaves.

3. The States Parties to this Convention shall exchange information in order to ensure the practical co-ordination of the measures taken by them in combating the slave trade and shall inform each other of every case of the slave trade, and of every attempt to commit this criminal offence, which comes to their notice.

Article 4

Any slave who takes refuge on board any vessel of a State Party to this Convention shall *ipso facto* be free.

Section III. Slavery and Institutions and Practices Similar to Slavery

Article 5

In a country where the abolition or abandonment of slavery, or of the institutions or practices mentioned in Article 1 of this Convention, is not yet complete, the act of mutilating, branding or otherwise marking a slave or a person of servile status in order to indicate his status, or as a punishment, or for any other reason, or of being accessory thereto, shall be a criminal offence under the laws of the States Parties to this Convention and persons convicted thereof shall be liable to punishment.

Article 6

1. The act of enslaving another person or of inducing another person to give himself or a person dependent upon him into slavery, or of attempting these acts, or being accessory thereto, or being a party to a conspiracy to accomplish any such acts, shall be a criminal offence under the laws of the States Parties to this Convention and persons convicted thereof shall be liable to punishment.

2. Subject to the provisions of the introductory paragraph of Article 1 of this Convention, the provisions of paragraph 1 of the present article shall also apply to the act of inducing another person to place himself or a person dependent upon him into the servile status resulting from any of the institutions or practices mentioned in Article 1, to any attempt to perform such acts, to being accessory thereto, and to being party to a conspiracy to accomplish any such acts.

Section IV. Definitions

Article 7

For the purposes of the present Convention:

(a) "Slavery" means, as defined in the Slavery Convention of 1926, the status or condition of a person over whom any or all of the powers attaching to the right of ownership are exercised, and "slave" means a person in such condition or status;

(b) "a person of servile status" means a person in the condition or status resulting from any of the institutions or practices mentioned in Article 1 of this Convention;

(c) "slave trade" means and includes all acts involved in the capture, acquisition or disposal of a person with intent to reduce him to slavery; all acts involved in the acquisition of a slave with a view to selling or exchanging him; all acts of disposal by sale or exchange of a person acquired with a view to being sold or exchanged; and, in general, every act of trade or transport in slaves by whatever means of conveyance.

Section V. Co-Operation Between States Parties and

Communication of Information

Article 8

1. The States Parties to this Convention undertake to co-operate with each other and with the United Nations to give effect to the foregoing provisions.

2. The Parties undertake to communicate to the Secretary-General of the United Nations copies of any laws, regulations and administrative measures enacted or put into effect to implement the provisions of this Convention.

3. The Secretary-General shall communicate the information received under paragraph 2 of this article to the other Parties and to the Economic and Social Council as part of the documentation for any discussion which the Council might undertake with a view to making further recommendations for the abolition of slavery, the slave trade or the institutions and practices which are the subject of this Convention.

Section VI. Final Clauses

Article 9

No reservations may be made to this Convention.

Article 10

Any dispute between States Parties to this Convention relating to its interpretation or application, which is not settled by negotiation, shall be referred to the International Court of Justice at the request of any one of the parties to the dispute, unless the parties concerned agree on another mode of settlement.

Article 11

1. This Convention shall be open until 1 July, 1957, for signature by any State Member of the United Nations or of a specialized agency. It shall be subject to ratification by the signatory States, and the instruments of ratification shall be deposited with the Secretary General of the United Nations, who shall inform each signatory and acceding State.

2. After 1 July, 1957, this Convention shall be open for accession by any State Member of the United Nations or of a specialized agency, or by any other State to which an invitation to accede has been addressed by the General Assembly of the United Nations. Accession shall be effected by the deposit of a formal instrument with the Secretary-General of the United Nations, who shall inform each signatory and acceding State.

Article 12

1. This Convention shall apply to all non-self-governing, trust, colonial and other non-metropolitan territories for the international relations of which any State Party is responsible; the Party concerned shall, subject to the provisions of paragraph 3 of this

article, at the time of signature, ratification or accession declare the non-metropolitan territory or territories to which the Convention shall apply *ipso facto* as a result of such signature, ratification or accession.

2. In any case in which the previous consent of a non-metropolitan territory is required by the constitutional laws or practices of the Party or of the non-metropolitan territory, the Party concerned shall endeavour to secure the needed consent of the non-metropolitan territory within the period of twelve months from the date of signature of the Convention by the metropolitan State, and when such consent has been obtained the Party shall notify the Secretary-General. This Convention shall apply to the territory or territories named in such notification from the date of its receipt by the Secretary-General.

3. After the expiry of the twelve-month period mentioned in the preceding paragraph, the States Parties concerned shall inform the Secretary-General of the results of the consultations with those non-metropolitan territories for whose international relations they are responsible and whose consent to the application of this Convention may have been withheld.

Article 13

1. This Convention shall enter into force on the date on which two States have become Parties thereto.

2. It shall thereafter enter into force with respect to each State and territory on the date of deposit of the instrument of ratification or accession of that State or notification of application to that territory.

Article 14

1. The application of this Convention shall be divided into successive periods of three years, of which the first shall begin on the date of entry into force of the Convention in accordance with paragraph 1 of Article 13.

2. Any State Party may denounce this Convention by a notice addressed by that State to the Secretary-General not less than six months before the expiration of the current three-year period. The Secretary-General shall notify all other Parties of each such notice and the date of receipt thereof.

3. Denunciations shall take effect at the expiration of the current three-year period.

4. In cases where, in accordance with the provisions of Article 12, this Convention has become applicable to a non-metropolitan territory of a Party, that Party may at any time thereafter, with the consent of the territory concerned, give notice to the Secretary-General of the United Nations denouncing this Convention separately in respect of that territory. The denunciation shall take effect one year after the date of the receipt of such notice by the Secretary-General, who shall notify all other Parties of such notice and the date of the receipt thereof.

Article 15

This Convention, of which the Chinese, English, French, Russian and Spanish texts are equally authentic, shall be deposited in the archives of the United Nations Secretariat. The Secretary-General shall prepare a certified copy thereof for communication to States Parties to this Convention, as well as to all other States Members of the United Nations and of the specialized agencies....

Vienna Convention on Diplomatic Relations

500 U.N.T.S. 95, 23 U.S.T. 3227, T.I.A.S. No. 7502 (1961)

The States Parties to the present Convention,

Recalling that people of all nations from ancient times have recognized the status of diplomatic agents,

Having in mind the purposes and principles of the Charter of the United Nations concerning the sovereign equality of States, the maintenance of international peace and security, and the promotion of friendly relations among nations,

Believing that an international convention on diplomatic intercourse, privileges and immunities would contribute to the development of friendly relations among nations, irrespective of their differing constitutional and social systems,

Realizing that the purpose of such privileges and immunities is not to benefit individuals but to ensure the efficient performance of the functions of diplomatic missions as representing States,

Affirming that the rules of customary international law should continue to govern questions not expressly regulated by the provisions of the present Convention,

Have agreed as follows:

Article 1

For the purpose of the present Convention, the following expressions shall have the meanings hereunder assigned to them:

(a) the "head of the mission" is the person charged by the sending State with the duty of acting in that capacity;

(b) the "members of the mission" are the head of the mission and the members of the staff of the mission;

(c) the "members of the staff of the mission" are the members of the diplomatic staff, of the administrative and technical staff and of the service staff of the mission;

(d) the "members of the diplomatic staff" are the members of the staff of the mission having diplomatic rank;

(e) a "diplomatic agent" is the head of the mission or a member of the diplomatic staff of the mission;

(f) the "members of the administrative and technical staff" are the members of the staff of the mission employed in the administrative and technical service of the mission;

(g) the "members of the service staff" are the members of the staff of the mission in the domestic service of the mission;

(h) a "private servant" is a person who is in the domestic service of a member of the mission and who is not an employee of the sending State;

(i) the "premises of the mission" are the buildings or parts of buildings and the land ancillary thereto, irrespective of ownership, used for the purposes of the mission including the residence of the head of the mission.

Article 2

The establishment of diplomatic relations between States, and of permanent diplomatic missions, takes place by mutual consent.

Article 3

1. The functions of a diplomatic mission consist *inter alia* in:

(a) representing the sending State in the receiving State;

(b) protecting in the receiving State the interests of the sending State and of its nationals, within the limits permitted by international law;

(c) negotiating with the Government of the receiving State;

(d) ascertaining by all lawful means conditions and developments in the receiving State, and reporting thereon to the Government of the sending State;

(e) promoting friendly relations between the sending State and the receiving State, and developing their economic, cultural and scientific relations.

2. Nothing in the present Convention shall be construed as preventing the performance of consular functions by a diplomatic mission.

Article 4

1. The sending State must make certain that the *agrément* of the receiving State has been given for the person it proposes to accredit as head of the mission to that State.

2. The receiving State is not obliged to give reasons to the sending State for a refusal of *agrément*.

Article 5

1. The sending State may, after it has given due notification to the receiving States concerned, accredit a head of mission or assign any member of the diplomatic staff, as the case may be, to more than one State, unless there is express objection by any of the receiving States.

2. If the sending State accredits a head of mission to one or more other States it may establish a diplomatic mission headed by a *chargé d'affaires ad interim* in each State where the head of mission has not his permanent seat.

3. A head of mission or any member of the diplomatic staff of the mission may act as representative of the sending State to any international organization.

Article 6

Two or more States may accredit the same person as head of mission to another State, unless objection is offered by the receiving State.

Article 7

Subject to the provisions of Articles 5, 8, 9 and 11, the sending State may freely appoint the members of the staff of the mission. In the case of military, naval or air *attachés*, the receiving State may require their names to be submitted beforehand, for its approval.

Article 8

1. Members of the diplomatic staff of the mission should in principle be of the nationality of the sending State.

2. Members of the diplomatic staff of the mission may not he appointed from among persons having the nationality of the receiving State, except with the consent of that State which may be withdrawn at any time.

3. The receiving State may reserve the same right with regard to nationals of a third State who are not also nationals of the sending State.

Article 9

1. The receiving State may at any time and without having to explain its decision, notify the sending State that the head of the mission or any member of the diplomatic staff of the mission is *persona non grata* or that any other member of the staff of the mission is not acceptable. In any such case, the sending State shall, as appropriate, either recall the person concerned or terminate his functions with the mission. A person may be declared *non grata* or not acceptable before arriving in the territory of the receiving State.

2. If the sending State refuses or fails within a reasonable period to carry out its obligations under paragraph 1 of this article, the receiving State may refuse to recognize the person concerned as a member of the mission.

Article 10

1. The Ministry for Foreign Affairs of the receiving State, or such other ministry as may be agreed, shall be notified of:

(a) the appointment of members of the mission, their arrival and their final departure or the termination of their functions with the mission;

(b) the arrival and final departure of a person belonging to the family of a member of the mission and, where appropriate, the fact that a person becomes or ceases to be a member of the family of a member of the mission;

(c) the arrival and final departure of private servants in the employ of persons referred to in sub-paragraph (a) of this paragraph and, where appropriate, the fact that they are leaving the employ of such persons;

(d) the engagement and discharge of persons resident in the receiving State as members of the mission or private servants entitled to privileges and immunities.

2. Where possible, prior notification of arrival and final departure shall also be given.

Article 11

1. In the absence of specific agreement as to the size of the mission, the receiving State may require that the size of a mission be kept within limits considered by it to be reasonable and normal, having regard to circumstances and conditions in the receiving State and to the needs of the particular mission.

2. The receiving State may equally, within similar bounds and on a nondiscriminatory basis, refuse to accept officials of a particular category.

Article 12

The sending State may not, without the prior express consent of the receiving State, establish offices forming part of the mission in localities other than those in which the mission itself is established.

Article 13

1. The head of the mission is considered as having taken up his functions in the receiving State either when he has presented his credentials or when he has notified his arrival and a true copy of his credentials has been presented to the Ministry for Foreign Affairs of the receiving State, or such other ministry as may be agreed, in accordance with the practice prevailing in the receiving State which shall be applied in a uniform manner.

2. The order of presentation of credentials or of a true copy thereof will be determined by the date and time of the arrival of the head of the mission.

Article 14

1. Heads of mission are divided into three classes, namely:

(a) that of ambassadors or nuncios accredited to Heads of State, and other heads of mission of equal rank;

(b) that of envoys, ministers and internuncios accredited to Heads of State;

(c) that of *chargés d'affaires* accredited to Ministers of Foreign Affairs.

2. Except as concerns precedence and etiquette, there shall be no differentiation between heads of mission by reason of their class.

Article 15

The class to which the heads of their missions are to be assigned shall be agreed between States.

Article 16

1. Heads of mission shall take precedence in their respective classes in the order of the date and time of taking up their functions in accordance with Article 13.

2. Alterations in the credentials of a head of mission not involving any change of class shall not affect his precedence.

3. This article is without prejudice to any practice accepted by the receiving State regarding the precedence of the representative of the Holy See.

Article 17

The precedence of the members of the diplomatic staff of the mission shall be notified by the head of the mission to the Ministry for Foreign Affairs or such other ministry as may be agreed.

Article 18

The procedure to be observed in each State for the reception of heads of mission shall be uniform in respect of each class.

Article 19

1. If the post of head of the mission is vacant, or if the head of the mission is unable to perform his functions, a *chargé d'affaires ad interim* shall act provisionally as head of the mission. The name of the *chargé d'affaires ad interim* shall be notified, either by the head of the mission or, in case he is unable to do so, by the Ministry for Foreign Affairs of the sending State to the Ministry for Foreign Affairs of the receiving State or such other ministry as may be agreed.

2. In cases where no member of the diplomatic staff of the mission is present in the receiving State, a member of the administrative and technical staff may, with the consent of the receiving State, be designated by the sending State to be in charge of the current administrative affairs of the mission.

Article 20

The mission and its head shall have the right to use the flag and emblem of the sending State on the premises of the mission, including the residence of the head of the mission, and on his means of transport.

Article 21

1. The receiving State shall either facilitate the acquisition on its territory, in accordance with its laws, by the sending State of premises necessary for its mission or assist the latter in obtaining accommodation in some other way.

2. It shall also, where necessary, assist missions in obtaining suitable accommodation for their members.

Article 22

1. The premises of the mission shall be inviolable. The agents of the receiving State may not enter them, except with the consent of the head of the mission.

2. The receiving State is under a special duty to take all appropriate steps to protect the premises of the mission against any intrusion or damage and to prevent any disturbance of the peace of the mission or impairment of its dignity.

3. The premises of the mission, their furnishings and other property thereon and the means of transport of the mission shall be immune from search, requisition, attachment or execution.

Article 23

1. The sending State and the head of the mission shall be exempt from all national, regional or municipal dues and taxes in respect of the premises of the mission, whether owned or leased, other than such as represent payment for specific services rendered.

2. The exemption from taxation referred to in this article shall not apply to such dues and taxes payable under the law of the receiving State by persons contracting with the sending State or the head of the mission.

Article 24

The archives and documents of the mission shall be inviolable at any time and wherever they may be.

Article 25

The receiving State shall accord full facilities for the performance of the functions of the mission.

Article 26

Subject to its laws and regulations concerning zones entry into which is prohibited or regulated for reasons of national security, the receiving State shall ensure to all members of the mission freedom of movement and travel in its territory.

Article 27

1. The receiving State shall permit and protect free communication on the part of the mission for all official purposes. In communicating with the Government and the other missions and consulates of the sending State, wherever situated, the mission may employ all appropriate means, including diplomatic couriers and messages in code or cipher. However, the mission may install and use a wireless transmitter only with the consent of the receiving State.

2. The official correspondence of the mission shall be inviolable. Official correspondence means all correspondence relating to the mission and its functions.

3. The diplomatic bag shall not be opened or detained.

4. The packages constituting the diplomatic bag must bear visible external marks of their character and may contain only diplomatic documents or articles intended for official use.

5. The diplomatic courier, who shall be provided with an official document indicating his status and the number of packages constituting the diplomatic bag, shall be protected by the receiving State in the performance of his functions. He shall enjoy personal inviolability and shall not be liable to any form of arrest or detention.

6. The sending State or the mission may designate diplomatic couriers ad hoc. In such cases the provisions of paragraph 5 of this article shall also apply, except that the immunities therein mentioned shall cease to apply when such a courier has delivered to the consignee the diplomatic bag in his charge.

7. A diplomatic bag may be entrusted to the captain of a commercial aircraft scheduled to land at an authorized port of entry. He shall be provided with an official document indicating the number of packages constituting the bag but he shall not be considered to be a diplomatic courier. The mission may send one of its members to take possession of the diplomatic bag directly and freely from the captain of the aircraft.

Article 28

The fees and charges levied by the mission in the course of its official duties shall be exempt from all dues and taxes.

Article 29

The person of a diplomatic agent shall be inviolable. He shall not be liable to any form of arrest or detention. The receiving State shall treat him with due respect and shall take all appropriate steps to prevent any attack on his person, freedom or dignity.

Article 30

1. The private residence of a diplomatic agent shall enjoy the same inviolability and protection as the premises of the mission.

2. His papers, correspondence and, except as provided in paragraph 3 of Article 31, his property, shall likewise enjoy inviolability.

Article 31

1. A diplomatic agent shall enjoy immunity from the criminal jurisdiction of the receiving State. He shall also enjoy immunity from its civil and administrative jurisdiction, except in the case of:

(a) a real action relating to private immovable property situated in the territory of the receiving State, unless he holds it on behalf of the sending State for the purposes of the mission;

(b) an action relating to succession in which the diplomatic agent is involved as executor, administrator, heir or legatee as a private person and not on behalf of the sending State;

(c) an action relating to any professional or commercial activity exercised by the diplomatic agent in the receiving State outside his official functions.

2. A diplomatic agent is not obliged to give evidence as a witness.

3. No measures of execution may be taken in respect of a diplomatic agent except in the cases coming under sub-paragraphs (a), (b) and (c) of paragraph 1 of this article, and provided that the measures concerned can be taken without infringing the inviolability of his person or of his residence.

4. The immunity of a diplomatic agent from the jurisdiction of the receiving State does not exempt him from the jurisdiction of the sending State.

Article 32

1. The immunity from jurisdiction of diplomatic agents and of persons enjoying immunity under Article 37 may be waived by the sending State.

2. Waiver must always be express.

3. The initiation of proceedings by a diplomatic agent or by a person enjoying immunity from jurisdiction under Article 37 shall preclude him from invoking immunity from jurisdiction in respect of any counter-claim directly connected with the principal claim.

4. Waiver of immunity from jurisdiction in respect of civil or administrative proceedings shall not be held to imply waiver of immunity in respect of the execution of the judgment, for which a separate waiver shall be necessary.

Article 33

1. Subject to the provisions of paragraph 3 of this article, a diplomatic agent shall with respect to services rendered for the sending State be exempt from social security provisions which may be in force in the receiving State.

2. The exemption provided for in paragraph 1 of this article shall also apply to private servants who are in the sole employ of a diplomatic agent, on condition:

(a) that they are not nationals of or permanently resident in the receiving State; and

(b) that they are covered by the social security provisions which may be in force in the sending State or a third State.

3. A diplomatic agent who employs persons to whom the exemption provided for in paragraph 2 of this article does not apply shall observe the obligations which the social security provisions of the receiving State impose upon employers.

4. The exemption provided for in paragraphs 1 and 2 of this article shall not preclude voluntary participation in the social security system of the receiving State provided that such participation is permitted by that State.

5. The provisions of this article shall not affect bilateral or multilateral agreements concerning social security concluded previously and shall not prevent the conclusion of such agreements in the future.

Article 34

A diplomatic agent shall be exempt from all dues and taxes, personal or real, national, regional or municipal, except:

(a) indirect taxes of a kind which are normally incorporated in the price of goods or services;

(b) dues and taxes on private immovable property situated in the territory of the receiving State, unless he holds it on behalf of the sending State for the purposes of the mission;

(c) estate, succession or inheritance duties levied by the receiving State, subject to the provisions of paragraph 4 of Article 39;

(d) dues and taxes on private income having its source in the receiving State and capital taxes on investments made in commercial undertakings in the receiving State;

(e) charges levied for specific services rendered;

(f) registration, court or record fees, mortgage dues and stamp duty, with respect to immovable property, subject to the provisions of Article 23.

Article 35

The receiving State shall exempt diplomatic agents from all personal services, from all public service of any kind whatsoever, and from military obligations such as those connected with requisitioning, military contributions and billeting.

Article 36

1. The receiving State shall, in accordance with such laws and regulations as it may adopt, permit entry of and grant exemption from all customs duties, taxes, and related charges other than charges for storage, cartage and similar services, on:

(a) articles for the official use of the mission;

(b) articles for the personal use of a diplomatic agent or members of his family forming part of his household, including articles intended for his establishment.

2. The personal baggage of a diplomatic agent shall be exempt from inspection, unless there are serious grounds for presuming that it contains articles not covered by the exemptions mentioned in paragraph 1 of this article, or articles the import or export of which is prohibited by the law or controlled by the quarantine regulations of the receiving State. Such inspection shall be conducted only in the presence of the diplomatic agent or of his authorized representative.

Article 37

1. The members of the family of a diplomatic agent forming part of his household shall, if they are not nationals of the receiving State, enjoy the privileges and immunities specified in Articles 29 to 36.

2. Members of the administrative and technical staff of the mission, together with members of their families forming part of their respective households, shall, if they are not nationals of or permanently resident in the receiving State, enjoy the privileges and immunities specified in Articles 29 to 35, except that the immunity from civil and administrative jurisdiction of the receiving State specified in paragraph 1 of Article 31 shall not extend to acts performed outside the course of their duties. They shall also enjoy the privileges specified in Article 36, paragraph 1, in respect of articles imported at the time of first installation.

3. Members of the service staff of the mission who are not nationals of or permanently resident in the receiving State shall enjoy immunity in respect of acts performed in the course of their duties, exemption from dues and taxes on the emoluments they receive by reason of their employment and the exemption contained in Article 33.

4. Private servants of members of the mission shall, if they are not nationals of or permanently resident in the receiving State, be exempt from dues and taxes on the emoluments they receive by reason of their employment. In other respects, they may enjoy privileges and immunities only to the extent admitted by the receiving State. However, the receiving State must exercise its jurisdiction over those persons in such a manner as not to interfere unduly with the performance of the functions of the mission.

Article 38

1. Except insofar as additional privileges and immunities may be granted by the receiving State, a diplomatic agent who is a national of or permanently resident in that State shall enjoy only immunity from jurisdiction, and inviolability, in respect of official acts performed in the exercise of his functions.

2. Other members of the staff of the mission and private servants who are nationals of or permanently resident in the receiving State shall enjoy privileges and immunities only to the extent admitted by the receiving State. However, the receiving State must exercise its jurisdiction over those persons in such a manner as not to interfere unduly with the performance of the functions of the mission.

Article 39

1. Every person entitled to privileges and immunities shall enjoy them from the moment he enters the territory of the receiving State on proceeding to take up his post or, if already in its territory, from the moment when his appointment is notified to the Ministry for Foreign Affairs or such other ministry as may be agreed.

2. When the functions of a person enjoying privileges and immunities have come to an end, such privileges and immunities shall normally cease at the moment when he leaves the country, or on expiry of a reasonable period in which to do so, but shall subsist until that time, even in case of armed conflict. However, with respect to acts performed by such a person in the exercise of his functions as a member of the mission, immunity shall continue to subsist.

3. In case of the death of a member of the mission, the members of his family shall continue to enjoy the privileges and immunities to which they are entitled until the expiry of a reasonable period in which to leave the country.

4. In the event of the death of a member of the mission not a national of or permanently resident in the receiving State or a member of his family forming part of his household, the receiving State shall permit the withdrawal of the movable property of the deceased, with the exception of any property acquired in the country the export of which was prohibited at the time of his death. Estate, succession and inheritance duties shall not be levied on movable property the presence of which in the receiving State was due solely to the presence there of the deceased as a member of the mission or as a member of the family of a member of the mission.

Article 40

1. If a diplomatic agent passes through or is in the territory of a third State, which has granted him a passport visa if such visa was necessary, while proceeding to take up or to return to his post, or when returning to his own country, the third State shall accord him inviolability and such other immunities as may be required to ensure his transit or return. The same shall apply in the case of any members of his family enjoying privileges or immunities who are accompanying the diplomatic agent, or traveling separately to join him or to return to their country.

2. In circumstances similar to those specified in paragraph 1 of this article, third States shall not hinder the passage of members of the administrative and technical or service staff of a mission, and of members of their families, through their territories.

3. Third States shall accord to official correspondence and other official communications in transit, including messages in code or cipher, the same freedom and protection as is accorded by the receiving State. They shall accord to diplomatic couriers, who have been granted a passport visa if such visa was necessary, and diplomatic bags in transit the same inviolability and protection as the receiving State is bound to accord.

4. The obligations of third States under paragraphs 1, 2 and 3 of this article shall also apply to the persons mentioned respectively in those paragraphs, and to official communications and diplomatic bags, whose presence in the territory of the third State is due to *force majeure*.

Article 41

1. Without prejudice to their privileges and immunities, it is the duty of all persons enjoying such privileges and immunities to respect the laws and regulations of the receiving State. They also have a duty not to interfere in the internal affairs of that State.

2. All official business with the receiving State entrusted to the mission by the sending shall be conducted with or through the Ministry for Foreign Affairs of the receiving or such other ministry as may be agreed.

3. The premises of the mission must not be used in any manner incompatible with the functions of the mission as laid down in the present Convention or by other rules of general international law or by any special agreements in force between the sending and the receiving State.

Article 42

A diplomatic agent shall not in the receiving State practice for personal profit any professional or commercial activity.

Article 43

The function of a diplomatic agent comes to an end, *inter alia*:

(a) on notification by the sending State to the receiving State that the function of the diplomatic agent has come to an end;

(b) on notification by the receiving State to the sending State that, in accordance with paragraph 2 of Article 9, it refuses to recognize the diplomatic agent as a member of the mission.

Article 44

The receiving State must, even in case of armed conflict, grant facilities in order to enable persons enjoying privileges and immunities, other than nationals of the receiving State, and members of the families of such persons irrespective of their nationality, to leave at the earliest possible moment. It must, in particular, in case of need, place at their disposal the necessary means of transport for themselves and their property.

Article 45

If diplomatic relations are broken off between two States, or if a mission is permanently or temporarily recalled:

(a) the receiving State must, even in case of armed conflict, respect and protect the premises of the mission, together with its property and archives;

(b) the sending State may entrust the custody of the premises of the mission, together with its property and archives, to a third State acceptable to the receiving State;

(c) the sending State may entrust the protection of its interests and those of its nationals to a third State acceptable to the receiving State.

Article 46

A sending State may with the prior consent of a receiving State, and at the request of a third State not represented in the receiving State, undertake the temporary protection of the interests of the third State and of its nationals.

Article 47

1. In the application of the provisions of the present Convention, the receiving State shall not discriminate as between States.

2. However, discrimination shall not be regarded as taking place:

(a) where the receiving State applies any of the provisions of the present Convention restrictively because of a restrictive application of that provision to its mission in the sending State;

(b) where by custom or agreement States extend to each other more favourable treatment than is required by the provisions of the present Convention.

Article 48

The present Convention shall be open for signature by all States Members of the United Nations or of any of the specialized agencies or Parties to the Statute of the International Court of Justice, and by any other State invited by the General Assembly of the United Nations to become a Party to the Convention, as follows: until 31 October 1961 at the Federal Ministry for Foreign Affairs of Austria and subsequently, until 31 March 1962, at the United Nations Headquarters in New York.

Article 49

The present Convention is subject to ratification. The instruments of ratification shall be deposited with the Secretary-General of the United Nations.

Article 50

The present Convention shall remain open for accession by any State belonging to any of the four categories mentioned in Article 48. The instruments of accession shall be deposited with the Secretary-General of the United Nations.

Article 51

1. The present Convention shall enter into force on the thirtieth day following the date of deposit of the twenty-second instrument of ratification or accession with the Secretary-General of the United Nations.

2. For each State ratifying or acceding to the Convention after the deposit of the twenty-second instrument of ratification or accession, the Convention shall enter into force on the thirtieth day after deposit by such State of its instrument of ratification or accession.

Article 52

The Secretary-General of the United Nations shall inform all States belonging to any of the four categories mentioned in Article 48:

(a) of signatures to the present Convention and of the deposit of instruments of ratification or accession, in accordance with Articles 48, 49 and 50;

(b) of the date on which the present Convention will enter into force, in accordance with Article 51.

Article 53

The original of the present Convention, of which the Chinese, English, French, Russian and Spanish texts are equally authentic, shall be deposited with the Secretary General of the United Nations, who shall send certified copies thereof to all States belonging to any of the four categories mentioned in Article 48.

Vienna Convention on Consular Relations (extracts)
596 U.N.T.S. 261 (1963)

Article 5
Consular Functions

Consular functions consist in:

(a) protecting in the receiving State the interests of the sending State and of its nationals, both individuals and bodies corporate, within the limits permitted by international law;

(b) furthering the development of commercial, economic, cultural and scientific relations between the sending State and the receiving State and otherwise promoting friendly relations between them in accordance with the provisions of the present Convention;

(c) assisting by all lawful means conditions and developments in the commercial, economic, cultural and scientific life of the receiving State, reporting thereon to the Government of the sending State and giving information to persons interested;

(d) issuing passports and travel documents to nationals of the sending State, and visas or appropriate documents to persons wishing to travel to the sending State;

(e) helping and assisting nationals, both individuals and bodies corporate, of the sending State; ...

(h) safeguarding, within the limits imposed by the laws and regulations of the receiving State, the interests of minors and other persons lacking full capacity who are nationals of the sending State, particularly where any guardianship or trusteeship is required with respect to such persons;

(i) subject to the practices and procedures obtaining in the receiving State, representing or arranging appropriate representation for nationals of the sending State before the tribunals and other authorities of the receiving State, for the purpose of obtaining, in accordance with the laws and regulations of the receiving State, provisional measures for the preservation of the rights and interests of these nationals, where, because of absence or any other reason, such nationals are unable at the proper time to assume the defense of their rights and interests;

(j) transmitting judicial and extra-judicial documents or executing letters rogatory or commissions to take evidence for the courts of the sending State in accordance with international agreements in force or, in the absence of such international agreements, in any other manner compatible with the laws and regulations of the receiving State;

(k) exercising rights of supervision and inspection provided for in the laws and regulations of the sending State in respect of vessels having the nationality of the sending State, and of aircraft registered in that State, and in respect of their crews;

(l) extending assistance to vessels and aircraft mentioned in sub-paragraph (k) of this article and to their crews, taking statements regarding the voyage of a vessel, examining and stamping the ship's papers, and, without prejudice to the powers of the authorities of the receiving State, conducting investigations into any incidents which occurred during the voyage, and settling disputes of any kind between the master, the officers and the seamen in so far as this may be authorized by the laws and regulations of the sending State;

(m) performing any other functions entrusted to a consular post by the sending State which are not prohibited by the laws and regulations of the receiving State or to which no objection is taken by the receiving State or which are referred to in the international agreements in force between the sending State and the receiving State.

Article 6
Exercise of Consular Functions Outside the Consular District

A consular officer may, in special circumstances, with the consent of the receiving State, exercise his functions outside his consular district.

Article 31
Inviolability of the Consular Premises

1. Consular premises shall be inviolable to the extent provided by this article.

2. The authorities of the receiving State shall not enter that part of the consular premises which is used exclusively for the purpose of the work of the consular post except with the consent of the head of the consular post or of his designee or of the head of the diplomatic mission of the sending State. The consent of the head of the consular post may, however, be assumed in case of fire or other disaster requiring prompt protective action.

3. Subject to the provisions of paragraph 2 of this article, the receiving State is under a special duty to take all appropriate steps to protect the consular premises against any intrusion or damage and to prevent any disturbance of the peace of the consular post or impairment of its dignity.

4. The consular premises, their furnishings, the property of the consular post and its means of transport shall be immune from any form of requisition for purposes of national defence or public utility. If expropriation is necessary for such purposes, all possible steps shall be taken to avoid impeding the performance of consular functions, and prompt, adequate and effective compensation shall be paid to the sending State.

Article 33
Inviolability of the Consular Archives and Documents

The consular archives and documents shall be inviolable at all times and wherever they may be.

Article 36
Communication and Contact with Nationals of the Sending State

1. With a view to facilitating the exercise of consular functions relating to nationals of the sending State:

(a) consular officers shall be free to communicate with nationals of the sending State and to have access to them. Nationals of the sending State shall have the same freedom with respect to communication with and access to consular officers of the sending State;

(b) if he so requests, the competent authorities of the receiving State shall, without delay, inform the consular post of the sending State if, within its consular district, a national of that State is arrested or committed to prison or to custody pending trial or is detained in any other manner. Any communication addressed to the consular post by the person arrested, in prison, custody or detention shall also be forwarded by the said authorities without delay. The said authorities shall inform the person concerned without delay of his rights under this subparagraph;

(c) consular officers shall have the right to visit a national of the sending State who is in prison, custody or detention, to converse and correspond with him and to arrange for his legal representation. They shall also have the right to visit any national of the sending State who is in prison, custody or detention in their district in pursuance of a judgment. Nevertheless, consular officers shall refrain from taking action on behalf of a national who is in prison, custody or detention if he expressly opposes such action.

2. The rights referred to in paragraph 1 of this article shall be exercised in conformity with the laws and regulations of the receiving State, subject to the proviso, however, that the said laws and regulations must enable full effect to be given to the purposes for which the rights accorded under this article are intended.

Article 40
Protection of Consular Officers

The receiving State shall treat consular officers with due respect and shall take all appropriate steps to prevent any attack on their person, freedom or dignity.

Article 41
Personal Inviolability of Consular Officers

1. Consular officers shall not be liable to arrest or detention pending trial, except in the case of a grave crime and pursuant to a decision by the competent judicial authority.

2. Except in the case specified in paragraph 1 of this article, consular officers shall not be committed to prison or liable to any other form of restriction on their personal freedom save in execution of a judicial decision of final effect.

3. If criminal proceedings are instituted against a consular officer, he must appear before the competent authorities. Nevertheless, the proceedings shall be conducted with the respect due to him by reason of his official position and, except in the case specified in paragraph 1 of this article, in a manner which will hamper the exercise of consular functions as little as possible. When, in the circumstances mentioned in paragraph 1 of this article, it has become necessary to detain a consular officer, the proceedings against him shall be instituted with the minimum of delay.

Article 42
Notification of Arrest, Detention or Prosecution

In the event of the arrest or detention, pending trial, of a member of the consular staff, or of criminal proceedings being instituted against him, the receiving State shall promptly notify the head of the consular post. Should the latter be himself the object of any such measure, the receiving State shall notify the sending State through the diplomatic channel.

Article 43
Immunity from Jurisdiction

1. Consular officers and consular employees shall not be amenable to the jurisdiction of the judicial or administrative authorities of the receiving State in respect of acts performed in the exercise of consular functions.

2. The provisions of paragraph 1 of this article shall not, however, apply in respect of a civil action either:

(a) arising out of a contract concluded by a consular officer or a consular employee in which he did not contract expressly or impliedly as an agent of the sending State; or

(b) by a third party for damage arising from an accident in the receiving State caused by a vehicle, vessel or aircraft.

Article 44
Liability to Give Evidence

1. Members of a consular post may be called upon to attend as witnesses in the course of judicial or administrative proceedings. A consular employee or a member of the service staff shall not, except in cases mentioned in paragraph 3 of this article, decline to give evidence. If a consular officer should decline to do so, no coercive measure or penalty may be applied to him.

2. The authority requiring the evidence of a consular officer shall avoid interference with the performance of his functions. It may, when possible, take such evidence at his residence or at the consular post or accept a statement from him in writing.

3. Members of a consular post are under no obligation to give evidence concerning matters connected with the exercise of their functions or to produce official correspondence and documents relating thereto. They are also entitled to decline to give evidence as expert witnesses with regard to the law of the sending State.

Article 45
Waiver of Privileges and Immunities

1. The sending State may waive, with regard to a member of the consular post, any of the privileges and immunities provided for in Articles 41, 43 and 44.

2. The waiver shall in all cases be express, except as provided for in paragraph 3 of this article, and shall be communicated to the receiving State in writing.

3. The initiation of proceedings by a consular officer or a consular employee in a matter where he might enjoy immunity from jurisdiction under Article 43 shall preclude him from invoking immunity from jurisdiction in respect of any counter-claim directly connected with the principal claim.

4. The waiver of immunity from jurisdiction for the purposes of civil or administrative proceedings shall not be deemed to imply waiver of immunity from the measures of execution resulting from the judicial decision; in respect of such measures, a separate waiver shall be necessary.

Article 55
Respect for the Laws and Regulations of the Receiving State

1. Without prejudice to their privileges and immunities, it is the duty of all persons enjoying such privileges and immunities to respect the laws and regulations of the receiving State. They also have a duty not to interfere in the internal affairs of that State.

2. The consular premises shall not be used in any manner incompatible with the exercise of consular functions.

3. The provisions of paragraph 2 of this article shall not exclude the possibility of offices or other institutions or agencies being installed in part of the building in which the consular premises are situated, provided that the premises assigned to them are separate from those used by the consular post. In that event, the said offices shall not, for the purposes of the present Convention, be considered to form part of the consular premises....

List of U.S. Bilateral Extradition Treaties

Treaties in Force, 2005
Section I: Bilateral Treaties and Other Agreements
http://www.state.gov/s/l/treaties/c15824.htm

Country	Entered into force
Albania	November 14, 1935
Antigua & Barbuda	July 1, 1999
Argentina	June 15, 2000
Australia	May 8, 1976
Austria	January 1, 2000
Bahamas	September 22, 1994
Barbados	March 3, 2000
Belgium	September 1, 1997
Belize	March 27, 2001
Bolivia	November 21, 1996
Brazil	December 17, 1964
Bulgaria	June 24, 1924
Burma	November 1, 1941
Canada	March 22, 1976
Chile	June 26, 1902
China	January 21, 1998
Colombia	March 4, 1982
Congo (France)	July 27, 1911
Costa Rica	October 11, 1991
Cuba	March 2, 1905
Cyprus	September 14, 1999
Czechoslovakia	March 29, 1926
Denmark	July 31, 1974
Dominica	May 25, 2000
Dominican Republic	August 2, 1910
Ecuador	November 12, 1873
Egypt	April 22, 1875
El Salvador	July 10, 1911
Estonia	November 15, 1924
Fuji	June 24, 1935
Finland	May 11, 1980
France	February 1, 2002

The Gambia	June 24, 1935
Germany (Federal Republic of)	August 29, 1980
Ghana	June 24, 1935
Greece	November 1, 1932
Grenada	September 14, 1999
Guatemala	August 15, 1903
Guyana	June 24, 1935
Haiti	June 28, 1905
Honduras	July 10, 1912
Hungary	March 18, 1997
Iceland	February 19, 1906
India	July 21, 1999
Iran	April 23, 1936
Ireland	December 15, 1984
Israel	December 5, 1963
Italy	September 24, 1984
Jamaica	July 7, 1991
Japan	March 26, 1980
Jordan	July 29, 1995
Kenya	June 24, 1935
Kiribati	January 21, 1977
Korea	December 20, 1999
Latvia	March 1, 1924
Lebanon	June 24, 1935
Liberia	November 21, 1939
Liechtenstein	June 28, 1937
Lithuania	March 31, 2003
Luxembourg	February 1, 2002
Malawi	June 24, 1935
Malaysia	June 2, 1997
Malta	June 24, 1935
Mauritius	June 24, 1935
Mexico	January 25, 1980
Moldova	March 28, 1940
Nauru	August 30, 1935
Netherlands	September 15, 1983
New Zealand	December 8, 1970

Nicaragua	July 14, 1907
Nigeria	June 24, 1935
Norway	March 7, 1980
Pakistan	March 9, 1942
Panama	May 8, 1905
Papua New Guinea	August 30, 1935
Paraguay	March 9, 2001
Peru	August 25, 2003
Philippines	November 22, 1996
Poland	September 17, 1999
Portugal	November 14, 1908
Romania	April 7, 1925
Saint Kitts & Nevis	February 23, 2000
Saint Lucia	February 2, 2000
Saint Vincent & The Grenadines	September 8, 1999
San Marino	July 8, 1908
Seychelles	June 24, 1935
Sierra Leone	June 24, 1935
Singapore	June 24, 1935
Solomon Islands	January 21, 1977
South Africa	June 25, 2001
Spain	June 16, 1971
Sri Lanka	January 12, 2001
Suriname	July 11, 1889
Swaziland	June 24, 1935
Sweden	December 3, 1963
Switzerland	September 10, 1997
Tanzania	June 24, 1935
Thailand	May 17, 1991
Tonga	June 24, 1935
Trinidad & Tobago	November 29, 1999
Turkey	January 1, 1981
Tuvalu	January 21, 1977
United Kingdom	January 21, 1977
Uruguay	April 11, 1984
Venezuela	April 14, 1923
Yugoslavia	June 12, 1902

Zambia   June 24, 1935
Zimbabwe   April 26, 2000
Compiled: February 10, 2006

Treaty on Extradition Between the Government of Canada and the Government of the United States of America

Washington, December 3, 1971; Instruments of Ratification exchanged
March 22, 1976; in force March 22, 1976, 1976 Can. T.S. No. 3
(amended by an Exchange of Notes)

Canada and the United States of America, desiring to make more effective the co-operation of the two countries in the repression of crime by making provision for the reciprocal extradition of offenders, agree as follows:

Article 1

Each contracting Party agrees to extradite to the other, in the circumstances and subject to the conditions described in this Treaty, persons found in its territory who have been charged with, or convicted of, any of the offenses covered by Article 2 of this Treaty committed within the territory of the other, or outside thereof under the conditions specified in Article 3(3) of this Treaty.

Article 2

(1) Persons shall be delivered up according to the provisions of this Treaty for any of the offenses listed in the Schedule annexed to this Treaty, which is an integral part of this Treaty, provided these offenses are punishable by the laws of both contracting Parties by a term of imprisonment exceeding one year.

(2) Extradition shall also be granted for attempts to commit, or conspiracy to commit or being party to any of the offenses listed in the annexed Schedule.

(3) Extradition shall also be granted for any offense against a federal law of the United States in which one of the offenses listed in the annexed Schedule, or made extraditable by paragraph (2) of this article, is a substantial element, even if transporting, transportation, the use of the mails or interstate facilities are also elements of the specific offense.

Article 3

(1) For the purpose of this Treaty the territory of a Contracting Party shall include all territory under the jurisdiction of that Contracting Party, including air space and territorial waters and vessels and aircraft registered in that principal place of business, or, if the lessee has no such place of business, his permanent residence in, that contracting Party if any such aircraft is in flight, or if any such vessel is on the high seas when the offense is committed. For the purposes of this treaty an aircraft shall be considered in flight from the moment when power is applied for the purpose of the take-of until the moment when the landing run ends.

(2) In a case when offense 23 of the annexed Schedule is committed on board an aircraft at any time form the moment when all its external doors are closed following embarkation until the moment when any such door is opened for disembarkation, such offense and any other offense covered by Article 2 committed against passengers or crew of that aircraft in connection with such offense shall be considered to have been committed within the territory of a Contracting Party if the aircraft was registered in that Contracting Party, if the aircraft landed in the territory of that contracting party with the alleged offender still on board, or if the aircraft was leased without crew to a lessee who has his principal place of business, or if the lessee has no such place of business, his permanent residence in that Contracting Party.

(3) When the offense of which extradition has been requested has been committed outside the territory of the requesting State, the executive or other appropriate authority of the requested State shall have the power to grant the extradition if the laws of the requested State provide for jurisdiction over such an offense committed in similar circumstances.

Article 4

(1) Extradition shall not be granted in any of the following circumstances:

(i) When the person whose surrender is sought is being proceeded against, or has been tried and discharged or punished in the territory of the requested State of the offense for which his extradition is requested.

(ii) When the prosecution for the offenses has become barred by lapse of time according to the laws of the requesting State.

(iii) When the offense in respect of which extradition is requested is of a political character, or the person whose extradition is requested proves that the extradition request has been made for the purpose of trying or punishing him for an offense of the above-mentioned character. If any question arises as to whether a case comes within the provisions of this subparagraph, the authorities of the Government on which the requisition is made shall decide.

(2) The provisions of subparagraph (iii) of paragraph (1) of this article shall not be applicable to the following:

(i) A kidnaping, murder or other assault against the life or physical integrity of a person to whom a Contracting Party has the duty according to international law to give special protection, or any attempt to commit such an offense with respect to any such person.

(ii) When offense 23 of the annexed Schedule, or an attempt to commit, or a conspiracy to commit, or being a party to the commission of that offense, has been committed on board an aircraft engaged in commercial services carrying passengers.

Article 5

If a request for extradition is made under this Treaty for a person who at the time of such request, or at the time of the commission of the offense for which extradition is sought, is under the age of eighteen years and is considered by the requested State to be one of its residents, the requested State, upon a determination that extradition would disrupt the social readjustment and rehabilitation of that person, may recommend to the requesting State that the request for extradition be withdrawn, specifying the reasons therefor.

Article 6

When the offense for which extradition is requested is punishable by death under the laws of the requesting State and the laws of the requested State do not permit such punishment for that offense, extradition may be refused unless the requesting State Provides such assurances as the requested State considers sufficient that the death penalty shall not be imposed, or, if imposed, shall not be executed.

Article 7

When the person whose extradition is requested is being proceeded against or is serving a sentence in the territory of the requested State for an offense other than for which extradition has been requested, his surrender may be deferred until the conclusion of the proceedings and the full execution of any punishment he may be or may have been awarded.

Article 8

The determination that extradition should or should not be granted shall be made in accordance with the law of the requested State and the person whose extradition is sought shall have the right to use all remedies and resources provided by such law.

Article 9

(1) The request for extradition shall be made through the diplomatic channel.

(2) The request shall be accompanied by a description of the person sought, a statement of the facts of the case, the text of the laws of the requesting State describing the offense and prescribing the punishment for the offense, and a statement of the law relating to the limitation of the legal proceedings.

(3) When the request relates to a person who has not yet been convicted, it must also be accompanied by a warrant of arrest issued by a judge or other judicial office of the requesting State and by such evidence as, according to the laws of the requested State, would justify his arrest and committal for trial if the offense had been committed there, including evidence proving the person requested is the person to whom the warrant of arrest refers.

(4) When the request relates to a person already convicted, it must be accompanied by the judgement of conviction and sentence passed against him in the territory of the requesting State, by a statement showing how much of the sentence has not been served, and by evidence proving that the person requested is the person to whom the sentence refers.

Article 10

(1) Extradition shall be granted only if the evidence be found sufficient, according to the laws of the place where the person sought shall be found, either to justify his committal for trial if the offense of which he is accused had been committed in its territory or to prove that he is the identical person convicted by the courts of the requesting State.

(2) The documentary evidence in support of a request for extradition or copies of these documents shall be admitted in evidence in the examination of the request for extradition when, in the case of a request emanating from Canada, they are authenticated by an officer of the Department of Justice of Canada and are certified by the principal diplomatic or consular officer of the United States in Canada, or when, in the case of a request emanating from the United States, they are authenticated by an officer of the Department of State of the United States and are certified by the principal diplomatic or consular officer of Canada in the United States.

Article 11

(1) In case of urgency a Contracting Party may apply for the provisional arrest of the person sought pending the presentation of the request for extradition through the diplomatic channel. Such application shall contain a description of the person sought, and indication of intention to request the extradition of the person sought and a statement of the existence of a warrant of arrest had the offense been committed, or the person sought been convicted, in the territory of the requested State.

(2) On receipt of such application the requested State shall take the necessary steps to secure the arrest of the person claimed.

(3) A person arrested shall be set at liberty upon the expiration of forty-five days from the date of his arrest pursuant to such application if a request for his extradition accom-

panied by the documents specified in Article 9 shall not have been received. This stipulation shall not prevent the institution of proceedings with a view to extraditing the person sought if the request is subsequently received.

Article 12

(1) A person extradited under the present treaty shall not be detained, tried or punished in the territory of the requesting State for an offense other than that for which extradition has been granted nor be extradited by that State to a third State unless:

(i) He has left the territory of the requesting State after his extradition and has voluntarily returned to it;

(ii) He has not left the territory of the requesting State within thirty days after being free to do so.

(iii) The requested State has consented to his detention, trial, punishment for an offense other than that for which extradition was granted or to his extradition to a third State, provided such other offense is covered by Article 2.

(2) The foregoing shall not apply to offenses committed after the extradition.

Article 13

(1) A requested State upon receiving two or more requests for the extradition of the same person either for the same offense, or for different offenses, shall determine to which of the requesting States it will extradite the person sought.

(2) Among the matters which the requested State may take into consideration are the possibility of a later extradition between the requesting States, the seriousness of each offense, the place where the offense was committed, the dates upon which the requests were received and the provisions of any extradition agreements between the requested State and the other requesting State or States.

Article 14

(1) The requested State shall promptly communicate to the requesting State through the diplomatic channel the decision on the request for extradition.

(2) If a warrant or order for the extradition of a person sought has been issued by the competent authority and he is not removed from the territory of the requested State within such time as may be prescribed by the laws of that State, he may be set at liberty and the requested State may subsequently refuse to extradite that person for the same offense.

Article 15

(1) To the extent permitted under the law of the requested State and subject to the rights of third parties, which shall be duly respected, all articles acquired as a result of the offense or which may be required as evidence shall, if found, be surrendered to the requesting State if extradition is granted.

(2) Subject to the qualifications of paragraph (1) of this article, the above-mentioned articles shall be returned to the requesting State even if the extradition, having been agreed to, cannot be carried out owing to the death or escape of the person sought.

Article 16

(1) The right to transport through the territory of one of the Contracting Parties a person surrendered to the other Contracting Party by a third State shall be granted on request made through the diplomatic channel, provided that conditions are present which

would warrant extradition of such person by the State of transit and reasons of public order are not opposed to the transit.

(2) The party to which the person has been extradited shall reimburse the Party through whose territory such person is transported for any expenses incurred by the latter in connection with such transportation.

Article 17

(1) Expenses related to the transportation of the person sought to the requesting State shall be paid by the requesting State. The appropriate legal officers of the State in which the extradition proceedings take place shall, by all legal means within their power, assist the requesting State before the respective judges and magistrates.

(2) No pecuniary claim, arising out of the arrest, detention, examination and surrender of persons sought under the terms of this Treaty, shall be made by the requested State against the requesting State.

Article 18

(1) This Treaty shall be ratified and the instruments of ratification shall be exchanged at Ottawa as soon as possible.

(2) This Treaty shall terminate and replace any extradition agreements and provisions on extradition in any other agreement in force between Canada and the United States; except that the crimes listed in such agreements and committed prior to entry into force of this Treaty shall be subject to extradition pursuant to the provisions of such agreements.

(3) This Treaty shall enter into force upon the exchange of ratifications. It may be terminated by either Contracting Party giving notice of termination to the other Contracting Party at any time and the termination shall be effective six months after the date of receipt of such notice.

Schedule

1. Murder; assault with intent to commit murder.
2. Manslaughter.
3. Wounding; maiming; or assault occasioning bodily harm.
4. Unlawful throwing or application of any corrosive substances at or upon the person of another.
5. Rape; indecent assault.
6. Unlawful sexual acts with or upon children under the age specified by the laws of both the requesting and requested States.
7. Willful nonsupport or willful abandonment of a minor when such minor is or is likely to be injured or his life is or is likely to be endangered.
8. Kidnapping; child stealing; abduction; false imprisonment.
9. Robbery; assault with intent to steal.
10. Burglary; housebreaking.
11. Larceny, theft or embezzlement.
12. Obtaining property, money or valuable securities by false pretenses or by threat of force or by defrauding the public or any person by deceit or falsehood or other fraudulent means, whether such deceit or falsehood or any fraudulent means would or would not amount to a false pretense.

13. Bribery, including soliciting, offering and accepting.

14. Extortion.

15. Receiving any money, valuable securities or other property knowing the same to have been unlawfully obtained.

16. Fraud by a banker, agent, or by a director of officer of any company.

17. Offenses against the laws relating to counterfeiting or forgery.

18. Perjury in any proceeding whatsoever.

19. Making a false affidavit or statutory declaration of any extrajudicial purpose.

20. Arson.

21. Any act done with intent to endanger the safety of any person traveling upon a railway, or in any aircraft or vessel or other means of transportation.

22. Piracy, by statute or by law of nations; mutiny or revolt on board a vessel against the authority of the captain or commander of such vessel.

23. Any unlawful seizure or exercise of control of an aircraft, by force or violence or threat of force or violence, or by any other form of intimidation, on board such aircraft.

24. Willful injury to property.

25. Offenses against the bankruptcy laws.

26. Offenses against the laws relating to the traffic in, production, manufacture, or importation of narcotic drugs, Cannabis sativa L., hallucinogenic drugs, amphetamines, barbiturates, cocaine and its derivatives.

27. Use of the mails or other means of communication in connection with schemes devised or intended to deceive or defraud the public or for the purpose of obtaining money or property by false pretenses.

28. Offenses against federal laws relating to the sale or purchase of securities.

29. Making or having in possession any explosive substance with intent to endanger life, or to cause severe damage to property.

30. Obstructing the course of justice in a judicial proceeding, existing or proposed, by:

   a) dissuading or attempting to dissuade a person by threats, bribes, or other corrupt means from giving evidence;

   b) influencing or attempting to influence by threat, bribes, or other corrupt means a person in his conduct as a juror; or

   c) accepting a bribe or other corrupt consideration to abstain from giving evidence or to do or to refrain from doing anything as a juror.

Protocol Amending the Treaty on Extradition
1991 Can. T.S. No. 37

The Government of the United States of America and the Government of Canada;

Desiring to make more effective the Extradition Treaty between the Contracting Parties, signed at Washington on December 3, 1971, as amended by the agreement effected by an Exchange of Notes on June 28 and July 9, 1974 (hereinafter referred to as "the Extradition Treaty");

Have agreed as follows:

Article I

Article 2 of the extradition Treaty is deleted and replaced by the following:

Article 2

"(1) Extradition shall be granted for conduct which constitutes an offense punishable by the laws of both Contracting Parties by imprisonment or other form of detention for a term exceeding one year or any greater punishment.

"(2) An offense is extraditable notwithstanding

"(i) that conduct such as interstate transportation or use of the mails or of other facilities affecting interstate or foreign commerce, required for the purpose of establishing jurisdiction, forms part of the offense in the United States, or,

"(ii) that it relates to taxation or revenue or is one of a purely fiscal character."

Article II

The Schedule to the Extradition Treaty, as amended, is deleted.

Article III

Paragraph (2) of Article 3 of the Extradition Treaty is deleted. Paragraph (3) of Article 3 of the Extradition Treaty is amended to read as follows:

"(2) When the offense for which extradition is requested was committed outside the territory of the requesting State, the executive or other appropriate authority of the requested State shall grant extradition if the laws of the requested State provide for jurisdiction over such an offense committed in similar circumstances. If the laws in the requested State do not so provide, the executive authority in the requested State may, in its discretion, grant extradition."

Article IV

Paragraph (2) of Article 4 of the Extradition Treaty, as amended, is deleted and replaced by the following:

"(2) For the purpose of this Treaty, the following offenses shall be deemed not to be offenses within subparagraph (iii) of paragraph 1 of this article:

"(i) An offense for which each Contracting Party has the obligation pursuant to a multilateral international agreement to extradite the person sought or to submit the case to its competent authorities for the purpose of prosecution;

"(ii) Murder, manslaughter or other culpable homicide, malicious wounding or inflicting grievous bodily harm;

"(iii) an offense involving kidnapping, abduction, or any form of unlawful detention, including taking a hostage;

"(iv) An offense involving the placing or use of explosives, incendiaries or destructive devices or substances capable of endangering life or of causing grievous bodily harm or substantial property damage; and

"(v) An attempt or conspiracy to commit, or counselling the commission of, any of the foregoing offenses, or aiding or abetting a person who commits or attempts to commit such offenses."

Article V

Article 7 of the Extradition Treaty is deleted and replaced by the following:

Article 7

"When the person sought is being proceeded against or is serving a sentence in the requested State for an offense other than that for which extradition is requested, the requested State may surrender the person sought or postpone surrender until the conclusion of the proceedings or the service of the whole or any part of the sentence imposed."

Article VI

Paragraph (3) of Article 11 of the Extradition treaty is deleted and replaced by the following:

"(3) A person arrested shall be set at liberty upon the expiration of sixty days from the date of arrest pursuant to such application if a request for extradition and the documents specified in Article 9 have not been received. This stipulation shall not prevent the institution of proceedings with a view to extraditing the person sought if the request and documents are subsequently received."

Article VII

The Extradition Treaty is amended by adding the following after Article 17:

Article 17 BIS

"If both contracting Parties have jurisdiction to prosecute the person for the offense for which extradition is sought, the executive authority of the requested State, after consulting with the executive authority of the requesting State, shall decide whether to extradite the person or to submit the case to its competent authorities for the purpose of prosecution. In making its decision, the requested State shall consider all relevant factors, including but not limited to:

"(i) the place where the act was committed or intended to be committed or the injury occurred or was intended to occur;

"(ii) the respective interests of the Contracting Parties;

"(iii) the nationality of the victim or the intended victim; and

"(iv) the availability and location of the evidence."

Article VIII

Notwithstanding paragraph (2) of Article 18 of the Extradition Treaty, this Protocol shall apply in all cases where the request for extradition is made after its entry into force regardless of whether the offense was committed before or after that date.

Article IX

(1) This Protocol shall be subject to ratification in accordance with the applicable procedures of the Government of the United States and the Government of Canada and instruments of ratification shall be exchanged as soon as possible.

(2) The Protocol shall enter into force upon the exchange of instruments of ratification.

In Witness Whereof, the undersigned, being duly authorized thereto by their respective Governments, have signed this Protocol.

Done in duplicate at Ottawa, this 11th day of January 1988, in the English and French languages, the two texts being equally authentic.

Treaty Between the Government of the United States of America and the Government of Canada on Mutual Legal Assistance in Criminal Matters

1990 Can. T.S. No. 19

The Government of the United States of America and the Government of Canada,

Desiring to improve the effectiveness of both countries in the investigation, prosecution and suppression of crime through cooperation and mutual assistance in law enforcement matters,

Have agreed as follows:

Article I
Definitions

For the purposes of this Treaty:

"Central Authority" means—

(a) for Canada, the Minister of Justice or officials designated by him;

"Competent Authority" means any law enforcement authority with responsibility for matter related to the investigation or prosecution of offenses;

"Offence" means—

(a) for Canada, an offense created by a law of Parliament that may be prosecuted upon indictment, or an offence created by the Legislature of a Province specified in the Annex;

(b) for the United States, an offence for which the statutory penalty is a term of imprisonment of one year or more, or an offence specified in the Annex;

"Public Interest" means any substantial interest related to a national security or other essential public policy;

"Request" means a request made under this Treaty.

Article II
Scope of Application

1. The Parties shall provide, in accordance with the provisions of this Treaty, mutual legal assistance in all matters relating to the investigation, prosecution and suppression of offences.

2. Assistance shall include:

(a) examining objects and sites;

(b) exchanging information and objects;

(c) locating or identifying persons;

(d) serving documents;

(e) taking the evidence of persons;

(f) providing documents and records;

(g) transferring persons in custody;

(h) executing requests for searches and seizures.

3. Assistance shall be provided without regard to whether the conduct under investigation or prosecution in the Requesting State constitutes an offence or may be prosecuted by the Requested State.

4. This Treaty is intended solely for mutual legal assistance between Parties. The provisions of this Treaty shall not give rise to a right on the part of a private party to obtain, suppress or exclude any evidence or impede the execution of a request.

Article III
Other Assistance

1. The Parties, including their competent authorities, may provide assistance pursuant to other agreements, arrangements or practices.

2. The Central Authorities may agree, in exceptional circumstances, to provide assistance pursuant to this Treaty in respect of illegal acts that do not constitute an offence within the definition of offence in Article I.

Article IV
Obligation To Request Assistance

1. A Party seeking to obtain documents, records or other articles known to be located in the territory of the other Party shall request assistance pursuant to Article III(1).

2. Where denial of a request or delay in its execution may jeopardize successful completion of an investigation or prosecution, the Parties shall promptly consult, at the instance of either Party, to consider alternative means of assistance.

3. Unless the Parties otherwise agree, the consultations shall be considered terminated 30 days after they have been requested, and the Parties' obligations under this article shall then be deemed to have been fulfilled.

Article V
Limitations on Compliance

1. The Requested State may deny assistance to the extent that—

(a) the request is not made in conformity with the provisions of this Treaty; or

(b) execution of the request is contrary to its public interest, as determined by its Central Authority.

2. The Requested State may postpone assistance if execution of the request would interfere with an ongoing investigation or prosecution in the Requested State.

3. Before denying or postponing assistance pursuant to this article, the Requested State, through its Central Authority—

(a) shall promptly inform the Requesting State of the reason for considering denial or postponement; and

(b) shall consult with the Requesting State to determine whether assistance may be given subject to such terms and conditions as the Requested State deems necessary.

4. If the Requesting State accepts assistance subject to the terms conditions referred to in paragraph 3(b), it shall comply with said terms and conditions.

Article VI
Requests

1. Requests shall be made by the Central Authority of the Requesting State directly to the Central Authority of the Requested State.

2. Requests shall be made in writing where compulsory process is required in the Requested State or where otherwise required by the Requested State. In urgent circumstances, such requests may be made orally, but shall be confirmed in writing forthwith.

3. A request shall contain such information as the Requested State requires to execute the request, including—

(a) the name of the competent authority conducting the investigation or proceeding to which the request relates;

(b) the subject matter and nature of the investigation or proceeding to which the request relates;

(c) a description of the evidence, information or other assistance sought;

(d) the purpose for which the evidence, information or other assistance is sought, and at any time limitations relevant thereto; and

(e) requirements for confidentiality.

4. The Courts of the Requesting State shall be authorized to order lawful disclosure of such information as is necessary to enable the Requested State to execute the request.

5. The Requested State shall use its best efforts to keep confidential a request and its contents except when otherwise authorized by the Requesting State.

Article VII
Execution of Requests

1. The Central Authority of the Requested State shall promptly execute the request or, when appropriate, transmit it to the competent authorities, who shall make best efforts to execute the request. The Courts of the Requested State shall have jurisdiction to issue subpoenas, search warrants or other orders necessary to execute the request.

2. A request shall be executed in accordance with the law of the Requested State and, to the extent not prohibited by law of the Requested State, in accordance with the directions stated in the request.

Article VIII
Costs

1. The Requested State shall assume all ordinary expenses of executing a request within its boundaries, except—

(a) fees of experts;

(b) expenses of translation and transcription; and

(c) travel and incidental expenses of persons traveling to the Requested State to attend the execution of a request.

2. The Requesting State shall assume all ordinary expenses required to present evidence from the Requested State in the requesting State, including—

(a) travel and incidental expenses of witnesses traveling to the Requesting State, including those of accompanying officials; and

(b) fees of experts.

3. If during the execution of the request it becomes apparent that expenses of an extraordinary nature are required to fulfill the request, the Parties shall consult to determine the terms and conditions under which the execution of the request may continue.

4. The Parties shall agree, pursuant to Article XVIII, on practical measures as appropriate for the reporting and payment of costs in conformity with this article.

Article IX
Limitations of Use

1. The Central Authority of the Requested State may require, after consultation with the Central Authority of the Requesting State, that information or evidence furnished be kept confidential or be disclosed or used only subject to terms and conditions it may specify.

2. The Requesting State shall not disclose or use information or evidence furnished for purposes other than those stated in the request without the prior consent of the Central Authority of the Requested State.

3. Information or evidence made public in the Requesting State in accordance with paragraph 2 may be used for any purpose.

Article X
Location or Identity of Persons

The competent authorities of the Requested State shall make best efforts to ascertain the location and identity of persons specified in the request.

Article XI
Service of Documents

1. The Requested State shall serve any document transmitted to it for the purpose of service.

2. The Requesting State shall transmit a request for the service of a document pertaining to a response or appearance in the Requesting State within a reasonable time before the scheduled response or appearance.

3. A request for the service of a document pertaining to an appearance in the Requesting State shall include such notice as the Central Authority of the Requesting State is reasonably able to provide of outstanding warrants or other judicial orders in criminal matters against the person to be served.

4. The Requested State shall return a proof of service in the manner required by the Requesting State or in any manner agreed upon pursuant to Article XVIII.

Article XII
Taking of Evidence in the Requested State

1. A person requested to testify and produce documents, records or other articles in the Requested State may be compelled by subpoena or order to appear and testify and produce such documents, records and other articles, in accordance with the requirements of the law of the Requested State.

2. Every person whose attendance is required for the purpose of giving testimony under this article is entitled to such fees and allowances as may be provided for by the law of the Requested State.

Article XIII
Government Documents and Records

1. The Requested State shall provide copies of publicly available documents and records of government departments and agencies.

2. The Requested State may provide copies of any document, record or information in the possession of a government department or agency, but not publicly available, to the same extent and under the same conditions as would be available to its own law enforcement and judicial authorities.

Article XIV
Certification and Authentication

1. Copies of documents and records provided under Article XII or Article XIII shall be certified or authenticated in the manner required by the Requesting State or in any manner agreed upon pursuant to Article XVIII.

2. No document or record otherwise admissible in evidence in the Requesting State, certified or authenticated under paragraph 2, shall require further certification or authentication.

Article XV
Transfer of Persons in Custody

1. A person in custody in the Requested State whose presence is requested in the Requesting State for the purposes of this Treaty shall be transferred from the Requested State to the Requesting State for that purpose, provided the person in custody consents and the Requested State has no reasonable basis to deny the request.

2. The Requesting State shall have the authority and duty to keep the person in custody at all times and return the person to the custody of the Requested State immediately after the execution of the request.

Article XVI
Search and Seizure

1. A request for search and seizure shall be executed in accordance with the requirements of the law of the Requested State.

2. The competent authority that has executed a request for search and seizure shall provide such certifications as may be required by the Requesting State concerning, but not limited to, the circumstances of the seizure, identity of the item seized and integrity of its condition, and continuity of possession thereof.

3. Such certifications may be admissible in evidence in a judicial proceeding in the Requesting State as proof of the truth of the matters certified therein, in accordance with the law of the Requesting State.

4. No item seized shall be provided to the Requesting State until that State has agreed to such terms and conditions as may be required by the Requested State to protect third party interests in the item to be transferred.

Article XVII
Proceeds of Crime

1. The Central Authority of either Party shall notify the Central Authority of the other Party of proceeds of crime believed to be located in the territory of the other party.

2. The Parties shall assist each other to the extent permitted by their respective laws in proceedings related to the forfeiture of the proceeds of crime, restitution to the victims of crime, and the collection of fines imposed as a sentence in a criminal prosecution.

Article XVIII
Improvement of Assistance

1. The Parties agree to consult as appropriate to develop other specific agreements or arrangements, formal or informal, on mutual legal assistance.

2. The Parties may agree on such practical measures as may be necessary to facilitate the implementation of this Treaty.

Article XIX
Ratification and Entry Into Force

1. This Treaty shall be ratified, and the instruments of ratification shall be exchanged at Washington, D.C., as soon as possible.

2. This Treaty shall enter into force upon the exchange of instruments of ratification.

Article XX
Termination

Either Party may terminate this Treaty by giving written notice to the other Party at any time. Termination shall become effective six months after receipt of such notice.

Annex

The definition of offence includes offenses created by the Legislature of Province of Canada or offenses under the law of the United States in the following categories:

(1) securities;

(2) wildlife protection;

(3) environmental protection; and

(4) consumer protection.

Council of Europe Convention on Action Against Trafficking in Human Beings
Council of Eur. T.S. No. 197 (2005)

Preamble

The member States of the Council of Europe and the other Signatories hereto,

Considering that the aim of the Council of Europe is to achieve a greater unity between its members;

Considering that trafficking in human beings constitutes a violation of human rights and an offence to the dignity and the integrity of the human being;

Considering that trafficking in human beings may result in slavery for victims;

Considering that respect for victims' rights, protection of victims and action to combat trafficking in human beings must be the paramount objectives;

Considering that all actions or initiatives against trafficking in human beings must be non-discriminatory, take gender equality into account as well as a child-rights approach;

Recalling the declarations by the Ministers for Foreign Affairs of the Member States at the 112th (14–15 May 2003) and the 114th (12–13 May 2004) Sessions of the Committee of Ministers calling for reinforced action by the Council of Europe on trafficking in human beings;

Bearing in mind the Convention for the Protection of Human Rights and Fundamental Freedoms (1950) and its protocols;

Bearing in mind the following recommendations of the Committee of Ministers to member states of the Council of Europe: Recommendation No. R (91) 11 on sexual exploitation, pornography and prostitution of, and trafficking in, children and young adults; Recommendation No. R (97) 13 concerning intimidation of witnesses and the rights of the defence; Recommendation No. R (2000) 11 on action against trafficking in human beings for the purpose of sexual exploitation; Recommendation Rec (2002 5 on the protection of women against violence;

Bearing in mind the following recommendations of the Parliamentary Assembly of the Council of Europe: Recommendation 1325 (1997) on traffic in women and forced prostitution in Council of Europe member states; Recommendation 1450 (2000) on violence against women in Europe; Recommendation 1545 (2002) on a campaign against trafficking in women; Recommendation 1610 (2003) on migration connected with trafficking in women and prostitution; Recommendation1611 (2003) on trafficking in organs in Europe: Recommendation 1663 (2004) Domestic slavery: servitude, au pairs and mail-order brides;

Bearing in mind the European Union Council Framework Decision of 19 July 2002 on combatting trafficking in human beings, the European Union Council Framework Decision of 15 March 2001 on the standing of victims in criminal proceedings and the European Union Council Directive of 29 April 2004 on the residence permit issued to third-country nationals who are victims of trafficking in human beings or who have been the subject of an action to facilitate illegal immigration, who cooperate with the competent authorities;

Taking due account of the United Nations Convention against Transnational Organized Crime and the Protocol thereto to Prevent, Suppress and Punish Trafficking in Persons, Especially Women and Children with a view to improving the protection which they afford and developing the standards established by them;

Taking due account of the other international legal instruments relevant in the field of action against trafficking in human beings;

Taking into account the need to prepare a comprehensive international legal instrument focusing on the human rights of victims of trafficking and setting up a specific monitoring mechanism,

Have agreed as follows:

Chapter I — Purposes, Scope, Non-discrimination Principle and Definitions

Article 1 — Purposes of the Convention

1. The purposes of this Convention are:

   a. to prevent and combat trafficking in human beings, while guaranteeing gender equality;

   b. to protect the human rights of the victims of trafficking, design a comprehensive framework for the protection and assistance of victims and witnesses, while guaranteeing gender equality, as well as to ensure effective investigation and prosecution;

   c. to promote international cooperation on action against trafficking in human beings.

2. In order to ensure effective implementation of its provisions by the Parties, this Convention sets up a specific monitoring mechanism.

Article 2 — Scope

This Convention shall apply to all forms trafficking in human beings, whether national or transnational, whether or not connected with organised crime.

Article 3 — Non-Discrimination Principle

The implementation of the provisions of this Convention by Parties, in particular the enjoyment of measures to protect and promote the rights of victims, shall be secured without discrimination on any ground such as sex, race, coulour, language, religion, political or other opinion, national or social origin, association with a national minority, property, birth or other status.

Article 4 — Definitions

For the purposes of this Convention:

a. "Trafficking in human beings" shall mean the recruitment, transportation, transfer, harbouring or receipt of persons, by means of the threat or use of force or other forms of coercion, of abduction, of fraud, of deception, of the abuse of power or of a position of vulnerability or of the giving or receiving of payments or benefits to achieve the consent of a person having control over anther person, for the purpose of exploitation. Exploitation shall include, at a minimum, the exploitation of the prostitution of others or other forms of sexual exploitation, forced labour or services, slavery or practices similar to slavery, servitude or the removal of organs;

b. The consent of a victim of "Trafficking in human beings" to the intended exploitation set forth in subparagraph (a) of this article shall be irrelevant where any of the means set forth in subparagraph (a) have been used;

c. The recruitment, transportation, transfer, harbouring or receipt of a child for the purpose of exploitation shall be considered "trafficking in human beings" even if this does not involve any of the means set forth in subparagraph (a) of this article;

d. "Child" shall mean any person under eighteen years of age;

e. "Victim" shall mean any natural person who is subject to trafficking in human beings as defined in this article.

Chapter II — Prevention, Co-Operation and Other Measures

Article 5 — Prevention of Trafficking in Human Beings

1. Each Party shall take measure to establish or strengthen national co-ordination between the various bodies responsible for preventing and combatting trafficking in human beings.

2. Each Party shall establish and/or strengthen effective policies and programmes to prevent trafficking in human beings, by such means as: research, information, awareness raising and education campaigns, social and economic initiatives and training programmes, in particular for persons vulnerable to trafficking and for professionals concerned with trafficking in human beings.

3. Each Party shall promote a Human Rights-based approach and shall use gender mainstreaming and a child-sensitive approach in the development, implementation and assessment of all the policies and programmes referred to in paragraph 2.

4. Each Party shall take appropriate measures as may be necessary, to enable migration to take place legally, in particular through dissemination of accurate information by relevant offices, on the conditions enabling the legal entry in and stay on its territory.

5. Each Party shall take specific measures to reduce children's vulnerability to trafficking, notably by creating a protective environment for them.

6. Measures established in accordance with this article shall involve, where appropriate, non-governmental organisations, other relevant organisations and other elements of civil society committed to the prevention of trafficking in human beings and victim protection or assistance.

Article 6 — Measure to Discourage the Demand

To discourage the demand that fosters all forms of exploitation of persons, especially women and children, that leads to trafficking, each Party shall adopt or strengthen legislative, administrative, educational, social, cultural or other measures including:

a. research on best practices, methods, and strategies;

b. raising awareness of the responsibility and important role of media and civil society in identifying the demand as one of th root causes of trafficking in human beings;

c. target information campaigns involving, as appropriate, inter alia, public authorities and policy makers;

d. preventive measures, including educational programmes for boys and girls during their schooling, which stress the unacceptable nature of discrimination based on sex, and its disastrous consequences, the importance of gender equality and the dignity and integrity of every human being.

Article 7 — Border Measures

1. Without prejudice to international commitments in relation to the free movement of persons, Parties shall strengthen, to the extent possible, such border controls as may be necessary to prevent and detect trafficking in human beings.

2. Each Party shall adopt legislative or other appropriate measure to prevent, to the extent possible, means of transport operated by commercial carriers from being used in the commission of offences established in accordance with this Convention.

3. Where appropriate, and without prejudice to applicable international conventions, such measures shall include establishing the obligation of commercial carriers, including any transportation company or the owner or operator of any means of transport, to ascertain that all passengers are in possession of travel documents required for entry into the receiving State.

4. Each Party shall take the necessary measures, in accordance with its internal law, to provide for sanctions in cases of violation of the obligation set forth in paragraph 3 of this article.

5. Each Party shall adopt such legislative or other measures as may be necessary to permit, in accordance with its internal law, the denial of entry or revocation of visas of person implicated in the commission of offences established in accordance with this Convention.

6. Parties shall strengthen co-operation among border control agencies by, *inter alia*, establishing and maintaining direct channels of communication.

Article 8 — Security and Control of Documents

Each Party shall adopt such measure as may be necessary:

a. To ensure that travel or identity documents issued by it are of such quality that they cannot easily be misused and cannot readily be falsified or unlawfully altered, replicated or issued; and

b. To ensure the integrity and security of travel or identity documents issued by or on behalf of the Party and to prevent their unlawful creation and issuance.

Article 9 — Legitimacy and Validity of Documents

At the request of another Party, a Party shall, in accordance with its internal law, verify within a reasonable time the legitimacy and validity of travel or identity documents issued or purported to have been issued in its name and suspected of being used for trafficking in human beings.

Chapter III—Measures to Protect and Promote the Rights of Victims, Guaranteeing Gender Equality

Article 10—Identification of the Victims

1. Each Party shall provide its competent authorities with persons who are trained and qualified in preventing and combatting trafficking in human beings, in identifying and helping victims, including children, and shall ensure that the different authorities collaborate with each other as well as with relevant support organisations, so that victims can be identified in a procedure duly taking into account the special situation of women and child victims and, in appropriate cases, issued with residence permits under the conditions provided for in Article 14 of the present Convention.

2. Each Party shall adopt such legislative or other measures as may be necessary to identify victims as appropriate in collaboration with other Parties and relevant support organisations. Each Party shall ensure that, if the competent authorities have reasonable grounds to believe that a person has been victim of trafficking in human beings, that person shall not be remove from its territory until the identification process as victim of an offence provided for in Article 18 of this Convention has been completed by the competent authorities and shall likewise ensure that that person receives the assistance provided for in Article 12, paragraphs 1 and 2.

3. When the age of the victim is uncertain and there are reasons to believe that the victim is a child, he or she shall be presumed to be a child and shall be accorded special protection measures pending verification of his/her age.

4. As soon as an unaccompanied child is identified as a victim, each Party shall:

a. provide for representation of the child by a legal guardian, organisation or authority which shall act in the best interest of that child;

b. take the necessary steps to establish his/her identity and nationality;

c. make every effort to locate his/her family when this is in the best interest of the child.

Article 11—Protection of Private Life

1. Each Party shall protect the private life and identity of victims. Personal data regarding them shall stored and used in conformity with the conditions provided for by the Convention for the Protection of Individuals with regard to Automatic Processing of Personal Data (ETS No. 108).

2. Each Party shall adopt measures to ensure, in particular, that the identity, or details allowing the identification, of a child victim of trafficking are not made publicly known, through the media or by any other means, except, in exceptional circumstances, in order to facilitate the tracing of family members or otherwise secure the well-being and protection of the child.

3. Each Party shall consider adopting, in accordance with Article 10 of the Convention for the Protection of Human Rights and Fundamental Freedoms as interpreted by the European Court of Human Rights, measures aimed at encouraging the media to protect the private life and identity of victims through self-regulation or through regulatory or co-regulatory measures.

Article 12 — Assistance to Victims

1. Each Party shall adopt such legislative or other measures as may be necessary to assist victims in their physical, psychological and social recovery. Such assistance shall include at least:

a. standards of living capable of ensuring their subsistence, through such measure as: appropriate and secure accommodation, psychological and material assistance;

b. access to emergency medical treatment;

c. translation and interpretation services, when appropriate;

d. counseling and information, in particular as regards their legal rights and the services available to them, in a language that they can understand;

e. assistance to enable their rights and interests to be presented and considered at appropriate stages of criminal proceedings against offenders;

f. access to education for children.

2. Each Party shall take due account of the victim's safety and protection needs.

3. In addition, each Party shall provide necessary medical or other assistance to victims lawfully resident within its territory who do not have adequate resources and need such help.

4. Each Party shall adopt the rules under which victims lawfully resident within its territory shall be authorised to have access to the labour market, to vocational training and education.

5. Each Party shall take measures, where appropriate and under the conditions provided for by its internal law, to co-operate with non-governmental organisations, other relevant organisations or other elements of civil society engaged in assistance to victims.

6. Each Party shall adopt such legislative or other measures as may be necessary to ensure that assistance to a victim is not made conditional on his or her willingness to act as a witness.

7. For the implementation of the provisions set out in this article, each Party shall ensure that services are provided on a consensual and informed basis, taking due account of the special needs of persons in a vulnerable position and the rights of children in terms of accommodation, education and appropriate health care.

Article 13 — Recovery and Reflection Period

1. Each Party shall provide in its internal law a recovery and reflection period of at least 30 days, when there are reasonable grounds to believe that the person concerned is a victim. Such a period shall be sufficient for the person concerned to recover and escape the influence of traffickers and/or to take an informed decision on cooperating with the competent authorities. During this period it shall not be possible to enforce any expulsion order against him or her. This provision is without prejudice to the activities carried out by the competent authorities in all phases of the relevant national proceedings, an in particular when investigating and prosecuting the offences concerned. During this period, the Parties shall authorize the persons concerned to stay in their territory.

2. During this period, the persons referred to in paragraph 1 of this Article shall be entitled to the measures contained in Article 12, paragraphs 1 and 2.

3. The parties are not bound to observe this period if grounds of public order prevent it or if it is found that victim status is being claimed improperly.

Article 14 — Residence Permit

1. Each Party shall issue a renewable residence permit to victims, in one or other of the two following situations or in both:

   a. the competent authority considers that their stay is necessary owing to their personal situation.

   b. the competent authority considers that their stay is necessary for the purpose of their co-operation with the competent authorities in investigation or criminal proceedings.

2. The residence permit for child victims, when legally necessary, shall be issued in accordance with the best interests of the child and, where appropriate, renewed under the same conditions.

3. The non-renewal or withdrawal of a residence permit is subject to the conditions provided for by the internal law of the Party.

4. If the victim submits an application of another kind of residence permit, the Party concerned shall take into account that he or she holds, or has held, a residence permit in conformity with paragraph 1.

5. Having regard to the obligations of Parties to which Article 40 of this Convention refers, each Party shall ensure that granting of a permit according to this provision shall be without prejudice to the right to seek and enjoy asylum.

Article 15 — Compensation and Legal Redress

1. Each Party shall ensure that victims have access, as from their first contact with the competent authorities, to information on relevant judicial and administrative proceedings in a language which they can understand.

2. Each Party shall provide, in its internal law, for the right to legal assistance and to free legal aid for victims under the conditions provided by its internal law.

3. Each Party shall provide, in its internal law, for the right of victims to compensation from the perpetrators.

4. Each Party shall adopt such legislative or other measures as may be necessary to guarantee compensation for victims in accordance with the conditions under its internal law, for instance through the establishment of a fund for victim compensation or measures or programmes aimed at social assistance and social integration of victims, which could be funded by the assets resulting from the application provided in Article 23.

Article 16 — Repatriation and Return of Victims

1. The Party of which a victim is a national or in which that person had the right of permanent residence at the time of entry into the territory of the receiving Party shall, with due regard for his or her rights, safety and dignity, facilitate and accept, his or her return without undue or unreasonable delay.

2. When a Party returns a victim to another State, such return shall be with due regard for the rights, safety and dignity of that person and for the status of any legal proceedings related to the fact that the person is a victim, and shall preferably be voluntary.

3. At the request of a receiving Party, a requested Party shall verify whether a person is its national or had the right of a permanent residence in its territory at the time of entry into the territory of the receiving Party.

4. In order to facilitate the return of a victim who is without proper documentation, the Party of which that person is a national or in which he or she had the right of a per-

manent residence at the time of entry into the territory of the receiving Party shall agree to issue, at the request of the receiving Party, such travel documents or other authorisation as may be necessary to enable the person to travel to and re-enter its territory.

5. Each Party shall adopt such legislative or other measures as may be necessary to establish repatriation programmes, involving relevant national or international institutions and non governmental ogranisations. Theses programmes aim at avoiding re-victimisation. Each party should make its best effort to favour the reintegration of victims into society of the State of return, including reintegration into the education system and the labour market, in particular through the acquisition and improvement of their professional skills. With regard to children, these programmes should include enjoyment of the right to education and measures to secure adequate care or receipt by the family or appropriate care structures.

6. Each Party shall adopt such legislative or other measures as may be necessary to make available to victims, where appropriate in co-operation with any other Party concerned, contact information of structures that can assist them in the country where they are returned or repatriated, such as law enforcement offices, non-governmental organisations, legal professions able to provide counseling and social welfare agencies.

7. Child victims shall not be returned to a State, if there is indication, following a risk and security assessment, that such return would not be in the best interest of the child.

Article 17 — Gender Equality

Each Party shall, in applying measures referred to in this chapter, aim to promote gender equality and use gender mainstreaming in the development, implementation and assessment of the measures.

Chapter IV — Substantive Criminal Law

Article 18 — Criminalisation of Trafficking in Human Beings

Each Party shall adopt such legislative and other measures as may be necessary to establish as criminal offences the conduct contained in article 4 of this Convention, when committed intentionally.

Article 19 — Criminalisation of the Use of Services of a Victim

Each Party shall consider adopting such legislative and other measures as may be necessary to establish as criminal offences under its internal law, the use of services which are the object of exploitation as referred to in Article 4 paragraph a of this Convention, with the knowledge that the person is a victim of trafficking in human beings.

Article 20 — Criminalisation of Acts Relating to Travel or Identity Documents

Each Party shall adopt such legislative and other measures as may be necessary to establish as criminal offences the following conducts, when committed intentionally and for the purpose of enabling the trafficking in human beings:

a. forging a travel or identity document;

b. procuring or providing such a document;

c. retaining, removing, concealing, damaging or destroying a travel or identity document of another person.

Article 21 — Attempt and Aiding or Abetting

1. Each Party shall adopt such legislative and other measures as may be necessary to establish as criminal offences when committed intentionally, aiding or abetting the com-

mission of any of the offences established in accordance with Articles 18 and 20 of the present Convention.

2. Each Party shall adopt such legislative and other measures as may be necessary to establish as criminal offences when committed intentionally, an attempt to commit the offences established in accordance with Articles 18 and 20, paragraph a, of this Convention.

Article 22 — Corporate Liability

1. Each Party shall adopt such legislative and other measures as may be necessary to ensure that a legal person can be held liable for a criminal offence established in accordance with this Convention, committed for its benefit by any natural person, acting either individually or as part of an organ of the legal person, who has a leading position within the legal person, based on:

    a. a power of representation of the legal person;

    b. an authority to take decisions on behalf of the legal person;

    c. an authority to exercise control within the legal person.

2. Apart from the cases already provided for in paragraph 1, each Party shall take the measures necessary to ensure that a legal person can be held liable where the lack of supervision or control by a natural person referred to in paragraph 1 has made possible the commission of a criminal offence established in accordance with this Convention for the benefit of that legal person by a natural person acting under its authority.

3. Subject to the legal principles of the Party, the liability of a legal person may be criminal, civil or administrative.

4. Such liability shall be without prejudice to the criminal liability of the natural persons who have committed the offence.

Article 23 — Sanctions and Measures

1. Each Party shall adopt such legislative and other measures as may be necessary to ensure that the criminal offences established in accordance with Articles 18 to 21 are punishable by effective, proportionate and dissuasive sanctions. These sanctions shall include, for criminal offences established in accordance with Article 18 when committed by natural persons, penalties involving deprivation of liberty which can give rise to extradition.

2. Each Party shall ensure that legal persons held liable in accordance with Article 22 shall be subject to effective, proportionate and dissuasive criminal or non-criminal sanctions or measures, including monetary sanctions.

3. Each Party shall adopt such legislative and other measures as may be necessary to enable it to confiscate or otherwise deprive the instrumentalities and proceeds of criminal offences established in accordance with Articles 18 and 20, paragraph a, of this Convention, or property the value of which corresponds to such proceeds.

4. Each Party shall adopt such legislative or other measures as may be necessary to enable the temporary or permanent closure of any establishment which was used to carry out trafficking in human beings, without prejudice to the rights of *bona fide* third parties or to deny the perpetrator, temporary or permanently, the exercise of the activity in the course of which this offence was committed.

Article 24 — Aggravating Circumstances

Each Party shall ensure that the following circumstances are regarded as aggravating circumstances in the determination of the penalty for offences established in accordance with Article 18 of this Convention:

a. the offence deliberately or by gross negligence endangered the life of the victim;

b. the offence was committed against a child;

c. the offence was committed by a public official in the performance of her/his duties;

d. the offence was committed within the framework of a criminal organisation.

Article 25 — Previous Convictions

Each Party shall adopt such legislative and other measures providing for the possibility to take into account final sentences passed by another Party in relation to offences established in accordance with this Convention when determining the penalty.

Article 26 — Non-Punishment Provision

Each Party shall, in accordance with the basic principles of its legal system, provide for the possibility of not imposing penalties on victims for their involvement in unlawful activities, to the extent that they have been compelled to do so.

Chapter V — Investigation, Prosecution and Procedural Law

Article 27 — *Ex Parte* and *Ex Officio* Applications

1. Each Party shall ensure that investigations into or prosecution of offences established in accordance with this Convention shall not be dependent upon the report or accusation made by a victim, at least when the offence was committed in whole or in part on its territory.

2. Each Party shall ensure that victims of an offence in the territory of a Party other than the one where they reside may make a complaint before the competent authorities of their State of residence. The competent authority to which the complaint is made, insofar as it does not itself have competence in this respect, shall transmit it without delay to the competent authority of the Party in the territory in which the offence was committed. The complaint shall be dealt with in accordance with the internal law of the Party in which the offence was committed.

3. Each Party shall ensure, by means of legislative or other measures, in accordance with the conditions provided for by its internal law, to any group, foundation, association or non-governmental organisations which aims at fighting trafficking in human beings or protection of human rights, the possibility to assist and/or support the victim with his or her consent during criminal proceedings concerning the offence established in accordance with Article 18 of this Convention.

Article 28 — Protection of Victims, Witnesses and Collaborators with the Judicial Authorities

1. Each Party shall adopt such legislative or other measures as may be necessary to provide effective and appropriate protection from potential retaliation or intimidation in particular during and after investigation and prosecution of perpetrators, for:

a. victims;

b. as appropriate, those who report the criminal offences established in accordance with Article 18 of this Convention or otherwise co-operate with the investigating or prosecuting authorities;

c. witnesses who give testimony concerning criminal offences established in accordance with Article 18 of this Convention;

d. when necessary, members of the family of persons referred to in subparagraphs a and c.

2. Each Party shall adopt such legislative or other measures as may be necessary to ensure and to offer various kinds of protection. This may include physical protection, relocation, identity change and assistance in obtaining jobs.

3. A child victim shall be afforded special protection measures taking into account the best interest of the child.

4. Each Party shall adopt such legislative or other measures as may be necessary to provide, when necessary, appropriate protection from potential retaliation or intimidation in particular during and after investigation and prosecution of perpetrators, for members or groups, foundations, associations or non-governmental organisations which carry out the activities set out in Article 27, paragraph 3.

5. Each party shall consider into agreements or arrangements with other States for the implementation of this article.

Article 29 — Specialised Authorities and Co-ordinating Bodies

1. Each Party shall adopt such measures as may be necessary to ensure that persons or entities are specialised in the fight against trafficking and the protection of victims. Such persons or entities shall have the necessary independence in accordance with the fundamental principles of the legal system of the Party, in order for them to be able to carry out their functions effectively and free from any undue pressure. Such persons or the staffs of such entities shall have adequate training and financial resources for their tasks.

2. Each Party shall adopt such measures as may be necessary to ensure co-ordination of the policies and actions of their governments' departments and other public agencies against trafficking in human beings, where appropriate, through setting up co-ordinating bodies.

3. Each Party shall provide or strengthen training for relevant officials in the prevention of and fight against trafficking in human beings, including Human Rights training. The training may be agency-specific and shall, as appropriate, focus on: methods used in preventing such trafficking, prosecuting the traffickers and protecting the rights of the victims, including protecting the victims from the traffickers.

4. Each Party shall consider appointing National Rapporteurs or other mechanisms for monitoring the anti-trafficking activities of State institutions and the implementation of national legislation requirements.

Article 30 — Court Proceedings

In accordance with the Convention for the Protection of Human Rights and Fundamental Freedoms, in particular Article 6, each Party shall adopt such legislative or other measures as may be necessary to ensure in the course of judicial proceedings:

a. the protection of victims' private life and, where appropriate, identity;

b. victims' safety and protection from intimidation.

In accordance with the conditions under its internal law and, in the case of child victims, by taking special care of children's needs and ensuring their right to special protection measures.

Article 31 — Jurisdiction

1. Each Party shall adopt such legislative and other measures as may be necessary to establish jurisdiction over any offence established in accordance with this Convention, when the offence is committed:

a. in its territory; or

b. on board ship flying the flag of that Party; or

c. on board an aircraft registered under the laws of that Party; or

d. by one of its nationals or by a stateless person who has his or her habitual residence in its territory, if the offence is punishable under criminal law where is was committed or if the offence is committed outside the territorial jurisdiction of any State; or

e. against one of its nationals.

2. Each Party may, at the time of signature or when depositing its instrument of ratification, acceptance, approval or accession, by a declaration addressed to the Secretary General of the Council of Europe, declare that it reserves the right not to apply or to apply only in specific cases or conditions the jurisdiction rules laid down in paragraphs 1 (d) and (e) of this article or any part thereof.

3. Each Party shall adopt such measures as may be necessary to establish jurisdiction over the offences referred to in this Convention, in cases where an alleged offender is present in its territory and it does not extradite him/her to another Party, solely on the basis of his/her nationality, after a request for extradition.

4. When more than one Party claims jurisdiction over an alleged offence established in accordance with this Convention, the Parties involved shall, where appropriate, consult with a view to determining the most appropriate jurisdiction for prosecution.

5. Without prejudice to the general norms of international law, this Convention does not exclude any criminal jurisdiction exercised by a Party in accordance with internal law.

Chapter VI — International Co-Operation and Co-Operation with Civil Society

Article 32 — General Principles and Measures for International Co-Operation

The Parties shall co-operate with each other, in accordance with the provisions of this Convention, and through application of relevant applicable international and regional instruments, arrangements agreed on the basis of uniform or reciprocal legislation and internal laws, to the widest extent possible, for the purpose of:

– preventing and combatting trafficking in human beings;

– protecting and providing assistance to victims;

– investigations or proceedings concerning criminal offences established in accordance with this Convention.

Article 33 — Measures Relating to Endangered or Missing Persons

1. When a Party, on the basis of information at its disposal has reasonable grounds to believe that the life, the freedom or the physical integrity of a person referred to in Article 28, paragraph 1, is in immediate danger on the territory of another Party, the Party that has the information shall, in such a case of emergency, transmit it without delay to the latter so as to take the appropriate protection measures.

2. The Parties to this Convention may consider reinforcing their co-operation in the search for missing people, in particular for missing children, if the information available leads them to believe that she/he is a victim of trafficking in human beings. To this end, the Parties may conclude bilateral or multilateral treaties with each other.

Article 34—Information

1. The requested Party shall promptly inform the requesting Party of the final result of the action taken under this chapter. The requested Party shall also promptly inform the requesting Party of any circumstances which render impossible the carrying out of the action sought or are likely to delay it significantly.

2. A Party may, within limits of its internal law, without prior request, forward to another Party information obtained within the framework of its own investigations when it considers that the disclosure of such information might assist the receiving Party in initiating or carrying out investigations or proceedings concerning criminal offences established in accordance with this Convention or might lead to a request for co-operation by that Party under this chapter.

3. Prior to providing such information, the providing Party may request that it be kept confidential or used subject to conditions. If the receiving Party cannot comply with such request, it shall notify the providing Party, which shall then determine whether the information should nevertheless be provided. If the receiving Party accepts the information subject to the conditions, it shall be bound by them.

4. All information requested concerning Articles 13, 14 and 16, necessary to provide the rights conferred by these Articles, shall be transmitted at the request of the Party concerned without delay with due respect to Article 11 of the present Convention.

Article 35—Co-Operation With Civil Society

Each Party shall encourage state authorities and public officials, to co-operate with non-governmental organisations, other relevant organisations and members of civil society, in establishing strategic partnerships with the aim of achieving the purpose of this Convention.

Chapter VII—Monitoring Mechanism

Article 36—Group of Experts on Action Against Trafficking in Human Beings

1. The Group of experts on action trafficking in human beings (hereinafter referred to as "GRETA"), shall monitor the implementation of this Convention by the Parties.

2. GRETA shall be composed of a minimum of 10 members and a maximum of 15 members, taking into account a gender and geographical balance, as well as the multi disciplinary expertise. They shall by elected by the Committee of the Parties for a terms of office of 4 years, renewable once, chosen from amongst nationals of the States Parties to this Convention.

3. The election of the members of GRETA shall be based on the following principles:

   a. they shall be chosen from among persons of high moral character, known for their recognised competence in the fields of Human Rights, assistance and protection of victims and of action against trafficking in human beings or having professional experience in the areas covered by this Convention;

   b. they shall sit in their individual capacity and shall be independent and impartial in the exercise of their functions and shall be available to carry out their duties in an effective manner;

   c no two members of GRETA may be nationals of the same State;

   d. they should represent the main legal systems.

4. The election of the members of GRETA shall be determined by the Committee of Ministers, after consulting with and obtaining the unanimous consent of the Parties to

the Convention, within a period of one year following the entry into force of this Convention. GRETA shall adopt its own rules of procedure.

Article 37 — Committee of the Parties

1. The Committee of the Parties shall be composed of the representatives on the Committee of Ministers of the Council of Europe of the member States Parties to the Convention and representatives of the Parties to the Convention, which are not members of the Council of Europe.

2. The Committee of the Parties shall be convened by the Secretary General of the Council of Europe. Its first meeting shall be held within a period of one year following the entry into force of this Convention in order to elect the members of GRETA. It shall subsequently meet whenever on third of the Parties, the President of GRETA or the Secretary General so requests.

3. The Committee of the Parties shall adopt its own rules of procedure.

Article 38 — Procedure

1. The evaluation procedure shall concern the Parties to the Convention and be divided in rounds, the length of which is determined by GRETA. At the beginning of each round GRETA shall select the specific provisions on which the evaluation procedure shall be based.

2. GRETA shall define the most appropriate means to carry out this evaluation. GRETA may in particular adopt a questionnaire for each evaluation round, which may serve as a basis for the evaluation of the implementation by the Parties of the present Convention. Such a questionnaire shall be addressed to all Parties. Parties shall respond to this questionnaire, as well as to any other request of information from GRETA.

3. GRETA may request information from civil society.

4. GRETA may subsidiarily organise, in co-operation with the national authorities and the "contact person" appointed by the latter, and, if necessary, with the assistance of independent national experts, country visits. During these visits, GRETA may be assisted by specialists in specific fields.

5. GRETA shall prepare a draft report containing its analysis concerning the implementation of the provisions on which the evaluation is based, as well as its suggestions and proposals concerning the way in which the Party concerned may deal with the problems which have been identified. The draft report shall be transmitted for comments to the Party which undergoes the evaluation. Its comments are taken into account by GRETA when establishing its report.

6. On this basis, GRETA shall adopt its report and conclusions concerning the measures taken by the Party concerned to implement the provisions of the present Convention. This report and conclusions shall be sent to the Party concerned and to the Committee of the Parties. The report and conclusions of GRETA shall be made public as from their adoption, together with eventual comments by the Party concerned.

7. Without prejudice to the procedure of paragraphs 1 to 6 of this article, the Committee of the Parties may adopt, on the basis of the report and conclusions of GRETA, recommendations addressed to this Party (a) concerning the measures to be taken to implement the conclusions of GRETA, if necessary setting a date for submitting information on their implementation, and (b) aiming at promoting co-operation with that Party for the proper implementation of the present Convention.

Chapter VIII — Relationship With Other International Instruments

Article 39 — Relationship with the Protocol to Prevent, Suppress and Punish Trafficking in Persons, Especially Women and Children, Supplementing the United Nations Convention Against Transnational Organised Crime

This Convention shall not affect the rights and obligations derived from the provisions of the Protocol to prevent, suppress and punish trafficking in persons, especially women and children, supplementing the United Nations Convention against transnational organised crime, and intended to enhance the protection afforded by it and develop the standards contained therein.

Article 40 — Relationship With Other International Instruments

1. This Convention shall not affect the rights and obligations derived from other international instruments to which Parties to the present Convention are Parties or shall become Parties and which contain provisions on matters governed by this Convention and which ensure greater protection and assistance for victims of trafficking.

2. The Parties to the Convention may conclude bilateral or multilateral agreements with one another on the matters dealt with in this Convention, for purposes of supplementing or strengthening its provisions or facilitating the application of the principles embodied in it.

3. Parties which are members of the European Union shall, in their mutual relations, apply Community and European Unions rules in so far as there are Community or European Union rules governing the particular subject concerned and applicable to the specific case, without prejudice to the object and purpose of the present Convention and without prejudice to its full application with other Parties.

4. Nothing in this Convention shall affect the rights, obligations and responsibilities of States and individuals under international law, including international humanitarian law and international human rights law and, in particular, where applicable, the 1951 Convention and the 1967 Protocol relating to the Status of Refugees and the principle of non-refoulment as contained therein.

Chapter IX — Amendments to the Convention

1. Any proposal for an amendment to this Convention presented by a Party shall be communicated to the Secretary General of the Council of Europe and forwarded by him or her to the member States of the Council of Europe, any signatory, any State Party, the European Community, to any State invited to sign this Convention in accordance with the provisions of Article 42 and to any State invited to accede to this Convention in accordance with the provisions of Article 43.

2. Any amendment proposed by a Party shall be communicated to GRETA, which shall submit to the Committee of Ministers its opinion on that proposed amendment.

3. The Committee of Ministers shall consider the proposed amendment and the opinion submitted by GRETA and, following consultation of the Parties to this Convention and after obtaining their unanimous consent, may adopt the amendment.

4. The text of any amendment adopted by the Committee of Ministers in accordance with paragraph 3 of this article shall be forwarded to the Parties for acceptance.

5. Any amendment adopted in accordance with paragraph 3 of this article shall enter into force on the first day of the month following the expiration of a period of one month after the date on which all Parties have informed the Secretary General that they have accepted it.

Chapter X—Final Clauses

1. This Convention shall be open for signature by the member States of the Council of Europe, the non member States which have participated in its elaboration and the European Community.

2. This Conventions is subject to ratification, acceptance or approval. Instruments of ratification, acceptance or approval shall be deposited with the Secretary General of the Council of Europe.

3. This Convention shall enter into force on the first day of the month following the expiration of a period fo three months after the date on which 10 Signatories, including at least 8 member States of the Council of Europe, have expressed their consent to be bound by the Convention in accordance with the provisions of the preceding paragraph.

4. In respect of any State mentioned in paragraph 1 or the European Community, which subsequently expresses its consent to be bound by it, the Convention shall enter into force on the first day of the month following the expiration of a period of three months after the date of the deposit of its instrument of ratification, acceptance or approval.

Article 43—Accession to the Convention

1. After entry into force of this Convention, the Committee of Ministers of the Council of Europe may, after consultation of the Parties to this Convention and obtaining their unanimous consent, invite any non-member State of the Council of Europe, which has not participated in the elaboration of the Convention, to accede to this Convention by a decision taken by the majority provided for in Article 20 d. of the Statute of the Council of Europe, and by unanimous vote of the representatives of the Contracting States entitled to sit on the Committee of Ministers.

2. In respect of any acceding State, the Convention shall enter into force on the first day of the month following the expiration of a period of three months after the date of deposit of the instrument of accession with the Secretary General fo the Council of Europe.

Article 44—Territorial Application

1. Any State or the European Community may, at the time of signature or when depositing its instrument of ratification, acceptance, approval or accession, specify the territory or territories to which this Convention shall apply.

2. Any Party may, at any later date, by a declaration addressed to the Secretary General of the Council of Europe, extend the application of this Convention to any other territory specified in the declaration and for whose international relations it is responsible or on whose behalf it is authorised to give undertakings. In respect of such territory, the Convention shall enter into force on the first day of the month following the expiration of a period of three months after the date of receipt of such declaration by the Secretary General.

3. Any declaration made under the two preceding paragraphs may, in respect of any territory specified in such declaration, be withdrawn by a notification addressed to the Secretary General of the Council of Europe. The withdrawal shall become effective on the first day of the month\ following the expiration of a period of three months after the date of receipt of such notification by the Secretary General.

Article 45—Reservations

No reservations may be made in respect of any provision of this Convention, with the exception of the reservation of Article 31, paragraph 2.

Article 46—Denunciation

1. Any Party, at any time, denounce this Convention by means of a notification addressed to the Secretary General of the Council of Europe.

2. Such denunciation shall become effective on the first day of the month following the expiration of a period of three months after the date of receipt of the notification by the Secretary General.

Article 47—Notification

The Secretary General of the Council of Europe shall notify the member States of the Council of Europe, any signatory, any State Party, the European Community, to any State invited to sign this Convention in accordance with the provisions of Article 42 and to any State invited to accede to this Convention in accordance with the provisions of Article 43 of:

   a. any signature;

   b. the deposit of any instrument of ratification, acceptance, approval or accession;

   c. any date of entry into force of this Convention in accordance with Articles 42 and 43;

   d. any amendment adopted in accordance with Article 41 and the date on which such an amendment enters into force;

   e. any denunciation made in pursuance of the provisions of Article 46;

   f. any other act, notification or communication relating to this Convention;

   g. any reservation made under Article 45.

In witness whereof the undersigned, being duly authorised thereto, have signed this Convention.

Done at Warsaw, this 16th day of May 2005, in English and in French, both texts being equally authentic, in a single copy which shall be deposited in the archives of the Council of Europe. The Secretary General of the Council of Europe shall transmit certified copies to each member State of the Council of Europe, to the non-member States which have participated in the elaboration of this Convention, to the European Community and to any State invited to accede to this Convention.

Council of Europe Convention on Laundering, Search, Seizure and Confiscation of the Proceeds from Crime
E.T.S. No. 141 (Nov. 8, 1990)

Preamble

The Member States of the Council of Europe and the other States signatory hereto,

Considering that the aim of the Council of Europe is to achieve a greater unity between its members;

Convinced of the need to pursue a common criminal policy aimed at the protection of society;

Considering that the fight against serious crime, which has become an increasingly international problem, calls for the use of modern and effective methods on an international scale;

Believing that one of these methods consists in depriving criminals of the proceeds from crime;

Considering that for the attainment of this aim a well-functioning system of international co-operation also must be established;

Have agreed as follows:

Chapter I — Use of terms

Article 1. Use of terms

For the purposes of this Convention:

a. "proceeds" means any economic advantage from criminal offences. It may consist of any property as defined in subparagraph b of this article;

b. "property" includes property of any description, whether corporeal or incorporeal, movable or immovable, and legal documents or instruments evidencing title to, or interest in such property;

c. "instrumentalities" means any property used or intended to be used, in any manner, wholly or in part, to commit a criminal offence or criminal offences;

d. "confiscation" means a penalty or a measure, ordered by a court following proceedings in relation to a criminal offence or criminal offences resulting in the final deprivation of property;

e. "predicate offence" means any criminal offence as a result of which proceeds where generated that may become the subject of an offence as defined in Article 6 of this Convention.

Chapter II — Measures to be taken at national level

Article 2. Confiscation measures

1. Each Party shall adopt such legislative and other measures as may be necessary to enable it to confiscate instrumentalities and proceeds or property the value of which corresponds to such proceeds.

2. Each Party may, at the time of signature or when depositing its instruments of ratification, acceptance, approval or accession, by a declaration addressed to the Secretary General of the Council of Europe, declare that paragraph 1 of this article apples only to offences or categories of offences specified in such declaration.

Article 3. Investigative and provisional measures

1. Each Party shall adopt such legislative and other measures as may be necessary to enable it to identify and trace property which is liable to confiscation pursuant to Article 2, paragraph 1, and to prevent any dealing in, transfer or disposal of such property.

Article 4. Special investigative powers and techniques

1. Each party shall adopt such legislative and other measures as may be necessary to empower its courts or other measures as may be necessary to empower its courts or other competent authorities to order that bank, financial or commercial records be made available or be seized in order to carry out the actions referred to in Articles 2 and 3. A Party shall not decline to act under the provisions of this article on grounds of bank secrecy.

2. Each party shall consider adopting such legislative and other measures as may be necessary to enable it to use special investigative techniques facilitating the identification and tracing of proceeds and the gathering of evidence related thereto. Such techniques may include monitoring orders, observation, interception of telecommunications, access to computer systems and orders to produce specific documents.

Article 5. Legal remedies

Each Party shall adopt such legislative and other measures as may be necessary to ensure that interested parties affected by measures under Articles 2 and 3 shall have effective legal remedies in order to preserve their rights.

Article 6. Laundering offences

1. Each Party shall adopt such legislative and other measures as may be necessary to establish as offences under its domestic law, when committed intentionally:

a. the conversion or transfer of property, knowing that such property is proceeds, for the purpose of concealing or disguising the illicit origin of the property or of assisting any person who is involved in the commission of the predicate offence to evade the legal consequences of his actions;

b. the concealment or disguise of the true nature, source, location, disposition, movement, rights with respect to, or ownership of, property, knowing that such property is proceeds; and, subject to its constitutional principles and the basic concepts of its legal system:

c. the acquisition, possession or use of property, knowing, at the time of receipt, that such property was proceeds;

d. participation in, association or conspiracy to commit, attempts to commit and aiding, abetting, facilitating and counseling the commission of any of the offences established in accordance with this article.

2. For the purposes of implementing or applying paragraph 1 of this article:

a. it shall not matter whether the predicate offence was subject to the criminal jurisdiction of the party;

b. it may not be provided that the offences set forth in that paragraph do not apply to the persons who committed the predicate offence;

c. knowledge, intent or purpose required as an element of an offence set forth in that paragraph may be inferred from objective, factual circumstances.

3. Each Party may adopt such measures as it considers necessary to establish also as offences under its domestic law all or some of the acts referred to in paragraph 1 of this article, in any or all of the following cases where the offender:

a. ought to have assumed that the property was proceeds;

b. acted for the purpose of making profit;

c. acted for the purpose of promoting the carrying on of further criminal activity.

4. Each Party may, at the time of signature or when depositing its instruments of ratification, acceptance, approval or accession, by declaration addressed to the Secretary General of the Council of Europe declare that paragraph 1 of this article applies only to predicate offences or categories of such offences specified in such declaration.

Chapter III — International co-operation

Section 1 — Principles of international co-operation

Article 7. General principles and measures for international co-operation

1. The Parties shall co-operate with each other to the widest extent possible for the purposes of investigations and proceedings aiming at the confiscation of instrumentalities and proceeds.

2. Each Party shall adopt such legislative or other measures as may be necessary to enable it to comply, under the conditions provided for in this chapter, with requests:

a. for confiscation of specific items of property representing proceeds or instrumentalities, as well as for confiscation of proceeds consisting in a requirement to pay a sum of money corresponding to the value of proceeds;

b. for investigation assistance and provisional measures with a view to either form of confiscation referred to under a. above.

Section 2 — Investigating assistance

Article 8. Obligation to assist

The Parties shall afford each other, upon request, the widest possible measure of assistance in the identification and tracing of instrumentalities, proceeds and other property liable to confiscation. Such assistance shall include any measure providing and securing evidence as to the existence, location or movement, nature, legal status or value of the aforementioned property.

Article 9. Execution of assistance

The assistance pursuant to Article 8 shall be carried out as permitted by and in accordance with the domestic law of the requested Party and, to the extent not compatible with such law, in accordance with the procedures specified in the request.

Article 10. Spontaneous information

Without prejudice to its own investigations or proceedings, a Party may without prior request forward to another Party information on instrumentalities and proceeds, when it considers that the disclosure of such information might assist the receiving Party in initiating or carrying out investigations or proceedings or might lead to a request by that Party under this chapter.

Section 3 — Provisional measures

Article 11. Obligation to take provisional measures

1. At the request of another Party which has instituted criminal proceedings or proceedings for the purpose of confiscation, a Party shall take the necessary provisional measures, such as freezing or seizing, to prevent any dealing in, transfer or disposal of property which, at a later stage, may be the subject of a request for confiscation or which might be such as to satisfy the request.

2. A Party which has received a request for confiscation pursuant to Article 13 shall, if so requested, take the measures mentioned in paragraph 1 of this article in respect of any property which is the subject of the request or which might be such as to satisfy the request.

Article 12. Execution of provisional measures

1. The provisional measures mentioned Article 11 shall be carried out as permitted by and in accordance with the domestic law of the requested Party and, to the extent not incompatible with such law, in accordance with the procedures specified in the request.

2. Before lifting any provisional measure taken pursuant to this article, the requested Party shall, wherever possible, give the requesting Party an opportunity to present its reasons in favor of continuing the measure.

Section 4 — Confiscation

Article 13. Obligation to confiscate

1. A Party, which has received a request made by another Party for confiscation concerning instrumentalities or proceeds, situated in its territory, shall:

a. enforce a confiscation order made by a court of a requesting Party in relation to such instrumentalities or proceeds; or

b. submit the request to its competent authorities for the purpose of obtaining an order of confiscation and, if such order is granted, enforce it.

2. For the purposes of applying paragraph 1.b. of this article, any Party shall whenever necessary have competence to institute confiscation proceedings under its own law.

3. The provisions of paragraph 1 of this article shall also apply to confiscation consisting in a requirement to pay a sum of money corresponding to the value of proceeds, if property on which the confiscation can be enforced is located in the requested Party. In such cases, when enforcing confiscation pursuant to paragraph 1, the requested Party shall, if payment is not obtained, realize the claim on any property available for that purpose.

4. If a request for confiscation concerns a specific item of property, the Parties may agree that the requested Party may enforce the confiscation in the form of a requirement to pay a sum of money corresponding to the value of the property.

Article 14. Execution of confiscation

1. The procedures for obtaining and enforcing the confiscation under Article 13 shall be governed by the law of the requested Party.

2. The requested Party shall be bound by the findings as to the facts in so far as they are stated in conviction or judicial decision of the requesting party or in so far as such conviction or judicial decisions implicitly based on them.

3. Each Party may, at the time of signature or when depositing its instrument of ratification, acceptance, approval or accession, by a declaration addressed to the Secretary General of the Council of Europe, declare that paragraph 2 of this article applies only subject to its constitutional principles and the basic concepts of its legal system.

4. If the confiscation consists in the requirement to pay a sum of money, the competent authority of the requested party shall concert the amount there of into the currency of that Party at the rate of exchange ruling at the time when the decision to enforce the confiscation is taken.

5. In the case of Article 13, paragraph 1.a., the requesting Party alone shall have the right to decide on any application for review of the confiscation order.

Article 15. Confiscated property

Any property confiscated by the requested Party shall be disposed of by that Party in accordance with its domestic law, unless otherwise agreed by the Parties concerned.

Article 16. Right of enforcement and maximum amount of confiscation

1. A request for confiscation made under Article 13 does not affect the right of the requesting Party to enforce itself the confiscation order.

2. Nothing in this Convention shall be so interpreted as to permit the total value of the confiscation to exceed the amount of the sum of money specified in the confiscation

order. If a Party finds that this might occur, the Parties concerned shall enter into consultations to avoid such an effect.

Article 17. Imprisonment in default

The requested Party shall not impose imprisonment in default or any other measure restricting the liberty of a person as a result of a request under Article 13, if the requesting Party has so specified in the request.

Section 5 — Refusal and postponement of co-operation

Article 18. Grounds for refusal

1. Co-operation under this chapter may be refused if:

a. the action sought would be contrary to the fundamental principles of the legal system of the requested party; or

b. the execution of the request is likely to prejudice the sovereignty, security, *ordre public* or other essential interests of the requested Party; or

c. in the opinion of the requested Party, the importance of the case to which the request relates does not justify the taking of the action sought; or

d. the offence to which the request relates is a political or fiscal offence; or

e. the requested Party considers that compliance with the action sought would be contrary to the principle of *ne bis in idem*; or

f. the offence to which the request relates would not be a offence under the law of the requested Party if committed within its jurisdiction. However, this ground for refusal applies to co-operation under Section 2 only in so far as the assistance sought involves coercive action.

2. Co-operation under Section 2, in so far as the assistance sought involves coercive action, and under Section 3 of this chapter, may also be refused if the measures sought could not be taken under the domestic law of the requested Party for the purposes of investigations or proceedings, had it been similar domestic case.

3. Where the law of the requested Party so requires, co-operation under Section 2, in so far as the assistance sought involves coercive action, and under Section 3 of this chapter may also be refused if the measures sought or any other measures having similar effects would not be permitted under the law of the requesting Party, or, as regards the competent authorities of the requesting Party, if the request is not authorized by either a judge or another judicial authority, including public prosecutors, any of these authorities acting in relation to criminal offences.

4. Co-operation under Section 4 of this chapter may also be refused if:

a. under the law of the requested Party confiscation is not provided for in respect of the type of offence to which the request relates; or

b. without prejudice to the obligation pursuant to Article 13, paragraph 3, it would be contrary to the principles of the domestic laws of the requested Party concerning the limits of confiscation in respect of the relationship between an offence and:

i. an economic advantage that might be qualified as its proceeds; or

ii. property that might be qualified as its instrumentalities; or

c. under the law of the requested Party confiscation may no longer be imposed or enforced because of the lapse of time; or

d. the request does not relate to a previous conviction, or a decision of a judicial nature or a statement in such a decision that an offence or several offences have been committed, on the bases of which the confiscation has been ordered or sought; or

e. confiscation is either not enforceable in the requesting Party, or it is still subject to ordinary means of appeal; or

f. the request relates to a confiscation order resulting from a decision rendered *in absentia* of the person against whom the order was issued and, in the opinion of the requested Party, the proceedings conducted by the requesting Party leading to such decision did not satisfy the minimum rights of defence recognized as due to everyone against whom a criminal charge is made.

5. For the purposes of paragraph 4.f. of this article a decision is not considered to have been rendered *in absentia* if:

a. it has been confirmed or pronounced after opposition by the person concerned; or

b. it has been rendered on appeal, provided that the appeal was lodged by the person concerned.

6. When considering, for the purposes of paragraph 4.f. of this article, if the minimum rights of defence have been satisfied, the requested Party shall take into account the fact that the person concerned has deliberately sought to evade justice or the fact that that person, having had the possibility of lodging a legal remedy against the decision made *in absentia*, elected not to do so nor to ask for adjournment.

7. A Party shall not invoke bank secrecy as a ground to refuse any co-operation under this chapter. Where its domestic law so requires, a Party may require that a request for co-operation which would involve the lifting of bank secrecy be authorized by either a judge or another judicial authority, including public prosecutors, any of these authorities acting in relation to criminal offences.

8. Without prejudice to the ground for refusal provided for in paragraph 1.a. of this article:

a. the fact that the person under investigation or subjected to a confiscation order by the authorities of the requesting Party is a legal person shall not be invoked by the requested Party as an obstacle to affording any co-operation under this chapter;

b. the fact that the natural person against whom an order of confiscation of proceeds has been issued has subsequently been dissolved shall not be invoked as an obstacle to render assistance in accordance with Article 13, paragraph 1.a.

Article 19. Postponement

The requested Party may postpone action on a request if such action would prejudice investigations or proceedings by its authorities.

Article 20. Partial or conditional granting of a request

Before refusing or postponing co-operation under this chapter, the requested Party shall, where appropriate after having consulted the requesting Party, consider whether the request may be granted partially or subject to such conditions as it deems necessary.

Section 6 — Notification and protection of third parties' rights

Article 21. Notification of documents

1. The Parties shall afford each other the widest measure of mutual assistance in the serving of judicial documents to persons affected by provisional measures and confiscation.

2. Nothing in this article is intended to interfere with:

a. the possibility of sending judicial documents, by postal channels, directly to persons abroad;

b. the possibility for judicial officers, officials or other competent authorities of the Party of origin to effect service of judicial documents directly through the consular authorities of that Party or through judicial officers, officials or other competent authorities of the Party of destination, unless the Party of destination makes a declaration to the contrary to the Secretary General of the Council of Europe at the time of signature or when depositing its instrument of ratification, acceptance, approval or accession.

3. When serving judicial documents to persons abroad affected by provisional measures or confiscation orders issued in the sending Party, this Party shall indicate what legal remedies are available under is law to such persons.

Article 22. Recognition of foreign decisions

1. When dealing with a request for co-operation under Sections 3 and 4, the requested Party shall recognize any judicial decision taken in the requesting Party regarding rights claimed by third parties.

2. Recognition may be refused if:

a. third parties did not have adequate opportunity to assert their right; or

b. the decision is incompatible with a decision already taken in the requested Party on the same matter; or

c. it is incompatible with the *ordre public* of the requested Party; or

d. the decision was taken contrary to provisions on exclusive jurisdiction provided for by the law of the requested Party.

Section 7 — Procedural and other general rules

Article 23. Central Authority

1. The Parties shall designate a central authority or, if necessary, authorities, which shall be responsible for sending and answering requests made under this chapter, the execution of such requests or the transmission of them to the authorities competent for their execution.

2. Each Party shall, at the time of signature or when depositing its instrument of ratification, acceptance, approval or accession, communicate to the Secretary General of the Council of Europe the names and addresses of the authorities designated in pursuance of paragraph 1 of this article.

Article 24. Direct communication

1. The central authorities shall communicate directly with one another.

2. In the event of urgency, requests or communications under this chapter may be sent directly by the judicial authorities, including public prosecutors, of the requesting Party to such authorities of the requested Party. In such cases a copy shall be sent at the same

time to the central authority of the requested Party through the central authority of the requesting Party.

3. Any request or communication under paragraphs 1 and 2 of this article may be made though the International Criminal Police Organization (Interpol).

4. Where a request is made pursuant to paragraph 2 of this article and the authority if not competent to deal with the request, it shall refer the request to the competent national authority and inform directly the requesting Party that it has done so.

5. Requests or communications under Section 2 of t his chapter, which do not involve coercive action, may be directly transmitted by the competent authorities of the requesting Party to the competent authorities of the requested Party.

Article 25. Form of request and languages

1. All requests under this chapter shall be made in writing. Modern means of telecommunications, such as telefax, may be used.

2. Subject to the provisions of paragraph 3 of this article, translations of the requests or supporting documents shall not be required.

3. At the time of signature or when depositing its instrument of ratification, acceptance, approval or accession, any Party may communicate to the Secretary General of the Council of Europe a declaration that it reserves the right to require that requests made to it and documents supporting such requests accompanied by a translation into its own language or into one of the official languages of the Council of Europe or into such one of these languages as it shall indicate. It may on that occasion declare its readiness to accept translations in any other language as it may specify. The other Parties may apply the reciprocity rule.

Article 26. Legalization

Documents transmitted in application of this chapter shall be exempt from all legalization formalities.

Article 27. Content of request

1. Any request for co-operation under this chapter shall specify:

a. the authority making the request and the authority carrying out the investigations or proceedings;

b. the object of and the reason for the request;

c. the matters, including the relevant facts (such as date, place and circumstances of the offence) to which the investigations or proceedings relate, except in the case of a request for notification;

d. in so far as the co-operation involves coercive action:

i. the text of the statutory provisions or, where this is not possible, statement of the relevant law applicable; and

ii. an indication that the measure sought or any other measures having similar effects could be taken in the territory of the requesting Party under its own law;

e. where necessary and in so far as possible:

i. details of the person or person concerned, including name, date and place of birth, nationality and location, and, in the case of a legal person, its seat; and

ii. the property in relation to which co-operation is ought, its location, its connection with the person or persons concerned, any connection with the offence, as well as any available information about other persons' interests in the property; and

f. any particular procedure the requesting Party wishes to be followed.

2. A request for provisional measures under Section 3 in relation to seizure of property on which a confiscation order consisting in the requirement to pay a sum of money may be realized shall also indicate a maximum amount for which recovery is sought in that property.

3. In addition to the indications mentioned in paragraph 1, any request under Section 4 shall contain:

a. in the case of Article 13, paragraph 1.a.:

i. a certified true copy of the confiscation order made by the court in the requesting Party and a statement of the grounds on the basis of which the order was made, if they are not indicated in the order itself;

ii. an attestation by the competent authority of the requesting Party that the confiscation order is enforceable and not subject to ordinary means of appeal

iii. information as to the extent to which the enforcement of the order is requested; and

iv. information as to the necessity of taking any provisional measures;

b. in the case of Article 13, paragraph 1.b., a statement of the facts relied upon by the requesting Party sufficient to enable the requested Party to seek the order under its domestic law;

c. when third parties have had the opportunity to claim rights, documents demonstrating that this has been the case.

Article 28. Defective requests

1. If a request does not comply with the provisions of this chapter or the information supplied is not sufficient to enable the requested Party to deal with the request, that Party may ask the requesting Party to amend the request or to complete it with additional information.

2. The requested Party may set a time-limit for the receipt of such amendments or information.

3. Pending receipt of the requested amendments or information in relation to a request under Section 4 of this chapter, the requested Party may take any of the measures referred to in Sections 2 or 3 of this chapter.

Article 29. Plurality of requests

1. Where the requested Party receives more than one request under Sections 3 or 4 of this chapter in respect of the same person or property, the plurality of requests shall not prevent that Party from dealing with the requests involving the taking of provisional measures.

2. In the case of plurality of requests under Section 4 of this chapter, the requested Party shall consider consulting the requesting Parties.

Article 30. Information

1. The requested Party shall promptly inform the requesting Party of:

a. the action initiated on a request under this chapter;

b. the final result of the action carried out on the basis of the request;

c. a decision to refuse, postpone or make conditional, in whole or in party, any co-operation under this chapter;

d. any circumstances which render impossible the carrying out of the action sought or are likely to delay it significantly; and

e. in the event of provisional measures taken pursuant to a request under Sections 2 or 3 of this chapter, such provisions of its domestic law as would automatically lead to the lifting of the provisional measure.

2. The requesting Party shall promptly inform the requested Party of:

a. any review, decision or any other fact by reason of which the confiscation order ceases to be wholly or partially enforceable; and

b. any development, factual or legal, by reason of which any action under this chapter is no longer justified.

3. Where a Party, on the basis of the same confiscation order, requests confiscation in more than one Party, it shall inform all Parties which are affected by an enforcement of the order about the request....

Article 32. Restriction of use

1. The requested Party may make the execution of a request dependent on the condition that the information or evidence obtained will not, without its prior consent, be used or transmitted by the authorities of the requesting Party for investigations or proceedings other than those specified in the request.

2. Each Party may, at the time of signature or when depositing its instrument of ratification, acceptance, approval or accession, by declaration addressed to the Secretary General of the Council of Europe, declare that, without its prior consent, information or evidence provided by it under this chapter may not be used or transmitted by the authorities of the requesting Party in investigations or proceedings other than those specified in the request.

Article 33. Confidentiality

1. The requesting Party may require that the requested Party keep confidential the facts and substance of the request, except to the extent necessary to execute the request. If the requested party cannot comply with the requirement of confidentiality, it shall promptly inform the requesting Party.

2. The requesting Party shall, if not contrary to basic principles of its national law and if so requested, keep confidential any evidence and information provided by the requested Party, except to the extent that its disclosure is necessary of the investigations or proceedings described in the request.

3. Subject to the provisions of its domestic law, a Party which has received spontaneous information under Article 10 shall comply with any requirement of confidentiality as required by the Party which supplies the information. If the other Party cannot comply with such requirement, is shall promptly inform the transmitting Party.

Article 34. Costs

The ordinary costs of complying with a request shall be borne by the requested Party. Where costs of a substantial or extraordinary nature are necessary to comply with a request, the Parties shall consult in order to agree the conditions on which the request is to be executed and how the costs shall be borne.

Article 35. Damages

1. When legal action on liability for damages resulting from an act or omission in relation to co-operation under this chapter has been initiated by a person, the Parties concerned shall consider consulting each other, where appropriate, to determine how to apportion any sum of damages due.

2. A Party which has become subject of a litigation for damages shall endeavor to inform the other Party of such litigation if that Party might have an interest in the case.

Chapter IV — Final provisions

Article 36. Signature and entry into force

1. This Convention shall be open for signature by the member States of the Council of Europe and non-Member States which have participated in its elaboration. Such States may express their consent to be bound by:

    a. signature without reservation as to ratification, acceptance or approval; or

    b. signature to ratification, acceptance or approval, followed by ratification, acceptance or approval.

2. Instruments of ratification, acceptance or approval shall be deposited with the Secretary General of the Council of Europe.

3. This Convention shall enter into force on the first day of the month following the expiration of a period of three months after the date on which three States, of which at least two are Member States of the Council of Europe, have expressed their consent to be bound by the Convention in accordance with the provisions of paragraph 1.

4. In respect of any signatory State which subsequently expresses its consent to be bound by it, the Convention shall enter into force on the first day of the month following the expiration of a period of three months after the date of the expression of its consent to be bound by the Convention in accordance with the provisions of paragraph 1.

Article 37. Accession to the Convention

1. After the entry into force of this Convention, the Committee of Ministers of the Council of Europe, after consulting the Contracting States to the Convention, may invite any State not a member of the Council and not having participated in its elaboration to accede to this Convention, by a decision taken by the majority provided for in Article 20.d. of the Statute of the Council of Europe and by the unanimous vote of the representatives of the Contracting States entitled to sit on the Committee.

2. In respect of any acceding State the Convention shall enter into force on the first day of the month following the expiration of a period of three months after the date of deposit of the instrument of accession with the Secretary General of the Council of Europe.

Article 38. Territorial application

1. Any State may, at the time of signature or when depositing its instrument of ratification, acceptance, approval or accession, specify the territory or territories to which this Convention shall apply.

2. Any state may, at any later date, by a declaration addressed to the Secretary General of the Council of Europe, expend the application of this Convention to any other territory specified in the declaration. In respect of such territory the Convention shall enter into force on the first day of the month following the expiration of a period of three months after the date of receipt of such declaration by the Secretary General.

3. Any declaration made under the two preceding paragraphs may, in respect of any territory specified in such declaration, be withdrawn by a notification addressed to the Secretary General. The withdrawal shall become effective on the first day of the month following the expiration of a period of three months after the date of receipt of such notification by the Secretary General.

Article 39. Relationship to other conventions and agreements

1. This Convention does not affect the rights and undertakings derived from international multilateral conventions concerning special matters.

2. The Parties to the Convention may conclude bilateral or multilateral agreements with one another on the matters dealt with in this Convention, for purposes of supplementing or strengthening its provisions or facilitating the application of the principles embodied in it.

3. If two or more Parties have already concluded an agreement or treaty in respect of a subject which is dealt with in this Convention or otherwise have established their relations in respect of that subject, they shall be entitled to apply that agreement or treaty or to regulate those relations accordingly, in lieu of the present convention, if it facilitates international co-operation.

Article 40. Reservations

1. Any State may, at the time of signature or when depositing its instrument of ratification, acceptance, approval or accession, declare that it avails itself of one or more of the reservations provided of in Article 2, paragraph 2, Article 6, paragraph 4, Article 14, paragraph 3, Article 21, paragraph 2, Article 25, paragraph 3 and Article 32, paragraph, 2. No other reservation may be made.

2. Any State which has made a reservation under the preceding paragraph may wholly or partly withdraw it by means of a fortification addressed to the Secretary General of the Council of Europe. The withdrawal shall take effect on the date of receipt of such notification by the Secretary General.

3. A Party which has made a reservation in respect of a provision of this Convention may not claim the application of that provision by any other Party; it may, however, it its reservation is partial or conditional, claim the application of that provision in so far as it has itself accepted it.

Article 41. Amendments

1. Amendments to this Convention may be proposed by and Party, and shall be communicated by the Secretary General of the Council of Europe to the Member States of the Council of Europe and to every non-Member State which has acceded to or has been invited to accede to this Convention in accordance with the provisions of Article 37.

2. Any amendment proposed by a Party shall be communicated to the Europe Committee on Crime Problems which shall submit to the Committee of Ministers its opinion on that proposed amendment.

3. The Committee of Ministers shall consider the proposed amendment and the opinion submitted by the European Committee on Crime Problems and may adopt the amendment.

4. The text of any amendment adopted by the Committee of Ministers in accordance with paragraph 3 of this article shall be forwarded to the Parties for acceptance.

5. Any amendments adopted in accordance with paragraph 3 of this article shall come into force on the thirtieth day after all Parties have informed the Secretary General of their acceptance thereof.

Article 42. Settlement of disputes

1. The European Committee on Crime Problems of the Council of Europe shall be kept informed regarding the interpretation and application of this Convention.

2. In case of a dispute between Parties as to the interpretation or application of this Convention, they shall seek a settlement of the dispute through negotiation or any other peaceful means of their choice, including submission of the dispute to the European Committee on Crime Problems, to an arbitral tribunal whose decisions shall be binding upon the Parties, or to the International court of Justice, as agreed upon by the Parties concerned.

Article 43. Denunciation

1. Any Party may, at any time, denounce this Convention by means of a notification addressed to the Secretary General of the Council of Europe.

2. Such denunciation shall become effective on the first day of the month following the expiration of a period of three months after the date of receipt of the notification by the Secretary General.

3. The present Convention shall, however, continue to apply to the enforcement under Article 14 of confiscation for which a request has been made in conformity with the provisions of this Convention before the date on which such a denunciation takes effect.

Article 44. Notifications

The Secretary General of the Council of Europe shall notify the Member States of the Council and any State which has acceded to this Convention of:

a. any signature;

b. the deposit of any instrument of ratification, acceptance, approval or accession;

c. any date of entry into force of this Convention in accordance with Articles 36 and 37;

d. any reservation made under Article 40, paragraph 1;

e. any other act, notification or communication relating to this Convention.

In witness whereof the undersigned, being duly authorized thereto, have signed this Convention.

Done at Strasbourg, this 8th day of November 1990, in English and in French, both texts being equally authentic, in a single copy which shall be deposited in the archives of the Council of Europe. The Secretary General of the Council of Europe shall transmit certified copies to each Member State of the Council of Europe, to the non-Member States which have participated in the elaboration of this Convention, and to any State invited to accede to it.

The 1991 European Communities Directive, Council Directive on Prevention of the Use of the Financial System for the Purpose of Money Laundering
91/308/EEC, 1991 O.J. (L 166) 77 (June 10, 1991)

The Council of the European Communities

Having regard to the Treaty establishing the European Economic Community, and in particular Article 57(2), first and third sentences, and Article 100a thereof,

Having regard to the proposal from the Commission,

In co-operation with the European Parliament,

Having regard to the opinion of the Economic and Social Committee,

Whereas when credit and financial institutions are used to launder proceeds from criminal activities (hereinafter referred to as "money laundering"), the soundness and stability of the institution concerned and confidence in the financial system as a whole could be seriously jeopardized, thereby losing the trust of the public;

Whereas lack of Community action against money laundering could lead Member States, for the purpose of protecting their financial systems, to adopt measures which could be inconsistent with completion of the Single Market;

Whereas, in order to facilitate their criminal activities, launderers could try to take advantage of the freedom of capital movement to supply financial services which the integrated financial area involves, if certain co-ordinating measures are not adopted at Community level;

Whereas money laundering has an evidence influence on the rise of organized crime in general and drug trafficking in particular;

Whereas there is more and more awareness that combating money laundering is one of the most effective means of opposing this form of criminal activity, which constitutes a particular threat to Member States societies;

Whereas money laundering must be combated mainly by penal means and within the framework of international co-operation among judicial and law enforcement authorities, as has been undertaken, in the field of drugs, by the United Nations Convention Against Illicit Traffic in Narcotic Drugs and Psychotropic Substances, adopted on 19 December 1988 in Vienna (hereinafter referred to as the "Vienna Convention") and more generally in relation to all criminal activities, by the council of Europe Convention on laundering tracing, seizure, and confiscation of proceeds of crime, opened for signature on 8 November 1990 in Strasbourg;

Whereas a penal approach should, however, not be the only way to combat money laundering, since the financial system can play a highly effective role; where as reference must be made in this context to the recommendation of the Council of Europe of 27 June 1980 and to the declaration of principles adopted in December 1988 in Basle by the banking supervisory authorities of the Group of Ten, both of which constitute major steps towards preventing the use of the financial system for money laundering;

Whereas money laundering is usually carried out in an international context so that the criminal origin of the funds can be better disguised;

Whereas measures exclusively adopted at a national level, without taking account of international co-ordination and co-operation would have very limited effects;

Whereas any measures adopted by the Community in this field should be consistent with other action undertaken in other international fora;

Whereas in this respect any Community action should take particular account of the recommendations adopted by the financial action task force on money laundering, set up in July 1989 by the Paris summer of the seven most developed countries;

Whereas the European Parliament has requested, in several resolutions, the establishment of a global Community programme to combat drug trafficking, including provisions on prevent of money laundering;

Whereas for the purposes of this Directive the definition of money laundering is taken from that adopted in the Vienna Convention; whereas, however, since money laundering occurs not only in relation to the proceeds of drug-related offences but also in relation to the proceeds of other criminal activities (such as organized crime and terrorism), the Member States should, within the meaning of their legislation, extend the effects of the Directive to include the proceeds of such activities, to the extent that they are likely to result in laundering operations justifying sanctions on that basis;

Whereas prohibition of money laundering in Member States' legislation backed by appropriate measures and penalties is a necessary condition for combating this phenomenon;

Whereas ensuring that credit and financial institutions require identification of their customers when entering into business relations or conducting transactions, exceeding certain thresholds, are necessary to avoid launderers taking advantage of anonymity to carry out their criminal activities;

Whereas such provisions must also be extended, as far as possible, to any beneficial owners;

Whereas credit and financial institutions must keep for at least five years copies or references of the identification documents required as well as supporting evidence and records consisting of documents relating to transactions or copies thereof similarly admissible in court proceedings under the applicable national legislation for use as evidence in any investigation into money laundering;

Whereas ensuring that credit and financial institutions examine with special attention any transaction which they regard as particularly likely, by its nature, to be related to money laundering is necessary in order to preserve the soundness and integrity of the financial system as well as to contribute to combating this phenomenon;

Whereas to this end they should pay special attention to transactions with third countries which do not apply comparable standards against money laundering to those established by the Community or to other equivalent standards set out by international fora and endorsed by the Community;

Whereas, for those purposes, Member States may ask credit and financial institutions to record in writing the results of the examination they are required to carry out and to ensure that hose results are available to the authorities responsible for efforts to eliminate money laundering;

Whereas preventing the financial system from being used for money laundering is a task which cannot be carried out by the authorities for combining this phenomenon without the co-operation of credit and financial institutions and their supervisory authorities;

Whereas banking secrecy must be lifted in such cases;

Whereas a mandatory system of reporting suspicious transactions which ensures that information is transmitted to the above mentioned authorities without alerting the customers concerned, is the most effective way to accomplish such co-operation;

Whereas a special protection clause is necessary to exempt credit and financial institutions, their employees and their directors from responsibility for breaching restrictions on disclosure of information;

Whereas the information received by the authorities pursuant to this Directive may be used only in connection with combating money laundering;

Whereas Member States may nevertheless provide that this information may be used for other purposes;

Whereas establishment by credit and financial institutions of procedures of internal control and training programmes in this field are complementary provisions without which the other measures contained in this Directive could become ineffective;

Whereas, since money laundering can be carried out not only through credit and financial institutions but also through other type of professionals and categories of undertakings, Member States must extend the provisions of this Directive in whole or in part, to include those professionals and undertakings whose activities are particularly likely to be used for money laundering purposes;

Whereas it is important that the Member States should take particular care to ensure that co-ordinated action is taken n the Community where there are strong grounds for believing that professions or activities the conditions governing the pursuit of which have been harmonized at Community level are being used for laundering money;

Whereas the effectiveness of efforts to eliminate money laundering is particularly dependent on the close co-ordination and harmonization of national implementing measures;

Whereas such co-ordination and harmonization which is being carried out in various interstate bodies requires, in the Community context, co-cooperation between Member States and the Commission in the framework of a contact committee;

Whereas it is for each Member State to adopt appropriate measures and to penalize infringement of such measures in an appropriate manner to ensure full application of this Directive;

Has adopted to this Directive

Article 1

For the purpose of this Directive:

— "credit institution" means a credit institution, as defined as in the first indent of Article 1 of Directive 77/780/EEC1, as last amended by Directive 89/646/EEC2, and includes branches within the meaning of the third indent of that Article and located in the Community, of credit institutions having their head offices outside the Community.

— "financial institution" means an undertaking other than a credit institution whose principal activity is to carry out one or more of the operations included in numbers 2 to 12 and number 14 of the list annexed to Directive 89/646/EEC, or an insurance company duly authorized in accordance with Directive 79/26EEC3 as last amended by Directive 90/619/EEC4, in so far as it carries out activities covered by that Directive; this definition includes branches located in the Community of financial institutions whose head offices are outside the Community.

— "money laundering" means the following conduct when committed intentionally:

— the conversion or transfer of property, knowing that such property is derived from criminal activity or from an act of participation in such activity, of the purpose of concealing or disguising the illicit origin of the property or of assisting any person who is involved in the commission of such activity to evade the legal consequences of his action.

— the concealment or disguise of the true nature, source, location, disposition, movement, rights with respect to, or ownership of property, knowing that such property is derived from criminal activity or from an act of participation in such activity.

— the acquisition, possession or use of property, knowing, at the time of receipt, that such property was derived from criminal activity or from an action of participation in such activity.

—participation in, association to commit, attempts to commit and aiding, abetting, facilitating and counselling the commission of any of the actions mentioned in the foregoing paragraphs.

Knowledge, intent or purpose required as an element of the above-mentioned activities may be inferred from objective factual circumstances.

Money laundering shall be regarded as such even where the activities which generated the property to be laundered were perpetrated in the territory of another Member state or in that of a third country.

—"Property" means assets of every kind, whether corporeal or incorporeal, movable or immovable, tangible or intangible, and legal documents or instruments evidencing title to or interests in such assets.

—"Criminal activity" means a crime specified in Article 3(1)(a) of the Vienna Convention and any other criminal activity designated as such for the purposes of this Directive by each Member State.

—"Competent authorities" means the national authorities empowered by law or regulation to supervise credit or financial institutions.

Article 2

Member States shall ensure that money laundering as defined in this directive is prohibited.

Article 3

1. Member States shall ensure that credit and financial institutions require identification of their customers by means of supporting evidence when entering into business relations, particularly when opening an account or savings accounts, or when offering safe custody facilities.

2. The identification requirement shall also apply for any transaction with customers other than those referred to in paragraph 1, involving a sum amounting to ECU 15 000 or more, whether the transaction is carried out in a single operation or in several operations which seem to be linked. Where the sum is now known at the time when the transaction is undertaken, the institution concerned shall proceed with identification as soon as it is apprised of the sum and establishes that the threshold has been reached.

3. By way of derogation from paragraphs 1 and 2, the identification requirements with regard to insurance policies written by insurance undertakings within he meaning of Directive 79.267/EEC, where they perform activities which fall within the scope of that Directive shall not be required where the period premium amount or amounts to be paid in any given year does nor do not exceed ECU 1 000 or where a single premium is paid amounting to ECU 2 5000 or less. If the periodic premium amount or amounts to be paid in any given year is or are increased so as to exceed the EC 1 000 threshold, identification shall be required.

4. Member States may provide that the identification requirement is not compulsory for insurance policies in respect of pension schemes taken out by virtue of a contract of employment or the insured's occupation, provided that such policies contain no surrender clause and may not be used as collateral for a loan.

5. In the event of doubt as to whether the customers referred in the above paragraphs are acting of their own behalf, or where it is certain that they are not acting on their own behalf, the credit and financial institutions shall take reasonable measures to obtain

information as to the real identity of the persons on whose behalf those customers are acting.

6. Credit and financial institutions shall carry out such identification, even where the amount of the transaction is lower than the threshold laid down, wherever there is suspicion of money laundering.

7. Credit and financial institutions shall not be subject to the identification requirements provided for in this article where the customer is also a credit or financial institution covered by this Directive.

8. Member States may provide that the identification requirements regarding transactions referred to in paragraphs 3 and 4 are fulfilled when it is established that the payment for the transaction is to be debited from an account opened in the customer's name with a credit institution subject to this Directive according to the requirements of paragraph 1.

Article 4

Member States shall ensure that credit and financial institution keep the following for use as evidence in any investigation into money laundering:

— in the case of identification, a copy of the references of the evidence required, for a period of at least five years after the relationship with their customer has ended,

— in the case of transactions, the supporting evidence and records consisting of the original documents or copies admissible in court proceedings under the applicable national legislation for a period of at least five years following execution of the transactions.

Article 5

Member States shall ensure that credit and financial institutions examine with special attention any transaction which they regard as particularly likely, by its nature, to be related to money laundering.

Article 6

Member States shall ensure that credit and financial institutions and their directors and employees co-operate fully with the authorities responsible for combating money laundering:

— by informing those authorities, on their own initiative, of any fact which might be an indicate of money laundering,

— by furnishing those authorities, at their request, with all necessary information, in accordance with the procedures established by the applicable legislation.

The information referred to in the first paragraph shall be forwarded to the authorities responsible for combating money laundering of the Member State in whose territory the institution forwarding the information is situated. The person or persons designated by the credit and financial institutions in accordance with the procedures provided for in Article II(1) shall normally forward the information. Information supplied to the authorities in accordance with the first paragraph may be used only in connection with the combating of money laundering. However, Member States may provide that such information may also be used for other purposes.

Article 7

Member States shall ensure that credit and financial institutions refrain from carrying out transactions which they know or suspect to be related to money laundering until they have apprised the authorities referred to in Article 6. Those authorities may, under conditions determined by their national legislation, give instructions not to execute the operation. Where such a transaction is suspected of giving rise to money laundering and where to refrain in such manner is impossible or is likely to frustrate efforts to pursue the beneficiaries of a suspected money laundering operation, the institutions concerned shall apprise the authorities immediately afterwards.

Article 8

Credit and financial institutions and their directors and employees shall not disclose to the customers concerned nor to there third persons that information has been transmitted to the authorities in accordance with Articles 6 and 7 or that money laundering investigation is being carried out.

Article 9

The disclosure in good faith to the authorities responsible for combating money laundering by an employee or director of a credit or financial institution of the information referred to in Articles 6 and 7 shall not constitute a breach of any restriction or disclosure of information imposed by contract or by an legislative, regulatory or administrative provision, and shall not involve the credit or financial institution, its directors or employees in liability of any kind.

Article 10

Member States ensure that if, in the course of inspections carried out in credit or financial institutions by the competent authorities, or in any other way, those authorities discover facts that could continue evidence of money laundering, they inform the authorities responsible for combating laundering.

Article 11

Member States shall ensure that credit and financial institutions:

1. establish adequate procedures of internal control and communication in order to forestall and prevent operations related to money laundering,

2. take appropriate measures so that their employees are aware of the provisions contained in this Directive. These measures shall include participation of their relevant employees in special training programmes to help them recognize operations which may be related to money laundering as well as to instruct them as to how to proceed in such cases....

Article 14

Each Member State shall take appropriate measures to ensure full application of all the provisions of this Directive and shall in particular determine the penalties to be applied for infringement of the measures adopted pursuant to this Directive.

Article 15

The Member States may adopt or retain in force stricter provision in the field covered by this Directive to prevent money laundering.

Article 16

1. Member States shall bring into force the laws, regulations and administrative decisions necessary to comply with this Directive before 1 January 1993 at the latest.

2. Where Member States adopt these measures, they shall contain a reference to this Directive or shall contain a reference to this Directive or shall be accompanied by such ref-

erence on the occasion of their official publication. The methods of making such a reference shall be laid down by the Member States.

3. Member States shall communicate to the Commission the text of the main provisions of national law which they adopting the field governed by this Directive.

Article 17

One year after 1 January 1993, whenever necessary and at least at three yearly intervals thereafter the Commission shall draw up a report on the implementation of this Directive and submit it to the European Parliament and the Council.

Article 18

This Directive is addressed to the Member States.

Done at Luxembourg, 10 June 1991.

European Convention on Transfer of Proceedings in Criminal Matters
(30 March 1978)

The member States of the Council of Europe, signatory hereto,

Considering that the aim of the Council of Europe is the achievement of greater unity between its Members;

Desiring to supplement the work which they have already accomplished in the field of criminal law with a view to arriving at more just and efficient sanctions;

Considering it useful to this end to ensure, in a spirit of mutual confidence, the organisation of criminal proceedings on the international level, in particular, by avoiding the disadvantages resulting from conflicts of competence;

Have agreed as follows:

PART I
Definitions

Article 1

For the purposes of this Convention:

(a) "offence" comprises acts dealt with under the criminal law and those dealt with under the legal provisions listed in Appendix III to this Convention on condition that where an administrative authority is competent to deal with the offence it must be possible for the person concerned to have the case tried by a court;

(b) "sanction" means any punishment or other measure incurred or pronounced in respect of an offence or in respect of a violation of the legal provisions listed in Appendix III.

PART II
Competence

Article 2

1. For the purposes of applying this Convention, any Contracting State shall have competence to prosecute under its own criminal law any offence to which the law of another Contracting State is applicable.

2. The competence conferred on a Contracting State exclusively by virtue of paragraph 1 of this article may be exercised only pursuant to a request for proceedings presented by another Contracting State.

Article 3

Any Contracting State having competence under its own law to prosecute an offence may, for the purposes of applying this Convention, waive or desist from proceedings against a suspected person who is being or will be prosecuted for the same offence by another Contracting State. Having regard to Article 21, paragraph 2, any such decision to waive or to desist from proceedings shall be provisional pending a final decision in the other Contracting State.

Article 4

The requested State shall discontinue proceedings exclusively grounded on Article 2 when to its knowledge the right of punishment is extinguished under the law of the requesting State for a reason other than time-limitation, to which Articles 10(c), 11(f) and (g), 22, 23 and 26 in particular apply.

Article 5

The provisions of Part II of this Convention do not limit the competence given to a requested State by its municipal law in regard to prosecutions.

PART III
Transfer of Proceedings

Section 1: Request for Proceedings

Article 6

1. When a person is suspected of having committed an offence under the law of a Contracting State, that State may request another Contracting State to take proceedings in the cases and under the conditions provided for in this Convention.

2. If under the provisions of this Convention a Contracting State may request another Contracting State to take proceedings, the competent authorities of the first State shall take that possibility into consideration.

Article 7

1. Proceedings may not be taken in the requested State unless the offence in respect of which the proceedings are requested would be an offence if committed in its territory and when, under these circumstances the offender would be liable to sanction under its own law also.

2. If the offence was committed by a person of public status or against a person, an institution or any thing of public status in the requesting State, it shall be considered in the requested State as having been committed by a person of public status or against such a person, an institution or any thing corresponding, in the latter State, to that against which it was actually committed.

Article 8

1. A Contracting State may request another Contracting State to take proceedings in any one or more of the following cases:

(a) if the suspected person is ordinarily resident in the requested State;

(b) if the suspected person is a national of the requested State or if that State is his State of origin;

(c) if the suspected person is undergoing or is to undergo a sentence involving deprivation of liberty in the requested State;

(d) if proceedings for the same or other offences are being taken against the suspected person in the requested State;

(e) if it considers that transfer of proceedings is warranted in the interests of arriving at the truth and in particular that the most important items of evidence are located in the requested State;

(f) if it considers that the enforcement in the requested State of a sentence if one were passed is likely to improve the prospects for social rehabilitation of the person sentenced; ...

(h) if it considers that it could not itself enforce a sentence if one were passed even by having recourse to extradition, and that the requested State could do so.

2. Where the suspected person has been finally sentenced in a Contracting State, that State may request the transfer of proceedings in one or more of the cases referred to in paragraph 1 of this article only if it cannot itself enforce the sentence, even by having recourse to extradition, and if the other Contracting State does not accept enforcement of a foreign judgment as a matter of principle or refuses to enforce such sentence.

Article 9

1. The competent authorities in the requested State shall examine the request for proceedings made in pursuance of the preceding articles. They shall decide, in accordance with their own law, what action to take thereon.

2. Where the law of the requested State provides for the punishment of the offence by an administrative authority, that State shall, as soon as possible, so inform the requesting State unless the requested State has made a declaration under paragraph 3 of this article.

3. Any Contracting State may at the time of signature, or when depositing its instrument of ratification, acceptance or accession, or at any later date indicate, by declaration addressed to the Secretary General of the Council of Europe, the conditions under which its domestic law permits the punishment of certain offences by an administrative authority. Such a declaration shall replace the notification envisaged in paragraph 2 of this article.

Article 10

The requested State shall not take action on the request:

(a) if the request does not comply with the provisions of Articles 6, paragraph 1, and 7, paragraph 1;

(b) if the institution of proceedings is contrary to the provisions of Article 35;

(c) if, at the date on the request, the time-limit for criminal proceedings has already expired in the requesting State under the legislation of that State.

Article 11

Save as provided for in Article 10 the requested State may not refuse acceptance of the request in whole or in part, except in any one or more of the following cases:

(a) if it considers that the grounds on which the request is based under Article 8 are not justified;

(b) if the suspected person is not ordinarily resident in the requested State;

(c) if the suspected person is not a national of the requested State and was not ordinarily resident in the territory of that State at the time of an offence;

(d) if it considers that the offence for which proceedings are requested is an offence of a political nature or a purely military or fiscal one;

(e) if it considers that there are substantial grounds for believing that the request for proceedings was motivated by considerations of race, religion, nationality or political opinion;

(f) if its own law is already applicable to the offence and if at the time of the receipt of the request proceedings were precluded by lapse of time according to that law; Article 26, paragraph 2, shall not apply in such a case;

(g) if its competence is exclusively grounded on Article 2 and if at the time of the receipt of the request proceedings would be precluded by lapse of time according to its law, the prolongation of the time-limit by six months under the terms of Article 23 being taken into consideration;

(h) if the offence was committed outside the territory of the requesting State;

(i) if proceedings would be contrary to the fundamental principles of the legal system of the requested State;

(j) if the requested State has violated a rule of procedure laid down in this Convention.

Article 12

1. The requested State shall withdraw its acceptance of the request if, subsequent to this acceptance, a ground mentioned in Article 10 of this Convention for not taking action on the request becomes apparent.

2. The requested State may withdraw its acceptance of the request:

(a) if it becomes apparent that the presence in person of the suspected person cannot be ensured at the hearing of proceedings in that State or that any sentence, which might be passed, could not be enforced in that State;

(b) if one of the grounds for refusal mentioned in Article 11 becomes apparent before the case is brought before a court; or

(c) in other cases, if the requesting State agrees.

Section 2: Transfer Procedure

Article 13

1. All requests specified in this Convention shall be made in writing. They, and all communications necessary for the application of this Convention, shall be sent either by the Ministry of Justice of the requesting State to the Ministry of Justice of the requested State or, by virtue of special mutual arrangement, direct by the authorities of the requesting State to those of the requested State; they shall be returned by the same channel.

2. In the urgent cases, requests and communications may be sent through the International Criminal Police Organisation (INTERPOL).

3. Any Contracting State may, by declaration addressed to the Secretary General of the Council of Europe, give notice of its intention to adopt insofar as it itself is concerned rules of transmission other than those laid down in paragraph 1 of this article.

Article 14

If a Contracting State considers that the information supplied by another Contracting State is not adequate to enable it to apply this Convention, it shall ask for the necessary additional information. It may prescribe a date for the receipt of such information.

Article 15

1. A request for proceedings shall be accompanied by the original, or a certified copy, of the criminal file and all other necessary documents. However, if the suspected person is remanded in custody in accordance with the provisions of Section 5 and if the requesting State is unable to transmit these documents at the same time as the request for proceedings, the documents may be sent subsequently.

2. The requesting State shall also inform the requested State in writing of any procedural acts performed or measures taken in the requesting State after the transmission of the request which have a bearing on the proceedings. The communication shall be accompanied by any relevant documents.

Article 16

1. The requested State shall promptly communicate its decision on the request for proceedings to the requesting State.

2. The requested State shall also inform the requesting State of a waiver of proceedings or of the decision taken as a result of proceedings. A certified copy of any written decision shall be transmitted to the requesting state.

Article 17

If the competence of the requested State is exclusively grounded on Article 2, that State shall inform the suspected person of the request for proceedings with a view to allowing him to present his views on the matter before that State has taken a decision on the request.

Article 18

1. Subject to paragraph 2 of this article, no translation of the documents relating to the application of this Convention shall be required.

2. Any Contracting State may, at the time of signature or when depositing its instrument of ratification, acceptance or accession, by declaration addressed to the Secretary General of the Council of Europe, reserve the right to require that, with the exception of the copy of the written decision referred to in Article 16, paragraph 2, the said documents be accompanied by a translation. The other Contracting States shall send the translations in either the national language of the receiving State or such of the official languages of the Council of Europe as the receiving State shall indicate. However, such an indication is not obligatory. The other Contracting State may claim reciprocity.

3. This article shall be without prejudice to any provisions concerning translation of requests and supporting documents that may be contained in agreements or arrangements now in force or that may be concluded between two or more Contracting States.

Article 19

Documents transmitted in application of this Convention need not be authenticated.

Article 20

Contracting Parties shall not claim from each other refund of any expenses resulting from the application of the Convention.

Section 3: Effects in the requesting State of a request for proceedings

Article 21

1. When the requesting State has requested proceedings, it can no longer prosecute the suspected person for the offence in respect of which the proceedings have been requested or enforce a judgement which has been pronounced previously in that State against him for that offence. Until the requested State's decision on the request for proceedings has been received, the requesting State shall, however, retain its right to take all steps in respect of prosecution, short of bringing the case to trial, or, as the case may be, allowing the competent administrative authority to decide the case.

2. The right of prosecution and of enforcement shall revert to the requesting State:

(a) if the requested State informs it of a decision in accordance with Article 10 not to take action on the request;

(b) if the requested State informs it of a decision in accordance with Article 11 to refuse acceptance of the request;

(c) if the requested State informs it of a decision in accordance with Article 12 to withdraw acceptance of the request;

(d) if the requested State informs it of a decision not to institute proceedings or discontinue them;

(e) if it withdraws its request before the requested State has informed it of a decision to take action on the request.

Article 22

A request for proceedings, made in accordance with the provisions of this Part, shall have the effect in the requesting State of prolonging the time-limit for proceedings by six months.

Section 4: Effects in the requested State of a request for proceedings

Article 23

If the competence of the requested State is exclusively grounded on Article 2, the time-limit for proceedings in that State shall be prolonged by six months.

Article 24

1. If proceedings are dependent on a complaint in both States the complaint brought in the requesting State shall have equal validity with that brought in the requested State.

2. If a complaint is necessary only in the requested State, that State may take proceedings even in the absence of a complaint if the person who is empowered to bring the complaint has not objected within a period of one month from the date of receipt by him of notice from the competent authority informing him of his right to object.

Article 25

In the requested State the sanction applicable to the offence shall be that prescribed by its own law unless that law provides otherwise. Where the competence of the requested State is exclusively grounded on Article 2, the sanction pronounced in that State shall not be more severe than that provided for in the law of the requesting State.

Article 26

1. Any act with a view of proceedings, taken in the requesting State in accordance with its law and regulations, shall have the same validity in the requested State as if it had been

taken by the authorities of that State, provided that assimilation does not give such act a greater evidential weight than it has in the requesting State.

2. Any act which interrupts time-limitation and which has been validly performed in the requesting State shall have the same effects in the requested State and vice versa.

Section 5: Provisional measures in the requested State

Article 27

1. When the requesting State announces its intention to transmit a request for proceedings, and if the competence of the requested State would be exclusively grounded on Article 2, the requested State may, on application by the requesting State and by virtue of this Convention, provisionally arrest the suspected person:

(a) if the law of the requested State authorises remand in custody for the offence, and

(b) if there are reasons to fear that the suspected person will abscond or that he will cause evidence to be suppressed.

2. The application for provisional arrest shall state that there exists a warrant of arrest or other order having the same effect, issued in accordance with the procedure laid down in the law of the requesting State; it shall also state for what offence proceedings will be requested and when and where such offence was committed and it shall contain as accurate a description of the suspected person as possible. It shall also contain a brief statement of the circumstances of the case.

3. An application for provisional arrest shall be sent direct by the authorities in the requesting State mentioned in Article 13 to the corresponding authorities in the requested State, by post or telegram or by any other means affording evidence in writing or accepted by the requested State. The requesting Sate shall be informed without delay of the result of its application.

Article 28

Upon receipt of a request for proceedings accompanied by the documents referred to in Article 15, paragraph 1, the requested State shall have jurisdiction to apply all such provisional measures, including remand in custody of the suspected person and seizure of property, as could be applied under its own law if the offence in respect of which proceedings are requested had been committed in its territory.

Article 29

1. The provisional measures provided in Articles 27 and 28 shall be governed by the provisions of this Convention and the law of the requested State. The law of the State, or the Convention shall also determine the conditions on which the measures may lapse.

2. These measures shall lapse in the cases referred to in Article 21, paragraph 2.

3. A person in custody shall in any event be released if he is arrested in pursuance of Article 27 and the requested State does not receive the request for proceedings within 18 days from the date of the arrest.

4. A person in custody shall in any event be released if he is arrested in pursuance of Article 27 and the documents which accompany the request for proceedings have not been received by the requested State within 15 days from the receipt of the request for proceedings.

5. The period of custody applied exclusively by virtue of Article 27 shall not in any event exceed 40 days.

PART IV
Plurality of Criminal Proceedings

Article 30

1. Any Contracting State which, before the institution or in the course of proceedings for an offence which it considers to be neither of a political nature nor a purely military one, is aware of proceedings pending in another Contracting State against the same person in respect of the same offence shall consider whether it can either waive or suspend its own proceedings, or transfer them to the other Sate.

2. If it deems it advisable in the circumstances not to waive or suspend its own proceedings it shall so notify the other State in good time and in any event before judgment is given on the merits.

Article 31

1. In the eventuality referred to in Article 30, paragraph 2, the States concerned shall endeavor as far as possible to determine, after evaluation in each case of the circumstances mentioned in Article 8, which of them alone shall continue to conduct proceedings. During this consultative procedure the States concerned shall postpone judgment on the merits without however being obliged to prolong such postponement beyond a period of 30 days as from the despatch of the notification provided for in Article 30, paragraph 2.

2. The provisions of paragraph 1 shall not be binding:

(a) on the State despatching the notification provided for in Article 30, paragraph 2, if the main trial has been declared open there in the presence of the accused before despatch of the notification;

(b) on the State to which the notification is addressed, if the main trial has been declared open there in the presence of the accused before receipt of the notification.

Article 32

In the interests of arriving at the truth and with a view of the application of an appropriate sanction, the State concerned shall examine whether it is expedient that one of them alone shall conduct proceedings and, if so, endeavor to determine which one, when:

(a) several offences which are materially distinct and which fall under the criminal law of each of those States are ascribed either to a single person or to several persons having acted in unison;

(b) a single offence under which falls under the criminal law of each of those States is ascribed to several persons having acted in unison.

Article 33

All decisions reached in accordance with Articles 31, paragraph 2, and 32 shall entail, as between the States concerned, all the consequences of a transfer of proceedings as provided for in this Convention. The State which waives its own proceedings shall be deemed to have transferred them to the other State.

Article 34

The transfer procedure provided for in Section 2 of Part III shall apply in so far as its provisions are compatible with those contained in the present Part.

PART V
Ne bis in idem

Article 35

1. A person in respect of whom a final and enforceable criminal judgment has been rendered may for same act neither be prosecuted nor sentenced nor subjected to enforcement of a sanction in another Contracting State:

(a) if he was acquitted;

(b) if the sanction imposed:

(i) has been completely enforced or is being enforced, or

(ii) has been wholly, or with respect to the part not enforced, the subject of a pardon or an amnesty, or

(iii) can no longer be enforced because of lapse of time;

(c) if the court convicted the offender without imposing a sanction.

2. Nevertheless, a Contracting State shall not, unless it has itself requested the proceedings, be obliged to recognise the effect of *ne bis in idem* if the act which gave rise to the judgment was directed against either a person or an institution or any thing having public status in that State, or if the subject of the judgment had himself a public status in that State.

3. Furthermore, a Contracting State where the act was committed or considered as such according to the law of that State shall not be obliged to recognise the effect of *ne bis in idem* unless that State has itself requested the proceedings.

Article 36

If new proceedings are instituted against a person who in another Contracting State has been sentenced for the same act, then any period of deprivation of liberty arising from the sentence enforced shall be deducted from the sanction which may be imposed.

Article 37

This Part shall not prevent the application of wider domestic provisions relating to the effect of *ne bis in idem* attached to foreign criminal judgments....

European Convention on the International Validity of Criminal Judgments
E.T.S. No. 70 (1970)

PART I
Definitions

Article I

For the purposes of this Convention:

(a) "European criminal judgment" means any final decision delivered by a criminal court of a Contracting State as a result of criminal proceedings;

(b) "Offence" comprises, apart from acts dealt with under the criminal law, those dealt with under the legal provisions listed in Appendix II to the present convention on condition that where these provisions give competence to an administrative authority there must be opportunity for the person concerned to have the case tried by a court;

(c) "Sentence" means the imposition of a sanction;

(d) "Sanction" means any punishment or other measure expressly imposed on a person, in respect of an offence, in a European criminal judgment, or in an "*ordonnance pénale*";

(e) "Disqualification" means any loss or suspension of a right or any prohibition or loss of legal capacity;

(f) "Judgment rendered *in absentia*" means any decision considered as such under Article 21, paragraph 2;

(g) "*Ordonnance pénale*" means any of the decisions delivered in another Contracting State and listed in Appendix III to this Convention.

PART II
Enforcement of European Criminal Judgments

SECTION 1
General provisions

(a) *General conditions of enforcement*

Article 2

This Part is applicable to:

(a) sanctions involving deprivation of liberty;

(b) fines or confiscation;

(c) disqualifications.

Article 3

1. A Contracting State shall be competent in the cases and under the conditions provided for in this Convention to enforce a sanction imposed in another Contracting State which is enforceable in the latter State.

2. This competence can only be exercised following a request by the other Contracting State.

Article 4

1. The sanction shall not be enforced by another Contracting State unless under its law the act for which the sanction was imposed would be an offence if committed on its territory and the person on whom the sanction was imposed liable to punishment if he had committed the act there.

2. If the sentence relates to two or more offences, not all of which fulfil the requirements of paragraph 1, the sentencing State shall specify which part of the sanction applies to the offences that satisfy those requirements.

Article 5

The sentencing State may request another Contracting State to enforce the sanction only if one or more of the following conditions are fulfilled:

(a) if the person sentenced is ordinarily resident in the other State;

(b) if the enforcement of the sanction in the other State is likely to improve the prospects for the social rehabilitation of the person sentenced;

(c) if, in the case of a sanction involving deprivation of liberty, the sanction could be enforced following the enforcement of another sanction involving deprivation of liberty which the person sentenced is undergoing or is to undergo in the other State;

(d) if the other State is the State of origin of the person sentenced and has declared itself willing to accept responsibility for the enforcement of that sanction;

(e) if it considers that it cannot itself enforce the sanction, even by having recourse to extradition, and that the other State can.

Article 6

Enforcement requested in accordance with the foregoing provisions may not be refused, in whole or in part, save:

(a) where enforcement would run counter to the fundamental principles of the legal system of the requested State;

(b) where the requested State considers the offence for which the sentence was passed to be of a political nature or a purely military one;

(c) where the requested State considers that there are substantial grounds for believing that the sentence was brought about or aggravated by considerations of race, religion, nationality or political opinion;

(d) where enforcement would be contrary to the international undertakings of the requested State;

(e) where the act is already the subject of proceedings in the requested State or where the requested State decides to institute proceedings in respect of the act;

(f) where the competent authorities in the requested State have decided not to take proceedings or to drop proceedings already begun, in respect of the same act;

(g) where the act was committed outside the territory of the requesting State;

(h) where the requested State is unable to enforce the sanction;

(i) where the request is grounded on Article 5(e) and none of the other conditions mentioned in that Article is fulfilled;

(j) where the requested State considers that the requesting State is itself able to enforce the sanction;

(k) where the age of the person sentenced at the time of the offence was such that he could not have been prosecuted in the requested State;

(l) where under the law of the requested State the sanction imposed can no longer be enforced because of the lapse of time;

(m) where and to the extent that the sentence imposes a disqualification.

Article 7

A request for enforcement shall not be complied with if enforcement would run counter to the principles recognized in the provisions of Section 1 of Part III of this Convention.

(b) *Effects of the transfer of enforcement*

Article 8

For the purposes of Article 6, paragraph 1 and the reservation mentioned under (c) of Appendix I of the present Convention any act which interrupts or suspends a time limitation validly performed by the authorities of the sentencing State shall be considered as having the same effect for the purpose of reckoning time limitation in the requested State in accordance with the law of that State.

Article 9

1. A sentenced person detained in the requesting State who has been surrendered to the requested State for the purpose of enforcement shall not be proceeded against, sentenced or detained with a view to the carrying out of a sentence or detention order for any offence committed prior to his surrender other than that for which the sentence to be enforced was imposed, nor shall he for any other reason be restricted in his personal freedom, except in the following cases:

(a) when the State which surrendered him consents. A request for consent shall be submitted, accompanied by all relevant documents and a legal record of any statement made by the convicted person in respect of the offence concerned. Consent shall be given when the offence for which it is requested would itself be subject to extradition under the law of the State requesting enforcement or when extradition would be excluded only by reason of the amount of the punishment;

(b) when the sentenced person, having had an opportunity to leave the territory of the State to which he has been surrendered, has not done so within 45 days of his final discharge, or if he has returned to that territory after leaving it.

2. The State requested to enforce the sentence may, however, take any measure necessary to remove the person from its territory, or any measures necessary under its law, including proceedings by default, to prevent any legal effects of lapse of time.

Article 10

1. The enforcement shall be governed by the law of the requested State and that State alone shall be competent to take all appropriate decisions, such as those concerning conditional release.

2. The requesting State alone shall have the right to decide on any application for review of sentence.

3. Either State may exercise the right of amnesty or pardon.

Article 11

1. When the sentencing State has requested enforcement it may no longer itself begin the enforcement of a sanction which is the subject of that request. The sentencing State may, however, begin enforcement of a sanction involving deprivation of liberty when the sentenced person is already detained on the territory of that State at the moment of the presentation of the request.

2. The right of enforcement shall revert to the requesting State:

(a) if it withdraws its request before the requested State has informed it of an intention to take action on the request;

(b) if the requested State notifies a refusal to take action on the request;

(c) if the requested State expressly relinquishes its right of enforcement. Such relinquishment shall only be possible if both the States concerned agree or if enforcement is no longer possible in the requested State. In the latter case, a relinquishment demanded by the requesting State shall be compulsory.

Article 12

1. The competent authorities of the requested State shall discontinue enforcement as soon as they have knowledge of any pardon, amnesty or application for review of sentence or any other decision by reason of which the sanction ceases to be enforceable. The same shall apply to the enforcement of a fine when the person sentenced has paid it to the competent authority in the requesting State.

2. The requesting State shall without delay inform the requested State of any decision or procedural measure taken on its territory that causes the right of enforcement to lapse in accordance with the preceding paragraph.

(c) *Miscellaneous provisions*

Article 13

1. The transit through the territory of a Contracting State of a detained person, who is to be transferred to a third Contracting State in application of this Convention, shall be granted at the request of the State in which the person is detained. The State of transit may require to be supplied with any appropriate document before taking a decision on the request. The person being transferred shall remain in custody in the territory of the State of transit, unless the State from which he is being transferred requests his release.

2. Except in cases where the transfer is requested under Article 34 any Contracting State may refuse transit:

(a) on one of the grounds mentioned in Article 6 (b) and (c);

(b) on the ground that the person concerned is one of its own nationals.

3. If air transport is used, the following provisions shall apply:

(a) when it is not intended to land, the State from which the person is to be transferred may notify the State over whose territory the flight is to be made that the person concerned is being transferred in application of this Convention. In the case of an unscheduled landing such notification shall have the effect of a request for provisional arrest as provided for in Article 32, paragraph 2, and a formal request for transit shall be made;

(b) where it is intended to land, a formal request for transit shall be made.

Article 14

Contracting States shall not claim from each other the refund of any expenses resulting from the application of this Convention.

SECTION 2
Requests for enforcement

Article 15

1. All requests specified in this Convention shall be made in writing. They, and all communications necessary for the application of this Convention, shall be sent either by the Ministry of Justice of the requesting State to the Ministry of Justice of the requested State or, if the Contracting States so agree, direct by the authorities of the requesting State to those of the requested State; they shall be returned by the same channel.

2. In urgent cases, requests and communications may be sent through the International Criminal Police Organization (INTERPOL).

3. Any Contracting State may, by declaration addressed to the Secretary General of the Council of Europe, give notice of its intention to adopt other rules in regard to the communications referred to in paragraph 1 of this article.

Article 16

The request for enforcement shall be accompanied by the original, or a certified copy, of the decision whose enforcement is requested and all other necessary documents. The original, or certified copy, of all or part of the criminal file shall be sent to the requested State, if it so requires. The competent authority of the requesting State shall certify the sanction enforceable.

Article 17

If the requested State considers that the information supplied by the requesting State is not adequate to enable it to apply this Convention, it shall ask for the necessary additional information. It may prescribe a date for the receipt of such information.

Article 18

The authorities of the requested State shall promptly inform those of the requesting State of the action taken on the request for enforcement.

The authorities of the requested State shall, where appropriate, transmit to those of the requesting State a document certifying that the sanction has been enforced.

Article 19

1. Subject to paragraph 2 of this article, no translation of requests or of supporting documents shall be required.

2. Any Contracting State may, at the time of signature or when depositing its instrument of ratification, acceptance or accession, by a declaration addressed to the Secretary General of the Council of Europe, reserve the right to require that requests and supporting documents be accompanied by a translation into its own language or into one of the official languages of the Council of Europe or into such one of those languages as it shall indicate. The other Contracting States may claim reciprocity.

3. This article shall be without prejudice to any provisions concerning translation of requests and supporting documents that may be contained in agreements or arrangements now in force or that may be concluded between two or more Contracting States.

Article 20

Evidence and documents transmitted in application of the Convention need not be authenticated....

SECTION 5
Enforcement of sanctions

(a) *General clauses*

Article 37

A sanction imposed in the requesting State shall not be enforced in the requested State except by a decision of the court of the requested State. Each Contracting State may, however, empower other authorities to take such decisions if the sanction to be enforced is only a fine or a confiscation and if these decisions are susceptible of appeal to a court.

Article 38

The case shall be brought before the court or the authority empowered under Article 37 if the requested State sees fit to take action on the request for enforcement.

Article 39

1. Before a court takes a decision upon a request for enforcement the sentenced person shall be given the opportunity to state his views. Upon application he shall be heard by the court either by letters rogatory or in person. A hearing in person must be granted following his express request to that effect.

2. The court may, however, decide on the acceptance of the request for enforcement in the absence of a sentenced person requesting a personal hearing if he is in custody in the requesting State. In these circumstances any decision as to the substitution of the sanction under Article 44 shall be adjourned until, following his transfer to the requested State, the sentenced person has been given the opportunity to appear before the court.

Article 40

1. The court, or in the cases referred to in Article 37, the authority empowered under the same Article, which is dealing with the case shall satisfy itself:

(a) that the sanction whose enforcement is requested was imposed in a European criminal judgment;

(b) that the requirements of Article 4 are met;

(c) that the condition laid down in Article 6(a) is not fulfilled or should not preclude enforcement;

(d) that enforcement is not precluded by Article 7;

(e) that, in case of a judgment rendered *in absentia* or an "*Ordonnance pénale*" the requirements of Section 3 of this Part are met.

2. Each Contracting State may entrust to the court or the authority empowered under Article 37 the examination of other conditions of enforcement provided for in this Convention.

Article 41

The judicial decisions taken in pursuance of the present section with respect to the requested enforcement and those taken on appeal from decisions by the administrative authority referred to in Article 37, shall be appealable.

Article 42

The requested State shall be bound by the findings as to the facts insofar as they are stated in the decision or insofar as it is impliedly based on them.

(b) *Clauses relating specifically to enforcement of sanctions involving deprivation of liberty*

Article 43

When the sentenced person is detained in the requesting State he shall, unless the law of that State otherwise provides, be transferred to the requested State as soon as the requesting State has been notified of the acceptance of the request for enforcement.

Article 44

1. If the request for enforcement is accepted, the court shall substitute for the sanction involving deprivation of liberty imposed in the requesting State a sanction prescribed by its own law for the same offence. This sanction may, subject to the limitations laid down in paragraph 2, be of a nature or duration other than that imposed by the requesting

State. If this latter sanction is less than the minimum which may be pronounced under the law of the requested State, the court shall not be bound by that minimum and shall impose a sanction corresponding to the sanction imposed in the requesting State.

2. In determining the sanction, the court shall not aggravate the penal situation of the person sentenced as it results from the decision delivered in the requesting State.

3. Any part of the sanction imposed in the requesting State and any term of provisional custody, served by the person sentenced shall be deducted in full. The same shall apply in respect of any period during which the person sentenced was remanded in custody in the requesting State before being sentenced insofar as the law of that State so requires.

4. Any Contracting State may, at any time, deposit with the Secretary General of the Council of Europe a declaration which confers on it in pursuance of the present Convention the right to enforce a sanction involving deprivation of liberty of the same nature as that imposed in the requesting State even if the duration of that sanction exceeds the maximum provided for by its national law for a sanction of the same nature. Nevertheless, this rule shall only by applied in cases where the national law of this State allows, in respect of the same offence, for the imposition of a sanction of at least the same duration that imposed in the requesting State but which is of a more severe nature. The sanction imposed under this paragraph may, if its duration and purpose so require, be enforced in a penal establishment intended for the enforcement of sanctions of another nature.

(c) *Clauses relating specifically to enforcement of fines and confiscations*

Article 45

1. If the request of enforcement of a fine or confiscation of a sum of money is accepted, the court or the authority empowered under Article 37 shall convert the amount thereof into the currency of the requested State at the rate of exchange ruling at the time when the decision is taken. It shall thus fix the amount of the fine, or the sum to be confiscated, which shall nevertheless not exceed the maximum sum fixed by its own law for the same offence, or failing such a maximum, shall not exceed the maximum amount customarily imposed in the requested State in respect of a like offence.

2. However, the court or the authority empowered under Article 37 may maintain up to the amount imposed in the requesting State the sentence of a fine or of a confiscation when such a sanction is not provided for by the law of the requested State for the same offence, but this law allows for the imposition of more severe sanctions. The same shall apply if the sanction imposed in the requesting State exceeds the maximum laid down in the law of the requested State for the same offence, but this law allows for the imposition of more severe sanctions.

3. Any facility as to time of payment or payment by installments, granted in the requesting State, shall be respected in the requested State.

Article 46

1. When the request for enforcement concerns the confiscation of a specific object, the court or the authority empowered under Article 37 may order the confiscation of that object only insofar as such confiscation is authorized by the law of the requested State for the same offence.

2. However, the court or the authority empowered under Article 37 may maintain the confiscation ordered in the requesting State when this sanction is not provided for in the law of the requested State for the same offence but this law allows for the imposition of more severe sanctions.

Article 47

1. The proceeds of fines and confiscations shall be paid into the public funds of the requested State without prejudice to any rights of third parties.

2. Property confiscated which is of special interest may be remitted to the requesting State if it so requires.

Article 48

If a fine cannot be exacted, a court of the requested State may impose an alternative sanction involving deprivation of liberty insofar as the laws of both States so provide in such cases unless the requesting State expressly limited its request to exacting of the fine alone. If the court decides to impose an alternative sanction involving deprivation of liberty, the following rules shall apply:

(a) If conversion of a fine into a sanction involving deprivation of liberty is already prescribed either in the sentence pronounced in the requesting State or directly in the law of that State, the court of the requested State shall determine the nature and length of such sanction in accordance with the rules laid down by its own law. If the sanction involving deprivation of liberty already prescribed in the requesting States is less than the minimum which may be imposed under the law of the requested State, the court shall not be bound by that minimum and shall impose a sanction corresponding to the sanction prescribed in the requesting State. In determining the sanction the court shall not aggravate the penal situation of the person sentenced as it results from the decision delivered in the requesting State.

(b) In all other cases the court of the requested State shall convert the fine in accordance with its own law, observing the limits prescribed by the law of the requesting State.

(d) *Clauses relating specifically to enforcement of disqualification*

Article 49

1. Where a request for enforcement of a disqualification is made such disqualification imposed in the requesting State may be given effect in the requested State only if the law of the latter State allows for disqualification for the offence in question.

2. The court dealing with the case shall appraise the expediency of enforcing the disqualification in the territory of its own State.

Article 50

1. If the court orders enforcement of the disqualification it shall determine the duration thereof within the limits prescribed by its own law, but may not exceed the limits laid down in the sentence imposed in the requesting State.

2. The court may order the disqualification to be enforced in respect of some only of the rights whose loss or suspension has been pronounced.

Article 51

Article 11 shall not apply to disqualifications.

Article 52

The requested State shall have the right to restore to the person sentenced the rights of which he has been deprived in accordance with a decision taken in application of this section.

PART III
International Effects of European Criminal Judgments

SECTION 1
Ne bis in idem

Article 53

1. A person in respect of whom a European criminal judgment has been rendered may for the same act neither be prosecuted nor sentenced nor subjected to enforcement of a sanction in another Contracting State:

(a) if he was acquitted;

(b) if the sanction imposed:

(i) has been completely enforced or is being enforced, or

(ii) has been wholly, or with respect to the part not enforced, the subject of a pardon or an amnesty, or

(iii) can no longer be enforced because of lapse of time;

(c) if the court convicted the offender without imposing a sanction.

2. Nevertheless, a Contracting State shall not, unless it has itself requested the proceedings, be obliged to recognize the effect of *ne bis in idem* if the act which gave rise to the judgment was directed against either a person or an institution or any thing having public status in that State, or if the subject of the judgment had himself a public status in that State.

3. Furthermore, any Contracting State where the act was committed or considered as such according to the law of that State shall not be obliged to recognise the effect of *ne bis in idem* unless that State has itself requested the proceedings.

Article 54

If new proceedings are instituted against a person who in another Contracting State has been sentenced for the same act, then any period of deprivation of liberty arising from the sentence enforced shall be deducted from the sanction which may be imposed.

Article 55

This Section shall not prevent the application of wider domestic provisions relating to the effect of *ne bis in idem* attached to foreign criminal judgments.

SECTION 2
Taking into consideration

Article 56

Each Contracting State shall legislate as it deems appropriate to enable its courts when rendering a judgment to take into consideration any previous European criminal judgment rendered for another offence after a hearing of the accused with a view to attaching to this judgment all or some of the effects which its law attaches to judgments rendered in its territory. It shall determine the conditions in which this judgment is taken into consideration.

Article 57

Each Contracting State shall legislate as it deems appropriate to allow the taking into consideration of any European criminal judgment rendered after a hearing of the accused so as to enable application of all or part of a disqualification attached by its law to judgments rendered in its territory. It shall determine the conditions in which this judgment is taken into consideration ...

Article 62

1. Any Contracting State may at any time, by declaration addressed to the Secretary General of the Council of Europe, set out the legal provisions to be included in Appendices II or III to this Convention.

2. Any change of the national provisions listed in Appendices II or III shall be notified to the Secretary General of the Council of Europe if such a change renders the information in these Appendices incorrect.

3. Any changes made in Appendices II or III in application of the preceding paragraphs shall take effect in each Contracting State one month after the date of their notification by the Secretary General of the Council of Europe.

APPENDIX I

Each Contracting State may declare that it reserves the right:

(a) to refuse enforcement, if it considers that the sentence relates to a fiscal or religious offence;

(b) to refuse enforcement of a sanction for an act which according to the law of the requested State could have been dealt with only by an administrative authority;

(c) to refuse enforcement of a European criminal judgment which the authorities of the requesting State rendered on a date when, under its own law, the criminal proceedings in respect of the offence punished by the judgment would have been precluded by the lapse of time;

(d) to refuse the enforcement of sanctions rendered *in absentia* and "*ordonnances pénales*" or of one of these categories of decisions only;

(e) to refuse the application of the provisions of Article 8 where this State has an original competence and to recognize in these cases only the equivalence of acts interrupting or suspending time limitation which have been accomplished in the requesting State;

(f) to accept the application of Part III in respect of one of its two sections only.

APPENDIX II

List of offences other than offences dealt with under criminal law

The following offences shall be assimilated to offences under criminal law:

— in France: Any unlawful behavior sanctioned by a "*contravention de grande voirie*".

— in the Federal Republic of Germany: Any unlawful behavior dealt with according to the procedure laid down in Act on violations of Regulations (*Gesetz über Ordnungswidrigkeiten*) of 24 May 1968 (BGBL 1968, I 481).

— in Italy: Any unlawful behavior to which is applicable Act. No. 317 of 3 March 1967.

The Constitution of Interpol

GENERAL PROVISIONS

Article 1

The Organization called the "INTERNATIONAL CRIMINAL POLICE COMMISSION" shall henceforth be entitled: "THE INTERNATIONAL CRIMINAL POLICE ORGANIZATION—INTERPOL". Its seat shall be in France.

Article 2

Its aims are:

(a) To ensure and promote the widest possible mutual assistance between the criminal police authorities within the limits of the laws existing in different countries and in the spirit of the "Universal Declaration of Human Rights";

(b) To establish and develop all institutions likely to contribute effectively to the prevention and suppression of ordinary law crimes.

Article 3

It is strictly forbidden for the Organization to undertake any intervention or activities of a political, military, religious or racial character.

Article 4

Any country may delegate as a Member to the Organization any police body whose functions come within the framework of activities of the Organization.

The request for membership shall be submitted to the Secretary General by the appropriate governmental authority.

Membership shall be subject to approval by a two-thirds majority of the General Assembly.

STRUCTURE AND ORGANIZATION

Article 5

The International Criminal Police Organization—Interpol shall comprise:

—The General Assembly

—The Executive Committee

—The General Secretariat

—The National Central Bureaus

—The Advisers.

THE GENERAL ASSEMBLY

Article 6

The General Assembly shall be the body of supreme authority in the Organization. It is composed of delegates appointed by the Members of the Organization.

Article 7

Each Member may be represented by one or several delegates; however, for each country there shall be only one delegation head, appointed by the competent governmental authority of that country.

Because of the technical nature of the Organization, Members should attempt to include the following in their delegations:

(a) High officials of departments dealing with police affairs,

(b) Officials whose normal duties are connected with the activities of the Organization,

(c) Specialists in the subjects on the agenda.

Article 8

The functions of the General Assembly shall be the following:

(a) To carry out the duties laid down in the Constitution;

(b) To determine principles and lay down the general measures suitable for attaining the objectives of the Organization as given in Article 2 of the Constitution;

(c) To examine and approve the general programme of activities prepared by the Secretary General for the coming year;

(d) To determine any other regulations deemed necessary;

(e) To elect persons to perform the functions mentioned in the Constitution;

(f) To adopt resolutions and make recommendations to Members on matters with which the Organization is competent to deal;

(g) To determine the financial policy of the Organization;

(h) To examine and approve any agreements to be made with other organizations.

Article 9

Members shall do all within their power, in so far as is compatible with their own obligations, to carry out the decisions of the General Assembly.

Article 10

The General Assembly of the Organization shall meet in ordinary session every year. It may meet in extraordinary session at the request of the Executive Committee or of the majority of Members.

Article 11

The General Assembly may, when in session, set up special committees for dealing with particular matters.

Article 12

During the final meeting of each session, the General Assembly shall choose the place of meeting for the following session. The date of this meeting shall be fixed by agreement between the inviting country and the President after consultation with the Secretary General.

Article 13

Only one delegate from each country shall have the right to vote in the General Assembly.

Article 14

Decisions shall be made by a simple majority except in those cases where a two-thirds majority is required by the Constitution.

THE EXECUTIVE COMMITTEE ...

THE GENERAL SECRETARIAT

Article 25

The permanent departments of the Organization shall constitute the General Secretariat.

Article 26

The General Secretariat shall:

(a) Put into application the decisions of the General Assembly and the Executive Committee;

(b) Serve as an international centre in the fight against ordinary crime;

(c) Serve as a technical and information centre;

(d) Ensure the efficient administration of the Organization;

(e) Maintain contact with national and international authorities, whereas questions relative to the search for criminals shall be dealt with through the National Central Bureaus;

(f) Produce any publications which may be considered useful;

(g) Organize and perform secretariat work at the sessions of the General Assembly, the Executive Committee and any other body of the Organization;

(h) Draw up a draft programme of work for the coming year for the consideration and approval of the General Assembly and the Executive Committee;

(i) Maintain as far as is possible direct and constant contact with the President of the Organization.

Article 27

The General Secretariat shall consist of the Secretary General and a technical and administrative staff entrusted with the work of the Organization.

Article 28

The appointment of the Secretary General shall be proposed by the Executive Committee and approved by the General Assembly for a period of five years. He may be reappointed for other terms but must lay down office on reaching the age of sixty-five, although he may be allowed to complete his term of office on reaching this age.

He must be chosen from among persons highly competent in police matters.

In exceptional circumstances, the Executive Committee may propose at a meeting of the General Assembly that the Secretary General be removed from office.

Article 29

The Secretary General shall engage and direct the staff, administer the budget, and organize and direct the permanent departments, according to the directives decided upon by the General Assembly or Executive Committee.

He shall submit to the Executive Committee or the General Assembly any propositions or projects concerning the work of the Organization.

He shall be responsible to the Executive Committee and the General Assembly.

He shall have the right to take part in the discussions of the General Assembly, the Executive Committee and all other dependent bodies.

In the exercise of his duties, he shall represent the organization and not any particular country.

Article 30

In the exercise of their duties, the Secretary General and the staff shall neither solicit nor accept instructions from any government or authority outside the Organization. They shall abstain from any action which might be prejudicial to their international task.

Each Member of the Organization shall undertake to respect the exclusively international character of the duties of the Secretary General and the staff, and abstain from influencing them in the discharge of their duties.

All Members of the Organization shall do their best to assist the Secretary General and the staff in the discharge of their functions.

NATIONAL CENTRAL BUREAUS

Article 31

In order to further its aims, the Organization needs the constant and active co-operation of its Members, who should do all within their power which is compatible with the legislations of their countries to participate diligently in its activities.

Article 32

In order to ensure the above co-operation, each country shall appoint a body which will serve as the National Central Bureau. It shall ensure liaison with:

(a) The various departments in the country;

(b) Those bodies in other countries serving as National Central Bureaus;

(c) The Organization's General Secretariat.

Article 33

In the case of those countries where the provisions of Article 32 are inapplicable or do not permit of effective centralized co-operation, the General Secretariat shall decide, with these countries, the most suitable alternative means of co-operation.

THE ADVISERS

Article 34

On scientific matters, the Organization may consult "Advisers".

Article 35

The role of the Advisers shall be purely advisory.

Article 36

Advisers shall be appointed for three years by the Executive Committee. Their appointment will become definite only after notification by the General Assembly.

They shall be chosen from among those who have a world-wide reputation in some field of interest to the Organization.

Article 37

An Adviser may be removed from office by decision of the General Assembly.

BUDGET AND RESOURCES

Article 38

The Organization's resources shall be provided by:

(a) The financial contributions from Members;

(b) Gifts, bequests, subsidies, grants and other resources after these have been accepted or approved by the Executive Committee.

Article 39

The General Assembly shall establish the basis of Members' subscriptions and the maximum annual expenditure according to the estimate provided by the Secretary General.

Article 40

The draft budget of the Organization shall be prepared by the Secretary General and submitted for approval to the executive Committee.

It shall come into force after acceptance by the General Assembly.

Should the General Assembly not have had the possibility of approving the budget, the Executive Committee shall take all necessary steps according to the general outlines of the preceding budget.

RELATIONS WITH OTHER ORGANIZATIONS

Article 41

Whenever it deems fit, having regard to the aims and objects provided in the Constitution, the Organization shall establish relations and collaborate with other intergovernmental or non-governmental organizations. The general provisions concerning the relations with international, inter-governmental or non-governmental organizations will only be valid after their approval by the General Assembly.

The Organization may, in connection with all matters in which it is competent, take the advice of non-governmental international, governmental national or non-governmental national organizations.

With the approval of the General Assembly, the Executive Committee or, in urgent cases, the Secretary General may accept duties within the scope of its activities and competence either from other international institutions or organizations or in application of international conventions....

Rules on Interpol Police Cooperation and Control of Its Archives

Part One: PROCESSING AND COMMUNICATION OF POLICE INFORMATION WITHIN THE ICPO-INTERPOL INTERNATIONAL POLICE CO-OPERATION SYSTEM

GENERAL PROVISIONS

Article 1

(1) International police co-operation within the ICPO-Interpol conforms to the Organization's aims set forth in Article 2 of its Constitution.

(2) The purpose of the present Rules is to protect police information processed and communicated within the ICPO-Interpol international police co-operation system against any misuse, especially in order to avoid any threat to individual rights. To this end, they specify the procedures to be used by the NCBs and the General Secretariat in processing and communicating police information within the system of co-operation.

Article 2

For the purpose of the present rules, the following expressions shall have the meanings hereunder assigned to them:

(a) "Processing of information" includes all the operations relating to the collection, registration, analysis, verification, modification, preservation and deletion of information, whatever the method used to perform such operations.

(b) "Police information" means any information pertaining to constituent elements of ordinary law crimes, as expressed in Article 2(b) of the Constitution and excluded by Article 3 of the Constitution, the investigation and prevention of such crimes, the prosecution and punishment of alleged offenders, and any information pertaining to missing persons and unidentified dead bodies; the term does not include information that is unrelated to specific criminal cases and that cannot under any circumstances be used to identify the private individuals or corporate bodies it may concern.

PROCESSING OF POLICE INFORMATION BY THE GENERAL SECRETARIAT

Article 3

(1) Under the terms of sub-paragraph (b) of Article 26 of the ICPO-Interpol Constitution, the General Secretariat shall serve as an international centre in the fight against ordinary law crimes. Its responsibility for processing police information derives from this provision.

(2) Without prejudice to the provisions of Article 22 (d) or Article 29(1) of the ICOP-Interpol Constitution, the Secretary General of the Organization shall decide on the type and structure of the General Secretariat's archives containing police information.

(3) Processing of police information by the General Secretariat within the buildings and premises of the ICPO-Interpol Headquarters shall not be subject to any national legislation. It shall be conducted in conformity with the provisions of the present Rules and of agreements concluded with the Headquarters country.

(4) The purposes for which the General Secretariat shall process police information are to prevent and investigate ordinary law crimes, as expressed in Article 2(b) of the Constitution and excluded by Article 3 of the Constitution, to bring alleged offenders to justice, to find missing persons, and to identify dead bodies. However, such information may also be used for internal management purposes.

(5) Items of police information may be processed for research and publication purposes, or for any other legitimate purpose. However, every precaution must be taken to ensure that it is not possible to identify any persons concerned. Any police information that has been published may also be processed for general reference purposes.

Article 4

(1) The General Secretariat shall take all necessary precautions to protect the safety and secrecy of police information and to prevent such information from being illicitly or improperly processed or communicated.

(2) General Secretariat staff shall be bound by rules of professional secrecy.

Article 5

(1) The General Secretariat shall process police information communicated to it by the NCBs, or communicated by other official institutions concerned with the enforcement of the criminal law, provided the NCB of the country concerned consents to such communication. NCBs may give general consent to the communication of police information by certain such institutions or to the communication of certain categories of police information by any such institution.

(2) NCBs shall take all appropriate measures to ensure that the police information communicated to the General Secretariat by them, or with their consent, is correct and up to date. In all such communications, factual information shall be clearly distinguished from deductions and conclusions drawn from the facts. If an NCB finds that police information which has been communicated to the General Secretariat is not correct or is no longer correct, it shall ask the General Secretariat to modify or, if appropriate, delete that information. To this end, NCBs shall keep records, for an appropriate period, of all communications sent by them, or with their consent, to the General Secretariat.

(3) The General Secretariat is only the depository of police information communicated to it by the NCBs or with their consent. It is not allowed to modify or delete such information on its own initiative except in the circumstances covered by paragraph (5) of the present article. It must modify or delete such information if asked to do so by the NCB by which, or with whose consent, the information was communicated; it may modify or delete such information if authorized to do so by that NCB.

(4) When the same item of police information has been communicated to the General Secretariat by, or with the consent of, several NCBs, one of which later asks that item be modified or deleted, the General Secretariat shall transmit the request to all the other NCBs concerned. If one of them does not consent to the modification or deletion of the item, the General Secretariat shall take note of the request, retain the item of information, and inform the other NCBs concerned and the NCBs to which the information has already been communicated by the General Secretariat, of the situation. Any subsequent communication by the General Secretariat of the item shall be accompanied by a copy of the request for modification or deletion.

(5) Deletion by the General Secretariat of police information considered on the basis of certain general criteria to be out of date shall be governed by special rules approved by the General Assembly.

Article 6

(1) The General Secretariat may process police information:

(a) obtained from sources accessible to the public;

(b) sent to it:

(aa) by an official institution concerned with the enforcement of the criminal law in a state that is not a member of the Organization, either on that institution's own initiative or in reply to an enquiry the Organization has addressed to a diplomatic mission of that state at the request of an NCB;

(bb) by an intergovernmental organization performing its official duties.

(2) When police information being processed by the General Secretariat has been received from one of the sources mentioned in paragraph (1) of the present article, it shall be modified or, if appropriate, deleted by the General Secretariat if it is found to be incorrect or no longer correct. If necessary, the General Secretariat shall take all appropriate measures to ensure that such information is correct and up to date.

(3) When the General Secretariat receives police information from private individuals or corporate bodies other than those mentioned in paragraph (1) of the present article (it being understood that the General Secretariat may not solicit police information from such individuals or bodies), it shall register such information and may communicate it, together with any relevant information in its possession, to the NCBs of any States concerned. Thereafter, those NCBs shall, if necessary, take all appropriate measures to ensure that the information is correct and up to date; processing and communication of that information shall be governed by the same rules as those that apply to police information communicated to the General Secretariat by those NCBs.

COMMUNICATION OF POLICE INFORMATION
BY THE GENERAL SECRETARIAT

Article 7

(1) The General Secretariat shall communicate or publish police information under the conditions set forth in the present Rules.

(2) It is assumed that NCBs communicating police information to the General Secretariat, or consenting to such communication (Article 5(1)), have given their consent to the subsequent communication, under the conditions set forth in the present Rules, of such information by the General Secretariat or by NCBs to which it has been communicated by the General Secretariat.

(3)Paragraph (2) of the present article does not apply to information expressly classified by the NCB or the official institution that sent it as being intended for the General Secretariat alone. When information is so classified, the General Secretariat may communicate only those parts of it that will enable the recipient of the communication to ask the NCB concerned for further particulars.

(4) When communicating police information, the General Secretariat shall not distort its contents shall specify its source. Furthermore, if the General Secretariat is communicating a summary of information it has processed, or the deductions or conclusions it has drawn from police information, it shall make the fact clear.

Article 8

(1) NCBs asking the General Secretariat to communicate police information shall give the reasons for their requests; the same applies to requests from official institutions concerned with the enforcement of the criminal law, transmitted with the consent of their countries' NCBs. General consent may be given by NCBs for the transmission of requests by certain such institutions or for the transmission of certain categories of request. The General Secretariat may require an account of the facts justifying access to the information. It shall refuse to communicate the information if sufficient justification is not provided or if the request is not in conformity with the aims set forth in Article 3(4) and (5); otherwise, it shall communicate the relevant information to the requesting NCB. When a request is received from an official institution acting with the consent of its country's NCB, the reply shall be forwarded to that NCB unless the latter has agreed that it may be sent directly to the institution concerned.

(2) The General Secretariat shall communicate police information to NCBs on its own initiative if it considers that the latter should take action in conformity with the purposes set forth in the first sentence of Article 3(4). With an NCB's prior authorization, whenever such cases occur, the General Secretariat may also communicate certain categories of information to certain other official institutions concerned with the enforcement of the criminal law in that NCB's country.

(3) In the circumstances described in paragraphs (1) and (2) of the present article, the General Secretariat shall send copies of the communication of the NCBs empowered to dispose of the information under the terms of Article 5(3) and (4). In the circumstances described in paragraph (1) of the present article, the General Secretariat shall also, if it considers such action appropriate, send the NCBs concerned copies of the request.

(4) Except in the circumstances inscribed in paragraphs (1) and (2) of the present article, the General Secretariat may not communicate or publish police information processed under the terms of Article 6(1)(b) without consulting the source of the information and taking its views into account.

(5) Otherwise, the General Secretariat shall not communicate or publish police information without prior authorization from the NCBs empowered to dispose of the information under the terms of Article 5(3) and (4). General authorization may be given by NCBs for certain categories of information and for certain categories of communication.

Article 9

(1) The General Secretariat shall keep records of requests it receives for the communication of police information and of its own communications of police information for the period specified in the rules referred to in Article 5(5).

(2) While it still has a record of such communications, the General Secretariat shall inform all the institutions, bodies and individuals to which the relevant information has been communicated of the deletion of substantial modification of any such information under the terms of Article 5(3) or those of Article 6(2).

(3) The special rules mentioned in Article 5(5) shall stipulate the conditions in which institutions, bodies and individuals that have received an item of police information from the General Secretariat, and the NCBs empowered to dispose of the information under the terms of Article 5(3) and (4), must be informed if the item concerned is deleted under those rules.

(4) While it still has a record of such communications, the General Secretariat shall inform the NCBs empowered to dispose of the information in accordance with the terms of Article 5(3) and (4), as well as all the institutions, bodies and individuals to which the relevant information has been communicated, of the modification of any item of personal police information made in accordance with the provisions of Article 25(1).

Article 10

Once police information has been published, the conditions set forth in Article 8(4) and (5) shall not apply to the communication of such information for general reference purposes or to its publication by the General Secretariat, nor shall the procedure set forth in Article 9 apply in such circumstances.

COMMUNICATION OF POLICE INFORMATION BY NCBs TO EACH OTHER PROCESSING OF POLICE INFORMATION BY NCBs

Article 11

NCBs shall process police information and communicate it to each other subject to their States' laws, to the international treaties their States have concluded, and the ICPO-Interpol Constitution. Such co-operation between NCBs shall also be governed by special rules approved by the General Assembly.

ELECTRONIC PROCESSING OF POLICE INFORMATION

Article 12

(1) Articles 3 to 10 of the present Rules shall apply to the processing of police information in an electronic data processing system consisting of a processing centre installed at the General Secretariat and peripherals and terminals operated by the General Secretariat; they shall also apply to the communication and publication of information so processed.

(2) The establishment of any international electronic data processing system for processing police information (other than the one mentioned in paragraph (1) of the present article), which includes a processing centre at the General Secretariat, can be authorized only by the General Assembly. Implementation of any such system shall be governed by special rules approved by the General Assembly.

PROCEDURE FOR SETTLEMENT OF PROBLEMS

Article 13

Problems that arise between NCBs or between an NCB and the General Secretariat in connection with the application of present Rules should be solved by concerted action. If this fails, the matter may be submitted to the Executive Committee and, if necessary, to the General Assembly.

COMMUNICATION OF POLICE INFORMATION
IN SPECIAL CIRCUMSTANCES

Article 14

Special circumstances may justify the communication of police information received from an Interpol member State to authorities in that State before which institutions concerned with the enforcement of the criminal law are legally answerable. No provisions of the present Rules shall affect the possibility of such communication.

Part Two: INTERNAL CONTROL OF INTERPOL'S ARCHIVES

Article 15

A Supervisory Board is hereby set up for the internal control of Interpol's archives. It shall be constituted and shall function in accordance with the terms of the Exchange of Letters between the Government of the French Republic and the ICPO-Interpol concerning organization of the internal control of Interpol's archives.

Article 16

The Supervisory Board shall be composed of five members of different nationalities, as follows:

(a) three persons appointed either on the basis of their impartiality and their competence in matters relating to data protection, or because they hold or have held senior judicial posts;

(b) a member of the Organization's executive Committee or his deputy, appointed by the Executive Committee;

(c) an electronic data processing expert or his deputy.

Article 17

(1) The persons mentioned in Article 16(a) and their deputies must be nationals of the Organization's member States.

(2) Then following procedure shall be adopted to appoint these persons: one of them shall be appointed by the Organization, another by Government of the Headquarters State, and the third shall be appointed jointly by the other two. This third person, who shall be Chairman of the Board, shall be chosen because of the senior judicial post he holds or has held. In case of disagreement regarding the appointment of the third person, that person shall be appointed by the Secretary General of the Permanent Court of Arbitration. Each of these persons shall have a deputy, appointed in the same way.

(3) The electronic data processing expert and his deputy, mentioned in Article 16(c), shall be appointed by the Chairman of the Board from a list of five candidates submitted by the Organization.

Article 18

(1) The person to be appointed by the Organization in accordance with Article 17(2), and that person's deputy, shall be appointed by the Executive Committee from a list of candidates nominated by the Organization's member States. Each nomination shall provide information about the candidate's suitability in the light of the conditions laid down in Article 16(a).

(2) The list of five candidates for the seat on the Board to be held by an expert in electronic data processing, which the Organization submits in accordance with Article 17(3), shall be drawn up by the Organization's Executive Committee. The candidates shall be selected from a list of electronic data processing experts nominated by the Organization's member States. Each nomination shall provide information about the candidate's qualifications as an electronic data processing expert.

(3) The members of the Supervisory Board shall be familiar with at least one of the working languages of the Organization's General Secretariat.

(4) The term of office of the members of the Board and their deputies shall be three years, commencing on the date on which the fifth member of the Board is appointed. Each member may be reappointed once.

(5) Deputies shall take the place of members of the Board who cannot attend meetings.

(6) If a member of the Board is no longer in a position to perform his duties, or has resigned, his deputy shall become a member of the Board in his place. A new deputy shall then be appointed for the remainder of the term of office. The same procedure shall be followed if a deputy is no longer in a position to perform his duties or has resigned.

Article 19

(1) In the exercise of their duties, the members of the Board shall neither solicit nor accept instructions from any persons or bodies.

(2) Without prejudice to the first sentence of Article 23, the members of the Board shall consider as confidential all facts that come to their knowledge as a consequence of, or in connection with, their membership of the Board.

Article 20

The Secretary General shall provide the Supervisory Board with a list of the computerized and other archives held, indicating the purposes for which they are maintained.

Article 21

(1) The Board shall meet at least once a year. Meetings shall be convened by the Chairman of the Board, after consultation with the Secretary General or his representative.

(2) The Board shall not sit unless at least four of its members, including the Chairman of or his deputy, are present.

(3) The decisions of the Board shall be taken by simple majority. If an equal number of votes is cast for and against a motion, the Chairman shall have a deciding vote.

(4) The Organization's Secretary General or his representative shall assist the Supervisory Board.

(5) The General Secretariat shall act as the Board's secretariat.

(6) The General Secretariat shall keep records, for an appropriate period, of all the Board's verifications, investigations and decisions.

Article 22

The Supervisory Board shall verify that personal information contained in the archives is:

(a) obtained and processed in accordance with the provisions of the Organization's Constitution and the interpretation thereof given by the appropriate organs of the Organization;

(b) recorded for specific purposes and not used in any way that is incompatible with those purposes;

(c) accurate;

(d) kept for a limited period in accordance with the conditions laid down by the Organization.

Article 23

The Supervisory Board shall make available to nationals or permanent residents of the Organization's member States a list of the archives mentioned in Article 20. At the request of such persons, it shall verify that any personal information held by the Organization about them complies with the conditions laid down in Article 22. It shall notify the requesting party that the verifications requested have been carried out.

Article 24

(1) For the purposes of the verifications provided for in Article 22, the Board shall have free access to the Organization's archives.

(2) In order to carry out the verifications provided for in Articles 22 and 23, the Board may consult the Secretary General, any member of the General Secretariat staff, the Executive Committee and the NCBs.

(3) Before asking the Executive Committee to have information modified under the terms of Article 25(1), the Board shall hear the Secretary General or his representative and consult the NCBs of any States concerned.

(4) When, in cases covered by the second sentence of Article 23, the requests made to the Board are clearly unreasonable, for instance because of their number or because of their repetitive or systematic nature, the Board may refrain from carrying out the verifications and shall not be compelled to reply to the person requesting them.

Article 25

(1) The Board shall notify the Executive Committee of the results of its investigations, and any necessary modifications shall be made by the appropriate organs of the Organization.

(2) The Board shall prepare an annual report on its activities for the information of the Executive Committee and possible transmission to the General Assembly.

Article 26

The Board shall decide on its own procedure, insofar as it is not laid down in the present Rules.

FINAL PROVISIONS

Article 27

(1) The present Rules shall constitute an Appendix to the General Regulations of the Organization.

(2) The present Rules shall enter into force on the same date as the entry into force of the Exchange of Letters between the Government of the French Republic and the ICPO-Interpol concerning organization of the internal control of Interpol's archives.

(3) Any of the Organization's internal provisions, insofar as they are incompatible with the present Rules, are hereby superseded.

Interpol's Resolutions on Terrorism
Sept. 1984
RESOLUTION

Subject: Violent Crime Commonly Referred to as Terrorism

TAKING INTO ACCOUNT Article 3 of the Organization's Constitution,

TAKING INTO ACCOUNT the Resolutions already adopted by the General Assembly and entitled:

— Requests for international enquiries

(Resolution No. 14, Lisbon, 1951)

— Unlawful acts against international civil aviation

(Resolution No. 3, Brussels, 1970)

— Hostages and blackmail

(Resolution No. 7, Frankfurt, 1972)

— Unlawful acts of international concern

(Resolution No. 5, Vienna, 1971)

— Safeguarding of international civil aviation

(Resolution No. 3, Cannes, 1974)

— Acts of violence committed by organized groups

(Resolution No. 8, Nairobi, 1979),

CONSIDERING THAT:

(a) in many countries there are organized groups engaging in violent criminal activities designed, by spreading terror or fear, to enable them to attain allegedly political objectives,

(b) such activities are commonly covered by the term "terrorism", that they constitute an international phenomenon and that they are connected with other forms of crime,

(c) the types of crimes committed in the context of terrorism include, in particular, attacks on human life and physical integrity, kidnapping, hostage-taking, unlawful interference with civil aviation and serious attacks on public or private property,

AWARE THAT several international conventions covering such matters (the European Convention on the suppression of terrorism, the Organization of American States' Convention to prevent and punish acts of terrorism, the League of Arab States' Extradition Convention) do not admit exceptions for political reasons in extradition cases where certain serious crimes have been committed in the context of terrorism,

ACKNOWLEDGING THAT:

(a) by virtue of the principle of national sovereignty, the political character of any offense can only be determined by national legislation,

(b) it is nonetheless essential to combat this type of crime which causes considerable damage in Member States.

The ICPO-Interpol General Assembly, meeting in Luxembourg from 4th to 11th September 1984 at its 53rd session:

ASKS the NCBs, while respecting the provisions of Article 3 of the Organization's Constitution, to cooperate as fully as possible to combat terrorism as far as their national laws permit.

RESOLUTION

Subject: APPLICATION OF ARTICLE 3 OF THE CONSTITUTION

TAKING INTO ACCOUNT Article 3 of the Organization's Constitution,

The ICPO-Interpol General Assembly, meeting in Luxembourg from 4th to 11th September 1984 at its 53rd Session:

RECOMMENDS THAT, in order to facilitate the interpretation of Article 3, the principles listed below should be circulated to all departments responsible for crime prevention and law enforcement, and that they should be applied by both the NCBs and the General Secretariat.

I. RULES AND PROCEDURE

1. Under Article 3 of the Constitution, the Organization is strictly forbidden "to undertake any intervention or activities of a political, military, religious or racial character".

2. A resolution adopted by the General Assembly in 1951 makes it clear that the scope of the Article covers "offenses of a predominantly political, racial or religious character ... even if—in the requesting country—the facts amount to an offense against the ordinary law".

3. It is impossible to give a more precise definition of a political, military, religious or racial case. Each case has to be examined separately, with due consideration for the specific context.

4. When the Secretary General is aware of a case in which it might be necessary to apply Article 3, he discusses it with the requesting NCB to determine whether Article 3 is in fact applicable.

5. If the NCB maintains its request for action, it assumes full responsibility for the specific nature of the case and the Secretariat gives the fullest possible details in any notice published about it.

6. When, in the light of the provision of Article 3, the Secretary General is in complete disagreement with an NCB over the interpretation to be given to certain facts, the Secretariat refuses to collaborate on the case.

7. When an NCB, acting on its own initiative, obviously infringes the provisions of Article 3, the Secretary General informs other NCBs of his point of view.

8. If, during a bilateral exchange between NCBs, a difference of opinion arises regarding the application of Article 3, the General Secretariat must be informed.

9. The refusal of one or more countries to act on a request circulated by an NCB or by the General Secretariat (an extradition request, for example), does not mean that the request itself is invalid and that it automatically comes under Article 3 of the Constitution. However, if certain countries refuse extradition, this is reported to the other NCBs in an addendum to the original notice indicating that the offender has been released. When a person is arrested with a view to extradition the wanted notice remains valid, unless the requesting country decides otherwise, until the person concerned has been extradited.

II. ANALYSIS OF POSITIONS ADOPTED IN SPECIFIC INSTANCES

1. Some of the acts included as offences in various national penal codes are by their very nature political, military, religious or racial (*e.g.*, membership of a prohibited organization, the expression of certain prohibited opinions, offences against the internal or external security of the State, desertion from the armed forces, treason, espionage, practicing a prohibited religion, recruitment or propaganda for particular religions, membership of a racial association). Such acts come within the scope of Article 3.

2. Article 3 covers any acts committed by politicians in connection with their political activities, even if those concerned are prosecuted after their fall from power and, in some cases, after they have fled abroad. The situation is different in the case of an offence committed by a politician acting as a private individual.

3. When offences are committed by persons with definite political motives but when the offences committed have no direct connection with the political life of the offenders' country or the cause for which they are fighting, the crime may no longer de deemed to come within the scope of Article 3. This is particularly true when offences are committed in countries which are not directly involved (*i.e.*, outside the "conflict area") and when the offences constitute a serious threat to personal freedom, life or property.

Examples are cases in which:

— police officers are killed or hostages are taken outside the conflict area, with a view to obtaining the release of an accomplice;

— there is an attack on members of the general public outside the conflict area (for instance by leaving a bomb in a bank or throwing a grenade into a café).

4. Offences committed outside the conflict area in order to draw attention to a particular cause (aircraft hijacking, the taking of hostages, kidnappings) do not come within the scope of Article 3.

5. Generally speaking, a valid criterion is whether or not there is anything to connect the victims directly or indirectly with the aims or objectives pursued by the offenders, and with the countries in the conflict area or with the relevant political situation.

6. When assessing a particular case in the light of the provisions of Article 3 of the Constitution, the type of cooperation requested by the NCB concerned also has to be considered. When prevention is involved there is nothing to hinder the circulation of technical information, even if this has been obtained in connection with politically motivated cases. Similarly it must be possible to circulate information about potential aircraft hijackers or offenders likely to take hostages, provided that such circulars are not based solely on the fact that the person in question belongs to a particular political movement.

U.N. General Assembly Resolution 46/152
(1991)

The General Assembly

Alarmed by the scope of criminality and by the dangers posed to the welfare of all nations by the rising incidence of crime generally and by the many forms of criminal activity that have international dimensions,

Also alarmed by the high cost of crime in both human and material terms, especially in its new and transnational forms, and aware of the effects of crime both on States and on individual victims,

Recalling that, in its resolution 45/108 of 14 December 1990, it decided to establish an intergovernmental working group to "produce a report elaborating proposals for an effective crime prevention and criminal justice programme and suggesting how that programme could most appropriately be implemented,"

Acknowledging with appreciation the work of the Intergovernmental Working Group on the Creation of an Effective International Crime and Justice Programme, which met at Vienna from 5 to 9 August 1991,

Acknowledging also with appreciation the work of the Ministerial Meeting on the Creation of an Effective United Nations Crime Prevention and Criminal Justice Programme, held in Paris from 21 to 23 November 1991,

Recognizing that criminality is a major concern of all nations and that it calls for a concerted response from the international community aimed at preventing crime and recidivism, improving the functioning of criminal justice and law enforcement, and increasing respect for individual rights,

Acknowledging that a United Nations programme devoted to crime prevention and criminal justice can only be effective with the direct involvement of Member States,

Convinced that the principal purpose of such a programme should be to provide practical assistance to States in combating both national and transnational crime,

Noting the principles contained in the Milan Plan of Action and the Guiding Principles for Crime Prevention and Criminal Justice in the Context of Development and a New International Economic Order, as well as other pertinent instruments formulated by United Nations congresses on the prevention of crime and the treatment of offenders and approved by the General Assembly,

Recalling the relevant resolutions in which it has stressed the importance of the Commission on Human Rights and the Centre for Human Rights at Geneva with regard to respect for human rights in the administration of justice,

Recognizing also the urgent need to promote and intensify international cooperation in crime prevention and criminal justice, and the fact that t this cooperation can be effective only if it is executed with the direct participation of the receiving States, with due respect for their needs and priorities,

1. *Takes note with appreciation* of the report of the Ministerial Meeting on the Creation of an Effective United Nations Crime Prevention and Criminal Justice Programme;

2. *Approves* the statement of principles and programme of action, annexed to the present resolution, recommending the establishment of a United Nations crime prevention and criminal justice programme;

3. *Supports* a clearer definition of its mandate with regard to crime prevention and criminal justice, under the aegis and guidance of the United Nations, whose aim will be to respond to the most pressing priorities and needs of the international community in the face of both national and transnational criminality;

4. *Requests* the Secretary-General to give a high level of priority within the United Nations framework, and within the overall existing United Nations resources, to the activities of the United Nations crime prevention and criminal justice programme;

5. *Decides* that the United Nations crime prevention and criminal justice programme shall be devoted to providing States with practical assistance, such as data collection, information and experience sharing, and training, in order to achieve the goals of preventing crime within and among States and of improving the response to crime;

6. *Invites* Member States to give their political and financial support and to take measures that will ensure the implementation of the provisions of the statement of principles and programme of action as they relate to the strengthening of the United Nations crime prevention and criminal justice programme in terms of its structure, content and priorities;

7. *Requests* the Secretary-General to take the necessary action within the overall existing United Nations resources in accordance with the financial rules and regulations of the United Nations and to provide appropriate resources for the effective functioning of the United Nations crime prevention and criminal justice programme in accordance with the principles outlined in the statement of principles and programme of action;

8. *Urges* all entities of the United Nations system, including the regional commissions, the United Nations congresses on the prevention of crime and the treatment of offenders, the United Nations institutes for the prevention of crime and the treatment of offenders, the specialized agencies and the relevant intergovernmental and non-governmental organizations, to assist the United Nations crime prevention and criminal justice programme in fulfilling its tasks;

9. *Encourages* all developed countries to review their aid programmes in order to ensure that there is a full and proper contribution in the field of criminal justice within the overall context for development priorities;

10. *Decides* to recommend that a commission on crime prevention and criminal justice be established as a functional commission of the Economic and Social Council, which would hold its inaugural meeting during 1992, and recommends that the meeting of the Committee on Crime Prevention and Control scheduled for February 1992 be canceled and to make available the funds necessary for the World of the new commission within the budget for the biennium 1992–1993;

11. *Requests* the Economic and Social Council at its organizational session of 1992:

(a) To dissolve the Committee on Crime Prevention and Control;

(b) To establish the commission on crime prevention and criminal justice as a new functional commission of the Economic and Social Council, in accordance with the recommendations contained in the statement of principles and programme of action;

(c) To endorse the role and functions of the United Nations congresses on the prevention of crime and the treatment of offenders, in accordance with the recommendations contained in the statement of principles and programme of action;

12. *Decides* that the present members of the Committee on Crime Prevention and Control should be invited to participate during the first two days of the inaugural session of the new commission, at the expense of their respective Governments, except in the case of Committee members from least developed countries, in order to facilitate an orderly transition;

13. *Also decides* to retain for the United Nations crime prevention and criminal justice programme, without prejudice to additional funds that may be made available by the Secretary-General, all funds currently allocated to the programme, as well as any savings realized by restructuring;

14. *Requests* the Secretary-General to report to the General Assembly at its forty-seventh session on measures taken to implement the statement of principles and programme of action....

I. STATEMENT OF PRINCIPLES

1. We recognize that the world is experiencing very important changes resulting in a political climate conducive to democracy, to international cooperation, to more widespread enjoyment of basic human rights and fundamental freedoms, and to the realization of the aspirations of all nations to economic development and social welfare. Notwithstanding these developments, the world today is still beset by violence and other forms of serious crime. These phenomena, wherever they occur, constitute a threat to the maintenance of the rule of law.

2. We believe that justice based on the rule of law is the pillar on which civilized society rests. We seek to improve its quality. A humane and efficient criminal justice system can be an instrument of equity, constructive social change and social justice, protecting basic values and peoples' inalienable rights. Every right of the individual should enjoy protection of the law against violation, a process in which the criminal justice system plays an essential role.

3. We have in mind the fact that the lowering of the world crime rate is related to, among other factors, the improvement of the social conditions for the population. The developed countries and the developing countries are experiencing difficult situations in this respect. Nevertheless, the specific problems encountered by the developing countries justify priority being given to dealing with the situation confronting these countries.

4. We believe that rising crime is impairing the process of development and the general well-being of humanity and is causing general disquiet within our societies. If this situation continues, progress and development will be the ultimate victims of crime.

5. We also believe that the growing internationalization of crime must generate new and commensurate responses. Organized crime is exploiting the relaxation of border controls designed to foster legitimate trade and, hence, development. The incidence and scope of such crimes may increase further in the coming years unless sound preventive measures are taken. It is thus particularly important to anticipate events and to assist Member States in mounting suitable preventive and control strategies.

6. We recognize that many criminal offences have international dimensions. In this context, there is an urgent need for States to address while respecting the sovereignty of States, problems arising in collecting evidence, extraditing offenders and promoting mutual legal assistance, for example, when such offences are committed across frontiers or when frontiers are used to escape detection or prosecution. Despite differences in legal systems, experience has shown that mutual assistance and cooperation can be effective countermeasures and can help to prevent conflicts of jurisdiction.

7. We also recognize that democracy and a better quality of life can flourish only in a context of peace and security for all. Crime poses a threat to stability and to a safe environment. Crime prevention and criminal justice, with due regard to the observance of human rights, is thus a direct contribution to the maintenance of peace and security.

8. We must ensure that any increases in the capacity and capabilities of perpetrators of crime are matched by similar increases in the capacity and capabilities of law enforcement and criminal justice authorities. By pooling our knowledge and developing suitable countermeasures, success in the prevention of crime and reduction of victimization can be maximized. We recognize in particular the need to improve and strengthen the means of the crime prevention and control authorities in the developing countries, whose critical economic and social situation is further increasing the difficulties in this area.

9. We call on the international community to increase its support of technical cooperation and assistance activities for the benefit of all countries, including developing and smaller countries, and for the purpose of expanding and strengthening the infrastructure needed for effective crime prevention and viable, fair and humane criminal justice systems.

10. We acknowledge the contributions of the United Nations crime prevention and criminal justice programme to the international community. We note that it is a long-recognized fact that inadequate resources have been devoted to the implementation of the program, which has in the past been inhibited from achieving its potential....

11. We accordingly recommend intensified international cooperation in crime prevention and criminal justice, including the creation of an effective United Nations crime prevention and criminal justice programme.

12. We are convinced that there is a need for Governments to define more clearly the role and functions of the United Nations crime prevention and criminal justice programme and the Secretariat and to determine priorities within that programme.

13. We strongly believe that the review of the programme should aim at strengthening its effectiveness, improving its efficiency and establishing an adequate Secretariat support structure.

II. PROGRAMME OF ACTION

A. DEFINITION

14. The United Nations crime prevention and criminal justice programme shall bring together the work of the commission on crime prevention and criminal justice, the inter-regional and regional institutes for the prevention of crime and the treatment of offenders, the network of government-appointed national correspondents in the field of crime prevention and criminal justice, the Global Crime and Criminal Justice Information Network and the United Nations congresses on the prevention of crime and the treatment of offenders in providing assistance to Member States in their efforts to reduce the incidence and costs of crime and in developing the proper functioning of the criminal justice system. The establishment of this programme will be effected in accordance with the procedures defined below and within the framework of the total available resources of the United Nations.

B. GOALS

15. The programme shall be designed to assist the international community in meeting its pressing needs in the field of crime prevention and criminal justice and to provide countries with timely and practical assistance in dealing with problems of both national and transnational crime.

16. The general goals of the programme shall be to contribute to the following:

(a) The prevention of crime within and among States;

(b) The control of crime both nationally and internationally;

(c) The strengthening of regional and international cooperation in crime prevention, criminal justice and the combating of transnational crime;

(d) The integration and consolidation of the efforts of Member States in preventing and combating transnational crime;

(e) More efficient and effective administration of justice, with due respect for the human rights of all those affected by crime and all those involved in the criminal justice system;

(f) The promotion of the highest standards of fairness, humanity, justice and professional conduct.

C. SCOPE OF THE UNITED NATIONS CRIME PREVENTION
AND CRIMINAL JUSTICE PROGRAMME

17. The programme shall include appropriate forms of cooperation for the purpose of assisting States in dealing with problems of both national and transnational crime. In particular, it may include:

(a) Research and studies at the national, regional and global levels on specific prevention issues and criminal justice measures;

(b) Regular international surveys to assess trends in crime and developments in the operation of criminal justice systems and in crime prevention strategies;

(c) Exchange and dissemination of information among States on crime prevention and criminal justice, particularly with regard to innovative measures and the results achieved in their application;

(d) Training and upgrading of the skills of personnel working in the various areas of crime prevention and criminal justice;

(e) Technical assistance, including advisory services, particularly in respect of the planning, implementation and evaluation of crime prevention and criminal justice programmes, training and the use of modern communication and information techniques; such assistance may be implemented by means of, for example, fellowships, study tours, consultancies, secondments, courses, seminars and demonstration and pilot projects.

18. Within the framework of the programme, the United Nations should directly carry out the above-mentioned forms of cooperation or should act as a coordinating or facilitating agent. Special attention should be paid to the creation of mechanisms to provide flexible and appropriate assistance and to respond to the needs of Member States at their request, without duplicating the activities of other existing mechanisms.

19. For the purpose of those forms of cooperation, Member States should establish and maintain reliable and effective channels of communication among themselves and with the United Nations.

20. The programme may also include, as appropriate, while respecting the sovereignty of States, a review of the effectiveness and application of and, where necessary, further development and promotion of international instruments on crime prevention and criminal justice.

D. PROGRAMME PRIORITIES

21. In developing the programme, areas of priority shall be determined in response to the needs and concerns of Member States, giving particular consideration to the following:

(a) Empirical evidence, including research findings and other information on the nature and extent of crime and on trends in crime;

(b) The social, financial and other costs of various forms of crimes and/or crime control to the individual, the local, national and international community, and to the development process;

(c) The need of developing or developed countries, which are confronting specific difficulties related to national or international circumstances, to have recourse to experts and other resources necessary for establishing and developing programmes for crime prevention and criminal justice that are appropriate at the national and local levels;

(d) The need for a balance within the programme of work between programme development and practical action;

(e) The protection of human rights in the administration of justice and the prevention and control of crime;

(f) The assessment of areas in which concerted action at the international level and within the framework of the programme would be most effective;

(g) Avoidance of overlapping with the activities of other entities of the United Nations system or of other organizations.

22. The commission on crime prevention and criminal justice shall not be bound by mandates conferred prior to its formation, but shall assess them on their merits by applying the above-mentioned principles.

E. STRUCTURE AND MANAGEMENT

1. Commission on crime prevention and criminal justice

23. A commission on crime prevention and criminal justice shall be established as a functional commission of the Economic and Social Council. The commission shall have the power to create ad hoc working groups to appoint special rapporteurs, as it deems necessary.

Membership

24. The Commission shall consist of forty Member States of the United Nations, elected by the Economic and Social Council on the basis of the principle of equitable geographical distribution. Its members shall serve for a term of three years, except that the terms of one half of the first elected members, whose names shall be chosen by lot, shall expire after two years.

Each Member State shall make every effort to ensure that its delegation includes experts and senior officials with special training and practical experience in crime prevention and criminal justice, preferably with policy responsibility in the field. Provisions should be made in the regular budget of the United Nations to defray the travel costs of the representatives of the least developed countries that are members for the Commission.

Sessions

25. The commission shall hold annual sessions of not more than ten working days.

Functions

26. The commission shall have the following functions:

(a) To provide policy guidance to the United Nations in the field of crime prevention and criminal justice;

(b) To develop, monitor and review the implementation of the programme on the basis of a system of medium-term planning in accordance with the priority principles provided in paragraph 21 above.

(c) To facilitate and help to coordinate the activities of the interregional and regional institutes;

(d) To mobilize the support of Member States for the United Nations crime prevention and criminal justice programme;

(e) To prepare the congresses and to consider suggestions regarding possible subjects for the programme of work as submitted by the congresses.

2. Committee on crime prevention and control

27. The Committee on Crime Prevention and Control should be dissolved by the Economic and Social Council upon the establishment by the Council of the commission on crime prevention and criminal justice. There will be a basic need for involving independent experts in the areas of crime prevention and control.

28. The commission shall, when necessary, use the services of a limited number of qualified and experienced experts, either as individual consultants or in working groups, in order to assist in the preparations for and follow-up work of the commission. Their advice shall be transmitted to the commission for consideration. The commission shall be encouraged to seek such advice whenever such expertise is needed. One of the major tasks of the experts shall be to assist in the preparations for the congresses.

3. United Nations congresses on the prevention of crime and the treatment of offenders

29. The United Nations congresses on the prevention of crime and the treatment of offenders, as a consultative body of the programme, shall provide a forum for:

(a) The exchange of views between States, intergovernmental organizations, non-governmental organizations and individual experts representing various professions and disciplines;

(b) The exchange of experiences in research, law and policy development;

(c) The identification of emerging trends and issues in crime prevention and criminal justice;

(d) The provision of advice and comments to the commission on crime prevention and criminal justice on selected matters submitted to it by the commission;

(e) The submission of suggestions, for the consideration of the commission, regarding possible subjects for the programme of work.

30. In order to enhance the effectiveness of the programme and to achieve optimal results, the following arrangements should be implemented:

(a) The congresses should be held every five years, for a period of between five and ten working days;

(b) The commission shall select precisely defined topics for the congresses in order to ensure a focused and productive discussion;

(c) Quinquennial regional meetings should be held under the guidance of the commission on issues related to the agenda of the commission or of the congresses, or on any other matters, except when a region does not consider it necessary to hold such a meeting. The interregional and regional institutes should be fully involved, as appropriate, in the organization of those meetings. The Commission shall give due consideration to the need to finance such meetings, in particular in developing regions, through the regular budget of the United Nations;

(d) Action-oriented research workshops on topics selected by the commission, as part of a congress programme, and ancillary meetings associated with the congresses should be encouraged.

4. Organizational structure of the secretariat and of the programme

31. The Secretariat shall be the permanent body responsible for facilitating the implementation of the programme, the priorities of which shall be established by the com-

mission, and for assisting the commission in conducting evaluations of the progress made and analyses of the difficulties encountered. For that purpose, the Secretariat shall:

(a) Mobilize existing resources, including institutes, intergovernmental organizations, non-governmental organizations and other competent authorities for the implementation of the programme;

(b) Coordinate research, training and the collection of data on crime and justice, and provide technical assistance and practical information for Member States, particularly through the global information network on crime and criminal justice;

(c) Assist the commission in the organization of its work and in the preparation, in accordance with the directions for the commission, of the congresses and any other events relating to the programme;

(d) Ensure that the potential donors of criminal justice assistance are put in touch with countries needing the help in question;

(e) Make the case for assistance in the field of criminal justice to the appropriate funding agencies.

32. It is recommended to the Secretary-General that, in recognition of the high priority that should be accorded to the programme, an upgrading of the Crime Prevention and Criminal Justice Branch into a division should be effected as soon as possible, under the conditions set out in paragraph 14, bearing in mind the structure of the United Nations Office at Vienna.

33. The Professional staff of the Secretariat of the programme shall be called "Crime Prevention and Criminal Justice Officers."

34. The Secretariat of the programme shall be directed by a senior official responsible for the overall day-today management and supervision of the programme, communicating with the relevant government officials, the specialized agencies and intergovernmental organizations whose activities are relevant to the programme.

F. PROGRAMME SUPPORT

1. Interregional and regional institutes for the prevention of crime and the treatment of offenders

35. The activities of the United Nations institutes for the prevention of crime and the treatment of offenders should be supported by Member States and the United Nations, giving particular attention to the needs of such institutes located in developing countries. Given the important role of such institutes, their contributions to policy development and implementation, and their resource requirements, should be fully integrated into the overall programme especially those of the African Regional Institute for the Prevention of Crime and treatment of Offenders.

2. Coordination among the interregional and regional institutes

36. The interregional and regional institutes should keep one another and the commission informed on a regular basis about their programme of work and its implementation.

37. The commission may request the interregional and regional institutes, subject to the availability of resources, to implement select elements of the programme. The commission may also suggest areas for inter-institute activities.

38. The commission shall seek to mobilize extra budgetary support for the activities of the interregional and regional institutes.

3. Network of government-appointed national correspondents in the field of crime prevention and criminal justice

39. Member States should designate one or more national correspondents in the field of crime prevention and criminal justice as focal points for the purpose of maintaining direct communication with the Secretariat and other elements of the programme.

40. The national correspondents shall facilitate contact with the Secretariat on matters of legal, scientific and technical cooperation, training, information on national laws and regulations, legal policy, organization of the criminal justice system, crime prevention measures and penitentiary matters.

4. Global information network on crime and criminal justice

41. Member States shall support the United Nations in the development and maintenance of the global information network on crime and criminal justice in order to facilitate the collection, analysis, exchange and dissemination, as appropriate, of information and the centralization of inputs from non-governmental organizations and scientific institutions in the field of crime prevention and criminal justice.

42. Member States shall undertake to provide the Secretary-General on a regular basis and upon request with data on the dynamics, structure and extent of crime and on the operation of crime prevention and criminal justice strategies in their respective countries.

5. Intergovernmental and non-governmental organizations

43. Intergovernmental and non-governmental organizations and scientific community are a valuable source of professional expertise, advocacy and assistance. Their contributions should be fully utilized in programme development and implementation.

G. FUNDING OF THE PROGRAMME

44. The programme shall be funded from the regular budge of the United Nations. Funds allocated for technical assistance may be supplemented by direct voluntary contributions from Member States and interested funding agencies. Member States are encouraged to make contributions to the United Nations Trust Fund for Social Defence, to be renamed the United Nations crime prevention and criminal justice fund. They are also encouraged to contribute in kind for the operational activities of the programme, particularly by seconding staff, organizing training courses and seminars, and providing the requisite equipment and services.

Convention Applying the Schengen Agreement of 14 June 1985

The Kingdom of Belgium, the Federal Republic of Germany, the French Republic, the Grand Duchy of Luxembourg and the Kingdom of the Netherlands, hereinafter called the Contracting Parties,

Taking as their basis the Schengen Agreement of 14 June 1985 on the gradual abolition of checks at their common borders,

Having decided to implement the intention expressed in that agreement of bringing about the abolition of checks at their common borders on the movement of persons and facilitating the transport and movement of goods,

Whereas the Treaty establishing the European Communities, supplemented by the Single European Act, provides that the internal market shall comprise a area without internal frontiers,

Whereas the aim pursued by the Contracting Parties coincides with that objective, without prejudice to the measures to be taken to implement the provisions of the Treaty,

Whereas the implementation of that intention requires a series of appropriate measures and close co-operation between the Contracting Parties,

Have agreed as follows:

TITLE I. DEFINITIONS

Art. 1. For the purpose of the Convention:

Internal borders shall mean the common land borders of the Contracting Parties, their airports for internal flights and their sea ports for regular trans-shipment connections exclusively from or to other ports within the territories of the Contracting Parties no calling at any ports outside those territories;

External borders shall mean the Contracting Parties' land and sea borders and their airport and sea ports, provided they are not internal borders;

Internal flights shall mean any flight exclusively to or from territories of the Contracting Parties not landing within the territory of a Third State;

Third State shall mean any State other than the Contracting Parties;

Alien shall mean any person other than a national of a Member State of the European Communities;

Alien reported as a person shall mean any alien listed reported as a person not to be permitted entry in the Schengen Information System in accordance with Article 96;

Border crossing point shall mean any crossing point authorized by the competent authorities for the crossing of external borders;

Border control shall mean a check made at a border in response solely to an intention to cross the border, regardless of any other consideration;

Carrier shall mean any natural or legal person whose occupation it is to provide passenger transport by air, sea or land;

Residence permit shall mean an authorization of any type issued by a Contracting Party giving the right of residence within its territory. This definition shall not include temporary admission to reside with the territory of a Contracting Party for the purpose of the processing of an application for asylum or an application for a residence permit;

Application for asylum shall mean any application submitted in writing, orally or otherwise by an alien at an external border or within the territory of a Contracting Party with a view to obtaining recognition as a refugee in accordance with the Geneva Convention of 28 July 1951 relating to the Status of Refugees, as amended by the New York Protocol of 31 January 1967 and as such obtaining the right of residence;

Processing of an shall mean all the procedures for examining and application for asylum taking a decision on an application for asylum, including measures taken in implementation of a final decision there on, with the exception of the determination of the Contracting Party responsible for the processing of an application for asylum under this Convention.

TITLE II. ABOLITION OF CHECKS AT INTERNAL BORDERS AND MOVEMENT OF PERSONS

CHAPTER 1. CROSSING INTERNAL FRONTIERS

Art. 2. 1. Internal borders may be crossed at any point without any checks on persons being carried out.

2. Where public policy or national security so require, however, a Contracting Party may, after consulting the other Contracting Parties, decide that for a limited period national border checks appropriate to the situation will be carried out at internal borders. If public policy or national security require immediate action, the Contracting Parties concerned shall take the necessary measures and shall inform the other Contracting Parties thereof at the earliest opportunity.

3. The abolition of checks on persons at internal borders shall not affect either Article 22 below or the exercise of police powers by the competent authorities under each Contracting Party's legislation throughout its territory, or the obligations to hold, carry and produce permits and documents provided for in its legislation.

4. Checks on goods shall be carried out in accordance with the relevant provisions of this Convention.

CHAPTER 2. CROSSING EXTERNAL BORDERS

Art. 3. 1. External borders may in principle be crossed only at border crossing points during the fixed opening hours. More detailed provisions, and exceptions and arrangements for minor border traffic, as well as the rules applicable to special categories of maritime traffic such as yachting and coastal fishing, shall be adopted by the Executive Committee.

2. The Contracting Parties undertake to introduce penalties for the unauthorized crossing of external borders at places other than crossing points or at times other than the fixed opening hours.

Art. 4. 1. The Contracting Parties guarantee that as from 1993 passengers on flights from Third States who board internal flights will first be subject, upon arrival, to person and hand baggage checks in the airport of arrival of their external flight. Passengers on internal flights who board flights bound for Third States will first be subject, on departure, to personal and hand baggage checks in the airport of departure of their external flight.

2. The Contracting Parties shall take the measures required for checks to be carried out in accordance with paragraph 1.

3. Neither paragraph 1 nor paragraph 2 shall affect checks on registered luggage; such checks shall be carried out either in the airport of final destination or in the airport of initial departure.

4. Until the date laid down in paragraph 1, airports shall, by way of derogation from the definition of internal borders, be considered as external borders for internal flights.

Art. 5. 1. For visits not exceeding three months entry into the territories of the Contracting Parties may be granted to an alien who fulfills the following conditions:

(a) in possession of a valid document or documents permitting him to cross the border, as determined by the Executive Committee;

(b) in possession of a valid visa if required;

(c) if applicable, submits documents substantiating the purpose and the conditions of the planned visit and has sufficient means of support, both for the period of the planned visit and to return to his country of origin or to travel in transit in a Third State, into which his admission is guaranteed, or is in a position to acquire such means legally;

(d) has not been reported as a person not to be permitted entry;

(e) is not considered to be a threat to public policy, national security or the international relations of any of the Contracting Parties.

2. Entry to the territories of the Contracting Parties must be refused to any alien who does not fulfil all the above conditions unless a Contracting Party considers it necessary to derogate from that principle on humanitarian grounds or in the national interest or because of international obligations. In such cases permission to enter will be restricted to the territory of the Contracting Party concerned, which must inform the other Contracting Parties accordingly. These rules shall not preclude the application of special provisions concerning the right of asylum or of the provisions of Article 18.

3. An alien who holds a residence permit or a return visa issued by one of the Contracting Parties or, if required, both documents, shall be permitted to enter in transit, unless his name is on the national list of persons reported as not to be permitted entry which is held by the Contracting Party at the external borders of which he arrives.

Art. 6. 1. Cross-border movement at external borders shall be subject to checks by the competent authorities. Checks shall be made in accordance with uniform principles, within the scope of national powers and national legislation, account being taken of the interest of all Contracting Parties throughout the Contracting Parties' territories.

2. The uniform principles referred to in paragraph 1 shall be as follows:

(a) Checks on person shall include not only the verification of travel documents and of the other conditions governing entry, residence, work and exit but also checks to detect and prevent threats to the national security and public policy of the Contracting Parties. Such checks shall also cover vehicles and objects in the possession of persons crossing the border. They shall be carried out by each Contracting Party in accordance with its legislation, in particular as regards searches.

(b) All persons must be subject to at least one check making it possible to establish their identities on the basis of their presentation of travel documents.

(c) On entry aliens must be subject to a thorough check as defined in (a).

(d) On exit checks shall be carried out as required in the interest of all Contracting Parties under the law on aliens in order to detect and prevent threats to the national security and public policy of the Contracting Parties. Such checks shall be made in all cases in respect of aliens.

(e) If such checks cannot be made because of particular circumstances priorities must be established. In this connection, entry checks shall in principle take priority over exit checks.

3. The competent authorities shall use mobile units to exercise surveillance on external borders between crossing points; the same shall apply to border crossing points outside normal opening hours. This surveillance shall be carried out in such a way as not to encourage people to circumvent the checks at crossing points. The surveillance procedures shall, where appropriate, be fixed by the Executive Committee.

4. The Contracting Parties undertake to deploy enough appropriate officers to conduct checks and maintain surveillance along external borders.

5. An equivalent level of control shall be exercised at external frontiers.

Art. 7. The Contracting Parties shall assist each other and shall maintain constant, close co-operation with a view to the effective exercise of checks and surveillance. They shall in particular exchange all relevant, important information, with the exception of data relating to named individuals, unless otherwise provided in this Convention, shall as far as possible harmonize the instructions given to officers manning checkpoints. Such co-operation may take the form of the exchange of liaison officers.

Art. 8. The Executive Committee shall take the necessary decisions relating to the practical procedures for implementing border checks and surveillance.

CHAPTER 3. VISAS

Section 1. Visas for short visits

Art. 9. 1. The Contracting Parties undertake to adopt a common policy on the movement of persons and in particular on the arrangements for visas. They shall give each other assistance to that end. The Contracting Parties undertake to pursue by common agreement the harmonization of their policies on visas.

2. The visa arrangements relating to Third States, the nationals of which are subject to visa arrangements common to all the Contracting Parties at the time when this Convention is signed or later, may be amended only by common agreement of all the Contracting Parties. A Contracting Party exceptionally derogate from the common visa arrangements with respect to a Third State for over-riding reasons of national policy that require an urgent decision. It must first consult the other Contracting Parties, and in its decision, must take account of their interests and of the consequences of that decision....

TITLE III. POLICY AND SECURITY

CHAPTER 1. POLICE CO-OPERATION

Art. 39. 1. The Contracting Parties undertake to ensure that their police authorities shall, in compliance with national legislation and within the limits of their responsibilities, assist each other for the purposes of preventing and detecting criminal offences, in so far as national law does not stipulate that the request is to be made to the legal authorities and provided the request or the implementation thereof does not involve the application of coercive measures by the requested Contracting Party. Where the requested police authorities do not have jurisdiction to implement a request, they shall forward it to the competent authorities.

2. The written information provided by the requested Contracting Party under paragraph 1 may not be used by the requesting Contracting Party as evidence of the criminal offence other than with the agreement of the relevant legal authorities of the requested Contracting Party.

3. Requests for assistance referred to in paragraph 1 and the replies to such requests may be exchanged between the central bodies responsible in each Contracting Party for international police co-operation. Where the request cannot be made in good time by the above procedure, it may be addressed by the police authorities of the requesting Contracting Party directly to the competent authorities of the requested Party, which may reply directly. In such cases, the requesting police authority shall as soon as possible inform the central body responsible in the requested Contracting Party for international police co-operation of its direct application.

4. In border regions, co-operation may be covered by arrangements between the responsible Ministers of the Contracting Parties.

5. The provisions of this article shall not preclude more detailed present or future bilateral agreements between Contracting Parties with a common border. The Contracting Parties shall inform each other of such agreements.

Art. 40. 1. Police officers of one of the Contracting Parties who, within the framework of a criminal investigation, are keeping under observation in their country, a person who is presumed to have taken part in a criminal offence to which extradition may apply, shall be authorized to continue their observation in the territory of another Contracting Party where the latter has authorized cross-border observations in response to a request for assistance which has previously been submitted. Conditions may be attached to the authorization.

On request the observation will be entrusted to officers of the Contracting Party in whose territory it is carried out.

The request for assistance referred to in the first subparagraph must be sent to an authority designated by each of the Contracting Parties and having jurisdiction to grant or to forward the requested authorization.

2. Where, for particularly urgent reasons, prior authorization of the other Contracting Party cannot be requested, the officers conducting the observation shall be authorized to continue beyond the border the observation of a person presumed to have committed offences listed in paragraph 7, provided that the following conditions are met:

(a) the authorities of the Contracting Party designated under paragraph 5, in whose territory the observation is to be continued, must be notified immediately, during the observation, that the border has been crossed;

(b) A request for assistance submitted in accordance with paragraph 1 and outlining the grounds for crossing the border without prior authorization shall be submitted without delay.

Observation shall cease as soon as the Contracting Party in whose territory it is taking place so requests, following the notification referred to in (a) or the request referred to in (b) or where authorization has not been obtained five hours after the border was crossed.

3. The observation referred to in paragraphs 1 and 2 shall be carried out only under the following general conditions:

(a) The officers conducting the observation must comply with the provisions of this article and with the law of the Contracting Party in whose territory they are operating; they must obey the instructions of the local responsible authorities.

(b) Except in the situations provided for in paragraph 2, the officers shall, during the observation, carry a document certifying that authorization has been granted.

(c) The officers conducting the observation must be able at all times to provide proof that they are acting in an official capacity.

(d) The officers conducting the observation may carry their service weapons during the observation save where specifically otherwise decided by the requested Party; their use shall be prohibited save in cases of legitimate self-defense.

(e) Entry into private homes and places not accessible to the public shall be prohibited.

(f) The officers conducting the observation may neither challenge nor arrest the person under observation.

(g) All operations shall be the subject of a report to the authorities of the Contracting Party in whose territory they took place; the officers conducting the observation may be required to appear in person.

(h) The authorities of the Contracting Party from which the observing officers have come shall, when requested by the authorities of the Contracting Party in whose territory the observation took place, assist the enquiry subsequent to the operation in which they took part, including legal proceedings.

4. The officers referred to in paragraph 1 and 2 shall be:

—as regards the Kingdom of Belgium: members of the *"police judiciaire près les Parquets"*, the *"gendarmerie"* and the *"police communale"* as well as customs officers, under the conditions laid down in appropriate bilateral agreements referred to in paragraph 6, with respect to their powers regarding illicit traffic in narcotic drugs and psychotropic substances, traffic in arms and explosives, and the illicit carriage of toxic and dangerous waste;

—as regards the Federal the Federal Republic of Germany, officers of the *"Polizeien des Bundes und der Länder"* as well as, with respect only to illegal traffic in narcotic drugs and psychotropic substances and arms traffic, officers of the *"Zollfahndungsdienst"* (customs investigation service) in their capacity as auxiliary officers of the public ministry;

—as regards the French Republic: officers and criminal police officers of the national police and national *"gendarmerie"* as well as customs officers, under conditions laid down in appropriate bilateral agreements referred to in paragraph 6, with respect to their powers regarding illicit traffic in narcotic drugs and psychotropic substances, traffic in arms and explosives, and the illicit carriage of toxic and dangerous waste;

—as regards the Grand Duchy of Luxembourg: officers of the *"gendarmerie"* and the police as well as customs officers, under conditions laid down in appropriate bilateral agreements referred to in paragraph 6, with respect to their powers regarding illicit traffic in narcotic drugs and psychotropic substances, traffic in arms and explosives, and the illicit carriage of toxic and dangerous waste;

—as regards the Kingdom of the Netherlands: officers of the *"Rijkspolitie"* and the *"Gemeentepolitie"* as well as, under the conditions laid down in appropriate bilateral agreements referred to in paragraph 6, with respect to their powers regarding illicit traffic in narcotic drugs and psychotropic substances, traffic in arms and explosives and the illicit carriage of toxic and dangerous waste, officers of the fiscal information and research service responsible for entry and excise duties.

5. The authority referred to in paragraph 1 and 2 shall be:

—as regards the Kingdom of Belgium: The *"Commissariat général de la Police judiciare"*;

—as regards the Federal Republic of Germany: the *"Bundeskriminalamt"*;

—as regards the French Republic: the *"Direction centrale de la Police judiciare"*;

—as regards the Grand Duchy of Luxembourg: the *"Procureur géneral d'Etat"*;

—as regards the Kingdom of the Netherlands: the *"Landelijk Officier van Justitie"* responsible for cross-border observation.

6. The Contracting Parties may, at bilateral level, extend the scope of this article and adopt additional measures in implementation thereof.

7. The observation referred to in paragraph 2 may take place only for one of the following criminal offences:

—assassination,

—murder,

—rape,

—arson,

—counterfeiting,

— armed robbery and receiving stolen goods,

— extortion,

— kidnapping and hostage taking,

— traffic in human beings,

— illicit traffic in narcotic drugs and psychotropic substances,

— breach of the laws on arms and explosives,

— use of explosives,

— illicit carriage of toxic and dangerous waste.

Art. 41. 1. Officers of one of the Contracting Parties following, in their country, an individual apprehended in the act of committing one of the offences referred to in paragraph 4 or participating in one of those offences, shall be authorized to continue pursuit in the territory of another Contracting Party without prior authorization where given the particular urgency of the situation it was not possible to notify the competent authorities of the other Contracting Party by one of the means provided for in Article 44 prior to entry into that territory or where these authorities have been unable to reach the scene in time to take over the pursuit.

The same shall apply where the person pursued has escaped from provisional custody or while serving a custodial sentence.

The pursuing officers shall, not later than when they cross the border, contact the competent authorities of the Contracting Party in whose territory the pursuit is to take place. The pursuit will cease as soon as the Contracting Party on the territory of which the pursuit is taking place so requests. At the request of the pursuing officers, the competent local authorities shall challenge the pursued person so as to establish his identity or to arrest him.

2. The pursuit shall be carried out in accordance with one of the following procedures, defined by the declaration provided for in paragraph 9:

(a) The pursuing officers shall not have the right to apprehend.

(b) If no request to cease the pursuit is made and if the competent local authorities are unable to intervene quickly enough, the pursuing officers may apprehend the person pursued until the officers of the Contracting Party in the territory of which the pursuit is taking place, who must be informed without delay, are able to establish his identity or arrest him.

3. Pursuit shall be carried out in accordance with paragraphs 1 and 2 in one of the following ways as defined by the declaration provided for in paragraph 9:

(a) in an area or during a period as from the crossing of the border, to be established in the declaration;

(b) without limit in space or time.

4. In a declaration referred to in paragraph 9, the Contracting Parties shall define the offences referred to in paragraph 1 in accordance with one of the following procedures:

(a) The following offences:

— assassination,

— murder,

— rape,

— arson,

— counterfeiting,

— armed robbery and receiving of stolen goods,

— extortion,

— kidnapping and hostage taking,

— traffic in human beings,

— illicit traffic in narcotic drugs and psychotropic substances,

— breach of the laws on arms and explosives,

— use of explosives,

— illicit carriage of toxic and dangerous waste,

— taking to flight after an accident which has resulted in death or serious injury.

(b) Extraditable offenses.

5. Pursuit shall be subject to the following general conditions:

(a) The pursuing officers may comply with the provisions of this article and with the law of the Contracting Party in whose territory they are operation; they must obey the instructions of the competent local authorities.

(b) Pursuit shall be solely over land borders.

(c) Entry intro private homes and places not accessible to the public shall be prohibited.

(d) The pursuing officers shall be easily identifiable, either by their uniform or by means of an armband or by accessories fitted to their vehicle; the use of civilian clothes combined with the use of unmarked vehicles without the aforementioned identification is prohibited; the pursuing officers must at all times be able to prove that they are acting in official capacity.

(e) The pursuing officers may carry their service weapons; their use shall be prohibited save in cases of legitimate self-defense.

(f) One the pursued person has been apprehended as provided for in paragraph 2(b), for the purpose of bringing him before the competent local authorities he may be subjected only to a security search; handcuffs may be used during his transfer; objects carried by the pursued person may be seized.

(g) After each operation mentioned in paragraphs 1,2, and 3, the pursuing officers shall present themselves before the local competent authorities of the Contracting Party in whose territory they were operating and shall give an account of their mission; at the request of those authorities, they must remain at their disposal until the circumstances of their action have been adequately elucidated; this condition shall apply even where the pursuit has not resulted in the arrest of the pursued person.

(h) The authorities of the Contracting Party from which the pursuing officers have come shall, when requested by the authorities of the Contracting Party in whose territory the pursuit took place, assist the enquiry subsequent to the operation in which they took part, including legal proceedings.

6. A person who, following the action provided for in paragraph 2, has been arrested by the competent local authorities may, whatever his nationality, be held for questioning. The relevant rules of national law shall apply by analogy.

If the person is not a national of the Contracting Party in the territory of which he was arrested, he shall be released no later than six hours after his arrest, not including the hours between midnight and 9.00 in the morning, unless the competent local authorities have previously received a request for his provisional arrest for the purposes of extradition in any form whatever.

7. The officers referred to in the previous paragraphs shall be:

— as regards the Kingdom of Belgium: members of the *"police judiciaire près les Parquets"* the *"gendarmerie"* and the *"police communale"* as well as customs officers, under the conditions laid down in appropriate bilateral agreements referred to in paragraph 10, with respect to their powers regarding illicit traffic in narcotic drugs and psychotropic substances, traffic in arms and explosives, and the illicit carriage of toxic and dangerous waste;

— as regards the Federal Republic of Germany: officers of the *"Polizeien des Bundes und der Länder"* as well as, with respect only to illegal traffic in narcotic drugs and psychotropic substances and arms traffic, officers of the *"Zollfahndungsdienst"* (customs investigation service) in their capacity as auxiliary officers of the public ministry;

— as regards the French Republic: officers and criminal police officers of the national police and national *"gendarmerie"* as well as customs officers, under the conditions laid down in the appropriate bilateral agreements referred to in paragraph 10, with respect to their powers regarding illicit traffic in narcotic drugs and psychotropic substances, traffic in arms or explosives, and the illicit carriage of toxic and dangerous waste;

— as regards the Grand Duchy of Luxembourg: officers of the *"gendarmerie"* and the police as well as customs officers, under the conditions laid down in the appropriate bilateral agreements referred to in paragraph 10, with respect to their powers regarding illicit traffic in narcotic drugs and psychotropic substances, traffic in arms and explosives, and the illicit carriage of toxic and dangerous waste;

— as regards the Kingdom of the Netherlands: officers of the *"Rijkspolitie"* and the *"Gemeentepolitie"* as well as, under the conditions laid down in the appropriate bilateral agreements referred to in paragraph 10, with respect to their powers regarding illicit traffic in narcotic drugs and psychotropic substances, traffic in arms and explosives and the illicit carriage of toxic and dangerous waste, officers of the fiscal information and research service responsible for entry and excise duties.

8. This article shall be without prejudice, where the Contracting Parties are concerned, to Article 27 of the Benelux Treaty of 27 June 1962 on Extradition and Mutual Assistance in Criminal Matters as amended by the Protocol of 11 May 1974.

9. On signing this Convention, each Contracting Party shall make a declaration in which it shall define, on the basis of paragraphs 2, 3 and 4 above, the procedures for implementing pursuit in it territory for each of the Contracting Parties with which it has a common border. A Contracting Party may at any moment replace its declaration by another declaration, provided the latter does not restrict the scope of the former.

Each declaration shall be made after consultations with each of the Contracting Parties concerned and with a view to obtaining equivalent arrangements on both sides of internal borders.

10. The Contracting Parties may, on a bilateral basis, extend the scope of paragraph 1 and adopt additional provisions in implementation of this article.

Art. 42. During the operations referred to in Articles 40 and 41, officers operating on the territory of another Contracting Party shall be regarded as officers of that Party with respect to offences committed against them or by them.

Art. 43. 1. Where, in accordance with Articles 40 and 41 of this Convention, officers of a Contracting Party are operating in the territory of another Contracting Party, the first Contracting party shall be responsible for any damage caused by them during the course of their mission, in accordance with the law of the Contracting Party in whose territory they are operating.

2. The Contracting Party in whose territory the damage referred to in paragraph 1 is caused shall repair such damage under the conditions applicable to damage caused by its own officers.

3. The Contracting Party whose officers have caused damage to whomsoever in the territory of another Contracting Party shall reimburse in full to the latter any sums it has paid out to the victims or other entitled persons.

4. Without prejudice to the exercise of its rights vis-à-vis third parties and without prejudice to paragraph 3, each Contracting Party shall refrain, in the case provided for in paragraph 1, from requesting reimbursement of the amount of damages it has sustained from another Contracting Party.

Art. 44. 1. In accordance with the relevant international agreements and account being taken of local circumstances and the technical possibilities, the Contracting Parties shall set up, in particular in border areas, telephone, radio, and telex lines and other direct links to facilitate police and customs co-operation, in particular for the transmission of information in good time for the purposes of cross-border observation and pursuit.

2. In addition to these short-term measures, they will in particular examine the following possibilities:

(a) the exchange of equipment or the assignment of liaison officials provided with appropriate radio equipment;

(b) the widening of the frequency bands used in border areas;

(c) the establishment of a common link for police and customs services operating in these areas;

(d) co-operation of their programmes for the procurement of communications equipment, with a view to achieving the introduction of standardized compatible communications systems.

Art. 45. 1. The Contracting Parties undertake to take the measures required to guarantee that:

(a) the managers of establishments providing lodging or their employees ensure that aliens accommodated therein, including nationals of the other Contracting Parties as well as those of other Member States of the European Communities, with the exception of accompanying spouses or minors or members of travel groups, personally complete and sign declaration forms and confirm their identity by the production of a valid identity document;

(b) the declaration forms thus completed will be kept for the competent authorities or forwarded to them where such authorities deem this necessary for the prevention of threats, for criminal proceedings or to ascertain what has happened to persons who have disappeared or who have been the victim of an accident, save were national law provides otherwise.

2. Paragraph 1 shall apply by analogy to persons staying in any accommodation provided by professional lessors, in particular tents, caravans and boats.

Art. 46. 1. In particular cases, each Contracting Party may, in compliance with its national legislation and without being asked, send the Contracting Party concerned any information which may be of interest to it in helping prevent future crime and to prevent offences against or threats to public order and security.

2. Information shall be exchanged, without prejudice to the arrangements for co-operation in border areas referred to in Article 39(4), through a central body to be designated. In particularly urgent cases, the exchange of information within the meaning of this article may take place directly between the police authorities concerned, save where national provisions provide otherwise. The central body shall be informed of this as soon as possible.

Art. 47. 1. The Contracting Parties may conclude bilateral agreements providing for the secondment, for a specified or unspecified period, of liaison officers from one Contracting Party to the police authorities of the other Contracting Party.

2. The secondment of liaison officers for a specified or unspecified period is intended to promote and to accelerate co-operation between the Contracting Parties, particularly by providing assistance

(a) in the form of the exchange of information for the purposes of fighting crime by means both of prevention and of punishment;

(b) in complying with requests for mutual police assistance and legal assistance in criminal matters;

(c) for the purposes of missions carried out by the authorities responsible for the surveillance of external borders.

3. Liaison officers shall have the task of giving advice and assistance. They shall not be competent to take independent police action. They shall supply information and perform their duties in accordance with the instructions given to them by the Contracting Party of origin and by the Contracting Party to which they are seconded. They shall make report regularly to the head of the police service to which they are seconded.

4. The Contracting Parties may agree within a bilateral or multilateral framework that liaison officers from a Contracting Party seconded to third States shall also represent the interests of one or more other Contracting Parties. Under such agreements, liaison officers seconded to third States shall supply information to other Contracting Parties when requested to do so or on their own initiative and shall, within the limits of their powers, perform duties on behalf of such Parties. The Contracting Parties shall inform one another of their intentions as regards the secondment of liaison officers to third States.

CHAPTER 2. MUTUAL ASSISTANCE IN CRIMINAL MATTERS

Art. 48. 1. The provisions of this Chapter are intended to supplement the European Convention of 20 April 1959 on Mutual Assistance in Criminal Matters as well as, in relations between the Contracting Parties which are members of the Benelux Economic Union, Chapter II of the Benelux Treaty on Extradition and Mutual Assistance in Criminal Matters of 27 June 1962, as amended by the Protocol of 11 May 1974, and to facilitate the implementation of these agreements.

2. Paragraph 1 shall not affect the application of the broader provisions of the bilateral agreements in force between the Contracting Parties.

Art. 49. Mutual assistance shall also be afforded:

(a) in proceedings brought by the administrative authorities in respect of offences which are punishable in one of the two Contracting Parties or in both Contracting parties by virtue of being infringements of the rules of law, where the decision may give rise to proceedings before a criminal court;

(b) in proceedings for compensation in respect of unjustified prosecution or conviction;

(c) in proceedings in non-contentious matters;

(d) in civil proceedings joined to criminal proceedings, as long as the criminal court has not yet given a final ruling in the criminal proceedings;

(e) to communicate legal statements relating to the execution of a sentence or measure, conditional release or the postponement or suspension of execution of a sentence or measure.

Art. 50. 1. The Contracting Parties undertake to afford each other, in accordance with the Convention and the Treaty referred to in Article 48, mutual assistance as regards infringements of their rules of law with respect to excise duty, value added tax and customs duties. Customs provisions are the rules laid down in Article 2 of the Convention of 7 September 1967 between Belgium, the Federal Republic of Germany, France, Italy, Luxembourg and the Netherlands on mutual assistance between customs administrations, as well as Article 2 of Council Regulation (EEC) No. 1468/81 of 19 May 1981.

2. Requests based on evasion of excise duties may not be rejected on the grounds that the country requested does not levy excise duties on the goods referred to in the request.

3. The requesting Contracting Party shall not forward or use information or evidence obtained from the requested Contracting Party for enquiries, proceedings or procedures other than those referred to in its request, without the prior assent of the requested Contracting Party.

4. The mutual assistance provided for in this article may be refused where the alleged amount of duty underpaid or evaded is no more than ECU 25 000 or where the presumed value of the goods exported or imported without authorization is no more than ECU 100 000, unless, given the circumstances or the identity of the accused, the case is deemed to be extremely serious by the requesting Contracting Party.

5. The provisions of this article shall also apply when the mutual assistance requested concerns infringements punishable only by a fine as infringements of the rules of law in proceedings brought by the administrative authorities, where the request for assistance emanates from a judicial authority.

Art. 51. The Contracting Parties may not make the admissibility of letters rogatory for search or seizure dependent on conditions other than the following:

(a) the offence giving rise to the letters rogatory is punishable under the law of both Contracting Parties by a custodial sentence or a security measure restricting liberty of a maximum of at least six months or is punishable under the law of one of the two Contracting Parties by an equivalent penalty and under the law of the other Contracting Party as an infringement of the regulations which is prosecuted by the administrative authorities where the decision may give rise to proceedings before a criminal court.

(b) execution of the letter rogatory is consistent with the law of the requested Contracting Party.

Art. 52. 1. Each Contracting Party may address procedural documents directly by post to persons who are in the territory of another Contracting Party. The Contracting Parties shall send the Executive Committee a list of the documents which may be forwarded in this way.

2. Where there is reason to believe that the addressee does not understand the language in which the document is drafted, the document—or at least the important passage in it—must be translated into (one of) the language(s) of the Contracting Party in the territory of which the addressee is staying. If the authority forwarding the document knows that the addressee speaks only another language, the document—or at least the important passages thereof—must be translated into that other language.

3. An expert or witness who has failed to answer a summons to appear, sent to him by post, shall not, even if the summons contains a notice of penalty, be subjected to any punishment or measure of restraint, unless subsequently he voluntarily enters the territory of the requesting Party and is there again duly summoned. The authority sending a summons to appear by post shall ensure that it does not involve penalties. This provision shall be without prejudice to Article 34 of the Benelux Treaty on Extradition and Mutual Assistance in Criminal Matters of 27 June 1962 as amended by the Protocol of 11 May 1974.

4. If the offence on which the request for assistance is based is punishable under the law of both Contracting Parties as an infringement of the regulations which is being prosecuted by the administrative authorities where the decision may give rise to proceedings before a criminal court, the procedure outlined in paragraph 1 must in principle be used for the forwarding of procedural documents.

5. Notwithstanding paragraph 1, procedural documents may be forwarded through the legal authorities of the requested Contracting Party where the addressee's address is unknown or where the requesting Contract Party requires a formal service.

Art. 53. 1. Requests for assistance may be made directly between legal authorities and returned through the same channels.

2. paragraph 1 shall not prejudice the possibility of requests being sent and returned between Ministries of Justice or though the intermediary of national central offices of the International Criminal Police Organization.

3. Requests for the temporary transfer or transit of persons provisionally under arrest or detained or who are the subject of a measure depriving them of their liberty, and the periodic or occasional exchange of data from the judicial records must be effected through the Ministries of Justice.

4. Within the meaning of the European Convention of 20 April 1959 on Mutual Assistance in Criminal Matters, Ministry of Justice means, where the Federal Republic of Germany is concerned, the Federal Minister of Justice and the Justice Ministers or Senators of the Federal States.

5. Information laid down with a view to proceedings in respect of infringement of the legislation on driving and rest time, in accordance with Article 21 of the European Convention of 20 April 1959 on Mutual Assistance in Criminal Matters of 27 June 1962, as amended by the Protocol of 11 May 1974, may be sent by the legal authorities of the requesting Contracting Party directly to the legal authorities of the requested Contracting Party.

CHAPTER 3. APPLICATION OF THE *NON BIS IN IDEM* PRINCIPLE

Art. 54. A person who has been finally judged by a Contracting Party may not be prosecuted by another Contracting Party for the same offences provided that, where he is sentenced, the sentence has been served or is currently being served or can no longer be carried out under the sentencing laws of the Contracting Party.

1. A Contracting Party may, when ratifying, accepting or approving this Convention, declare that it is not bound by Article 54 in one or more of the following cases:

(a) where the acts to which the foreign judgment relates took place in whole or in part in its own territory; in the latter case, this exception shall not however apply if the acts took place in part in the territory of the Contracting Party where the judgment was given;

(b) where the acts to which the foreign judgment relates constitute an offense against State security or other equally essential interests of that Contracting Party;

(c) where the acts to which to foreign judgment relates were committed by an official of that Contracting Party in violation of the obligations of his office.

2. A Contracting Party which has made a declaration regarding the exception referred to in paragraph 1(b) shall specify the categories of offenses to which this exception may apply.

3. A Contracting Party may at any moment withdraw a declaration relating to one or more of the exceptions referred to in paragraph 1.

4. The exceptions which were the subject of a declaration under paragraph 1 shall not apply where the Contracting Party concerned has, in respect of the same acts, requested the other Contracting Party to prosecute or has granted the extradition of the person concerned....

Art. 56. If further proceedings are brought by a Contracting Party against a person, who has been finally judged for the same offences by another Contracting Party, any period of deprivation of liberty served on the territory of the latter Contracting Party on account of the offences in question must be deducted from any sentence handed down. Account will also be taken, to the extent that national legislation permits, of sentences other than periods of imprisonment already undergone.

Art. 57. 1. Where a Contracting Party accuses an individual of an offence and the competent authorities of that Contracting Party have reason to believe that the accusation relates to the same offenses as those for which the individual has already been finally judged by another Contracting Party, these authorities shall, if they deem it necessary, request the relevant information from the competent authorities of the contracting Party in whose territory judgment has already been delivered.

2. The information requested shall be provided as soon as possible and shall be taken into consideration as regards further action to be taken in the proceedings in progress.

3. At the time of ratification, acceptance or approval of this Convention, each Contracting Party will nominate the authorities which will be authorized to request and receive the information provided for in this article.

Art. 58. The above provisions shall not preclude the application of wider national provisions on the "*non bis in idem*" effect attached to legal decisions taken abroad.

CHAPTER 4. EXTRADITION

Art. 59. 1. The provisions of this Chapter are intended to supplement the European Convention of 13 September 1957 on Extradition as well as, in relations between the

Contracting Parties which are members of the Benelux Economic Union, Chapter I of the Benelux Treaty on Extradition and Mutual Assistance in criminal Matters of 27 June 1962, as amended by the Protocol of 11 May 1974, and to facilitate the implementation of these agreements.

2. Paragraph 1 shall not affect the application of the broader provisions of the bilateral agreements in force between Contracting Parties.

Art. 60. In relations between two Contracting Parties, one of which is not a party to the European Convention on Extradition of 13 September 197, the provisions of the said Convention shall apply, subject to the reservations and declarations made at the time of ratifying this Convention or, for Contracting Parties which are not parties to the Convention, at the time of ratifying, approving or accepting the present Convention.

Art. 61. The French Republic undertakes to extradite, at the request of one of the Contracting Parties, persons against whom proceedings are being taken for offences punishable under French law by deprivation of liberty or under a detention order for a maximum period of at least two years and under the law of the requesting Contracting Party by deprivation of liberty or under a detention order for a maximum period of at least a year.

Art. 62. 1. As regards interruption of prescription, only the provisions of the requesting Contract Party shall apply.

2. An amnesty granted by the requested Contracting Party shall not prevent extradition unless the offence falls within the jurisdiction of that Contracting Party.

3. The absence of a charge or an official notice authorizing proceedings, necessary only under the legislation of the requested Contracting Party, shall not affect the obligation to extradite.

Art. 63. The Contracting Parties undertake, in accordance with the Convention and the Treaty referred to in Article 59, to extradite between themselves persons being prosecuted by the legal authorities of the requesting Contracting Party for one of the offences referred to in Article 50(1), or being sought by them for the purposes of execution of a sentence or detention order imposed in respect of such an offence.

Art. 64. A report included in the Schengen Information System in accordance with Article 95 shall have the same force as a request for provisional arrest under Article 16 of the European Convention on Extradition of 13 September 1957 or Article 15 of the Benelux Treaty on Extradition and Mutual Assistance in Criminal Matters of 27 June 1962, as amended by the Protocol of 11 May 1974.

Art. 65. 1. Without prejudice to the option to use the diplomatic channel, requests for extradition and transit shall be sent by the relevant Ministry of the requesting Contracting Party to the relevant Ministry of the requested Contracting Party.

2. The relevant Ministries shall be:

— as regards the Kingdom of Belgium: the Ministry of Justice;

— as regards the Federal Republic of Germany: the Federal Ministry of Justice and the Justice Ministers or Senators of the Federal States;

— as regards the French Republic: the Ministry of Foreign Affairs;

— as regards the Grand Duchy of Luxembourg: the Ministry of Justice;

— as regards the Kingdom of the Netherlands: the Ministry of Justice.

Art. 66. 1. If the extradition of a wanted person is not obviously prohibited under the laws of the requested Contracting Party, that Contracting Party may authorize extradition without formal extradition proceedings, provided that the wanted person agrees thereto in a statement made before a member of the judiciary after being examined by the latter and informed of his right to formal extradition proceedings. The wanted person may have access to a lawyer during such examination.

2. In cases of extradition under paragraph 1, a wanted person who explicitly states that he will not invoke the rule of speciality may not revoke that statement.

CHAPTER 5. TRANSFER OF THE EXECUTION OF CRIMINAL JUDGMENTS

Art. 67. The following provisions shall apply between the Contracting Parties who are parties to the Council of Europe Convention of 21 March 1983 on the Transfer of Sentenced Persons, for the proposes of supplementing that Convention.

Art. 68. 1. The Contracting Party in whose territory a sentence of deprivation of liberty or a detention order has been imposed in a judgment which has obtained the force of res judicata in respect of a national of another Contracting Party who, by escaping to his own country, has avoided the execution of that sentence or detention order, may request the latter Contracting Party, if the escaped person is in its territory, to take over the execution of the sentence or of the detention order.

2. The requested Contracting Party may, at the request of the requesting Contracting Party, prior to the arrival of the documents supporting the request that the execution of the sentence or of the detention order or part of the sentence be taken over, and prior to the decision on that request, take the convicted person into police custody or take other measures to ensure that he remains in the territory of the requested Contracting Party.

Art. 69. The transfer of execution under Article 68 shall not require the consent of the person on whom the sentence or the detention order has been imposed. The other provisions of the Council of Europe Convention of 21 March 1983 on the Transfer of Sentenced Person shall apply by analogy.

CHAPTER 6. NARCOTIC DRUGS

Art. 70. 1. The Contracting Parties shall set up a permanent working party to examine problems relating to the combating of offences involving narcotic drugs and to draw up proposals, where necessary, to improve the practical and technical aspects of co-operation between the Contracting Parties. The working party shall submit its proposals to the Executive Committee.

2. The working party referred to in paragraph 1, the members of which are nominated by the relevant national authorities, shall include representatives of the police and of the customs authorities.

Art. 71. 1. The Contracting Parties undertake as regards the direct or indirect sale of narcotic drugs and psychotropic substances of whatever type, including cannabis, and the possession of such products and substances for sale or export, to take, in compliance with the existing United Nations Conventions,1 all measures necessary for the prevention and punishment of the illicit traffic in narcotic drugs and psychotropic substances.

2. The Contracting Parties undertake to prevent and to punish by administrative and penal measures the illegal export of narcotic drugs and psychotropic substances, including cannabis, as well as the sale, supply and handling of such products and substances, without prejudice to the relevant provisions of Articles 74, 75 and 76.

3. To combat the illegal importation of narcotic drugs and psychotropic substances, including cannabis, the Contracting Parties shall strengthen the checks on the movement of persons and goods and of means of transport at their external borders. Such measures

shall be drawn up by the working party provided for in Article 70. This working party shall consider *inter alia* the reassignment of some of the police and customs staff released from internal border duty, as well as recourse to modern drug-detection methods and sniffer dogs.

4. To ensure compliance with this article, the Contracting Parties shall specifically maintain surveillance on places known to be used for drugs trafficking.

5. The Contracting Parties shall do all in their power to prevent and combat the negative effects of the illicit demand for narcotic drugs and psychotropic substances of whatever kind, including cannabis. The measures adopted to this end shall be the responsibility of each Contracting Party.

Art. 72. The Contracting Parties shall, in accordance with their constitution and their national legal system, ensure that legislation is enacted to permit the seizure and confiscation of assets from illicit traffic in narcotic drugs and psychotropic substances.

Art. 73. 1. The Contracting Parties shall, in accordance with their constitution and their national legal system, to take measures to allow monitored deliveries to take place in the illicit traffic in narcotic drugs and psychotropic substances.

2. In each individual case, a decision to allow monitored deliveries will be taken on the basis of prior authorization by each of the Contracting Parties concerned.

3. Each Contracting Party shall retain responsibility for and control over the operation on its own territory and shall be empowered to intervene.

Art. 74. With respect to legal trade in narcotic drugs and psychotropic substances, the Contracting Parties agree to transfer inside the country, wherever possible, checks conducted at the border and arising from obligations under the United Nations Conventions listed in Article 71.

Art. 75. 1. As regards the movement of travellers to the territory of the Contracting Parties or within such territory, individuals may carry narcotic drugs and psychotropic substances in connection with medical treatment, provided they produce at any check a certificate issued or authenticated by a competent authority of the State of residence.

2. The Executive Committee shall adopt the form and content of the certificate referred to in paragraph 1 and issued by one of the Contracting Parties, with particular reference to the data regarding the nature and quantity of the products and substances and the duration of the journey.

3. The Contracting Parties shall notify each other of the authorities responsible for the issue and authentication of the certificate referred to in paragraph 2.

Art. 76. 1. The Contracting Parties shall, if necessary, and in accordance with their medical, ethical and practical usage, adopt the appropriate measures for the monitoring of narcotic drugs and psychotropic substances subjected in the territory of one or more Contracting Party to more rigorous checks than in their own territory so that the effectiveness of such checks is not prejudiced.

2. Paragraph 1 shall also apply to substances frequently used for the manufacture of narcotic drugs and psychotropic substances.

3. The Contracting Parties shall notify each other of the measures taken in order to monitor the legal trade in the substances referred to in paragraphs 1 and 2.

4. Problems experienced in this connection shall be regularly raised in the Executive Committee.

CHAPTER 7. FIREARMS AND AMMUNITION

Art. 77. The Contracting Parties undertake to bring into line with the provisions of this Chapter their national laws, regulations and administrative provisions relating to the purchase, possession, sale and surrender of firearms and ammunition.

2. This Chapter covers the purchase, possession, sale and surrender of firearms and ammunition by natural and legal persons; it does not cover their supply to the central and territorial authorities, the armed forces or the police, nor the purchase or possession by them of firearms and ammunition for the manufacture of firearms and ammunition by public undertakings....

TITLE IV. THE SCHENGEN INFORMATION SYSTEM

CHAPTER 1. SETTING UP OF THE SCHENGEN INFORMATION SYSTEM

Art. 92. 1. The Contracting Parties shall set up and maintain a joint information system, hereinafter referred to as the Schengen Information System, consisting of a national section in each of the Contracting Parties and a technical support function. The Schengen Information System shall enable the authorities designated by the Contracting Parties, by means of an automated search procedure, to have access to reports on persons and objects for the purposes of border checks and controls and other police and customs checks carried out within the country in accordance with national law and, in the case of the single category of report referred to in Article 96, for the purposes of issuing visas, the issue of residence permits and the administration of aliens in the context of the application of the provisions of this Convention relating to the movement of persons.

2. Each Contracting Party shall set up and maintain, for its own account and at its own risk, its national section of the Schengen Information System, the data file of which shall be made materially identical to the data files of the national sections of each of the other Contracting Parties using the technical support function. To ensure the rapid and effective transmission of data as referred to in paragraph 3, each Contracting Party shall observe when creating its national section, the protocols and procedures which the Contracting Parties have jointly established for the technical support function. Each national sections' data file shall be available for the purposes of automated search in the territory of each of the Contracting Parties. It shall not be possible to search the data files of other Contracting Parties' national sections.

3. The Contracting Parties shall set up and maintain jointly and with joint liability for risks, the technical support function of the Schengen Information System, the responsibility for which shall be assumed by the French Republic; the technical support function shall be located in Strasbourg. The technical support function shall comprise a data file which ensures that the date files of the national sections are kept identical by the on-line transmission of information. The data file of the technical support function shall contain reports on persons and objects where these concern all the Contracting Parties. The data file of the technical support function shall contain no data other than those referred to in this paragraph and in Article 113(2).

CHAPTER 2. OPERATION AND UTILIZATION OF THE SCHENGEN INFORMATION SYSTEM

Art. 93. The purpose of the Schengen Information System shall be in accordance with this Convention to maintain public order and security, including State security, and to apply the provisions of this Convention relating to the movement of persons, in the territories of the Contracting Parties, using information transmitted by the system.

Art. 94. 1. The Schengen Information System shall contain only the categories of data which are supplied by each of the Contracting Parties and are required for the purposes laid down in Articles 95 to 100. The Contracting Party providing a report shall determine whether the importance of the case warrants the inclusion of the report in the Schengen System.

2. The categories of data shall be as follow:

(a) persons reported

(b) objects referred to in Article 100 and vehicles referred to in Article 99.

3. The items included in respect of persons, shall be no more than the following:

(a) name and forename, any aliases possibly registered separately;

(b) any particular objective and permanent physical features;

(c) first letter of second forename;

(d) date and place of birth;

(e) sex;

(f) nationality;

(g) whether the persons concerned are armed;

(h) whether the persons concerned are violent;

(i) reason for the report;

(j) action to be taken;

Other references, in particular the date listed in Article 6, first sentence of the Council of Europe Convention of 28 January 1981 for the Protection of Individuals with regard to Automatic Processing of Personal Data, shall not be authorized.

4. In so far as a Contracting Party considers that a report in accordance with Articles 95, 97 or 99 is incompatible with its national law, its international obligations or essential national interests, it may subsequently add to the report in the data file of the national section of the Schengen Information System a note to the effect that the action referred to will not be taken in its territory in connection with the report. Consultations must be held in this connection with the other Contracting Parties. If the reporting Contracting Party does not withdraw the report it will continue to apply in full for the other Contracting Parties.

Art. 95. 1. Data relating to persons wanted for arrest for extradition purposes shall be included at the request of the judicial authority of the requesting Contracting Party.

2. Prior to making a report, the reporting Contracting Party shall check whether the arrest is authorized by the national law of the requested Contracting Parties. If the reporting Contracting Party has doubts, it must consult the other Contracting Parties concerned.

The reporting Contracting Party shall send the requested Contracting Parties together with the report, by swiftest means, the following essential information relating to the case:

(a) the authority which issued the request for arrest;

(b) whether there is an arrest warrant or a document having the same force, or an enforceable judgment;

(c) the nature and legal classification of the offence;

(d) a description of the circumstances in which the offence was committed, including the time, place and degree of participation in the offence by the person reported;

(e) as far as possible, the consequence of the offence.

3. A requested Contracting Party may add to the report in the file of the national section of the Schengen Information System a note prohibiting arrest in a connection with the report, until such time as the note is deleted. The note shall be deleted no later than 254 hours after the report is included, unless the Contracting Party refuses to make the requested arrest on legal grounds or for special reasons of expediency. Where, in particularly exceptional cases, this is justified by the complexity of the facts underlying the report, the above time limit may be extended to one week. Without prejudice to a qualifying note or a decision to refuse arrest, the other Contracting Parties may make the arrest requested in the report.

4. If, for particularly urgent reasons, a Contracting Party requests an immediate search, the Party requested shall examine whether it is able to withdraw its note. The Contracting Party requested shall take the necessary steps to ensure tat the action to be taken can be carried out without delay if the report is validated.

5. If the arrest cannot be made because an investigation has not been completed or owing to a refusal by the requested Contracting Party, the latter must regard the report as being a report for the purposes of communicating the place of residence of the person concerned.

6. The requested Contracting Parties shall carry out the action to be taken as requested in the report in compliance with extradition Conventions in force and with national law. They shall not be required to carry our the action requested where one of their nationals is involved, without prejudice to the possibility of making the arrest in accordance with national law.

Art. 96. 1. Data relating to aliens who are reported for the propose of being refused entry shall be included on the bases of a national report resulting from decisions taken, in compliance with the rules of procedure laid down by national legislation, by the administrative authorities or courts responsible.

2. Decisions may be based on a threat to public order or national security and safety which the presence of an alien in national territory may pose. Such may in particular be the case with:

(a) an alien who has been convicted of an offence carrying a custodial sentence of at least one year;

(b) an alien who, there are serious grounds for believing, has committed serious offences, including those referred to in Article 71, or against whom there is genuine evidence of an intention to commit such offences in the territory or a Contracting Party.

3. Decisions may also be based on the fact that the alien has been the subject of a deportation, removal or expulsion measure which has not been rescinded or suspended, including or accompanied by a prohibition on entry or, where appropriate, residence, based on non-compliance with national regulations on the entry or residence of aliens.

Art. 97. Data relating to persons who have disappeared or to persons who, in the interest of their own protection or in order to prevent threats, need to be placed provisionally in a place of safety at the request of the competent authority or the competent judicial authority of the reporting Party, shall be included in order that the policy authorities can communicate their whereabouts to the reporting Party or can remove the person to a place of safety for the purposes of preventing him from continuing his journey, if so authorized by national legislation. This shall apply in particular to minors and to persons who must be interned by decision of a competent authority. Communication of the information shall be subject to the consent of the person who has disappeared, if of full age.

Art. 98. 1. Data relating to witnesses, to persons summoned to appear before the judicial authorities in connection with criminal proceedings in order to account for acts for which are being prosecuted, or to persons who are to be notified of a sentence, shall be included, at the request of the competent judicial authorities, for the purposes of communicating their place of residence or domicile.

2. Information requested shall be communicated to the requesting Party in accordance with national legislation and with the Conventions in force concerning mutual judicial assistance in criminal matters.

Art. 99. 1. Data relating to persons or vehicles shall be included, in compliance with national law of the reporting Contracting Party, for the purposes of discreet surveillance or specific checks, in accordance with paragraph 5.

2. Such a report may be made for the purposes of prosecuting criminal offences and for the prevention of threats to public safety:

(a) where there are real indications to suggest that the person concerned intends to commit or is committing numerous and extremely serious offences, or

(b) where an overall evaluation of the person concerned, in particular on the basis of offences committed hitherto, gives reason to suppose that he will also commit extremely serious offences in future.

3. In addition, a report may be made in accordance with national law, at the request of the authorities responsible for State security, where concrete evidence gives reason to suppose the information referred to in paragraph 4 is necessary for the prevention of a serious threat by the person or other serious threats to internal or external State security. The reporting Contracting Party shall be required to consult the other Contracting Party before hand.

4. For purposes of discreet surveillance, the following information may in whole or in part be collected and transmitted to the reporting authority when border checks or other police and customs checks are carried out within the country:

(a) the fact that the person or the vehicle reported has been found;

(b) the place, time or reason for the check;

(c) the route and destination of the journey;

(d) persons accompanying the person concerned or occupants of the vehicle;

(e) the vehicle used;

(f) objects carried;

(g) the circumstances under which the person or vehicle was found.

When such information is collected, steps must be taken to ensure that the discreet nature of the surveillance is not jeopardized.

5. In the context of the specific checks referred to in paragraph 1, persons, vehicles and objects carried may be searched in accordance with national law, in order to achieve the purpose referred to in paragraphs 2 and 3. If the specific check is not authorized in accordance with the law of a Contracting Party, it shall automatically be converted, for that Contracting Party, into discreet surveillance.

6. A requested Contracting Party may add to the report in the file of the national section of the Schengen Information System a note prohibiting, until the note is deleted, performance of the action to be taken pursuant to the report for the purpose of discreet

surveillance or specific checks. The note must be deleted no later than 24 hours after the report has been included unless the Contracting Party refuses to take the action requested on legal groups or for special reasons of expediency. Without prejudice to a qualifying note or a refusal decision, the other Contracting Parties may carry out the action requested in the report.

Art. 100. 1. Data relating to objects sought for the purposes of seizure or of evidence in criminal proceedings shall be included in the Schengen Information System.

2. If a search brings to light the existence of a report on a item which has been found the authority noticing the report shall contact the reporting authority in order to agree on the requisite measures. For this purpose, personal data may also be transmitted in accordance with this Convention. The measures to be taken by the Contracting Party which found the object must comply with its national law.

3. The categories of objects listed below shall be included:

(a) motor vehicles with a capacity in excess of 50 cc which have been stolen, misappropriated or lost;

(b) trailers and caravans with an unladen weight in excess of 750 kg which have been stolen, misappropriated or lost;

(c) firearms which have been stolen, misappropriated or lost;

(d) blank documents which have been stolen, misappropriated or lost;

(e) identification documents issued (passports, identity cards, driving licensees which have been stolen, misappropriated or lost;

(f) bank notes (registered notes).

Art. 101. 1. Access to data included in the Schengen Information System and the right to search such data directly shall be reserved exclusively for the authorities responsible for

(a) border checks;

(b) other police and customs checks carried out within the country, and the coordination of such checks.

2. In addition, access to data included in accordance with Article 96 and the right to search such data directly may be exercised by the authorities responsible for issuing visas, the central responsible for examining visa applications and the authorities responsible for issuing residence permits and the administration of aliens within the framework of the application of the provisions on the movement of persons under this Convention. Access to data shall be governed by the national law of each Contracting Party.

3. Users may only search data which are necessary for the performance of their tasks.

4. Each of the Contracting Parties shall communicate to the Executive Committee a list of the competent authorities which are authorized to search the data included in the Schengen Information System directly. The list shall indicate for each authority the data which it may search, and for what purposes.

CHAPTER 3. PROTECTION OF PERSONAL DATA AND SECURITY DATA UNDER THE SCHENGEN INFORMATION SYSTEM

Art. 102. 1. The Contracting Parties may use the data provided for in Articles 95 to 100 only for the purposes laid down for each type of report referred to in those Articles.

2. Data may be duplicated only for technical purposes, provided that such duplication is necessary for direct searching by the authorities referred to in Article 101. Reports

by other Contracting Parties may not be copied from the national section of the Schengen Information System in other national data files.

3. In connection with the types of report provided for in Articles 95 to 100 of this Convention, any derogation from paragraph 1 in order to change from one type of report to another must be justified by the need to prevent an imminent serious threat to public order and safety, for serious reasons of State security or for the purposes of preventing a serious offence. The prior authorization of the reporting Contracting Party must be obtained for this purpose.

4. Data may not be used for administrative purposes. By way of derogation, data included in accordance with Article 96 may be used, in accordance with the national law of each of the Contracting Parties, only for the purposes of Article 101(2).

5. Any use of data which does not comply with paragraphs 1 to 4 shall be considered as a misuse in relation to the national law of each Contracting Party.

Art. 103. Each Contracting Party shall ensure that, on average, every tenth transmission of personal data is recorded in the national section of the Schengen Information System by the data file managing authority for the purposes of checking the admissibility of searching. The recording may be used only for this purpose and shall be deleted after six months.

Art. 104. 1. The law apply to reports shall be the national law of the reporting Contracting Party, unless more rigorous conditions are laid down in this Convention.

2. In so far as this Convention does not lay down specific provisions, the law of each Contracting Party shall apply to data included in the national section of the Schengen Information System.

3. In so far as this Convention does not lay down specific provisions concerning performance of the action requested in the report, the national law of the Contracting Party requested which carries out the action shall apply. In so far as this Convention lays down specific provisions concerning performance of the action requested in the report, responsibility for the action to be taken shall be governed by the national law of the requested Contracting Party. If the action requested cannot be performed, the requested Contracting Party shall inform the reporting Contracting Party without delay.

Art. 105. The reporting Contracting Party shall be responsible for the accuracy, up-to-datedness and lawfulness of the inclusion of data in the Schengen Information System.

Art. 106. 1. Only the reporting Contracting Party shall be authorized to amend, supplement, correct or delete data which it has introduced.

2. If one of the Contracting Parties which has not made the report has evidence to suggest that an item of data is legally or factually inaccurate, it shall advise the reporting Contracting Party thereof as soon as possible; the latter must check the communication and, if necessary, correct or delete the item in question without delay.

3. If the Contracting Parties are unable to reach agreement, the Contracting Party which did not generate the report shall submit the case to the joint supervisory authority referred to in Article 115(1) for its opinion.

Art. 107. Where a person has already been the subject of a report in the Schengen Information System, a Contracting Party which introduces a further report shall come to an agreement on the inclusion of the reports with the Contracting Party which introduced the first report. The Contracting Parties may also adopt general provisions to this end.

Art. 108. 1. Each of the Contracting Parties shall designate an authority which shall have central responsibility for the national section of the Schengen Information System.

2. Each of the Contracting Parties shall make its report via that authority.

3. The said authority shall be responsible for the correct operation of the national section of the Schengen Information System and shall take the measures necessary to ensure compliance with the provisions of this Convention.

4. The Contracting Parties shall inform one another, via the Depositary, of the authority referred to in paragraph 1.

Art. 109. 1. The right of any person to have access to data relating to him which are included in the Schengen Information System shall be exercised in accordance with the law of the Contracting Party before which it invokes that right. If the national law so provides, the national supervisory authority provided for in Article 114(1) shall decide whether information shall be communicated and by what procedures. A Contracting Party which has not made the report may communicate information concerning such data only if it has previously given the reporting Contracting Party an opportunity to state its position.

2. Communication of information to the person concerned shall be refused if it may undermine the performance of the legal task specified in the report, or in order to protect the rights and freedoms of others. It shall be refused in any event during the period of reporting for the purposes of discreet surveillance.

Art. 110. Any person may have factually inaccurate data relating him corrected or have legal inaccurate data relating to him deleted.

Art. 111. 1. Any person may, in the territory of each Contracting Party, bring before the courts or the authority competent under national law an action to correct, delete or provide information or obtain compensation in connection with a report concerning him.

2. The Contracting Parties shall under amongst themselves to execute final decisions taken by the courts of authorities referred to in paragraph 1, without prejudice to the provisions of Article 16....

Art. 116. 1. Each Contracting Party shall be responsible in accordance with its national law, for any injury caused to a person through the use of the national data file of the Schengen Information System. This shall also be the case where the injury was caused by the reporting Contracting Party, where the latter included legally or factually inaccurate data.

2. If the Contracting Party against which an action is brought is not the reporting Contracting party, the latter shall be required to reimburse, on request, sums paid out as compensation, unless the data were sued by the requested Contracting Party in contravention of this Convention.

Art. 117. 1. With regard to the automatic processing of personal data which are transmitted pursuant to this Title, each Contracting party shall, not later than when this Convention enters into force, make the national arrangements necessary to achieve a level of protection of personal data at least equal to that resulting from the principles of the Council of Europe Convention of 28 January 1981 for the Protection of Individuals with regard to the Automatic Processing of Personal Data, and in compliance with Recommendation R (87) 15 of 17 September 1987 of the Committee of Ministers of the Council of Europe regulating the sue of personal data in the police sector.

2. The transmission of personal data provided for in this Title may take place only where the arrangements for the protection of personal data provided for in paragraph 1 have entered into force in the territory of the Contracting Parties concerned by the transmission.

Art. 118. 1. Each of the Contracting Parties shall undertake, in respect of the national section of the Schengen Information System, to take the measures necessary to:

(a) prevent any unauthorized person from having access to installations used for the processing of personal data (checks at the entrance to installations);

(b) prevent data media from being read, copied, modified or removed by unauthorized persons (control of data media);

(c) prevent the unauthorized entry of data into the file and any unauthorized consultation, modification or deletion of personal data included in the file (control of data entry);

(d) prevent automated data processing systems from being used by unauthorized persons by means of data transmission equipment (control of utilization);

(e) guarantee that, with respect to the sue of an automated data processing system, authorized persons have access only to data for which they are responsible (control of access);

(g) guarantee that it is possible to check and establish a posteriori what personal data has been introduced into automated data processing systems, when and by whom (control of data introduction);

(h) prevent the unauthorized reading, copying, modification or deletion of personal data during the transmission of data and the transport of data media (control of transport).

2. Each Contracting party must take special measures to ensure the security of data when it is being transmitted to services located outside the territories of the Contracting Parties. Such measures must be communicated to the joint supervisory authority.

3. Each Contracting Party may designate for the processing of data in its national section of the Schengen Information System only specially qualified persons subject to security checks.

4. The Contracting Party responsible for the technical support function of the Schengen Information System shall take the measures laid down in paragraphs 1 to 3 in respect of the latter....

Treaty on European Union and Final Act

(1992)

TITLE VI

PROVISIONS ON COOPERATION IN THE FIELDS OF JUSTICE AND HOME AFFAIRS

Article K

Cooperation in the fields of justice and home affairs shall be governed by the following provisions.

Article K.1

For the purposes of achieving the objectives of the Union, in particular the free movement of persons, and without prejudice to the powers of the European Community, Member States shall regarding the following areas as matters of common interest:

1. asylum policy;

2. rules governing the crossing by persons of the external borders of the Member States and the exercise of controls thereon;

3. immigration policy and policy regarding nationals of third countries:

(a) conditions of entry and movement by nationals of third countries on the territory of Member States;

(b) conditions of residence by nationals of third countries on the territory of Member States, including family reunion and access to employment;

(c) combatting unauthorized immigration, residence and work by nationals of third countries on the territory of Member States;

4. combatting drug addiction in so far as this is not covered by 7 to 9;

5. combatting fraud on an international scale in so far as this is not covered by 7 to 9;

6. judicial cooperation in civil matters;

7. judicial cooperation in criminal matters;

8. customs cooperation;

9. police cooperation for the purposes of preventing and combatting terrorism, unlawful drug trafficking and other serious forms of international crime, including if necessary certain aspects of customs cooperation, in connection with the organization of a Union-wide system of exchanging information within a European Police Office (Europol).

Article K.2

1. The matters referred to in Article K.1 shall be dealt with in compliance with the European Convention for the protection of Human Rights and Fundamental Freedoms of 4 November 1950 and the Convention relating to the Status of Refugees of 28 July 1951 and having regard to the protect afforded by Member States to persons persecuted on political grounds.

2. This Title shall not affect the exercise of the responsibilities incumbent upon Member States with regard to the maintenance of law and order and the safeguarding of internal security.

Article K.3

1. In the areas referred to in Article 1.1, Member States shall inform and consult one another within the Council with a view to co-ordinating their action. To that end, they shall establish collaboration between the relevant departments of their administrations.

2. The Council may:

— on the initiative of any Member State or of the Commission, in the areas referred to in Article K.1(1) to (6);

— on the initiative of any Member State, in the areas referred to in Article K1(7) to (9);

(a) adopt joint positions and promote, using the appropriate form and procedures, any cooperation contributing to the pursuit of the objectives of the Union;

(b) adopt joint action in so far as the objectives of the Union can be attained better by joint action than by the Member States acting individually on account of the scale or effects of the action envisaged; it may decide that measures implementing joint action are to be adopted by a qualified majority;

(c) without prejudice to Article 220 of the Treaty establishing the European Community, draw up conventions which it shall recommend to the Member States for adoption in accordance with their respective constitutional requirements.

Unless otherwise provided by such conventions, measures implementing them shall be adopted within the Council by a majority of two-thirds of the High Contracting Parties.

Such conventions may stipulate that the Court of Justice shall have jurisdiction to interpret their provisions and to rule on any disputes regarding their application, in accordance with such arrangements as they may lay down.

Article K.4

1. A Coordinating Committee shall be set up consisting of senior officials. In addition to its coordinating role, it shall be the task of the Committee to:

—give opinions for the attention of the Council, either at the Council's request or on its own initiative;

—contribute, without prejudice to Article 151 of the Treaty establishing the European Community, to the preparation of the Council's discussions in the areas referred to in Article K.1 and, in accordance with the conditions laid down in Article 100d of the Treaty establishing the European Community, in the areas referred to in Article 100c of that Treaty.

2. The Commission shall be fully associated with the work in the areas referred to in this Title.

3. The Council shall act unanimously, except on matters of procedure and in cases where Article K.3 expressly provides for other voting rules.

Where the Council is required to act by a qualified majority, the votes of its members shall be weighted as laid down in Article 148(2) of the Treaty establishing the European Community, and for their adoption, acts of the Council shall require at least fifty-four votes in favor, case by at least eight members.

Article K.5

Within international organizations and at international conferences in which they take part, Member States shall defend the common positions under the provisions of this Title.

Article K.6

The Presidency and the Commission shall regularly inform the European Parliament of discussions in the areas covered by this Title.

The President shall consult the European Parliament on the principal aspects of activities in the areas referred to in this Title and shall ensure that the views of the European Parliament are duly taken into consideration.

Article K.7

The provisions of this Title shall not prevent the establishment or development of closer cooperation between two or more Member States in so far as such cooperation does not conflict with, or impeded, that provided for in this Title....